Family Law and Practice

Family Law and Practice

Fifth Edition

Grace A. Luppino, Esq.

Justine FitzGerald Miller, Esq.

 **Pearson**

Vice President, Portfolio Management: Andrew Gilfillan
Portfolio Manager: Gary Bauer
Editorial Assistant: Lynda Cramer
Vice President, Product Marketing: Brad Parkins
Product Marketing Manager: Heather Taylor
Product Marketing Assistant: Liz Bennett
Director, Digital Studio and Content Production: Brian Hyland
Managing Producer: Jennifer Sargunar
Content Producer: Rinki Kaur
Manager, Rights Management: Johanna Burke

Manufacturing Buyer: Deidra Headlee
Creative Digital Lead: Mary Siener
Full-Service Management and Composition: Integra Software Services Pvt. Ltd.
Full-Service Project Manager: Gowthaman Sadhanandham
Cover Design: Studio Montage
Cover Photos: Ariel Skelle/Digitalvision/Getty Images, Monkey Business Images/Shutterstock, Rido/Shutterstock
Printer/Binder: LSC Communications, Inc.
Text Font: Times LT Pro Roman
Cover Printer: LSC Communications

Library of Congress Cataloging-in-Publication Data

Names: Luppino, Grace A., author. | Miller, Justine FitzGerald, author.
Title: Family law and practice/Grace A. Luppino, Justine FitzGerald Miller.
Description: Fifth edition. | Upper Saddle River, New Jersey: Pearson Education, Inc., [2020] | Includes index.
Identifiers: LCCN 2018028125 | ISBN 9780133495188 (alk. paper) | ISBN 0135186315
Subjects: LCSH: Domestic relations—United States. | Legal assistants—United States—Handbooks, manuals, etc. | LCGFT: Textbooks.
Classification: LCC KF505.Z9 L87 2020 | DDC 346.7301/5—dc23
    LC record available at https://lccn.loc.gov/2018028125

1 18

ISBN 10:   0-13-518631-5
ISBN 13: 978-0-13-518631-2

Dedication

This book is dedicated to my family . . .
those related by blood, by marriage, and by love.

Grace A. Luppino

Dedicated to Justine, George, and Emma.

Justine FitzGerald Miller

Brief Contents

Contents

CHAPTER 6

Preface

This fifth edition of *Family Law and Practice*, is a comprehensive textbook for students in paralegal studies programs and broader legal studies programs, as well as those majoring in criminal justice, social work, and education.

Our goal remains to prepare students to enter the workplace possessing a solid knowledge of the various aspects of family law and a firm grasp of the procedural components used in a family law practice, including the documents filed with the court and the information-gathering tools utilized to resolve financial issues as well as custody and visitation dispositions. To meet our challenge, this edition includes a division of the book into two parts. With this new edition, we hope to realize our goal of first introducing the student to the principles of family law, then with this background in place, presenting a section that demonstrates how the theory is then translated into practice.

ORGANIZATION

- **Chapter 1, Introduction to Family Law and Practice** addresses issues critical to family law practice in the twenty-first century and eliminates less relevant sections. Although somewhat condensed, there is still a section providing a historical perspective on the evolution of family law and the changing views regarding marriage, the roles and responsibilities of each spouse, the status of children in the family, and, last but not least, what constitutes a family.

Part One: Family Law

- **Chapter 2, Marriage and Marriage Alternatives**, begins with a look at marriage, as we once knew it, a union between one man and one woman, and how recent legal efforts have redefined this institution in several jurisdictions. We also discuss how to create a valid marriage, the legal benefits of the marital union, and the prohibitions that make some marriages invalid. We have included a section on the legal prosecution of bigamists and polygamists along with a discussion of the hit television series, *Sister Wives*, and the legal case that arose from the attempted criminal prosecution of the cast members. The chapter ends with an overview of "marriage alternatives," which present a different approach to relationships outside the traditional bounds of marriage. This chapter also gives updates on the status of same-sex marriage and contains a discussion of *Obergefell v. Hodges*, the U.S. Supreme Court case legalizing same-sex marriage in the United States. Because of the increase in cohabitation, with many couples opting out of traditional marriage, we have gone into detail on the legal remedies available to cohabiting couples according to the landmark decision of *Marvin v. Marvin*. In light of these changes in modern society, we have included a new section on drafting cohabitation agreements to protect the rights of unmarried couples.
- **Chapter 3, Premarital and Postmarital Agreements**, contains new information on the now generally accepted criteria for determining the validity of a premarital and postmarital agreement, as many jurisdictions have adopted some version of the Uniform Premarital Agreement Act, and on how to prepare and execute an agreement that will be legally enforceable. Other practical aspects of the chapter also include identifying which documents must be reviewed before drafting a premarital and postmarital agreement. We have

expanded the section on postmarital agreements and, to make the subject more interesting, included examples of cases where premarital agreements that were invalidated by the courts as well as a look at some of the more popular celebrity prenups.

- **Chapter 4, Divorce, Separation, and Annulment**, is devoted solely to an explanation of the three options married couples have for ending their marriages: dissolution, legal separation, and annulment. We discuss the factors that help legal practitioners differentiate whether the circumstances call for a divorce or dissolution, a legal separation, or an annulment. We also explain the advantages and disadvantages of non-fault divorce.

- **Chapter 5, Alimony, Support, and Maintenance.** In this chapter, we address the statutory factors considered by family court judges in evaluating the issue of alimony. The student learns how to identify and describe the various types of alimony, the circumstances that trigger the termination of alimony, and how and when alimony may be modified. We have also included a section on alimony reform and current efforts around the country to eliminate permanent or lifetime alimony.

- **Chapter 6, Property and Debt Distribution.** While the purpose of alimony is to provide a needy spouse with support or "maintenance," the goal of property and debt distribution is to fairly distribute the marital assets and debts between the spouses. Property and debt division are some of the most contested issues in modern divorce cases, second only to custody disputes. We have included an expanded explanation of the difference between individual property and marital property and more intensive coverage of the "hows" and "whys" of property distribution and debt allocation in community property and equitable distribution states. We also address the issue of marital debt, because in many marriages, distribution of debts may be the only financial issue to resolve. The chapter also includes a brief introduction to bankruptcy law, changes in the federal bankruptcy law that impact divorce cases, means testing, timing the filing of the bankruptcy petition before or after the divorce, and whether alimony, child support, and property distribution may be discharged in bankruptcy. The chapter concludes with an expanded section on the tax consequences of divorce and the innocent spouse rule.

- **Chapter 7, Child Custody, Visitation, and Rights of Third Parties**, lays out the traditional and nontraditional arrangements for custody and visitation, including the requirement many states now impose on the parties to agree upon a parenting plan and present it to the court for evaluation and approval. In this chapter, we introduce the concept of "nesting" as an access alternative in which the child stays in the home while the parents are the ones who are required to move on a rotating basis. The chapter contains an update on grandparents' rights and the emergence of a movement advocating the expansion of those rights despite the restrictions imposed by the United States Supreme Court case of *Troxel v. Granville*. This chapter also discusses the difference between the standard applied in many jurisdictions to determine either granting access/visitation or custody to grandparents or third parties. This edition also includes a discussion on parental alienation, allegations of parental sexual abuse of children, and custody disputes over extra embryos produced to facilitate in vitro fertilization.

- **Chapter 8, Child Support**, introduces information regarding the latest computerized methods of locating and keeping track of delinquent payer parents as well as more effective methods of collection of arrearages. This chapter includes a discussion on the rationale behind implementation of the child support guidelines, the purpose of deviation criteria and identification of factors a court may take into consideration when deviating from the guidelines, the basis for modification of child support orders, and a description of the child support enforcement process. This edition includes a hypothetical child support case as well as a step-by-step calculation of the amount of child support due. It also gives the student a basic approach to addressing the child support calculation issue in their respective jurisdiction, and the resources necessary in completing this task.

- **Chapter 9, Paternity and the Rights and Responsibilities of Unmarried Parents.** This chapter addresses the multitude of issues arising from the dramatic increase of unmarried couples who either intentionally or unexpectedly become parents and choose to remain single, either as cohabitants or individually living separate lives. A new addition to this chapter is a discussion of verification of paternity actions, along with a sample form used in the court system to formally recognize paternal identity and allow the court to enter orders for paternal access/visitation, child support, and transfers of custody to the father. This chapter also includes a new sample parenting plan.
- **Chapter 10, Family Violence and State Intervention.** This chapter covers the legal issues that arise when children and spouses are victims of domestic violence and how the state intervenes. From the antiquated historical perceptions of victims to modern-day changes, this chapter includes an overview of child protection laws, the protection of abused and neglected children, civil restraining orders and criminal orders of protection, mandatory arrests, and the Violence Against Women Act of 1994 and its current amendments. The section on domestic violence also includes the various legal options paralegals must be aware of, as well as a section on how to represent both the victim and the alleged abuser in these types of cases.
- **Chapter 11, Adoption and Surrogacy Contracts.** This chapter contains a subsection on the lengthy and intricate process of stepparent adoption, and a subsection on the "second parent" adoption process through which some states confer co-parent status on the same-sex partner of an adoptive parent. The topic of open adoption is discussed extensively, and a sample open adoption agreement is provided. We have also included a section on surrogacy contracts, including the landmark case of Baby M.

Part Two: Family Practice

- **Chapter 12, Ethics in Family Law**, continues to provide the practical basis for rules of professional responsibility and examples of their practical application. Again, the paralegal's ethical responsibilities are emphasized. Also discussed is the ever-expanding impetus to license paralegals and the recent efforts of some lawmakers to promote legislation that would extend liability for ethical breaches to the paralegal when warranted. This chapter also includes a section on the ethical considerations involving the use of technology, particularly the impact of electronic mail and the precautions that must be taken to avoid breaches of client confidentiality. This chapter addresses other practical issues impacting a paralegal's daily work environment. For example, family courts are increasingly seeing more and more self-represented, or *pro se*, litigants; this book addresses the ethical considerations and precautions one must take when dealing with an opposing party who is representing himself or herself. The book also addresses the resources available to parties who are representing themselves, including the availability of useful and affordable "unbundled legal services."
- **Chapter 13, The Client Interview**, begins by addressing the practical aspects of family law practice. Most family lawyers will tell you that family law is less law and more hand-holding. Here, we focus on helping the student understand the

emotional aspects of family law practice. In this chapter, the student also learns to identify the steps in the client interview and the essential information that must be obtained from a client. The importance of referring clients to appropriate support services when necessary is also stressed. Because family law is the most emotionally charged practice specialty, this chapter concludes with a section on workplace violence as well as safety tips for those working in the field.

- **Chapter 14, Initial and Responsive Pleadings.** Following the client interview and the signing of the retainer letter, the supervising attorney on the file will delegate to an appropriate staff member the responsibility of preparing the documents that must be filed with the court to initiate the divorce proceeding or other desired family-related suit. In this chapter the student learns the basics of drafting a dissolution of marriage complaint or petition for the plaintiff and the defendant's answer and cross-complaint. We have updated the section entitled **The Electronic Courthouse**, which reflects the nationwide trend toward implementing the electronic filing of documents in family matters. The chapter discusses the e-filing process, and the precautions and repercussions that must be observed when filing documents electronically. Protecting privacy is also stressed with sections on federal and state rules governing the redacting of personal information from electronic documents.

- **Chapter 15, Temporary Relief**, describes the purpose of temporary relief or *pendente lite* relief, the basic components of a temporary relief motion, and the paralegal's role in facilitating these matters. In this fifth edition, we emphasize the changes in technology that have eliminated the use of paper calendars and filing of paper motions. In this edition, we also list and define the most frequently used family law motions.

- **Chapter 16, Discovery in the Electronic Age.** The name of this chapter has been changed to reflect our fast-paced and ever-changing age of information. It is imperative for the family law professional to be aware of how technology can both aid and hinder the discovery process. We have added a section on E-discovery that deals with the process of obtaining, collecting, preparing, reviewing, and distributing information from the opposing party in a legal case that has been electronically stored. In this new edition, we have expanded how social networking websites such as Facebook are revolutionizing discovery in family-related cases. In many cases, hiring a private investigator is no longer necessary when vital information can be obtained with the click of a mouse! We also discuss the uses of self-help surveillance technology in catching a spouse in the act with spyware and GPS tracking devices and the limitations on the admissibility of such evidence in a court of law.

- **Chapter 17, Separation Agreements**, focuses on the practical skills needed in assisting the attorney in the separation agreement process. This includes not only how to draft a proposal letter for the client's review, but also how to prepare a separation agreement and the most common standard clauses. This chapter includes a section on parenting plans. These are detailed agreements regarding access to the children and some sample provisions specifying particular days, times, transportation, place of pickup and drop-off, holidays, summer vacations, and birthdays.

- **Chapter 18, Alternative Dispute Resolution and the Divorce Trial**, includes a comprehensive section on mediation and other alternative methods of dispute resolution used to diminish the instances of protracted and unpleasant litigation arising from custody and property disputes. This chapter also includes a section on how the family courts use technology and how important it is for legal professionals to become familiar with their jurisdiction's court rules surrounding this issue.

- **Chapter 19, Postjudgment Divorce Matters**, identifies the various methods used to facilitate enforcement of court orders, especially support enforcement methods and remedies. This chapter also includes a discussion of instances where courts may modify "nonmodifiable" sections of a settlement agreement.

To make this edition relevant and interesting to more students throughout the country, we have included cases, statutes, and legal forms from a variety of states.

NEW TO THIS EDITION

Chapter 2

Updated status of same-sex marriages in the United States, including the legal effect of *U.S. v. Windsor* and *Obergefell v. Hodges* on the issue.

Chapter 3

Additional cases on testing the validity of premarital and postnuptial agreements
Updated celebrity premarital agreement section

Chapter 7

Updated section on grandparents' rights and the emergence of a movement advocating the expansion of those rights despite the restrictions imposed by the United States Supreme Court case of *Troxel v. Granville*.

Chapter 8

Streamlined child support chapter

Chapter 9

Updated court forms to include a sample parenting plan
Updated discussion on verification of paternity actions

Chapter 11

Updated section on gay adoption in light of the *Obergefell v. Hodges* decision
Updated section on surrogacy contracts

Chapter 14

Updated court form exhibits
Updated privacy protection statutes

Chapter 15

Updated court form exhibits
Modernized language from pendente lite to temporary relief

Chapter 16

Updated section on the legal consequences of the use of social networking website

Chapter 18

Expanded section on contemporary uses of technology in the family law courtroom and cell phones in the courtroom

Chapter 19

Revised section on the enforcement of family court orders, which includes a new section on civil and criminal contempt

BUILDING PARALEGAL WORKPLACE SKILLS

End-of-chapter material has been organized into three sections: *Chapter Review and Reinforcement*, *Building Your Paralegal Skills*, and *Building Your Professional Portfolio*.

- **Chapter Review and Reinforcement:** This section of activities is designed to confirm that the student understands basic terms and concepts presented in the chapter. It contains sections on the **Key Terms** and **Review of Key Concepts**, which guides the student's review by reemphasizing the main points of law covered in the chapter.
- **Building Your Paralegal Skills:** In this section the student performs activities that build the analytical and functional workplace skills that they will need in practice. First, students read and brief a relevant case—**Case for Briefing**—that showcases one of the key topics covered in the chapter. The student is then directed in **Critical Thinking and Legal Analysis Applications** to apply the legal principles learned in the case to a problem they may confront on any given day in a family law practice and determine how the law in the student's own home state would resolve the issue as applied to the same facts.
- **Building Your Professional Portfolio** presents the student with a fact scenario. Based on the scenario, the student is asked to generate a sample legal document. The goal is for the paralegal student to steadily build a family law practice portfolio throughout the course to show prospective employers during their job search.

In conclusion, we hope that our revisions, updates, and additions to this, our third edition, offer our students greater knowledge, understanding, and skill development in the area of family law and practice.

INSTRUCTOR SUPPLEMENTS

Instructor's Manual with Test Bank. Includes content outlines for classroom discussion, teaching suggestions, and answers to selected end-of-chapter questions from the text. This also contains a Word document version of the test bank.

TestGen. This computerized test generation system gives you maximum flexibility in creating and administering tests on paper, electronically, or online. It provides state-of-the-art features for viewing and editing test bank questions, dragging a selected question into a test you are creating, and printing sleek, formatted tests in a variety of layouts. Select test items from test banks included with TestGen for quick test creation, or write your own questions from scratch. TestGen's random generator provides the option to display different text or calculated number values each time questions are used.

PowerPoint Presentations. Our presentations are clear and straightforward. Photos, illustrations, charts, and tables from the book are included in the presentations when applicable.

To access supplementary materials online, instructors need to request an instructor access code. Go to www.pearsonhighered.com/irc, where you can register for an instructor access code. Within 48 hours after registering, you will receive a confirming e-mail, including an instructor access code. Once you have received your code, go to the site and log on for full instructions on downloading the materials you wish to use.

ALTERNATE VERSIONS

eBooks. This text is also available in multiple eBook formats. These are an exciting new choice for students looking to save money. As an alternative to purchasing the printed textbook students can purchase an electronic version of the same content. With an eTextbook, students can search the text, make notes online, print out reading assignments that incorporate lecture notes, and bookmark important passages for later review. For more information, visit your favorite online eBook reseller or visit www.mypearsonstore.com.

Acknowledgments

We wish to thank reviewers of this book who provided many helpful comments and insights that have been incorporated into the fifth edition:

Carina Aguirre, Platt College
Laura Drake, Cincinnati State Technical and Community College
Patricia Greer, Berkeley College
Rebecca Whitcombe, College of Lake County

We would also like to thank the reviewers of the fourth edition:

Robert Diotalevi, Florida Gulf Coast University
Gary W. Tamaeker, Greenville Technical College
Karen McGuffee, University of Tennessee at Chattanooga

We wish to thank the following people for their support and encouragement in making this book a reality:
Gary Bauer, Rinki Kaur, Linda Cramer, and Gowthaman Sadhanandham at Pearson; our special thanks to paralegal Pamela Robicheau for her countless hours of legal research, editing, and preparation of the original manuscript. This book could not have been completed without her hard work, expertise, and devotion to this project.

Grace A. Luppino
Justine FitzGerald Miller

Family Law and Practice

Chapter **one**

INTRODUCTION TO FAMILY LAW AND PRACTICE

Family law is one of the most interesting, exciting, and dynamic areas of legal practice. If you like boxing, wrestling, or any of the other pugilistic arts, you will certainly enjoy being part of a legal team that tackles the knotty problems and ever-changing cultural, social, and economic issues that affect the American family.

LEARNING OBJECTIVES

After studying this chapter, you should be able to:

1. Identify the sources of law used to resolve family matters.

2. List the procedures courts use to address disputed family law issues.

3. List the procedures law firms use within the office to handle family law cases.

4. Describe the role of societal values in the history and development of family law.

5. Describe the impact of the Industrial Revolution on the family as an economic unit.

6. Discuss the factors that precipitate changes in family law.

Figure 1-1 A paralegal who is both competent and enthusiastic can provide valuable assistance to attorneys.

Stephen Coburn/Shutterstock

Family law as a specialty evolved slowly, but now, in most jurisdictions, family law cases occupy more space on the civil court docket than does any other type of matter. This increase has occurred because of changes in our society during the past fifty years that have affected attitudes toward marriage, family, divorce, and parenting.

During the first half of the twentieth century in the United States, divorce was far less common than it is today. At the turn of the twentieth century, fewer than one in twenty marriages ended in divorce; since the mid-1970s, for every two marriages that took place in a given year, one divorce has occurred. Today, more than one-half of children under the age of eighteen are growing up in one-parent homes. As a result of this trend, many law firms devote their practice exclusively to family law; for other firms, the practice of family law comprises a large segment of the work produced. Both types of law firms increasingly employ paralegals in their family law department. These paraprofessionals, with the guidance of their supervisory attorneys, complete the myriad of tasks needed to provide thorough, effective representation to clients on family matters.

A paralegal who is both competent in and enthusiastic about family law practice can provide valuable assistance to attorneys who spend all or most of their time practicing family law. Employment opportunities for paralegals in this field of law will abound as long as individuals continue to seek attorneys to help them resolve their marital and family conflicts, and as long as there are paralegals whose training has provided them with a solid background in both family law theory and practice. The goal of this book is to provide the paralegal student, in a comprehensive and understandable manner, with just that type of theoretical and practical education.

FAMILY LAW THEORY

Family law theory provides the analytical framework for the body of substantive law used in courts to decide marital and other family-related matters. These laws determine, regulate, and enforce the obligations of marriage and parenthood. They are made by the legislative branches of state governments and interpreted and applied by members of the states' judicial branches, as judges make decisions in the courtroom. In some instances, where there are no statutory guidelines, judges make the law. These common law and statutory decisions are not made arbitrarily, nor are they made in a vacuum without considering what is taking place in the society in which the laws will be enforced. When a law is being made, it is fashioned in a way that promotes the dominant views of the time on the proper, fair, or most enlightened way to handle the issues at hand. Legislation and judicial opinions reflect the values and attitudes of society. These values and attitudes produce the ideas that provide the theory or underlying rationale for resolving a legal issue in a particular manner. As values and attitudes change and as society acquires new information and knowledge related to various aspects of family law issues, new theories emerge and replace the earlier rationales for resolving disputes.

In the area of family law, courts and legislatures use many different approaches to address marital disputes and the issues arising from such disputes. These issues include:

- support and maintenance of family members,
- care and custody of minor children, and
- division of property upon the breakup of the marital unit.

Over time, family law theory has grown and evolved as society has changed. The history of American family law presented in this chapter demonstrates how differently family law issues have been treated during different time periods.

FAMILY LAW PRACTICE

Court Systems

The United States has a dual court system. There is a federal court system and a state court system. Each system has trial courts, intermediate courts of appeal, and courts of final appeal where the decisions of the intermediate appeal courts may be reviewed. Federal courts address violations of the federal criminal and civil statutes and violations of the U.S. Constitution. Federal courts also hear civil disputes between parties who reside in different states. State courts address violations of state criminal and civil laws and violations of the state constitution, and they may hear cases involving violations of the U.S. Constitution. State courts also hear civil disputes between parties when at least one party resides in the state.

State courts have *exclusive jurisdiction* to try disputes between parties in the area of family law. In most states, there are specialized family trial courts that decide both simple and complex family law issues. A decision of a state's family trial court may be appealed to that state's intermediate and highest appellate courts. In some rare instances, when an appeal involves a new and previously unsettled family law question that could involve a violation of the U.S. Constitution, it may go as far as the U.S. Supreme Court for resolution. For example, as will be discussed in a later chapter, the U.S. Supreme Court has heard and ruled on such issues as the rights of grandparents to visit their grandchildren when a parent opposes such contact.

Exclusive jurisdiction
A court's power to hear certain actions of classes of actions to the exclusion of all other courts.

Court Procedures

In every state and jurisdiction, the judicial system provides specific procedures for bringing disputed substantive family law issues before the court. These include procedures for:

- initiating family-related actions in a court,
- acquiring and presenting evidentiary information,
- providing temporary solutions to issues of support, custody, and visitation while a matter is pending,

- enforcing or modifying a court's orders,
- conducting alternative dispute resolution,
- processing uncontested matters by streamlining process, and
- litigating contested matters.

Every state or jurisdiction has its own particular set of procedural rules to follow in the practice of family law. These rules are part of the jurisdiction's larger body of civil procedural law that governs how private parties may enforce their substantive legal rights through the court system. In the practice of family law, knowledge of the family court's procedural rules is essential.

Office Procedures

It is equally essential to know the procedures that a law firm uses within its office to handle family law matters. Every law office has its own particular methods and practices for the following aspects of managing family law cases:

- obtaining and recording information from clients,
- setting up files,
- preparing legal documents for filing in court,
- docketing court dates,
- recording the amount of time spent working on each file, and
- billing clients for work done.

APPLYING FAMILY LAW THEORY TO FAMILY LAW PRACTICE

It is also very important to understand how family law theory is actually applied in the real world of family law practice. In many instances in a marital dispute, issues such as property division, alimony, child support, and even child custody are worked out by the parties in a manner that is consistent with the prevailing theoretical view and the substantive statutory or common law guidelines. When this happens, formal adversarial proceedings such as contested hearings on certain preliminary matters or a full-blown divorce trial are not necessary. This can happen when the parties work out an agreement to settle their differences through *settlement*, *mediation*, or *collaborative lawyering*. These forms of *alternative dispute resolution* will be discussed in Chapter 14.

THE FAMILY PRACTITIONER'S ROLE IN THE DISSOLUTION PROCESS

The practice of family law involves as much negotiating as it does litigating. For instance, a common saying is that there are no winners in a divorce, and the children are the biggest losers. The family law practice firm that strives toward and achieves the most favorable outcomes for its clients with the least amount of emotional and financial pain to all the individuals affected provides the highest degree of service to the client. Whether the service involves the initial divorce proceeding or a subsequent need to enforce or modify the alimony, child support, or custody order, the family practice lawyer who can meet the client's objectives with the least amount of court intervention will serve a client well, both financially and emotionally.

All litigation is adversarial, by its nature, and can only escalate hostility between the adverse parties.

In a family law practice, the clients' need for legal assistance arises from discord in the most personal and intimate areas of their lives. Much attention and concern should be given to the manner in which the controversy is handled and the

Settlement
The practice of negotiating areas of disagreement and, through compromise, reaching an agreement to present to the court.

Mediation
Where the parties meet and attempt to resolve the pending issues surrounding their dissolution of marriage action with the assistance of a trained third party, either court-provided and free or privately engaged and paid.

Collaborative lawyering
A form of dispute resolution designed to bring together the respective parties, their attorneys, and other professionals with the goal of reaching an amicable settlement, thus avoiding costly litigation in family court.

Alternative dispute resolution
A method of resolving disputes between parties without resorting to a trial.

Figure 1-2 With the assistance of a trained mediator, the parties attempt to resolve the issues surrounding the dissolution of their marriage.

Kzenon/Shutterstock

consequences for all concerned of mishandling or insensitively handling the issues underlying the dispute. All staff members of the law office should be aware of the need to handle delicate matters with great care. With the very high divorce rate that exists today, many members of the court system and the attorneys who specialize in family law have become adept at treating all parties with respect and with an understanding of the turmoil that accompanies the breakup of a marriage.

Divorces are much easier to obtain in the new millennium than they were in the 1890s. Most of the stigma attached to divorce has disappeared, and today's communities offer many resources to help divorcing spouses and their children deal with the difficult changes taking place. Community support for families going through this type of crisis is readily available today because of our society's acceptance of divorce. This was not always the case. For many centuries and for a number of decades in the twentieth century, there was enormous pressure from social, cultural, and certain religious institutions to preserve the marital union and nuclear family at almost any cost. We now turn to a historical glimpse of the nature of marriage and divorce over time and the values and attitudes that contributed to past and present views of both marriage and divorce.

THE ROOTS AND TRADITIONS OF AMERICAN FAMILY LAW

Much of American legal tradition has its roots in the common law decisions of England. However, centuries before the creation of the English common law, ancient legal systems developed rules to govern the rights and responsibilities of spouses and other family members. These ancient rules left their mark on later legal systems. In ancient Greece, a married woman was a ***chattel***, the legal property of her husband with no rights of her own. For centuries afterward, marriage was a formal arrangement in society in which women were subservient to men.

Chattel
A tangible, movable piece of personal property.

Although in various cultures, at different points in history, women did possess some legal rights, they generally occupied a legal status that was inferior to that of men. In the United States, it was not until the passage of the Married Women's Property Acts that American women were allowed to own property in their own name. For this and many other equally compelling reasons, women were often reluctant to initiate legal proceedings to end their marriages.

Marriage, for many centuries, was a very strong social institution that contributed to the stability of society. Christianity transformed marriage from a mere social institution into a sacrament, a holy union lasting for eternity—"What God has brought together, let no man put asunder." Marriage was a legally and morally sanctioned relationship between a man and a woman, functioning as one social and economic unit. Spouses were responsible for the care of each other and jointly responsible for the care and maintenance of their children, the issue of their union. However, divorce was not unheard of even in the earliest of times. In ancient times, a form of divorce took place when a woman left her husband or when a husband cast out his wife. In both instances, the husband remained in the family home and retained possession and control of the children of the marriage since they were regarded as chattel, pieces of personal property owned by the husband. In the Christian Western European civilizations of the Middle Ages, church and state were intertwined and the state enforced the doctrines of the Christian church, including the proscription against divorce.

Until the mid-1500s, there was one Christian church for all of Western Europe. This was the Roman Catholic Church with its seat of power vested in the pope in Rome. In the 1530s when King Henry VIII wished to divorce his queen, Catherine of Aragon, and marry Anne Boleyn, the Roman Catholic Church refused to give Henry VIII a dispensation to divorce and remarry. Henry VIII, as the head of the church in England, broke from Rome and established the Church of England. During the second half of the sixteenth century, several different religious groups arose in England, Scotland, Germany, and France, eventually resulting in the establishment of many new Christian sects, separate from the Church of Rome, which became branches of the Protestant movement. Originally, in the European countries where Protestantism prevailed, the church and state continued their close connection and the national religion became the prevailing Protestant denomination in the country. For instance, in Scotland, the established religion was Presbyterianism. In the American colonies settled by the Puritans, such as the Massachusetts Bay Colony, Puritanism became the state religion. In other of the thirteen original American colonies such as Virginia and the Carolinas, which were settled by Englishmen who remained loyal to the established Church of England, the Anglican religion became the official religion of the colony. However, despite the continuing connection of church and state, many of the now largely Protestant European nations and the Protestant colonies in America allowed at least what came to be called civil divorce. On the other hand, in the European countries where Roman Catholicism remained either the state religion or the religion embraced by the majority of inhabitants, civil divorce was much slower in coming. In Italy and the Republic of Ireland, civil divorce was not legally authorized until the second half of the twentieth century!

MARRIAGE, DIVORCE, AND FAMILY LAW FROM COLONIAL AMERICA TO THE TWENTIETH CENTURY

In colonial America, although marriage was regarded as a sacred union, the Puritans who had settled the New England colonies recognized and allowed divorce. They also sanctioned a form of legal separation known as "divorce of bed and board" under which the couple's sacred union remained intact but they no longer cohabited. When a couple divorced or separated, colonial governments imposed on the husband the continuing obligation of economic support of his wife and their children.

When the thirteen original colonies broke away from England and formed a new nation, the state governments assumed the power to legally authorize and legally dissolve marriages. The new American nation provided specifically for the separation of church and state in its Constitution. There was to be no national religion, nor were any of the new states allowed to establish any one religion as the official religion of that state. Henceforth, marriage and divorce as civil matters became separated from marriage and divorce as religious issues. In the eyes of the state, marriage was now viewed as a civil contract between two parties.

Under the marriage contract, each party had obligations to the other party. When one of the parties failed to perform an obligation of the marriage, he or she had breached the marital contract. The nonbreaching party could sue for a termination of the marriage contract and for damages from the other party as compensation for the harm caused by the breach. If the nonbreaching or "innocent" party proved that the marital contract had been breached, the court could terminate the marriage and, under the civil law, both parties were free to remarry. The state, through its court system, could order the offending or breaching party to compensate the other party and enter orders for the continuing support of the minor children of the marriage.

When each state government established either legislative or common law grounds for establishing breach of the marriage contract, these were commonly referred to as the grounds for divorce. When the female spouse alleged and proved grounds for divorce, the court almost always ordered the male spouse to continue to provide financial support to his former wife and his children. In many instances, even when a husband brought and won a divorce action against his wife, if the wife had been financially dependent on her husband for subsistence, the court ordered the husband to continue to provide for her financial support. However, enforcing these obligations was not always possible. Many ex-husbands disappeared from the court's jurisdiction, and many divorced women and their children suffered economic deprivation and frequently social isolation as well. As long as women lacked the ability to support themselves, divorce was not a practical alternative. Societal pressures from many avenues, including the church, the extended family, and the local community, were also exerted to keep the family intact.

Political and economic forces also promoted the advantages of staying married. During the eighteenth century and for a good part of the nineteenth century, the intact family was the basic economic unit of the new American nation. When the United States was mainly an agrarian society, its financial health and political strength depended on the production and sale of agricultural products from thousands of small family farms. All family members were essential to the operation of these farms. Family members, even young children, contributed to the economic advancement of their family and the nation by performing one or more of the many chores needed to keep the farm running.

The Industrial Revolution and the Family

The Industrial Revolution of the nineteenth century gave rise to the factory system in the United States and shifted the centers of economic activity from the country towns to the cities. In the early and middle years of the nineteenth century, many individuals left the family farms in the New England and Middle Atlantic states

Figure 1-3 As time went by, respectable married women were not expected to work but rather to stay home, do housework, and take care of their children.

Everett Collection/Shutterstock

to work in the cities. Throughout the second half of the 1800s, the large influx of immigrants from Europe added to the population of urban centers. Frequently, mothers, fathers, and even young children worked in city factories. Eventually, laws were passed to protect children from working at early ages.

Some women then began to stay at home to care for their children. When this occurred, the husband became the person primarily responsible for the family's financial support. He also usually became the family member with predominant economic power. Men had the ability to obtain credit in their own names, whereas women could only obtain credit under their husband's, father's, or brother's signature. Even married women who continued to work in mills and factories and later in offices and stores had inferior economic power because these women were frequently paid far less than their male counterparts. Single women fared no better in the workplace. In fact, except for low-paying jobs in factories or low-paying positions as domestic servants, there were few employment opportunities for women in nineteenth-century America.

As time went by, "respectable" married women were not expected to work. Even well-educated, married women who, when single, had held positions as school teachers or nursing professionals had few or no opportunities to work for pay. Many school systems prohibited married women from working as teachers; other school systems would not hire women with young children. Hospitals frequently instituted similar exclusionary policies for staff nurses.

As a result of these constraints, married women did not often consider divorce as a solution to a failing or unhappy marriage. Many women feared that they would have no means of supporting themselves or their children. Further, divorce carried a social stigma. Divorced women were not well accepted in many communities. The children of divorced mothers were often excluded from neighborhood play and not welcome in the homes of their friends who came from intact families.

Despite the many negative consequences of divorce for both women and men, and especially for children, the divorce rates rose at a slow but steady pace throughout the nineteenth century and into the early decades of the twentieth century. In the 1880s, one out of sixteen American marriages ended in divorce.

FAMILY LAW FROM THE DAWN OF THE TWENTIETH CENTURY TO THE PRESENT DAY

By 1900, there was one divorce for every twelve marriages. Undoubtedly, industrialization and urbanization played some part in this increase. These social and economic developments decreased the value of the intact family as an economic unit, while providing women a meager increase in opportunities for paid employment outside the home.

When divorce did occur during the first half of the twentieth century, courts usually ordered the husband to make weekly alimony payments and support payments for the maintenance of his former spouse and his children. Mothers were always awarded custody of children unless they were deemed in some way unfit or unless they abandoned the children and did not seek custody. Society continued to frown on divorce. To get a legal divorce, one party had to bring a civil suit and prove one of a limited number of grounds before the court would grant a decree of divorce. Typically, most states granted a divorce if one party proved the other committed adultery, abandoned them, or was a habitual drunkard. Eventually, many states added grounds known as intolerable cruelty and mental cruelty. Even if parties agreed to divorce, one party had to sue the other party alleging one of these grounds. If the other party did not challenge the allegations, the judge would grant a divorce.

By the 1960s, attitudes toward divorce were changing. Many young people no longer feared the severe sanctions imposed by their religious faith. Also, some religious groups took a more compassionate view of couples in a bad marriage. Traditional religious institutions lost much influence over individuals and society in the 1960s when people began to question all aspects of American culture, including women's roles and women's rights, constraints on employment opportunities for women, and constraints on sexual freedom and reproductive choices.

Prior to the 1960s, *fault* played a central role both in the granting of divorce and in the determination of the amounts set for alimony awards and the distribution of marital property. For instance, a spouse who alleged and proved the ground of adultery or habitual drunkenness in a divorce proceeding not only was granted relief in the form of a divorce but also received a larger share of the marital assets, a hefty amount of alimony and child support, and almost always sole custody of the children.

Fault
The responsibility for or cause of wrongdoing or failure; the wrongful conduct responsible for the failure or breakdown of a marriage.

Beginning in the mid-1960s and growing strong in the 1970s, public support emerged for what came to be known as *no-fault divorce*. Beginning in the 1970s, a number of state legislatures modified existing divorce laws to include the ground that the marital union or marital relationship had broken down irretrievably. This ground did not place fault for the breakdown on either party. The spouse seeking the divorce and bringing the legal action had merely to testify under oath that the marriage had broken down irretrievably and that there was no possibility of reconciliation. This change plus the many societal changes mentioned earlier resulted in many more divorces than previously.

No-fault divorce
In order to obtain a divorce, a litigant traditionally had to prove one of the statutory fault grounds or no divorce was granted; in 1969, the California legislature enacted the first no-fault divorce, which required parties only to prove that they had irreconcilable differences and there was no hope of reconciliation; currently, all fifty states have some form of no-fault divorce provisions where one of the parties only has to allege that the marriage has broken down and that there is no hope of reconciliation in order for the court to dissolve a marriage.

In addition, the 1970s witnessed the beginnings of a trend toward awarding custody to fathers even when mothers were not deemed unfit. Many custody battles ensued as mothers' work schedules paralleled fathers' in terms of time spent away from home. The 1970s also saw the advent of joint custody arrangements in which parents shared the child-rearing responsibilities, and children sometimes "commuted" from one parent's household to the other's on a weekly or biweekly basis!

Divorce actions also increased dramatically in segments of the married population where individuals previously never considered severing their marital ties. Older women, frequently with the support of and at the urging of their adult children, sought divorces after decades of troubled marriages. These women demanded a fair share of what they and their husbands had acquired during the marriage. Another development arising from new social conditions dealt with health-care provisions. With the advent of comprehensive health insurance and the skyrocketing costs of health care, courts routinely ordered the noncustodial spouse, often the father, to maintain his minor children and sometimes his former spouse on his health plan—or pay her Consolidated Omnibus Budget Reconciliation Act (COBRA) premium. Women with superior health plans through their employers also sometimes were required to cover their children even if they were not the children's custodial parent. Further, with women making large salaries, men began to seek alimony from former wives and courts began awarding it to them!

The increase in the number of divorces gave rise to an increase in second and third marriages. With this higher rate of divorce and remarriage, prenuptial agreements also increased in both number and complexity. The trend toward easy and frequent divorce continued through the 1980s and 1990s. The mid-1990s saw the beginnings of social and political action to once again make divorces harder to obtain. Initially, it looked as though the laws surrounding the severing of the marital relationship would be on their way to coming full circle by the beginning of the millennium. However, this was not to be the case. So far, the efforts to tighten the granting of marital dissolutions have produced little change. Apparently, no-fault divorce remains the most desirable default option for a marriage that falters and then fails.

FAMILY LAW—YESTERDAY, TODAY, AND TOMORROW

High Divorce Rates

Cohabitation
Unmarried parties living together as if married.

Tremendous changes have taken place in American family law and practice over the last half century. Divorced persons and their children are no longer stigmatized in the eyes of society. The prevailing view is that it is better for all parties involved to get divorced than remain in a bad marriage. Accordingly, the most significant change over the past fifty years has been the high divorce rate, which is currently twice as high as it was in the 1960s. It reached its peak in the 1980s and has been slowly declining. The reason for this decline, however, is related to the fact that marriage, itself, is declining. More couples are choosing **cohabitation** rather than marriage. Many of those who do marry may have a firm commitment to stay married. For the cohabitating couples, it is hard to discern the failure rate of these relationships because they are severed by mutual agreement and not by judicial intervention. However, when cohabitating couples have produced or at least conceived a child prior to ending their cohabitation, courts frequently do become involved. One or both of the unmarried parents may initiate a legal action to determine their respective parental rights and responsibilities. Therefore, even as divorce numbers decline, family courts and family law practitioners continue to be very busy with the issues confronting unmarried parents, not just initially, but throughout the eighteen years of their children's minority.

Most marriages entered into today still have only a forty to fifty percent chance of surviving. If you ask the question, "Why is there such a high divorce rate?" in legal circles, the answer is the shift from fault to no-fault divorce. In order to obtain a divorce, a litigant traditionally had to prove one of the statutory fault grounds, or no divorce was granted. Traditional fault grounds included physical or mental cruelty, adultery, desertion, confinement to a prison or mental institution for a specified period of time, commission of a felony, and intemperance. Because fault grounds were difficult to prove, parties often colluded for the sole purpose of obtaining a divorce. Where the state fault grounds included mental and physical cruelty, mental cruelty was the easiest fault ground to fabricate. The parties understood that in order to get divorced, they had to play by the state's rules, and that a certain amount of lying was necessary if the goal was to dissolve a marriage. In 1969, the California legislature enacted the first no-fault divorce, which required parties only to prove that they had irreconcilable differences and there was no hope of reconciliation. The concept of no-fault divorce spread throughout the entire United States. Currently, all fifty states have some form of no-fault divorce provisions. Statutes vary from jurisdiction to jurisdiction, so it is important for attorneys and paralegals practicing family law to be familiar with their state requirements. New York State, for example, has one of the strictest no-fault statutes in the country. New York law requires a one-year period of separation as well as the filing of a written, notarized separation agreement. If the parties cannot resolve matters amicably, they must file for a divorce under the fault system and allege one of the statutory fault grounds.

Women in the Workplace

Changes have also occurred in the American family with the advent of the women's movement. Prior to this era, fathers financially supported their daughters until the responsibility was passed on to husbands. In a traditional marriage, the husband was the head of the household and worked to support the family. The wife's function was to tend to the needs of the husband, home, and children. She was subordinate to her husband and dependent upon him for fulfilment of all her needs. The women's movement not only raised women's consciousness regarding the elevation of their status in society to that of men, but it also helped open doors for economic opportunity. Many women have pursued the goal of becoming financially independent by working outside the home, with some making more money than their husbands and commanding more status in the workplace. With more opportunities open to women, they are less likely to stay in unhappy marriages because they know they can take care of themselves and their children.

Changes in How Custody Is Decided

The second most significant change occurring in family law in the last fifty years concerns the custody of the minor children. With women working outside the home as many and sometimes more hours than men, granting custody to the children's mother is no longer the firm rule it once was. Courts now apply the "best interests of the child" standard to settling custody disputes. When the father is more available, both physically and emotionally, can provide a more stable home, and is more than willing to become "Mr. Mom," the courts now give Dad and the kids an opportunity to reside together while the mother usually receives liberal visitation, or *access*, as it is newly termed. Frequently, when this occurs, the parents have joint legal custody, with physical custody vested in the father.

Marriage as an Economic Enterprise

With the exception of resolving child custody and visitation issues, modern divorce law requires a shift in focus from proving fault to determining property and debt division; divorces are increasingly becoming financial accountings. For a couple with substantial assets, not only must they have attorneys representing them, but they also must rely on the assistance of accountants, pension valuation experts, appraisers, and other professionals. Those without substantial assets must learn how to live on what they have or work harder and longer to make ends meet. Most jurisdictions rely on the system of equitable distribution to divide property. Under the common law system of the past, judges looked at who actually held title to the property and determined its division in a divorce case based on who owned it. This system was extremely unfair to the traditional homemaker spouse, whose noneconomic contributions were not recognized. Many courts today look at the marital property of the parties, its value, and who has contributed to its acquisition, preservation, appreciation, or depreciation. The concept of equitable distribution assumes that marriage is an *economic partnership*, valuing not only the contributions of the employer spouse but also the efforts of the homemaker spouse.

Changes have also occurred in spousal support awards. Traditionally, wives who were married for over ten years were awarded permanent or lifetime alimony. This was because of the financial position of women. They did not work outside the home and did not acquire Social Security or pension benefits. Without permanent alimony, a woman would become a charge on the taxpayers. The concept of alimony shifted as attitudes toward men, women, and social mores changed. Permanent alimony currently is a dying horse, and it is not awarded to a spouse unless it was a long-term marriage of over twenty years, the spouse suffers from ill health, or the spouse has been out of the workforce for so long that climbing any kind of corporate ladder is not possible. Permanent alimony was replaced by rehabilitative alimony, which afforded the wife alimony in the short term for the purpose of becoming self-sufficient. Additionally, husbands may now ask for alimony from their wives, whereas in the past, this was legally and socially unacceptable.

The reality of divorce, however, is that women usually fare much worse economically after a divorce. Women are most likely to be awarded custody of the children and must pick up the slack when the child support enforcement system fails to provide a solution. The amount of child support awarded was traditionally left up to the discretion of the trial court judge. It wasn't until the early 1990s that federal intervention prompted states to enact standard formulas to determine the amount of child support subject to strict deviation criteria. In 1984, Congress passed the ***Child Support Enforcement Amendments*** to enable mothers to collect child support and ease the social welfare burden on taxpayers. Some of these measures include federal and state income tax refund interception, wage withholding, revocation of professional licenses, and interstate enforcement. Despite these efforts, most women still find the system frustrating.

Relaxed Residency Requirements

Changes in residency requirements in the last half century have also impacted divorce in the United States. Historically, in many jurisdictions, a prospective divorce litigant had to wait either one or two years before a divorce could be filed. The purpose behind these requirements was that the state had to have a vested interest in the marriage before the courts would intervene in the divorce. States wanted to prevent ***migratory divorces***—people flocking to a particular jurisdiction because of the short divorce residency requirements. The trend today is shorter residency requirements, making divorces easier to obtain.

Streamlined and Simplified Divorce Procedures

Another recent trend is the increased number of ***pro se litigants*** dominating the divorce dockets due to the high cost of divorce. Many jurisdictions are creating *pro se* resource centers in courthouses, posting forms and instructions online, and enlisting lawyers from the private bar to take on cases *pro bono* or at reduced rates to alleviate the burden. Paralegals, under lawyer supervision, may also assist in helping prepare documents. Courts are also simplifying and streamlining the process for uncontested divorces and requiring parties involved in contested cases to participate in alternative dispute resolution as opposed to knock-down, drag-out divorce trials. In cases where the parties have little or no assets, no children, were married for a relatively short period of time, and both want the divorce, simplified procedures are being adopted by many jurisdictions. Many states have enacted ***summary dissolution of marriage***. All that is required in these jurisdictions, if you meet the requirements, is the filing of official documents with the appropriate court without the assistance of attorneys. Another form of low-cost divorce enacted by a number of states is a ***simplified divorce procedure***, which is sometimes referred to as summary

Child Support Enforcement Amendments
Federal laws passed to enable mothers to collect child support and ease the social welfare burden on the taxpayers.

Migratory divorces
People flocking to a particular jurisdiction to get divorced because of the short divorce residency requirements.

***Pro se* litigants**
Individuals who represent themselves in legal proceedings; see *pro per*.

Summary dissolution of marriage
Simplified procedures for obtaining a divorce in cases where the parties have little or no assets, have no children, were married for a relatively short period of time, and both want the divorce; all that is required in these jurisdictions, if you meet the requirements, is the filing of official documents with the appropriate court without the assistance of attorneys.

Simplified divorce procedure
A form of low-cost divorce enacted by a number of states that is sometimes referred to as summary process or divorce by mutual consent; the parties in these states must appear before the court to dissolve their marriage.

process or divorce by mutual consent. Unlike the summary dissolution of marriage, the parties in these states must appear before the court to dissolve their marriage. The process, however, is simplified and the courts make user-friendly forms and guidebooks available.

THE "MODERN FAMILY"—THE WAVE OF THE FUTURE?

The past few decades have witnessed various departures from what in the twentieth century had come to be considered the "typical American family," namely, a *nuclear family* consisting of a married couple—mom and dad—and their offspring. Now in the twenty-first century, more couples are choosing to become parents first and marry later—or not. Couples marrying for the second time are creating *blended families* that include the children of each spouse from a previous marriage and, frequently, a child or children the couple have had together. Same-sex couples are openly living together as legally married spouses or as *domestic partners* where the law allows. Many of these couples are parenting children as well. Now, also, more grandparents have become the *primary caretakers* and legal guardians of their children's sons and daughters and are raising these grandchildren.

All of these changes in the nature and structure of the family present issues, actual and potential, some of which have already found their way to family court. If these trends continue, and there is no reason to believe they will not, the substantive body of family law will expand to encompass these new and interesting family forms.

Nuclear family
A term used to refer to the "typical American family," consisting of a mother, father, and their offspring.

Blended families
A term used to refer to couples marrying for the second time where the family comprises children of each spouse from a previous marriage or relationship and children the couple have had together.

Domestic partners
A committed relationship between two persons of the same gender, who reside together and support each other, in a mutually exclusive partnership.

Primary caretaker
The individual who has taken on the main responsibility for the daily care, rearing, and nurturing of a child.

Concept Review and Reinforcement

KEY TERMS

alternative dispute resolution	domestic partners	primary caretaker
blended family	exclusive jurisdiction	*pro se* litigants
chattel	fault	settlement
Child Support Enforcement Amendments	mediation	simplified divorce procedure
cohabitation	migratory divorce	summary dissolution of marriage
collaborative lawyering	no-fault divorces	
	nuclear family	

REVIEW OF KEY CONCEPTS

1. What are some of the changes in American society over the past fifty years that have affected substantive family law?

2. Why is marriage described as an economic partnership?

3. How has the great increase in the number of women in the workforce affected courts' decisions on alimony, child support, and custody?

4. What is meant by the term *pro se* litigant, and in how many different ways can the increase in *pro se* litigants affect a family law practice?

5. How has no-fault divorce affected our society?

BUILDING YOUR PARALEGAL SKILLS

CASE FOR BRIEFING

HOWARD v. LILLIAN, 62 A.D. 3D 187 (1ST DEPT 2009)

Critical Thinking and Legal Analysis Applications

1. You work for a high-powered family law firm in New York City. The firm's client, Mrs. Andrews, wants to bring a dissolution action alleging mental cruelty and adultery. Mr. and Mrs. Andrews have been married for twenty years and have two teenage children. Both Mr. and Mrs. Andrews have worked throughout the marriage at high-powered, high-earning jobs in advertising and public relations. During their marriage, together they have equally contributed to the accumulation of many assets, including a high-priced Manhattan co-op apartment, a country home in upstate New York, condos in Vail and Aruba, and a very large stock portfolio.

   Mrs. Andrews has disclosed that during their marriage Mr. Andrews has had numerous adulterous affairs. He has fathered two children with former mistresses. He has paid large amounts of child support for these children and, in fact, although not obligated to do so, he currently pays private school tuition and summer camp expenses for each child. Mrs. Andrews has suffered enormous emotional distress, anger, and feelings of betrayal because of her husband's blatant adulterous conduct. She also claims that the marital partnership has sustained great financial loss due to the exorbitant amounts Mr. Andrews has paid in child support and "extras" for the children of his adulterous affairs. She wants a divorce settlement that provides her with at least three-fourths of the marital assets and also wants child support for her teenagers that will allow them to live as lavishly as their father's other children. Because she now earns slightly more than her husband, she is not seeking any alimony, but she certainly does not want him to receive alimony from her!

   Your supervising attorney is concerned that under New York law, Mr. Andrews' conduct has not been sufficiently unconscionable to constitute the "egregious fault" that New York law seems to require to justify awarding Mrs. Andrews the bulk of the marital estate. He wants you to review New York case law, especially the recent case *Howard v. Lillian,* to see if his concern is warranted and present your conclusions in a brief interoffice memorandum. You can find this case by using one of the online legal research services the office subscribes to.

   You may also use your favorite search engine, by entering "New York family law cases," and go to one of the many sites that will pop up. When you arrive at your site of choice, select the section entitled "CASE LAW" and either enter the case name: *Howard v. Lillian* or the case site: 62 A.D. 3rd 187 [1st Dept 2009].

Building a Professional Portfolio

PORTFOLIO **EXERCISES**

1. As you begin your portfolio, create a section for Substantive Law, with subsections for Statutory Law and Case Law. Then, either go online or to your local state law library. Find and copy your state's section on statutes relating to family law. Insert these documents into your portfolio notebook. As time goes by, you will add case law from your state on various issues.

2. As you begin your portfolio, also create a section for Procedural Law. Either online or at your state law library, find the "rules of practice" for your state. If there is a separate section for Family Law Procedure, copy that section for insertion into your portfolio.

Part one

INTRODUCTION TO PART ONE: FAMILY LAW

It is essential to have a solid foundation in the principles of family law. The creation of a family through traditional marriage or marriage alternatives gives rise to a host of rights and responsibilities while the relationships are intact and when they are dissolved. The pages that follow identify the basic legal concepts underlying the creation of the family and the obligations imposed upon the adult members during its existence and which endure beyond its demise.

Chapter **two**

MARRIAGE AND MARRIAGE ALTERNATIVES

We live in a time where the traditional views of marriage are facing many challenges. This chapter begins with a look at marriage as we once knew it—a union between one man and one woman—and how a United States Supreme Court decision redefined this institution. The chapter ends with an overview of "marriage alternatives," which present a different approach to relationships outside the traditional bounds of marriage. They may include "civil unions" or "domestic partnerships," created by courts and legislatures as legally sanctioned relationships for same-sex couples, and, in some jurisdictions, opposite-sex couples. We will also learn that many couples in the United States are opting out of legal marriage altogether, choosing to "cohabitate" or live together.

LEARNING OBJECTIVES

After studying this chapter, you should be able to:

1. Understand the different types of marriages and marriage alternatives.

2. Identify the legal benefits of marriage.

3. Understand how to create common law marriage.

4. Explain the legal effect of *Obergefell v. Hodges*.

5. Determine the requirements for creating a valid marriage.

6. Define the legal remedies available to cohabitating couples according to the landmark decision of *Marvin v. Marvin*.

MARRIAGE

Marriage Defined

Marriage
A marriage is defined as the joining together of two adult individuals in a civil contract.

The traditional definition of marriage as we have known it for centuries has been the legal union of one man and one woman. In the United States, a marriage is now defined as the joining together of two adult individuals in a civil contract called *marriage*.

CIVIL AND RELIGIOUS MARRIAGE

The institution of marriage is regulated on a state level, and this status confers state and federal rights and responsibilities on the married couple. Couples who wish to marry may choose either a civil or religious marriage, or both. A *civil marriage*—or a *civil ceremony*, as it is sometimes called—is a legal status created by a state government when a state official, such as a judge or justice of the peace, performs a ceremony joining two single adults who have met the state's statutory qualifications in a marital union. A civil marriage imposes various legal rights and responsibilities on the married couple.

Civil marriage or civil ceremony
A legal status created by a state government when a state official, such as a judge or justice of the peace, performs a ceremony joining two single adults who have met the state's statutory qualifications in a marital union.

Religious marriage
The religious solemnization of the union of two individuals according to the requirements of the particular faith in question.

A *religious marriage* is the religious solemnization of the union of two individuals according to the requirements of the particular faith in question. State statutes allow ministers, priests, rabbis, and other members of the clergy who perform the religious marriage to execute and file a couple's marriage license, thus satisfying the state's civil marriage requirements by making the marriage legal in the eyes of the law.

In addition to its role as a social and religious institution, marriage affords the couple important rights in the eyes of the law. The legal benefits of marriage include:

- Elective share protection
- Estate and gift tax exemptions benefits
- Family court jurisdiction for dissolving marital relationship and obtaining orders in the area of alimony, property and debt division, child custody, visitation, and child support
- Family leave
- The ability to file joint income tax returns for state and federal tax purposes
- Guardianship rights
- Hospital visitation rights
- Immigration benefits
- Insurance benefits
- Intestate succession protection
- Joint adoptions
- Military benefits
- Appointment as conservator for a disabled spouse
- Decision-making power for an incapacitated spouse
- Retirement benefits
- Spousal or marital communications privilege in court proceedings
- Loss of consortium claims in personal injury suits
- Right to file wrongful death lawsuits
- Possession of deceased spouse's remains at death
- Social Security, Medicare, and disability benefits
- Spousal or widow's allowance
- Stepparent adoptions
- Veterans' benefits
- Workers' compensation benefits

Figure 2-1 A religious marriage is the religious solemnization of the union of two individuals according to the requirements of the particular faith in question.

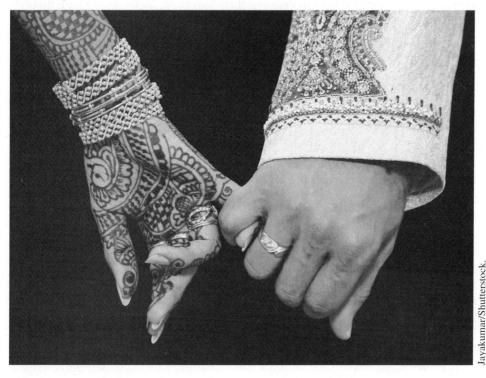

Jayakumar/Shutterstock.

COVENANT MARRIAGE

Covenant marriage is a response to the rising divorce rate in the United States as a result of the change from fault to no-fault divorce. In addition, the U.S. Census of 2000 reveals that many couples are avoiding marriage and opting to cohabitate instead. Our society has also accepted divorce as another adult passage. Many go into marriage with the feeling that if it doesn't work out, divorce is always an option. Social stigma is no longer attached to divorce. Some feel that opposite-sex marriages are too easy to get into and too easy to terminate. Covenant marriage is an alternative type of marriage that can be summarized as requiring premarital counseling, a return to fault-based grounds in order to dissolve the marriage, counseling before going through divorce, adherence to a covenant contract, and a longer mandatory waiting period. This type of marriage is supported by religious groups who view marriage as a covenant between God and the spouses.

The end result is to reduce the divorce rate and make marriages harder to dissolve. People will be discouraged from going into marriage too quickly and divorcing too quickly. Covenant marriage is intended to reinforce the commitment to marriage. Three states have covenant marriage as an option. Louisiana was the first to enact covenant marriage in 1997, followed by Arizona in 1998 and Arkansas in 2001. Covenant marriage has not "caught on" and has not become popular even in the jurisdictions that enacted it.

Covenant marriage
An alternative type of marriage that can be summarized as requiring premarital counseling, a return to fault-based grounds in order to dissolve the marriage, counseling before going through divorce, the signing of a covenant contract, and longer mandatory waiting periods.

Louisiana Covenant Marriage Act

Under Louisiana's covenant marriage law, the couple must sign a statement of intent, recite a declaration, and provide proof of participation in a premarital course. In the event the parties wish to dissolve their marriage, they can obtain a divorce by proving the fault grounds of adultery, imprisonment for a felony, abandoning the marital home for a period of at least one year, or physically or sexually abusing a family member. If such fault grounds are not available, the parties may be divorced if they have lived separately and apart for a specified period of time. There is a provision in the law that allows couples who are already married to convert to a covenant marriage.

> **DECLARATION, LOUISIANA CIVIL CODE ANNOTATED; TITLE V, ARTICLE 103 AND LOUISIANA REVISED STATUTES, SECTION 9–308**
>
> We do solemnly declare that marriage is a covenant between a man and a woman who agree to live together as husband and wife for so long as they both may live. We have chosen each other carefully and disclosed to one another everything which could adversely affect the decision to enter into this marriage. We have received premarital counseling on the nature, purposes, and responsibilities of marriage. We have read the Covenant Marriage Act, and we understand that a Covenant Marriage is for life. If we experience martial difficulties, we commit ourselves to take all reasonable efforts to preserve our marriage, including marital counseling.
>
> With full knowledge of what this commitment means, we do hereby declare that our marriage will be bound by Louisiana law on Covenant Marriages and we promise to love, honor, and care for one another as husband and wife for the rest of our lives.[1]

COMMON LAW MARRIAGE

By the end of the nineteenth century, the institution known as common law marriage was recognized in most states in the United States as a legal form of marriage that carried with it all of the rights and obligations of a ceremonial and statutorily memorialized union. Common law marriages were numerous in frontier states and in rural areas where the parties were often geographically distant from the county or municipal offices that issued marriage licenses. However, common law marriages also existed in urban areas. Today, many states have statutorily abolished common law marriage. Legal proceedings that affect common law marriages are becoming increasingly rare because very few states permit or recognize the formation of a common law marriage within their boundaries. However, states that do recognize common law marriages do adjudicate their dissolution. In addition, some states do not recognize the formation of a common law marriage within the state, but will recognize as legally valid a common law marriage formed in a state where common law marriage is legal. In these states, the courts will adjudicate the dissolution of these marriages as long as other jurisdictional requirements have been met.

---

[1]§273. Covenant Marriage; Contents of Declaration of Intent, Louisiana State Legislature.

Figure 2-2 Requirements vary from state to state, but creating a common law marriage requires more than living with someone.

Merzzie/Shutterstock.

What Is a Common Law Marriage?

A *common law marriage* is a marriage created without a license or ceremony. According to popular myth, simply living with a member of the opposite gender for a period of time creates this form of marriage. Requirements vary from state to state, but creating a common law marriage requires more than living with someone.

In general, the requirements for a valid common law marriage are as follows:

Common law marriage
A marriage created without a license or ceremony.

- The parties must live together for a significant period of time.
- There must be a "holding out" as husband and wife. This means that they refer to each other as "my wife" and "my husband," hold assets in joint name, file tax returns together, and so on. In many common law marriages, the female may also adopt the usage of her common law husband's surname. For a "holding out" to exist, the couple's actions and representations must give the general public the impression that they are married.
- The parties intend to be married.

States That Recognize Common Law Marriage

Alabama, Colorado, District of Columbia, Iowa, Kansas, Montana, Oklahoma, Rhode Island, South Carolina, Texas, and Utah all recognize common law marriage. New Hampshire recognizes common law marriage for inheritance purposes only. Georgia, Idaho, Ohio, and Pennsylvania recognize common law marriages created before certain dates in an effort to phase them out over time.

Love Hurts It sure does, especially when you're trying to claim that a common law marriage exists between you and one of the stars of *The Big Chill* and *Syriana.*

SANDRA JENNINGS v. WILLIAM M. HURT

160 A.D.2D 576, 554 N.Y.S.2D 220 (1990)
APPELLATE DIVISION OF THE SUPREME COURT OF NEW YORK, FIRST DEPARTMENT

SILBERMANN, J

In her amended complaint, plaintiff alleged that she and defendant had entered into a common-law marriage by virtue of having held themselves out as husband and wife in South Carolina from October 31, 1982, to January 10, 1983. After meeting in 1981, the parties began living together in New York City. On October 31, 1982, plaintiff joined defendant in South Carolina where he was filming a movie. When plaintiff became pregnant in 1982, defendant, who was married to another woman, commenced divorce proceedings with the divorce becoming final on December 3, 1982. During that same year, defendant's counsel drafted a financial agreement for the parties. The relationship between the parties in South Carolina became somewhat volatile but plaintiff alleged that during one of their arguments, defendant told her that "as far as he was concerned, we were married in the eyes of God" and that they had "a spiritual marriage." He also purportedly told her that "[w]e were more married than married people." Plaintiff's claim that she is defendant's common-law wife is based on these events. Defendant's testimony directly contradicted that of plaintiff.

The record fails to support plaintiff's claim that she is defendant's common law wife. Notably, plaintiff never mentioned the conversation regarding the "spiritual marriage" at her deposition. The record also reveals that a statement in which plaintiff allegedly signed her name as "Sandra Cronsberg Hurt" was an altered copy in which the name "Hurt" had been inserted.

In 1983, defendant filed an affidavit with the Putative Fathers' Registry in New York which acknowledged his paternity of plaintiff's child. Filing this document, designed to ensure the child's legitimacy, would have been unnecessary had the parties in fact been married. Moreover, in 1984, one year after the parties left South Carolina, drafts of a relationship agreement continued to state "whether or not the parties hereafter marry each other." Other documents introduced into evidence listed defendant as single and plaintiff as his "friend" rather than his spouse. Of the many witnesses who testified and of the numerous affidavits offered into evidence, almost all demonstrated that the parties never held themselves out as being married nor were they perceived as husband and wife.

To establish a common-law marriage in South Carolina, the proponent must establish "an intention on the part of both parties to enter into a marriage contract" (*Ex Parte Blizzard*, 185 S.C. 131, 133, 193. S.E. 633, 635). The mutual agreement necessary to create such a marriage "must be conveyed with such a demonstration of intent and with such clarity on the part of the parties that marriage does not creep up on either of them and catch them unawares. One cannot be married unwittingly or accidentally" (Collier v. City of Milford, 206 Conn. 242, 251, 537 A.2d 474, 479). The evidence in the instant case clearly demonstrates that there was neither a mutual intent nor an agreement to enter into a marriage contract. Consequently, there was no common-law marriage.

We further find that the Supreme Court properly denied plaintiff's motion for leave to amend her complaint to allege three new causes of action since these causes of action were insufficient as a matter of law (see, East Asiatic Co. v. Corash, 34 A.D.2d 432). The first proposed cause of action, to impose a constructive trust on an apartment owned by defendant, cannot stand since plaintiff failed to establish that she had a property interest in the apartment. Nor did she establish all of the necessary elements for a constructive trust (see, Onorato v. Lupoli, 135 A.D.2d 693).

The second proposed cause of action, relating to defendant's alleged breach of a promise to support plaintiff in the future, is too vague to sufficiently state a cause of action (see, Dombrowski v. Somers, 41 N.Y.2d 858). Moreover, while plaintiff claims that this cause of action sounds in fraud, it arose directly from the breach of contract and is therefore a contract claim instead of a cause of action in fraud (Marks v. Nassau County Assn. for Help of Retarded Children, 135 A.D.2d 512). The third proposed cause of action, that defendant falsely promised to support plaintiff if she would have his child and give up her career, is void as against public policy (see, McCall v. Frampton, 81 A.D.2d 607). The law does not recognize a cause of action for sacrificing career opportunities in order to act as a "wife" (see, Baron v. Jeffer, 98 A.D.2d 810). Concur—Sullivan, J.P., Carro, Milonas, Rosenberger and Smith, J.J.

Source: Sandra Jennings v. William M. Hurt, 160 A.D.2D 576, 554 N.Y.S.2D 220 (1990), Appellate Division of the Supreme Court of New York, First Department, New York State Unified Court System.

Why Choose Common Law Marriage?

People may opt for a common law marriage for these reasons:

- **Convenience.** In the nineteenth century, while the frontier was being settled, parties pledged themselves to each other without benefit of clergy or state officials because they were miles away from either religious or governmental institutions.
- **Personal preference.** Some couples opposed and wished to avoid intrusion by either church or state. For instance, in the early decades of the twentieth century, many free-spirited individuals known as *Bohemians* lived in the Greenwich Village section of New York and scorned the legal and religious trappings of conventional society as bourgeois and artificial. Their common law marriages were often political or societal statements. Some Bohemians went even further with their protests and embraced living together instead of any legally binding arrangement.
- **Poverty.** Some couples simply had no money for a church wedding or for an official ceremony and the attendant costs of a marriage license and blood tests.

SAME-SEX MARRIAGE

Same-Sex Marriage in the United States

The sexual revolution brought about many social changes, one of which has been in the area of same-sex marriage. Recent headlines chronicle the successful efforts of the LGBT community for not only social acceptance and equal rights but also the right to enter into marital relationships. Despite these victories and the legal protections that ensued, many still wish to preserve the traditional definition of marriage—a union between one man and one woman.

The Legal Battle for Recognition of Same-Sex Marriage

Marriage is considered a fundamental right in our system of jurisprudence. For many years, same-sex marriage advocates argued that denying same-sex couples the right to marry on the basis of gender violated the Fourteenth Amendment and Establishment Clause of the U.S. Constitution because the state was establishing a religion (i.e., the prohibition reflects Judeo-Christian biblical views against homosexual conduct). Courts in the past rejected this argument, ruling that a legitimate

Figure 2-3 The United States Supreme Court decision of *Obergefell v. Hodges* established the nationwide right to marry for same-sex couples.

Govicinity/Shutterstock

governmental interest is served by prohibiting marriages between members of the same sex. Many courts held that states should sanction only marriages that are capable of procreating—reproducing children. A classification resulting in the denial of a fundamental right may only be upheld where it is necessary to accomplish a compelling state interest, and achieving that goal cannot be done by less restrictive means.

In 1967, the U.S. Supreme Court struck down a Virginia statute that prohibited interracial marriages. This statute and similar legislation were known as miscegenation laws and were enforced in many states. The Virginia statute at the time read as follows:

> All marriages between a white person and a colored person shall be absolutely void without any decree of divorce or other legal process. (Virginia Code Ann. 750–57)

In *Loving v. Virginia,* 388 U.S. 1 (1967), the Supreme Court held that marriage is a fundamental right that cannot be restricted by states unless there is a compelling state interest. Until recently, courts rejected the application of this holding when deciding the legality of same-sex marriage and routinely upheld laws passed by state legislatures that prohibited same-sex marriage.

Defense of Marriage Act

Defense of Marriage Act (DOMA)

A federal law passed in response to attempts on the part of gay-rights activists to require states to recognize same-sex marriages; DOMA defines marriage for federal purposes.

In May 1996, the U.S. Congress enacted the *Defense of Marriage Act (DOMA)*. The act protected the traditional definition of marriage as a union between a man and a woman in the U.S. Code and barred same-sex couples from enjoying federal benefits, regardless of how their states redefined marriage, either through statute or judicial act. Marriage was referenced in many federal laws such as tax, bankruptcy, immigration, Social Security, and military justice statutes. DOMA also ensured that states would not be forced to recognize same-sex marriages performed in other states that sanctioned such unions.

DEFENSE OF MARRIAGE ACT, 28 U.S.C. SECTION 1738C (1996)

SEC. 2. POWERS RESERVED TO THE STATES.

(a) IN GENERAL—Chapter 115 of title 28 United States Code, is amended by adding after section 1738B the following:

"Sec. 1738C. Certain acts, records, and proceedings and the effect thereof

No State, territory, or possession of the United States, or Indian tribe, shall be required to give effect to any public act, record, or judicial proceeding of any other State, territory, possession, or tribe respecting a relationship between person of the same sex that is treated as a marriage under the laws of such other State, territory, possession, or tribe, or a right or claim arising from such relationship."[2]

SEC. 3. DEFINITION OF MARRIAGE

IN GENERAL—Chapter 1 of Title 1, United States Code, is amended by adding at the end the following:

"Sec. 7. Definition of 'marriage' and 'spouse'
In determining the meaning of any Act of Congress, or of any ruling, regulation, or interpretation of the various administrative bureaus and agencies of the United States, the word 'marriage' means only a legal union between one man and one woman as husband and wife, and the word 'spouse' refers only to a person of the opposite sex who is a husband or a wife."[3]

Another tactic used by advocates of same-sex marriage was to attack bans based on the states' Equal Rights Amendments (ERAs). In the case of *Baehr v. Miike* (formerly *Baehr v. Lewin*), 74 Haw. 530, 852 P.2d 44 (1993), Hawaii was the first state in the country in which a court of law was asked to determine if same-sex couples had the right to a legally recognized marriage. In December 1990, several same-sex couples applied for marriage licenses and were denied. The couples filed a lawsuit against the Hawaii State Department of Health contending that the marriage statute was unconstitutional because it prohibited same-sex couples from obtaining marriage licenses on the basis of sex and sexual orientation. In October 1991, the plaintiffs' complaint was dismissed by the trial court on the grounds of failure to state a claim on which relief could be granted. The plaintiffs appealed this decision to the Supreme Court of Hawaii. On May 1, 1993, Hawaii's highest court stunned the nation when it reversed the trial court's ruling and remanded the case for a new trial. The court held that restrictions on same-sex marriages may violate the Equal Protection Clause of Hawaii's state constitution because they prohibit same-sex couples from obtaining a marriage license on the basis of gender. Couples were entitled to protection under the state's ERA and could not be denied a marriage license based on compelling state interests. This would require the legal test of strict scrutiny.

On remand, it was up to the Hawaii state attorney general to prove a compelling state interest—that the state of Hawaii was justified in its restrictions. The state's position was that marriage is for the procreation and rearing of children by heterosexuals only. It is in the children's best interest to be raised by their biological parents, and states have interests in promoting the development of children.

---

[2]28 USC Sec. 1738C—Certain Acts, Records, and Proceedings and the Effect Thereof, Office of the Law Revision Counsel.

[3]Title 1—General Provisions, Chapter 1—Rules of Construction, Section 7—Definition of Marriage and Spouse, Office of the Law Revision Counsel.

The plaintiffs presented expert testimony that confirmed that children of gay parents are no different developmentally than children raised by heterosexual couples. In addition, the plaintiffs argued that the state's argument is flawed because the state places children in foster care and because many children are raised in single-parent homes.

While the *Baehr* case progressed through the Hawaiian court system, the Hawaii legislature in 1994 reacted to the decision by amending its marriage statute to expressly state that marriage is between a man and a woman.

In December 1996, the trial court ruled in favor of the plaintiffs and issued an injunction ordering the state to issue marriage licenses to the same-sex couples. The next day, the state filed a motion to stay the injunctions until the state had the opportunity to appeal the case. The motion was granted, and no licenses were issued to the plaintiffs.

In April 1997, the Hawaii legislature closed this issue by passing a constitutional amendment stating that the legislature could limit marriage to a man and a woman.

Baehr sent shockwaves throughout the country. In response, many jurisdictions amended their marriage statutes, defining marriage as a union between a man and a woman. States feared that if Hawaii legalized gay marriage, same-sex partners would go to Hawaii, get married, and then return to their state of domicile and demand that their marriage be recognized under the full faith and credit clause of the U.S. Constitution. The full faith and credit clause states that states must honor the public acts, records, and judicial proceedings of every other state (U.S. Const. Art. IV, § 1). If a heterosexual couple marries in Hawaii, then moves to Ohio, the state of Ohio must legally recognize the marriage.

In addition to passage of DOMA, other federal efforts included a proposed amendment to the U.S. Constitution that would ban same-sex marriage. Attempts to pass the Federal Marriage Amendment in 2005 were unsuccessful. The proposed act read as follows:

> Marriage in the United States of America shall consist only of the union of a man and a woman.
>
> Neither this constitution or the constitution of any state, nor state or federal law, shall be construed to require that marital status or the legal incidents thereof be conferred upon unmarried couples or groups.

Most states banned same-sex marriage by enactment of either state statute or state constitutional amendments. In addition, most states refused to recognize same-sex marriages legally created in other jurisdictions by either state statute or constitutional amendment.

In 2003, the Massachusetts Supreme Court held in *Goodridge v. Department of Public Health*, 440 Mass. 309 (2003) that a state law barring same-sex marriage was unconstitutional under the Massachusetts constitution and that same-sex couples should have the right to enter into a civil marriage. The court reasoned that a civil union relegates same-sex couples to a different status, opposing the concept of "separate but equal," making Massachusetts the first jurisdiction in the United States to legalize same-sex marriage.

Numerous court challenges and legislative actions over the years were responsible for turning the tide in the United States in favor of same-sex marriage. In October of 2012, the Second U.S. Circuit Court of Appeals held that the Defense of Marriage Act violated the U.S. Constitution's Equal Protection Clause, ruling in favor of a widow named Edith Windsor, an eighty-three-year-old lesbian who sued the federal government for charging her more than $363,000 in estate taxes after being denied the benefit of spousal deductions. Edith Windsor appealed her case all the way to the U.S. Supreme Court, and on June 26, 2013, the Defense of Marriage Act was struck down in *U.S. v. Windsor,* 133 S.Ct. 2675, 570 *U.S.*

_____ (2013) on the grounds that the federal government could not discriminate against same-sex couples when determining federal protections and benefits. The *Windsor* decision however, did not resolve the issue of state recognition of same-sex marriages. If a same-sex couple married in a state where gay marriage was legalized and then moved to a state that did not recognize such unions, the couple was deemed unmarried in the eyes of that state's law.

UNITED STATES v. WINDSOR

In this case, the U.S. Supreme Court determined the constitutionality of DOMA and its application to federal estate tax law. If one spouse dies, the surviving spouse's estate passes to the surviving spouse free from federal taxes. This federal tax benefit, however, was only available to married heterosexual couples because DOMA defined marriage as the union of one man and one woman. As a result, Edith Windsor, the surviving spouse of a same-sex marriage recognized in New York, had to pay the sum of $363,053 in federal estate taxes.

Windsor sued in federal district court, where she argued that DOMA's treatment of legally married couples violates equal protection guarantees in the Fifth Amendment's Due Process Clause. The Department of Justice refused to defend the U.S. government in this case on the grounds that the Obama administration found DOMA to be unconstitutional. DOMA was defended by the Bipartisan Legal Advisory Group of the United States House of Representatives. The court agreed, ruling on behalf of Windsor and awarding her a refund. The Second Circuit Court of Appeals affirmed the district court's decision in favor of Windsor.

The case was appealed to the U.S. Supreme Court, and oral arguments were heard on March 27, 2013. On June 26, 2013, in a much anticipated decision, the U.S. Supreme Court, in a 5–4 decision, ruled that the Defense of Marriage Act is unconstitutional. The Court struck down the provision in DOMA that restricted the definition of marriage for federal purposes to a union between one man and one woman. Justice Anthony Kennedy (retired) wrote:

"The federal statute is invalid, for no legitimate purpose overcomes the purpose and effect to disparage and to injure those whom the state, by its marriage laws, sought to protect in personhood and dignity."

The Court held that this provision violates the U.S. Constitution's guarantee of the right to due process and equal protection under the law. The effect of this decision is that same-sex couples who are married in states that have legalized same-sex marriage are now entitled to the same federal benefits and burdens as married heterosexual couples. So for Edith Windsor, she will now be entitled to the federal estate tax deduction, the denial of which sparked this entire case. The Court's decision, however, did not affect the provision of DOMA that allows individual states not to recognize same-sex marriages created in another jurisdiction. Bans on same-sex marriage in states that have imposed them still remain intact. Same-sex couples moving out of states that formerly recognized their marriages have to proceed with caution and good legal advice regarding the applicability of the law in their new home state.

Source: United States V. Windsor, Executor Of The Estate Of Spyer, et Al., 133 S.Ct. 2675, 570 U.S, 2013.

In 2015, the U.S. Supreme Court delivered the final blow in a long-fought battle for marriage rights in the case of ***Obergefell v. Hodges***, 135 S. Ct. 2584, 576 U.S. ____ (2015). By the time the decision was handed down in this case, thirty-six states and the District of Columbia had already legalized gay marriage. In a historic 5–4 landmark decision, the Court finally resolved the issue of same-sex marriage by holding that state bans on same-sex marriage or refusals to recognize same-sex marriages legally recognized in other jurisdictions violated the Equal Protection Clause and Due Process Clause of the Fourteenth Amendment.

OBERGEFELL et al. v. HODGES, DIRECTOR, OHIO DEPARTMENT OF HEALTH, et al.

...Michigan, Kentucky, Ohio, and Tennessee define marriage as a union between one man and one woman. The petitioners, fourteen same-sex couples and two men whose same-sex partners are deceased, filed suits in Federal District Courts in their home states, claiming that respondent state officials violate the Fourteenth Amendment by denying them the right to marry or to have marriages lawfully performed in another state given full recognition...

...The history of marriage as a union between two persons of the opposite sex marks the beginning of these cases. To the respondents, it would demean a timeless institution if marriage were extended to same-sex couples. But the petitioners, far from seeking to devalue marriage, seek it for themselves because of their respect— and need—for its privileges and responsibilities, as illustrated by the petitioners' own experiences....

...Well into the twentieth century, many states condemned same-sex intimacy as immoral, and homosexuality was treated as an illness. Later in the century, cultural and political developments allowed same-sex couples to lead more open and public lives. Extensive public and private dialogue followed, along with shifts in public attitudes. Questions about the legal treatment of gays and lesbians soon reached the courts, where they could be discussed in the formal discourse of the law. In 2003, this Court overruled its 1986 decision in *Bowers* v. *Hardwick*, 478 U. S. 186, which upheld a Georgia law that criminalized certain homosexual acts, concluding laws making same-sex intimacy a crime "demea[n] the lives of homosexual persons." *Lawrence* v. *Texas*, 539 U. S. 558. In 2012, the federal Defense of Marriage Act was also struck down. *United States* v. *Windsor*, 570 U. S. ____. Numerous same-sex marriage cases reaching the federal courts and state supreme courts have added to the dialogue.

...The Fourteenth Amendment requires a State to license a marriage between two people of the same sex...

...The fundamental liberties protected by the Fourteenth Amendment's Due Process Clause extend to certain personal choices central to individual dignity and autonomy, including intimate choices defining personal identity and beliefs. See, for example, *Eisenstadt* v. *Baird*, 405 U. S. 438; *Griswold* v. *Connecticut*, 381 U. S. 479–486...

...Four principles and traditions demonstrate that the reasons marriage is fundamental under the Constitution apply with equal force to same-sex couples. The first premise of this Court's relevant precedents is that the right to personal choice regarding marriage is inherent in the concept of individual autonomy. This abiding connection between marriage and liberty is why *Loving* invalidated interracial marriage bans under the Due Process Clause. See 388 U. S., at 12. Decisions about marriage are among the most intimate that an individual can make. See *Lawrence, supra,* at 574. This is true for all persons, whatever their sexual orientation.

A second principle in this Court's jurisprudence is that the right to marry is fundamental because it supports a two-person union unlike any other in its importance to the committed individuals. The intimate association protected by this right was central to *Griswold* v. *Connecticut*, which held the Constitution protects the right of married couples to use contraception, 381 U. S., at 485, and was acknowledged in *Turner, supra,* at 95. Same-sex couples have the same right as opposite-sex couples to enjoy intimate association, a right extending beyond mere freedom from laws making same-sex intimacy a criminal offense. See *Lawrence, supra,* at 567.

A third basis for protecting the right to marry is that it safeguards children and families and thus draws meaning from related rights of childrearing, procreation, and education. See, for example, *Pierce* v. *Society of Sisters*, 268 U. S. 510. Without the recognition, stability, and predictability marriage offers, children suffer the stigma of knowing their families are somehow lesser. They also suffer the significant material costs of being raised by unmarried parents, relegated to a more difficult and uncertain family life. The marriage laws at issue thus harm and humiliate the children of same-sex couples. See *Windsor, supra,* at _____. This does not mean that the right to marry is less meaningful for those who do not or cannot have children. Precedent protects the right of a married couple not to procreate, so the right to marry cannot be conditioned on the capacity or commitment to procreate.

Finally, this Court's cases and the Nation's traditions make clear that marriage is a keystone of the Nation's social order. See *Maynard* v. *Hill,* 125 U. S. 190. States have contributed to the fundamental character of marriage by placing it at the center of many facets of the legal and social order. There is no difference between same- and opposite-sex couples with respect to this principle, yet same-sex couples are denied the constellation of benefits that the States have linked to marriage and are consigned to an instability many opposite-sex couples would find intolerable. It is demeaning to lock same-sex couples out of a central institution of the Nation's society, for they, too, may aspire to the transcendent purposes of marriage.

The limitation of marriage to opposite-sex couples may long have seemed natural and just, but its inconsistency with the central meaning of the fundamental right to marry is now manifest...

...The right to marry is a fundamental right inherent in the liberty of the person, and under the Due Process and Equal Protection Clauses of the Fourteenth Amendment couples of the same sex may not be deprived of that right and that liberty. Same-sex couples may exercise the fundamental right to marry. *Baker* v. *Nelson* is overruled. The state laws challenged by the petitioners in these cases are held invalid to the extent they exclude same-sex couples from civil marriage on the same terms and conditions as opposite-sex couples....

Reversed.

Source: Obergefell v. Hodges, 135 S.Ct. 2584 (2015).

Creating a Valid Marriage

In order to create a valid marriage, a couple must comply with the laws of their jurisdiction. Barring some variations, most jurisdictions impose the following requirements:

Age Requirement: Anyone who has reached the age of majority in their state, usually age eighteen, may marry without the consent of their parents. If one or both of the individuals seeking to marry are under the age of eighteen, state law may require parental consent or ***emancipation*** by a court. Youths may be emancipated by operation of law, that is, on their birthday, by reaching the age of majority or by court order at a younger age, usually age sixteen or seventeen. Emancipation by court order is where a judge declares a minor an adult in the eyes of the law.

Emancipation

Acquiring adult status; a youth may be emancipated by operation of law—that is, on his or her birthday by reaching the age of majority or by court order at a younger age.

Blood Test Requirement: Most states, except for Indiana and Montana, have repealed mandatory blood tests for couples planning to marry. The original purpose for premarital blood testing was to screen for syphilis, rubella, and genetic disorders such as sickle-cell anemia or Tay-Sachs disease. In October of 2003, the State of Connecticut repealed premarital blood tests on the advice of the Centers for Disease Control and Prevention. Testifying in support of the repeal, Norma Gayle, Connecticut's Department of Public Health commissioner, said that premarital blood tests are expensive, inconvenient, and have little impact on prevention.

Marriage License Requirement: To get married, many state laws require both parties to personally appear before the county clerk in the county in which the wedding will take place, fill out and sign an application, and

Marriage license
A document issued by the county clerk that authorizes a couple to get married.

Marriage certificate
A document prepared by the official performing the marriage; most jurisdictions require the bride and groom, the person officiating the marriage, and one or two witnesses to sign the marriage certificate after the completion of the ceremony; in some jurisdictions, the marriage certificate is filed with the clerk upon completion of the marriage and in others it is incorporated into the marriage license.

pay a nominal fee. The prospective bride and groom swear under oath on issues regarding age, prior marriages, and the legal relationship between the spouses, if any. The clerk then issues a *marriage license*. A marriage license is a document issued by the county clerk that authorizes a couple to get married. It is important to differentiate between a marriage license and a *marriage certificate*. While a marriage license is a legal document issued by the clerk that will eventually be filed with the state once the marriage is performed, the marriage certificate is a document prepared by the official performing the marriage. Most jurisdictions require the bride and groom, the person officiating the marriage, and one or two witnesses to sign the marriage certificate after the completion of the ceremony. In some jurisdictions, the marriage certificate is filed with the clerk upon completion of the marriage, and in others it is incorporated into the marriage license. All states now require the parties to disclose their respective Social Security numbers so that in the event of divorce they may be located for child-support enforcement purposes.

Solemnization Requirement: The marriage must be solemnized by a person authorized under state law. Clergy and justices of the peace generally carry out this function in most jurisdictions.

Connecticut General Statutes Sec. 46b-22

(a) All judges and retired judges, either elected or appointed and including federal judges and judges of other states who may legally join persons in marriage in their jurisdictions, family support magistrates, state referees, and justices of the peace may join persons in marriage in any town in the state and all ordained or licensed clergymen, belonging to this state or any other state, so long as they continue in the work of the ministry may join persons in marriage. All marriages solemnized according to the forms and usages of any religious denomination in this state, including marriages witnessed by a duly constituted Spiritual Assembly of the Baha'is, are valid. All marriages attempted to be celebrated by any other person are void.[4]

Recording Requirement: The person officiating the wedding ceremony has the responsibility of recording the marriage license and the marriage certificate with the county clerk within a specific statutory period. The couple may then obtain an official copy of the marriage license from the appropriate state agency.

Marriages Performed Abroad

Most jurisdictions recognize marriages created in other states or foreign countries as long as the marriage was validly created in the state or country of origin and does not violate the public policy of the state. Same-sex marriages created in foreign countries where such unions are valid will probably not be recognized given the effect of DOMA.

No Steps, No Marriage In *Singh v. Singh,* Mrs. Singh's refusal to take the traditional seven steps called the "saptapadi" invalidated her marriage under India's Hindu Marriage Act of 1955 and New York law as well. The *Singh* case illustrates that the validity of foreign marriages will be considered and enforced even if the married couple seeks a divorce in the United States.

---

[4]Sec. 46b-22. Who may join persons in marriage. Penalty for unauthorized performance, Connecticut General Assembly.

VIJAI P. SINGH v. VIMLA SINGH

67 MISC.2D 878, 325 N.Y.S.2D 590 (1971)
SUPREME COURT, SPECIAL TERM, TOMPKINS COUNTY

FREDERICK B. BRYANT, J.

This is an action brought by the plaintiff to have his purported marriage to the defendant declared null and void pursuant to section 5 of the Hindu Marriage Act (Act. No. 25 of the Laws of India, 1955).

The complaint alleges that the purported marriage took place in Allahabad, India, on January 19, 1964, when both parties were residents of India. The plaintiff asserts that he is now and has been for more than two years prior to the commencement of this action a resident of the State of New York. The complaint and the evidence submitted show that the marriage was arranged by the respective parents of the plaintiff and the defendant without the consent of either of the parties and that certain ceremonies and rites customary and essential in marriages performed according to the Hindu Marriage Act were not observed. The plaintiff asserts that because of this the purported marriage was a nullity. These ceremonies include the invocation before the sacred fire and the "saptapadi"—that is, the taking of seven steps by the bride and bridegroom before the sacred fire. The plaintiff alleges that the defendant refused to participate in these two rites and that the purported marriage was never consummated. The parties have never lived together as husband and wife.

Service of the summons in the action by personal service upon the defendant in India is shown by affidavit in accordance with Section 232 Dom. Rel. of the Domestic Relations Law. The plaintiff appeared and testified before the court together with a cooperating witness and the proof required by Section 144 Dom. Rel. of the Domestic Relations Law has been completed. The defendant has not appeared in the action nor answered the complaint. The court finds that it has jurisdiction of the subject matter of the action by reason of the plaintiff's uncontested allegation of residence in the State required by subdivision 5 of section 230 Dom. Rel. of the Domestic Relations Law.

Section 7 of the Hindu Marriage Act of 1955 reads as follows:

"Ceremonies for a Hindu marriage: (1) A Hindu marriage may be solemnized in accordance with the customary rites and ceremonies of either party thereto."
"(2) Where such rites and ceremonies include the Saptapadi (that is, the taking of seven steps by the bridegroom and the bride jointly before the sacred fire), the marriage becomes complete and binding when the seventh step is taken."

The meaning and effect of the quoted section is the principal question before this court. Plainly, where the customary ceremonies of either party to the marriage include the saptapadi the marriage is complete when the saptapadi is performed. But when the saptapadi is not performed the question arises as to whether the marriage is thereby invalid. Numerous Indian authorities on this point have been studied, including "The Hindu Marriage Act of 1955" by D.H. Chandhari; "Hindu Law of Marriage" by S.V. Gupte; "Indian Law of Marriage and Divorce" by Kumaid Desai; "The Hindu Marriage Act" by P.V. Deolalkar; "The Hindu Marriage Act" by Kashi Prasad; "The Hindu Marriage Act" by P.S.B. Bendra; "The Hindu Code" by Shiva Gopal; "The Hindu Law and Usage" by Nirmal Kumar Roy; and "The Hindu Marriage Act, 1955" by S.K. Shanglo. While these writers are not completely unanimous in their view as to the absolute necessity for performance of the saptapadi in order that a valid marriage be contracted, it seems to be the consensus that if the saptapadi is included among the customary rites and ceremonies of the parties to a marriage without the saptapadi, it is invalid and no marriage at all. Apparently, the customary beliefs and practices of the parties are determinative on this issue.

In the present case the plaintiff established that his purported marriage to the defendant was to be a Hindu marriage, solemnized by a Hindu priest. In such circumstances the saptapadi was an essential part of the rite. The refusal of the defendant to take the seven steps, although urged by the priest and her father several times to do so, amounted in effect to a refusal of her consent to the marriage. The plaintiff later learned that the reason for this refusal was that the defendant was in love with someone else and did not want to marry the plaintiff. She told the plaintiff she was not his wife and did not consider him to be her husband and another witness testified to the defendant's failure to perform the saptapadi and to her present refusal to acknowledge herself the plaintiff's wife.

Under all of these circumstances it is this court's opinion that the defendant's failure to perform the saptapadi—an essential element in the marriage rites—makes the marriage invalid under New York law and likewise invalid under the Hindu Marriage Act of 1955. This is not a situation of a ***voidable marriage***. The marriage in the present case was void ab initio in accordance with the Hindu Marriage Act and this annulment action merely declares that to be the fact.

Source: Vijai P. Singh v. Vimla Singh, 67 MISC.2D 878, 325 N.Y.S.2D 590 (1971), U.S. Supreme Court.

Voidable marriage
A marriage that is invalid at its inception but remains in effect unless the court terminates it. The plaintiff is therefore entitled to a decree declaring his purported marriage to the defendant on January 19, 1964, to be null and void.

MARRIAGE PROHIBITIONS

Restricting Marriage between Family Members

Consanguinity
Related by blood.

Affinity
Related by marriage.

Void ab initio
Invalid from its inception.

A marriage between family members related by ***consanguinity*** (blood) or ***affinity*** (marriage) is ***void ab initio***, or from its inception. All jurisdictions prohibit marriage between close relatives related by blood or consanguinity and do not allow marriage to a parent, grandparent, child, grandchild, aunt, uncle, niece, or nephew. States regulate intrafamilial relationships through marriage statutes and criminal statutes prohibiting incest. From a public policy standpoint, states justify such laws based on claims that children conceived in an incestuous relationship are born with genetic defects. The image of the uncivilized hillbilly who marries his sister and produces cross-eyed children is widely frowned upon in our society and is a source of ridicule on daytime talk shows. More important, laws prohibiting incest prevent the exploitation of children and establish a social order within the family unit. Intrafamilial relationships are also prohibited because they disrupt family harmony and violate social norms. From a religious perspective, incest is considered a sin under biblical law and is strictly prohibited in Judeo-Christian traditions.

Marriage laws also restrict unions between family members related by affinity or marriage. Laws regarding marriage between cousins, in-laws, and step-relatives, however, vary from state to state. In 1957, rock legend Jerry Lee Lewis created a scandal when he married his first cousin, and such marriages are still considered taboo today. Marriage between first cousins is banned in twenty-four states. Nineteen states have no restrictions, and the others place either a sterility requirement or mandate genetic counseling to ensure that the couple is well aware of the risks of reproducing children who may be born with genetic abnormalities. New scientific evidence, however, may support repealing laws that prohibit marriage between cousins. A report in the *Journal of Genetic Counseling,* published in April of 2002, entitled "Genetic Counseling and Screening of Consanguineous Couples and Their Offspring: Recommendations of the National Society of Genetic Counselors," concluded that children born of first cousins have a two to three percent greater risk of birth defects and a slightly over four percent greater risk of early death than the general population, and such risks may be detected early through genetic testing.

CALIFORNIA FAMILY CODE, SECTION 2200[5]

Marriages between parents and children, ancestors and descendants of every degree, and between brothers and sisters of the half as well as the whole blood, and between uncles and nieces or aunts and nephews, are incestuous, and void from the beginning, whether the relationship is legitimate or illegitimate.

FLORIDA STATUTE SEC. 741.21[6]

Incestuous marriages prohibited. A man may not marry any woman to whom he is related by lineal consanguinity, nor his sister, nor his aunt, nor his niece. A woman may not marry any man to whom she is related by lineal consanguinity, nor her brother, nor her uncle, nor her nephew.

TEXAS FAMILY CODE SEC. 6.201[7]

Consanguinity. A marriage is void if one party to the marriage is related to the other as:

1. an ancestor or descendant, by blood or adoption;
2. a brother or sister, of the whole or half blood or by adoption;
3. a parent's brother or sister, of the whole or half blood or by adoption; or
4. a son or daughter of a brother or sister, of the whole or half blood or by adoption.

Bigamous or Polygamous Marriages

Bigamy is defined as being married to two people at the same time. **Polygamy** is defined as having multiple spouses. All jurisdictions prohibit bigamous and polygamous marriages. Contrary to popular belief, Utah also prohibits polygamous and bigamous marriages, which were once sanctioned by the Mormon Church many years ago. These practices are punishable under criminal law throughout the country.

Bigamy
Being married to two people at the same time.

Polygamy
Having multiple spouses.

We live in a culture where getting married two to three times in a lifetime is not unheard of. Once a client is legally divorced, he or she is free to remarry immediately, as long as state requirements are satisfied. Divorced persons who wish to remarry should make sure that they are legally divorced from their previous spouse. If this is overlooked or the person lies to the city official and is granted a marriage license and goes through a ceremony, the second marriage may be declared invalid. The second spouse is referred to as a **putative spouse**. The first spouse is in a stronger legal position. If a previous marriage was not legally dissolved, this may be "cured" by legally dissolving the first marriage. Once the divorce to the first spouse is final, the second marriage has been "cured" and is now valid.

Putative spouse
The spouse in a second marriage where the first marriage has not yet been legally dissolved.

Legal Prosecution of Bigamists and Polygamists

All fifty states have statutes that criminalize bigamy with some classifying it as a felony and others a misdemeanor. The purpose of the bigamy statute is to outlaw being legally married to more than one person at the same time. In the classical

---

[5]Family Code Section 2200–2201, State of California.

[6]2011 Florida Statutes, Chapter 741—Marriage; Domestic Violence, Sec 741.21—Incestuous Marriages Prohibited, State of Florida.

[7]Title 1—The Marriage Relationship, Chapter 6—Suit for Dissolution of Marriage, Subchapter C—Declaring a Marriage Void, Sec. 6.201—Consanguinity, Texas Constitution and Statutes.

bigamy case, the offender enters into a legal marriage with the first spouse and then, without legally severing the first marriage, marries a second person. Both of these marriages require marriage licenses issued by the state. Some states go even further in their statutes by criminalizing situations where the offender cohabits with someone other than a spouse, or by deeming the second relationship a common law marriage in states that recognize this status.

The terms *polygamy* and *bigamy* are often used interchangeably. For legal purposes, once that second "marriage" is created through a license, common law marriage, or in some states cohabitation, the activity falls under the definition of bigamy. Polygamists who are "married" to multiple spouses may not always be subject to prosecution under the bigamy statute. Take the case of *Sister Wives*. For those of you who are familiar with the TLC Network hit television series *Sister Wives*, it is a reality show that follows the lives of Kody Brown; his four wives Meri, Janelle, Christine, and Robyn; and their seventeen children. The Brown family belongs to the Apostolic United Brethren, a polygamous fundamentalist branch of the Mormon religion.

Sister Wives debuted on September 27, 2010, and was filmed in Lehi, Utah, where the family resided. Local police opened an investigation seeking to prosecute Brown under Utah's bigamy statute once the show aired. Brown, however, was legally married only to Meri, the first wife. The arrangement with the other "wives" is not a legal marriage but rather a spiritual union created in a religious ceremony where no additional marriage license existed. Prosecutors could potentially present two arguments against Brown's defense. One would be to claim that the subsequent relationships were common law marriages, recognized in Utah. The other is arguing that under Utah's bigamy statute, illustrated below, cohabitation while being married to a first spouse is a crime.

UTAH CRIMINAL CODE SECTION 76-7-101[8]

1. A person is guilty of bigamy when, knowing he has a husband or wife or knowing the other person has a husband or wife, the person purports to marry another person or cohabits with another person.
2. Bigamy is a felony of the third degree.
3. It shall be a defense to bigamy that the accused reasonably believed he and the other person were legally eligible to remarry.

The Brown family moved to Las Vegas, Nevada, in January 2011. They also hired attorney Jonathan Turley, professor of law at the George Washington University Law School, to prepare a legal defense in the event of arrest. The case was dropped on June 1, 2012, because the investigation revealed that there were no crimes committed other than the polygamous arrangement.

While there is no federal statute prohibiting polygamy, federal agencies have the power to send in inspectors from agencies like the Internal Revenue Service, Federal Bureau of Investigation, and Bureau of Alcohol, Tobacco, and Firearms for underlying offenses. States do not often prosecute polygamy cases unless there is another crime being committed such as child abuse, welfare fraud, or tax evasion. Many states lack the financial resources to mount numerous prosecutions where the only crime is consensual activity between adults. Pursuing such cases could potentially open the door to legal challenges regarding the validity of such statutes on constitutional grounds.

Enter the *Sister Wives* and the case of *Brown v. Herbert,* Case No. 2:11-CV-0652-CW, 2012 WL 380110 (D. Utah Feb. 3, 2012). Brown filed a

---

[8]Title 76—Utah Criminal Code, Chapter 7—Offenses against the Family, Sec 101—Bigamy-Defense, Utah State Legislature.

lawsuit in federal district court challenging the constitutionality of the Utah bigamy statute. The federal court first held that the Browns had standing to challenge the law even though the criminal case was dropped. The case was argued in U.S. District Court on January 17, 2013. The Browns argued that polygamist arrangements are consensual and deserve protection under the U.S. Constitution's right to privacy unless governmental intrusion is justified because there are other crimes being committed. The attorney for the state argued that the law should be upheld on public policy grounds because the law is there to protect the social harm that results from polygamous marriages. This would include the sexual abuse and exploitation of girls, some as young as thirteen, who are forced into "spiritual" marriages with older men, and the exiling of young boys to eliminate competition with older men for young brides. The Browns are relying on the landmark U.S. Supreme Court case of *Lawrence v. Texas,* 539 U.S. 558 (2003). In *Lawrence,* the Court struck down a Texas sodomy statute that criminalized private sexual relations between consenting adults on the grounds that such activity was protected under the U.S. Constitution's right to privacy.

MARRIAGE ALTERNATIVES

Domestic Partnership

A *domestic partnership* is a legal relationship between two individuals, whether they are of the same or opposite gender, who reside together and provide one another with mutual support. The legal benefits of domestic partnership status vary from state to state and in the various local governments where this marriage alternative is available. Legal rights afforded to domestic partners are not as extensive as those available to couples joined together by either a civil union or civil marriage. Domestic partnership laws providing all or some state spousal rights to same-sex couples include California, Oregon, Washington, Maine, Hawaii, District of Columbia, Nevada, and Wisconsin.

Domestic partnership
A committed relationship between two persons of the same gender, who reside together and support each other, in a mutually exclusive partnership.

CALIFORNIA DOMESTIC PARTNERSHIP ACT

California Family Code Section 297.5[9]

(a) Registered domestic partners shall have the same rights, protections, and benefits, and shall be subject to the same responsibilities, obligations, and duties under law, whether they derive from statutes, administrative regulations, court rules, government policies, common law, or any other provisions or sources of law, as are granted to and imposed upon spouses.

(b) Former registered domestic partners shall have the same rights, protections, and benefits, and shall be subject to the same responsibilities, obligations, and duties under law, whether they derive from statutes, administrative regulations, court rules, government policies, common law, or any other provisions or sources of law, as are granted to and imposed upon former spouses.

(c) A surviving registered domestic partner, following the death of the other partner, shall have the same rights, protections, and benefits, and shall be subject to the same responsibilities, obligations, and duties under

---

[9]Title 76—Utah Criminal Code, Chapter 7—Offenses against the Family, Sec 101–Bigamy—Defense, Utah State Legislature.

law, whether they derive from statutes, administrative regulations, court rules, government policies, common law, or any other provisions or sources of law, as are granted to and imposed upon a widow or a widower.

(d) The rights and obligations of registered domestic partners with respect to a child of either of them shall be the same as those of spouses. The rights and obligations of former or surviving registered domestic partners with respect to a child of either of them shall be the same as those of former or surviving spouses.

(e) To the extent that provisions of California law adopt, refer to, or rely upon, provisions of federal law in a way that otherwise would cause registered domestic partners to be treated differently than spouses, registered domestic partners shall be treated by California law as if federal law recognized a domestic partnership in the same manner as California law.

(f) Registered domestic partners shall have the same rights regarding nondiscrimination as those provided to spouses.

(g) No public agency in this state may discriminate against any person or couple on the ground that the person is a registered domestic partner rather than a spouse or that the couple are registered domestic partners rather than spouses, except that nothing in this section applies to modify eligibility for long-term care plans pursuant to Chapter 15 (commencing with Section 21660) of Part 3 of Division 5 of Title 2 of the Government Code.

(h) This act does not preclude any state or local agency from exercising its regulatory authority to implement statutes providing rights to, or imposing responsibilities upon, domestic partners.

(i) This section does not amend or modify any provision of the California Constitution or any provision of any statute that was adopted by initiative.

(j) Where necessary to implement the rights of registered domestic partners under this act, gender-specific terms referring to spouses shall be construed to include domestic partners.

(k) (1) For purposes of the statutes, administrative regulations, court rules, government policies, common law, and any other provision or source of law governing the rights, protections, and benefits, and the responsibilities, obligations, and duties of registered domestic partners in this state, as effectuated by this section, with respect to community property, mutual responsibility for debts to third parties, the right in particular circumstances of either partner to seek financial support from the other following the dissolution of the partnership, and other rights and duties as between the partners concerning ownership of property, any reference to the date of a marriage shall be deemed to refer to the date of registration of a domestic partnership with the state.

(2) Notwithstanding paragraph (1), for domestic partnerships registered with the state before January 1, 2005, an agreement between the domestic partners that the partners intend to be governed by the requirements set forth in Sections 1600 to 1620, inclusive, and which complies with those sections, except for the agreement's effective date, shall be enforceable as provided by Sections 1600 to 1620, inclusive, if that agreement was fully executed and in force as of June 30, 2005.

Civil Unions

A *civil union* was a legal status created by a state granting same-sex couples who chose this option the same legal rights as married opposite-sex couples in their jurisdiction. Vermont was the first state in the country to create civil unions. On December 20, 1999, the Vermont Supreme Court, in *Baker v. Vermont,* held that same-sex couples were entitled the same rights as their heterosexual counterparts under the Common Benefits Clause of the Vermont state constitution, which included the right to marry. The court ordered the Vermont legislature to either grant same-sex couples the same rights by legalizing gay marriage or devise a marriage alternative. The legislature opted to preserve Vermont's traditional definition of marriage as a legally recognized union between one man and one woman. Alternatively, the Vermont legislature extended all the rights, responsibilities, and privileges granted to opposite-sex couples to same-sex couples, but instead of calling it marriage, the legislature called it a civil union. The rights afforded to couples who entered into civil unions were far more comprehensive than those in jurisdictions that grant domestic partnership status. Civil unions have been phased out in the United States after the *Obergefell v. Hodges* decision removed the impediments to same-sex marriage.

Civil union

A separate category of legal recognition that grants same-sex couples marriage rights available to heterosexual couples, in the states of Vermont and Connecticut; civil unions are a way for same-sex couples to formalize their relationship and take advantage of the same state rights afforded to heterosexual couples.

COHABITATION

Introduction

According to the U.S. Census, the unmarried partner population numbered 7.7 million in 2010 and grew forty-one percent between 2000 and 2010, four times as fast as the overall household population. These statistics indicate that more and more people view cohabitation either as a trial marriage or as an alternative to getting married. The emergence of cohabitation as a marriage alternative presents new challenges for family law practitioners and paralegals.

Couples who plan to live together should have a cohabitation agreement in writing that specifically delineates their respective rights and responsibilities. While matters regarding the custody and support of children may be resolved in the family courts by unmarried parents, issues involving property, debts, and other obligations must be dealt with in civil court. Our population has become familiar with the term *palimony,* a lawsuit for support filed against a cohabiting partner. Palimony is not a legal concept but rather a term coined by the media describing lawsuits for compensation in cohabitation cases—a cross between the words *pal* and *alimony.* In palimony cases, one partner may have agreed to cohabitate with someone who was financially well off. They may have quit their job or career on the promise that their partner would take care of them. If the relationship terminates, this promise could result in a court granting support or property division by virtue of a contractual arrangement. A cohabitation agreement would outline the parties' rights and obligations and possibly avoid unnecessary litigation.

A cohabitation agreement should be in writing, be signed by both parties, and include the terms of the parties' cohabitation arrangement and how they will deal with their finances. Both parties should hire their own independent attorneys who may assist in negotiating an agreement and drafting and reviewing the finished product. Very often, the paralegal will be asked to draft a cohabitation agreement.

Begin the drafting of the agreement by clarifying the client's expectations and terms of the agreement with the partner. It is best that the parties specifically determine their financial obligations. Remember that agreements where sexual acts or relations are used as consideration are unenforceable. Therefore, a well-drafted

Figure 2-4Couples who plan to live together should have a cohabitation agreement in writing that specifically delineates their respective rights and responsibilities.

Mangostock/Shutterstock.

cohabitation agreement should contain a clause stating that the providing of sexual services in no way shall be construed as consideration. The following are some points that should be considered when drafting a cohabitation agreement.

- How will property acquired during the course of the relationship be distributed upon death or dissolution of the parties' union? Remember that a last will and testament is an absolute necessity to supplement the cohabitation agreement.
- How will the parties address the issue of financial support during the relationship and will either be obligated to provide such support upon dissolution?
- How will the household expenses and debts be paid? Who will be responsible?
- If the parties own property, will it be held in joint tenancy with right of survivorship so the surviving partner will inherit the property? What about other joint accounts? Will the surviving partner have access to assets in the event the other dies?
- How will these assets and debts be divided in the event of dissolution of the relationship?
- How will the parties resolve issues involving the principal residence, whether it is an apartment, condominium, or house?
- Who will make health-care decisions in the event either of the parties becomes ill or incapacitated? It is crucial that cohabitating couples not only draft wills, but also living wills, health-care proxies, and durable powers of attorney.
- Is health insurance coverage available for domestic partners through an employer? If so, who will pay for the extra premium, as well as any income taxes imputed on the employee partner for tax purposes?
- While not binding and always subject to the evaluation of a court on best interest standards, how will the parties define child support, custody, and visitation?

Marvin v. Marvin In response to the very sharp increase in cohabitation arrangements that occurred in the late 1960s and early 1970s, the law had to change to make some accommodations for resolving disputes between cohabiting partners. The first case to recognize the rights of cohabitants was *Marvin v. Marvin*, 18 Cal. 3d 660, 557 P.2d 106, 134 Cal. Rptr. 815 (1976). In *Marvin*, the plaintiff and the defendant had lived together for a period of seven years. During this period, the plaintiff agreed to give up her career and provide domestic services for the defendant. In exchange, the defendant agreed to financially support the plaintiff and share any assets that were accumulated. This agreement was *not* memorialized in writing.

When the relationship ended, the plaintiff sued the defendant on a contractual basis for support and a division of the assets. The trial court dismissed her case and she appealed. On appeal, the California Supreme Court held that the contract between the parties was valid and remanded the case to the trial court to be judged on its merits. The parties had accumulated approximately one million dollars in assets. However, these assets were titled in the name of the defendant.

The defendant attacked the validity of the contract by raising the long-standing public policy argument. According to the defendant, a contract that included sexual relations was void. The California Supreme Court held that as long as sexual relations were not the sole consideration, the court should disregard that provision and enforce the lawful provisions of the agreement.

Marvin Lays Foundation for Cohabitation Remedies

While the California Supreme Court addressed the validity of the parties' contract on public policy grounds, it also concluded that the plaintiff's complaint stated a cause of action based on an express contract theory, and in addition, could be amended to state a cause of action founded upon theories of implied contract or equitable relief. *Marvin v. Marvin*, 18 Cal. 3D, 660 (1976) is a landmark case in the area of cohabitation, but these remedies vary from state to state. Here is a basic overview of the express and implied remedies cohabitants in conflict often relied upon, followed by excerpts from the *Marvin* case laying the groundwork for such relief:

1. **Express contract.** This would require an express agreement between the parties regarding the specific terms. The high court recognized that in a romantic relationship, parties do not generally negotiate the terms of their roles and expectations, let alone reduce them to a written document.
2. **Implied-in-fact contract.** In an implied-in-fact contract, the intention of the parties is inferred by their conduct. In supporting an implied contract argument in a cohabitation case, examining the conduct of the parties is essential. How did the parties conduct themselves during their relationship? What contributions, both monetary and nonmonetary, did the parties bring to the relationship? Were assets commingled in joint accounts?
3. **Quasi-contract.** Quasi-contracts are contractual obligations that the court imposes on the parties. No actual contract has been entered into by the parties. The court takes this position when it appears that one party has been so unjustly enriched that the court creates a contract to avoid unfairness to the other party.
4. **Implied partnership.** When a cohabiting couple works on a business enterprise that is owned by one of the parties, the court creates an implied partnership. The court assesses the financial status of the business and distributes the assets and liabilities just as such a distribution would occur upon the dissolution of a business partnership.

5. **Implied trust.** A trust is a legal relationship where one party, the trustee, holds legal title to property for the benefit of the beneficiary. Most trusts are expressed trusts, in which the parties have negotiated the terms. Implied trusts are legal fictions, created by the court, and not by the parties, to avoid an injustice. One type of trust is a resulting trust. In a resulting trust, one party provides the funds for property, while title is in the other party's name. Here, the courts created a trust where the parties did not.

EXAMPLE 1

Mary has enough money for a down payment on a house but has poor credit. John has excellent credit and can qualify for a mortgage in his sole name. With Mary's down payment, John agrees to split the mortgage payments and purchases the house, which is titled in his name only. John and Mary move into the house and live there for ten years together. During this time, Mary contributes to the mortgage payments and household expenses. The relationship deteriorates, and Mary and John break up. Mary moves out of the house because John has become verbally abusive. Mary may sue for her interest in the house on a resulting trust theory.

Another type of implied trust is a constructive trust. A constructive trust is also a legal fiction. A judge who feels that it is necessary to impose such an obligation in order to avoid the unjust enrichment of one cohabitant at the expense of the other creates it. A constructive trust is different from a resulting trust. A constructive trust is created when a person in a fiduciary position is engaged in fraud, wrongdoing, or other unconscionable conduct and is unjustly enriched as a result of this behavior.

EXAMPLE 2

Mary moves into John's house and spends over $125,000 renovating the kitchen and two bathrooms. John and Mary break up and Mary moves out. She demands compensation for the thousands she put into improving John's house, but John refuses. A court of law may require John to reimburse Mary through the imposition of a constructive trust.

While the *Marvin* court established a variety of legal remedies for litigating cohabitants, it did not approve of treating cohabiting couples as married couples:

> … [W]e take this occasion to point out that the structure of society itself largely depends upon the institution of marriage and nothing we have said in this opinion should be taken to derogate from that institution. [*Marvin v. Marvin,* 557 P.2d 106, 122 (1976)]

MICHELLE MARVIN v. LEE MARVIN

18 CAL. 3D 660 (1976)
SUPREME COURT OF CALIFORNIA

Plaintiff's complaint states a cause of action for breach of an express contract.

In Trutalli v. Meraviglia (1932) 215 Cal. 698 [12 P.2d 430] we established the principle that nonmarital partners may lawfully contract concerning the ownership of property acquired during the relationship. We reaffirmed this principle in Vallera v. Vallera (1943) 21

Cal.2d 681, 685 [134 P.2d 761], stating that "If a man and woman [who are not married] live together as husband and wife under an agreement to pool their earnings and share equally in their joint accumulations, equity will protect the interests of each in such property."

In the case before us plaintiff, basing her cause of action in contract upon these precedents, maintains that the trial court erred in denying her a trial on the merits of her contention. Although that court did not specify the ground for its conclusion that plaintiff's contractual allegations stated no cause of action, defendant offers some four theories to sustain the ruling; we proceed to examine them.

Defendant first and principally relies on the contention that the alleged contract is so closely related to the supposed "immoral" character of the relationship between plaintiff and himself that the enforcement of the contract would violate public policy. He points to cases asserting that a contract between nonmarital partners is unenforceable if it is "involved in" an illicit relationship, or made in "contemplation" of such a relationship. A review of the numerous California decisions concerning contracts between nonmarital partners, however, reveals that the courts have not employed such broad and uncertain standards to strike down contracts. The decisions instead disclose a narrower and more precise standard: a contract between nonmarital partners is unenforceable only to the extent that it explicitly rests upon the immoral and illicit consideration of meretricious sexual services.

Although the past decisions hover over the issue in the somewhat wispy form of the figures of a Chagall painting, we can abstract from those decisions a clear and simple rule. The fact that a man and woman live together without marriage, and engage in a sexual relationship, does not in itself invalidate agreements between them relating to their earnings, property, or expenses. Neither is such an agreement invalid merely because the parties may have contemplated the creation or continuation of a nonmarital relationship when they entered into it. Agreements between nonmarital partners fail only to the extent that they rest upon a consideration of meretricious sexual services. Thus the rule asserted by defendant, that a contract fails if it is "involved in" or made "in contemplation" of a nonmarital relationship, cannot be reconciled with the decisions.

The decisions ... thus demonstrate that a contract between nonmarital partners, even if expressly made in contemplation of a common living arrangement, is invalid only if sexual acts form an inseparable part of the consideration for the agreement. In sum, a court will not enforce a contract for the pooling of property and earnings if it is explicitly and inseparably based upon services as a paramour. The Court of Appeal opinion in Hill, however, indicates that even if sexual services are part of the contractual consideration, any severable portion of the contract supported by independent consideration will still be enforced.

In summary, we base our opinion on the principle that adults who voluntarily live together and engage in sexual relations are nonetheless as competent as any other persons to contract respecting their earnings and property rights. Of course, they cannot lawfully contract to pay for the performance of sexual services, for such a contract is, in essence, an agreement for prostitution and unlawful for that reason. But they may agree to pool their earnings and to hold all property acquired during the relationship in accord with the law governing community property; conversely they may agree that each partner's earnings and the property acquired from those earnings remains the separate property of the earning partner. So long as the agreement does not rest upon illicit meretricious consideration, the parties may order their economic affairs as they choose, and no policy precludes the courts from enforcing such agreements.

In the present instance, plaintiff alleges that the parties agreed to pool their earnings, that they contracted to share equally in all property acquired, and that defendant agreed to support plaintiff. The terms of the contract as alleged do not rest upon any unlawful consideration. We therefore conclude that the complaint furnishes a suitable basis upon which the trial court can render declaratory relief. The trial court consequently erred in granting defendant's motion for judgment on the pleadings.

Plaintiff's complaint can be amended to state a cause of action founded upon theories of implied contract or equitable relief.

Source: Michelle Marvin v. Lee Marvin, 18 Cal. 3d 660 (1976), Supreme Court of California.

As we have noted, both causes of action in plaintiff's complaint allege an express contract; neither assert any basis for relief independent from the contract. We are aware that many young couples live together without the solemnization of marriage, in order to make sure that they can successfully later undertake marriage. This trial period, preliminary to marriage, serves as some assurance that the marriage will not subsequently end in dissolution to the harm of both parties. We are aware, as we have stated, of the pervasiveness of nonmarital relationships in other situations.

The mores of the society have indeed changed so radically in regard to cohabitation that we cannot impose a standard based on alleged moral considerations that have apparently been so widely abandoned by so many. Lest we be misunderstood, however, we take this occasion to point out that the structure of society itself largely depends upon the institution of marriage, and nothing we have said in this opinion should be taken to derogate from that institution. The joining of the man and woman in marriage is at once the most socially productive and individually fulfilling relationship that one can enjoy in the course of a lifetime.

We conclude that the judicial barriers that may stand in the way of a policy based upon the fulfillment of the reasonable expectations of the parties to a nonmarital relationship should be removed. As we have explained, the courts now hold that express agreements will be enforced unless they rest on an unlawful meretricious consideration. We add that in the absence of an express agreement, the courts may look to a variety of other remedies in order to protect the parties' lawful expectations.

The courts may inquire into the conduct of the parties to determine whether that conduct demonstrates an implied contract or implied agreement of partnership or joint venture ... or some other tacit understanding between the parties. The courts may, when appropriate, employ principles of constructive trust... or resulting trust... Finally, a nonmarital partner may recover in quantum meruit for the reasonable value of household services rendered less the reasonable value of support received if he can show that he rendered services with the expectation of monetary reward.

Since we have determined that plaintiff's complaint states a cause of action for breach of an express contract, and, as we have explained, can be amended to state a cause of action independent of allegations of express contract, we must conclude that the trial court erred in granting defendant a judgment on the pleadings.

The judgment is reversed and the cause remanded for further proceedings consistent with the views expressed herein.

Marvin Aftermath: Upon remand, the Superior Court, on hearing the evidence, found that Lee Marvin never agreed to support Michelle Marvin and that they never had an agreement to share any property accumulated during the course of their relationship. Michelle Marvin was, however, awarded the sum of $104,000 so that she could learn some new skills and become self-sufficient enough to support herself.

Example Cohabitation Complaint On November 11, 2004, political comedian Bill Maher was served with a $9 million palimony lawsuit which was later dismissed. See **Appendix D, Bill Maher Palimony Complaint**, which illustrates the contractual grounds often filed by cohabitants seeking legal relief outside the family courts. Some of the *Marvin* grounds raised in the plaintiff's complaint include breach of contract, promissory estoppel, and promissory fraud, along with a few intentional torts.

Concept Review and Reinforcement

KEY **TERMS**

affinity
bigamy
civil marriage or civil ceremony
civil union
common law marriage
consanguinity

covenant marriage
Defense of Marriage Act (DOMA)
domestic partnership
emancipation
marriage
marriage certificate

marriage license
polygamy
putative spouse
religious marriage
void ab initio
voidable marriage

REVIEW OF **KEY CONCEPTS**

Use the Internet to find the answers to state-specific questions.

1. What are the requirements for a valid marriage in your state?
2. What are the legal benefits of marriage?
3. Is living together with a partner for a period of years enough to establish a common law marriage?
4. Do you live in a common law jurisdiction? If so, what are the requirements for a valid common law marriage in your state?
5. Why do you think covenant marriages have not become popular in this country despite the high divorce rate?

6. What was the legal effect of the federal Defense of Marriage Act on same-sex couples?
7. What was the effect of *Obergefell v. Hodges* on the issue of same-sex marriage?
8. Why do you think so many couples are choosing cohabitation instead of traditional marriage?
9. What remedies are available to cohabiting couples according to the landmark decision by the California Supreme Court in *Marvin v. Marvin*?

BUILDING YOUR PARALEGAL SKILLS

CASE FOR BRIEFING

LITTLETON v. PRANGE, 9 S.W.3D 223 (TEX.APP. (4TH) 1999)

Critical Thinking and Legal Analysis Applications

1. Research your state statutes and court decisions and determine how your jurisdiction would respond to the facts as set forth in *Littleton v. Prange*. How would your state answer the question addressed by the Court of Appeals in Texas in *Littleton*: "Can there be a valid marriage between a man and a person born as a man, but surgically altered to have the physical characteristics of a woman?" You may wish to start your research by determining whether your jurisdiction amends sex designations on birth certificates by conducting a search on the Internet.

Building a Professional Portfolio

PORTFOLIO **EXERCISES**

For this exercise, you will need to team up with a classmate, friend, or adult member of your family. Assume that the two of you are a couple that is planning to move in together. Based on the specific circumstances of your case, draft a cohabitation agreement by using a cohabitation agreement form found on the Internet.

Chapter **three**

PREMARITAL AND POSTMARITAL AGREEMENTS

LEARNING OBJECTIVES

After studying this chapter, you should be able to:

1. Define the term *premarital agreement.*

2. Understand the historical evolution of premarital agreements.

3. Determine what documents must be acquired before drafting a premarital agreement.

4. List and explain the requirements for drafting and executing a valid premarital agreement.

5. Identify the unenforceable provisions of a premarital agreement.

6. Define "postmarital agreement."

7. Understand the reasons for entering into a postmarital agreement.

8. Understand the importance of state law.

Prior to marriage, the parties involved may choose to enter into a contract that determines their respective rights upon dissolution of the marriage or the death of one of the parties. These arrangements are called antenuptial agreements, premarital agreements, or prenuptial agreements. The term premarital agreement is most commonly used today since many jurisdictions have adopted some version of the Uniform Premarital Agreement Act (UPAA), which will be discussed later in this chapter. It is important, however, to know the other terms historically used to identify this contract since they may appear in older statutes, cases, or literature regarding this issue. For purposes of this text, the term premarital agreement is used. The parties also have the option of entering into similar agreements during the course of the marriage. These contracts are called postmarital or postnuptial agreements and have increased in popularity over recent years. The enforceability of these contracts is dependent on state law.

PREMARITAL AGREEMENTS

Introduction

A *premarital agreement* is a contract entered into between two parties who intend to marry. Occasionally, this document addresses how the responsibilities and property rights will be handled during the marriage—who will pay the bills, who will support children from a prior marriage, who will pay the mortgage, how the children's upbringing will be handled, and who will care for the children's day-to-day needs. Frequently, the premarital agreement focuses on the disposition of the parties' estates in the event of divorce or death.

Once exclusively a staple in the legal arsenal of the rich and famous, more and more couples are now considering premarital agreements. These contracts were historically entered into by older men who married younger women. These men wished to protect their assets from potential "gold diggers" who were arguably marrying them for their money. Today, premarital agreements are popular among people who are entering into second or third marriages. In these cases, one or both parties may come with baggage. The husband, for instance, may be obligated to pay alimony and child support to the former wife. The wife may have children from a previous relationship. Premarital agreements are also used by parties who have more assets or income than their spouse-to-be and by those who wish to protect the inheritance rights of their adult children. Premarital agreements are also considered a means of financial and emotional self-defense in a society with a high divorce rate. In addition, young professionals who have postponed marriage until their thirties or forties resort to *prenuptial agreements* to protect assets they have accumulated.

Some parties enter into such agreements *after* the marriage has been performed. These contracts are called postnuptial agreements, and the elements are similar to those of premarital agreements. The only difference is that a postnuptial agreement is entered into during the marriage, especially in cases where one of the spouses has received or is about to receive an inheritance. Drafting a postnuptial agreement essentially requires adherence to the same legal elements that apply to drafting a premarital agreement.

A premarital agreement is not a very romantic topic to discuss with a prospective partner, even if it can save the parties a great deal of grief in the long run. Money is also a very delicate topic to discuss under any circumstances and even more difficult to interject into a personal relationship. Talk of money can dredge up old childhood wounds and expose embarrassing habits that have formed in adulthood.

Prior to 1970, premarital agreements were frowned on by the courts. Judges often found these contracts void against public policy because they contemplated the end of the marital relationship. The state government had an interest in preserving the institution of marriage. The prevailing view was that premarital agreements facilitated divorce because they encouraged the spouse in the position to benefit most from the contract to put less effort into preserving the marital relationship. Courts were also protective of women's interests, fearing that men, who traditionally had more assets and business savvy, would leave women destitute in the event of divorce. For many centuries, a woman's traditional position was that of homemaker and child rearer. Many women lacked the education and finances to negotiate on an equal level with men. Premarital agreements were introduced into our legal system by men who had greater assets and greater business sophistication in legal matters. The courts feared that if premarital agreements were enforced, women would be unable to support themselves and would have to rely on public assistance.

Premarital agreement
A contract entered into by the prospective spouses regarding their rights during the marriage and in the event of a divorce; also known as an antenuptial agreement or prenuptial agreement.

Prenuptial agreement
A contract entered into by the prospective spouses regarding their rights during the marriage and in the event of a divorce; also known as an antenuptial agreement or premarital agreement.

Figure 3-1 A premarital agreement can be a very delicate subject to discuss with a prospective spouse.

Martin Novak/Shutterstock.

The 1960s and 1970s brought many social changes to the institution of marriage, such as the advent of the women's liberation movement and no-fault divorce. No-fault divorce removed the traditional fault grounds that were once required to be proven by the moving spouse in order to obtain a divorce (i.e., abandonment, adultery, intemperance). The changing role of women propelled them to pursue higher education, greater opportunities in the workplace, and, as a result, economic independence. The women's liberation movement also demanded equal treatment under the law. Courts eventually did away with the legal presumptions that aimed to protect women in the legal system. Judicial attitudes progressed to the point where premarital agreements are enforced because it made sense in this era. Premarital agreements allow prospective spouses to enter into a marriage with more predictability since they can now get their legal and financial house in order.

In 1970, the Florida Supreme Court, in *Posner v. Posner,* 233 So.2d 381 (Fla. 1970), paved the way for family courts around the country to hold that premarital agreements made in contemplation of marriage were not invalid *per se.*[1] While the premarital agreement in this case was invalidated because of nondisclosure of assets, it was not struck down on public policy grounds.

Legal Requirements of a Valid Premarital Agreement

The content of a premarital agreement, as well as any other contract, will depend on the intent of the parties. Some are very detailed documents covering specific aspects of married life, such as who will pay the bills and who will do the household chores. Exhibit 3-1 shows a sample premarital agreement. Premarital agreements, however, cannot bind parties during the marriage. For example, assume the parties agree in a premarital agreement that the husband will wash the dishes and take out the trash. This provision will not be enforced by the court. The court will not

[1] *Victor Posner, Petitioner v. Sari Posner, Respondent, 233 SO.2D 381 (1970), Supreme Court of Florida.*

enforce those portions of a premarital agreement that govern the spouse's respective duties during an intact marriage. These provisions are useful only to provide the couple with guidelines as to how they wish to conduct their day-to-day affairs.

Exhibit 3-1 Sample Premarital Agreement (author unknown)

WHEREAS, the parties are contemplating a legal marriage under the laws of the State of Connecticut; and

WHEREAS, it is their mutual desire to enter into this Agreement whereby they will regulate their relationship toward each other with respect to the property each of them own and in which each of them has an interest;

NOW, therefore, it is agreed as follows:

1. That the properties of any kind or nature, real, personal or mixed, wherever the same may be found, which belong to each party, shall be and forever remain the separate estate of said party, including all interests, rents, and profits which may accrue therefrom.
2. That each party shall have at all times the full right and authority, in all respects, the same as each would have if not married, to use, enjoy, mortgage, convey, and encumber such property as may belong to him or her.
3. That each party may make such disposition of his or her property as the case may be, by gift or will during his or her lifetime, as each sees fit; and in the event of the decease of one of the parties, the survivor shall have no interest in the property of the estate of the other, either by way of inheritance, succession, family allowance or homestead.
4. That each party, in the event of a legal separation or dissolution of marriage, shall have no right as against the other by way of claims for support, alimony, property division, attorney's fees, and costs.
5. This Prenuptial Agreement shall be construed under the laws of the State of Connecticut.

Dated this 10th day of May, 2018

(Name)	Witness
(Date)	Witness
(Name)	
(Date)	

Acquiring the Necessary Documentation

The following information should be obtained from the client for review, whether the office is representing the spouse seeking the premarital agreement or the spouse reviewing the agreement. Some of the terms and concepts listed in this chapter are discussed in detail in other chapters. A brief definition is included where needed for the convenience of the reader. For each party, obtain information regarding:

1. Assets and their current fair market value
2. Income, both earned and unearned
3. Debts and liabilities

4. Previous divorce obligations owed to a former spouse, such as the following:

- Alimony (Alimony is financial support, often in the form of money, paid to a former spouse.)—What is the amount and duration of payments?
- Child support (Child support is financial support, often in the form of money, that is paid to a custodial parent for the support of the minor children of the marriage.)—What is the amount, and what are the ages of the children?
- College expenses—Is the party obligated to pay higher education costs?
- Insurance premiums—Must the party pay health, life, or disability insurance premiums?
- Qualified domestic relations orders (QDROs) (A QDRO is a court order served on a pension administrator ordering the plan to distribute a specified portion of the employee spouse's pension funds to the nonemployee spouse.)—Are there any future rights to an employee pension that the client will receive or be required to pay out?
- Tax obligations—Does either of the parties owe money to a local, state, or federal tax entity?
- Lawsuits—Does either party anticipate receiving money damages or a settlement amount from a pending lawsuit?
- Legal judgments—Have any legal judgments been entered against the parties requiring payment of damages?
- Credit history—Have there been previous or pending bankruptcies?

Who Should Have a Premarital Agreement?

The following parties should consider having a premarital agreement prepared:

- parties who have children from a previous marriage whose financial interests they wish to protect,
- parties who have significant assets or are very well compensated,
- parties who anticipate a family inheritance, and
- parties who wish to protect their separate property (property acquired prior to marriage).

If a party wants to ensure that assets pass to the children of a previous marriage, a premarital agreement is essential. A spouse enjoys statutory protections, such as:

- an elective statutory share of the deceased spouse's estate (this share is usually elected if the deceased spouse left the surviving spouse nothing or very little in the will);
- intestacy succession rights;
- homestead rights in the principal; and
- widow's allowance.

These rights are automatically conferred on the spouse by virtue of the legal marital status. A spouse may, however, waive these rights in the prenuptial agreement. Without a properly executed premarital agreement in effect, a surviving spouse is legally entitled to claim a portion of the deceased spouse's estate. An attorney may advise a client to sign a qualified terminal interest trust (QTIP). A QTIP is a trust naming the children as beneficiaries of the client's estate, while allowing the surviving spouse access to the assets acquired during his or the deceased spouse's lifetime. In addition, the attorney should also advise the client to write a new will and change beneficiary designations on insurance policies, trusts, annuities, and other retirement plans to safeguard the current spouse.

Parties who are well compensated or have significant assets may also seek the protection of a premarital agreement. The client may be well advised by the attorney to keep the money he or she has already amassed in a separate account and not to commingle these funds with marital property.

Premarital Agreements—Post *Posner*

As the landmark case upholding premarital agreements that included provisions contemplating divorce, *Posner* was cited as precedent in other states in determining the validity of such contracts. In 1976, the ***Uniform Premarital Agreement Act (UPAA)***, a model act, was drafted by the National Conference of Commissioners on Uniform State Laws. It provides states with model legislation that addresses the issues necessary to create a valid premarital agreement. States have the option of whether to adopt the model act as is, adopt a revised version, or ignore it. Remember that a premarital agreement is a contract and all contracts require some type of consideration. The consideration in a premarital agreement, as recognized in all jurisdictions, is the marriage. A *promise* to marry, on the other hand, is not valid consideration.

Uniform Premarital Agreement Act (UPAA) A model act drafted by the National Conference of Commissioners on Uniform State Laws that provides states with model legislation addressing the issues necessary to create a valid premarital agreement.

The UPAA states that to be enforceable, a premarital agreement must:

- be in writing,
- be signed by both parties,
- be signed by parties who have the contractual capacity to enter into a contract and do so voluntarily,
- require that each spouse provide a fair and reasonable disclosure of their financial assets and obligations prior to execution, and
- not be unconscionable at the time of execution.

The UPAA states that a premarital agreement may address issues such as waiver or modification of alimony and the disposition of property upon divorce, death, or separation. Generally, parties are free to contract regarding these issues as long as the agreement does not violate public policy or involve the commission of a crime. When it comes to matters dealing with the custody of children and their support, the court always retains jurisdiction to override the agreement based on the best interest of the children. For example, while the parties may agree that children will be raised within a certain religion, an agreement that gives the mother sole custody in the event of divorce is unenforceable. It is up to the courts to decide the custody issue based on what is in the best interest of the children.

Drafting and Executing Valid Premarital Agreements

1. **Checking State Law.** When drafting a premarital agreement, paralegals must check state law to determine whether their state has adopted some version of the UPAA, permits premarital agreements through statutory or case law, or has no definitive case law or statute on the issue. The following states have passed a state version of the UPAA:

     Arizona, Arkansas, California, Connecticut, Delaware, District of Columbia, Hawaii, Idaho, Illinois, Indiana, Iowa, Kansas, Maine, Montana, Nebraska, Nevada, New Jersey, New Mexico, North Carolina, North Dakota, Oregon, Rhode Island, South Dakota, Texas, Utah, Virginia, and Wisconsin.

The text of Arizona's *UPAA* and California's Premarital Agreement Act is located in Appendix A.

2. **Determining Intent of the Parties.** When drafting a premarital agreement, it is important to be very clear on the intention of the party or parties. It may be necessary to prepare and review several drafts of the agreement before the final document is ready for execution. If your client is proposing the agreement to his or her prospective spouse, it is important for the attorney to review a draft with the client to determine if the client's objectives have been met and to explain legal terms so they are fully understood. If your client is on the receiving end of the agreement, it may be possible that portions of the proposed agreement may have to be negotiated and that several drafts will have to be written until the intent of the parties is clearly indicated.

3. **Document Must Be in Writing.** Promises made in contemplation of marriage must be made in writing and signed by the parties.

4. **Adequate Financial Disclosure.** Prospective spouses entering into a premarital agreement have a duty to fully disclose their property and financial obligations. Clients may want to hide, falsify, or misrepresent their financial information; however, if the jurisdiction requires disclosure, the agreement may be rendered unenforceable if this requirement is not satisfied. Many jurisdictions require the parties to attach an accurate financial statement to the agreement. The extent of disclosure is different from one jurisdiction to another, so it is important to review state law.

5. **Advice of Independent Counsel.** The proponent of a premarital agreement must give his or her prospective spouse the opportunity to have an independent attorney of his or her choice review the agreement. The reviewing attorney will advise the client of the rights he or she is relinquishing by signing the premarital agreement and may also be involved in renegotiating certain provisions. It is not advisable for the attorney drafting

Figure 3-2 The advice of independent counsel who will look out for the client's interests is crucial before signing a premarital agreement.

the premarital agreement to refer the opposing party to an attorney or draft a premarital agreement on behalf of both parties, as this would present a conflict of interest. Additionally, a prospective spouse should be given ample time to find an attorney and to consider the ramifications of the agreement. The bride, for example, should not be accosted in the vestibule of the church on the day of the wedding and forced to sign a document she has not been able to review with her own attorney. If a party waives the right to seek independent counsel, this waiver should be obtained in writing to avoid any future problems.

6. **Fairness.** A basic principle of contract law is that *unconscionable* contracts will not be enforced. Premarital agreements are no exception to the general rule. An agreement is unconscionable when it is so unfair to one party that the court will refuse to enforce it. Courts regularly review contracts on the basis of "fairness." In business environments, the parties enter into contracts as arm's-length transactions. Prospective spouses, however, are in a confidential relationship and may be pressured into signing for fear that the marriage will not go forward. Therefore, prospective spouses are more susceptible to undue influence, thus alerting the courts to the possibility of unconscionability.

> **Unconscionable**
> An agreement that is so unfair to one party that the court will refuse to enforce it.

Courts will generally enforce a premarital agreement unless one party can prove that it promotes divorce (e.g., a large, enticing property settlement upon divorce) or the contract was entered into with the intent to divorce.

A court will determine fairness at the time the agreement was executed and at the time of enforcement. Provisions that seemed fair at the time of drafting may be invalid at the time of execution. For example, it would be unconscionable to enforce an agreement where a spouse who has become recently disabled waived alimony at the time of the signing of the agreement. In this case, the spouse's health and the unwillingness on the part of many courts to allow the spouse to become a charge on the taxpayers may render the agreement unenforceable due to unconscionability. Unconscionability is determined by the courts based on the particular facts and circumstances of the case.

A proponent spouse may wish to include a provision in the prenuptial agreement that will give the prospective spouse some type of support or property in the event of a divorce. The courts may frown upon agreements that leave the less economically disadvantaged spouse without any reasonable means of support.

7. **Voluntariness.** Another principle of contract law applicable to premarital agreements is a "meeting of the minds." This means that each party must understand and agree to the terms of a contract. If a person is forced or pressured to sign, or signs for fear that the marriage will be called off, the contract may later be declared unenforceable by the court.

8. **Choice of Governing Law.** A premarital agreement should include a clause indicating which state law controls in the event of a dispute. Language such as "this premarital agreement shall be construed under the laws of the State of" should be incorporated into the document. Under traditional contract law, an agreement that is silent regarding governing law will be construed under the laws of the jurisdiction where the agreement was originally signed. The UPAA, however, allows the parties to choose the governing law as long as there is some type of connection to the chosen state—one of the parties either lives, plans to live, or plans to marry in that particular state.

9. **Unenforceable Provisions.** Parties are generally free to waive or modify the financial rights and obligations affecting the adults in the relationship. Provisions dealing with child custody or child support, however, are always within the control of the court and cannot be contracted away by the parties. The court decides these issues based on what is in the best interest of the child. Let's say, for example, the agreement read that in the event of divorce, the wife shall have custody of the minor children. The couple marries and divorces ten years later. The mother is now addicted to drugs but still seeks to enforce the provision in the premarital agreement giving her custody of the minor children. This provision is unenforceable, and the question regarding child custody will be determined by the court.

Provisions that are illegal or against **public policy** will also be deemed unenforceable. For example, a provision stating that the wife will agree to a ménage à trois at least once a month will be deemed void against public policy as it promotes adultery. Here is the California judicial definition of "public policy," cited from the case of *Noble v. City of Palo Alto*, 89 Cal. App. 47, 50-51 (1928):

> By "public policy" is intended that principle of law which holds that no citizen can lawfully do that which has a tendency to be injurious to the public or against the public good, which may be termed the policy of the law. Likewise, it has been defined as the principles under which freedom of contract or private dealing are restricted by law for the good of the community ... Public policy means the public good. Anything which tends to undermine that sense of security for individual rights, whether of personal liberty or private property, which any citizen ought to feel is against public policy. It is the evil tendency and not the actual result which is the test of illegality (*Maryland Trust Co. v. National Bank*, 102 Md. 608 [62 Atl. 79]).

Public policy
A belief generally held by a majority of the public as to the desirability or rightness or wrongness of certain behavior.

Testing the Validity of a Premarital Agreement

The unconscionability radar of the Court of Appeals of Indiana was on high alert in this case where a sixteen-year-old minor was asked by a man twice her age to sign a premarital agreement without the benefit of legal counsel. The facts in this case are a perfect example of a contract that is unfair and most definitely unenforceable in the eyes of the law.

> ### JULIE M. FETTERS v. JAY M. FETTERS
>
> 26 N.E.3d 1016 (2015)
> COURT OF APPEALS OF INDIANA
> FEBRUARY 26, 2015.
> REHEARING DENIED APRIL 28, 2015.
>
> BARNES, JUDGE.
>
> ... The restated issue before us is whether the premarital agreement is unconscionable....
>
> #### Facts
>
> Julie and Jay began having a sexual relationship in 1994, when Julie was fourteen years old and Jay was twenty-nine. Jay was a school janitor at the time, but Julie did not go to his school. In the summer of 1995, when Julie was fifteen, she became

pregnant by Jay, who was then thirty. Police began investigating Jay for sexual misconduct with a minor. Jay believed he could avoid prosecution if he married Julie, and Julie agreed to do so.

Before getting married, Jay asked Julie, who had just turned sixteen, to sign a premarital agreement prepared by his attorney. Among other things, the agreement provided that each party would retain their own separate property in the event of divorce. Julie went to Jay's attorney's office with her mother, where Jay's attorney went over the document with her. Despite not being able to read very well and not understanding the agreement, Julie agreed to sign it; her mother also signed it. Julie did not have an attorney of her own review the document. Jay was never prosecuted for his relationship with Julie.

Julie dropped out of school when she got married, and she had the couple's first child in the spring of 1996. The couple had a second child in 2003. Julie never obtained her GED and worked in various low-wage jobs during about half the marriage and exclusively cared for the children during the other half. In 2011, Julie filed a petition for dissolution of the marriage. She sought to disavow the premarital agreement and have it declared void by the trial court.

Jay has continued working as janitor, earning approximately $590 per week and accumulating a PERF pension worth approximately $38,000. Julie works as a nurses' aide, earning approximately $9.85 per hour and working fifteen to thirty-five hours per week, and has no retirement plan. During the marriage, the couple lived in a home Jay had acquired before marriage and which had a value at the time of separation of $62,000. Julie, who owned no property at the time of the marriage, had acquired two vehicles in her name during it worth a total of $13,900; Jay owned two vehicles and one motorcycle in his own name, worth a total of $8,500.

The trial court denied Julie's request to invalidate the premarital agreement. Thus, in accordance with the agreement, it entered a final dissolution decree awarding the full value of the marital residence and Jay's PERF pension to him, along with his vehicles, while awarding Julie her own vehicles. Julie now appeals.

Analysis

… Premarital agreements have long been recognized as valid contracts in Indiana, "as long as they are entered into freely and without fraud, duress, or misrepresentation, and are not unconscionable." *Rider v. Rider,* 669 N.E.2d 160, 162 (Ind.1996). Our legislature codified this caselaw approval of premarital agreements with its adoption in 1995 of a version of the Uniform Premarital Agreement Act ("the Act"), now found at Indiana Code Chapter 31-11-3.[1] The Act went into effect in Indiana on July 1, 1995, and so it applies to this case. *See id.* at 164. In part, the Act states:

(a) A premarital agreement is not enforceable if a party against whom enforcement is sought proves that:
   (1) the party did not execute the agreement voluntarily; or
   (2) the agreement was unconscionable when the agreement was executed.
   * * * * *
(b) A court shall decide an issue of unconscionability of a premarital agreement as a matter of law.

… We also observe that the Act makes the issue of unconscionability a question of law. This means that our review of the trial court's ultimate ruling on unconscionability is de novo…. Underlying that legal determination may be factual determinations regarding the circumstances surrounding execution of the agreement, which we review for clear error as we would any other factual determination….

… We readily conclude that this premarital agreement is unconscionable as a matter of law. Although it does not appear Jay is highly educated, there still was a gross disparity in life experience between him and Julie. Indeed, Jay apparently violated criminal laws intended to protect minors by carrying out his illicit sexual relationship

continued

with Julie.... And, he personally benefitted greatly by marrying Julie and avoiding prosecution, with no comparable benefit to Julie. Rather, Julie dropped out of school and did not further her education, while either caring for the couple's children or working at low-wage jobs. Also, the property division portion of the agreement was entirely one-sided in Jay's favor, as he was the only party bringing any assets into the marriage.

Furthermore, Indiana law has long held that contracts entered into by a minor are voidable at the option of the minor while he or she remains a minor, or within a reasonable time after reaching majority.... This reflects the law's view that minors are not always entirely competent to enter into contracts with adults and are deserving of special protection in that regard. Although Julie was permitted to marry Jay at age sixteen, she still was a minor for purposes of contract formation....

... Finally, we note Julie's lack of education, her difficulty reading, her stated lack of understanding of the premarital agreement, and the fact that she did not receive independent legal advice. It is true that Jay likewise appears not to be highly educated and it is possible he also did not understand all of the agreement's intricacies. But, it was his attorney who prepared the agreement, and it is entirely in his favor. We also do not believe that Julie's mother's advice and consent regarding the premarital agreement was an adequate substitute for professional legal advice.

In sum, after considering all of the circumstances surrounding the premarital agreement's execution and its one-sided nature in favor of the dominant party, Jay, we conclude that the agreement was unconscionable at the time of its execution. Premarital agreements traditionally have been looked upon favorably in Indiana.... However, we refuse to accept that this agreement is conscionable....

Conclusion

... We conclude that the agreement is unconscionable, Julie is not barred from challenging it, and it therefore is void. We reverse the trial court's division of property in the parties' dissolution and remand for the trial court to divide the marital property in a manner consistent with the general laws governing such division.

Reversed and remanded.

Assessing the Client's Position regarding the Enforceability of the Premarital Agreement

The law office will either be representing the party who originally proposed that a premarital agreement be prepared and executed and now seeks its enforcement or the party who agreed to its execution but who now seeks legal representation to oppose the enforcement. In either case, the first aspect to review is what circumstances existed during the formation of the contract. The court will generally uphold a premarital agreement unless the parties possessed unequal bargaining power. If both parties had similar financial and educational backgrounds at the time of the execution, the court will most likely uphold the agreement.

Second glance doctrine
Consideration of what circumstances exist at the time of enforcement of a prenuptial agreement in order to protect spouses from changes in circumstances that occurred since the date of the formation of the prenuptial agreement.

The second aspect to consider is what circumstances exist at the time one of the parties seeks enforcement of the agreement. The courts apply the *second glance doctrine* in order to protect spouses from changes in circumstances that occurred since the date of the formation of the premarital agreement. Provisions may not take effect for years. Fairness and reasonableness are subjective tests to be determined by the courts after reviewing the totality of circumstances, such as the parties' health, financial status, intellectual and business savvy, existence of dependent children, and current standard of living.

Figure 3-3 The onset of a serious illness or medical condition may be considered a substantial change of circumstances and render a waiver of alimony in a premarital agreement unenforceable.

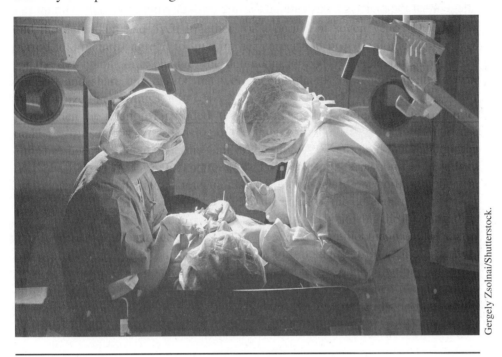

Gergely Zsolnai/Shutterstock.

CELEBRITY PREMARITAL AGREEMENTS

The short shelf life of celebrity marriages and the fact that many of them are domiciled in community property jurisdictions, like California for instance, make the execution of a premarital agreement a must. Taken straight from the popular press, here is some "news" on celebrity prenuptials.

Brad Pitt and Angelina Jolie

In September of 2016, Angelina Jolie filed for divorce from Brad Pitt, signaling the end of one of Hollywood's royal couples. While no one really knows the intimate details of another's marriage, divorce papers were filed after Pitt was involved in a much-publicized altercation that took place on the couple's private plane between Pitt and their teenage son, Maddox. The FBI and Los Angeles County Department of Children and Family Services investigated the matter and cleared Pitt of any child-abuse–related charges. The couple had already resolved their financial matters in a premarital agreement executed prior to their marriage in 2014, which laid the foundation for dividing their reported $400 million combined fortune. What is left are matters related to their six children which the couple is currently working on.

Kim Kardashian and Kris Humphries

The Kardashian sisters are very astute when it comes to legal matters. Daughters of a famous celebrity attorney, the late Robert Kardashian, both know that an iron-clad premarital agreement is a must in a Hollywood marriage. Kim Kardashian, star of *Keeping Up with the Kardashians,* filed for divorce just seventy-two days after her heavily marketed and televised wedding to NBA player Kris Humphries. The

Confidentiality clause

A clause found in an agreement where the parties agree not to discuss the details of their relationship with the press.

celebrity press reported that the Kardashian/Humphries premarital agreement allegedly included something called a *confidentiality clause* where the parties agreed not to discuss the details of their relationship with the press.

Humphries, who was seeking an annulment of the marriage on fraud grounds, alleged that the marriage was entered into for publicity purposes only. Humphries also wanted to invalidate the premarital agreement so he would be free to discuss what happened during this short-lived marriage. His claim was that the marriage was basically a publicity stunt, designed by Kardashian to make millions by televising the wedding. The premarital agreement protected Kardashian's earnings from Humphries' reach. Humphries also wanted Kardashian to return the $2 million engagement ring; however, it was reported that the premarital agreement stated that she was entitled to keep the ring in the event of divorce. In 2013, the parties reached a settlement, dissolving their marriage on the grounds of "irreconcilable differences" rather than an annulment. Even though Humphries was seeking a reported $7 million from Kardashian, he received nothing and was responsible for his own attorney's fees.

Kim Kardashian and Kanye West

Kardashian and West allegedly entered into what the popular press called a "midnup," described as a prenuptial agreement executed in the middle of a marriage. The couple was reportedly considering such a contract for the purpose of protecting Kardashian from West's alleged financial issues. This is nothing new in legal circles where the legal profession refers to such contracts as postnuptial or postmarital agreements.

Khloe Kardashian and Lamar Odom

Khloe Kardashian, star of *Kourtney & Khloe Take Miami* and *Keeping Up with the Kardashians*, and Los Angeles Clippers star Lamar Odom allegedly signed a premarital agreement three weeks after their celebrity wedding. Apparently, the couple agreed that the marriage would not be legally binding until the contract was signed. Reported clauses included Kardashian asking for $500,000 for each year of marriage and $25,000 a month in spousal support. Odom, on the other hand, would keep his $33 million Lakers' salary for the next four years and the couple's seven-bedroom, nine-bathroom house. Unfortunately, the couple divorced in December of 2016.

Deion Sanders and Pilar Sanders

Former Dallas Cowboy and sports analyst Deion Sanders scored a touchdown when a Texas court ruled against his wife, Pilar, who argued that the premarital agreement she signed twelve years earlier was invalid. Pilar claimed that she did not initial the agreement and that the initials on the actual document were not hers. She also claimed that Deion failed to fully disclose the extent of his estate, which rendered the agreement void. A paralegal working for Deion's attorney, however, testified that Pilar had forgotten to initial a few sections of the agreement and did so at a later date with another pen. The court found that she signed the agreement voluntarily, which included a $100,000 "signing bonus" and a million dollars when the divorce was final.

Jessica Biel and Justin Timberlake

Star of *7th Heaven* and *The Texas Chainsaw Massacre*, Jessica Biel allegedly initiated her pending nuptials to Justin Timberlake with a proposed premarital agreement that includes an *infidelity clause*. An infidelity clause is triggered if one of the spouses commits adultery. Its purpose is to penalize the cheating spouse by affecting the divorce settlement. Reportedly, Biel wants $500,000 if Timberlake ever strays.

Infidelity clause
An infidelity clause is triggered if one of the spouses commits adultery. Its purpose is to penalize the cheating spouse by affecting the divorce settlement.

Nicole Kidman and Keith Urban

Nicole Kidman and country singer Keith Urban allegedly signed a premarital agreement stating that in the event of divorce, Urban would receive approximately $600,000 for every year married. The use of illegal drugs on the part of Urban, however, would leave him with nothing under the terms of the agreement.

Barry Bonds and Sun Bonds

While San Francisco Giants All-Star player Barry Bonds may always be remembered in baseball history as the player who was indicted on perjury and obstruction of justice charges in 2007 for his involvement in a steroid scandal, his name has different connotations in family law circles. In 1988, Bonds asked Sun, his wife-to-be, to sign a premarital agreement. Bonds was earning $106,000 a year at the time the agreement was executed. While Bonds was represented by an attorney, his wife was not. The premarital agreement included a clause where the wife agreed to waive any interest in his future earnings. Little did she know that eventually he would be earning in the millions. When the marriage broke down, Sun challenged the validity of the agreement on the grounds that she was not represented by an attorney at the time she signed the agreement.

The California Appellate Court ruled in favor of Sun, even though it was not unusual for parties to sign a premarital without the benefit of legal counsel. The Bonds decision challenged the validity of many previously executed agreements, sending shockwaves in legal circles. In 2000, the California Supreme Court upheld the agreement on the ground that Sun had entered into it voluntarily, thus making it an enforceable document. Legal cases are a lot like fairy tales. There is always some moral to the story. The Bonds decision suggests that before signing a premarital agreement, clients should have it thoroughly reviewed by independent counsel. Litigating a case all the way up to the state Supreme Court level is expensive, time consuming, and stressful.

If I Knew Back Then What I Know Now ...

Here are some celebrities who probably wish that they had their prospective spouse execute a premarital agreement. Instead, they had to pull out the checkbook.

Camille Grammer and Kelsey Grammer

Fans of Bravo's *The Real Housewives of Beverly Hills* are all too familiar with the breakdown of the marriage between Camille and Kelsey Grammer. Grammer, the star of *Cheers* and *Frasier* as well as one of Hollywood's highest-paid actors, failed to convince a divorce court that some of his earnings should be considered separate property. Only a portion of his earnings were earned prior to his marriage to Camille, leaving a total of seven years subject to marital property distribution. The couple was married for thirteen years but failed to enter into a premarital agreement. The couple settled their divorce case with the Real Housewife receiving $30 million.

Mel Gibson and Robyn Gibson

After twenty-six years of marriage, seven children, and no premarital agreement, Mel Gibson and his wife Robyn called it quits. Without a premarital agreement, California community property law entitled Robyn to a 50/50 division of the approximately $900 million earned by the famous actor.

Paul McCartney and Heather Mills

Former Beatle Paul McCartney ignored a chorus of good advice and married Heather Mills, a woman over twenty years his junior, without the benefit of a premarital agreement. Unfortunately, the marriage broke down, and a London family court ordered McCartney to pay Mills a lump sum of $33 million, as well as $70,000 a year in child support in addition to paying for a nanny and a private school education.

POSTMARITAL AGREEMENTS

Postnuptial agreement
Agreement made *after* the marriage has been performed in which the elements are similar to those of prenuptial agreements.

A 2012 survey published by the American Academy of Matrimonial Lawyers revealed that almost half of its members have seen an increase in the demand for postmarital agreements. A postmarital agreement (also known as a ***postnuptial agreement***) is a contract between spouses who wish to remain married but want to alter or confirm the legal rights and responsibilities inherent in the marital relationship.

Under common law, a husband and wife could not enter into a contractual agreement because upon marriage a husband and wife merged into one legal entity. Unfortunately, you need two parties to create a contract, so spouses were barred from doing so because of this common law principle. The law started to change in the 1980s when courts were more willing to enforce such contracts as long as they adhered to the same requirements as premarital agreements.

Reasons for Entering into a Postmarital Agreement

Spouses may consider entering into a postmarital agreement for a variety of reasons:

Contractual Afterthought Some couples may have just forgotten to take care of the matter before the wedding, or they may have discussed the issue but failed to actually get down to the business of having one drafted. In cases of second and third marriages, the parties may wish to protect children and grandchildren from previous relationships in the event of divorce or death. A postmarital agreement may also be considered where the parties executed a premarital agreement and new issues emerge or matters covered under the premarital agreement require some update, adjustment, or clarification.

Addressing Conflicts The parties may wish to execute a postmarital agreement to deal with conflicts that arise during the course of the marriage. There may be a situation where one spouse has committed adultery and the other spouse wants to create a postmarital agreement that contains an infidelity clause that would punish the cheating spouse in the event of another transgression that would lead to divorce.

Substantial Change in Circumstances In other cases, there may be a substantial change in circumstances where one or both of the spouses seek to protect his or her interest in writing. For example, a spouse gets a new job or promotion and seeks to protect the increase in his or her earnings, or a spouse may be promoted to partner in a business and may wish to secure his or her partnership interest. Some private companies may even require partners to enter into a postmarital agreement as a condition of employment. This protects the partnership from having a divorce court award part of the spouse's partnership interest as part of the proceedings or intermeddling family members in probate court in the event of death. On the other hand, a spouse may give up his or her career for the purpose of staying home with the children or taking care of a sick or elderly relative. This is not uncommon, especially in situations where day care is too expensive or where multigenerational families are living together. Arrangements such as these put the stay-at-home spouses at an economic disadvantage, and they may wish to protect themselves in the event the marriage dissolves.

Inheritances/New Assets Postmarital inheritances or acquiring new or unanticipated assets can also be the catalyst. A spouse may want to secure his or her inheritance from being categorized as marital property and subject to distribution in the event of a divorce. A spouse may also inherit an interest in a family-owned business or something of sentimental value that needs to be kept "in the family." A situation may also exist where the spouses started a business together and may want to address its distribution in the event of a divorce or death of one of the spouses. Protection may also be necessary in situations where one spouse provides the initial investment from his or her funds for the purposes of purchasing a house, business, vacation home, or other asset. The postmarital agreement may specify that in the event of divorce or death, the spouse may recoup his or her initial contribution.

Testing the Validity of a Postnuptial Agreement

In this case, the wife's extramarital affair with a man she met online prompted her husband to negotiate a reconciliation on the condition that she would sign a postmarital agreement. Once the husband filed for divorce, the wife challenged the postmarital agreement on the grounds of fraud in the inducement. The Court of Civil Appeals of Alabama, however, did not agree and determined that this agreement was valid and enforceable, especially after twenty years of marriage and the wife's familiarity with the assets of the marriage and ample opportunity to investigate their value.

TAHNYA B. NORTHINGTON v. DAVID S. NORTHINGTON

Docket No. 2160352.
Court of Civil Appeals of Alabama
November 9, 2017

Thompson, Presiding Judge.

Tahnya B. Northington ("the wife") appeals from a judgment of the Tuscaloosa Circuit Court ("the trial court") that, among other things, upheld the validity of a postnuptial agreement ("the agreement") she had entered into with David S. Northington ("the husband").

The only issue presented on appeal in this matter is whether the trial court erred in determining that the agreement was valid and enforceable. The evidence relevant to that issue indicated the following. The parties married in March 1995. Two children were born during the marriage; the wife had a child from a previous marriage, but the husband helped rear that child as his own. In late March 2012, the husband discovered that the wife was engaged in an extramarital affair. The wife of the man with whom the wife in this case was having the affair notified the husband. On April 2 or 3, 2012, the husband confronted the wife, who admitted that she had engaged in a physical sexual affair with the man, who lived on the West Coast. The wife conceded that she had met the man online and had engaged in "phone sex" and "Skype sex,"

continued

that is, via computer using a web camera, with him before the man traveled to Alabama. The wife and the man met in Birmingham and carried out a physical affair.

When the husband confronted the wife, he gave her the option of divorcing or reconciling, with the condition that, if she chose reconciliation, she would sign a postnuptial agreement. The wife chose reconciliation, and the parties began marriage counseling. The parties also spent a considerable time—more than two years—crafting the agreement. The wife consulted with three attorneys during the course of negotiations and testified that she had made changes to various drafts of the agreement before executing it. The wife signed the agreement on June 23, 2014; the husband signed it on June 25, 2014. On December 8, 2015, the husband filed a complaint for a divorce in the trial court. The wife answered and filed a counterclaim alleging that the agreement was not fair or equitable and that it was obtained in a fraudulent manner because, she said, in making the agreement, the husband had withheld from her the value of his assets. The trial court held a bifurcated trial so that it could first determine the enforceability of the agreement. . . .

. . . The wife contends that the agreement is not valid and enforceable because, she says, the "undisputed evidence" indicates that there was fraud in the inducement of her execution of the agreement. Specifically, the wife argues that the husband's refusal to disclose the values of the real estate and Bama Exterminating was a violation of what she said was his legal duty to fully and fairly disclose not only his assets, but also the value of those assets. . . .

. . . In the instant case, the undisputed evidence indicates that the wife, although perhaps reluctant to do so, agreed to sign the postnuptial agreement rather than end the marriage after the husband discovered her affair. The negotiations regarding the agreement lasted some 27 months, and the wife consulted with 3 attorneys. She was represented by an attorney at the time she executed the agreement. The agreement listed all of the real estate the wife was agreeing to relinquish, as well as Bama Exterminating. The wife had been married to the husband for almost 20 years at the time the agreement was signed, and she was familiar with the real estate, as well as the income derived from Bama Exterminating. Although the husband did not provide the wife with the market values of the real estate as she had requested, he did provide her with methods she could use to learn the values of the properties. Some of the real estate on the husband's list had been in the wife's family and had been purchased from one of her family members. Nonetheless, during the 27 months of negotiating the agreement, the wife was aware that she did not know the market values of the properties at issue, yet she chose not to avail herself of any of the husband's suggestions for learning those values.

The evidence presented supports a conclusion that the wife knew specifically which real-estate properties she would be giving up pursuant to the agreement, she was familiar with those properties, she consulted with attorneys during the negotiations regarding the agreement and was represented by counsel at the time she signed the agreement, and she had more than a general knowledge of the extent of the husband's estate at the time the agreement was signed. Additionally, there is no evidence indicating that she was under duress at the time she signed the agreement.

Based on the foregoing, we conclude that the evidence demonstrated that the agreement was fair, just, and equitable from the wife's point of view. Accordingly, the trial court's determination that the postnuptial agreement was valid and enforceable is due to be affirmed.

AFFIRMED.

Know Your State Law

While a majority of states recognize postmarital agreements, it is important to learn the rules in your particular jurisdiction. For example, Michigan prohibits spouses from entering into postnuptial agreements that encourage or anticipate the breakdown of the marriage on public policy grounds.

In some states, postnuptial agreements are governed by case law. In *Bratton v. Bratton*, 136 S.W.3d 595 (2004), for example, the Tennessee Supreme Court held that a postnuptial agreement will be enforced when the following three criteria are met: (1) the agreement is supported by consideration; (2) the agreement was entered into freely, knowledgeably, in good faith, and without the exertion of duress or undue influence; and (3) the agreement is fair and equitable.

In other jurisdictions, such as Arkansas, Hawaii, Illinois, and North Carolina, postnuptial agreements are governed by standard contract principles, while other states have no clear rules on their enforceability. States like Minnesota have codified the requirements for drafting an enforceable postnuptial agreement in their state statutes.

MINN. STAT. 519.11 ANTENUPTIAL AND POSTNUPTIAL CONTRACTS[2]

Subdivision 1.Antenuptial contract.

A man and woman of legal age may enter into an antenuptial contract or settlement prior to solemnization of marriage which shall be valid and enforceable if (a) there is a full and fair disclosure of the earnings and property of each party, and (b) the parties have had an opportunity to consult with legal counsel of their own choice. An antenuptial contract or settlement made in conformity with this section may determine what rights each party has in the nonmarital property, defined in section 518.003, subdivision 3b, upon dissolution of marriage, legal separation, or after its termination by death and may bar each other of all rights in the respective estates not so secured to them by their agreement. This section shall not be construed to make invalid or unenforceable any antenuptial agreement or settlement made and executed in conformity with this section because the agreement or settlement covers or includes marital property, if the agreement or settlement would be valid and enforceable without regard to this section.

Subd. 1a.Postnuptial contract.

(a) Spouses who are legally married under the laws of this state may enter into a postnuptial contract or settlement which is valid and enforceable if it:
  (1) complies with the requirements for antenuptial contracts or settlements in this section and in the law of this state, including, but not limited to, the requirement that it be procedurally and substantively fair and equitable both at the time of its execution and at the time of its enforcement; and
  (2) complies with the requirements for postnuptial contracts or settlements in this section.

(b) A postnuptial contract or settlement that conforms with this section may determine all matters that may be determined by an antenuptial contract or settlement under the law of this state, except that a postnuptial contract or settlement may not determine the rights of any child of the spouses to child support from either spouse or rights of child custody or parenting time.

(c) A postnuptial contract or settlement is valid and enforceable only if at the time of its execution each spouse is represented by separate legal counsel.

---

[2]2012 Minnesota Statutes, Chapter 519, Section 11, Minnesota State Legislature.

(d) A postnuptial contract or settlement is presumed to be unenforceable if either party commences an action for a legal separation or dissolution within two years of the date of its execution, unless the spouse seeking to enforce the postnuptial contract or settlement can establish that the postnuptial contract or settlement is fair and equitable.

(e) Nothing in this section shall impair the validity or enforceability of a contract, agreement, or waiver which is entered into after marriage and which is described in chapter 524, article 2, part 2, further, a conveyance permitted by section 500.19 is not a postnuptial contract or settlement under this section....

Fair and Reasonable

In *Ansin v. Craven-Ansin*, the Massachusetts Supreme Judicial Court held that postnuptial agreements are not automatically unenforceable as a matter of public policy and are subject to a five-part test in order to determine whether the agreement is "fair and reasonable."

KENNETH S. ANSIN VS. CHERYL A. CRAVEN-ANSIN

457 Mass. 283 (2010)
Massachusetts Supreme Judicial Court
April 5, 2010–July 16, 2010

MARSHALL, C.J. We granted direct appellate review in this divorce proceeding to determine whether so-called "postnuptial" or "marital" agreements are contrary to public policy and, if not, whether the marital agreement at issue is enforceable.... The dispute is between Kenneth S. Ansin (husband) and Cheryl A. Craven-Ansin (wife) concerning the validity of their 2004 written agreement "settling all rights and obligations arising from their marital relationship" in the event of a divorce. Two years after the agreement was executed, in November, 2006, the husband filed a complaint for divorce and sought to enforce the terms of the agreement. At the time of the complaint, the parties had been married for twenty-one years and had two sons.

... We briefly summarize key provisions of the marital agreement. The agreement sets forth the parties' intent that, in the event of a divorce, the terms of the agreement are to be "valid and enforceable" against them, and "limit the rights" that "otherwise arise by reason of their marriage." ... The agreement recites that the parties are aware of the rights to which they may be entitled under Massachusetts law, that each has retained independent legal counsel, and that each executed the agreement "freely and voluntarily." The agreement states that the parties are "aware of the other's income," warrants that each has been provided with "all information requested by the other," and affirms that each "waives his or her rights to further inquiry, discovery and investigation." The agreement further recites that each is "fully satisfied" that the agreement "will promote marital harmony" and "will ensure the treatment of Husband's property to which the parties agreed before their marriage and since their separation."

As for the distribution of property in the event of a divorce, the agreement states that the wife "disclaims any and all interest she now has or ever may have" in the husband's interest in the Florida real estate and other marital assets. The husband agreed to pay the wife $5 million, and thirty percent of the appreciation of all marital property held by the couple from the time of the agreement to the time of the divorce.... The agreement provides that the wife could remain in the marital home for one year after any divorce, with the husband paying all reasonable expenses of that household. The husband agreed to pay for the wife's medical insurance until her death or remarriage, and he agreed to maintain a life insurance policy to the exclusive benefit of the wife in the amount of $2.5 million while the parties remained married.

... Whether a marital agreement should be recognized in Massachusetts is a long-deferred question of first impression.... Consistent with the majority of States to address the issue... we conclude that such agreements may be enforced... Our decision is consistent with our established recognition that a marital relationship need not vitiate contractual rights between the parties...

... The wife argues that marital agreements are different in kind and should be declared void against public policy because they are "innately coercive," "usually" arise when the marriage is already failing, and may "encourage" divorce. The wife provides no support for, and we reject, any assumption that marital agreements are typically executed amid threats of divorce or induced by illusory promises of remaining in a failing marriage. Marital contracts are not the product of classic arm's-length bargaining, but that does not make them necessarily coercive. Such contracts may inhibit the dissolution of a marriage or may protect the interests of third parties such as children from a prior relationship. In any event, a marital agreement will always be reviewed by a judge to ensure that coercion or fraud played no part in its execution...

... Before a marital agreement is sanctioned by a court, careful scrutiny by the judge should determine at a minimum whether (1) each party has had an opportunity to obtain separate legal counsel of each party's own choosing; ... (2) there was fraud or coercion in obtaining the agreement; (3) all assets were fully disclosed by both parties before the agreement was executed; (4) each spouse knowingly and explicitly agreed in writing to waive the right to a judicial equitable division of assets and all marital rights in the event of a divorce; and (5) the terms of the agreement are fair and reasonable at the time of execution and at the time of divorce... Where one spouse challenges the enforceability of the agreement, the spouse seeking to enforce the agreement shall bear the burden of satisfying these criteria...

... In evaluating whether a marital agreement is fair and reasonable at the time of execution, a judge should accordingly consider the entire context in which the agreement was reached, allowing greater latitude for agreements reached where each party is represented by separate counsel of their own choosing.... A judge may consider "the magnitude of the disparity between the outcome under the agreement and the outcome under otherwise prevailing legal principles," whether "the purpose of the agreement was to benefit or protect the interests of third parties (such as the children from a prior relationship)," and "the impact of the agreement's enforcement upon the children of the parties."... Other factors may include the length of the marriage, the motives of the contracting spouses, their respective bargaining positions, the circumstances giving rise to the marital agreement, the degree of the pressure, if any, experienced by the contesting spouse, and other circumstances the judge finds relevant.

Viewed at the time of execution, we agree with the judge that the marital agreement at issue here was fair and reasonable. As noted earlier, the wife was represented by experienced, independent counsel throughout the negotiations. In the event of a divorce, the wife was to receive a substantial fixed sum payment from her husband. If the marital estate appreciated in value after execution of the agreement, she would receive, in addition, a percentage of the increase in value; she did not forgo the fixed payment if the marital assets, including the husband's interest in the Florida real estate, declined substantially. There is no basis to the wife's claim that the judge "ignore[d]" the husband's "legal obligation of disclosure of value" of the Florida real estate. As we discussed in detail earlier, the basis of the valuation was known to and accepted by the wife and her lawyer. We see no reason to disturb the judge's ruling on this point.

... Conclusion. Enforcement of a marital agreement is not contrary to public policy. We agree with the judge in the Probate and Family Court that the marital agreement in this case should be specifically enforced.

Source: Kenneth S. Ansin v. Cheryl A. Craven-Ansin, 457 MASS. 283 (2010), Massachusetts Judicial Court.

JUDGMENT AFFIRMED

Drafting Considerations

As indicated earlier in this chapter, it is crucial to know your state law before beginning the task of drafting a postmarital agreement. While a boilerplate document may be a good starting point, failure to research and incorporate your jurisdiction's requirements when drafting may lead to a malpractice lawsuit. Courts tend to scrutinize postmarital agreements with greater care than they do premarital contracts. A prospective spouse who does not want to sign a premarital agreement has the option of saying "No thanks" and walking away. Married spouses may not have this luxury; in fact, walking away may not be an option, and a spouse's bargaining power is limited.

In general, a postmarital agreement should include all of the requirements necessary for drafting a premarital agreement. There are two additional requirements that are important to address with postmarital agreements.

(1) **Consideration:** Each party to a contract must give up something of value, for example, money, property, or a promise. This is called consideration. Marriage is the consideration in a premarital agreement. For postmarital agreements, however, the parties fulfill the consideration requirement by mutually relinquishing marital property rights or transferring some property from one spouse to the other.

   Example: Husband has just completed six months of an alcohol rehabilitation program. During this time the wife went through great hardship to care for the family. The wife may ask the husband to sign a postnuptial agreement in which he promises to pay her a sum of money (consideration) in the event of a relapse.

(2) **The Agreement Does Not Contemplate or Encourage Divorce:** It is important that the language used in a postmarital agreement clearly demonstrates that the purpose of the contract is for the spouses to agree to an amicable settlement of their property disputes. Postmarital agreements that contemplate or encourage divorce may be considered unenforceable in the eyes of the court.

Concept Review and Reinforcement

KEY **TERMS**

confidentiality clause
infidelity clause
postnuptial agreement

premarital agreement
prenuptial agreement
public policy

second glance doctrine
unconscionable
Uniform Premarital Agreement Act (UPAA)

REVIEW OF **KEY CONCEPTS**

1. Using Internet legal research resources such as Westlaw or Loislaw, what are the requirements in your state for drafting a valid premarital agreement? Does case law or statutory law govern the subject of premarital agreements in your state? Has your jurisdiction adopted the UPAA?

2. Based on the historical explanation included in the *Posner* case, explain why premarital agreements were once considered void contracts and what changed according to the court's decision.

3. Based on your reading of this chapter, why are premarital agreements no longer just for the rich and famous?

4. Explain why the advice of independent counsel is so important for the purpose of reviewing a premarital agreement.

5. Discuss the issues involving the enforceability of premarital agreements during the dissolution process and how an opponent spouse may challenge a premarital agreement.

6. Using Internet legal research resources such as Westlaw or Loislaw, what are the requirements in your state for drafting postmarital agreements?

BUILDING YOUR PARALEGAL SKILLS

CASES FOR BRIEFING

BILIOURIS v. BILIOURIS, 67 MASS. APP. CT. 149 (2006)

Critical Thinking and Legal Analysis Applications

Sandra Evans and Felipe Gonzalez are to be married this morning at St. John the Baptist Church. This is Felipe's second marriage and Sandra's first. Sandra arrives at the church in a limousine, and before exiting the luxury car, Felipe slides into the backseat holding a document that he asks Sandra to sign. Looking confused, she asks him what it is. Felipe tells her that it is a premarital agreement and that if she loves him she will sign it. With two hundred guests waiting in the church and the stress of the wedding, Sandra reluctantly signs the document and says to Felipe, "I guess we'll have to talk about this later." Felipe reassures her not to worry and that it is just a formality. Two years and a baby later, the marriage falls apart, and Sandra is questioning the validity of the document she signed on her wedding day.

Based on the case of *Biliouris v. Biliouris,* 67 Mass. App. Ct. 149 (2006), how would the Massachusetts courts decide this case?

Based on the premarital agreement laws in your jurisdiction, how would the courts in your state decide this case?

Building a Professional Portfolio

PORTFOLIO EXERCISES

1. You work as a paralegal for the law firm of Cocco, Cocco & Cocco in your state. Your supervisor, Attorney Rocco Cocco, asks you to review a premarital agreement drafted by the client, Frank Holloway, and to draft a letter on his behalf, which he will sign, explaining the enforceability of the following clause:

   The parties agree not to have children. In the event the wife becomes pregnant, she shall terminate the pregnancy. If for any reason she shall fail to terminate the pregnancy, the husband shall not be liable for child support.

2. You work as a paralegal in the State of Connecticut for the law office of Emanuel Perez. Paula White has just retained the firm to represent her in the drafting and execution of a premarital agreement. She plans to marry her long-time boyfriend, James Meyerson, later this year. Both are residents of Branford, Connecticut.

She lives at 121 Westway Drive, and he lives at 231 Summit Place. Ms. White owns two apartment buildings located on 501 and 503 Main Street in Branford. Each building has twenty tenants in it and generates $750 per month per unit. Both properties were recently appraised at a fair market value of $1,000,000 each. These two properties have been in the White family for many years, and Ms. White wants to keep it that way. She heard that a divorce court in the State of Connecticut may award any part of either party's estate in a divorce case regardless of whether it was acquired before or during the marriage. She is concerned that in the event of divorce, her husband may make a claim to this property. She would like to have a premarital agreement drafted to prevent this from happening. Using a form found on the Internet, draft a premarital agreement that will achieve Ms. White's objectives.

Chapter **four**

DIVORCE, SEPARATION, AND ANNULMENT

LEARNING OBJECTIVES

After studying this chapter, you should be able to:

1. Define "dissolution of marriage."

2. Define "legal separation."

3. Describe the situations that favor a legal separation over a divorce.

4. Define "annulment."

5. Identify the grounds that justify an annulment.

The end of a relationship is like the rupture of a once-beautiful dream. When the relationship has been formalized as a marriage, the legal task of ending the marriage is never pleasant, but it need not be an ugly nightmare, provided competent and caring family law professionals skillfully shepherd the client through the process. The first order of the day is to determine if the circumstances call for a divorce or dissolution, a legal separation, or an annulment.

DISSOLVING THE MARITAL UNION

Excluding the death of a spouse, there are three ways to end a marital relationship: (1) dissolution of marriage, (2) legal separation, and (3) annulment.

Dissolution of Marriage

Dissolution of marriage is the phrase many jurisdictions use to formally define the word ***divorce***. It is the complete legal severance of the marital relationship. After the conclusion of the divorce proceeding, the parties are legally free to remarry if they so choose. Be it a ceremonial or common law marriage, it is the state that must legally dissolve the marital union. State intervention is required to protect the rights of the parties, provide a forum where grievances can be aired instead of encouraging couples to resort to self-help, and formally end a legal status that carries many rights and obligations. Major issues such as child support, custody, visitation, alimony, and property and debt division must be resolved either by mutual agreement of the parties, with assistance from attorneys or mediators, or by judicial order.

Divorce is a drastic measure. An individual who believes his or her marriage has failed or is in the process of falling apart should investigate all options available so that he or she can make an informed decision on how to proceed.

Family Counseling ***Family counseling*** is a service that enables couples to evaluate the viability of their marital relationship. A spouse or spouses who still possess the desire to salvage their marital relationship may wish to consider family counseling before making the final break. There are counselors in private practice who offer this service. If that alternative is too expensive, some community agencies offer marriage counseling at affordable prices. In a therapeutic setting, spouses can air their differences and explore ways to resolve them. If one of the

Dissolution of marriage
The phrase many jurisdictions use to formally define the complete legal severance of the marital relationship.

Divorce
The complete legal severance of the marital relationship.

Family counseling
A service that enables couples to evaluate the viability of their marital relationship.

Figure 4-1 A spouse or spouses who still possess the desire to salvage their marriage may wish to consider family counseling before making the final break.

Anton Gvozdikov/Shutterstock.

two spouses will not consider counseling or if that process is tried but fails, the next step is to dissolve the marriage.

Mediation
A form of alternative dispute resolution, conducted by a neutral person, designed to avoid undue litigation and lessen the emotional trauma involved in a divorce.

Mediation *Mediation* is a process, conducted by a neutral person, designed to avoid undue litigation and lessen the emotional trauma involved in a divorce. Once the decision is made to divorce, the parties may consider engaging the services of an attorney or certified family law mediator whose role is to facilitate a dialogue between the spouses on the many issues that must be resolved before a divorce is granted. These issues frequently include the custody, visitation, and support of any minor children; alimony; and the division of marital property and marital debt. Even if mediation is successful, the parties must still go to court. One of the parties will bring a dissolution of marriage action against the other spouse. Then the court will review the agreement drawn up in the mediation sessions. If the court determines that the agreement is fair and freely entered into by both parties, the court will incorporate their agreement into a court decree, give full force to each provision as an order of the court, and legally dissolve the marriage. If the mediation process is not employed or has not resulted in an agreement, other options must be pursued.

Collaborative Lawyering Collaborative lawyering is another alternative to protracted litigation. When one spouse tells the other spouse of his or her intention to divorce before actually bringing the action, or when both spouses have discussed their differences and agree to disagree, each spouse may retain his or her own attorney but authorize their respective lawyers to negotiate an agreement. This process, known as collaborative lawyering, differs from the mediation process because each party's lawyer acts as an advocate for his or her client and tries to achieve the best possible outcome for the client while recognizing that concessions and compromise on the part of each spouse will be necessary to forge an agreement without going to trial. Collaborative lawyering may be a desirable alternative for some couples but not others. Success depends on the attorneys' negotiating skills and each party's ability to be forthcoming, realistic, and reasonable. If each spouse acknowledges the other's rights to be involved with and have a say in the minor children's upbringing, and if the marital property and debts can be easily identified and reasonably divided, this process can result in an agreement. As with successful mediation, one of the parties must still bring a dissolution action and the court must review and approve the agreement before incorporating it into a divorce decree and dissolving the marriage. Collaborative lawyering will not be successful if one or both of the spouses are extremely hostile to the other, if they are involved in a vicious custody dispute, or if one or both of the spouses fail to disclose all of their financial information to prevent a fair and equitable property distribution. When this is the case, the only remaining alternative is for one spouse to institute dissolution proceedings and anticipate a vigorous adversarial proceeding.

Grounds for Dissolution As mentioned in Chapter One, in order to get a divorce, the party who is bringing the action must state the grounds for divorce. With the advent of no-fault divorce, the "irretrievable breakdown of the marriage" ground, also known as "irreconcilable differences" ground, has become the most popular and frequently asserted ground as it obviates the need to place the blame for the failure of the marriage on either party. Previously, typical grounds included intolerable cruelty—mental, physical, or both—abandonment, habitual drunkenness, and adultery. These grounds still exist and may be asserted when appropriate. Additionally, in certain states, not only are these grounds available, but there are also other grounds to raise. For instance, in Tennessee, the statute governing grounds for divorce offers a more comprehensive array of options.

Statutes

TENNESSEE CIVIL CODE ANNOTATED § 36-4-101 GROUNDS FOR DIVORCE FROM BONDS OF MATRIMONY

(a) The following are causes of divorce from the bonds of matrimony:

(1) Either party, at the time of the contract, was and still is naturally impotent and incapable of procreation;

(2) Either party has knowingly entered into a second marriage, in violation of a previous marriage, still subsisting;

(3) Either party has committed adultery;

(4) Willful or malicious desertion or absence of either party, without a reasonable cause, for one (1) whole year;

(5) Being convicted of any crime that, by the laws of the state, renders the party infamous;

(6) Being convicted of a crime that, by the laws of the state, is declared to be a felony, and sentenced to confinement in the penitentiary;

(7) Either party has attempted the life of the other, by poison or any other means showing malice;

(8) Refusal, on the part of a spouse, to remove with that person's spouse to this state, without a reasonable cause, and being willfully absent from the spouse residing in Tennessee for two (2) years;

(9) The woman was pregnant at the time of the marriage, by another person, without the knowledge of the husband;

(10) Habitual drunkenness or abuse of narcotic drugs of either party, when the spouse has contracted either such habit after marriage;

(11) The husband or wife is guilty of such cruel and inhuman treatment or conduct towards the spouse as renders cohabitation unsafe and improper, which may also be referred to in pleadings as inappropriate marital conduct;

(12) The husband or wife has offered such indignities to the spouse's person as to render the spouse's position intolerable, and thereby forced the spouse to withdraw;

(13) The husband or wife has abandoned the spouse or turned the spouse out of doors for no just cause, and has refused or neglected to provide for the spouse while having the ability to so provide;

(14) Irreconcilable differences between the parties; and

(15) For a continuous period of two (2) or more years that commenced prior to or after April 18, 1985, both parties have lived in separate residences, have not cohabited as man and wife during such period, and there are no minor children of the parties.

Source: Title 36 Domestic Relations, Chapter 4 Divorce and Annulment, § 36-4-101 Grounds for Divorce from Bonds of Matrimony, TN.Gov.

The Dissolution Action

1. **The Initial Pleadings and Responsive Pleadings**

To initiate dissolution proceedings, the person seeking the divorce, the plaintiff spouse, will file a complaint or petition with the proper court and will have a copy served on the defendant spouse. The defendant spouse, in response, will enter an appearance and file an answer. The defendant may also wish to file a counterclaim or cross-claim and any special defenses, if appropriate. These documents comprise the initial and responsive pleadings filed in a dissolution matter. Later in this book, Chapter Eleven is devoted to these pleadings; it covers, in detail, all of the sections contained in the complaint and also discusses some other documents that may be filed during this initial period if additional circumstances exist. The following is a brief description of the usual initial and responsive pleadings and the purpose of each document:

- **The Complaint (Petition).** The complaint or petition will recite the grounds justifying the dissolution and the relief requested. Each state has statutes or common law decisions which establish what grounds for granting a divorce exist in that state. The traditional grounds in most states are fault based. These grounds typically include adultery, abandonment, physical cruelty, mental cruelty, habitual intemperance (drunkenness), and incarceration for the conviction of a felony. In addition, most states now allow ***no-fault divorce*** on the ground of irretrievable breakdown of the marriage or irreconcilable differences. The plaintiff spouse must allege at least one ground, but may allege additional grounds if appropriate.

- **The Appearance and the Answer.** Following this, the other spouse, known as the defendant, will have a specified time period within which he or she has to respond to the allegations of the complaint. The defendant spouse must first enter an appearance. This is usually a one-page preprinted, fillable court form which the defendant spouse or his or her attorney must sign. The appearance will contain necessary contact information and usually is filed at the same time as the answer. The answer is the defendant's formal response to the complaint. In the answer, the defendant spouse will either admit or deny the allegations articulating the grounds or will leave the plaintiff spouse to his or her proof. If the defendant denies the allegations, she or he is in effect contesting the divorce, meaning that the plaintiff spouse will have to prove at least one of the grounds in a divorce trial unless an agreement is reached in the pretrial period.

- **The Cross-Complaint (Counterclaim).** With his or her answer, the defendant spouse may, if he or she wishes, file a cross-complaint. This is a document in which the defendant spouse seeks a divorce against the plaintiff spouse and alleges his or her grounds upon which if proven the court may grant a divorce in his or her favor. They may be the same as alleged by the plaintiff, such as irreconcilable differences, or may be completely different.

- **Special Defenses.** A special defense introduces a new fact whereby the defendant does not merely deny the facts alleged but also offers new evidence to invalidate the plaintiff's case and avoid a judgment. Special defenses are very rare but not unheard of in dissolution cases. For instance, a defendant spouse could raise the special defense that a valid marriage never existed and hence cannot be dissolved!

2. **Discovery**

The purpose of a divorce proceeding is to have the court legally end the marriage, and enter orders for custody, alimony, child support, and division of the marital property and debts. The discovery phase of a dissolution matter gives each spouse the opportunity to gather information and documents from the other spouse for use in their case against the other party and support their requests for relief. Each spouse will be required to disclose all information sought in the other spouse's discovery requests and must do so by certain deadlines. Chapter Thirteen, which specifically

---

No-fault divorce
In order to obtain a divorce, a litigant traditionally had to prove one of the statutory fault grounds or no divorce was granted; in 1969, the California legislature enacted the first no-fault divorce, which required parties only to prove that they had irreconcilable differences and there was no hope of reconciliation; currently, all fifty states have some form of no-fault divorce provisions where one of the parties only has to allege that the marriage has broken down and that there is no hope of reconciliation in order for the court to dissolve a marriage.

addresses discovery, explores this process in depth. What follows is a brief description of the discovery tools available to parties and examples of their use:

- **Interrogatories** are written questions served on the opposing party to be answered in writing and under oath. These questions may concern financial matters such as employment or possibly unknown real-estate holdings or more personal matters such as the names of medical doctors, therapists, or past or present lovers.
- **Requests for Production of Documents** are formal requests for documents such as earnings information, income tax returns, W-2s, 1099 forms, deeds, pension plan documents, bank statements, and statements of investment holdings such as stocks, bonds, and mutual funds.
- **Requests for Physical and Mental Examination** arise in situations where physical or mental health issues could affect the ability of either spouse to properly parent the children or to contribute to the support of the children.
- **Requests for Admission** in which one spouse formally requests that the other spouse formally admit relevant facts or events that inevitably can be proved at trial. Such admissions might include acknowledgment of promotion to a higher pay grade at work, an arrest on a driving while intoxicated charge, or the recent birth of a spouse's child with his or her paramour.
- **Depositions** are procedures where one party orders the other party or a person who may be called as a witness at trial to appear and answer questions under oath, which are transcribed by a court reporter. This discovery tool is expensive and is necessary in limited circumstances such as when there are serious concerns that one spouse is withholding important financial information or when the testimony of school personnel or a mental health professional may be required to settle custody or visitation.

3. **Pretrial Proceedings**

Some jurisdictions, upon a motion from one or both of the parties, permit *preliminary hearings* to enter temporary custody, child support, and alimony matters during the pendency of the divorce proceedings. Other pretrial events may include a court referral to the family relations division for a *custody study and evaluation*. If there is a custody dispute, a family relations officer will meet with each of the parents and may also speak with the children and possibly with school officials and any mental health professionals involved with the family. Following this study or evaluation, the family relations officer will make a recommendation to the court. Either party may dispute this recommendation and offer evidence supporting their own position at a trial. In another pretrial proceeding, the court, on its own initiative or upon request from one of the spouses, may order the parties to mediation by a family court officer regarding a parenting plan and each party's access to the children. Sometimes when a dissolution proceeding is placed on the trial list, the court may automatically order that the parties first attend a ***settlement conference*** in an attempt to settle all or some of the unresolved issues, thereby eliminating the need for a trial or shortening its scope and duration. In some jurisdictions, a judge conducts the settlement conference, while other states appoint two experienced attorneys, sometimes referred to as special masters, to conduct the conference.

Settlement conference
A meeting with both lawyers and their respective clients with the specific goal of settling the case without court intervention.

Figure 4-2 Sometimes when a dissolution proceeding is placed on the trial list, the court may automatically order that the parties first attend a settlement conference in an attempt to settle all or some of the unresolved issues, thereby eliminating the need for a trial or shortening its scope and duration.

Alexander Raths/Shutterstock.

4. **Trial**

At trial, the party bringing the action has the burden of proving the ground or grounds that are alleged to constitute a breach of the marriage contract. That party may present witnesses supporting his or her case and will testify himself or herself. Depending on the grounds alleged and the issues contested, these witnesses may be family members, friends, neighbors, and also professionals such as accountants, real-estate appraisers, social workers, therapists, and school personnel. When the plaintiff spouse finishes, he or she will rest his or her case. The defendant spouse then has an opportunity to present his or her own witnesses to rebut the plaintiff. After trial, the court will make a decision on contested matters and enter orders with the court's opinion. The divorce trial is discussed in greater detail in Chapter Fourteen.

5. **Appeal**

Either party may appeal all or part of the court's decision. A majority of appeals deal with custody decisions, alimony awards, and property division. When an appeal is timely filed, the contested portion of the divorce decree may be stayed until the appellate court issues its decision.

6. **Post-Judgment Matters**

When divorce proceedings are concluded, some parties never return to court. However, as time passes, many spouses will see a need to revisit issues previously resolved. While orders affecting the division of property are almost always final and not subject to modification, provisions for custody, alimony, and child support are modifiable if changed circumstances so warrant. For instance, if either spouse experiences an increase or decrease in income, the court, upon the filing of a proper motion, may raise or lower the amount for support. Similarly, if a parent alleges and proves that the custody or access/visitation determination is no longer in the child's best interest, the court will modify the order. Additionally, if either spouse fails to comply with any of the court's orders, the other spouse may file a motion for contempt and seek reimbursement for the attorney's fees incurred in bringing the matter back to court. All of these possibilities are addressed in greater detail in a later chapter devoted to post-judgment matters.

Legal Separation

Clients inquiring about a divorce will very often ask about a *legal separation*, or *separate maintenance*, as it is known in some jurisdictions. Instead of asking for a dissolution of marriage, the client's petition or complaint requests a legal separation: a status that allows the parties to live separate and apart, but unable to remarry. Once clients hear that they cannot remarry, many abandon the idea.

While not as common today, legal separations are available in most jurisdictions and may be chosen for some of the following reasons:

Religious: If the client's religion objects to divorce, a legal separation may be an option.

Medical Insurance Coverage: If a client has serious health problems, is the non-employee spouse, and is currently covered under a spouse's health insurance, it is important to examine whether a divorce or legal separation is in the client's best interest. Most insurance coverage ceases upon divorce; however, some policies may allow continued coverage in cases of legal separation. Ask for a copy of the client's group policy to determine when coverage ceases.

Financial: Parties may want to delay obtaining a formal divorce in order to qualify for certain Social Security and pension rights. If a couple has been married for ten years, for example, they qualify for a divorced spouse benefit under federal Social Security law. Therefore, reaching the ten-year mark is important, especially in cases where they may be very close. If this is the situation, the couple may obtain a legal separation and later convert it to a divorce, while preserving their rights.

Trial Separation: The parties may wish to enter into a trial separation and live separate and apart during this interim period. They may view the legal separation as a cooling-off period with the prospect of reconciling in the near future. A legal separation may be a solution, especially if they want a formal agreement on issues of custody, support, and property division. There are procedural mechanisms available to convert legal separations to dissolutions in cases where the parties wish to change their status later on.

An action for a legal separation is similar to a divorce or dissolution action in that specific grounds must be alleged and proven. The grounds that can be alleged are usually the same grounds that can be alleged in a divorce proceeding. Historically, an action for legal separation was brought by a spouse who desired to avoid the legal, social, or religious ramifications of a divorce but nevertheless wished to live apart from the other spouse. Legal separations are not as common today, but the action has survived and is still available to the spouse who wishes to pursue that course of action rather than divorce.

Courts granting legal separations may, when appropriate, order one spouse to provide financial support for the other spouse by making periodic payments to the spouse. Most courts will order the noncustodial spouse to pay child support to

Legal separation
An action brought by a spouse who wishes to avoid the legal, social, or religious ramifications of a divorce but nevertheless wishes to live apart from his or her spouse.

Separate maintenance
An action that affirms the continuation of a marriage and enforces the legal obligations of each spouse in the marriage.

the custodial spouse for the minor children. Courts may also order an equitable distribution of marital property or may incorporate into the separation decree the parties' separation agreement in which the parties themselves have negotiated a division of the marital estate.

After a legal separation, both parties retain certain marital rights and obligations that are extinguished after a divorce is final. For instance, a spouse may still have to provide medical insurance coverage for the other spouse and will still be able to have that spouse covered under any family policy. Similarly, a spouse may have more favorable rights under the other spouse's pension plan if legally separated rather than divorced. For instance, some pension plans, upon an individual's death, call for either the payment of a lump sum or partial or full periodic pension payments to the person's spouse. A spouse who has obtained a legal separation rather than a divorce will be eligible for such a benefit. In addition, if one party to a legal separation dies intestate, his or her spouse will be entitled to a statutory spousal share of the estate. If the deceased spouse had a will, then the other spouse may elect either to receive what was bequeathed to him or her in the will or to receive the statutory spousal share, and will usually select whichever amount is greater.

A legal separation also places limitations on spouses. The most restrictive limitation is that because the parties are still legally married, neither party is free to remarry.

Separate Maintenance

An action for separate maintenance is similar to a legal separation. The marriage is still intact and neither party is legally free to remarry. In addition, an action for separate maintenance affirms the continuation of the marriage and enforces the legal obligations of each spouse in the marriage. An action for separate maintenance does not expressly or necessarily authorize a husband or wife to live apart; however, a wife's refusal to cohabit with her husband is sanctioned and authorized. Actions for separate maintenance are less common today than in the nineteenth century and during the first half of the twentieth century. Sometimes they were initiated by a wife whose husband was about to go abroad or to another part of this country to work or to perform military service. On other occasions, the action for separation was a precursor to a divorce action brought during a period of marital discord or during a trial separation.

Annulments

Annulment
A judicial decision that a valid marriage does not exist or never existed between a person and another party.

An **annulment** is a court order terminating a marriage by declaring it void from its inception. There are two types of annulments. A civil annulment is obtained through a court order, and laws vary from state to state. A religious annulment is obtained through a religious body and is separate and distinct from a civil annulment. For example, Roman Catholics who divorce must obtain a religious annulment or an "ecclesiastical declaration of nullity" in accordance with church law before they can remarry or receive Holy Communion. A religious annulment does not affect issues such as legal dissolution of the marriage, alimony, child custody, property division, and child support. These matters must be dealt with in a civil court, through either a divorce or civil annulment, *before* an ecclesiastical declaration of nullity may be obtained in the Roman Catholic Church. If there is no civil divorce or annulment, the church tribunal will most likely encourage the parties to reconcile their differences.

In order to obtain a civil annulment, the moving party must prove that a defect existed at the time of the marriage that rendered it invalid. Some clients think that annulments are easier to obtain than divorces, especially if they were in a short-term marriage. This could not be further from the truth, as the grounds for obtaining an annulment may be very difficult to prove. In addition, annulments cannot be obtained simply because one or both of the parties feel as though they made a horrible mistake.

Grounds for Annulment—Void versus Voidable Marriage

A *void marriage* is invalid at the time of its creation. A *voidable marriage* is invalid at its inception but remains in effect unless the court terminates it. When a court is satisfied that the petitioning party has proven that a legal impediment existed at the time the marriage ceremony took place, the court may declare a marriage null and void. In some jurisdictions, the court may be limited to declaring the marriage "voidable" rather than void. The invalid marriage may become valid once the impediment to marriage has been removed. For instance, where a petitioning party has brought an annulment action based on legal incapacity due to *minority* age, if both parties are now of legal age, the court may issue a decision giving the petitioning party the legal right to void the marriage if he or she wishes. However, if that party has reconsidered the decision to annul the marriage, the marriage may continue on its own initiative. Conversely, a court will always declare a marriage null and void on proof that one or both parties entered into a prior valid marriage and is (are) still legally married to the party of the prior marriage. Existence of the following grounds on the part of one or both parties allows a court to declare a marriage null and void or voidable, under some circumstances:

- A valid prior existing marriage that was never legally terminated. If the previous marriage is legally terminated, and the couple is still cohabitating, the void marriage may become valid.
- Close relation by blood, or *consanguinity*.
- One or both of the parties lacked the mental capacity or were mentally disabled to the extent of not being able to understand or appreciate the nature of the marriage.
- One or both of the parties entered the marriage with no intention of living in a marital relationship or residing together as husband and wife. For example, at one time in the United States, a noncitizen could acquire U.S. citizenship by marrying a U.S. citizen, in what is known as a *sham or green card marriage*. In many cases, the citizen agreed to the marriage for monetary compensation, and sometimes did not meet the person until the day of the ceremony and never saw the person again.
- Under the legal age of consent in their jurisdiction. In many states, parents may consent to the marriage of a sixteen- or seventeen-year-old child. Teenagers who are legally emancipated by a court of law may also marry without parental consent. If one or both of the parties were underage at the time of the marriage, reach the age of majority, and then continue to cohabitate, the once void marriage may be valid.
- One or both parties were forced to enter into the marriage through fraud, duress, or coercion. An example of a marriage entered into under duress is the "shotgun wedding." There was a time in the history of our country when getting pregnant out of wedlock was not acceptable. Many men were forced into what became known as a "shotgun wedding" in order to protect the honor of the woman and her family. Fraud is also a basis for annulment. Failure to disclose infertility, a criminal history of felonious

Void marriage
A marriage that is invalid at the time of its creation.

Voidable marriage
A marriage that is invalid at its inception but remains in effect unless the court terminates it.

Consanguinity
Related by blood.

Sham or green card marriage
A U.S. citizen agrees to a marriage for monetary compensation.

conduct, an incurable illness, or a history of severe mental illness to a pro-spective spouse may be grounds for an annulment if such vital information disclosed prior to the marriage would have resulted in a refusal to enter into the marriage.

- One or both parties were under the influence of drugs or alcohol.
- One or both parties are physically unable to consummate the marriage.

Annulments are alive and well in the United States today, as the accompany-ing recent, much-publicized case illustrates.

On May 9, 2005, after having known each other for a brief four months, Renee Zellweger, star of *Jerry McGuire* and *The Bridget Jones Diary,* married country singer Kenny Chesney on a trip to the Virgin Islands. As with many celeb-rity marriages, blink and you'll miss it. On September 15, 2005, Zellweger filed papers with the Los Angeles Superior Court asking for an annulment and citing fraud as grounds. In later statements, Zellweger clarified the term *fraud* as only a legal term, having no reflection on Chesney's character. A later statement by both parties released to the public said that they both had different objectives at the start of the marriage, but these conflicting objectives were not specified. Another celebrity marriage with an extremely short shelf life concerns pop star Britney Spears. On January 5, 2004, a Clark County family court judge granted Spears an annulment, declaring her five-hour marriage to childhood friend Jason Allen Alexander null and void. Spears and Alexander entered into marriage at the Little White Chapel in Las Vegas, Nevada, only to regret it five hours later. In her an-nulment petition, Spears alleged the following grounds: "... Plaintiff Spears lacked understanding of her actions to the extent that she was incapable of agreeing to the marriage because before entering into the marriage the Plaintiff and Defendant did not know each others' likes and dislikes, each others' desires to have or not have children, and each others' desires as to state of residency. Upon learning of each others' desires, they are so incompatible that there was a want of understanding of each others' actions in entering into this marriage."

Although *annulment* is not a totally unfamiliar term to a layperson, most peo-ple do not know how an annulment differs from a marital dissolution or divorce action. The legal theory underlying an annulment action is quite different from the action for divorce or dissolution of marriage. A person institutes a divorce or dis-solution of marriage action to end a valid existing marriage. A person initiates an annulment proceeding to obtain a judicial decision that a valid marriage does not exist nor ever existed between that person and another party.

Just as a common law marriage may be legally formed without a formal cer-emony, a formal ceremony does not always establish legal marriage. In an annul-ment action, the court is called on to legally declare that despite ceremonial and state procedures, no legal marriage was formed or exists. A court may grant an annulment even if the parties obtained a marriage license and went through a mar-riage ceremony, provided that the petitioning party alleges and proves that at the time of the marriage ceremony, an impediment existed to the forming of a legally valid marriage. The petitioning party must introduce evidence of facts or circum-stance that the state legislature or state common law has determined constitute an impediment to the forming of a valid marital union.

Typical grounds for annulment can include incapacity because of minority age status, mental incompetence, one or both parties' involvement in the existence of a still legally valid marriage, the inability of one party to consummate the mari-tal union through sexual intercourse, and fraud that is material to the decision to marry (such as lying about one's reproductive ability, withholding knowledge of

Figure 4-3 Just as a common law marriage may be legally formed without a formal ceremony, a formal ceremony does not always establish legal marriage.

Blend Images/Shutterstock.

one's own infertility, or withholding material information about one's criminal history or the state of one's health).

A person seeking an annulment must be one of the parties to the marriage, unless a party is legally a minor or mentally incompetent. In such instance, the party's parent, legal guardian, or conservator can bring the action. The person bringing the annulment action must institute an annulment proceeding in a family court.

Concept Review and Reinforcement

KEY TERMS

annulment
consanguinity
dissolution of marriage
divorce
family counseling

legal separation
mediation
no-fault divorce
separate maintenance
settlement conference

sham or green card marriage
voidable marriage
void marriage

REVIEW OF KEY CONCEPTS

1. What is meant by the term *grounds for divorce*, and what were some of the traditional grounds in the United States?

2. What is the difference between a void marriage and a voidable marriage?

3. Explain the difference between a divorce and a legal separation.

4. What are some of the impediments to a valid marriage?

BUILDING YOUR PARALEGAL SKILLS

CASE FOR BRIEFING

L.K. V. F.K., 10 (2-22-2010) 2010 NY SLIP OP 50920 (U)

Critical Thinking and Legal Analysis Applications

1. You work for Bright & Bright, a small law firm in Buffalo, New York. Joe Carter, a forty-seven-year-old, very successful electrical contractor, has asked Richard Bright, his old high school buddy, to represent him in a divorce. Joe wants to divorce Lynda Carter, his wife of twenty-six years, and marry Nadine, his twenty-seven-year-old secretary with whom he now lives. Joe is willing to give Lynda Carter the house, alimony for life, and a generous cash settlement. Richard Bright first suggested that Joe bring the dissolution action based on the no-fault ground of irreconcilable differences. However, Joe did not want to deal with the one-year waiting period New York requires, and he also told Richard that Lynda Carter is furious and has told him that hell will freeze over before she agrees to a divorce. Richard Bright has filed the divorce papers alleging the ground of cruel and inhumane treatment.

   Lynda has retained counsel, and her lawyer has filed an answer denying the allegations and further asserting an affirmative defense. The affirmative defense calls for a dismissal of the action based on the fact that Joe previously moved out of the house and is in an adulterous relationship and that this behavior justifies and excuses her angry and "so-called cruel" behavior toward Joe. Richard Bright, at first, laughed at this defense and told Joe that it was the silliest defense he ever saw. However, his older brother, Elliot, the brighter of the Bright brothers, has voiced concerns and told Richard that Lynda Carter may have a winning argument. He has told Richard that New York courts have dealt with this issue before and that he better do some research on the subject. Richard Bright has found a recent case that not only addresses the issue but also reviews prior decisions on the subject.

   (a) Richard hands you the case of *L.K. v. F.K.* and tells you to review it and also review the prior cases cited to see if any of the fact patterns described are similar to Joe's situation. He then wants you to prepare an interoffice memorandum in which you analyze these cases, identify the current state of the law on this subject, and determine whether this defense is viable.

   (b) If you were Lynda Carter's lawyer and had some concerns that your affirmative defense strategy might fail, what pleadings would you suggest Lynda Carter file if the affirmative defense is not granted?

2. It was a dull day in the law firm of Applegate Law Firm, where you work as a family law paralegal, until Precious Pendergast walked in. Ms. Pendergast is an action film star who recently married the famous televangelist Reverend Billy Bullion. The wedding took place several months ago, and on the same day that Ms. Pendergast converted and was baptized by the Reverend himself in a highly televised ceremony. After the baptism, they were overcome with emotion and ran off to Las Vegas for a quickie marriage. They returned to the State of California, where they currently reside in his large mansion in Beverly Hills.

   Sobbing uncontrollably, Ms. Pendergast, who is pushing thirty-five, said that despite his countless sermons on family and encouraging his flock to "be fruitful and multiply," Reverend Bullion hates kids and doesn't want to be a father. He refers to children as "rugrats" and believes they should be seen, in someone else's house, and not heard. Upon learning of his true feelings toward children, she immediately made an appointment to see Attorney Applegate, who came highly recommended by Ms. Pendergast's Pilates teacher, Baby Atia. Ms. Pendergast would like to have this marriage annulled and hopes to resume her film career until either her biological clock stops ticking or the right man comes along.

Attorney Applegate has asked you to review the statute on annulments in California and prepare a client opinion letter regarding the feasibility of obtaining an annulment in the case of *Pendergast v. Bullion*. He has provided you with the appropriate statute, which is reprinted here. After you review it, he also wants you to review the most recent California case law available to determine how the state family court has interpreted the relevant sections of the statute and what leeway, if any, the judges exercise in their interpretation of these sections.

CALIFORNIA FAMILY CODE §2210[1]

A marriage is voidable and may be adjudged a nullity if any of the following conditions existed at the time of the marriage:

(a) The party who commences the proceeding or on whose behalf the proceeding is commenced was without the capability of consenting to the marriage as provided in Section 301 or 302, unless, after attaining the age of consent, the party for any time freely cohabited with the other as his or her spouse.

(b) The spouse of either party was living and the marriage with that spouse was then in force and that spouse (1) was absent and not known to the party commencing the proceeding to be living for a period of five successive years immediately preceding the subsequent marriage for which the judgment of nullity is sought or (2) was generally reputed or believed by the party commencing the proceeding to be dead at the time the subsequent marriage was contracted.

(c) Either party was of unsound mind, unless the party of unsound mind, after coming to reason, freely cohabited with the other as his or her spouse.

(d) The consent of either party was obtained by fraud, unless the party whose consent was obtained by fraud afterward, with full knowledge of the facts constituting the fraud, freely cohabited with the other as his or her spouse.

(e) The consent of either party was obtained by force, unless the party whose consent was obtained by force afterward freely cohabited with the other as his or her spouse.

(f) Either party was, at the time of marriage, physically incapable of entering into the marriage state, and that incapacity continues, and appears to be incurable.

---

[1] Family Code Section 2200–2201, State of California.

Building a Professional Portfolio

PORTFOLIO **EXERCISES**

1. Obtain a copy of your state's statute listing the fault-based grounds upon which a dissolution of marriage action may be brought. Prepare a memorandum to your supervising attorney listing these grounds.

2. If your state also statutorily authorizes no-fault divorce, find that statute and include in your memorandum how the no-fault grounds are phrased (e.g., "irretrievable breakdown," "irreconcilable differences") and if there are any conditions imposed for obtaining a dissolution of marriage on no-fault grounds, such as a waiting period or other preliminary requirements such as mandatory family counseling or mediation.

Hint: If you use an online legal research site to find the statutes, you may proceed by clicking on "statutes" and entering the name of your state; then try putting in the words *family law code*, *dissolution*, or *divorce* to get you to where you want more quickly.

Chapter **five**

ALIMONY, SPOUSAL SUPPORT, AND MAINTENANCE

LEARNING OBJECTIVES

After studying this chapter, you should be able to:

1. Understand the statutory factors considered by family court judges in evaluating the issue of alimony.

2. Identify and describe the various types of alimony.

3. Understand how and when alimony may be modified.

4. Explain the circumstances that trigger the termination of alimony.

Alimony *is the term given to a sum of money, or other property, paid by a former spouse to the other former spouse for financial support, pursuant to a court order, temporary or final, in a divorce proceeding. Terms such as* spousal support *and* spousal maintenance *are synonyms for alimony, and any one or all of these terms may be used by different jurisdictions in statutory or case law.*

HISTORY OF ALIMONY

Historically, married women had no rights to property in their own name or independent of their husbands. They could not control their own income, enter into contracts, buy and sell land, or sue or be sued. Since the United States inherited its legal system from England, we must look to early English law to trace the history of alimony. In England, the ecclesiastical courts or church courts had the power to grant divorces.

Ecclesiastical Courts

For many centuries throughout Western Europe, ***ecclesiastical courts***, or church courts, coexisted with secular courts, or courts administered by the state. In many European countries, there was an official state church, and it was this church that controlled ecclesiastical courts. In England, eventually it was the Church of England or Anglican Church that administered the church courts. These courts had the jurisdiction to hear some matters that could also be heard in the general state courts. In certain areas, however, the ecclesiastical or church court was the exclusive forum for addressing disputes.

    Ecclesiastical courts had exclusive jurisdiction over all family-related legal matters. In these matters, the church courts applied ***canon law***. The term *canon law* refers to the church's body of law or rules that determine man's moral obligations to man, to woman, and to God. In England, the Anglican Church retained much of the doctrine and dogma of the Roman Catholic Church, including the proscription against divorce as we know it and the status of matrimony as a sacrament. The "divorces" granted by these courts were not the divorces we are accustomed to today. Our definition of divorce, or divorce *a vinculo matrimonii*, is the complete severance of the marital relationship, allowing the parties to go their separate ways. This includes the right to remarry. The ecclesiastical courts only granted divorce *a mensa et thoro*, which means divorce from bed and board. The result of a divorce *a mensa et thoro* did not sever the marriage; it merely enabled the spouses to live separate and apart. In many religions, marriage is a sacrament not to be entered into lightly. In the eyes of God and the church, only the death of one of the two spouses ended a marriage. The church allowed only widowed persons to enter into new or second marriages.

    The church also changed the status of individuals upon marriage in that they were viewed as one entity. This concept influenced the secular law regarding the economic positions of spouses at common law. Upon marriage, husband and wife merged into "one body," the "one" being the husband. By virtue of the marriage ceremony, the spouses entered into a marital contract that imposed the duty of support on the husband. In turn, the wife gave up her rights to control or possess property or earnings that belonged to her. Women did not work outside the home and upon marriage took on the traditional roles of homemaking and rearing the children. This enabled the husband to focus on his career and increase his earning capacity.

Origins of the Alimony Award

Upon granting a divorce *a mensa et thoro*, the ecclesiastical courts ordered the husband to pay ***alimony***, or support to the wife. Not only was the husband obligated to support the wife during the marriage, but this duty also was ongoing, even through the separation period. The husband's duty to support the wife upon divorce was not absolute. The wife was entitled to alimony as long as she was

Ecclesiastical courts
Courts that had the jurisdiction to hear some matters that could also be heard in the general state courts; however, they had exclusive jurisdiction over all family-related legal matters; also known as church courts.

Canon law
The church's body of law or rules that determine man's moral obligations to man, to woman, and to God.

Alimony
A sum of money, or other property, paid by a former spouse to the other former spouse for financial support, pursuant to a court order, temporary or final, in a divorce proceeding; also known as spousal maintenance or spousal support.

Figure 5-1 In early times, a married couple was viewed as "one body" by the church.

Lloyd Smith/Shutterstock.

Married Women's Property Acts
Statutes that eliminated the disadvantages of married women and gave them the right to control their own earnings, bring lawsuits, be sued, own their own property, enter into contracts, and function in a legal capacity.

No-fault divorce laws
A modification of existing divorce laws to include the ground that the marital union or marital relationship had broken down irretrievably.

an "innocent spouse." If she had caused the breakdown of the marriage, she would get nothing. This would leave the wife with no monetary support. If the husband were at fault for the breakup of the marriage, his punishment obligated him to pay for his fault. Historically, both the theoretical and practical basis for the creation of alimony was to provide compensation for the wife and punish the husband for his wrongdoing.

Alimony in Early America

The English common law system was adopted by the settlers of America, and along with it came the laws regarding the severing of a marriage and the legal disadvantages suffered by married women. The duty of the husband to pay alimony upon divorce was codified in statutes of many American jurisdictions. In the late 1830s, American jurisdictions began passing the *Married Women's Property Acts*. These statutes eliminated the disadvantages of married women and gave them the right to control their own earnings, bring lawsuits, be sued, own their own property, enter into contracts, and function in a legal capacity. As time passed, societal attitudes toward women changed. Women were increasingly joining the workforce and gaining the ability to support themselves. Even though times were changing and more opportunities opened up to women, the American legal system still held on to the husband's duty to support his former wife.

When initiating a divorce action, the plaintiff spouse had to allege a legal reason or ground for requesting a divorce in the complaint or petition for dissolution of marriage. In the early 1970s, many jurisdictions began passing *no-fault divorce laws*. Prior to the passage of no-fault laws, a spouse seeking a divorce was required to have legal grounds—that is, facts proving that the other spouse was at fault. Some of the fault grounds included:

- adultery,
- habitual intemperance,
- desertion,
- mental cruelty,
- physical cruelty,
- incarceration in a penal institution, and
- institutionalization for mental illness.

The plaintiff spouse was required to produce evidence to prove his case. If the wife was responsible for the breakdown of the marriage, she lost alimony and property. If the husband were at fault, he would probably have to pay alimony and give the wife a considerable portion of property. If the plaintiff spouse could not meet the burden of proof, no divorce would be granted. Parties seeking divorces colluded or conspired together to commit perjury in cases where no fault existed and the parties merely wished to go their separate ways and end an unhappy marriage. The frequency of this type of charade was one of many factors that prompted state legislatures to consider and eventually enact laws that made divorce easier in most circumstances. In 1969, California led the nation in the passage of this country's first no-fault divorce law.

ALIMONY AWARDS IN A NO-FAULT SETTING

Prior to the 1970s, a party filing for divorce was required to prove "fault" grounds in order to have the marriage dissolved by the court. Under a fault-based system, the moving party was required to allege some type of wrongdoing that resulted in the breakdown of the marriage and to prove such allegations by presenting sufficient evidence to the court. The respondent spouse could also countersue for divorce and raise his or her own fault grounds. Under our current system of no-fault divorce, the courts must first dissolve the marriage. After the marriage is dissolved, the court will then render orders regarding alimony, property division, child support, child custody, and attorney's fees. No-fault divorce means that in order for the court to dissolve a marriage, one of the parties only has to allege that the marriage has broken down and that there is no hope of reconciliation.

Depending on the jurisdiction, the no-fault ground may be referred to as one of the following:

- irreconcilable differences,
- incompatibility,
- irretrievable breakdown, and
- irremediable breakdown.

While all states have some form of no-fault divorce law, many jurisdictions also allow spouses to allege a fault ground in their divorce pleadings. Whether the issue of fault may be raised in determining alimony or property division depends on the jurisdiction.

The 1960s and 1970s also saw a change in society's view of men, women, and marriage. More opportunities were available to women so they could become economically self-sufficient. In addition, marriage was now considered an economic partnership, where the contributions of the wife as homemaker were also gaining a new respect.

The modern view of marriage is much like that of a business partnership, where, upon dissolution of the entity, the partners are entitled to a fair division of the marital assets. The courts prefer property division awards as opposed to alimony because the parties can make a "clean break" and go their separate ways, much like business partners. Alimony does not coincide with this modern view of marriage because there is still a legal tie between former spouses.

While most states gender-neutralized their alimony statutes on their own initiative, other states resisted until court intervention required such a change. For instance, the Supreme Court of the United States in *Orr v. Orr*, 440 U.S. 268 (1979), held that an Alabama statute imposing the obligation on the husband alone to pay alimony was unconstitutional in that it violated the Fourteenth Amendment's Equal Protection Clause. While the court may impose the duty to pay alimony on either spouse, the reality is that women are still earning less than men and comprise the majority of alimony recipients today. Spouses most likely to obtain alimony for a significant period of time are those who have been in long-term marriages (over ten years), have given up career opportunities to raise their family and care for the home, or are ill or have a disability and cannot work. Alimony may also be awarded to a spouse for a limited period of time, allowing the opportunity to become self-sufficient. Alimony is also appropriate if the parties do not have substantial assets and periodic payments would provide for the needs of a spouse. It is also crucial that the payor spouse be employed and have a stable work record. When substantial property is involved, property division is preferred for the purpose of allowing parties to make a clean break. From the ecclesiastical view to present, we have seen alimony evolve from a punishment to compensate a spouse for the bad acts of another to a vehicle for providing economic support for a spouse.

Parties are free to negotiate an agreement regarding the amount of alimony to be paid. If the parties cannot agree, the court must make that decision. The determination of alimony is within the discretion of the court pursuant to state law. This means that the court has the power to make the alimony decision and that an appellate court will not reverse that decision unless the judge somehow abused his discretion. The parties are also free to agree to a waiver, meaning that they will not seek an alimony award in the divorce case.

Alimony Reform

Alimony reform advocacy groups have emerged in states like Arkansas, Connecticut, Florida, Georgia, Massachusetts, New Jersey, and Oregon and are calling for an overhaul of their jurisdictions' alimony statutes. Proponents argue that laws once protecting uneducated and unemployed women from the financial consequences of divorce deserve a second look in the twenty-first century where women make up a large portion of the workforce, and in many cases, are also the main wage earners. Here are some specific reforms being sought by various groups:

- Elimination of permanent alimony
- Creation of an income-based formula, much like the child support guidelines to calculate alimony
- Imposition of limits on the duration of alimony
- Inclusion of retroactivity provisions in new statutes so payor spouses can petition for a modification
- Exclusion of assets and income of payor spouse's new spouse/cohabitant in calculating modifications of alimony
- Termination of alimony payments upon payor spouse reaching Social Security retirement age
- Termination of alimony upon marriage or cohabitation

Massachusetts recently passed one of the most dramatic alimony reform statutes in recent history. Massachusetts was the first state in the American legal system to reference alimony in its laws, in 1785, with a carryover of English common law that required a husband to support the wife after the marriage was dissolved. While the Massachusetts statutes were updated in the 1970s with the passage of no-fault divorce, sweeping changes did not take place until enactment of the ***Massachusetts Alimony Reform Act of 2011*** that went into effect on March 1, 2012.

Bill H.3617 187th (2011 - 2012), An Act Reforming Alimony in the Commonwealth

Massachusetts Alimony Reform Act of 2011
A Massachusetts statute which became effective on March 1, 2012, for the purpose of reforming its alimony statute, taking into account women's increased participation in the workforce.

DETERMINING ALIMONY

Child support payments are based on state-enacted child support guidelines that provide a mathematical formula for determining the amount based on the income of the spouse. On the contrary, alimony is not calculated in such a precise manner. State alimony statutes set forth a list of criteria to be weighed by the judge in evaluating whether or not an award of alimony is appropriate. If alimony is awarded, the amount is determined by the judge after an assessment of the specific facts of the case and the statutory factors, unless the parties reached a mutual agreement without the court's intervention. Although the court considers each statutory factor, it does not have to give each factor equal weight. The court may focus on any number of factors depending on the circumstances of the case.

The California and Florida statutes presented next outline an example of statutory criteria considered by the family courts in determining whether an alimony award is appropriate.

Statutes

CALIFORNIA FAMILY CODE § 4320 FAM.*

Factors to be Considered in Ordering Support

In ordering spousal support under this part, the court shall consider all of the following circumstances:

(a) The extent to which the earning capacity of each party is sufficient to maintain the standard of living established during the marriage, taking into account all of the following:

    (1) The marketable skills of the supported party; the job market for those skills; the time and expenses required for the supported party to acquire the appropriate education or training to develop those skills; and the possible need for retraining or education to acquire other, more marketable skills or employment.

    (2) The extent to which the supported party's present or future earning capacity is impaired by periods of unemployment that were incurred during the marriage to permit the supported party to devote time to domestic duties.

(b) The extent to which the supported party contributed to the attainment of an education, training, a career position, or a license by the supporting party.

(c) The ability of the supporting party to pay spousal support, taking into account the supporting party's earning capacity, earned and unearned income, assets, and standard of living.

(d) The needs of each party based on the standard of living established during the marriage.

(e) The obligations and assets, including the separate property, of each party.

(f) The duration of the marriage.

(g) The ability of the supported party to engage in gainful employment without unduly interfering with the interests of dependent children in the custody of the party.

(h) The age and health of the parties.

(i) Documented evidence, including a plea of nolo contendere, of any history of domestic violence, as defined in Section 6211, between the parties or perpetrated by either party against either party's child, including, but not limited to, consideration of emotional distress resulting from domestic violence perpetrated against the supported party by the supporting party, and consideration of any history of violence against the supporting party by the supported party.

(j) The immediate and specific tax consequences to each party.

(k) The balance of the hardships to each party.

(l) The goal that the supported party shall be self-supporting within a reasonable period of time. Except in the case of a marriage of long duration as described in Section 4336, a "reasonable period of time" for purposes of this section generally shall be one-half the length of the marriage. However, nothing in this section is intended to limit the court's discretion to order support for a greater or lesser length of time, based on any of the other factors listed in this section, Section 4336, and the circumstances of the parties.

(m) The criminal conviction of an abusive spouse shall be considered in making a reduction or elimination of a spousal support award in accordance with Section 4324.5 or 4325.

(n) Any other factors the court determines are just and equitable.

---

*Part 3 - Spousal Support, Chapter 3 - Factors to be Considered in Ordering Support, State of California.

continued

FLORIDA STATUTES*

61.08 Alimony

(1) In a proceeding for dissolution of marriage, the court may grant alimony to either party, which alimony may be bridge-the-gap, rehabilitative, durational, or permanent in nature or any combination of these forms of alimony. In any award of alimony, the court may order periodic payments or payments in lump sum or both. The court may consider the adultery of either spouse and the circumstances thereof in determining the amount of alimony, if any, to be awarded. In all dissolution actions, the court shall include findings of fact relative to the factors enumerated in subsection (2) supporting an award or denial of alimony.

(2) In determining whether to award alimony or maintenance, the court shall first make a specific factual determination as to whether either party has an actual need for alimony or maintenance and whether either party has the ability to pay alimony or maintenance. If the court finds that a party has a need for alimony or maintenance and that the other party has the ability to pay alimony or maintenance, then in determining the proper type and amount of alimony or maintenance under subsections (5)-(8), the court shall consider all relevant factors, including, but not limited to:

   (a) The standard of living established during the marriage.

   (b) The duration of the marriage.

   (c) The age and the physical and emotional condition of each party.

   (d) The financial resources of each party, including the nonmarital and the marital assets and liabilities distributed to each.

   (e) The earning capacities, educational levels, vocational skills, and employability of the parties and, when applicable, the time necessary for either party to acquire sufficient education or training to enable such party to find appropriate employment.

   (f) The contribution of each party to the marriage, including, but not limited to, services rendered in homemaking, child care, education, and career building of the other party.

   (g) The responsibilities each party will have with regard to any minor children they have in common.

   (h) The tax treatment and consequences to both parties of any alimony award, including the designation of all or a portion of the payment as a nontaxable, nondeductible payment.

   (i) All sources of income available to either party, including income available to either party through investments of any asset held by that party.

   (j) Any other factor necessary to do equity and justice between the parties.

Upon the application of either party, unless the provisions of paragraph (c) or paragraph (d) apply, the court shall modify the terms of the order as necessary to direct that payments of alimony be made through the appropriate depository as provided in s. 61.181.

---

*The 2012 Florida Statutes - Title VI - Civil Practice and Procedure, Chapter 61- Dissolution of Marriage; Support; Time Sharing, State of Florida.

Spousal support

See *spousal maintenance*.

Spousal maintenance

A sum of money, or other property, paid by a former spouse to the other former spouse for financial support, pursuant to a court order, temporary or final, in a divorce proceeding; also known as alimony or spousal support.

RESOURCES FOR ALIMONY

Ability to pay involves an evaluation of the resources available to the payor spouse. The court looks at the following resources of a payor spouse:

- income from principal employment;
- income from any additional employment;

- income from rental property;
- investment income;
- income from royalties, copyrights, patents, and trademark rights; and
- pension income.

To determine the amount of resources available, the court looks at the payor spouse's net income. Taxes, debts, and allowable expenses must be deducted from the spouse's gross income. Gross income refers to the sum of all available sources of income. Net income is the dollar amount remaining after allowable deductions have been subtracted. These amounts must be carefully scrutinized because manipulation of these figures may occur during the course of the dissolution action. Some spouses intentionally reduce their income during the pendency of the case. They may refrain from taking promotions or raises, purposely cut down hours, drastically reduce commissions, get rid of a part-time job, or seek employment where they are paid cash "under the table." The payor spouse may also negotiate more fringe benefits from an employer for the purpose of showing less monetary compensation. The challenge for the payee spouse is to produce enough evidence to prove that the reduction in income was intentionally manipulated for the purpose of showing a smaller income. In this situation, it is essential that the discovery materials be reviewed carefully to determine whether the payor is living far beyond his or her means. Debts and expenses should also be scrutinized. Transfers to third parties, such as loans to family members and relatives, should also be looked on with suspicion. The question that must be asked is whether this debt or expense was acquired in good faith.

DETERMINING SPOUSAL NEED

A spouse is entitled to an alimony award sufficient enough to support him or her in the standard of living to which he or she had grown accustomed during the marriage. If the office represents the spouse seeking alimony, instruct the client to keep a log of attempts to find work. It may be very crucial to preserve that information for trial later. Has spouse had difficulty finding work due to lack of marketable skills or age discrimination?

The client should also keep a log of all expenses during the course of the divorce case. Later on, the paralegal may review and help clarify how much money the client needs to live. As stated earlier in this chapter, more and more frequently women are perfectly able to reenter the workforce and become self-supporting. Family courts take this into consideration when making alimony awards. The trend is to award no alimony at all or alimony that is short in duration. The courts will also look at the property available for division between the spouses. If there is a sufficient amount of property to distribute, then the courts are less likely to award alimony.

Alimony may also be awarded where the payee spouse has custody of small children and cannot work full time. Because day care can be very expensive, it may make more economic sense for the courts to make an alimony award at least until the children have reached the age where they are in school full time. The custodial parent will then have more opportunities to seek employment outside the home.

An award of alimony is highly probable in the case of an older homemaker who lacks the skills to go into the workforce or in the case of a spouse who is in poor health. The courts want to prevent a spouse from becoming a "charge on the state," that is, from having to apply for welfare and be supported by the taxpayers.

Figure 5-2 A court may reduce an alimony award once a payee spouse has entered the workforce and is gainfully employed.

iofoto/Shutterstock.

BALANCING PROPERTY DIVISION, CHILD SUPPORT, AND ALIMONY

Courts do not make alimony awards in a vacuum. Judges balance property division, child support, and alimony in order to reach an adequate resolution given the resources of the parties and their particular circumstances. Property awards divide the marital assets. Child support awards provide money paid to the custodial spouse for the benefit of the children. When there is an adequate amount of property, a property award may be more attractive, especially if the payor spouse's income or employment is unstable. If a spouse is steadily employed and income is stable, alimony may be a better choice. Some jurisdictions have even codified consideration of the property award in their alimony statutes. A higher child support award may be preferable in certain cases because the custodial parent does not have to declare child support payments as income for tax purposes. On the other hand, child support terminates when the child reaches the age of majority. The spouse is then left only with the more modest alimony payment.

TYPES OF ALIMONY

The court may order alimony during the pendency of the divorce action and at the time that it renders its final orders at the divorce trial or other judgment. At the time of making the final orders, the court may award or the parties may agree to either permanent, rehabilitative, or reimbursement alimony. Furthermore, these payments may be made in a lump sum or on a periodic basis. This section describes the different types of alimony with which the paralegal should become familiar.

Temporary Alimony

Pendente lite alimony
Payments made during the pendency of the divorce with the purpose of providing temporary financial support for the spouse; also known as temporary alimony.

Temporary alimony awards, also known as ***pendente lite alimony*** in some jurisdictions, are payments made during the pendency of the divorce with the purpose of providing temporary financial support for the spouse. In order for a court to make a temporary alimony award, the payor spouse must be served with notice, be physically present in court, and be given the opportunity to be heard and present his or her side of the case.

> ### *Statutes*
>
> ### FLORIDA STATUTES
>
> ### 61.071   Alimony pendente lite; suit money*
>
> In every proceeding for dissolution of the marriage, a party may claim alimony and suit money in the petition or by motion, and if the petition is well founded, the court shall allow a reasonable sum therefor. If a party in any proceeding for dissolution of marriage claims alimony or suit money in his or her answer or by motion, and the answer or motion is well founded, the court shall allow a reasonable sum therefor.

ALABAMA STATUTES

§ 30-2-50 Allowance for support during pendency of action[1]

Pending an action for divorce, the court may make an allowance for the support of either spouse out of the estate of the other spouse, suitable to the spouse's estate and the condition in life of the parties, for a period of time not longer than necessary for the prosecution of the complaint for divorce.

GENERAL LAWS OF MASSACHUSETTS

G.L.C. 208, § 17. Pendency of action; allowance; alimony[2]

The court may require either party to pay into court for the use of the other party during the pendency of the action an amount to enable him to maintain or defend the action, and to pay to him alimony during the pendency of the action. When the court makes an order for alimony on behalf of a party, and such party is not a member of a private group health insurance plan, the court shall include in such order for alimony a provision relating to health insurance, which provision shall be in accordance with section thirty-four.

The Florida, Massachusetts, and Alabama statutes cited next are examples of the family courts' statutory power to provide temporary support for spouses.

---

[1]Code of Alabama—Title 30: Marital and Domestic Relations—2—Divorce and Alimony, State of Alabama.

[2]Title III—Domestic Relations, Chapter 208—Divorce, Section 17—Pendency of Action; Allowance; Alimony, State of Massachusetts.

Alimony Waiver

On the day of the final divorce hearing, one or both of the spouses may wish to waive or relinquish their right to ask for alimony. If alimony is not awarded in the original divorce decree, the parties may not return to court to seek a modification later should the need arise. The same is true if the judgment is silent on the issue of alimony. Judges often canvass each spouse during the final divorce trial to determine if they have full knowledge of the *waiver of alimony* and its consequences. Lawyers should also advise clients of the effect of a waiver, making sure that they understand the legal implications long before going in front of a judge.

Waiver of alimony
One or both of the spouses may wish to waive or relinquish their right to ask for alimony.

Nominal Alimony

Instead of waiving alimony, a spouse may ask for **nominal alimony** in the amount of $1.00 per year. The purpose of nominal alimony is to allow the spouse to preserve his or her right to return to court in the event there is a change in circumstances and obtain alimony at a future date, even though it was not necessary at the time the original decree was entered. Obtaining an order of nominal alimony will ensure that the court has continuing jurisdiction to make modifications in the future.

A Picture Is Worth $1.00 A husband's midlife-crisis decision to abandon his job in sales in exchange for an uncertain career in photography did not elicit sympathy from the court when it came to supporting his ex-wife. The District Court of Appeal of Florida reversed the trial court's decision refusing to award the wife $1 in permanent periodic alimony in the event husband's new career didn't pay off. This case also refers to *bridge-the-gap alimony*, or *transitional alimony* as it is known in some states, which is defined as short-term, lump-sum alimony awarded to a spouse for the purpose of transitioning from married to single status. It is awarded based on the traditional concepts of alimony—need versus ability to pay—and does not terminate

Nominal alimony
Alimony in the amount of $1.00 per year; the purpose of nominal alimony is to allow the spouse to preserve his or her right to return to court in the event there is a change in circumstances.

Bridge-the-gap alimony
Short-term, lump-sum alimony awarded to a spouse for the purpose of transitioning from married to single status.

transitional alimony
Short-term, lump-sum alimony awarded to a spouse for the purpose of transitioning from married to single status.

upon death or remarriage. It is designed to pay for short-term, one-time expenses such as a rental security deposit, moving expenses, buying a car to get to and from work, or deposits for utilities, which may be necessary when the spouse does not have credit.

ROBERTA C. BLANCHARD v. MARAN L. BLANCHARD

793 So.2d 989 (Fla.App. 2 Dist. 2001)
District Court of Appeal of Florida, Second District

Altenbernd, Judge.

Roberta C. Blanchard, the wife, appeals a final judgment dissolving her marriage to Maran L. Blanchard, the husband. We reverse the judgment to the extent that it required the wife to pay to the husband bridge-the-gap alimony because the evidence did not support the award. In addition, we conclude that the trial court abused its discretion when it failed to award the wife $1 in permanent periodic alimony to reserve her future right to alimony in light of the husband's work history during this long-term marriage. We affirm the remaining provisions of the final judgment.

The Blanchards were married over thirty years, during which time they raised three children to adulthood. The wife worked as a teacher throughout the marriage. For most of this marriage, the husband sold recreational vehicles and earned significantly more income than his wife.

In 1997, the husband believed his sales position was in jeopardy. Rather than seek reemployment in the same industry, he decided to leave that field and develop a career in photography. This was a rather high-risk decision in light of the parties' modest standard of living and the husband's limited experience with photography.

The parties discussed this career change before the husband embarked on the venture. At trial, however, they disagreed about the wife's level of support for her husband's proposed career change. The wife admitted that she did not initially object to the plan, and that she permitted the investment of approximately $12,000 in marital funds to start the business. Although the husband perceived that the wife eagerly supported his decision, she testified that she privately hoped the husband would soon give up and return to his prior sales career. In essence, she believed that she was supporting her husband through a temporary mid-life crisis.

Both parties testified that they discussed the length of time the husband would pursue his new career to determine whether it would be profitable. The wife alleged that this "trial period" was three to six months, whereas the husband asserted that the parties talked about a time frame of a year. From May 1997, until the time of trial in September 1998, the wife financially supported the couple while they continued to live in the marital home. At the time of trial, the husband had been in the photography business for sixteen months, but still was not making any significant profit from the business. He testified that while his wife paid the household expenses, he was supporting himself on only a $100-per-week "draw" from the business account.

The trial court acknowledged that if the parties had divorced before 1997, the wife would have been entitled to permanent periodic alimony because of the length of the marriage, the historical incomes of the parties, and the other factors set forth in section 61.08, Florida Statutes (1999). Nevertheless, the trial court found that the wife acquiesced in the husband's decision to change careers, making this a marital decision that she could not, thereafter, unilaterally retract. As a result, the trial court granted the husband's request for "bridge-the-gap" alimony and required the wife pay him $500 per month for one year. The trial court did not grant the wife any amount of permanent periodic alimony because her current income far exceeded the husband's. In the final judgment, however, the trial court acknowledged that the husband might need to reconsider his options if his photography business did not soon become profitable.

Although we concur with much of the trial court's reasoning, we cannot affirm the trial court's decisions regarding the alimony requested by each party. Based upon the evidence presented, the trial court erred in awarding the husband bridge-the-gap alimony. In addition, the trial court abused its discretion by failing to reserve jurisdiction to potentially award the wife permanent alimony in the future.

In *Borchard v. Borchard*, 730 So.2d 748 (Fla. 2d DCA 1999), this court recognized that a trial court has the authority to fashion an award of permanent, lump-sum alimony, paid over a set period, to ease a party's transition from married life to single life. We cautioned, however, that "bridge-the-gap alimony is not a tool to compromise adversarial positions but to assist a spouse with any legitimate, identifiable, short-term need under circumstances where a lump sum award is reasonable and when the other spouse has the ability to pay the award. . . . It is a useful tool in a relatively small category of divorces." *Id.* at 753.

In *Borchard,* we envisioned a scenario in which a spouse was unable, through his or her own best efforts, to provide for the essentials of a transition from married life to single life. We emphasized that in some cases, a spouse may be unable to afford "basic living requirements" because of a divorce, particularly when there is a "meager" distribution of assets. *See id.* at 752-53. Here, there was no evidence that the husband lacked his basic needs. He received over $60,000 in marital assets, and these assets happened to be the more liquid of the parties' holdings. The trial court's equitable distribution scheme relieved him of all responsibility for the parties' marital debts. In truth, the husband is trying to receive rehabilitative alimony, disguised as bridge-the-gap alimony, to assist him in a risky, new business venture when he already has considerable experience and skill in another field. An award of rehabilitative alimony, however, generally requires a rehabilitative plan that will result in an increase in the party's income. See *Ingram v. Ingram*, 750 So.2d 130 (Fla. 2d DCA 2000). We decline to extend the purpose of bridge-the-gap alimony to meet the "needs" the husband pursues in this case.

We recognize that the wife participated, even if by acquiescence, in this career change. In addition, although she asserted the husband could become immediately reemployed in the recreational vehicle sales field, she offered no competent, substantial evidence sufficient to support imputing income to the husband. As a result, the trial court was correct in finding that no income should be imputed to the husband at this time, and that an award of any significant amount of permanent alimony to the wife was not appropriate. *See Gildea v. Gildea*, 593 So.2d 1212 (Fla. 2d DCA 1992).

Nevertheless, the trial court acknowledged that the husband's venture was likely either to become successful or to force him into a more profitable career sometime in the next few years. Because the business was new and the parties' circumstances were evolving, there was no means by which the trial court could judge the future viability of the wife's permanent periodic alimony claim. The historic incomes of the parties, the length of the marriage, the moderate marital assets, and the wife's needs, however, required an award of a nominal amount of permanent alimony to permit the wife to pursue a future increase should the husband's full earning potential materialize. See *Wing v. Wing*, 429 So.2d 782 (Fla. 3d DCA 1983); *Moore v. Moore*, 401 So.2d 841 (Fla. 5th DCA 1981). See also *Stock v. Stock*, 693 So.2d 1080 (Fla. 2d DCA 1997). Under these circumstances, the trial court abused its discretion in failing to award the wife a nominal amount of permanent periodic alimony, thus reserving jurisdiction to revisit this claim as the parties' new lives develop. See *Strahan v. Strahan*, 605 So.2d 1316 (Fla. 4th DCA 1992). See also *Fusco v. Fusco*, 616 So.2d 86 (Fla. 4th DCA 1993).

Source: 793 SO.2D 989 (FLA.APP. 2 DIST. 2001), District Court Of Appeal Of Florida, Second District, State of Florida.

Figure 5-3 Judges can exercise their discretion when awarding rehabilitative alimony while the payee spouse gets back on his or her feet.

Junial Enterprises/Shutterstock.

Permanent alimony

The term applied to court-ordered payments that are to be made to a spouse on a regular and periodic basis and that terminate only on the death, remarriage, or cohabitation of the other spouse or on court order.

Rehabilitative alimony

Spousal support that is awarded for a limited period of time to give the spouse the opportunity to become self-sufficient.

Permanent Alimony ***Permanent alimony*** is the term applied to court-ordered payments that are to be made to a spouse on a regular and periodic basis and that terminate only upon the death, remarriage, or cohabitation of the other spouse or upon court order. Permanent alimony is awarded with less frequency today. Women have increasingly joined the workforce and developed marketable employment skills to help them become self-sufficient. If you recall the historical discussion regarding the extension of the husband's duty to support after awarding divorce *a mensa et thoro*, you will see that the expanded role of women in the workplace has made permanent alimony a rare disposition in today's divorce courts. Spouses who are more likely to receive permanent alimony awards are those who have been in long-term marriages, those unable to acquire marketable skills, and those who are ill or have a disability. It is highly unlikely for spouses in these cases to be able to go to work and earn enough to adequately support themselves.

Rehabilitative Alimony The frequency of ***rehabilitative alimony*** awards reflects the current legal trend of providing short-term financial support to a former spouse. Rehabilitative alimony is awarded for a limited period of time to give the spouse the opportunity to become self-sufficient. In determining whether this type of alimony is appropriate, the crucial question to be answered is whether this spouse has the *ability* to become self-sufficient. For the traditional housewife who finds herself divorced after many years of marriage and has never worked outside the home, this may not be possible; nor is it feasible for a disabled or ill spouse. In many cases, however, the spouse either has marketable skills or has the ability to obtain them within a reasonable period of time. Under these circumstances, an award of rehabilitative alimony would provide the spouse with some financial assistance while she gets back on her feet.

Tennis Wife Gets Rehabilitative Alimony The wife worked on more than her backhand in this marriage! In the end, Mrs. Evans had to join the workforce and establish a plan to become self-sufficient.

EDWIN E. EVANS v. CYNTHIA S. EVANS

559 N.W. 2d 240 (S.D. 1997)
SOUTH DAKOTA SUPREME COURT

GILBERTSON, JUSTICE.

Facts and Procedure

Ed and Cyndy were married in June 1973, following completion of Ed's first year of law school. Cyndy had completed her college degree and worked full time from the beginning of the marriage until the parties moved to Sioux Falls in June 1977. At that time, Cyndy was expecting her first child. She did not return to the work force.

The parties' lifestyle was such that they belonged to a country club, had household help, and dined out frequently. They generally took two family vacations a year. The record reflects Ed worked many hours, including evenings and some weekends, and was often required to be out of town for days to weeks at a time. Cyndy volunteered her time in community, church, and school-related activities.

The parties have two children, Ashley and Kelsey, who were ages 17 and 14, respectively, at the time of the divorce trial. They attend parochial school and participate in many school and extracurricular activities. They drive late model cars and wear the best brand-named clothing. Cyndy has largely been responsible for coordinating the children's activities. While Ed was not available as much as Cyndy, he too took an interest in their children, assisting them with their homework and driving them to out-of-town functions.

In 1990, the parties began construction of a new home in Sioux Falls which ultimately cost considerably more money than had been originally planned. Around this time, Cyndy discontinued her volunteer activities and devoted her time instead to tennis and other personal interests. The parties admit they had problems with communication; the marriage began to deteriorate. In 1993, Cyndy invited a twenty-seven-year-old male tennis friend to move into the family's residence without discussing it with Ed and without his knowledge. When Ed learned of his wife's houseguest, he left home for a few days but returned at the childrens' request. He attempted to improve his relationship with Cyndy, but she showed little interest in attempts and spent evenings out with her friends, returning home in the early morning hours. Ed moved into a separate bedroom to show his displeasure, but the couple did not discuss their problems. By the summer of 1994, Cyndy had ceased attending family vacations, preferring instead to spend time with her friends at Lake Okoboji, while Ed and the children took family vacations without her. In the fall of 1994, Ed learned Cyndy was having an affair with a man who owned a home in Lake Okoboji. Although Cyndy initially denied the affair, she eventually admitted it was true. Upon learning this, Ed moved out of the parties' home.

Ed and Cyndy attempted a reconciliation, Cyndy promising to discontinue the affair and Ed promising to spend less time at work and more time with Cyndy and the children. Ed returned home, bought Cyndy a new car that she wanted, planned a family vacation in Jamaica for Thanksgiving, and purchased tickets for a concert Cyndy wanted to attend in Minneapolis. Within four days of Ed's return home, Cyndy announced she did not intend to stop seeing other men. Ed left home for the last time.

He continued spending time with Cyndy, however, and the family went on the planned vacation and to the concert and shopping trips in Minneapolis. Ed continued to provide spending money and paid the household expenses. He reduced his hours at work. Ed sought counseling and encouraged Cyndy to attend counseling sessions with him, or alone. She refused. Ed eventually gave up trying to reconcile the marriage.

During this period of separation, Ed paid Cyndy $10,000 per month to support her and their children. She stated they could not live on this amount. Ed suggested she sell the house. Cyndy refused and Ed filed the divorce action.

The trial court heard the matter over a four-day period, October 30–31, 1995, and on December 12–13, 1995. The trial court determined issues involving child support, property division, alimony award, and attorney fees. On February 16, 1996, the trial court awarded Ed a divorce on grounds of adultery and dismissed Cyndy's counterclaim. Both parties appealed the judgment of the trial court.

Cyndy raises . . . issues as follows. . . .

continued

Analysis and Decision

...3. Whether the trial court erred in determining the amount of alimony awarded?

The trial court awarded Cyndy rehabilitative alimony of $2,500 per month for six months, and $1,000 per month for five years thereafter. Cyndy's vocational expert opined, and the trial court found, that she would be able to earn $25,000 per year within three to five years, after retraining and reentering the work force. Cyndy appeals this award, arguing she is entitled to substantially more alimony. She bases her argument on her years of service to the marriage as a wife and homemaker and the vast discrepancy between earning capabilities of the parties.

Our standard of review of challenges to a trial court's award of alimony is well established. *Dussart v. Dussart*, 1996 S.D. 41, 546 NW2d 109, 111; *DeVries v. DeVries*, 519 N.W.2d 73, 77 (S.D. 1994).

A trial court is vested with discretion in awarding alimony and its decision will not be disturbed unless it clearly appears the trial court abused its discretion. Trial courts must consider the following factors when setting an alimony award: (1) the length of the marriage; (2) the parties' respective ages and health; (3) the earning capacity of each party; (4) their financial situations after the property division; (5) their station in life or social standing; and (6) the relative fault in the termination of the marriage. A trial court's findings on these factors must support its legal conclusions. As often stated, an abuse of discretion exists only where discretion has been "exercised to an end or purpose not justified by, and clearly against, reason and evidence."

Additional factors must be considered when the trial court makes an award of rehabilitative alimony. *Saint Pierre v. Saint Pierre*, 357 N.W.2d 250, 252 (S.D. 1984). In awarding rehabilitative or reimbursement alimony, the trial court should be guided by "the amount of supporting spouse's contributions, his or her foregone [sic] opportunities to enhance or improve professional or vocational skills, and the duration of the marriage following completion of the nonsupporting spouse's professional education." *Id.* An award of rehabilitative alimony must be designed to meet an educational need or plan of action whose existence finds some support in the record. *Radigan*, 465 N.W.2d at 486; *Ryken v. Ryken*, 440 N.W.2d 300, 303 (S.D. 1989) (*Ryken I*). "[T]he decision to award 'reimbursement' or 'rehabilitative' alimony, and, if so, in what amount and for what length of time, is committed to the sound discretion of the trial court. The purpose of rehabilitative alimony is to put the supporting spouse in a position to likewise upgrade their own economic marketability." *Studt v. Studt*, 443 N.W.2d 639, 643 (S.D. 1989) (internal citations omitted).

A review of the record in this case demonstrates the trial court's consideration of all the necessary factors, including Cyndy's traditional role of homemaker {4} and the parties discrepancy in earning capabilities. {5} The trial court also considered Cyndy's financial situation after the property division and her fault in the dissolution of the parties' marriage and lack of cooperation in Ed's efforts to save the marriage. In granting a divorce in favor of Ed on the basis of adultery, the trial court had before it numerous examples of uncontested marital misconduct by Cyndy upon which to base its finding of fault:

1. Moving into the family home a twenty-seven-year-old male tennis friend without Ed's prior knowledge or consent;
2. Refusing to attend family vacations as in the past, but rather vacationing at Lake Okoboji with friends;
3. Having an affair with a man who owned a home at Lake Okoboji;
4. Refusing to stop seeing other men after Ed found out about the affair, and when Ed attempted reconciliation, and

5. Refusing to attend when Ed sought counseling and encouraged Cyndy to attend either with him or alone.

The trial court properly concluded that Cyndy's fault was a factor to be taken into account in deciding alimony.

Following division of the marital property, Cyndy leaves the marriage with over one million dollars in assets. Approximately $400,000 of these assets are in the form of cash payments to be paid to Cyndy by Ed either immediately or over a period of the next five years at seven percent interest on the unpaid balance. The trial court found that, through conservative investment, Cyndy's liquid assets would provide annual income to her of $40,792, or $3,399 per month, without invading the principal. Following three to five years of wage-earning, this monthly income would rise to $4,782 per month. The trial court specifically noted that Cyndy would not be able to live in the luxurious lifestyle she enjoyed while married to Ed but, at the same time, should not be able to demand excessive long-term support from the husband to whom she did not wish to be married. The trial court concluded Cyndy should be able to live comfortably on the amount awarded. The court acknowledged Cyndy's contribution to the family's accumulation of wealth and her husband's success, and further noted the award was justified due to Cyndy's forgone employment opportunities during the parties' twenty-two year marriage. We cannot say the trial court's award was against reason and the evidence.

Regarding "educational need or plan of action" that must be evidenced from the record for an award of rehabilitative alimony, *Radigan,* 465 N.W.2d at 486, Cyndy presented herself for evaluation by the vocational rehabilitation specialist who testified on her behalf. Following his evaluation, which included a personal interview with Cyndy, taking her educational and work history, and submitting her to various vocational and personality-type testing, this expert concluded Cyndy's best course of action for reentering the work force would be to complete approximately six months of select computer courses at a vocational school and begin work in an entry-level position in the banking field. Cyndy had worked in banking before the parties moved to Sioux Falls in 1977 and her test scores in the vocational evaluation demonstrated a high interest and ability in this area. Her test scores also were high in the fields of business and sales. Although Cyndy did not express to this specialist any specific plans for employment or retraining during their interview, it was noted by the expert at trial that this is not unusual for a person who had not been career-minded during a long marriage and is presently going through a divorce

We affirm on this issue. . . .

Source: Edwin E. Evans v. Cynthia S. Evans, 559 N.W. 2D 240 (S.D. 1997), South Dakota Supreme Court, State of South Dakota.

Reimbursement Alimony As the following chapter illustrates, some jurisdictions have categorized a professional or advanced degree acquired during the marriage as marital property. This categorization has enabled the courts to put a monetary value on the degree and to award the nondegreed spouse either money or other property for his or her contributions made during the marriage that enabled the other spouse to obtain the degree. Many jurisdictions, however, do not categorize a degree as property. This would leave the nondegreed spouse uncompensated for the sacrifices endured in hopes that their family would have a better future. Courts, however, have responded to this injustice by creating the ***reimbursement alimony*** award. Here, the nondegreed spouse may be "reimbursed" for his or her contribution to the student spouse's attainment of the advanced degree, which results in an enhanced earning capacity. The nondegreed spouse may have helped pay the student spouse's tuition, supported the family while the student spouse was

Reimbursement alimony
Where a nondegreed spouse may be compensated for his or her contribution to the student spouse's attainment of an advanced degree that results in an enhanced earning capacity.

in school, or relocated or put off pursuing his or her own education in hopes that these sacrifices would later pay off in an increased standard of living. In these jurisdictions, the nondegreed spouse is reimbursed for the monetary and nonmonetary efforts that enhanced the other spouse's earning capacity. Reimbursement alimony awards are generally nonmodifiable and nonterminable so as to fully compensate the nondegreed spouse.

Durational Alimony

Durational alimony
A type of alimony that provides a spouse with financial assistance for a limited period of time following a short- or moderate-term marriage. The length of time of the support cannot exceed the length of the marriage.

On July 1, 2010, Florida created a new type of spousal support called *durational alimony*, making it the sixth type of alimony recognized in the state along with permanent alimony, rehabilitative alimony, bridge-the-gap alimony, temporary alimony, and lump-sum alimony. The statute also defines short-term, moderate-term, and long-term marriage.

Durational alimony is a statutory option where bridge-the-gap alimony, limited to two years under Florida law, is inadequate in helping the spouse become self-sufficient, but the spouse does not qualify for permanent alimony. The purpose of durational alimony is to provide a spouse with financial assistance for a limited period of time following a short- or moderate-term marriage, and the length of the support cannot exceed the length of the marriage.

Florida 61.08   Florida Statute Alimony

"(4)   For purposes of determining alimony, there is a rebuttable presumption that a short-term marriage is a marriage having a duration of less than 7 years, a moderate-term marriage is a marriage having a duration of greater than 7 years but less than 17 years, and long-term marriage is a marriage having a duration of 17 years or greater. The length of a marriage is the period of time from the date of marriage until the date of filing of an action for dissolution of marriage."

"(7)   Durational alimony may be awarded when permanent periodic alimony is inappropriate. The purpose of durational alimony is to provide a party with economic assistance for a set period of time following a marriage of short or moderate duration or following a marriage of long duration if there is no ongoing need for support on a permanent basis. An award of durational alimony terminates upon the death of either party or upon the remarriage of the party receiving alimony. The amount of an award of durational alimony may be modified or terminated based upon a substantial change in circumstances in accordance with s. 61.14. However, the length of an award of durational alimony may not be modified except under exceptional circumstances and may not exceed the length of the marriage."

The 2012 Florida Statutes - Title VI - Civil Practice and Procedure, Chapter 61 - Dissolution of Marriage; Support; Time Sharing

MODIFICATION OF ALIMONY

Modification of alimony
The issue of whether spousal support may be either increased or decreased after the original order has been entered due to a substantial change in one spouse's circumstances.

Modification of alimony addresses the issue of whether alimony may be either increased or decreased after the original order has been entered. To change or "modify" an alimony award, the party seeking the modification must go back to court and request that the court modify the original order. The moving party must prove that a substantial change of circumstances occurred since the date of the original order and that the change was involuntary. Because the court made the original order, only the court can change the obligations of the parties. For example, *pendente lite* orders may be modified during the *pendente lite* phase as long as the moving party can satisfy his or her burden of proof.

LUMP-SUM ALIMONY

Lump-sum alimony, or ***alimony in gross or alimony in* solido** as it is referred to in some states, is a form of support made to a spouse in one single payment. Once a spouse receives an award of lump-sum alimony, his or her interest has "vested." This means that he or she is entitled to the entire amount. This amount may be made in installments, if agreed upon by the parties or ordered by the court. It is important to check with state law as many jurisdictions do not allow lump-sum alimony payments as they trigger serious tax consequences.

Alimony in gross or alimony in solido
A support payment made in one single payment; also known as lump sum alimony.

Periodic Alimony

Periodic alimony, or alimony in future as it is referred to in some states, requires the payor spouse to make alimony payments on a weekly, bi-weekly, or monthly basis. The time period for making such payments often depends on the frequency at which the payor spouse receives his or her employment income.

Periodic alimony, or alimony in future
A term applied to court-ordered payments that are to be made to a spouse on a regular basis.

EXAMPLE 1

John, who is employed at a factory, files for divorce. His wife Mary files a motion for pendente lite or temporary alimony. Based on her need and John's ability to pay, she is awarded $100 a week. John loses his job and does not pay Mary for ten weeks. John owes Mary $1,000 in alimony arrearages or "back alimony."

Upon losing his job, John should have immediately filed a motion for modification with the court. He would then have been able to get the original $100 order modified because of a substantial change in circumstances, that is, the loss of his job. Once Mary stops receiving payments, she has the right to the arrearage, or amounts due by court order but unpaid. Mary may seek to enforce the original order by returning to court.

Final orders may also be modified upon showing of a substantial change in circumstances. A party may request an order of $1.00 of alimony per year. Obviously, this is only a nominal alimony amount; however, a request for such an award is necessary so the party may seek a modification after the entering of a final judgment. If no alimony is awarded to the spouse at the time the divorce decree is entered, he or she will be prohibited from coming back to court and seeking an alimony award in the future because no basis exists for modifying it. The reason for the $1.00 award is so that a nominal amount of alimony will leave the issue of alimony modifiable in the future in the event of a substantial change in circumstances.

Remember that an alimony award may be achieved in one of two ways: by agreement of the parties or by order of the court. When the parties are drafting an agreement, the modifiability of the alimony award must be addressed in the settlement agreement. While the parties may have agreed to the nonmodifiability of alimony and included such a clause in the separation agreement, the court may not enforce such a provision if a spouse would have to go on public assistance and be supported at taxpayers' expense.

Permanent alimony may be modified if there is a substantial change in circumstances. Remarriage automatically terminates permanent alimony in some jurisdictions, and in others, the party seeking the modification must do so through the court. When a former spouse remarries, the new spouse is legally obligated to provide spousal support. ***Cohabitation***, which means unmarried parties living together, may also terminate alimony. While cohabiting parties do not have a legal obligation to support each other, sharing expenses may improve the financial position of the divorced spouse; in other cases, it may not. The court must look at requests for modification on a case-by-case basis.

Cohabitation
Unmarried parties living together as if married.

Rehabilitative alimony is generally nonmodifiable; however, some courts retain jurisdiction for the purpose of modification. Lump-sum alimony awards are generally not modifiable. This means that the lump-sum alimony award is not affected by remarriage or cohabitation, and at the death of the payor spouse, the payee spouse may sue the payor's estate for any payments due. Because reimbursement alimony is awarded on the basis of the amount contributed by the non-degreed spouse, it is commonly nonmodifiable.

ESCALATION CLAUSES AND COST-OF-LIVING INCREASE CLAUSES

Escalation clause
Provides for increases in alimony payments due to the increase of payor's income and an increase in the cost of living, obviating the need for the parties to go back to court for modifications; also known as a cost-of-living clause.

In drafting settlement agreement provisions regarding alimony, the parties may include an *escalation clause* or *cost-of-living clause*. An escalation clause provides for increases in the alimony payments due to the increase of payor's income and an increase in the cost of living. The escalation clause obviates the need for the parties to go back to court for modifications, which will save parties time and money.

SUPPORT-RELATED COSTS—MEDICAL INSURANCE, ATTORNEY'S FEES, AND LIFE INSURANCE

Medical Insurance

Cost-of-living clause
Provides for increases in the alimony payments due to the increase of payor's income and an increase in the cost of living, which obviates the need for the parties to go back to court for modifications; also known as an escalation clause.

Because alimony involves the support of a former spouse, this chapter would not be complete without a brief discussion of medical insurance. The *Consolidated Omnibus Budget Reconciliation Act (COBRA), 26 U.S.C. sec. 4980B(f)*, is a federal law that enables a nonemployee spouse to continue his health insurance coverage provided by his spouse's employer, for a period of three years after the divorce, as long as the nonemployee spouse pays the premium. The children of the marriage may also be covered under COBRA during their dependency on their parents. Either one parent or both will be responsible for providing medical insurance coverage for the children.

Consolidated Omnibus Budget Reconciliation Act (COBRA), 26 U.S.C. sec. 4980B(f)
A federal law that enables a nonemployee spouse to continue his or her health insurance coverage provided by his or her spouse's employer for a period of three years after a divorce, as long as the nonemployee spouse pays the premium.

State laws also have an impact on medical insurance coverage. Some jurisdictions require a divorced spouse to provide coverage for former spouses who are not able to provide coverage for themselves.

Sometimes the COBRA payments are too high and a spouse may seek health insurance through their employer or other resource.

Statutes

MASSACHUSETTS GENERAL LAWS

§ 34. *Alimony or assignment of estate; determination of amount; health insurance.*

When the court makes an order for alimony on behalf of a spouse, said court shall determine whether the obligor under such order has health insurance or other health coverage available to him through an employer or organization or has health insurance or other health coverage available to him at reasonable cost that may be extended to cover the spouse for whom support is ordered. When said court has determined that the obligor has such insurance or coverage available to him, said court shall include in the support order a requirement that the obligor do one of the following: exercise the option of additional coverage in favor of the spouse, obtain coverage for the spouse, or reimburse the spouse for the cost of health insurance. In no event shall the order for alimony be reduced as a result of the obligor's cost for health insurance coverage for the spouse.

Source: Title III—Domestic Relations, Chapter 208—Divorce, Section 34—Alimony or Assignment of Estate; Determination of Amount; Health Insurance, State of Massachusetts.

ATTORNEY'S FEES

It is the responsibility of the respective parties to pay their **attorney's fees**. A common myth still held by many women is that the husband is required to pay her attorney's fees. The case of *Orr v. Orr*, 440 U.S. 268 (1979), declared this statutory requirement unconstitutional. Either party, however, may seek attorney's fees from the other spouse. The standard the court applies in determining attorney's fees is the need of one spouse and the ability to pay of the other spouse.

Most attorneys require clients to pay a retainer before taking on their divorce case and will later seek an award of attorney's fees to reimburse their client. For those who cannot afford a retainer, some attorneys may motion the court at the beginning of the proceedings for an advance award of legal fees to represent the needy spouse. In these cases, it is advisable that the representation of the spouse be contingent upon the granting of the motion for attorney's fees by the court and the receipt of payment. The rules of ethics require that an attorney's fee must be *reasonable*. It is within the court's discretion to determine what is reasonable. When defending the moving party's motion for attorney's fees, it is essential that an itemized bill be requested and that the charges be reviewed.

Attorney's fees
The amount charged by a lawyer to a client for undertaking his or her case.

Securing Alimony Payments with Life Insurance

A recipient spouse may request, and a payor spouse may be ordered to obtain, life insurance to secure alimony or child support payments for the duration of the support obligation, in the event of the payor spouse's death. If the recipient spouse is receiving permanent alimony and the duration of the obligation cannot be determined because it terminates upon death, remarriage, or cohabitation, the parties will agree to, or the courts will set, a specific amount. The payor spouse names the recipient spouse as beneficiary under the policy.

It is also important for the recipient spouse to obtain verification that the policy is in force and that premiums have been paid. The recipient spouse should request, either in court or pursuant to a separation agreement, the payor spouse's consent to receive notification from the insurance company if the payor fails to pay the premium. If this occurs, the recipient spouse may pay the premium and file a motion for contempt with the court to recover the unpaid premium and possibly attorney's fees. If the premium is not paid and the payor spouse dies, the recipient spouse may file a claim against his or her estate.

In *Parley v. Parley*, the Connecticut Appellate Court held that when making orders to obtain life insurance, a court should consider the cost and availability of such coverage as well as the spouse's ability to pay in light of other financial obligations.

GAIL A. PARLEY v. JON A. PARLEY

72 CONN. APP. 742, 807 A.2D 982 (2002)
APPELLATE COURT OF CONNECTICUT

MIHALAKOS, J.

The defendant, Jon A. Parley, appeals from the judgment of the trial court dissolving the parties' marriage. On appeal, the defendant claims that the court improperly (1) ordered him to obtain life insurance to secure the court's alimony order . . .

continued

...We reverse the judgment of the trial court as to its financial orders only and remand the matter to that court for a new trial as to the financial matters.

The following facts and procedural history are relevant to our consideration of the defendant's claims on appeal. The parties were married on August 10, 1979. Five children were born to the marriage, two of whom reached the age of majority prior to the dissolution action. On April 20, 1999, the plaintiff, Gail A. Parley, brought an action seeking dissolution of the marriage, claiming that it had irretrievably broken down.

The court entered orders regarding property distribution, alimony, child support and other miscellaneous matters. As part of the dissolution decree, the court ordered the defendant to pay to the plaintiff alimony in the amount of $50 per week. At the time of the dissolution, the defendant held a life insurance policy. To secure the alimony payment, the court ordered the defendant to obtain additional life insurance. . . .

. . . This appeal followed. . . .

. . . The defendant first claims that the court improperly ordered him to obtain additional life insurance to secure his alimony obligation. Specifically, he argues that the court failed to inquire regarding the cost and availability of such insurance, and, therefore, improperly ordered him to obtain the insurance. We agree and vacate the order of the court regarding the additional insurance to secure the alimony payments.

"The ordering of security for alimony by a trial court is discretionary under [General Statutes § 46b-82]." *Cordone v. Cordone*, supra, 51 Conn. App. 534; General Statutes § 46B-82. The court's discretion, however, is not without limits. This court has held that the trial court must delve into certain matters before ordering a party to obtain life insurance to secure the payment of alimony. See *Michel v. Michel*, 31 Conn. App.338, 341, 624 A.2d 914 (1993). Specifically, the court must engage in a search and inquiry into the cost and availability of such insurance. *Id.*; see also *Lake v. Lake*, 49 Conn. App. 89, 92, 712 A.2d 989, cert. denied, 246 Conn. 902, 719 A.2d 1166 (1998).

In the present case, the defendant held a life insurance policy at the time of the dissolution. The court ordered him to obtain additional life insurance to secure his alimony payments without inquiring into the cost or availability of the additional insurance. As in *Michel*, the court in the present case "has entered . . . financial orders that may be inappropriate, that is, too high or too low depending on the funds required to obtain such [additional] insurance." *Michel v. Michel, supra*, 31 Conn. App. 341. Although the charged party in *Michel* held no insurance at the time of the dissolution; *id.*, 340; we conclude that the same analysis is necessary in cases in which a party is ordered to obtain additional insurance. Because the court did not inquire as to the cost and availability of the additional life insurance, the court's order lacks a reasonable basis in the facts, and, therefore, constitutes an abuse of the court's discretion.

Although every improper financial order in a dissolution of marriage action does not necessarily merit a reconsideration of all of the court's financial orders; see, e.g., *Smith v. Smith*, 249 Conn. 265, 277, 752 A.2d 1023 (1999); in this case, the court's order that the defendant obtain additional life insurance is interdependent with its other financial orders and may not be severed from them. We must, therefore, remand the case to the trial court on all financial matters . . .

Source: Gail A. Parley v. Jon A. Parley, 72 CONN. APP. 742, 807 A.2D 982 (2002), Appellate Court of Connecticut, State of Connecticut.

TERMINATION OF ALIMONY

Remarriage

Alimony usually terminates on remarriage. The underlying policy is that upon re-marriage, the new spouse has a duty to support. It would be unfair to allow a divorced spouse, who has now remarried, to receive support from two sources. In some states, alimony automatically terminates upon remarriage and the payor spouse simply ceases payments. In other states, the parties petition the court for termination of alimony.

Cohabitation

In many jurisdictions, cohabitation results in the termination or modification of an alimony obligation. The problem with cohabitation as opposed to remarriage is that a cohabitant has no legal duty to support and can terminate the relationship at any time with little or no legal repercussions. It is important when drafting the settlement agreement to specifically indicate what type of conduct gives rise to a modification or termination of the alimony obligation.

Cohabitation Nation In *Rester*, the Court of Appeals of Mississippi finds the trial court judge committed a reversible error when he declined to terminate the husband's obligation to pay his wife alimony when the evidence clearly showed that his wife was cohabitating with another man and benefiting financially from this arrangement.

JOHN RESTER v. BETH HERRINGTON RESTER

5 So.3d 1132 (Miss. App. 2008)
Court of Appeals of Mississippi

Roberts, K., for the Court.

Summary of the Case

. . . John and Beth Rester divorced and executed a property settlement agreement. Within that agreement, John agreed to pay Beth $2,500 in monthly periodic ali-mony. Approximately ten years later, John claimed Beth had been cohabitating with a man named Al Cabrera as though they were married. Consequently, John sought to terminate his obligation to pay Beth alimony. In response, Beth filed a request for additional alimony. After conducting a hearing, the chancellor de-nied John's request for termination of alimony. Though the chancellor found that Cabrera and Beth had substantial contact for approximately five years, the chan-cellor also found that the facts were "just shy" of meriting termination of ali-mony. However, the chancellor also denied Beth's request for additional alimony. Aggrieved, John now appeals, and Beth cross-appeals. After careful consideration, we conclude that the chancellor committed reversible error when he declined to terminate John's obligation to pay Beth alimony. Accordingly, we affirm the chan-cellor's judgment to decline to increase John's alimony payments to Beth.

Analysis

. . . In *Schunvath v. Sckarwath*, 702 So.2d 1210, 1211 (§ 7) (Miss. 1997), the Missis-sippi Supreme Court adopted the rule that "proof of cohabitation creates a presump-tion that a material change in circumstances has occurred." The rationale behind the Supreme Court's implementation of this presumption is the "difficulty a providing

continued

spouse faces in presenting direct evidence of mutual financial support between cohabiting parties." *Id.* The Supreme Court went on to state that "parties who live in cohabitation can easily and purposely keep their condition of mutual financial support concealed from the paying spouse, as well as from courts seeking only financial documentation before it will grant a modification." *Id.* Accordingly, upon proof of cohabitation, the burden of proof shifts "to the recipient spouse to come forward with evidence suggesting that there is no mutual support." *Id.*

. . . In summary, there is no doubt that Beth failed to rebut the presumption of mutual support. In fact, the evidence overwhelmingly demonstrated the presence of mutual support. Cabrera bought groceries for Beth. By Beth's testimony, Cabrera gave her money for clothes and when she went on trips. Beth had access to Cabrera's debit card PIN number. Cabrera left money with Beth when he went out of town. During those times, Beth checked Cabrera's mail, opened it, and paid his bills. Beth testified that Cabrera never gave her money specifically for utilities, but she nonetheless testified that he "helped" her with her utilities. Cabrera helped Beth with projects around her home. Cabrera had a place to leave his personal vehicle when he went out of town for work, and Beth had the benefit of access to Cabrera's personal vehicle whenever she wanted to use it. Despite characterizing Harrison County as a whole as his home, it was at Beth's house that Cabrera stayed when he returned "home." Through Beth's family, Cabrera had a place to live after Hurricane Katrina devastated the Mississippi Gulf Coast.

. . . Because Beth admitted that she and Cabrera cohabited, and failed to rebut the presumption of mutual support, we must conclude that the chancellor was clearly wrong when he declined to terminate alimony. Accordingly, we are compelled to reverse the judgment of the chancellor and render judgment for John. Thus, John's obligation to pay Beth monthly periodic alimony is hereby terminated.

Source: John Rester v. Beth Herrington Rester, 5 SO.3D 1132 (MISS. APP. 2008), State of Mississippi Judiciary.

Death

Alimony terminates on the death of either party unless otherwise stated in the settlement agreement or the divorce decree. If support is to be extended beyond death, it can be accomplished by an irrevocable insurance policy on the payor's life, naming the payee spouse as beneficiary. Lump-sum alimony paid in installments and property division awards does not terminate upon the death of the payor spouse.

The Pitfalls of a May–December Marriage In *Schwartz*, the Supreme Court of Nevada found that the trial court should have looked at the husband's medical

ABIGAIL RICHLIN SCHWARTZ, APPELLANT, v. JONATHAN SCHWARTZ, AS THE PERSONAL REPRESENTATIVE OF MILTON I. SCHWARTZ, DECEASED, RESPONDENT

126 Nev. Adv. Op. No. 8, 49313 (2010)
Supreme Court of Nevada

by the court, Cherry, J.

Opinion

This appeal concerns a divorce and the awarding of assets by the district court to appellant Abigail Schwartz based on several agreements entered into by Abigail and

Milton Schwartz before Milton's death. The several agreements were entered into by Abigail and Milton before and during their marriage and include a reconciliation agreement entered into after a separation period.

In this opinion, we examine whether the district court abused its discretion in failing to award Abigail lump-sum alimony.

We conclude that the district court abused its discretion in failing to conduct a full and proper analysis of whether lump-sum alimony was appropriate in this case and hold that a district court should assess not only age disparity as set forth in *Daniel v. Baker*, 106 Nev. 412, 794 P.2d 345 (1990), but should also assess whether the life expectancy of the payor makes the award illusory. Accordingly, we reverse the district court's order regarding the award of alimony and remand for the district court to make a determination as to whether an award of lump-sum alimony was appropriate in this case.

Facts and Procedural History

Milton and Abigail met in May 1992. At the time of their meeting, Abigail was a registered nurse practicing in Las Vegas. Abigail stopped working as a registered nurse at Milton's request in order for the couple to be able to travel.

Milton and Abigail were married in 1993. At the time of their marriage, Milton was 71 years old and Abigail was 41 years old. Prior to their marriage, Abigail and Milton entered into a premarital agreement.

In December 1994, Milton filed for divorce against Abigail. On December 24, 1996, after 19 months of separation, Milton and Abigail reconciled and certain promises were made by both spouses, and these promises were memorialized in a reconciliation agreement.

On April 19, 2006, Milton filed a second complaint for divorce against Abigail. Abigail filed an answer and counterclaim against Milton seeking equitable relief and damages. After a two-day bench trial, the district court entered its findings of fact, conclusions of law, and divorce decree. In part, the district court ordered Milton to pay Abigail spousal support in the amount of $5,000 per month for a period of seven years.

Shortly after the district court entered its divorce decree, Milton and Abigail had dinner together at a restaurant in Las Vegas. During this dinner, Milton told Abigail that he was unhappy that they had obtained a divorce. Milton also expressed to Abigail that he was considering reconciling and that if he was to marry again, Abigail was the only wife for him. In the days following this dinner, Milton and Abigail spoke several more times about possibly reconciling and remarrying.

After the reconciliation dinner, Abigail filed a motion to alter and amend the district court's findings of fact, conclusions of law, and decree of divorce based on Milton's statements at the reconciliation dinner. Included in Abigail's motion was a motion for a new trial. The district court denied Abigail's motion to alter and amend its findings of fact, conclusions of law, and decree of divorce and for a new trial in its entirety. This appeal follows.

Discussion

Abigail argues that the district court abused its discretion in the amount of alimony it awarded to her and in failing to award her lump-sum alimony since Milton was in poor health at the time of the divorce proceedings and the alimony awarded her terminated at the time of Milton's death. Abigail contends that the district court erred in finding that this case was distinguishable from *Daniel v. Baker*, 106 Nev. 412, 794 P.2d 345 (1990), in which we reversed the district court's decision to award a monthly alimony payment that terminated upon the death of the payor and remanded with instructions to award permanent or lump-sum alimony. Abigail contends that, because of the age disparity between her and Milton, a lump-sum alimony award

continued

was required, and, thus, the district court abused its discretion in awarding alimony by not making such an award.

. . . We conclude that the district court did not abuse its discretion in the amount of alimony it awarded to Abigail. The district court analyzed the factors set out in *Sprenger* in making its alimony award. In making its alimony award, the district court specifically looked at: (1) the financial condition of the parties; (2) the nature and value of the parties' respective property; (3) the contribution of each party to property held by them; (4) the duration of the marriage; (5) Milton's income, earning capacity, age, health, and ability to labor; (6) Abigail's income, earning capacity, age, health, and ability to labor; (7) Abigail's reasonable post-divorce needs; and (8) the parties' station in life and gap in income. The district court was in the best position to hear and decide the facts of this case, and we will not substitute our judgment for that of the district court on this issue.

However . . . [w]e must conclude that the district court abused its discretion in failing to do a full and proper analysis of whether lump-sum alimony was appropriate in this case, as the district court did not take Milton's health into account. Milton testified at trial, at which time he was 85 years old and Abigail was 55 years old, that he had end-stage kidney disease, was on dialysis three times a week, and was in poor health. The district court should have taken Milton's poor health into account when making its determination of whether a lump-sum alimony award would have been proper in this case.

We thus hold that a district court should assess not only age disparity as set forth in *Daniel*, but also whether the life expectancy of the payor will make a non-lump-sum alimony award illusory. Along with the analysis set out in *Daniel*, the age and health of the payor should be taken into consideration when undertaking an analysis of whether lump-sum alimony is appropriate. *Id.* Specifically, a district court should look at the life expectancy of the payor at the time of making the alimony determination and take into account the payor's medical condition and prospects for healthy living. This analysis will help avoid an illusory alimony award when a payor is known to be terminally ill or known to have low prospects for continued healthy living since it will allow the payee to continue to receive alimony in a manner that will assure they are supported past the payor's death. As such, we remand this case back to the district court to complete its analysis of whether a lump-sum alimony award is appropriate in this case, taking into account Milton's age, health, and life expectancy in relation to the length of the alimony award.

We therefore reverse the district court's order with regard to the award of alimony and remand for the district court to perform a complete analysis of whether lump-sum alimony is appropriate in this case, consistent with our holding. We have carefully reviewed all other issues raised on appeal and determine that they lack merit. Accordingly, we affirm all other aspects of the district court's decision.

HARDESTY, J., SAITTA, J., concur

Source: Abigail Richlin Schwartz, Appellant, v. Jonathan Schwartz, as the Personal Representative of Milton I. Schwartz, Deceased, Respondent, 126 NEV. ADV. OP. NO. 8, 49313 (2010), Supreme Court of Nevada.

conditions at the time of making the alimony determination. The bottom line when divorcing an older spouse is that it is best to "get your money up front" since you never know what can happen!

ENFORCEMENT OF COURT-ORDERED PAYMENTS

When a party entitled to alimony payments pursuant to a court order is not paid, that party may commence a civil **contempt proceeding** to force the payor spouse to comply with the court's order. This process begins with the recipient spouse filing the appropriate paperwork within that jurisdiction (e.g., a motion for contempt or a citation with an order to show cause). In the proper document, the recipient will state what was awarded in the original order, that the payor spouse has not paid since a specific date, and include a request that the delinquent spouse be found in contempt of court. These documents are served on the payor and filed in the court where the original alimony award was entered. A contempt is an extension of the divorce matter; therefore, it is unnecessary to assert personal jurisdiction over the payor spouse. The only requirement is service, notice of the proceedings, and the opportunity to be heard.

> **Contempt proceeding**
> A civil proceeding that a party may commence to force the payor spouse to comply with the court's order when the party entitled to alimony is not paid.

Once the parties are in court, it is the payor spouse's burden to prove that she has, in fact, kept up the alimony payments and has the canceled checks or receipts to prove it. If the payor spouse cannot provide such proof, the court will order the payor spouse to pay the arrearage. If the arrearage cannot be paid in a lump sum, the court will make the arrearage payable in installments. The payor will then find herself obligated to make weekly payments on the arrearage in addition to the weekly payments authorized by the original court order.

The filing of a contempt action by the recipient spouse or payee spouse will often precipitate the filing of a modification motion by the payor spouse. This is especially true in cases where the payor spouse has failed to discharge his or her alimony or child support obligation because of unfavorably changed financial circumstances.

EXAMPLE 2

On August 1, John is ordered by the court to pay $100 per week as alimony to his wife Linda. On October 1, John loses his job due to a layoff at the plant where he works. Four weeks pass and Linda is not paid her court-ordered alimony award. Linda files a contempt action. John is properly served. He meets with his lawyer, who immediately files a modification on the basis that there has been a significant change in John's circumstances since the entering of the original alimony order— that is, John's being laid off.

In this scenario, John will probably not be able to modify his obligation for the arrearage because in most jurisdictions, past alimony amounts due may not be increased or decreased retroactively. Some states *do* allow for retroactive modifications of arrearages, but they are the exception, not the rule. Most courts, however, can always modify an alimony order for prospective payments. In John's case, his substantiated showing of his changed circumstances and its negative financial consequences should be sufficient good cause for the court to lower his alimony obligation.

ATTORNEY'S FEES IN CONTEMPT ACTIONS

The recipient spouse who is forced to bring a contempt action may also demand attorney's fees from the delinquent spouse. The recipient spouse will prevail if the payor is found to be in **willful contempt**. The court is likely to find willful

> **Willful contempt**
> When the recipient spouse proves that the payor spouse has the means to make weekly payments but purposefully and deliberately fails to do so.

contempt if the recipient spouse proves that the payor spouse has the means to make the payments but purposefully and deliberately fails to do so. The court may also find willful contempt if the recipient spouse demonstrates that although financial problems now prevent the payor from complying with the court-ordered alimony obligation, the payor, himself or herself, caused the financial setback either by spending too much, voluntarily leaving his or her employment, defrauding the recipient spouse, or engaging in some other type of irresponsible conduct.

Concept Review and Reinforcement

KEY **TERMS**

alimony
alimony in gross or alimony
    in solido
attorney's fees
bridge-the-gap alimony
canon law
cohabitation
Consolidated Omnibus Budget
    Reconciliation Act (COBRA)
contempt proceeding
cost-of-living clause

durational alimony
ecclesiastical courts
escalation clause
Married Women's Property Acts
Massachusetts Alimony Reform
    Act of 2011
modification of alimony
no-fault divorce laws
nominal alimony
pendente lite alimony
periodic alimony, or alimony in future

permanent alimony
rehabilitative alimony
reimbursement alimony
spousal maintenance
spousal support
temporary alimony
transitional alimony
waiver of alimony
willful contempt

REVIEW OF **KEY CONCEPTS**

1. Discuss the two interests that must be balanced by a family court before awarding alimony to a spouse.

2. Using Internet legal research resources such as Westlaw or Loislaw, or your state's legislative branch website, what are the statutory factors the courts must consider in your jurisdiction when evaluating the issue of alimony?

3. What are the different types of alimony that may be awarded in a divorce case?

4. In your opinion, do you believe that the issue of fault or wrongdoing by one spouse should be considered when awarding spousal support?

5. Based on your reading of this chapter, do you believe that a former spouse who is ordered to pay alimony should be allowed to modify or terminate said order when he or she has voluntarily left their place of employment or been discharged due to wrongdoing on the job?

BUILDING YOUR PARALEGAL SKILLS

CASES FOR BRIEFING

CROSBY V. LEBERT, 285 GA. 297, 676 S.E.2D 192 (2009)

Critical Thinking and Legal Analysis Applications

You work for a paralegal in the law office of Silva and Silva. Your supervisor, Adelia Silva, asks you to research a post-judgment alimony modification matter in the case of your client, Jonas Black. Mr. Black's former wife was ordered to pay the following in their divorce settlement:

"The Wife agrees to pay to the Husband, permanent periodic alimony in the sum of $300.00 (three-hundred dollars) per week. Wife also agrees to pay all monthly installment payments of Husband's 2009 Harley Davidson Full

Dresser motorcycle until the vehicle is paid in full and shall do so in the form of permanent periodic alimony. Wife hereby waives any and all interest she may have in the 2009 Harley Davidson Full Dresser the Husband is currently using. Husband's motorcycle is financed and titled in Wife's name. Wife shall timely pay all monthly installment payments of Husband's vehicle until the vehicle is paid in full and shall do so in the form of permanent periodic alimony. Once Husband's vehicle is paid in full, Wife shall sign title of the vehicle over to Husband."

Mr. Black really loves his Harley. He also loves his new girlfriend whom he intends to marry. He would like some advice on the effect that his pending remarriage will have on his alimony award and beloved motorcycle. It is the client's opinion that while he risks losing his $300 per week alimony award if he remarries, the motorcycle should be safe since it is really part of the property settlement.

Based on the case of *Crosby v. Lebert,* 285 Ga. 297, 676 S.E.2d 192 (2009), how would the Georgia courts decide this case?

Based on the family law in your jurisdiction, how would the courts in your state decide this case?

Building a Professional Portfolio

PORTFOLIO **EXERCISES**

Brian Smith has been paying permanent periodic alimony to his former wife in the sum of $250.00 per week for the last six months. His wife, Allison, recently moved her friend Judith and her two children into her home when Judith was displaced from her apartment after a recent hurricane. Allison and Judith are just friends and are not involved in a sexual relationship. Judith and her children sleep in one of the extra rooms in Allison's home. Judith contributes $175.00 per week toward the household expenses and does chores around the house. She also babysits for Allison and Brian's daughter, Aimee, when Allison has to work late. Judith is also very handy and enjoys working outdoors. She mows the lawn and takes care of the gardening for Allison, who has a "brown thumb." The two women and their children eat dinner and attend church together.

Brian wants to motion the court to terminate alimony on the grounds that his former wife is cohabitating. Their separation agreement states that alimony shall terminate in the event of wife's death, remarriage, or cohabitation. The question here is whether a sexually intimate relationship is a requirement in terminating alimony on the basis of cohabitation. Prepare an interoffice memo for your supervising attorney based on the relevant statutory and case law in your state.

Chapter **six**

PROPERTY AND DEBT DISTRIBUTION

LEARNING OBJECTIVES

After studying this chapter, you should be able to:

1. List and describe the various forms of ownership of real property.

2. Distinguish marital property from separate property.

3. Understand the concept of property transmutation.

4. Provide examples of the conversion of separate property into marital property.

5. Describe the concepts of equitable distribution and community property.

6. Define dissipation of marital assets and give examples.

7. Explain the effect of bankruptcy on a property settlement.

W hile the purpose of alimony is to provide a needy spouse with support or "maintenance," the goal of property and debt distribution is to fairly distribute the marital assets and debts between the spouses. Property and debt division is one of the most contested issues in modern divorce cases, second only to custody disputes. Spouses generally accumulate a myriad of assets and debts during a marriage, which may take center stage at a divorce hearing where the central issue is "Who gets what?" While asset accumulation is one of the goals of the married couple—especially fulfilling the American dream of home ownership—debts are unfortunately also part of the equation. In some marriages, distribution of debt may be the only financial issue to resolve. This chapter also introduces the reader to the effects of bankruptcy and the ever-present tax consequences in dissolving the family unit.

BASIC PRINCIPLES OF PROPERTY

This chapter focuses on the issue of property and debts and how they are divided at the time of divorce; therefore, an understanding of basic property principles is essential before proceeding any further.

Property can be classified as either *real* or *personal*. **Real property** is land and anything affixed to it (e.g., house, garage, barn, condominium). **Personal property** is anything other than real property that can be touched and is movable (e.g., cash, automobiles, bank accounts, jewelry, furniture, clothing, stocks, bonds).

Property can be owned by an individual alone; this is known as sole ownership. Property also can be held by two or more persons together; this is known as **concurrent ownership** or joint ownership. A sole owner has the right to give, sell, will, encumber, and lease her property. In other words, a sole owner can do anything legal with her property without another's approval. Concurrent owners have rights and responsibilities vis-à-vis each other that differ from jurisdiction to jurisdiction. The most common forms of concurrent or joint ownership are as follows:

- tenancy in common,
- joint tenancy with right of survivorship,
- tenancy by the entirety, and
- community property.

Real property
Land and anything affixed to it.

Personal property
Anything other than real property that can be touched and is movable.

Concurrent ownership
When property is held by two or more persons together; also known as joint ownership.

Tenancy in Common

Tenants in common each own an undivided interest in the property, have equal rights to use and enjoyment, and may dispose of their share by gift, will, or sale. At the time of a co-owner's death, his share passes to his beneficiaries, if he left a will, or to his heirs under the intestacy succession laws of his state if he dies without a will. Tenancy in common as a form of joint ownership is frequently used by individuals who are not related to one another. It may be used by persons joining together to purchase real property as a business investment, or it may be used by friends who buy a property to live in together.

Joint Tenancy

Joint tenants own equal interests in property, and at the death of one of the joint tenants, her interest automatically passes to the remaining joint tenant through what is known as the right of survivorship. A joint tenant also has the right to sell her interest in the jointly owned property. The sale of one co-owner's interest destroys the right of survivorship; the new co-owner and the remaining tenant now hold the property as tenants in common.

Joint tenancy is chosen as a form of ownership most often when the parties are married, are related, or are friends who have a very close relationship. This is probably so because joint tenancy includes the right of survivorship, and it also allows a tenant to sell her interest without obtaining the other tenant's permission.

Tenancy by the Entirety

Tenancy by the entirety is a form of co-ownership that can only exist between a husband and wife. It is similar to joint tenancy in that it carries with it the right of survivorship. The main difference, however, is that one tenant may not severe tenancy by the entirety without the permission of the other co-tenant.

Tenancy by the entirety affords both spouses a greater say in whether or not the tenancy will continue. It protects a spouse from the consequences of the other spouse selling his or her interest without any discussion or notice.

Community Property

In community property states, all property and income acquired during the marriage are deemed to be owned equally by both spouses, subject to certain exceptions. Community property is discussed in more detail later in this chapter.

Community property states have statutes providing that real estate purchased during the marriage is to be held by the spouses as community property. Exceptions to this rule are recognized when the real estate was purchased solely with funds that one of the spouses possessed prior to the marriage or had received as a gift or an inheritance.

PROPERTY AND DEBT DISTRIBUTION UPON MARITAL DISSOLUTION

Marital assets

The property acquired during a marriage.

It is the responsibility of each party's attorney to determine the extent and value of the property owned and what the client should be entitled to at the time of divorce. This process begins with the task of determining what property the client and his spouse own, either solely or jointly, regardless of how the property is titled. Title indicates a party's ownership interest in property—that is, "Whose name is the property in?" A list of property can be developed from information obtained from the client interview and through the formal discovery devices. The term *marital assets* refers to property acquired during a marriage. Here are some examples:

antiques	appliances	artwork
automobiles	bank accounts	boats
bonds	business interests	cash
clothing	collectibles (stamps, coins, etc.)	condominiums
copyrights	credit union accounts	goodwill
heirlooms	household furnishings	insurance
jewelry	judgments	lottery winnings
marital gifts	marital home	mutual funds
pending lawsuits	pension plans (401k, SEP, IRA)	pets
professional degrees	profit-sharing plans	silverware
stocks	tax refunds	time shares
trademarks	trailers	vacation homes

The next two cases presented in this chapter illustrate that marital property is not limited to traditional assets such as the marital home, bank accounts, and automobiles. Marital assets exist in many surprising forms. All it takes is a good legal eye to spot them and a good legal argument to toss them into the marital property pot. In *Campbell*, the court affirmed a long-standing rule defining lottery winnings as marital assets. In *Bennett*, the court determines the legal status of the family dog.

KIMBERLY A. CAMPBELL v. TERRY M. CAMPBELL

213 A.2D 1027, 624 N.Y.S.2D 493 (A.D. 4 DEPT. 1995
SUPREME COURT, APPELLATE DIVISION, FOURTH DEPARTMENT)

Memorandum: Plaintiff and 10 co-workers agreed that they would take turns purchasing a lottery ticket and that, if any one of them purchased a winning ticket, the proceeds would be shared in 11 equal shares. Plaintiff purchased a lottery ticket on

continued

at least one prior occasion, but it was not a winner. A co-worker purchased a winning lottery ticket on October 7, 1992. The jackpot prize was $4.5 million. Because of the policy of the New York State Lotto Commission to recognize only one winner per ticket, the co-worker obtained a Federal taxpayer identification number in the name of a trust and prepared a trust agreement for the disbursement of the lottery proceeds to all 11 co-workers. The trust agreement acknowledges the prior agreement of the parties, and all 11 co-workers executed the trust agreement.

Plaintiff commenced this action for divorce in 1993. Defendant counterclaimed for divorce and moved for an order enjoining and restraining plaintiff from spending or transferring her interest in the lottery proceeds. Defendant maintained that the lottery proceeds were marital property subject to equitable distribution. Supreme Court determined that the co-worker who purchased the winning lottery ticket was under no legal duty to share the proceeds with her co-workers, that the agreement to disburse a share of the proceeds to plaintiff constituted a gift, and that gift constituted plaintiff's separate property.

An agreement to share the proceeds of a lottery is a valid and enforceable agreement (citations omitted). An oral agreement to share proceeds that will be paid over a period of several years does not contravene the Statute of Frauds (citations omitted). The oral agreement to the co-workers was sufficiently definite to be enforced (citation omitted), and the court erred in concluding that the co-worker who purchased the winning ticket was under no legal duty to share the proceeds. Moreover, there is no evidence in the record of donative intent. It is undisputed that the co-worker acted pursuant to the oral agreement.

Domestic Relations Law § 236(B)(1)(c) defines marital property as "all property acquired by either or both spouses during the marriage and before . . . commencement of a matrimonial action, regardless of the form in which title is held." Thus, property acquired during the marriage is presumptively marital property, and plaintiff had the burden of showing that it was separate property (citations omitted). Courts have universally held that the proceeds of a winning lottery ticket acquired by a spouse during the marriage constitute marital property (citations omitted). That principle applies to instances where one spouse contributed with third persons to a pool of funds used to purchase lottery tickets and one of the tickets was a winner (citations omitted). The agreement of the co-workers constituted a pooling arrangement, and plaintiff's share of the proceeds constitutes marital property (citations omitted). Thus, we modify the order on appeal by vacating that part denying defendant's motion and by determining that plaintiff's share of the lottery proceeds constitutes marital property.

Because the court determined that the proceeds were separate property, it did not consider whether plaintiff should be enjoined from transferring or otherwise disposing of the proceeds and whether the proceeds should be placed in escrow pending the distribution of marital property. We remit this matter to Supreme Court for determination of defendant's motion.

Order unanimously modified on the law and as modified affirmed without costs and matter remitted to Supreme Court for further proceedings.

Source: Kimberly A. Campbell v. Terry M. Campbell, 213 A.2D 1027, 624 N.Y.S.2D 493 (A.D. 4 DEPT. 1995), United States Supreme Court.

Dog Visitation? Enforcement and supervision of pet visitation clauses would open the floodgates to litigation over pet-related problems. Traditionally, the courts have held that pets are personal property and will award the pet to either spouse at the time of the dissolution.

RONALD GREG BENNETT v. KATHRYN R. BENNETT

655 SO. 2D 109 (FLA. APP. 1 DIST. 1995)
DISTRICT COURT OF APPEAL OF FLORIDA, FIRST DISTRICT

WOLF, JUDGE.

Husband, Ronald Greg Bennett, appeals from a final judgment of dissolution of marriage which, among other things, awarded custody of the parties' dog, "Roddy." The husband asserts that (1) the trial court erred in awarding the former wife visitation with the parties' dog, and (2) the trial court erred in modifying the final judgment to increase the former wife's visitation rights with the dog. We find that the trial court lacked authority to order visitation with personal property; the dog would properly be dealt with through the equitable distribution process.

A brief recitation of the procedural history will demonstrate the morass a trial court may find itself in by extending the right of visitation to personal property. The parties stipulated to all issues in the final judgment of dissolution of marriage except which party would receive possession of the parties' dog, "Roddy." After a hearing, the trial court found that the husband should have possession of the dog and that the wife should be able to take the dog for visitation every other weekend and every other Christmas.

The former husband contested this decision and filed a motion for rehearing alleging that the dog was a premarital asset. He also filed a motion for relief from final judgment and an amended motion for rehearing. The wife replied and filed a motion to strike former husband's amended motion for rehearing and a motion for contempt. The former wife requested that the trial court transfer custody of the dog because the former husband was refusing to comply with the trial court's order concerning visitation with the dog.

A hearing on these motions was held on September 27, 1993. The wife's counsel filed an ore tenus motion requesting the trial court to change custody, or in the alternative, change visitation. The trial court denied the former husband's motion for rehearing and granted the former wife's ore tenus motion to change visitation. Thus, the trial court's ruling on visitation now reads:

7. *Dog, Roddy:* The former husband, RONALD GREGORY BENNETT, shall have custody of the parties' dog "Roddy" and the former wife, KATHRYN R. BENNETT n/k/a KATHRYN R. ROGERS, shall have visitation every other month beginning October 1, 1993. The visitation shall begin on the first day of the month and end on the last day of the month.

Based on the history of this case, there is every reason to believe that there will be continued squabbling between the parties concerning the dog.

While a dog may be considered by many to be a member of the family, under Florida law, animals are considered to be personal property. *County of Pasco v. Riehl,* 620 So. 2d 229 (Fla.2d DCA 1993), and *Levine v. Knowles,* 197 So. 2d 329 (Fla.3d DCA 1967). There is no authority which provides for a trial court to grant custody or visitation pertaining to personal property. § 61.075, Fla.Stat. (1993).

While several states have given family pets special status within dissolution proceedings (for example, *see Arrington v. Arrington,* 613 S.W.2d 565 (Tex. Civ. App. 1981)), we think such a course is unwise. Determinations as to custody and visitation lead to continuing enforcement and supervision problems (as evidenced by the proceedings in the instant case). Our courts are overwhelmed with the supervision of custody, visitation, and support matters related to the protection of our children. We cannot undertake the same responsibility as to animals.

While the trial judge was endeavoring to reach a fair solution under difficult circumstances, we must reverse the order relating to the custody of "Roddy," and remand for the trial court to award the animal pursuant to the dictates or the equitable distribution statute.

WEBSTER and MICKLE, J.J., concur.

Source: Ronald Greg Bennett v. Kathryn R.Bennett, 655 SO. 2D 109 (FLA. APP. 1 DIST. 1995), Florida First District Court of Appeal, State of Florida.

. . . BUT WHAT ABOUT THE DOG'S "BEST INTERESTS"?

Although most courts and legal scholars tend to view pets as property, this trend has not stopped at least one court from applying the legal standards used to determine child custody and visitation to decide the fate of the family dog.

In *Juelfs v. Gough,* 41 P.3d 593 (2002), the Alaska Supreme Court affirmed an award of "sole custody" of the family's pet to the husband. In 1993, the trial court, in its original divorce decree, using terms which applied to personal property, provided for shared ownership of the couple's chocolate Labrador retriever, Coho. This arrangement worked for several years. However, in 2000, the former wife, Julie, filed a motion to have the agreement incorporated in the divorce decree reviewed because her former husband, Stephen, refused to allow her agreed-upon time with Coho. Stephen opposed the motion, alleging that Julie's other two dogs posed a threat to Coho's life. He asserted that when the dogs were fighting, an attempt to separate the dogs resulted in an injury to Coho's leg, dislocating it at the elbow. This required the dog to be under "constant care and medication." After a hearing, the court awarded "legal and physical custody of Coho" to Steve and allowed Julie "reasonable visitation rights as determined" by Steve. Immediately, Julie sought unsuccessfully to have the order reviewed. Visitation arrangements apparently did not go smoothly. Within three months, the parties were back in court seeking reciprocal restraining orders against each other arising from an altercation that occurred when Stephen tried to retrieve Coho after Julie had taken the pet for a visit without permission.

Julie again filed a request to review the custody arrangement. This court reaffirmed its grant of Coho's custody to Stephen and sternly proclaimed that "Ms. Gough has no rights whatsoever to Coho and may not demand visitation or take the dog from Mr. Gough." Julie then filed for a change of custody and requested the matter be heard by a different judge. Ultimately, her efforts, even after review by another judge, were unsuccessful. She then appealed the ruling.

In her appeal, Julie questioned whether the trial court could modify a final divorce decree regarding property division.

The Alaska Supreme Court found that the trial court did not abuse its discretion in modifying the divorce decree to give Stephen sole custody of Coho. The Court noted that the custody of Coho *was* part of the property settlement agreed upon by both parties and incorporated into the divorce decree which is a final judgment, and that such final judgment could only be modified according to the controlling statute by "extraordinary circumstances." However, the situation regarding Coho constituted extraordinary circumstances.

The Court noted that Stephen's argument at the trial level against enforcement of the original agreement included the assertion that it is "in the best interests of Coho that the property settlement agreement provide that Coho be awarded to Steve Gough solely."

The Court found that such language was enough to warrant the trial court's action and agreed with the trial court's assessment that modification was warranted because the arrangement between the parties had assumed a state of facts, namely cooperation between them that proved not to exist: "The parties were unable to share custody of Coho without severe contention."

This case is interesting not only for its posture on pet sharing but also for its holding that a final divorce judgment is not so final that it may not be modified for equitable reasons. In this opinion, the Court noted that assumption of a state of facts that did not exist was akin to *fraud,* one of the circumstances the Alaska statute considered an *extraordinary circumstance.*

MARITAL DEBTS

Marital debts
Marital debts are the liabilities incurred by either spouse during the course of the marriage.

Debts are also part of the marital acquisition equation and must be identified as well as assets. *Marital debts* are the liabilities incurred by either spouse during the marriage. Examples of marital debts are as follows:

assessments	court judgments	credit card balances
loans	mortgages	tuitions
unpaid taxes	unreimbursed medical expenses	

THE DISTINCTION BETWEEN SEPARATE AND MARITAL PROPERTY

Separate property
Property acquired by a spouse *prior* to the marriage, or after the marriage by a gift, inheritance, or will, designated to that particular spouse alone.

Marital property
Real and personal property acquired during a marriage.

Once a list of a client's property and debts has been prepared, the next step is to divide the property into two categories: separate property and marital property. *Separate property* is property acquired by a spouse *prior* to the marriage or after the marriage by a gift, inheritance, or will, designated to that particular spouse alone. *Marital property* can be defined as property or income acquired during the marriage.

A common struggle in many divorce cases such as *Cohen v. Cohen* involves the down payment on the marital home. Kind parents who sometimes give money for the purchase of the home may find themselves in the middle of the separate versus marital property dilemma.

Remember that the definition of marital property excludes separate property. The issue of title or "whose name property is in" is unimportant. For instance, if the marital home was purchased during the marriage but title is solely in the wife's name as evidenced by the deed, it is still considered marital property. Both wife *and* husband have an interest in the home, regardless of whose name is on the deed. The family courts have statutory power to award property in a divorce matter regardless of the title interest.

The underlying policy behind the judicial authority statutes is that marriage is a partnership. In a business partnership, the partners pool their expertise, efforts, and resources to make the business operative and profitable. Similarly, during a marriage, the efforts and personal and financial resources of the parties are pooled for the benefit of the marital partnership. When the marriage has ended, each spouse has an interest in whatever has accumulated during the course of this partnership.

The task of defining separate and marital property is an important part of the divorce process. The court will award separate property to the spouse entitled to its ownership. Once the separate property is parceled out to respective spouses, the marital property becomes one of the focal points of the divorce litigation. Whatever goes into the marital property pot is up for grabs. In some states, such as Connecticut, the court may award *any* of the spouses' property, separate or marital, in the course of the divorce proceedings to either spouse, regardless of whether the property is separate or marital.

SHIRLEY R. COHEN v. HAROLD L. COHEN

474 P.2D 792 (1970)
SUPREME COURT OF COLORADO

GROVES, JUSTICE.

This proceeding arises out of a divorce action brought by the wife. The parties appear here in the same order as in the trial court and are referred to as plaintiff and defendant. The alleged error relates to the division of property and the award of alimony and attorney's fees to the plaintiff. We affirm.

continued

The plaintiff's principal contention is that the court erred in finding that a monetary gift made by the defendant's parents was a gift to the defendant rather than to the plaintiff. Prior to the marriage the defendant's father executed two checks payable to the plaintiff in the respective amounts of $6,000 and $5,000. The defendant's parents specified that the proceeds were to be applied towards the purchase of a home to be occupied by the parties, and the money was so applied. After executing the checks the father gave them to the defendant, who presented them to the plaintiff. The plaintiff endorsed the checks to the defendant and returned them to him. The defendant's father testified that he made the checks payable to the plaintiff on the advice of his accountant, who apparently thought this might cause a saving of gift tax. (The gift tax of $11,000 was later declared to the taxing authorities as having been made to the defendant.)

The court found that this was a gift by the defendant's parents to the defendant and that the plaintiff was not entitled to any portion of the $11,000 in the property division. The testimony was in conflict, but there is ample evidence to support the finding of the trial court as to the intent with respect to the gifts, and we should not and will not disturb that finding.

Judgment affirmed.

HODGES, KELLEY and LEE, JJ., concur.

Source: Shirley R. Cohen v. Harold L. Cohen, 474 P.2D 792 (1970), Supreme Court of Colorado.

Statutes

Relief is also provided in jurisdictions that make distinctions between separate and marital property, if doing so would result in an unjust or unfair result.

CONNECTICUT GENERAL STATUTES ANNOTATED (WEST) § 46B-81.

(a) At the time of entering a decree of annulling or dissolving a marriage or for legal separation pursuant to a complaint under section 46b-45, the superior court may assign to either the husband or wife all or any part of the estate of the other. The court may pass title to real property to either party or to a third person or may order the sale of such real property, without any act by either the husband or the wife, when in the judgment of the court it is the proper mode to carry the decree into effect. . .

(c) In fixing the nature and value of the property, if any, to be assigned, the court, after hearing the witnesses, if any, of each party, except as provided in subsection (a) of section 46b-51, shall consider the length of marriage, the causes for the annulment, dissolution of the marriage or legal separation, the age, health, station, occupation, amount and sources of income, vocational skills, employability, estate, liabilities and needs of each of the parties and the opportunity of each for future acquisition of capital assets and income. The court shall also consider the contribution of each of the parties in the acquisition, preservation or appreciation in value of their respective estates.

Source: Connecticut General Statutes 46b-81—Assignment of Property and Transfer of Title, State of Connecticut.

Frequently it is easy to determine what property belongs in the separate property category and what belongs in the marital property category; in other instances, the distinctions are not as clear. Separate property loses its separate classification and attains the marital property distinction when it is

- titled jointly,
- used for the purpose of supporting the marriage, *or*
- becomes so commingled with marital property that its separate origin cannot be traced.

Transmutation

The transformation of separate property to marital property.

Tracing

The process of tracking property during the course of a marriage so it retains its definition as separate property.

This transformation of separate property to marital property is known as *transmutation*. The process of determining when the asset was acquired by tracking its origin is called *tracing*. Tracing helps determine whether the property is separate or marital property. Tracing is not as easy as it sounds. The determination of what is separate or marital property may depend on whom your office is representing and may ultimately have to be decided by the courts if the parties cannot agree.

Whenever separate property is transmuted, the attempts at making a solid distinction between separate and marital property become blurry and tracing will be problematic. Determining when a separate asset exactly makes the transition to marital property may be very difficult. When a couple marries, it is usually their intent to share their resources and work in unison for the benefit of the marital partnership. Marriages are not entered into with the intent of tracking and recording every penny or every hour of labor performed in the acquisition of those marital assets. Therefore, the issue of whether a questionable asset is classified as separate or marital property may have to be resolved by the family court.

The Pitfalls of Commingling of Property and Assets As mentioned, one reason why it may be hard to distinguish between separate property and marital property is that separate and marital property or the income from such property may be *commingled*.

For instance, when a husband inherits real property from a parent, that property is separate property. However, the property is rental property and the rental income goes into the spouses' checking account from which marital bills are paid.

After a few years, the husband wishes to mortgage the property to take out some funds to buy a vacation home for the family. Although the property is worth a lot (i.e., has a lot of equity), the husband cannot get the loan amount he needs because his income is not high enough. With his wife's income added in, however, together they can qualify for the mortgage they need. Since the wife is going in on the mortgage, she wants to be on the deed also, so the husband quit claims a half interest to her. The couple pays cash for a vacation condo in another state with the proceeds from the mortgage on the rental property. They are both on the deed, having taken title in tenancy by the entirety. Six years later, the wife files for divorce and, as part of her property settlement proposal, asks for money equal to one-half the market value of the vacation home, the rental property, and the parties' principal residence.

All of the bills for all the properties and other household expenses have been paid out of the joint checking account. Both parties' paychecks go into this account as well as the rent payments from the rental property.

The husband agrees to sell the family home and split the sale proceeds, but he does not wish to share the vacation home with his wife because the cash payment for the vacation home came from the equity in the rental property. He sees both as separate property.

In this case the assets have been confusingly commingled. The wife argues that the property taxes for both the rental property and the condo have been paid out of the joint checking account and that the condo fee for the vacation condo also is paid from that account. She also notes that while both of these properties have been maintained through funds from the joint checking account, and both the properties have appreciated considerably, she is entitled to a percentage of the appreciation.

To avoid this type of commingling, it would have been better if the husband had a second checking account into which he put the rental income and then used the rental income to pay for the property taxes for that piece of real estate and for other related expenses such as insurance, maintenance, and any utilities not paid by tenants. To avoid having the wife on the rental property mortgage, he could have taken a second mortgage on the primary residence and made up any deficiency by taking a smaller mortgage on the rental property, which he could pay himself. Both parties would own the vacation condo and pay the condo fee and property taxes from the marital joint account. Upon the dissolution of their marriage, each spouse would be entitled to half the net value of the marital residence and the vacation home. The husband would have all of his separate rental property. If he could demonstrate that the rental income covered all of the property's expenses and that no marital assets were used nor any spousal effort expended for the property's upkeep, then he might not have to share any of the appreciation with his wife. On the other hand, if his spouse helped with caring for the property and if sometimes the marital funds had to be used for shortfalls due to inadequate rental income, then she would be entitled to a share of the appreciation in accordance with the amount of marital funds and her personal resources dedicated to maintaining that property. As will be discussed shortly, this type of outcome can and may occur in either a community property state or in what is termed as an *equitable distribution jurisdiction.*

VALUATION OF ASSETS

Once the property has been classified as either separate or marital property, the next step is to determine its value; that is, what is the marital property worth? What is the property's fair market value? Fair market value is the price a buyer is willing to pay a seller in exchange for the property.

Several methods are available to determine the value of marital property. Sometimes the parties are in agreement with the value of an asset and will mutually agree to a monetary figure. This consensus is very common with automobiles and the marital home. While many family homes are owned outright, others have outstanding mortgages and taxes due. Here, it is important to determine how much *equity* the parties have in the property. Equity is the fair market value of the property minus any encumbrances (i.e., mortgages, taxes, and liens) (see Figure 6-1).

Figure 6-1 A family home is often part of the marital property and attorneys need to determine how much equity the parties have in it.

Andy Dean Photography/Shutterstock.

EXAMPLE 1

John and Mary are married and they own a four-bedroom house. The fair market value of the marital home is $250,000. The outstanding mortgage due is $125,000, and property taxes due are $5,000. The equity is determined as follows:

FMV	*$250,000*
(less) Outstanding Mortgage & Property Taxes	*$130,000*
Equity	*$120,000*

RETAINING EXPERTS FOR VALUATION OF PROPERTY

If the parties cannot agree or are unable to determine the value of a marital asset, an expert can be retained. A family practice should always keep at its disposal a list of experts commonly used in family matters. The paralegal may assume the responsibility of maintaining a file folder on each expert, which should include an up-to-date resumé, list of fees, and area of expertise. Experts include accountants, appraisers, actuaries, bank counselors, domestic violence counselors, financial planners, pension valuators, social workers, psychiatrists, and psychologists.

If an expert is needed, either spouse or both should file a motion for appointment of an expert with the court. If the parties are in agreement, they can present the agreement to the court and put it on the record.

If they are not in agreement, the court will decide. The court will order the appointment of a disinterested expert, identify the specific property to be assessed, and determine who will pay the expert.

EFFECT OF PREMARITAL AGREEMENTS ON PROPERTY DISTRIBUTION

Prenuptial agreement
A contract entered into by the prospective spouses regarding their rights during the marriage and in the event of a divorce; also known as an antenuptial agreement or premarital agreement.

Premarital agreement
A contract entered into by the prospective spouses regarding their rights during the marriage and in the event of a divorce; also known as an antenuptial agreement or prenuptial agreement.

Antenuptial agreement
A contract entered into by the prospective spouses regarding their rights during the marriage and in the event of a divorce; also known as a premarital or prenuptial agreement.

Prior to marriage, the parties may have determined their respective property rights in a written document called a ***prenuptial***, ***premarital***, or ***antenuptial agreement*** (see Chapter 5). This is a contract entered into by the prospective spouses regarding their rights during the marriage and in the event of a divorce. It is essential to determine whether a client has entered into one of these agreements and to obtain a copy. Most courts will enforce these agreements provided that certain conditions existed at the time of their execution and circumstances have not substantially changed since the signing of the agreement. Premarital agreements must be in writing. There must be a full disclosure of all assets. This means that the parties must disclose the full extent and current values of all assets. The parties must also have an adequate opportunity to seek independent counsel before signing a premarital agreement.

As the *Parker* case illustrates, there are instances in which a court may find that the limiting language in a prenuptial agreement as to what constitutes marital assets may be overcome by evidence showing that certain property acquired during the marriage but held in only one spouse's name is nevertheless a jointly held marital asset.

Parker v. Parker, 773 N.Y.S.2d 518, 2 Misc.3d 484 (2003)

In *Parker,* a husband, in a dissolution proceeding, sought his share of his wife's extensive lottery winnings that she claimed was separate property as the ticket was only in her name. The court held that although in New York, it is settled law that a lottery prize won during a marriage is generally considered property acquired during the marriage subject to equitable distribution, "the specific language of the parties' prenuptial 'opting-out' agreement, which clearly defines marital assets as those held in joint name, renders the general inapplicable in this case, unless the husband can show that he and his wife should be declared joint title owners of the lottery winnings. The husband could show this if he produced evidence that the parties orally agreed to share any lottery winnings, and/or the lottery ticket purchases of either spouse were part of a joint venture."

In the absence of a premarital or prenuptial agreement, divorcing spouses are free to negotiate between themselves how property is to be distributed and then enter into a mutually consensual agreement regarding the division of their marital assets and marital debts, as well as child custody and support, alimony, visitation, and attorney's fees. If the parties are unwilling to negotiate, or if negotiation on some or all aspects of the marital dissolution fails, the court will decide the outcome of the unresolved issues. In some jurisdictions, the court will not allow a matter to be scheduled for trial unless the parties have first engaged in the mediation process conducted by a court-approved mediator.

RESOLVING THE ISSUE OF PROPERTY DISTRIBUTION: CONTESTED OR UNCONTESTED

When the parties are able to negotiate a plan they find mutually acceptable, a settlement or separation agreement is drafted and signed by both parties, thus obviating the need for a long court battle. Courts prefer agreements because the parties are more likely to be content with a settlement they have voluntarily negotiated and crafted. The court will not change or question an agreement unless it appears to be unfair or against public policy. The court will generally approve the agreement upon determining that it was entered into voluntarily and that it is fair and equitable. Courts also prefer agreements because it keeps the court docket moving by disposing of cases without protracted judicial proceedings and thus conserves judicial resources.

When the parties are unable to reach an agreement, it is up to the court to resolve the property dispute. Trial courts have great discretion in their decision-making powers. A trial court is in the best position to observe the demeanor of the parties. A trial court's decision will not be reversed on appeal unless the appellant can convince the higher court that the trial court abused its discretion by either misapplying the law or by making erroneous rulings regarding the admission of evidence.

When resolving disputes over the division of property, the courts will first make an award of separate property to the owner spouse. The definition of separate versus marital property may be one of the first areas of contention in the trial. Once the marital property pot has been defined, the court will divide the property according to the jurisdiction's property distribution statute. Family law paralegals must become familiar with their jurisdictions' statutes and the case law interpreting those statutes.

Equitable distribution
A system allowing family courts to distribute property acquired during marriage on the basis of fairness, as opposed to ownership.

Community property distribution
A system of property division that assumes that both husband and wife contributed to the accumulation of marital assets.

JURISDICTIONAL APPROACHES TO PROPERTY DISTRIBUTION

In the United States, two systems are used to dictate the division of marital property upon the dissolution of marriage: *equitable distribution* and *community property distribution*.

Equitable Distribution

As mentioned in earlier sections of this book we know, our system of jurisprudence is based on the English common law. The English common law system was also the approach used to determine the division of marital property upon dissolution of a marriage. Upon marriage, a husband and wife merged into a single legal entity—the husband. This was known as the *unity of spouses*. At common law, married women had a separate legal identity. A married woman could not own or manage her own property, she could not sue or be sued, nor could she control her wages. As time passed and attitudes toward married women changed, state legislatures in the United States, toward the end of the 1800s, enacted the Married Women's Property Acts. These statutes removed the common law strictures that prevented married women from owning and managing their own resources.

Although these statutes made it possible for women to own their own property, the divorce law did not change along with the new status of married women. Property acquired during the marriage was divided on the basis of who supplied the funds to purchase the property and possessed title. Traditionally, married women did not work outside the home. Husbands bought the property, retained title and ownership, and upon divorce, walked away with the lion's share of the assets. While jointly held property was divided between the spouses, the courts had no power to award property solely owned by one spouse to the nontitle spouse. State legislatures eventually saw the inequity and harshness of this method of property division and enacted statutes allowing family courts to distribute property acquired during marriage on the basis of equity or fairness, as opposed to ownership. This is known as the equitable distribution system of dividing marital property. Family courts in equitable distribution states, in determining how property is to be divided between a divorcing couple, must evaluate each spouse's interest in the marital property on an individual or case-by-case basis. Equitable distribution state statutes enumerate statutory factors that the courts must consider in the division of marital assets and debts. These factors commonly include the length of the marriage, the work history and job prospects of each spouse, the physical and mental health of each spouse, the source of particular assets, and the expenses of the children. Some of these factors are listed in the Connecticut statute. The courts, however, are not required to give equal weight to each factor and have the discretion to make decisions based on the merits of the particular case before them.

Most jurisdictions in the United States follow the equitable distribution system of property division. However, several states, particularly those located in the American Southwest and originally settled by Spanish and French colonists, adhere to the distribution system known as community property.

WAIVER OF THE RIGHT TO EQUITABLE DISTRIBUTION

As the *Haynes* case illustrates, a spouse may waive her right to equitable distribution of the marital estate, and the court will uphold the waiver even if the spouse did not realize the size of the share that she was entitled to, at the time she executed the waiver.

Haynes v. Haynes, 2003-50867 (New York Supreme Court 2003)

In *Haynes,* the court had to decide which of the wives of Keith Haynes, now deceased, should enjoy his lottery winnings. Haynes and his first wife, Yvonne, were married in 1974, separated amicably in March 1987 but were not divorced until the entry of judgment in August 1997. In January 1997 while the parties

Unity of spouses

The English common law system used to determine the division of marital property on dissolution of a marriage, which stated that, on marriage, a husband and wife merged into a single legal entity—the husband.

were still married, Mr. Haynes won $3,000,000.00 in the New York State lottery. Although Haynes originally told Yvonne Haynes that he would give her some of the proceeds, he later refused to do so. In Spring of 1997, Mr. Haynes told Yvonne Haynes that he wanted a divorce, and that he had retained an attorney. Yvonne Haynes had no desire to contest the divorce. When the divorce papers were delivered to her for her signature, she signed them as requested but did not read them first. One of the papers she signed was an affidavit in which she waived any equitable distribution claim she may have had. Keith Haynes subsequently remarried in December 2000 to Andrea Haynes. In January 2001, Yvonne Haynes moved to set aside the 1997 divorce judgment, alleging that it was procured by fraudulent means. She also moved for leave to institute a new divorce action in which she alleged abandonment and sought an equitable share of her husband's lottery winnings. During the pendency of the action, Mr. Haynes died. His current wife, Andrea Haynes, was named as administratrix of his estate and was eventually substituted for Mr. Haynes in the action. At the hearing on theses motions, Yvonne Haynes testified that at the time she signed the divorce papers, she did not know that she had a potential equitable distribution claim regarding a share of the lottery proceeds, and if she had known, she never would have signed the documents.

The court denied the motions based on the finding that the signing of the contested waiver was not the result of fraud, collusion, mutual mistake, or accident. The court noted that Ms. Haynes signed the documents without questioning their content or even reading the papers, and cited the well-established law that "[w]hen a party signs a document without having read its contents and without any valid excuse, such party is chargeable with knowledge of its terms . . . and is conclusively bound thereby."

Yvonne Haynes's motion to set aside the judgment of her divorce was denied, and the second Mrs. Haynes was the recipient of the spousal share of her husband's estate, which included all of the next proceeds of his lottery winnings.

Community Property

In community property jurisdictions, property acquired during the marriage belongs equally to each spouse, unless it has been excluded as separate property. California's property division statute provides that the court will "equally" divide the community estate of the parties.

The community property arrangement is based on Spanish and French concepts of marital property as codified in the *code civile* or **civil code**, the system of law existing on the European mainland, as opposed to the common law system of England.

Civil code
The system of Spanish and French concepts of marital property law existing on the European mainland; also known as the *code civile*.

Statutes

CALIFORNIA CIVIL CODE ANNOTATED (WEST)

§ 2550. Manner of Division of Community.

Except upon the written agreement of the parties, or on oral stipulation of the parties in open court, or as otherwise provided in this division, in a proceeding for dissolution of marriage or for legal separation of the parties, the court shall, either in its judgment of dissolution of the marriage, in its judgment of legal separation of the parties, or at a later time if it expressly reserves jurisdiction to make such a property division, divide the community estate of the parties equally.

Source: Family Code, Division 7—Division of Property, Part 2—General Provisions, § 2550. Manner of Division of Community, State of California.

Figure 6-2 Most of the community property states are located in the West and Southwest.

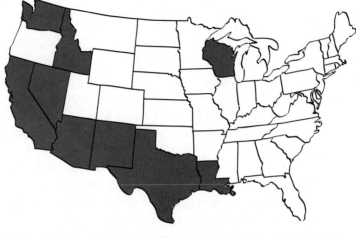

Community Property States: Arizona, Nevada, California, Washington, Wisconsin, Idaho, Louisiana, New Mexico, Texas

The nine states that use the community property system are mostly situated in the West and Southwest region of the United States. The community property states are (see Figure 6-2):

Arizona	New Mexico
California	Texas
Idaho	Washington
Louisiana	Wisconsin
Nevada	

The community property system assumes that both husband and wife contribute to the accumulation of marital assets. This concept values the work of the husband who traditionally worked outside the home as well as that of the stay-at-home spouse who took care of the home and the children. The husband, however, had the right to control the community property until such statutory provisions were found to violate the Equal Protection Clause of the U.S. Constitution. Upon acquisition of any asset or income during the marriage, both spouses acquire an equal interest in the property, regardless of who supplied the funds for its acquisition. Because each spouse is deemed to have contributed to the acquisition of the marital assets (and also the marital debts), the assets and debts are divided on a 50/50 basis upon divorce. The various community property states allow for deviations or application of the equitable distribution system after the property has been divided on a 50/50 basis.

Statutes

Arizona and California also recognize what is known as *quasi-community*. If a married couple acquires property in a noncommunity property state and then moves to a community property jurisdiction, upon divorce, the property is considered community property. Therefore, community property carries its distinctiveness over state lines.

continued

NEVADA REVISED STATUTES ANNOTATED

ALIMONY AND ADJUDICATION OF PROPERTY RIGHTS; AWARD OF ATTORNEY'S FEE; Except as otherwise provided in NRS 125, 155 and unless the action is contrary to a premarital agreement between the parties which is enforceable pursuant to chapter 123A of NRS]

1. In granting a divorce, the court: (b) Shall, to the extent practicable, make an equal disposition of the community property of the parties, except that the court may make an unequal disposition of the community property in such proportions as it deems just if the court finds a compelling reason to do so and sets forth in writing the reasons for making the unequal disposition.

2. Except as otherwise provided in this subsection, in granting a divorce, the court shall dispose of any property held in joint tenancy in the manner set forth in subsection 1 for the disposition of community property. If a party has made a contribution of separate property to the acquisition or improvement of property held in joint tenancy, the court may provide for the reimbursement of that party for his contribution. The amount of reimbursement must not exceed the amount of the contribution of separate property that can be traced to the acquisition or improvement of property held in joint tenancy, without interest of any adjustment because of an increase in the value of the property held in joint tenancy. The amount of the reimbursement must not exceed the value, at the time of the disposition of the property held in joint tenancy for which the contribution of separate property was made. In determining whether to provide for the reimbursement, in whole or in part, of a party who has contributed separate property, the court shall consider:

    (a) The intention of the parties in placing the property in joint tenancy;

    (b) The length of the marriage;

    (c) Any other factor which the court deems relevant in making a just and equitable disposition of that property.

    As used in this subsection, "contribution" includes a down payment, a payment for the acquisition or improvement of property, and a payment reducing the principal of a loan used to finance the purchase or improvement of property. The term does not include a payment of interest on a loan used to finance the purchase or improvement of property, or a payment made for maintenance, insurance or taxes on property.

3. Whether or not application for suit money has been made under the provisions of NRS 125.040, the court may award a reasonable attorney's fee to either party to an action for divorce if those fees are in issue under the pleadings.

4. In granting a divorce, the court may also set apart such portion of the husband's separate property for the wife's support, the wife's separate property for the husband's support or the separate property of either spouses for the support of their children as is deemed just and equitable.

Source: Nevada Revised Statutes Annotated Alimony and Adjudication of Property Rights; Award of Attorney's Fee, State of Nevada.

If you are a practicing paralegal in a community property state, it is essential that you become familiar with the intricacies of the community property laws in your state, as they differ from jurisdiction to jurisdiction.

Community Property Rules and Exceptions

The general rule is that anything a married couple accumulates during marriage is community property. Both spouses own an undivided share of the whole. There are some exceptions to this rule. Property owned by a spouse before marriage or property acquired during the marriage through a gift or an inheritance remains the separate property of that spouse. However, if the separate property is commingled with community property, such as when a cash gift to one spouse is deposited into a joint checking account, that money may be transmuted into property of the community's estate.

Although the general rule and the exceptions seem clear and straightforward, many issues can arise in a dissolution action that must be decided by more complicated rules. For instance, if a couple resides in a community property state, and one spouse buys a piece of real estate in an equitable distribution state and puts title in his name only, how do the courts of the community property state treat this asset in a dissolution proceeding? Similarly, when a couple is married and resides in a community property state for several years, then moves to an equitable distribution state and subsequently decides to divorce, how do the courts in equitable distribution states treat property acquired during the marriage while the couple were living in the community property state? Issues also arise on the death of one spouse. In a community property state, again the general rule is that upon the death of one spouse, one-half of the community property becomes the deceased person's (decedent's) estate and it passes through devise (will) or descent (state inheritance statutes) to the heirs. The other half of the community property estate is retained by the surviving spouse. In an equitable distribution state, if, for instance, a married couple owned a home as tenants by the entirety, when one spouse died a full interest in the house would automatically pass to the surviving spouse and the heirs would have no claim to that part of the decedent's estate.

Calculation of the Community Property Marital Estate Most community property states determine the value of the community estate by ascertaining the fair market value of the community assets minus the joint debts and other obligations of the parties. The figure obtained is the net community estate.

Characterization of Community Debts In a community property state, all debts incurred from the beginning of the marriage to the date the parties separate are community debts. Each spouse is equally responsible for these debts regardless of which party incurred the debt and regardless of whether it was with or without the other spouse's knowledge. During the marriage, each spouse is responsible for 100 percent of the debt, and upon dissolution, the law is that each spouse will assume one-half of that debt.

Exceptions to the Community Property Rules Even though the community property states are well known for their rule of an equal division of all marital assets and no division of separate assets, there are instances in which these rules are modified to prevent unfairness or injustice. Several community property states have enacted legislation to authorize a deviation from the community property strictures and spell out under what circumstances such a deviation may occur.

For instance, in Arizona, while the general practice is to equally distribute the community assets, if one spouse has dissipated the assets of the community estate through gambling, drugs, or frivolous spending or has hidden community property from the other spouse, the court will address this inequity by awarding the other spouse more of the community estate.

In Louisiana, state law allows prospective spouses to opt for the same separate property status they had as single persons. This alternative allows spouses to claim all assets, including already acquired retirement benefits, as separate property without accounting to the other spouse regarding the accrual, treatment, or disposal of assets. However, any contributions to a retirement plan made during the marriage will be considered community property and subject to division.

In Texas, when a married couple moves to Texas from an equitable distribution state, the status of property deeded or titled to only one spouse does not change. However, in a dissolution proceeding, if the parties cannot agree on how assets are to be divided, the court will step in and in this instance can and may divide property acquired while living outside the state in a manner that is fair and equitable. Such property could be divided equally regardless of in which spouse's name the title is vested, or a percentage of the property could be allocated to the other spouse.

In Nevada, community property is divided equally between divorcing spouses unless a court determines that such division is unjust. In that case, the court will divide property in a manner it deems equitable. Two of the factors the court will consider include the length of the marriage and the contribution either spouse made from separate property in acquiring or maintaining such property.

In California, the law requires that the community estate be divided equally if there is no written agreement to the contrary. Spouses may enter into an agreement where they can modify the division of assets, and if the agreement is entered into freely and knowingly, the court will allow it.

In California, equal ownership of assets does not depend on the quality or quantity of a spouse's contribution. Each spouse shares ownership of the marital property regardless of whether the assets were earned by one or the other.

Probate Issues in Community Property States and Equitable Distribution States

Spouses in a community property state receive one-half of the community estate upon the death of the other spouse. A spouse may leave separate property to anyone.

Several community property states have statutes that allow married couples to hold title to assets such as their home or investment accounts as "community property with the right of survivorship." Under this arrangement, when one spouse dies, the other spouse receives all of the assets held this way, and these assets are not subject to probate proceedings.

In an equitable distribution state, each spouse owns what their name is on, whether it be a deed, automobile or boat registration document, stock certificate, or other paper conferring title. In an equitable distribution jurisdiction, a husband or wife may leave whatever property he or she owns to whomever he or she wishes provided the other spouse receives at least what the state legislature or state common law has determined is the minimal spousal share.

In an equitable jurisdiction state, there are statutes of succession to ensure that a nonworking spouse will have at the minimum a fixed percentage of their deceased spouse's estate so that upon his death they will not be divested of all property acquired during marriage. California, because of the community property system of marital property ownership, does not have these types of statutes. Therefore, the quasi-community property system remedies the situation. Other states—Texas, for example—do not change the status of property that was acquired while living elsewhere. When a married couple moves to Texas, the status of property acquired elsewhere does not change. Texas does not have laws providing each spouse with a statutory share of the other's assets. Hence the nonworking spouse who would be entitled to one-half or one-third of her husband's estate despite his testamentary disposition in an equitable distribution state is out in the cold in Texas, where she has no statutory right to her husband's estate and may be disinherited under his will.

States with quasi-community property systems differ in various aspects. For instance, some states disagree about whether the nonworking spouse is entitled to one-half of the quasi-community property or to one-half of each asset.

Moving from a Community Property State to an Equitable Distribution State In general, equitable distribution states treat property acquired during marriage in a community property state as jointly held property in which each spouse has an undivided one-half interest. However, to the extent the common law states also have an elective or forced statutory share in a surviving spouse, that right is usually not extended to the undivided one-half interest owned by the deceased spouse. That one-half interest will fall outside the estate.

Distinctions between Separate and Marital Property in Community Property States as Compared with Distinctions in Equitable Distribution States In community property states as in equitable distribution states, the courts make a distinction between separate property and marital property.

In a community property state, a spouse's separate property is not included in the community estate before the estate is divided. Therefore, the spouse owning that property will leave the marriage with one-half of the community property and all of his or her separate property.

In an equitable distribution state, where the goal is equitable or fair division of the marital estate, one spouse's separate property may or may not be included in the marital estate. For instance, if either or both of the parties purchased cars during the marriage and each spouse has title to one car, these assets will be considered part of the marital estate. This will be especially beneficial to a spouse who purchased a car several years ago. That car will be included in the marital estate. If the other spouse recently purchased an expensive new car during the marital partnership, that will also be included in the marital estate. The assets of the marital estate will be totaled up and then divided in a manner that the court deems equitable. This division need not be 50/50 to be equitable. If the court finds that both parties contributed significantly to the economic partnership, the assets may be equally divided. However, if the court finds or if the parties agree that one spouse's effort was far greater than the other's effort, the property division will reflect that situation. If, for instance, for several years a woman holds down a very demanding job that is the only source of income to the household, and she also provides all of the care for the couple's three children and does the housework, while the husband does not work and assumes no household or child-care responsibilities, the court may distribute the bulk of the marital estate to the woman, especially if she has physical custody of the children. On the other hand, if the nonworking husband was a stay-at-home dad and took care of the household chores, including meals, laundry, and cleaning, and also functioned as the children's *primary caregiver*, the division would more likely be equal distribution, or close to it.

Primary caregiver
The individual who has done most of the significant parenting of the child since birth or for the several preceding years.

Treatment of the Appreciation of Separate Property during the Marriage

In many states, where a spouse owns an asset at the time of marriage, the spouse will be entitled to an amount equal to the entire value of that asset at the time of the marriage. If the asset has appreciated, the other spouse may be entitled to an amount that can be as much as one-half of the value of the appreciation. The court may look at the contributions the other spouse made to the marital partnership and how these contributions facilitated the maintenance of this asset.

There are instances where a spouse who has an investment fund at the time of the marriage lets it sit and neither contributes more to it nor makes any withdrawals from it. During the marriage, the value appreciates considerably and there was little or no maintenance needed while this asset grew. In such a case, this asset remains separate property and is not figured into the marital estate.

There are other times when a spouse will share in the appreciation of an investment product. If one spouse brings to the marriage a 401k plan worth $15,000, and during the course of the marriage makes contributions from his earnings, which increase the amount of the fund, the other spouse will be entitled to a share of the appreciation of the portion of the fund made up of the first spouse's post-marriage contributions.

THE NOT-SO-OBVIOUS ASSETS OF MARRIAGE—GOODWILL, PENSIONS, AND PROFESSIONAL DEGREES

Introduction

Some marital assets are not so obvious because they are not present in tangible form—that is, something we can see and touch. These intangible assets, however, may have substantial value, and it would be considered legal malpractice not to identify, valuate, and seek a fair division for the client. Some of the major intangible marital assets include goodwill, pensions, and the professional degree.

Goodwill *Goodwill* is a term used to describe the ability of a business or professional to attract future customers and repeat business due to a good reputation in the community. A dollar value on goodwill can be determined by an expert. Many states identify goodwill as marital property if a business or career has been enhanced during the marriage. A spouse who assists the other spouse in achieving that reputation may be entitled to share in the enhanced earning capacity that reputation will bring. Even where a spouse has stayed at home as a traditional homemaker, her contribution to the marital partnership has enabled her husband to pursue his business endeavors and create the goodwill that has enhanced his business reputation in the community. Therefore, in many states, she is entitled to a portion of the goodwill value of the business. Similarly, even where each spouse has his or her own business or professional practice, each spouse, as a member of the marital economic partnership, will have a financial interest in the other spouse's enterprise if it was initiated or expanded during the marriage, and in many states, may be entitled to a portion of the goodwill value of that business.

Calculating Goodwill

In calculating goodwill, it is essential that an expert be obtained to valuate this asset. In California, a community property state, all types of goodwill are included as marital property. Elsewhere, this is not always the case. Some states, including most of the other community property states, embrace California's approach. In other states, such as Indiana, Illinois, and Tennessee, the reputation or "name" of the principal in a business or professional practice is frequently not deemed marital property, while other intangible assets are included. A few states, such as Mississippi, exclude goodwill entirely from the marital estate.

Enterprise Goodwill versus Personal Goodwill

Many states divide goodwill into two components, *enterprise goodwill* and *personal goodwill*, and they use this distinction when deciding whether the goodwill in question is part of the marital estate subject to distribution upon divorce.

Enterprise goodwill refers to the intangible but usually marketable existence in a business of established relations with employees, customers, and suppliers. Factors that affect this type of goodwill include the location of the business, the reputation of the business, and the anticipated future profitability of the business, which will outlast any

Enterprise goodwill
The intangible but usually marketable existence in a business of established relationships with employees, customers, and suppliers.

Personal goodwill
The goodwill attributable to an individual's personal skill, training, or reputation.

particular person's involvement in the business. Enterprise goodwill usually continues to be an asset of the business when the business is sold. It is transferable to a subsequent owner and has a value to future owners. Because it arises from the business as a whole rather than being due to the prior owner's personal reputation, enterprise goodwill is considered an asset of the business to be valued and included in the marital estate.

Personal goodwill is solely attributable to an individual's personal skill, training, or reputation. Courts in many states have held that the goodwill that depends on the continued presence of a particular individual is a personal asset that represents nothing more than the future earning capacity of that person and is not divisible as part of a marital estate. Other states view personal goodwill as an intangible asset that is "salable" and therefore can be a part of the marital estate.

Goodwill of Bethany Foot Clinic

In this case of first impression, the Supreme Court of Oklahoma held that the goodwill of a medical sole proprietorship was a marital asset and its value subject to division by the family courts. The court did so because the wife's expert witness provided information that when similar types of medical practices were sold that a significant percentage of patients remained with the practice after the sale despite the absence of the prior principal practitioner.

ROBERT J. TRACZYK v. KATHLEEN M. TRACZYK

891 P.2D 1277 (OKLA. 1995)
SUPREME COURT OF OKLAHOMA

SIMMS, JUSTICE.

Husband first takes issue with the trial court considering the goodwill of his medical practice as marital property. He testified that there was no goodwill because he was the reason the patients came to the Bethany Foot Clinic and "not very many" of the patients would stay at the Bethany Foot Clinic with a new doctor if Husband sold it.

The professional practice of one spouse is an appropriate element of the marital property to be divided between the parties where it is jointly-acquired property. *Ford v. Ford*, 766 P.2d 950 (Okla. 1988); *Carpenter v. Carpenter*, 657 P.2d 646 (Okla. 1983). The issue before us is whether goodwill of Husband's podiatry practice may be considered in determining the value of the practice. . . .

. . . Pursuant to 60 O.S.1991, §§ 315 and 316, goodwill of a business is defined as "the expectation of continued public patronage," and is considered property transferable like any other property. *See also Freeling v. Wood*, 361 P.2d 1061, 1063 (Okla. 1961). ("The 'good will' value of any business is the value that results from the *probability that old customers will continue to trade with an established concern.* . . .[Such] good will of a business may be sold.") (Emphasis supplied); *Travis v. Travis*, 795 P.2d 96, 97 (Okla. 1990) (quoting *Freeling); Mocnik v. Mocnik*, 838 P.2d 500, 504 (Okla. 1992) (quoting *Travis*). . . .

In determining the value of the Bethany Foot Clinic, the expert witness consulted the Goodwill Registry, "an accumulation of information concerning sales of medical related practices by experts." From this publication, the expert determined that of the most recent purchases of podiatry clinics, an average of thirty-two percent (32%) of the podiatry patients stay with the clinic after it is sold to a new doctor. The range from which he obtained the average was 21% to 44% of clients staying. Noting that the traditional method used in valuing a medical practice is the previous year's gross income, the expert then took the previous year's gross income

continued

at the clinic ($324,201.51) and multiplied it by the 32% figure to arrive at a good-will value of $103,744.00. Adding this to the value of the remaining business assets, the expert found the total value of the Bethany Foot Clinic to be $152,605.44. The trial court accepted this valuation and used it in determining how much alimony in lieu of property division to award.

We find that the trial court did not err in considering the goodwill of the Bethany Foot Clinic as a factor in determining the value of the clinic as marital property. The goodwill of the Bethany Foot Clinic is distinct from the personal reputation of Dr. Traczyk. Although many of Dr. Traczyk's patients would not continue to patronize the Bethany Foot Clinic were Dr. Traczyk to sell to another podiatrist, competent evidence indicates that many would stay. Indeed, Dr. Traczyk may use the goodwill as a selling point to potential purchasers.

"If goodwill is to be divided as an asset, its value should be determined either by an agreement or *by its fair market value*. Both of these methods are widely accepted for valuing goodwill. *See* annotation, 78 A.L.R.4th 853, 860–71 (1987). *Mocnik*, 838 P.2d at 505."

Husband further argues that by both allowing goodwill to be divided as marital property and awarding support alimony, the trial court has charged him twice for his future income. We first reiterate that the goodwill of the Bethany Foot Clinic is not properly characterized as future income. Rather, it is an asset of the clinic.

Husband, though, disagrees with the distinction between future income and assets. He asserts two cases cited in *Travis* resolve the issue of "double-dipping" in to his future income. However, we find these cases, *Holbrook v. Holbrook*, 103 Wis. 2d327, 309 N.W.2d 343 (1981) and *Beasley v. Beasley*, 359 Pa. Super. 20, 518 A.2d 545 (1986), *allocatur denied*, 516 Pa. 631, 533 A.2d 90 (1987), unpersuasive because, as *Travis* indicates, they both concerned the goodwill of law practices where such goodwill was related to the reputation of the lawyer. In other words, *Holbrook* and *Beasley* are distinguishable because they did not involve a professional practice with transferable goodwill as the case at bar did.

The goodwill of the Bethany Foot Clinic was valued as an asset and was a factor in determining the total value of the business for property division purposes. This goodwill was part of the property which should be divided between the parties; Wife had a right to receive her share of the property. 43 O.S.1991, § 121. On the other hand, the award of *support alimony* was a separate determination based upon Husband's ability to pay and Wife's demonstrated need. *Johnson v. Johnson*, 674 P.2d 539 (Okla. 1983). Although the property division is permanent and irrevocable, the award of support alimony is subject to modification upon a showing of substantial change in circumstances, i.e. Husband's ability and/or Wife's demonstrated need. 43 O.S.1991, § 134; *Clifton v. Clifton*, 801 P.2d 693 (Okla. 1990).

"[S]upport alimony is not alimony in lieu of a division. Support alimony is exactly what its name implies, alimony for support and maintenance. Alimony *in lieu of a division* is given for satisfaction of a property division obligation. These are distinct obligations and the acceptance of one does not by implication waive the right of the other." *Greer v. Greer*, 807 P.2d 791, 794 (Okla. 1991) (Emphasis in original). By awarding support alimony and including goodwill in the value of the business for property division purposes, the trial court did not "double dip" into Husband's future income. Both awards, one for support alimony and one for alimony in lieu of property division, were proper and distinct from the other. We find no error in the trial court's valuation of the marital property and award of alimony in lieu of property division. . .

Source: Robert J. Traczyk v. Kathleen M. Traczyk, 891 P.2D 1277 (OKLA. 1995), Supreme Court of Oklahoma.

Notably, in the preceding case, the court viewed the clinic as a business, and it found the goodwill value of that business to be distinct from any goodwill arising from the doctor's personal reputation that was not included in the expert's valuation. In doing so, the court implied that it did not consider personal goodwill to be part of the marital estate. Subsequent holdings in Oklahoma cases confirmed that in Oklahoma, personal goodwill is not considered a marital asset subject to distribution upon divorce. Wisconsin, a community property state, on the other hand, recently established personal goodwill as a marital asset. Wisconsin courts, as a rule, strive to divide marital assets equally or on a fifty-fifty basis. In the case of *McReath v. McReath,* the Wisconsin Supreme Court found a professional's reputation to be a salable asset, the value of which was to be credited to each of the divorcing spouses on an equal basis. *In Re: The Marriage of Tracy J. McReath v. Timothy J. McReath,* 800 N.W. 399.[1]

In *McReath,* the Wisconsin Supreme Court, departing from an earlier ruling, confirmed that the personal goodwill of a medical professional created while carrying on his practice was to be considered an asset of his marriage. Further, the Supreme Court ruled that, henceforth, lower courts in Wisconsin were not to draw a distinction between enterprise goodwill and personal good will when dividing a marital estate that included a professional practice.

We disagreed, holding that there need not be an actual sale in order to determine the existence and value of a business's goodwill. *Id.*

Pensions

Next to the marital home, a pension may very often be the largest asset available for distribution upon divorce. At the time of retirement, the employee is entitled to receive the pension funds, either by periodic payments or in a lump sum. The pension may be funded through contributions from either the employer, employee, or a combination of both. A spouse seeking a portion of the employee spouse's pension is only entitled to the portion of the pension acquired during the marriage.

A pension is either vested or nonvested. While an employee is entitled to walk away from her job with the contribution made by her during her period of employment, she will only be entitled to the funds contributed by the employer if her pension has vested. A vested pension entitles the employee to the employer's contribution portion provided that the employee has worked for the employer for an enumerated number of years. Once the employee has reached the specific benchmark, her right to the employer contribution attaches and she is entitled to the pension. If she leaves her employment with an unvested pension, the right to the employer portion of the funds has not yet attached. In a divorce case, a vested pension should be considered marital property. An unvested pension represents a future expectancy interest. If an unvested employee leaves her employer before the vesting period, a divorcing spouse may only be entitled to a portion of the employee spouse's contributions.

Whether your office is representing the employee spouse or the nonemployee spouse, it is necessary to obtain the following information, either through discovery or the client interview:

1. Name, address, and telephone number of the plan administrator
2. Copy of the pension plan
3. A computer printout of monies paid into the plan by the client

---

[1] In Re The Marriage of Tracy J. McReath v. Timothy J. McReath, 335 Wis.2d 643, 800 N.W. 399, Supreme Court of Wisconsin.

A pension must be valuated. This means that the value or worth of the pension must be determined. Valuation will provide the attorney with a dollar amount attached to the pension so that the client's interests in marital property can be adequately protected. Numerous pension valuation services are available to family law attorneys. Many advertise in professional publications directed at the family bar. These services employ experts trained at valuing pensions and determining their fair market value. If the parties wish to forgo the valuation of the pension because of the added expense, a clause in the settlement agreement indicating that the valuation was waived is essential to protect the attorney from a malpractice claim.

Once a pension has been valuated, the attorneys for the parties must determine how this asset will be divided. This will depend on what other types of marital assets are available for distribution. If there is very little cash or other assets to distribute, the parties may seek to obtain a **qualified domestic relations order (QDRO)**. This is a court order served on the pension administrator ordering the plan to distribute a specified portion of the pension funds to the nonemployee spouse.

Qualified Domestic Relations Order (QDRO)
A court order served on the pension administrator ordering the plan to distribute a specified portion of the pension funds to the nonemployee spouse.

While state law dictates property division, federal law controls retirement benefits. When addressing the distribution of pension funds, employers must comply with the **Employee Retirement Income Security Act (ERISA)**. ERISA is a federal statute passed in 1974 to protect employees and their pensions in case an employer declares bankruptcy or goes out of business. This law governs retirement pay and pension benefits. ERISA was amended by the Retirement Equity Act (REA) of 1984. This federal statute determines the manner in which states may divide a pension at the time of divorce, and its requirements must be complied with in order for the QDRO to be valid. If the QDRO is invalid, the plan will not release any funds.

Employee Retirement Income Security Act (ERISA)
A federal statute passed in 1974 to protect employees and their pensions in case an employer declares bankruptcy or goes out of business. This law also governs retirement pay and pension benefits.

Pensions, either through an employer or self-directed (i.e., an IRA a spouse may have started on his own at a local bank), are tax deferred. This means that taxes on the income produced by the pension will not be paid until the monies are withdrawn at the time of retirement. If these funds are withdrawn prior to retirement, tax penalties will be imposed. An accountant should be consulted to determine the tax liability of liquidating any deferred compensation plan. The tax liability should be determined in advance so as to negotiate a payment of taxes due between the spouses. If the tax consequences are overlooked, the employee spouse could be in for a big surprise come tax time.

An employee spouse may not wish to have her pension distributed. If there are ample funds, the parties may agree to a buyout. In this scenario, the pension will be valuated, and the employee spouse will give cash to the nonemployee spouse in exchange for any interest he may have in her pension. This would allow the employee spouse's pension to remain untouched. The parties may also agree to *offset* the pension with other assets. For example, the employee spouse may agree to transfer her interest in the marital home or other marital assets in exchange for the full ownership of her pension benefits. However, this arrangement should be clearly spelled out in the parties' separation (settlement) agreement because the court may not allow a party to waive their interest in a pension without compensation to offset this loss.

Federal law requires that the employee spouse name the nonemployee spouse as a beneficiary of his retirement benefits. Once the marriage has been severed by a court, the client should be advised to change the beneficiary designation immediately. A certified copy of the judgment or certificate of dissolution complete with a court seal should be filed with the pension plan along with any necessary form required by the particular plan.

Pensions and Other Deferred Compensation Plans as a Part of Property Distribution Under the federal Employment Retirement Income Act (ERISA), a spouse must be named as a beneficiary on the other spouse's pension. When the parties divorce, each spouse will have an interest in the other spouse's holdings if the pension increased during the marriage through the spouse's employment.

If prior to marriage a spouse works for an employer for several years and becomes vested in a pension, then leaves that employer and makes no more contribution to that pension but will receive the value of the pension at retirement, that pension is the spouse's separate property.

Similarly, if before marriage a person contributes to a pension, 401k plan, or other type of retirement plan, the amount in that plan at the time of marriage is the person's separate property. During the marital partnership, if the person continues to make payments and the amount in the plan grows, the other spouse at the time of dissolution is entitled to one-half the amount by which the account has grown since the date of the marriage.

Sometimes, if there are other assets of the marriage in addition to the pensions, a spouse may choose not to disrupt the other spouse's pension plan but may take another asset of the marriage that equals what would be his or her share of the pension. If both spouses have pension plans, a property distribution scheme may be worked out whereby each spouse keeps his or her own pension, and if one spouse's pension is greater than the other, the spouse with the lesser pension will get another asset to offset the disparity. This type of arrangement can be implemented in both community property states and equitable distribution states. Theoretically, in a community property state each pension should be divided down the middle, but if the parties agree that an alternate plan will keep both pensions intact and still facilitate an equal division of the marital community property, the court will not object.

The Sanitation Worker's Disability Pension In 1991, the New York Court of Appeals held that a portion of a Department of Sanitation worker's disability pension was marital property and thus subject to equitable distribution.

GERALD A. DOLAN v. LOIS A. DOLAN

583 N.E.2d 908, 577 N.Y.S.2d 195 (N.Y. 1991)
NEW YORK COURT OF APPEALS

ALEXANDER, J.

On this appeal, plaintiff-husband challenges the Appellate Division's affirmance of Supreme Court's determination that a portion of his ordinary disability pension received from the New York City Employee's Retirement System is marital property and thus subject to equitable distribution pursuant to Part B Section 236 of the Domestic Relations Law. We conclude that inasmuch as a portion of that ordinary disability pension represents deferred compensation related to length of employment occurring during the marriage, it constitutes marital property subject to equitable distribution. Thus, there should be an affirmance.

The parties to this litigation were married on July 23, 1966. Three children were born of the union. In 1969, plaintiff became employed by the New York City Department of Sanitation. Nine years later he injured his back when he fell from a sanitation truck. He could not work at all for approximately five weeks and was unable to perform his normal work routine when he returned to work. Eventually, he was retired on an ordinary disability pension pursuant to Section 13-167 of New York City Administrative Code, effective April 17, 1980. At the time of his retirement, he had accumulated approximately eleven years of service with the Department of Sanitation, thus entitling him to pension benefits of $811.84 per month from the New York City Employee's Retirement System. He subsequently

continued

became employed by Marist College where he then enrolled as a full-time student.

The court concluded that 47.62% of plaintiff's ordinary disability pension was marital property subject to equitable distribution and that the remaining 52.38% was disability payment, and thus, was separate property not subject to equitable distribution. In order to determine the allocation between retirement benefits and disability benefits, the court compared the pension benefit plaintiff would have received had he retired normally with the allowance plaintiff received under the ordinary disability retirement provision. If plaintiff had fifteen years of service, he would have had vested regular pension benefits (see, NYS Admin Code § 13-173.1) computed under the formula for determining normal retirement allowances, and his pension would have been considerably less—it would have equaled 47.62% of what he received under the ordinary disability plan. Supreme Court concluded that 47.62% of the ordinary disability was pure pension, and thus was marital property of which defendant was entitled to 50%. The court also determined that defendant was entitled to 23.81% of any future increase in the monthly pension payment as well as retroactive pension payments from the date of the commencement of the action.

The Appellate Division affirmed Supreme Court's determination in all respects concluding that because the ordinary disability pension benefits plaintiff was receiving has a ten-year service requirement, such benefits were not solely compensation for injuries but were, in part, an award for length of service. It also concluded that the method used by Supreme Court to determine defendant's award was proper (— AD2d—). For reasons set forth below, we affirm.

The New York Legislature has determined that marital property shall include "all property acquired by either or both spouses during the marriage and before the execution of a separate agreement or the commencement of a matrimonial action" (Domestic Relations Law § 236 [B][1][d]). This Court has previously determined that pension benefits or vested rights to those benefits, except to the extent that they are earned or acquired before marriage or after commencement of a matrimonial action, constitute marital property (see, *Majauskas v. Majauskas,* 61 NY2d 481, 490). That determination was consistent with the intent of the Legislature as embodied in DRL § 236(B)(5)(d)(4) and accords with our understanding that a pension benefit is, in essence, a form of deferred compensation derived from employment and an asset of the marriage that both spouses expect to enjoy at a future date (*Damiano v. Damiano,* 94 AD2d 132, 137). Allowing one spouse to share the pension benefit the other obtains through employment and considering such benefits to be marital property is also consistent with the concept of equitable distribution which rests largely on the view that marriage is, among other things, an economic partnership to which each party has made a contribution (id. at 138).

However, any compensation a spouse receives for personal injuries is not considered marital property and is not subject to equitable distribution (DRL § 236 [B][1][d][2]). Thus a number of courts in this state have distinguished a "retirement pension" from a pure "disability pension" noting that the former is subject to equitable distribution whereas the latter, received as compensation for personal injuries, is not (see *Mylette v. Mylette,* 163 AD2d 43m revg, 140 Misc 2d 607; *West v. West,* 101 AD2d 834, after remittur, 115 AD2d 601; *Newell v. Newell,* 121 Misc 2d 586).

Plaintiff argues that his disability pension should not be subject to equitable distribution. He points to the fact that he was not eligible to receive a normal retirement pension because he had not been employed a sufficient number of years to be vested. Thus, had he retired without a disability in April 1980, he would have received no pension benefit. He contends that the pension benefits he receives are based merely upon his disability and should not be considered marital property. These arguments are unavailing.

Plaintiff was retired pursuant to the retirement for ordinary disability provision of Section 13-167 of the New York City Administrative Code, which entitles a member of the city civil service to receive an ordinary disability pension if he or she "is physically or mentally incapacitated for the performance of duty and ought to be retired," provided he or she "has had ten or more years of duty-service and was a member or otherwise in city-service in each of the ten years next preceding his or her retirement" (NYC Admin Code § 13-167 [a][1]). Thus, an employee may receive an ordinary disability pension even if the disability was not the result of a job-related accident, provided the employee satisfies the length of service requirement. By contrast, a civil service member qualifying for a pension for "accident disability" does not have to satisfy a length of service requirement. Rather, the only requirement for entitlement to an "accident disability" pension is that the employee be "physically or mentally incapacitated for the performance of city-service, as a natural and proximate result of such city-service," and that the "disability was not the result of willful negligence" on the part of the employee (NYC Admin Code § 113-168). Thus, the statutory scheme distinguishes between eligibility for "regular," "ordinary disability" and "accidental disability" pensions on the basis of length of service; entitlement to a "regular" pension vests upon 15 years of service (NYC Admin Code § 13-173.1) and an "ordinary disability" pension upon 10 years of service (NYC Admin Code § 13-167[a][1]), while there exists no length of service requirement for an "accidental disability" pension.

As indicated previously, it is firmly established in our jurisprudence that an employee's interest in "'pension rights', the rights commonly accorded an employee and his or her spouse in a pension plan, except to the extent that [that interest] is earned before marriage or after commencement of a matrimonial action, is marital property" (*Majauskas v. Majauskas,* 61 NY2d 481, 490, supra), the pension benefits constituting a form of deferred compensation derived from employment (*West v. West,* 101 AD2d 834, supra). In the typical pension plan, the employees' rights are incremental in that for each month or year of service, the employee receives credit which will enter into the computation of what the pension plan will pay to the employee (*Majauskas v. Majauskas,* supra at 490). It is clear from the length of service requirement for the ordinary disability pension at issue here that plaintiff is being compensated for his length of service to the Department of Sanitation in addition to being compensated for the injuries he sustained. Indeed, implicit in the service requirement for this ordinary disability pension is the desire to provide employees whose injuries have prevented them from working until normal retirement age with some form of compensation for their injuries while also awarding them a portion of the deferred compensation to which they would have been entitled but for the injuries (see e.g. *Mylette v. Mylette,* 163 AD2d 463, 465 supra). Thus, to the extent plaintiff's ordinary disability pension represents deferred compensation, it is indistinguishable from a retirement pension and therefore, to that extent, is subject to equitable distribution (see e.g. *Mylette v. Mylette,* 163 AD2d 463, 463 supra; *West v. West,* 101 AD2d 834, supra; *Newell v. Newell,* 121 Misc 2d 586, supra; see generally, Annotation, Pension or Retirement Benefits as Subject to Award or Division by Court in Settlement of Property Rights Between Spouses, 94 ALR3d 176 § 13).

Accordingly, the order of the Appellate Division should be affirmed, with costs.

Order affirmed with costs. Opinion by Judge Alexander. Chief Judge Wachtler and Judges Simons, Kaye, Titone, Hancock, and Bellacosa concur.

Source: Gerald A. Dolan v. Lois A. Dolan, 583 N.E.2D 908, 577 N.Y.S.2D 195 (N.Y. 1991), New York Court of Appeals.

Professional Degrees

In a marital partnership, spouses often make sacrifices of time, energy, and financial resources for the future good of the partnership. One of the sacrifices often made is putting a spouse through school. Many spouses who make the decision to seek a professional degree or license do so with the commitment and support of the other spouse. This decision may require moving to another city or town or sometimes another country. It also may require the nonstudent spouse to give up, either permanently or temporarily, his or her own professional goals while the student spouse pursues his or her goals. Frequently the nonstudent spouse may become the family's sole breadwinner to allow the student spouse time to focus on scholastic endeavors. The family's lifestyle may suffer a drastic change in lifestyle as the student spouse focuses on studies and spends time outside the classroom both studying and socializing with fellow students. Quality time with the family greatly decreases. The return to school can also involve financial sacrifices in terms of money needed for books and tuition (see Figure 6-3).

While all of these sacrifices are made in hopes that a professional or advanced degree will provide the family unit with a more prosperous future, more than a few nonstudent spouses have found themselves served with divorce papers while the student spouse, upon graduation, moves on with a new career, newfound friends, and, sometimes, a new romantic love interest!

Some states have classified a professional degree as marital property if it was obtained during the marriage. In these jurisdictions, a nonstudent spouse who makes monetary and nonmonetary contributions that enhance the other spouse's earning potential may claim a portion of the value of the professional degree as marital property. An expert can provide a monetary figure representing the value of a professional degree. The court will then award a portion of the value to the nonstudent spouse pursuant to the state's property division laws.

Figure 6-3 Some jurisdictions consider an advanced degree to be marital property if it was obtained during the marriage.

Hxdbzxy/Shutterstock.

New York has steadfastly recognized professional degrees and professional licenses as marital property beginning with the 1985 landmark case of *O'Brien v. O'Brien*:

- ### *O'Brien v. O'Brien*, 489 N.E. 2d 712

  In *O'Brien,* the New York Court of Appeals overturned the Appellate Division's finding that a professional medical license was not marital property. The higher court reinstated the trial court's judgment. The wife had been gainfully employed throughout the parties' nine-year marriage, in addition to performing household work and managing the family finances. She relinquished the opportunity to obtain permanent teaching certification while her husband pursued his education and contributed all of her earnings to the couple's living expenses and her husband's educational costs. Her husband received his medical license in October 1980, and served her with divorce papers two months later.

  At trial, the wife provided expert testimony that the present value of the medical license was $472,000.00 and that the present value of the wife's contribution to her husband's medical school education was $103,000. The trial court after considering the lifestyle the student spouse would enjoy from the enhanced earning potential his medical license would bring and the nonstudent's contributions and efforts toward attainment of it, made a distributive award to her of $188,800 representing forty percent of the value of the license and ordered it to be given in annual installments over a period of eleven years.

  New York courts have consistently applied the reasoning used in *O'Brien* to award a spouse a percentage of the value of a professional license based on the percentage of their contribution. These courts will also deny awarding any amount where the nonstudent spouse has made a minimal effect or contribution. The Appellate Division of the Supreme Court of New York, overturned the trial court's judgment in the 2008 case, *Higgins v. Higgins:*

- ### *Higgins v. Higgins*, 50 A.D. 3rd 852 [2d Dept. 2008]

  In *Higgins,* the Appellate Division held that the trial court improvidently exercised its discretion in awarding the defendant spouse thirty percent of the plaintiff spouse's enhanced earning capacity where the defendant offered no evidence that he made career sacrifices or assumed a disproportionate share of the housework as a consequence of the plaintiff's return to school as the plaintiff spouse worked full-time while attending school, funded some of her own education costs, and was still the primary caregiver for the parties' children.

  Many states do not recognize the professional degree or license as a marital asset. However, courts in those states frequently acknowledge the enhanced earning ability of a spouse who has earned a degree during the marriage and take that into consideration when making an alimony or maintenance and child support award. In *Lackey v. Lackey,* the Alabama Court of Civil Appeals upheld the trial court's award of a hefty amount of permanent periodic alimony to the nonstudent wife who persevered with her husband as he completed not one but two medical residencies during their marriage.

- ### *Lackey v. Lackey*, 2070603 (Ala, Civ. App. 3-6-2009)

  In *Lackey,* the husband appealed the trial court's troublesome alimony award arguing that his wife had the ability to earn a good salary and that any alimony award should be temporary. The appeals court firmly rejected this argument. While the marriage was only of six years duration—usually too brief a period to justify permanent alimony—the wife had to leave her career as a registered nurse while her husband completed the two residencies. Her husband's long hours and frequent absences from the home left the wife with most of the responsibility for caring for the parties' children. During that period, the family struggled to live on the husband's meager salary, credit cards, and financial assistance from the wife's parents. The wife, who had returned to work when the parties separated, was earning considerably less than she would have had if she kept on working, and her earning capacity would always be considerably less than her husband's enhanced ability.

Some courts have also extended the professional degree as property theory to any artistic or athletic skill developed during the marriage that enhances the participant spouse's earning capacity.

Wife's Slam Dunk In *Marriage of Anderson,* the court held that an NBA player's contract signed by the husband for the 1988–1989 season was marital property and subject to equitable distribution.

IN RE THE MARRIAGE OF BERNADETTE K. ANDERSON AND RICHARD A. ANDERSON

811 P.2d 419 (Colo.App. 1990)
Colorado Court of Appeals, Div. II.

Opinion By Judge Rothenberg.

In this dissolution of marriage action, Bernadette K. Anderson (wife) appeals from permanent orders entered relating to distribution of property and maintenance. We reverse and remand with directions.

The principal issue on appeal is whether husband's player contract with a professional basketball team constitutes marital property subject to division.

At the time of the decree on March 1, 1989, husband was currently under a three-year contract with the Portland Trail Blazers for the 1988–89, 1989–90 and 1990–91 seasons. According to the contract, he was to receive three yearly lump-sum payments totaling 1.5 million dollars. On October 5, 1988, and December 1, 1988, he received the first payment, which totaled $267,000 after taxes. Remaining payments of $475,000 and $575,000 were payable December 1989 and December 1990, respectively.

The NBA player contract in issue was never made part of the trial court record, but testimony of both husband and his attorney-agent indicated that the contract guaranteed payment: (1) if he died; (2) if he sustained injury during an NBA game or an official practice session; (3) if he had a mental breakdown or disability; (4) if he was terminated for lack of skill; or (5) if he were traded or waived by the team. Payment was not guaranteed if he sustained a physical disability from an injury unrelated to an NBA game or practice, or if he failed to pass a physical exam at the beginning of each season.

Husband testified that he used part of the $267,000 received to pay marital debts, child support maintenance and mortgage payments on the parties' townhouse. At the time of the permanent orders, however, he still had $150,000 in treasury securities and $14,000 in his checking account.

The trial court ruled that husband's NBA contract including the $267,000 payment already received by husband was not marital property, but was income belonging to the husband for husband's future services. On appeal, wife argues that husband's NBA contract is marital property, and she relies heavily on cases holding that a spouse's compensation which is deferred until after the dissolution, but fully earned during the marriage, is marital property (citations omitted). . . .

In our view, the money already received by husband during the marriage is not future income. It is cash on hand and therefore marital property subject to division. Accordingly, we hold that the money paid under the contract for the 1988–89 season and not expended for marital purposes as of the date of the dissolution *is* marital property subject to equitable distribution, and the trial court erred in ruling otherwise.

However, as to the final two years of husband's contract, we hold that those payments to be received for the 1989–90 and 1990–91 seasons do not constitute property; rather, they constitute future income. *See In re Marriage of Faulkner, supra.*

Section 14-10-113, C.R.S. (1987 Rel.Vol.6B) requires a trial court to consider three separate issues regarding the equitable distribution of assets in a dissolution: (1) It must characterize the asset and determine whether it is property; (2) it must then allocate the asset as separate property of one spouse or as marital property; and (3) finally, it must distribute the property equitably (citation omitted). . . .

On remand, the court should consider all relevant factors in distributing the marital property here including the contribution of each spouse during the marriage, the fact of their separation, and any dissipation of marital property (citation omitted). . . .

. . . The judgment as to maintenance and division of property is reversed, and the cause is remanded to the trial court for further proceedings not inconsistent with the views expressed herein.

TURSI and HUME, J.J., concur.

Source: In Re The Marriage of Bernadette K. Anderson and Richard A. Anderson, 811 P.2D 419 (COLO. APP. 1990), Colorado Court of Appeals, State of Colorado.

DISTRIBUTION OF THE MARITAL DEBTS

Division of the marital debts is as important as division of the marital assets. Many failed marriages have no assets but only debts to parcel out between the parties. A debt is a sum of money owed to a party called a creditor. The party responsible for the debt is called a debtor.

Debts must be identified and classified as either separate or marital debt. Then the obligation to pay is imposed on the respective spouses according to state law. Like separate property, debts incurred by a spouse prior to marriage belong to that spouse. A creditor in this case may only attach separate property to satisfy a debt incurred before the marriage. If no separate property exists, the creditor may then seek to attach marital property for satisfaction of the debt.

Debts incurred during the course of the marriage are considered marital debts. Just as spouses are jointly entitled to share in the fruits of the marriage, they will also be jointly responsible for the debts incurred during the marriage, regardless of whether the debt was incurred by one spouse or both. During the course of the marriage, couples will incur debts for necessaries such as food, clothing, shelter, and medical care. As long as a debt for necessaries is incurred during the marriage, both spouses are responsible for the debt. This obligation to provide for the necessaries of the family was historically imposed on the husband. Today, both husbands and wives are mutually responsible for providing the essentials to their families. A creditor due an obligation regarding a necessary may seek an attachment of marital property. Note that in the *Szesny* case, illustrated earlier in this chapter, the husband was held responsible for debts incurred during the marriage that were not classified as necessaries. Husband had dissipated the marital assets, and it would have been unfair for the court to hold the wife responsible for the husband's wrongdoing.

During the divorce process, the parties are free to negotiate regarding which spouse will assume a particular debt. If there is no dispute, a separation agreement will be drafted and the debt clauses will specify the debts to be assumed by the respective parties. The debt section should also include a hold harmless clause. A hold harmless clause indicates that a particular spouse will be responsible for a debt incurred during the marriage, that he will be solely responsible for its payment, and that the other spouse shall be free and clear of any obligation regarding that debt. This agreement, however, is not binding on a creditor. A creditor who is due a debt incurred during the marriage may sue one or both spouses regardless of what the separation agreement indicates. The hold harmless clause allows the spouse who got "stuck" paying the debt to turn around and seek repayment from the spouse initially obligated under the separation agreement. Remember also that although the creditor may only sue the spouse who incurred the debt during marriage, if judgment is granted in favor of the creditor, the creditor may seek to enforce the judgment against the marital assets of the marriage, assets in which the other spouse has an interest. After a divorce, a creditor can still seek to satisfy the debt by pursuing the spouse most able to pay the debt.

If the court must determine the allocation of debts, the spouse's ability to pay and assets available will be considered.

DISSIPATION OF MARITAL ASSETS

Just as each spouse during the period of a marriage may contribute to the acquisition, enhancement, preservation, and appreciation of the marital estate, so either or both spouses may *dissipate* or waste away marital assets. ***Dissipation***, or depletion of the marital assets, can occur in one or more of the following ways:

- overspending during the course of an intact marriage,
- overspending in contemplation of divorce,
- overspending upon formal or informal notice of impending divorce, and
- destroying, giving away, or selling a spouse's property.

Activities that constitute dissipation include running up credit card debt, depleting or closing out joint checking and savings accounts, making suspicious loans to relatives, purchasing "big-ticket" items with cash, gambling, and making high-risk or highly speculative investments.

When making property distribution awards in a dissolution proceeding, the court will take into consideration each spouse's role in and responsibility for the dissipation of marital assets. The court may punish the wrongdoing spouse by requiring the spouse to compensate the other spouse for the waste. This may be accomplished either by awarding the innocent spouse a larger percentage of the marital property or by ordering the wrongdoing spouse to pay to the other spouse an amount of cash equal to the monetary value of the assets depleted.

Motorcycle Madness Let's discuss the *Click* case. In defiance of a court order, Mr. Click took the Clicks' Gold Wing motorcycle and had an accident, which left him comatose. The Gold Wing was destroyed in the accident, leaving Mrs. Click to argue that her husband had dissipated a marital asset.

IN RE MARRIAGE OF WANDA CLICK AND ROBERT CLICK

169 Ill. App. 3d 48, 119 Ill. Dec. 701, 523 N.E.2d 169 (Ill. App. 2 Dist. 1988)
Appellate Court of Illinois, Second District

Justice Unverzagt Delivered the Opinion of the Court.

Petitioner, Wanda Click, appeals from the property distribution portion of an order entered by the circuit court of Kane County dissolving her marriage to Robert Click. While petitioner's action was pending, Robert was critically injured in a motorcycle accident. He has been in a coma since May 4, 1986. The trial court consolidated the dissolution action with an action by Robert's mother, Jacquelyn Click, to have Robert adjudicated a disabled adult and to have a guardian appointed for him. Jacquelyn was subsequently appointed guardian of Robert's person and estate, and she participated in the property division portion of the dissolution proceeding on his behalf.

Wanda initially sought to enforce a settlement agreement which she alleged the parties had reached before Robert's accident. The court rejected that claim, however, concluding that Wanda had not sufficiently established the terms of the alleged agreement to allow it to be enforced. On March 19, 1987, the court entered an order dissolving the marriage and dividing the marital property. The court noted that, according to Wanda, Robert was a professional thief who had only occasionally been "gainfully employed" during the marriage. Wanda worked only part-time during the marriage. The court found the testimony regarding the parties' earnings to be incredible as the evidence demonstrated that they had acquired assets far in excess of their reported income. The property division portion of the order directed the sale of the marital residence, in which Wanda was residing, and an equal distribution of the proceeds between the parties. It awarded Robert the proceeds of a worker's compensation claim involving an employment related injury he had received, the proceeds of a pending action concerning his motorcycle accident, the salvage value of the Gold Wing motorcycle on which he was injured, a motorcycle trailer, and a number of personal items. It awarded Wanda a 1983 automobile, a smaller motorcycle, an aluminum boat, and some personal items. Wanda was additionally required to reimburse Robert for some of his furnishings which she sold after his accident, and for some charges she made to his credit cards. The court also ordered the equal division of any property contained in a safe deposit box and an equal division of the sale proceeds of a speedboat "if it is ever located," which Wanda claimed Robert had bought. The court directed the guardian to sell all of the assets assigned to Robert and to use the proceeds for his care. The court reserved the issue of future maintenance for Robert.

On appeal, Wanda alleges that: (2) the evidence demonstrated that Robert had dissipated a marital asset by destroying the Gold Wing motorcycle. . . . Petitioner next contends that the court erred in rejecting her claim that Robert dissipated a marital asset when he took the Gold Wing motorcycle in contravention of a court order and then destroyed it in the accident that left him comatose. Dissipation of marital assets is generally defined as "the use of marital property for the sole benefit of one of the spouses for a purpose unrelated to the marriage at a time that the marriage is undergoing an irreconcilable breakdown" (citations omitted). While petitioner correctly asserts that courts have occasionally found a dissipation of assets where the dissipating spouse has derived no personal benefit from his or her actions (see, *e.g., In re Marriage of Siegel* (1984), 123 Ill. App. 3d 710, 719, 79 Ill. Dec. 219, 463 N.E.2d 773), we know of no authority, nor has petitioner cited any, which would permit a party to be held accountable for a dissipation which is not only detrimental to both parties, but purely unintentional as well. Robert violated a court order in taking the motorcycle—conduct which would ordinarily have resulted in the court's imposition of contempt sanctions against him. (See generally *In re G.B.* (1981), 88 Ill. 2d 36, 41, 58 Ill. Dec. 845, 420 N.E.2d 1096 (regarding a court's inherent contempt power).) There was no evidence to suggest that his injury and the destruction of the motorcycle were anything other than accidental, however, and we therefore conclude that the court correctly found that he did not dissipate a marital asset. . . .

. . . Judgment affirmed.

NASH and REINHARD, JJ., concur.

Source: In Re Marriage Of Wanda Click And Robert Click, 169 ILL. APP. 3D 48, 119 ILL. DEC. 701, 523 N.E.2D 169 (ILL. APP. 2 DIST. 1988), Illinois Courts.

During the pendency of a divorce or dissolution action, each spouse may have some access to the marital assets. During that period, each spouse has the right to use some portion of marital funds to pay for legitimate expense including the payment of reasonable legal fees in conjunction with the divorce action. Divorcing spouses may also use marital funds to pay certain personal expenses that they always paid from the funds during the course of the marriage. Such expenses may include individual property tax bills for each spouse's automobile, automobile insurance and health insurance premiums, expenses for unexpected or emergency home repairs, dental work, reasonable expenses of the minor children, and, of course, reasonable expenditures for necessaries such as food, clothing, and shelter.

But When Does the Dissipation Begin?

As outlined earlier, dissipation of marital assets may occur during the course of the marriage. However, some states limit compensating one spouse for the other spouse's improvident financial behavior only to the dissipation occurring once the marriage began to break down irretrievably. Determining when the irretrievable breakdown has occurred is an issue upon which reasonable minds—even reasonable judicial minds—may differ. As the following case illustrates, determining on which date the dissipation begins can have a substantial effect on the amount of monetary compensation the court awards to the "innocent" spouse.

In Illinois, the statute defines the dissipation period as beginning when the marriage is undergoing an irreconcilable breakdown.

Casino Crazy In the case of *In re Marriage of Holthaus*, the Illinois Appellate Court addressed, among other issues, the determination of when the parties' marriage began this process.

IN RE MARRIAGE OF ANGELINE HOLTHAUS AND NICHOLAS HOLTHAUS

377 Ill. App. 3d 397 (2008) 899 N.E. 2.d 355

PRESIDING JUSTICE BENOFF DELIVERED THE OPINION OF THE COURT

On May 10, 2007, the circuit court of Du Page County entered a judgment dissolving the marriage between petitioner, Angeline Holthaus, and respondent, Nicholas Holthaus. Angeline appealed, arguing that the trial court erred in . . . (2) finding that she dissipated $118,688 . . . Nicholas filed a cross-appeal, arguing that the trial court erred in finding that Angelina dissipated only $118,688. For the following reasons, we reverse and remand for further proceedings.

BACKGROUND

Angelina and Nicholas were married on June 21, 1961. They had two children during the marriage, both of whom were emancipated by the time of trial. . . .

According to Nicholas, in 1997 the parties ceased having a "romantic relationship" and in 1998 the parties ceased sharing a bedroom. Nicholas began to sleep in the "rec" room while Angeline slept upstairs in the master bedroom. Nicholas described the environment at the time as hostile. In 2001, the parties were no longer sharing meals. Although Angeline would cook the meals or the parties would order food in, Nicholas would take his plate and eat in the "rec" room, away from Angeline. Further, in 2001, the parties not only slept in separate parts of the house but also lived in separate parts of the house. Nicholas testified that the parties lived and ate separately because every conversation between them ended in an argument. Although there were times he thought things might get better, they always became worse and there was eventually a point when the parties "just didn't communicate at all."

At trial, Nicholas described an incident that occurred in October 2001. After discovering two ATM withdrawals made at the Grand Victoria Casino in Elgin, totaling $6,000, he confronted Angeline. Her only response at the time was that she wanted a divorce. The following months, Angeline gave Nicholas a letter in which she outlined her "plan" for the future. She stated she wanted the house and that she would be responsible for paying the equity loan if Nicholas did not want to contribute. In addition, she stated that she would be responsible for all the credit card debt. She asked Nicholas to inform her of his plans for paying other household and car expenses and asked that, in any case, he continue paying such expenses until March 2002 so that she could get her "affairs in order." Angeline further stated in the letter that she and Nicholas could use the time "as a cooling off period or a settling of affairs period, whichever would apply," depending upon whether they chose to stay together or separate. She concluded the letter by asking Nicholas to communicate with her in writing, "as communication [had] completely broken down between [them]."

After 2001, the parties together attended their son's wedding, made appearances at family events, and went out to dinner several times. In addition, Nicholas testified that he went to casinos with Angeline several times in order to help with Angeline's mother, who accompanied them. . . .

. . . In November 2004, Nicholas began to move some of his personal effects out of the marital home. Angeline testified that, as of January 2005, she was doing the cooking, cleaning, and shopping for the household. In February 2005, the parties got into an argument after which Nicholas left the marital home permanently. He returned several times in the weeks following his departure, to retrieve some of his personal items.

Nicholas testified that he believed "irreconcilable differences happened" as of October 2001. Angeline testified that she believed the marriage was "irretrievably broken" as of February 2005, when Nicholas moved out of the marital home. When presented with her deposition transcript in which she stated that she believed the marriage was irreconcilably broken as of 1999 and that there was no hope for rehabilitation at that time, Angeline admitted that she had made those statements during the deposition. Angeline filed a petition for dissolution of the parties' marriage on March 10, 2005. . . . Four days later, on March 14, 2005, Nicholas filed his own petition for dissolution of marriage. . . . The court consolidated the two cases on April 13, 2005. . . .

. . . Following trial, on April 24, 2007, the trial court issued a letter order announcing its decision on the issues presented at trial. The letter stated in relevant part:

"Elemental to the disposition of this case is the issue of dissipation, the date on which the marriage was irretrievably broken. . . ."

. . . [T]he court fixes the date of irretrievable breakdown as February 2005, the date of physical separation. It may be true that the irretrievable breakdown need not be the date of physical separation or filing. Yet whenever dissipation is claimed the court hears mostly self-serving testimony about how the relationship deteriorated years in advance. A more objective determinant, though not required, is certainly helpful. Here, for instance, despite Mr. Holthaus's testimony concerning the irretrievable breakdown occurring in 2001, he and Ms. Holthaus worked together (actually he says he did the work) to remodel/repair her mother's house well into 2003. So when was the breakdown? There was no testimony of any 'triggering' event after the 2003 joint effort to repair Ms. Holthaus's mother's house. Under the circumstances, February 2005 is the date that the marriage was irretrievably broken, Therefore the amount of dissipation set forth in the Request to Admit Facts (and coincidentally supported) is $118,668.00. . . .

continued

. . . The trial court entered a judgment of dissolution on May 10, 2007. The judgment stated that the trial court found Angeline had dissipated $118,688, and the trial court "allocated" that amount to her in its distribution of the marital estate. Angeline timely appealed, and Nicholas filed a timely cross-appeal.

ANALYSIS

On appeal, Angeline argues that the trial court erred in . . . (2) finding that she dissipated $118,688. . . . In his cross-appeal, Nicholas argues that the trial court erred in finding that Angeline dissipated only $118,688. We address each of these issues in turn. . . .

B. Dissipation

Both Angeline and Nicholas argue that the trial court erred in finding that Angeline dissipated $118,688. Angela contends that the trial court erroneously included $86,000 that Angeline withdrew before February 2005, which the trial court determined was the date of the irretrievable breakdown of the parties' marriage. Nicholas, on the other hand, contends that the trial court erred in calculating the dissipation only as of February 2005. We agree with Nicholas.

Section 503 9 (d) of the Illinois Marriage and Dissolution of Marriage Act lists the relevant factors a trial court should consider in determining how to distribute marital property in a dissolution proceeding. . . . Included in the factors is "the dissipation by each party of the marital or non-marital property." . . . Dissipation is the "'use of marital property for the sole benefit of one of the spouses for a purpose unrelated to the marriage at a time that the marriage is undergoing an irreconcilable breakdown.'" *In re Marriage of O'Neill*, . . . (1990), quoting in *re Marriage of Petrovich* . . . (1987). . . . Before addressing the trial court's finding, we first note that Angeline argues that dissipation applies to improper expenditures that are made only *after* the marriage has undergone an irreconcilable breakdown. In support of this position, Angeline relies on three cases: *In re Marriage of DeLarco*, . . . (2000), *In re Marriage of Toole* . . . (1995), and *O'Neill*, . . .

. . . In *DeLarco*, the appellate court, citing *Toole*, stated that dissipation "applies to allegedly improper expenditures of marital funds for purposes unrelated to the marriage, at a time *after* the marriage has irretrievably or irreconcilably broken down." (Emphasis added.) *DeLarco*. . . . In *Toole*, the appellate court had defined it the same way, relying on the Supreme Court case of *O'Neill*. *Toole*, . . . The court in *Toole*, however, applied the holding in *O'Neill* to a situation where, at the time of the alleged dissipation, the marriage had undergone an irreconcilable breakdown as established by the parties' separation. As noted, in *O'Neill*, the Supreme Court held that dissipation is the "use of marital property for the sole benefit of one of the spouses for a purpose unrelated to the marriage at a time when the marriage is *undergoing* an irreconcilable breakdown.'" (emphasis added) (*O'Neill*, . . . quoting *Petrovich*, . . .), not after the marriage is irreconcilably broken.

The cases of *Toole* and *DeLarco* are distinguishable from the present case. In *Toole*, the dissipation occurred when the marriage had irreconcilably broken down, rather than when the marriage was in the process of irreconcilably breaking down. The court in *Toole* merely applied the definition contained in *O'Neill* to include within its coverage the period from the beginning of the breakdown through the entry of the final judgment. Additionally, Angeline's citation to *DiLorco* references *dicta*. There the appellate court held simply that the trial court had miscalculated the attorney fees the petitioner had paid out of the marital assets. The appellate court directed the trial court, upon remand, to redistribute the marital estate in light of the correct amount, which was considered to be an advance on the petitioner's share. *DeLarco*, ... In our view, none of the cases we have reviewed, including *DeLarco* and *Toole,* are in conflict with the holding in *O'Neill.* According, we disagree with Angeline's contention that dissipation occurs only after an irreconcilable breakdown has occurred, and we turn now to the trial court's specific finding.

It appears that the trial court calculated dissipation, not from when the parties' marriage began undergoing an irreconcilable breakdown, but rather from when the parties' marriage had completed the process of breaking down. This is apparent from the trial court's language in its letter order: '[T] he court fixes the date of irretrievable breakdown as February 2005, the date of physical separation." So when was the breakdown? Under the circumstances February 2005 is the date that the marriage "was irretrievably broken." This language demonstrates that the trial court was attempting to pinpoint the date on which the parties' marriage "was irretrievably broken" rather than attempting to determine when the marriage began to irreconcilably break down. As previously discussed, dissipation is to be calculated from the time the parties' marriage begins to undergo an irreconcilable breakdown, not from a date after which it is irreconcilably broken. *In re Marriage of Olson,* . . . (1992).

Before reversing the trial court, however, we must first determine whether the trial's error in applying the incorrect standard for calculating dissipation was harmless. See *In re Marriage of Wilder,* (1983) ("not every error committed by the trial court in civil cases leads to reversal and reversal is required only when it appears that the outcome might have been different had the error not occurred"). If the parties' marriage began undergoing an irreconcilable breakdown in February 5, 2005, then the trial court's error was harmless. If, on the other hand, the parties' marriage began undergoing an irreconcilable breakdown prior to February 2005, then the trial court's error was not harmless, and we must reverse and remand to the trial court for a recalculation of dissipation.

Although the February 2005 argument between the parties does appear to be the final straw in the process of the irreconcilable breakdown of the parties' marriage, the evidence presented at trial by both Angeline and Nicholas strongly indicates that the parties' marriage was undergoing an irreconcilable breakdown long before then. Between 1997 and 2001, the parties stopped having marital relations, sleeping in the same bedroom, living in the same part of the house, sharing meals, and communicating. They were living in an environment that Nicholas testified, and Angeline did not contest, was hostile. In October 2001, following a confrontation between the parties regarding $6,000 Angeline had withdrawn at a casino, Angeline told Nicholas she wanted a divorce. The following month, she went so far as to write him a letter detailing her "plan" for the future, which included a suggested division of responsibility between the parties for their financial obligations and which indicated that Angeline wanted to keep the marital home. In November 2004, Nicholas began to move personal belongings out of the marital home, and he finally moved out permanently in February 2005. From this evidence, we conclude that the parties' were undergoing an irreconcilable breakdown long before February 2005. . . .

. . . According to the trial court's letter order, its determination of February 2005 was based, at least in part, on the fact that the parties "worked together" on Marie's home in 2003. The evidence presented at trial by both parties regarding the repair of Marie's home, however, fails to indicate that the parties' marriage was not undergoing an irreconcilable breakdown in 2003, despite their cooperation on the repairs. Although the evidence did establish that both parties participated in the repair of Marie's house, it appears that each did so apart from the other, much like they lived the rest of their lives. Angeline argues that the trial court could have found that the marriage was undergoing an irreconcilable breakdown only as of February 2005, because prior to that date Nicholas continued to live in the marital home, the parties attended family events together such as their son's wedding, the

continued

parties went out to dinner together a few times, Nicholas helped Angeline take Marie to the casino, and Angeline did the shopping, cooking, and cleaning for the parties. We do believe that these facts, either individually or together, negate the obvious irreconcilable breakdown that was taking place in the parties' marriage prior to February 2005. None of these facts indicates that the parties were attempting to reconcile or were even getting along. Taken with the facts that the parties lived in separate parts of the house, slept in separate rooms, did not communicate, and rarely ate meals together, the facts cited by Angeline indicate, at most, an effort by the parties to maintain a minimum level of civility in front of third parties and to keep the household operating.

As the parties' marriage was undergoing an irreconcilable breakdown prior to February 2005, we hold that the trial court's error in applying the incorrect standard in calculating dissipation was not harmless. Accordingly, we must reverse and remand this matter to the trial court. We do not fix a specific date for when the irreconcilable breakdown began. Rather we determine only that the irreconcilable breakdown occurred sometime prior to February 2005. Whether it began in the late 1990s when the parties ceased having marital relations and sharing a bedroom or in 2001 when Angeline stated she wanted a divorce and made a plan for separating the parties' financial responsibilities or at some other time supported by the evidence is a question of fact to be answered by the trial court. *See Vancura*, 356 Ill. App. 3d at 204. Accordingly, the trial court's decision on the issue of dissipation is reversed and the matter is remanded for future proceedings in accordance with this opinion. . . .

CONCLUSION

For the foregoing reasons, the judgment of the Du Page County Circuit Court is reversed and the matter is remanded for further proceedings.

Reversed and remanded.

McLAREN and SCHOSTOK, J. J., concur.

Source: In Re Marriage Of Angeline Holthaus And Nicholas Holthaus, 377 ILL. APP. 3D 397 (2008) 899 N.E. 2.D 355, State of Illinois.

TORT AWARDS AND OTHER JUDGMENTS AS MARITAL PROPERTY

If during the course of the marriage one party seeks relief through an administrative agency (e.g., a claim for workers' compensation or a discrimination claim that is settled or adjudicated at the level of the Commission on Human Rights and Opportunity/Equal Employment Opportunities Commission) or the courts due to the tortious or statutory misconduct of a third party, any settlement, award, or judgment shall be deemed an asset of the marriage. This is based on the theory that had the parties remained married, the family unit would have enjoyed the benefits of the settlement, award, or judgment and that the family unit, which includes the former or soon-to-be-former spouse, suffered economic losses or emotional distress as a result of the third party's misconduct. Despite the fact that all or a portion of any settlement, award, or judgment may be taxable as income to the injured spouse, any portion of any award that is given, by judgment of the agreement, to the uninjured spouse is deemed as *property settlement* and is therefore nontaxable.

Property settlement
A contract between spouses who are in the process of obtaining a divorce or a legal separation resolving the various legal issues that arise when a marriage is dissolving; also known as a marital settlement agreement, separation agreement, or settlement agreement.

BANKRUPTCY

Bankruptcy
A legal proceeding in federal court that allows individuals or businesses that are unable to pay their debts to either discharge their obligations or reorganize them to be paid over a period of time.

Exemptions
The amount and type of property that a debtor may keep despite the bankruptcy proceedings.

Chapter 7
A form of bankruptcy that allows a debtor to discharge or liquidate a majority of their debts.

Chapter 13
A form of bankruptcy where instead of liquidating of the debt, the debtor is subject to reorganization. Reorganization requires the debtor to pay back their creditors under a plan approved by the Bankruptcy Court over a period of three to five years.

Liquidate
To sell off assets and pay creditors with the proceeds.

Means test
A calculation under bankruptcy law that determines whether a debtor has the ability to pay back debts. Debtors have to pass the test in order to determine if they can pay back their debts.

Bankruptcy Abuse Prevention and Consumer Protection Act (BAPCPA)
New federal bankruptcy law passed on April 20, 2005 (with most provisions effective October 17, 2005), legislating significant changes impacting divorce litigation.

Families who are faced with divorce, insurmountable debt, and the inability to make ends meet often seek bankruptcy relief. **Bankruptcy** is a legal proceeding in federal court that allows individuals or businesses that are unable to pay their debts to either discharge their obligations or reorganize them to be paid over a period of time. The purpose of filing for bankruptcy is to get a fresh start. It is important to ask clients whether they are contemplating or have already filed for bankruptcy protection. If the answer is "yes" to either of these questions, issues regarding the bankruptcy need to be dealt with in the early stages of the case.

The federal courts in the United States have jurisdiction over bankruptcy cases. State law applies in bankruptcy cases when determining **exemptions**. This is the amount and type of property that a debtor may keep despite the bankruptcy proceedings.

Because the federal government has retained exclusive jurisdiction in the area of bankruptcy, the United States Congress regulates this area of the law under chapters in the Bankruptcy Code. There are several types of bankruptcy that a party seeking relief may wish to file depending on his or her circumstances. There are two basic types of bankruptcy relief chapters most commonly encountered in a divorce situation: **Chapter 7** and **Chapter 13**. Furthermore, a very important issue when parties to a divorce wish to file for bankruptcy is not only the type of Chapter to file but also when to file.

Chapter 7 allows a debtor to discharge or liquidate a majority of their debts; however, the downside of a Chapter 7 is that they will have to relinquish some of their assets. When debtors **liquidate** their assets, this means that they sell them off and pay their creditors with the proceeds. Debtors have to pass what is called a **means test** in order to determine if they can pay back their debts. The means test was established as a result of a major revision to the Bankruptcy Code in 2005 called the **Bankruptcy Abuse Prevention and Consumer Protection Act (BAPCPA)**. The purpose of the means test is to prevent debtors with high income from liquidating their debts in a Chapter 7 bankruptcy. Instead, the means test compares the debtor's income and expenses to the median income in the debtor's state for a household of the same size and determines their financial ability to pay off their debt. If a debtor makes less than the median income, they can qualify for Chapter 7 protection and can liquidate their debt. If the debtor's income in comparison to expenses is too high, then Chapter 7 is not an option. Instead, they must file for Chapter 13. Under Chapter 13, instead of liquidating of the debt, the debtor is subject to reorganization. Reorganization requires the debtor to pay back their creditors under a plan approved by the Bankruptcy Court over a period of three to five years. Chapter 13 allows a debtor to keep some of their assets and have their debts cancelled upon complying with the reorganization plan.

Timing the Bankruptcy Filing—before the Divorce

There are many advantages for couples contemplating both divorce and bankruptcy to filing before the divorce. The first advantage is that if the couple qualifies for Chapter 7, they can expect to have their bankruptcy case processed within four months, so the waiting period is not that long. On the other hand, a Chapter 13 filing takes three to five years to work its way through the reorganization process, and this may not be practical given the fact that the marriage has broken down and the relationship between the spouses may be strained. Married couples filing jointly pay only one filing fee to the bankruptcy court, one fee for the attorney, and one fee for credit counseling. Also, the attorney only has to file one bankruptcy petition and accompanying schedules because the parties are filing jointly. More important, the parties may be able to double their exemptions depending on state exemption law. The prospect of doubling exemptions may help save the marital residence, for example, under what is known as the homestead exemption if they reside in the home at the time of filing. A **homestead exemption** determines the amount of equity the parties can keep in their homes and shield from the bankruptcy proceedings. A big advantage to filing jointly before the divorce is filed is that the bankruptcy proceeding resolves all of the debt issues. It allows the divorce case to proceed with a clean slate and the parties to make a clean break.

Homestead exemption
Determines the amount of equity the parties can keep in their homes and shield from the bankruptcy proceedings.

Filing for Bankruptcy after the Divorce Is Final

There are circumstances that make filing for bankruptcy *after* the divorce more advantageous. This would require an assessment of the means test by reviewing the couple's income for the six months prior to the bankruptcy filing and, in a separate calculation, the client's income under a similar test. If a client earns much less than the spouse, then it may be advisable for them to wait until after the divorce is over so they could qualify for Chapter 7 instead of Chapter 13. Another reason to file after the divorce is if the client's state does not allow the doubling of exemptions. In this case, it may make more sense to file separately.

The Automatic Stay

Once the bankruptcy petition is filed, the individual who administers the bankruptcy estate, known as the **bankruptcy trustee**, issues an **automatic stay**. This is an injunction issued by the court that prohibits any collection activity against the debtor, and it can only be lifted by an order of the bankruptcy court. The automatic stay stops:

- Harassing phone calls and letters from creditors
- Foreclosures
- Credit card, medical and other bill collections
- Judgments
- Garnishments
- Property repossessions
- Reinstatement of disconnected utilities

Bankruptcy trustee
Individual who administers the bankruptcy estate.

Automatic stay
An injunction issued by the bankruptcy court that prohibits any collection activity against the debtor and that can only be lifted by an order of the bankruptcy court.

What the automatic stay does not stop is the debtor's obligation to pay tax debts, child support, and alimony. The stay also does not affect evictions and criminal prosecutions. This is particularly important to know in matters involving the prosecution of domestic violence cases that may arise in family-related matters. These obligations remain intact and enforceable. If the divorce has been filed already, and then an automatic stay is issued, then any property that is part of the bankruptcy estate is subject to the automatic stay. For example, Jillian and David are in the process of divorce. They have been unable to pay their mortgage, so the bank is seeking to foreclose on the property, which has no equity. The automatic stay, however, prohibits any action on the property without an order from the bankruptcy court. Under these circumstances, the bank could petition to have the stay lifted and proceed with the bankruptcy proceedings since there is nothing to save on property that is basically "underwater."

The Effect of Bankruptcy on Alimony, Child Support, and Property Distribution

Prior to the passage of BAPCPA, debtors used bankruptcy as a means of "discharging" or avoiding financial responsibilities such as court-ordered alimony, child support, and property distribution. BAPCPA remedied this practice by

Domestic support obligations (DSOs)

Under bankruptcy law, the classification of alimony, maintenance, and child support payments as first priority in bankruptcy proceedings, which means that other creditors cannot receive any payments owed to them by the creditor until the DSOs are fulfilled and that these obligations cannot be discharged in bankruptcy under either Chapter 7 or Chapter 13.

classifying alimony, maintenance, and child support payments as *domestic support obligations (DSOs)* and subject to "first priority" in bankruptcy proceedings. This means that other creditors cannot receive any payments owed to them by the creditor until the domestic support obligations are fulfilled and that these obligations cannot be discharged in bankruptcy under either Chapter 7 or Chapter 13. The debtor is responsible for paying DSOs even after receiving a discharge in bankruptcy.

The ability to discharge debts that are the result of a property settlement, however, depends on whether the debtor has filed for Chapter 7 or Chapter 13. Property settlement obligations are not dischargeable in a Chapter 7 bankruptcy but may be discharged in a Chapter 13 case.

Student Loans

Paying back a student loan may be a challenge, especially if both spouses have incurred these educational expenses. In 2012 during a speech on rising education costs, President Obama revealed to the audience that he and the first lady had finally finished paying off their loans only eight years prior. Both came from modest means, but fortunately for them, their careers enabled them to make their payments. Some are not so lucky. Both parties could have student loan debts in their separate names, or their respective loans may have been consolidated. Married couples were once able to consolidate their student loans into one loan with a more affordable rate. In 2006, Congress did away with consolidation of federal student loans, but some private lenders continued the practice. Regardless of what is in the divorce decree, both parties are responsible for the payment of a consolidated student loan. The divorce decree may say that both parties have to pay an equal share on the debt; however, if one spouse fails to make payments, the lender will go after the other—and this includes disability or death. The only option here is to take the spouse to court for civil contempt, which may be futile.

Discharging a student loan in bankruptcy is extremely difficult. Student loans are not dischargeable in bankruptcy unless the debtor can prove undue hardship. In a Chapter 7 case, the debtor has to prove to the bankruptcy court that failure to discharge the student loan would result in an undue hardship to the debtor and his or her dependents. (If the debtor cannot prove undue hardship, then filing for a Chapter 13 bankruptcy may be the best option to at least reorganize payment of the student loan.) Depending on the federal circuits, there are different tests for establishing undue hardship, some more stringent than others. On April 10, 2013, the Seventh Circuit Court ruled on what is considered a landmark case in this area of the law. In *Krieger vs. Educational Credit Management Association*, No. 12-3592, Seventh Circuit, April 10, 2013, the court discharged Krieger's student loan under the "hardship exception." Krieger, a poor woman in her 50s, lives in rural Illinois with her elderly mother. She obtained a student loan and went to school to become a paralegal. She financed her bachelor's degree with five student loans. She paid a portion of the debt off with the money she received in a divorce settlement, but still owed $25,000. Her only income is in the form of food assistance which amounts to $200 per month. Krieger has no access to reliable transportation and no Internet access—two very important resources when looking for work. Over a period of ten years, Krieger applied for approximately 180 jobs but was unable to find employment. The Educational Credit Management Association admitted that under her current circumstances, Krieger could not even afford to pay $1.00 per month toward the student loan. The case of *Brunner v. New York State Higher Educ. Servs. Corp.*, 831 F. 2d 395

(2d Cir. 1987), established the *Brunner test,* three conditions that must be met for the undue hardship exception to apply:

1. In light of the debtor's current income and expenses, the debtor will be unable to maintain even a minimal standard of living if forced to pay back the student loan.
2. The debtor's financial circumstances will most likely persist for a significant portion of the student loan's repayment period.
3. Good faith efforts were made by the debtor to pay the student loan.

The bankruptcy judge granted Krieger a discharge on her student loan and Educational Credit Management Association appealed to the U.S. District Court for the Central District of Illinois. Here, the district judge reversed the bankruptcy court's decision, finding that Krieger could have tried harder to find a job and should have taken advantage of an income-based repayment program. The judge determined that the good faith prong of the undue hardship could not be satisfied. The Seventh Circuit's first sentence in the opinion simply reads "Susan Krieger is destitute." The Court reversed the District Court's decision, holding that (1) the "good faith" test does not involve a commitment to future efforts to repay because if this were true, "no educational loan could ever be discharged, because it is always possible to pay in the future should prospects improve," and (2) Krieger should not have to look for employment in jobs that pay less than paralegal work, nor she have to enter into a twenty-five-year income-based repayment program. The Seventh Circuit also refused to disrupt the bankruptcy court's finding of fact regarding the likelihood of Krieger's circumstances persisting indefinitely.

There are many, many Kriegers out there who are so financially strapped with insurmountable debt and special circumstances who may wish to seek a bankruptcy discharge on their student loans. What is important about the *Krieger* case is that while it is only binding in the Seventh Circuit, it is encouraging to clients who are in dire financial straits, compounded by divorce, to seek for a discharge of student loan debt.

If a Former Spouse Has Filed for Bankruptcy

A situation may arise where a divorce client contacts the office to inform the attorney that they have received a notice from a bankruptcy court informing them that their former spouse has filed for bankruptcy. While DSOs are not dischargeable, some property settlements are subject to discharge and the debtor may be seeking to do away with these obligations. This notice should not be ignored and requires immediate action to preserve the client's rights. The client should file what is known as an ***adversary proceeding complaint*** in the bankruptcy case. This is a civil case filed with the bankruptcy court, and filing it will permit the client to argue to the judge that discharging nonsupport obligations will have an adverse effect on the client.

Adversary proceeding complaint
A civil case filed within a bankruptcy case; filing it will permit the client to argue to the judge that discharging nonsupport obligations will have an adverse effect on the client.

Added Protection in Property Settlement Agreement Clauses

While property division and nonsupport orders for the benefit of a spouse are not dischargeable in Chapter 7, they are in Chapter 13. The client may wish to add a clause to the property settlement portion of the separation agreement that acknowledges that property division and the support obligations of alimony and child support are connected and that any property settlement arrangement for the transfers of assets and payment of debts are to be considered domestic support obligations under the Bankruptcy Code. Basically, the clause establishes that if either of the parties files for bankruptcy, the purpose behind it is to seek relief from creditors, not to avoid obligations to the spouse. Furthermore, the parties would agree in writing that no obligations owed to the family pursuant to the agreement are dischargeable in the event of either spouse filing for post-divorce bankruptcy. This will give the client fodder to dispute attempts by the former spouse to discharge property or debt settlement arrangements in a Chapter 13 bankruptcy.

Tax Consequences

A basic knowledge of the tax consequences of dissolving a marriage is important for both attorneys and paralegals working in a family law practice. A working relationship with the client's bookkeeper, accountant, and other financial advisors should be established early on in the case, not only for the purpose of verifying the client's financial status, but also to engage their services in assessing the tax consequences of any proposed settlement and how it will impact the client's total financial health. Involving tax professionals early on in the divorce process will allow time for applying the appropriate strategies to minimize the client's tax burden.

As a starter, it is important to read *IRS Publication 504 Divorced or Separated Individuals.* The IRS publishes one every year, and it includes an overview of basic tax principles that all paralegals and legal office staff working on family matters should know. This publication and the others cited in this section may be accessed online through any search engine such as Google or Bing.

Deducting the Cost of Getting Divorced

According to an article published in *Forbes* magazine titled "To Have and To Hold," the average cost of getting a divorce is estimated to be $15,000 to $30,000. This obviously does not include any payouts to the spouse in the form of alimony, child support, or property division. This cost is just to pay the attorney for his or her legal services and, of course, any necessary court fees and expenses. Given the high price tag, clients often ask if they are allowed to "write off" the cost of the divorce on their taxes. The general rule is that legal fees incurred in a divorce are not deductible. The IRS prohibits any deduction for the cost of personal advice, counseling, and legal action in a divorce. However, there are expenses that may be deducted if they qualify under these special rules.

If the attorney is providing a client with tax advice in connection with a divorce case, then those fees may be deducted. The attorney, however, will have to specifically indicate on the client's statement how much of the fee is for tax advice and how much is for legal services. For example, the attorney has to research a tax question in the client's case regarding exemptions for dependents and spends half an hour doing so. The attorney bills her client at $300 an hour. The attorney must specifically indicate on the client's statement that $150 is for tax advice. Breaking down the fees for tax advice versus legal advice is important for purposes of deducting these expenses. The client may also deduct a portion of the legal fees incurred to collect alimony. This includes a portion of the fees for obtaining alimony in the course of the dissolution of the marriage, as well as any subsequent contempt or modification proceedings. Because alimony is a taxable event, the IRS allows a deduction for fees paid to obtain or collect alimony, as long as the fee for doing so is separately stated on the client's statement. Both of these fees are deductible as miscellaneous itemized deduction on *Form 1040 Schedule A.*

Jointly and severally liable
Where one or both parties may be held responsible for taxes due as well as any additions, penalties, or interest.

Innocent Spouse Rule

Spouses who file a joint tax return are ***jointly and severally liable*** for taxes due as well as any additions, penalties, or interest. This means that the IRS can seek payment of taxes due from either spouse or both. This obligation remains even if the couple divorces. As long as the parties filed a joint tax return, both spouses are legally responsible for the entire tax bill regardless of who earned the income, who claimed a disallowed deduction or credit, or who miscalculated the tax liability. The IRS does not care what the divorce decree or settlement agreement states regarding who is responsible for tax liabilities. The agency will seek payment from either spouse, usually the one with resources and/or employment. It is then up to that spouse to pursue the funds under the terms of the divorce agreement and recover those funds in family court.

The aggrieved party, however, may avoid full or partial liability if he or she qualifies for what is known as ***innocent spouse relief***. (*IRS Publication 971 Innocent Spouse Relief* is a helpful resource.) The spouse seeking relief must file *IRS Form 8857 Request for Innocent Spouse Relief* as well as meet all of the following criteria to qualify for innocent spouse relief:

Innocent spouse relief
An IRS rule that allows an aggrieved spouse to avoid full or partial liability arising from a joint tax return where a tax is assessed against his or her spouse.

- The parties must have filed a joint return where there was an understatement (or deficiency) in the tax due;
- The understatement must be due to the other spouse's "erroneous item." This means that the spouse must have either excluded income from the joint return, took deductions or credits that were disallowed, or incorrectly reported other information on the joint tax return; and
- At the time of signing the joint return, the spouse seeking relief did not know or should have known that the return contained an understatement of tax.

When taking all of the facts and circumstances of the case, it would be unfair to hold the spouse seeking relief liable.

Prior to 2011, the spouse seeking relief had to file Form 8857 no later than two years after the first IRS attempt to collect the tax. The IRS has eliminated this time limit to help more innocent spouses seek relief. Once a spouse files Form 8857, the IRS must contact the spouse or former spouse and involve them in the process. There are no exceptions even in cases of domestic violence. The IRS does protect the personal information of the spouse seeking relief, and does not disclose names, addresses, phone numbers, employer information, financial information, and any other matters that are not relevant to the issue of innocent spouse relief. Private information, however, will be disclosed in cases where the spouse seeking relief exhausts all of his or her administrative remedies with the IRS and then files the case in federal tax court. The tax court may be petitioned to keep this information confidential.

Property Division

According to the ***non-recognition rule***, the division or transfer of property made from an individual to a former spouse is not considered a taxable event as long as the transfer is "incident to divorce." This means that the transfer occurs no more than one year after the date in which the marriage ends or the transfer is related to the ending of the marriage. So parties who get divorced may transfer ownership of the house, bank accounts, stock, or other assets without triggering any tax consequences. Problems do arise, however, depending on the class of the property, whether it is the personal residence, retirement plan, or family business interest.

Non-recognition rule
Federal tax rule where the division or transfer of property made from an individual to a former spouse is not considered a taxable event as long as the transfer is incident to divorce.

Personal Residence

Of particular concern is the issue of the cost basis of the property. The cost basis is the price paid for the property plus the cost of any improvements. For example, let's say that Madeline and Alberto are now married and jointly buy a

Taxpayer Relief Act of 1997
A federal tax law, as amended by subsequent legislation enacted in 1998, that allows homeowners who live in a home no fewer than two years in the five-year period prior to sale to deduct a gain of $250,000 each or $500,000 for couples before any tax on gain must be paid.

house worth $450,000. During the course of the marriage, they made $25,000 worth of improvements. The cost basis of the house now is $475,000 (original cost $450,000 plus improvements $25,000 = $475,000). Suppose Alberto and Madeline live in the house for fifteen years and then sell it for $800,000. They are still married and the home is in joint ownership. The *Taxpayer Relief Act of 1997*, as amended by subsequent legislation enacted in 1998, allows homeowners who live in a home no fewer than two years in the five-year period prior to sale to deduct a gain of $250,000 each or $500,000 for couples before any tax on gain must be paid. So in this scenario, the selling price of $800,000 minus the cost basis $475,000 equals a gain of $325,000. Now subtract the $500,000 exclusion and there is no tax due since the gain of $325,000 is less than the $500,000 allowed by the IRS. Changing the facts slightly, let's assume Madeline and Alberto divorce and Madeline transfers her interest in the house to Alberto, who now has sole title as part of the divorce settlement. The selling price of $800,000 minus the cost basis $475,000 equals a gain of $325,000. Now subtract Alberto's exclusion of $250,000 as an individual owner, and he is now stuck with a taxable gain of $75,000. So even though the transfer of the house pursuant to a divorce decree is a nontaxable event, selling the house post divorce may trigger tax consequences.

Many couples solve this issue by agreeing that instead of transferring his or her interest in the home, the nonresident spouse vacates the marital home so that when the house is sold at a future date, the parties may retain the $500,000 combined exclusion in their interest in jointly held property, rather than the $250,000 single exclusion if the property is held in sole ownership. Here, the property settlement agreement should reflect the nonresident spouse's interest in the property. While protecting the $500,000 combined exclusion may be protected by this arrangement, it may not be possible in some cases depending on the specific needs and circumstances of the parties.

Retirement Plans

Family courts have the authority to divide retirement plans such as 401(k) plans, pensions, profit-sharing, and stock bonus plans between the spouses. The best way of doing this is for the parties to have a qualified domestic relations order, or QDRO. A QDRO ensures that the nonemployee spouse is responsible for the payment of taxes when he or she starts receiving payments from the plan. The nonemployee spouse also has the option of withdrawing his or her percentage and transferring it directly into their own individual retirement account (IRA) without incurring a tax penalty. Withdrawing funds from a retirement plan without the benefit of a QDRO for the purpose of satisfying a nonemployee spouse in a divorce matter will trigger heavy tax consequences for the employee spouse.

A QDRO is not necessary when dividing traditional or Roth IRAs, or Simplified Employee Pension Plan (SEP) accounts, as part of a divorce settlement. It is important that a distribution of an IRA not be considered a distribution to the owner spouse. For example, if the husband withdraws $50,000 from his IRA and pays the wife cash, this would be considered a distribution to the owner, and he would have to pay taxes and penalties on the funds withdrawn. A transfer, however, is not considered a distribution to the owner if it is done so pursuant to a divorce decree or other instrument incident to a divorce. So while a QDRO is not necessary, some type of writing or order in conjunction with the divorce is required for purposes of not incurring a tax liability. The transfer should take place after the divorce is final and should be specifically addressed in the divorce decree so it is not considered a distribution to the owner spouse. If the spouses are dividing portions of the IRA, then the recipient spouse should transfer his or her portion into a separate temporary IRA at the same company as the owner spouse. Once this transfer is made, the owner spouse's portion remains intact and the recipient spouse is now free to transfer the funds to an IRA company of their choosing. If one hundred percent of the IRA is being transferred from the owner spouse to the recipient spouse, then simply changing the name on the account is advisable. Once transfers are properly made, the recipient spouse is now the new owner. At this time, the parties may also wish to change their beneficiary designations on the account since many IRA owners often name the surviving spouse as the primary beneficiary.

Family Business Interests

Dividing the family business has complicated tax consequences as well as personal ramifications of having a former spouse as a business partner. There may be a situation where one spouse has spent a lot of time building the business and running its day-to-day operations while the other spouse is merely a joint owner in name only. When the marriage fails, the spouse managing the business may wish to own the business outright without any involvement of the former spouse. Accomplishing this involves a valuation of the business, accountings, and very careful tax and business planning. The division and transferability of the business interests are further complicated depending on whether one is dealing with a partnership or corporation. Here, the advice and involvement of tax professionals and attorneys specializing in business organization law is very important at the early stages of the divorce case.

Alimony

Alimony payments made pursuant to a divorce decree are considered ordinary income to the recipient and deductible to the payer spouse. According to *IRS Publication 504,* alimony is a payment to or for a former spouse under a divorce or separation instrument—if the spouses do not file a joint return with each other and all of the following requirements are met:

- Payment is in cash or cash equivalents like checks or money orders.
- Instrument (divorce or separate maintenance decree, separation agreement, support decree, or other court order) does not designate the payment as not alimony.
- Payment is not treated as child support.
- Spouses are not members of the same household at time when payments are made.

Clients receiving alimony payments should pay estimated quarterly taxes to avoid a hefty tax bill at the end of the year.

Alimony Recapture Rule

The best way to explain the alimony recapture rule is to begin with a scenario that is destined to trigger this tax consequence. Clarice and Edward are in the process of divorcing and have assets totaling $500,000. Shortly after they were married, Edward started a karate school now valued at $300,000. As part of the divorce settlement, Edward keeps his pension worth $100,000 and $150,000, which represents a one-half interest in the karate school. Clarice will keep the house worth $100,000 and will take $150,000 as the other half interest in the karate business. Edward agrees to pay her the interest in the school over the next three years, and his lawyer advised him to categorize it as alimony, so he could deduct the payments on his taxes. Both attorneys involved in the divorce were inexperienced and did not understand the tax ramifications of labeling property division as alimony for the purpose of deducting property distribution payments. The breakdown of "property division" payments Edward and Clarice agreed to looks like this:

Year	Amount Paid
2018	$60,000
2019	$55,000
2020	$35,000
Total	**$150,000**

While the division of the karate school is in reality a division of marital property, it has been disguised as alimony so that Edward could take the deduction on his taxes. If there is excess "front loading" of support payments during the first three years of the divorce, the IRS assumes that the parties really intended a transfer of property interest and called it alimony so that the payer spouse could take advantage of the tax deduction. The IRS now wants its money and will seek to "recapture" the taxes that are actually owed for deducted alimony payments. This is known as the **IRS recapture rule**. In this case, Edward will owe the IRS for the deductions he has taken, and Clarice, who paid taxes on the alimony as income, may receive a refund.

The IRS limits the amount of alimony that can be deducted in the first three years after the divorce. If alimony payments total $15,000 or less per year, they are deductible. If they exceed $15,000, as they do in year three in Edward and Clarice's case, the payer must satisfy complex tax rules for this deduction. The majority of property settlements in a divorce case are made in the first three years after the divorce. This is known as *front loading*, and the lawyers were structuring property settlements by classifying them as alimony. By calling a property settlement alimony the payer client could deduct the amount from income taxes. The IRS monitors alimony payments for front loading. If the majority of payments are made in a period of years, at the year-three mark this will indicate that front loading has occurred. The IRS will then seek to *recapture* the tax deduction. To be safe, payments in year one should not exceed payments made in year two or year three by more than fifteen percent.

IRS recapture rule
Applies when the parties do not wish to have alimony taxed as income or deducted; should be indicated in the settlement agreement.

Front loading
Where the majority of property settlements in a divorce case are made in the first three years after the divorce.

Child Support and Dependent Exemptions

While the payment of child support is not deductible to the payer spouse nor is it treated as income to the recipient spouse, one of the most contentious issues between divorcing parents is who will get to claim the children as dependents on their tax return since they are no longer filing a joint return. Claiming a child as a dependent, as well as the right to take advantage of available federal and state tax credits, results in significant tax savings to parents. While the custodial parent has the right to claim deductions and credits because the child resides with him or her, some parents share the deductions and credits by alternating years, or the right is transferred to the noncustodial parent as part of the negotiations. The noncustodial parent may claim the children as long as the custodial parent has officially released his or her right to claim these tax benefits by executing *IRS Form 8332 Release of Claim to Exemption for Child by Custodial Parent*. This issue should be clearly negotiated in the settlement agreement or delineated in the divorce decree so there is no confusion.

Family Support Payments versus Separate Payments of Alimony and Child Support

Family support payments or *unallocated support* are the terms given to regular, periodic payments a payer spouse makes to the other spouse for the financial maintenance of both the ex-spouse and children. This amount is not delineated into a portion that comprises spousal alimony and a portion for child support, but rather is one sum deemed "family support." Care should be taken so that a reduction of the amount of the family support payment does not occur upon the happening of a child-support-related event such as emancipation, employment, or the end of schooling.

> **Family support payments (or unallocated support)**
>
> Terms given to regular, periodic payments made by a payer spouse for the financial maintenance of both the ex-spouse and children.

The problem lies in determining what is alimony and what is child support. The IRS watches unallocated family support payments carefully. If the unallocated support payment is reduced due to changes in a child's age or needs, the IRS will be able to determine how much has been allocated for alimony and how much has been allocated for child support. If, previously, the payer spouse was deducting alimony payments in an amount greater than the IRS's subsequent determination of what constituted alimony, the payer spouse will have to pay a back tax and possibly a fine. If a payee spouse claimed as income a lesser amount of the family support payment than was actually allocated for alimony, the payee spouse will owe the IRS back taxes and also probably be subject to a fine.

Concept Review and Reinforcement

KEY **TERMS**

adversary proceeding complaint
antenuptial agreement
automatic stay
bankruptcy
Bankruptcy Abuse Prevention and Consumer Protection Act of 2005 (BAPCPA)
bankruptcy trustee
Chapter 7
Chapter 13
civil code
community property distribution
concurrent ownership
dissipation
domestic support obligations (DSO)

Employee Retirement Income Security Act (ERISA)
enterprise goodwill
equitable distribution
exemptions
family support payments or unallocated support
front loading
homestead exemption
innocent spouse relief
IRS recapture rule
jointly and severally liable
liquidate
marital assets
marital debts
marital property

means test
non-recognition rule
personal goodwill
personal property
premarital agreement
prenuptial agreement
primary caregiver
property settlement
Qualified Domestic Relations Order (QDRO)
real property
separate property
Taxpayer Relief Act of 1997
tracing
transmutation
unity of spouses

REVIEW OF **KEY CONCEPTS**

1. Define marital property and separate property, and identify the factors used to place property into one category or the other.

2. When is a spouse's pension a marital asset, when is it not, and why?

3. What is the relationship between the Employment Retirement Income Security Act and a qualified domestic relations order, and how do they protect the financial position of the nonpensioner spouse when the other spouse has a pension?

4. In a community property state, what property is considered community property and what property is considered separate property?

5. If a couple is getting divorced in a community property state, what are the factors or circumstances that could result in one party getting a greater share of the marital estate than the other party?

6. A woman is injured in a car accident and brings a lawsuit. Two years later and six months after her husband has begun dissolution proceedings, the case is settled and the woman receives a check for $75,000. Is this settlement money part of the marital estate in either an equitable distribution state or a community property state? If so, how would this property be distributed under each distribution system?

7. Explain why timing is important when married couples contemplating divorce are also considering bankruptcy.

8. What are the advantages of filing a joint bankruptcy petition?

9. What is the effect of bankruptcy on alimony, child support, and property distribution? What about attorney's fees or fees owed to a guardian ad litem?

10. When preparing a client invoice, why is it important to separately indicate the charges for tax advice and legal services?

11. Explain innocent spouse relief and how a client may qualify under this rule.

12. Briefly explain the tax consequences of alimony, child support, and property division.

BUILDING YOUR PARALEGAL SKILLS

CASES FOR BRIEFING

KRAFICK v. KRAFICK 234 CONN. 783 (1995)

Critical Thinking and Legal Analysis Applications

1. You work for a boutique law firm in Connecticut that specializes in family matters. Your supervising attorney has asked you to draft an opinion letter to be sent to his client, Mr. Brewster.

   The Brewsters are ending their marriage of thirty years upon mutual agreement. They have agreed to split their tangible assets equally. These include the family home and its contents as well as two mutual funds in which they have a joint interest. They will each keep their own vehicles.

   Mrs. Brewster has been employed as a teacher in the same school district for twenty-three years. She is fifty-five years old and plans to teach until she is sixty-two, when she will be able to retire after thirty years with the highest percentage of her salary she can receive as a pension. However, she has indicated that if the school district offers an attractive earlier pension distribution offer when she has taught for twenty-five years, she may take the offer. Mrs. Brewster recently inherited her mother's beach cottage, which has no mortgage. Upon selling the family home, Mrs. Brewster will live in the cottage, which is actually closer to where she works.

   Mr. Brewster is sixty years old. He worked for the local phone company for twenty-five years and took a lump sum early retirement benefit when he was fifty-five and the company was bought out. The parties used that money to pay for most of their daughter's college education. The Brewsters also took a small home equity loan to defray her college costs. Mr. Brewster is now self-employed as a telecommunications consultant. He is covered under his wife's health insurance and will have to provide his own health insurance once they are divorced. His consulting work was paying well until the recent economic downturn. Now, he is suffering financially and is looking for regular employment. He has a few small IRAs in his own name but no other retirement savings.

   Mrs. Brewster does not dispute that her husband has an interest in the value of her pension to date, but she wants to ensure that he will not share in the future appreciation of this asset. Mr. Brewster cannot decide whether he wants to receive his interest in the pension now or wait until Mrs. Brewster retires, especially if

continued

she does so in two years. Because of his current financial situation, he is leaning toward obtaining his interest now. Also, he also does not want to wait until he is sixty-seven years old to see any of the pension interest that could be obtained if his wife stays until she has been teaching for thirty years.

In the opinion letter, your supervising attorney wants you to discuss the three methods of dividing interests in spouses' pension benefits, discuss the advantages and disadvantages of each method, and recommend which method to pursue based on Mr. Brewster's circumstances. He also wants you to assess whether Mrs. Brewster will be amenable to the recommendation.

Krafick v. Krafick, 234 Conn. 783 articulates the law in Connecticut regarding pension division. After briefing this case, use it to identify the three approved methods of pension distribution and use the court's analysis of the advantages and disadvantages of each method to recommend what method would best suit Mr. Brewster's needs.

2. As part of your duties in the family law division of a medium-size firm, you have to research issues pertaining to separate property and marital property. Your firm's client is a stay-at-home mom and full-time homemaker who for the last twenty years has belonged to a stock club with four other women. She always used what she referred to as her own money to invest with the club. She got her own money from gifts from her husband and, earlier in her life, from her parents. Over the years, the stock club has made money, lost money, and made money again. Currently in the club fund there is $250,000.

The client's husband claims that he is entitled to one-half of his wife's share, which is approximately $50,000. Your client does not think he is entitled to any of this because she used her own money to invest and never used any joint assets to buy stocks. You are in a community property state. Your supervisor wants you to find a case in your state or, if there is nothing on point, in one of the other community property states that will be helpful to the client. Brief this case—apply the facts and present your conclusions to your supervising attorney in an interoffice memorandum.

To find a similar fact pattern, go to a legal research site, click on the case law site, enter your state, and enter a word or phrase having to do with marriage as a legal partnership. You can also check out family law court websites on the Internet for assistance with this activity.

Go to Westlaw, Lexis, Loislaw, or any other search engine dealing with case law and statutes to find if your state has a rule or made laws covering this issue. Review the cases applying this law to see how courts in your jurisdiction have applied the pertinent statutes.

Building a Professional Portfolio

PORTFOLIO **EXERCISES**

1. Design a client checklist form listing all possible types of real property and personal property. Divide the personal property part into tangible and intangible sections.

Chapter **seven**

CHILD CUSTODY, VISITATION, AND RIGHTS OF THIRD PARTIES

LEARNING OBJECTIVES

After studying this chapter, you should be able to:

1. Identify the factors considered in determining the child's best interest.

2. Understand the role family relations play in the determination of custody.

3. Be able to draw up a typical parenting plan.

4. Define the term *psychological parent*.

5. Describe the joint legal custody arrangement.

When a family unit is intact, the children reside with the parents in the family home and both parents share the right to make decisions regarding their children's health, education, and welfare. If the family unit dissolves, and husband and wife begin living separately, formal arrangements must be made for the care and custody of the children. This is done either through a stipulated agreement by the parents that is approved of by the court and made an order or through a determination made and ordered by the court when a mutually agreed-on arrangement is not possible. In either case, court orders will be entered and will address the issues of where the children will reside and who will be responsible for making decisions regarding their health, education, and welfare.

A HISTORICAL PERSPECTIVE ON CUSTODY

Throughout history, society's legal systems have used various methods to decide child custody issues. At times, societies and their legal systems have had very "cut and dry" and inflexible rules for awarding custody to one parent or the other upon a marital dissolution.

THE AGE OF PATERNAL DOMINANCE

In ancient civilizations, fathers possessed absolute right to the possession of their children. This right was known as *patria potestas*. Centuries later, at English common law, the father's right of possession still prevailed. In both England and the United States, until the early nineteenth century, according to the law, children were chattels, the private property of their fathers, and if a marriage broke down, the father's superior right to custody was undisputed.

Patria potestas
In ancient civilizations, where fathers possessed absolute right to the possession of their children and could even sell the children or put them to death if desired.

THE TENDER YEARS DOCTRINE

Beginning and throughout the nineteenth century, however, many societal changes took place that shifted the preference from father to mother in custody determinations. The theoretical justification for this preference came to be known as the *tender years doctrine*. The Industrial Revolution played a significant role in this shift. While families lived on and operated the family farm as their source of income, the father occupied the leadership role. The father was almost always physically present with the children and able to supervise their upbringing. With the coming of the factory system, many families moved to cities. The father began to work outside the home and the mother became the manager of the household and the children. By the end of the nineteenth century, with the mother dominant at home and responsible for meeting the children's needs throughout the day, the view developed that a mother's continuing presence was indispensable for the children's physical and emotional well-being. For many years, courts, applying the tender years doctrine, routinely awarded custody to the mother unless the father or another relative seeking custody could establish that the mother was unfit to care for the child.

Tender years doctrine
The theoretical justification for the placing of children with their mother.

The tender years doctrine was based on the assumption that young children were better off being cared for by their mothers. Fathers were not deemed capable of caring for infants and young children and, because of their work, were usually not available. Children of tender years included children age twelve and under, but custody of older children was also usually awarded to the mother. Occasionally, custody of an older child, particularly a son, was placed with the father if that was the child's preference and the mother had difficulty controlling the child.

The practice of routinely granting custody to the mother prevailed throughout the first half of the twentieth century and into the 1960s. However, beginning in the early 1970s, there was a great increase in custody awards to the father. The 1970s also saw the advent of joint custody and split custody rather than *sole custody* by either parent. These changes reflected the decline of the tender years doctrine and the acceptance of the gender-neutral *best interest of the child* standard.

Sole custody
Where one parent has exclusive custody of a child.

Best interest of the child
Standard that opened the contest for custody not only to fathers but also to other potential caregivers when the child's well-being or interests could be best served by such a custody determination.

THE BEST INTEREST STANDARD

The best interest standard began to emerge in the 1960s and 1970s as many societal changes occurred, including an increase in the number of mothers working outside the home. Prior to these decades, when a marriage broke up, the mother was most often a nonworking spouse who in many instances had never held a paying job. The father worked outside the home and was the family's only source of economic support. Upon dissolution of the marriage, the court usually awarded the nonworking spouse alimony. This enabled the wife to maintain the household and remain at home to raise the children to adulthood. Giving custody to fathers was not a viable option as fathers had to work to support themselves, their former spouses, and the minor children.

With the advent of greater and better-paying job opportunities for women, many mothers went to work. In situations where both the husband and wife were considered fit parents, if both worked outside the home, the wife was no longer the undisputed choice for custody. Courts had adhered to the belief that children of tender years always belonged with their mothers because young children needed personal care throughout the day and stay-at-home mothers were available to provide this care. Once mothers went to work and left the children's care to a nanny, a relative, or a day-care center, they no longer presented a more favorable choice for custody than the working father who could engage similar resources to care for the child. The child's interests were no longer necessarily best served by awarding sole custody to the mother. Fathers, who desired custody and who were aware of the changed societal conditions, began to present logical and very persuasive arguments to the court that frequently resulted in custody awards to fathers. At the heart of the successful father's argument was the contention that the children would be better off with their father. Fathers' attorneys, phrasing this concept in a more intellectually sophisticated manner, reminded the court that the best interests of the child should determine the custody disposition and that the interests of their client's child would be best served by placing the child with his or her father.

Figure 7-1 Until the 1970s, custody was traditionally awarded to mothers as a result of the tender years doctrine.

ESB Professional/Shutterstock.

Figure 7-2 After the shift from the tender years doctrine to the best interest standard, fathers began to be awarded custody more often than in the past.

Monkey Business Images/Shutterstock.

By the end of the 1970s the best interest of the child had become a significant factor that most jurisdictions considered. This trend continued and by the 1990s virtually all jurisdictions had abandoned the automatic tender years presumption of maternal custody in favor of identifying what disposition would promote the child's best interests.

Determining the Child's Best Interest

While the best interest of the children remains the preferred standard today, legal and psychological experts differ on the factor or factors to apply in determining best interest.

The discipline of child development and child psychology grew tremendously during the 1960s and 1970s. The knowledge gained from these fields and the criteria that emerged were applied to the making of custodial decisions on a regular basis. Courts increasingly referred the issue of custody to the court's *family relations unit* or *family services division*. In this unit, trained social workers and mental health professionals conducted studies and applied child development and child psychology concepts to make custody and visitation recommendations. Further, working parents frequently employed their own psychologists and psychiatrists to evaluate their children and testify on their behalf in court as ***expert witnesses***.

Family relations unit
Trained social workers who work for the court and conduct studies and apply child development and child psychology concepts to make custody and visitation recommendations; also known as the family services division.

Family services division
See *family relations unit.*

Expert witness
A person with specialized knowledge who is called to testify in court.

The gender-neutral best interest standard may be difficult to define. Some courts have used the primary caretaker rule, or psychological parent, while other jurisdictions have enacted specific factors to be considered when determining best interest in custody cases.

Statutory Factors

State statutory schemes articulate the factors family court judges use in determining the preferable placement of a child in a disputed custody action. An excerpt of Arizona's custody statute illustrates the factors considered in determining the best interest of the child.

Family court judges have broad discretion in resolving issues of child custody and visitation. The court must assess not only a parent's ability to provide a child with the necessities of life such as food, clothing, and shelter, but also their ability to provide nurturing, love, and affection. Certain factors have emerged as essential indicators of whether a certain custodial disposition is in the child's best interest.

Statutes

ARIZONA REVISED STATUTES ANNOTATED (WEST)

25.403. Custody; Best Interest of Child. . . .

A. The court shall determine custody, either originally or upon petition for modification, in accordance with the best interests of the child. The court shall consider all relevant factors, including:

1. The wishes of the child's parent or parents as to custody.
2. The wishes of the child as to the custodian.
3. The interaction and interrelationship of the child with the child's parent or parents, the child's siblings and any other person who may significantly affect the child's best interest.
4. The child's adjustment to home, school and community.
5. The mental and physical health of all individuals involved.
6. Which parent is more likely to allow the child frequent and meaningful continuing contact with the other parent.
7. If one parent, both parents, or neither parent has provided primary care of the child.
8. The nature and extent of coercion or duress used by a parent in obtaining an agreement regarding custody.
9. Whether a parent has complied with Chapter 3 article 5 of this title. . . .

Source: Chapter 4—Legal Decision-Making and Parenting Time, Article 1, Sec 25.403, State of Arizona.

Psychological Parent

Psychological parent
The parent who has had the child since the child's birth and/or who has spent the most meaningful time with the child, has bonded most fully with the child, and who has provided the most psychological nurturing of the child.

Where both parties are equally fit, a court may order a custody study to ascertain which parent is the child's *psychological parent*. Often, the parent who has had the child since the child's birth and/or who has spent the most meaningful time with the child, has bonded most fully with the child, and who has provided the most psychological nurturance to the child is considered the psychological parent. Custody is frequently awarded to the psychological parent because it is considered harmful to wrest the child away from the individual whom the child considers his psychological parent, the one with whom he has the strongest bonds.

Primary Caretaker

Courts frequently decide that custody should be awarded to the child's ***primary caretaker***. The primary caretaker is the individual who has done most of the significant parenting of the child since birth or for the several preceding years. The primary caretaker is usually the child's psychological parent.

Primary caretaker
The individual who has taken on the main responsibility for the daily care, rearing, and nurturing of a child.

The Primary Caretaker Rule An excerpt from the following case illustrates the factors used by courts in identifying a child's "primary caretaker."

DEBRA PASCALE v. JAMES PASCALE

660 A.2D 485 (N.J. 1995)
SUPREME COURT OF NEW JERSEY

. . . In cases of only joint legal custody, the roles that both parents play in their children's lives differ depending on their custodial functions. In common parlance, a parent who does not have physical custody over her child is the "noncustodial parent" and the one with sole residential or physical custody is the "custodial parent." Because those terms fail to describe custodial functions accurately, we adopt today the term *primary caretaker* to refer to the "custodial parent" and the term *secondary caretaker* to refer to the "noncustodial parent." Although both roles create responsibility over children of divorce, the primary caretaker has the greater physical and emotional role. Because the role of "primary caretaker" can be filled by men or women, the concept has gained widespread acceptance in custody determination. . . . Indeed, many state courts often determine custody based on the concept of "primary caretaker.". . .

In one of the earliest cases using the concept of "primary caretaker," the Supreme Court of Appeals of West Virginia articulated the many tasks that make one parent the primary, rather than secondary, caretaker: preparing and planning of meals; bathing, grooming, and dressing; purchasing, cleaning and caring for clothes; medical care, including nursing and general trips to physicians; arranging for social interaction among peers; arranging alternative care, i.e., babysitting or daycare; putting child to bed at night, attending to child in the middle of the night and waking the child in the morning; disciplining; and educating the child in a religious or cultural manner. *Garska, supra,* 278 S.E.2d at 363. . . .

Source: Debra Pascale v. James Pascale, 660 A.2D 485 (N.J. 1995), Supreme Court of New Jersey.

Once the tender years doctrine lost favor and the shift away from always awarding sole custody to the mother occurred, there was another shift, as well, from always awarding custody to only one parent. When both parents worked, sometimes courts believed that both parents should be jointly responsible for the children's financial maintenance and for the children's physical and emotional care, and the joint custody practice began to emerge.

Parents having ***joint custody*** are jointly or equally responsible for the financial, emotional, educational, and health-related needs of their children. They have an equal responsibility and an equal degree of say in deciding how to meet the various needs of their children. Joint custody will only be successful if the parents can communicate effectively, be flexible enough to compromise, and be able to negotiate to arrive at an adequate solution when conflicts arise.

Joint custody
Arrangement in which parents are equally responsible for the financial, emotional, educational, and health-related needs of their children.

All jurisdictions now prefer the belief or presume that joint or shared custody is in the best interest of the children. This preference rests on the presumption that despite the breakdown of the parents' marriage, both parents play a significant role in the well-being of the children.

The trend toward a presumption in favor of joint custody raised concerns among advocates for victims of domestic violence regarding the appropriateness of this arrangement. Under these circumstances, joint custody is not in the children's best interest as it may have an extremely detrimental effect on their emotional and physical health and well-being. States have responded by enacting statutes requiring the court to consider evidence of domestic violence as a factor in custody or access disputes. Some states have even legislated consideration of domestic violence in custody or visitation cases, as illustrated by the following Arizona statute.

Statutes

ARIZONA REVISED STATUTES ANNOTATED (WEST)

25-403 (B) . . . The court shall consider evidence of domestic violence being contrary to the best interests of the child. If the court finds that domestic violence has occurred, the court shall make arrangements for visitation that best protects the child and the abused spouse from further harm. The person who has committed an act of domestic violence has the burden of proving that visitation will not endanger the child or significantly impair the child's emotional development. . . .

Source: Chapter 4—Legal Decision-Making and Parenting Time, Article 1, Sec 25.403B, State of Arizona.

TRADITIONAL CUSTODY ARRANGEMENTS

Physical custody
When a parent has actual bodily possession of the children.

Legal custody
Where both parents are the children's legal guardians and, as such, have the right to make decisions regarding their children's health, education, and welfare.

Parents who reside together enjoy the right to *physical custody* of their children. This right, sometimes referred to as *residential or domiciliary custody*, means that the children live with the parents. The parents also have *legal custody* of the children, which means they have the right to make major decisions on behalf of their children regarding health, education, and religious upbringing. When the marital relationship breaks down, the parents no longer enjoy these rights simultaneously. Crafting a custody arrangement involves structuring the rights of the parents in arrangements that are in the children's best interest.

If the parties cannot reach an agreement on custody, the court will decide what is in the children's best interest based on the testimony of the parties, lay witnesses, and experts such as mental health counselors who perform *custody evaluations*. A custody evaluation is conducted by either a psychologist or psychiatrist who will interview both parties and the children and make a recommendation regarding what type of custody arrangement is in the children's best interest. The following custody arrangements address a combination of these rights. The court may award a custody evaluation or the parties may request one by filing a motion with the court. Typically, both parents share the cost of the evaluation.

If cost is an issue for the clients, most family courts have state-employed counselors available to conduct such evaluations, the cost of which is paid by the taxpayers. They are often referred to a family relations, family services, or other equivalent counselor used in a particular jurisdiction. They conduct custody and visitation evaluations and make them available to the court and the parties once they are completed. Very often, cases are resolved after reviewing the evaluations. If there is no resolution, the evaluation is admitted into evidence at trial; the family services officer is called to the witness stand and is subject to questioning by the parties.

In cases involving child custody, the court may appoint or the parties may request the appointment of an attorney for the minor children or a guardian ad litem. The attorney for the children represents their wishes and the guardian ad litem represents what is in the children's best interest. When a guardian ad litem has not been appointed, the attorney for the children represents not only the children's wishes but also their best interests. When these two roles conflict, the attorney must ask for the appointment of a guardian ad litem, or guardian for the legal proceedings, to represent the children's best interest. An example would be a child's attorney representing an abused child who wished to live with the abusive parent. In this case, the lawyer must advocate the child's wishes but ask for a guardian ad litem to advance the best interest of the child.

Joint Legal Custody

Joint legal custody is presumed to be in the best interest of the children because both parents are involved in their lives. When parents have joint legal custody, they both share in making the major decisions in the lives of the children. This is especially important for fathers. Mothers are often awarded custody of the children, and fathers often feel left out of the decision-making process. While both parents share in making decisions regarding the children's upbringing, the child resides with one parent. The noncustodial parent has visitation or access, frequently during the week as well as weekends and summer and school vacations. *Access* is the child's right to see the noncustodial parent. Nevertheless, the children's primary residence is with the custodial parent. In this instance, because the custodial parent has expenses for the children's daily needs, the joint but noncustodial parent will be ordered to pay child support to the custodial parent for the financial maintenance of the children.

Access
The child's right to see the noncustodial parent.

When parents have joint legal custody with the child or children's primary residence vested with one parent, sometimes the access rights of the other parent are exercised under an arrangement known as *nesting*. Under nesting, when the noncustodial parent has access to the child or children through overnight visits, on alternating weekends, and for some part of the school and summer vacations, the child or children remain in their primary residence and the noncustodial parent moves in for the designated period of time, while the custodial parent leaves the home and resides elsewhere during that time. While nesting is a wonderful way to keep the child grounded and in a stable physical environment, it takes two special parents to make this arrangement both pleasant and practical for all concerned.

Nesting
An arrangement where the access afforded to the noncustodial parent occurs at the child or children's primary residence. During the access period, the noncustodial parent moves in with the child or children while the custodial parent leaves the residence for that period of time.

Joint Legal and Physical Custody (Shared Custody)

In *joint legal and physical custody* (sometimes referred to as *shared physical custody*), both parents make the major decisions regarding the children's upbringing and they share residential custody. This means that the children reside with each parent approximately half of the time. This arrangement succeeds most often when the parents reside geographically close to each other and close to the children's school, church, doctor, and site of recreational activities. Under shared custody arrangements, the children reside with one parent for a certain amount of days per week and a certain number of days with the other. Typically, neither parent pays the other parent child support because both parents share expenses. When one parent's income is significantly higher than the other, however, the more affluent parent may give the other parent money to cover the children's needs or assume a greater share of the more expensive of the children's needs.

Joint legal and physical custody
Arrangement in which parents are equally responsible for the financial, emotional, educational, and health-related needs of their children.

Shared physical custody
An arrangement where parents have both joint legal custody and joint physical custody and the child resides with one parent for a certain number of days a week and a certain number of days with the other parent.

Sole Legal and Physical Custody

Parents with sole custody, or *custodial parents*, have the right to make all major decisions regarding the children's health, education, and religious upbringing as

Custodial parent
The parent with whom the child primarily resides.

Noncustodial parent
The parent who does not have the child living with him or her on a full-time basis.

well as have the children living in the home with them. *Noncustodial parents* have visitation or access rights as well as the ability to make day-to-day decisions when the children are in their care.

As stated earlier, all states presume that a joint custody arrangement is in the best interest of the children. A parent who can present strong evidence to the court that joint custody is not in the children's best interest may rebut this presumption. If there is child abuse or substance abuse or the parents harbor great animosity toward each other, making every decision a struggle, joint custody will not serve the children's best interest. In these types of situations, the best interest of the children will be better served by awarding one parent sole custody and the other parent visitation or access, provided that the custodial parent's authority will not thwart or impair the noncustodial parent's relationship with the children.

Split Custody

Split custody
A custody arrangement where one parent has sole custody for part of the calendar year each year, and the other parent has sole custody for the remaining part of the year.

A split custodial arrangement is less frequently used than other types of custody dispositions, and most often occurs when parents live geographically distant from one another, such as when one parent lives in New York while the other parent resides in California. Under the practice of *split custody*, one parent has sole custody of the child for a part of the calendar year each year, and the other parent has sole custody for the remaining portion of the year. Sometimes under a split custody arrangement, the split will be equal; each parent will have custody of the child for six months. During that time period, the parent will have sole and complete physical custody of the child.

Sometimes split custody means that one parent has sole physical custody of the child during the school year and the other parent has sole physical custody of the child for the summer months. Each parent has full authority to make decisions regarding the child's health, education, discipline, recreation, and welfare. This arrangement differs from joint custody with shared physical custody in that parents with joint custody with shared physical custody must consult the other custodial parent regarding at least major decisions regarding health, education, and welfare. For instance, if while a child was residing for the school year with the mother under joint custody, physical or otherwise, the mother decided to have the child undergo elective surgery for removal of tonsils and adenoids, and if the father who had joint custody did not agree with this decision, the parents would have to reach some type of agreement before surgery could be performed. Under a split custodial arrangement, the parent enjoying physical custody time could have the child undergo elective surgery without the legal consent of the other parent.

Split custody was actually a compromise before the 1970s. For several decades during the first half of the twentieth century, courts entered orders for a split custodial arrangement in instances either where both parents requested it or where the court felt that such a "Solomon" type of disposition was the fairest under the circumstances. In 1960s and 1970s, this arrangement occurred mainly when parents lived in different parts of the country or in different countries. Split custody can be very disruptive and undermine the child's need for continuity and stability in his or her relationships and environment. This type of arrangement is used very little today. Today, most, if not all, courts apply the best interest of the child standard to decisions regarding custody, and the current prevailing view is that split custody is detrimental to a child's best interest.

Another type of split custody arrangement may involve the splitting of siblings. One parent would be awarded custody of one or more children, and the other parent would have custody of the others. Courts generally frown on splitting up siblings. Keeping brothers and sisters together provides the children with some

Figure 7-3 Courts prefer not to break up siblings when a marriage dissolves because keeping brothers and sisters together provides children with some level of stability during this rough period.

Wong sze yuen/Shutterstock.

level of stability at a time when the breakup of their parents is traumatic for them to handle. There are some instances, however, where splitting the siblings may actually be in the best interest of the children, as one parent may be better able to control, discipline, or care for a particular child.

RIGHTS OF ACCESS

A noncustodial parent has the right to frequently spend time with the child unless the court finds that the access, formerly known as visitation, in some way endangers the child's emotional, mental, moral, or physical health. Family courts will award *access rights* to a parent in this position. The parties may agree to an access schedule, or it may be determined by the courts if the parties reach a stalemate.

There are two types of access schedules: *reasonable rights of access* and a *fixed schedule*. Reasonable access is a very flexible arrangement that requires the parties to work out their own schedule. This works best when the parties can reasonably coordinate access periods between themselves. This requires the ability to communicate and the willingness to put aside their differences for the benefit of the children. Some divorce decrees will include this provision, and as soon as the ink dries, the parties are back in court. Sometimes the custodial parent will set up obstacles to the noncustodial parent's access rights. The noncustodial parent may also disrupt the "reasonable" access schedule by showing up at the custodial parent's home on inconvenient days and times (especially when the custodial parent becomes romantically involved with someone else!). At this point, one of the

Access Rights
The right of a noncustodial parent to frequently spend time with the child unless the court finds that visitation in some way endangers the child's emotional, mental, moral, or physical health.

Reasonable rights of access
A very flexible arrangement that requires the parties to work out their own schedule for visitation with children.

Fixed schedule
Definite dates and time frames set aside for the purpose of allowing a noncustodial parent access to the child.

parties returns to court for the purpose of enforcing access or modifying the existing "reasonable" rights of access to a more definite schedule.

Fixed schedules are definite dates and time frames set aside for the purpose of allowing a noncustodial parent to spend time the child. Fixed schedules should spell out the days and hours on which a noncustodial parent may see the child. In addition, it is also a good idea to deal with holidays, birthdays, vacations, reasonable hours for phone calls, and other details so as to avoid conflict between the parties.

In some hostile divorces, the law office will often hear complaints from the client on the day following an access period. For example, custodial parents may call screaming about the noncustodial parent's failure to either pick up or return the child on time. In the latter scenario, some custodial parents will go so far as to call the police when the noncustodial parent is only delayed by several minutes! Custodial parents may also complain that the child looks dirty, has not eaten, or acts out when returning home. Some go further by making allegations regarding child sexual abuse. Noncustodial parents may raise similar concerns, in addition to complaints about the child not being available for access because the custodial parent has taken it upon himself not to make the child available.

Unsupervised access

A type of visitation that permits a noncustodial parent to freely visit with the child without others present.

Supervised access

A type of visitation that limits or restricts a parent's visitation rights.

There is also a difference between unsupervised access and supervised access. *Unsupervised access* permits a noncustodial parent to freely visit the child without others present, wherever the parent reasonably wishes to take the child and engage in child-appropriate activities. *Supervised access* limits a parent's rights in that it dictates restrictions surrounding the periods of access. Supervised access may be ordered in cases where a noncustodial parent has certain problems that bring into question the parent's ability to properly supervise the child. Parents who have substance abuse problems, mental or physical issues, a history of domestic violence, or are too immature to care for the child on their own may be required to have another person present during the access periods at a designated time and place. This person can sometimes be the custodial parent unless there is a history of domestic violence or problems with the parents' interaction. In this case, a neutral third party would be the best solution.

Virtual Access

Utah was the first jurisdiction, and Wisconsin the second, to enact virtual visitation or access legislation. Other states are in the process of drafting or proposing similar legislation. *Virtual visitation* is a court order allowing a parent in a divorce to communicate and maintain a relationship with the children through the use of technologies such as Internet video conferencing, web cams, e-mail, instant messaging, or any other type of wired or wireless technology, such as video phone calls like FaceTime on iPhones and iPads. In cases where the parents are divorced, it allows the noncustodial parent to maintain contact with the child between actual physical periods of access.

Virtual access is used as a supplement to live visitation and telephone contact. It is also not a justification for relocating a child to another state or for reducing the amount of live access with a noncustodial parent. Opponents feel that it will be used as a replacement for live access/visitation as technology becomes more popular. Virtual access is not for everyone, as it requires a certain amount of technological savvy. A family court that orders virtual access/visitation will also have to determine who will pay for the equipment and installation.

Governor Jim Doyle signed Wisconsin's virtual visitation statute into law on March 22, 2006. The Wisconsin statute includes a legislative preamble explaining the new statute, which reads as follows:

Wisconsin Senate Bill 244[1]

ANALYSIS BY THE LEGISLATIVE REFERENCE BUREAU

Under current law, in a divorce or legal separation in which a minor child is involved, and in a paternity action, the court must grant sole legal custody of the child to one parent or joint legal custody to both parents together. In addition, the court must allocate between the parents periods of physical placement, which is the condition under which the child is physically placed with the parent and the parent has the right and responsibility during that time to care for, and make routine daily decisions concerning, the child. The court may deny parent periods of physical placement with the child only if being physically placed with the parent would endanger the child's physical, mental, or emotional health.

This bill provides that, if the court grants periods of physical placement to both parents, the court may grant to a parent a reasonable amount of electronic communication at reasonable hours during the other parent's periods of physical placement with the child. Electronic communication is defined as time during which a parent and his or her child communicate by using various types of communication tools, such as the telephone, electronic mail, instant messaging, and video conferencing or other wired or wireless technologies via the Internet. The basis for granting electronic communication is whether it is in the child's best interest and whether equipment for providing electronic communication is reasonably available to both parents. Electronic communication may be used only to supplement, and not as a substitute or replacement for, the physical placement that a parent has with the child.

The bill provides that a parenting plan that a party files with the court before a pretrial conference when legal custody or physical placement is contested must include any electronic communication a parent is requesting and must indicate whether equipment for providing electronic communication is reasonably available to both parents. The bill also provides that, if a parent is proposing to move with the child and the other parent objects to the move, the court may not use the availability of electronic communication as a factor in support of a modification of physical placement or a refusal to prohibit the parent from moving with the child.

The people of the state of Wisconsin, represented in senate and assembly, do enact as follows:

SECTION 1. 767.001 (1g) of the statutes is created to read:

767.001 **(1g)** "Electronic communication" means time during which a parent and his or her child communicate by using communication tools such as the telephone, electronic mail, instant messaging, video conferencing or other wired or wireless technologies via the Internet, or another medium of communication.

SECTION 2. 767.23 (1) (ap) of the statutes is created to read:

767.23 **(1)** (ap) Upon the request of a party, granting periods of electronic communication to a party in a manner consistent with s. 767.24. The court or circuit court commissioner shall make a determination under this paragraph within 30 days after the request for a temporary order regarding periods of electronic communication is filed.

SECTION 3. 767.24 (1m) (L) of the statutes is amended to read:

767.24 **(1m)** (L) Whether and how the child will be able to contact the other parent when the child has physical placement with the parent providing the parenting plan, and what electronic communication, if any, the parent is seeking.

---

[1] 2005 Senate Bill 244, State of Wisconsin.

SECTION 4. 767.24 (1m) (Lm) of the statutes is created to read:

767.24 **(1m)** (Lm) Whether equipment for providing electronic communication is reasonably available to both parents.

SECTION 5. 767.24 (4) (e) of the statutes is created to read:

767.24 **(4)** (e) If the court grants periods of physical placement to more than one parent, the court may grant to either or both parents a reasonable amount of electronic communication at reasonable hours during the other parent's periods of physical placement with the child. Electronic communication with the child may be used only to supplement a parent's periods of physical placement with the child. Electronic communication may not be used as a replacement or as a substitute for a parent's periods of physical placement with the child. Granting a parent electronic communication with the child during the other parent's periods of physical placement shall be based on whether it is in the child's best interest and whether equipment for providing electronic communication is reasonably available to both parents.

SECTION 6. 767.327 (5m) of the statutes is renumbered 767.327 (5m) (intro.) and amended to read:

767.327 **(5m)** DISCRETIONARY Other FACTORS TO CONSIDER. (intro.) In making a determination under sub. (3), the: (a) The court may consider the child's adjustment to the home, school, religion and community.

SECTION 7. 767.327 (5m) (b) of the statutes is created to read:

767.327 **(5m)** (b) The court may not use the availability of electronic communication as a factor in support of a modification of a physical placement order or in support of a refusal to prohibit a move.

SECTION 8. Initial applicability.

(1) PARENTING PLANS. The treatment of section 767.24 (1m) (Lm) of the statutes first applies to parenting plans filed with the court on the effective date of this subsection.

Parenting Plans

Studies from the mental health community conclude that the children of divorce benefit tremendously when the parents work together. Even though the parties can no longer live together as husband and wife, they still are in a co-parenting relationship if the marriage produced children. When parties share children in common, it will be impossible for them to go their separate ways unless it is a case of complete abandonment. The current trend in the United States is to encourage divorcing parents to work together in their children's best interest and focus their attention on the children's needs.

More states are requiring parents to submit parenting plans to the court. A *parenting plan* is an agreement created by both parents detailing how they will continue their parenting responsibilities toward their children after their marriage is dissolved. A parenting plan addresses the following:

Parenting plan
An agreement created by both parents detailing how they will continue their parenting responsibilities toward their children after their marriage is dissolved.

1. **Decision Making.** This section delineates which parent will make the major decisions in the lives of the children. States are beginning to use the term *decision-making responsibility* in place of the word *custody* and the terms *access* or *parenting time* in place of the term *visitation*. Parenting plans reflect this new language, so it is important to become familiar with these terms.

2. **Children's Schedule.** In this section, the parents structure the children's schedule, defining how, where, and with whom the children will spend their week, including weekends, vacations, and holidays. This section may

also include details as to pickup and drop-off responsibilities, telephone access, notifying the other parent when changes need to be made in the schedule, giving the other parent right of first refusal when a babysitter is needed, and provisions on dealing with school cancellations, teacher conferences, or illness.

3. **Resolving Future Disputes.** The answer to custody and visitation disputes has often been to resolve them in a court of law. States that have adopted parenting plans discourage litigation and encourage mediation or counseling before intervening in a postjudgment dispute. In this section of the plan, the parties must outline how they will resolve future disputes regarding custody and visitation as well as who will assist them in the process. Will they seek a mediator, mental health counselor, minister, or other third party to help them resolve their differences amicably? Litigation is viewed as a last resort.

4. **Modification and Periodic Review.** Children's needs change as they age. A parenting plan that addresses the needs of an infant will be inadequate for a teenager. The parties may wish to build in provisions for periodic review of the plan to accommodate the changing needs of growing children. The parties should also address how they will deal with changes in life circumstances such as remarriage, cohabitation, relocation, and child-related issues. The plan may also include a general statement of cooperation and mutual respect between the parents.

Once the parenting plan is complete and signed by the parties, the court reviews it to determine if it is in the best interest of the children. While courts are in favor of parties reaching an agreement by their own accord, any provisions dealing with the welfare of the children must pass court scrutiny.

Mandatory Parenting Education Programs

Most states require divorcing parents with minor children to attend *mandatory parenting education programs*. They generally consist of several group sessions with a mental health professional approved by the state, which mandates attendance by the parents in divorce cases. The goal of the program is to educate parents on the effects of divorce on the children. They also focus on the children's emotional well-being and how the parents promote the children's emotional health by reassuring them that the divorce was not their fault and that their parents still love them. Parents are also educated on how to help the children through the transition and how to avoid hurtful or negative behaviors that may scar the children emotionally, and they are advised to keep children out of their conflicts. Following is an example of Minnesota's parenting education program statute:

Minnesota Statutes 518.157—Parent Education Program In Proceedings Involving Children[2]

- **Subdivision 1.** Implementation; administration. By January 1, 1998, the chief judge of each judicial district or a designee shall implement one or more parent education programs within the judicial district for the purpose of educating parents about the impact that divorce, the restructuring of families, and judicial proceedings have upon children and families; methods for preventing parenting time conflicts; and dispute

---

[2]2012 Minnesota Statutes, Chapter 518, Section 157, Minnesota State Legislature.

resolution options. The chief judge of each judicial district or a designee may require that children attend a separate education program designed to deal with the impact of divorce upon children as part of the parent education program. Each parent education program must enable persons to have timely and reasonable access to education sessions.

- **Subd. 2.** Minimum standards; plan. The Minnesota Supreme Court should promulgate minimum standards for the implementation and administration of a parent education program. The chief judge of each judicial district or a designee shall submit a plan to the Minnesota conference of chief judges for their approval that is designed to implement and administer a parent education program in the judicial district. The plan must be consistent with the minimum standards promulgated by the Minnesota Supreme Court.

- **Subd. 3.** Attendance. In a proceeding under this chapter where custody or parenting time is contested, the parents of a minor child shall attend a minimum of eight hours in an orientation and education program that meets the minimum standards promulgated by the Minnesota Supreme Court. In all other proceedings involving custody, support, or parenting time the court may order the parents of a minor child to attend a parent education program. The program shall provide the court with names of persons who fail to attend the parent education program as ordered by the court. Persons who are separated or contemplating involvement in a dissolution, paternity, custody, or parenting time proceeding may attend a parent education program without a court order. Unless otherwise ordered by the court, participation in a parent education program must begin within 30 days after the first filing with the court or as soon as practicable after that time based on the reasonable availability of classes for the program for the parent. Parent education programs must offer an opportunity to participate at all phases of a pending or postdecree proceeding. Upon request of a party and a showing of good cause, the court may excuse the party from attending the program. If past or present domestic abuse, as defined in chapter 518B, is alleged, the court shall not require the parties to attend the same parent education sessions and shall enter an order setting forth the manner in which the parties may safely participate in the program.

- **Subd. 4.** Sanctions. The court may impose sanctions upon a parent for failure to attend or complete a parent education program as ordered.

- **Subd. 5.** Confidentiality. Unless all parties agree in writing, statements made by a party during participation in a parent education program are inadmissible as evidence for any purpose, including impeachment. No record may be made regarding a party's participation in a parent education program, except a record of attendance at and completion of the program as required under this section. Instructors shall not disclose information regarding an individual participant obtained as a result of participation in a parent education program. Parent education instructors may not be subpoenaed or called as witnesses in court proceedings.

- **Subd. 6.** Fee. Except as provided in this subdivision, each person who attends a parent education program shall pay a fee to defray the cost of the program. A party who qualifies for waiver of filing fees under section 563.01 is exempt from paying the parent education program fee and the court shall waive the fee or direct its payment under section 563.01. Program providers shall implement a sliding fee scale.

Child's Preference

Some parents have the mistaken belief that a child's preference is the determining factor in a custody dispute. Courts are well aware that parents may pressure children, shower them with gifts, or avoid disciplining them in an effort to win their favor in a custody fight. While courts will consider the child's wishes as to whom she would prefer as a custodian, this is only one factor in a list of many that must be balanced in the best interest equation. States vary in terms of the age at which they will consider the child's wishes or the maturity level necessary for the child to form an intelligent decision.

The Right to Decide The *Harbin* case illustrates Georgia's child preference statute, which allows a child of fourteen years of age the right to decide his custodian, unless that custodian is deemed to be unfit.

ALICE JACKSON HARBIN v. ALLEN THOMAS HARBIN

238 Ga. 109, 230 S.E.2d 889 (Ga. 1976)
Supreme Court of Georgia

Per curiam.

This is an appeal from the denial of a petition to change custody. It was brought by the appellant-mother against the appellee-father who had been granted custody in a divorce action in 1972. There are three sons aged 15, 14 and 12 years. This appeal involves only the elder two children who have elected to live with the appellant. . . .

In the divorce action the mother was found to be unfit to have custody. A previous petition to change custody was denied in 1974 with a finding that there was no evidence of the mother's rehabilitation. . . .

Appellant contends that since her children over 14 years of age had elected to live with her, the trial court erred in ruling that she had the burden of persuasion as to her fitness to have custody. Appellant concedes that absent such an election by a child over 14 years of age, the moving party has the burden of showing a change of conditions materially affecting the welfare of the child. However, it is argued that once a 14-year-old child makes an election to live with one parent, the other parent has the burden of showing the selected parent is unfit to have custody. Appellant relies on Code Ann. § 74-107 which provides, ". . . where the child has reached the age of 14 years, such child shall have the right to select the parent with whom such child desires to live and such selection shall be controlling unless the parent so selected is determined not to be a fit and proper person to have the custody of said child." Code Ann. § 30-127 contains the same provision. . . .

. . . The mother who was the parent selected by the children presented evidence of her fitness to have custody. The father who has custody of the children presented evidence of the mother's unfitness by introducing the record of their 1972 divorce action and the 1974 judgment finding no evidence of rehabilitation. In our opinion the critical issue here is whether the 1972 divorce record and the later 1974 decree are, as contended in enumeration of error #3, inadmissible as evidence of the mother's unfitness. If this evidence is inadmissible then there is no evidence of the mother's unfitness and she is entitled to custody under Code Ann.§ 74-107 and Code Ann.§ 30-127.

In *Adams v. Adams,* supra, it is stated, "It is not a new or novel concept that a minor child may well be capable of making a wise selection. . . . Under the Act of 1962 (Ga.L.1962, pp. 713–715) [Amendment to Code Ann. § 74-107 and Code Ann. § 30-127] no parental right of custody by judgment or decree can defeat the right of a child reaching 14 years of age 'to select the parent with whom such child desires to live.' " This case together with a careful reading of the 1962 Act, which is now

continued

incorporated into Code Ann. § 30-127, persuades us that a child of 14 years or more was mature enough to select the parent with whom he desired to live and that this right of selection was controlling despite previous adjudications of unfitness. Therefore, it is our conclusion that such child's right of selection can only be defeated by a showing of present unfitness. . . . Accordingly, there is no evidence of the present unfitness of the appellant-mother to have custody. The judgment of the trial court must be reversed. The case is remanded for further hearing to permit the appellee to present evidence of appellant's present unfitness to have custody of her two children over 14 years of age.

Judgment reversed.

Source: Alice Jackson Harbin v. Allen Thomas Harbin, 238 GA. 109, 230 S.E.2D 889 (GA. 1976), Supreme Court of Georgia.

Parental Misconduct

Parental fault or misconduct is not a factor in deciding custody unless the parent's behavior affects the best interest of the children. The court looks at the parent's conduct and determines if such conduct is a danger to the health and welfare of the children. For example:

- A parent's religious beliefs are not a basis for granting or denying custody unless religious practices such as excessive corporal punishment, prolonged prayer or meditation services, excessive door-to-door solicitation, or avoidance of medical treatment are involved.
- An adulterous parent may not be a very good spouse, but the act of adultery alone is not enough to deny a parent custody or visitation.
- A particular mental or physical health problem does not automatically render a parent unfit. The court will focus on how the parent's particular condition affects his or her ability to provide the necessary care and supervision for the child. In cases of a parent coping with mental health issues, it is not enough to claim that a parent is unfit because he or she takes medication or sees a therapist. The opposing parent must prove that the emotional and psychiatric disorder affects the best interest of the children. An allegation that a parent is unfit because they take medication or see a therapist may backfire; the court may view this as a responsible act on behalf of a parent dealing with mental health issues.
- Cohabitation, remarriage, or a parent's dating may not be grounds for terminating custody or visitation unless the parent's new partner abuses the child or the parent or engages in other behavior that puts the child at risk.
- A parent's consumption of drugs, alcohol, or other addictive substances may result in loss of custody if the behavior presents a danger to the children. In the case of *DeMatteo v. DeMatteo*, 194 Misc.2d 640, 749 N.Y.S.2d 671 (2002), a 14-year-old child requested that his mother be prohibited from exposing him to cigarette smoking during her court-ordered visitation. The issue before the court was:

  Should the court take judicial notice: (1) that environmental tobacco smoke is a carcinogen; (2) that environmental tobacco smoke causes respiratory infections in children; (3) that environmental tobacco smoke causes asthma; (4) that environmental tobacco smoke causes coronary heart disease; and (5) that childhood exposure to environmental tobacco smoke causes increased risk of lung cancer? (Case of DeMatteo v. DeMatteo, 194 Misc.2d 640, 749 N.Y.S.2d 671 (2002), 641)

The New York Supreme Court held:

(1) The court takes judicial notice that environmental tobacco smoke is a carcinogen and causes lung cancer in otherwise healthy nonsmokers and that the children of smoking parents suffer a higher incidence of respiratory infections and smaller rates of increases in lung functions. The court declines to take judicial notice of any other questions presented.

(2) The plaintiff or any other party may introduce evidence to refute this holding at a hearing or trial. Any party seeking to refute the matter judicially noticed will have the burden of proof. Each party will have the burden of proof regarding any proposed visitation scheme that they propound.

(3) Pending a hearing or trial, the defendant's house where the child spends the majority of his time will remain a smoke-free home. The plaintiff will not smoke in her home 24 hours prior to scheduled visitations. There shall be no smoking in either parties' residence or automobile in Nicholas' presence. All parties shall have thirty days to request a hearing/trial; if no such request is received, this further decision/second interim order shall become final. (DeMatteo v. DeMatteo, 194 Misc.2d 640, 749 N.Y.S.2d 671 (2002), 642)

- A parent's sexual preference may impact a court's decision regarding custody depending on the jurisdiction and the personal views of the presiding judge as well as attorneys involved in the case. Many gay parents all over the country have lost custody of their children due to their sexual preference, on the basis that their sexual preference in and of itself is contrary to the best interest of the children. Denying gay parents custody still takes place even in states that do not condone such discriminatory standards. Many courts, however, focus on whether the parent's conduct has a detrimental impact on the children.

Mother's Sexual Preference In the *Charpentier* case, although the mother did not contest a decree granting custody to the father, she did dispute the financial orders entered by the trial court, claiming that the lower court was unduly influenced by her lifestyle. This case illustrates the trial court's concern with the effect of the mother's lifestyle and her same-sex partner's mental illness on the children.

REAL J. F. CHARPENTIER v. CATHY A. CHARPENTIER

206 CONN. 150, 536 A.2D 948 (CONN. 1998)
SUPREME COURT OF CONNECTICUT

SHEA, J.

. . . The parties were married on October 2, 1967. During the marriage five children were born, ranging in age from five to twelve at the time of judgment. The marriage was dissolved on August 22, 1986, by the Honorable Joseph Bogdanski, state trial referee, acting as the trial court. The trial court awarded the plaintiff husband, Real J. F. Charpentier, custody of the five children, and granted a right of reasonable visitation to the defendant wife. The defendant has not contested the custody decree. . . .

. . . A major contention of the defendant is that the trial court's financial orders were impermissibly influenced by her admitted lesbian sexual preference. We conclude that the trial court's financial orders were not so premised, but instead

continued

reasonably reflected the economic burden imposed on the plaintiff by the custody decree as the parent primarily responsible for raising five young children.

The defendant does not dispute engaging in an adulterous relationship with another woman, M, before the parties' separation. In December, 1984, while the plaintiff was hospitalized for seven days for viral pneumonia, the defendant moved M into the family home to live there amidst the five children. When the plaintiff returned home to recuperate, the defendant would leave each night to spend time with M. In February, 1985, the plaintiff moved out of the house. Within one day, the defendant had invited M again to live in the house with her and the children.

There is some indication in the record that the trial court might have been influenced by the defendant's lesbian sexual preference when it awarded custody of the children to their father, although the trial court was also much concerned with the abusive behavior of M toward the children. The trial court stated: "In spite of the dissolution action, there does not appear to be hostility or anger displayed by the parties to each other, and it is apparent that both parents deeply love their children. It further appears that both parents are capable of raising five children alone. The problem here is the presence in the homestead of a third party. The children all blame her for the breakup of their parent's marriage. They feel they are second best to her, and feel that their mother prefers to spend more time with her than with them. They have spoken of their concerns regarding the open display of affection between two lesbian women in the home and their desire not to have this done in front of their friends. As the children grow older they will have to struggle with a home life that is quite different from those of their peers. M has displayed difficulty in dealing with stress by impulsively attempting suicide or requesting in-patient hospitalization. The children have complained of her yelling at them and slapping them. It is not clear at this time how much stress and tension she can tolerate, and a household of five children can produce a chaotic environment."

We construe the references in the memorandum of decision to the defendant's lesbian relationship as indicating concern of the trial court not with her sexual orientation per se but with its effect upon the children, who had observed in the home inappropriate displays of physical affection between their mother and M, who had twice been institutionalized for mental problems, had been diagnosed as a schizophrenic, and had a history of suicide attempts, to continue to reside in the home with the children, especially when left alone to care for them. In awarding custody, the trial court ordered that M not be present during the defendant's visitation. . . .

Source: 206 CONN. 150, 536 A.2D 948. (CONN. 1998), Supreme Court of Connecticut.

Parental alienation
Psychological manipulation that destroys the child's once-positive relationship with that parent.

Parental Alienation Syndrome (PAS)
A child's response to this psychological manipulation that destroys the child's once-positive relationship with that parent.

- Behaviors such as speaking badly about the other parent in front of the child; discussing the reasons behind the breakdown of the marital relationship; false allegations of child sexual, physical, and emotional abuse; blaming the other parent for the financial problems now encountered by the custodial parent; using the child to carry negative messages to the other parent; and asking the child to choose between parents are called *parental alienation*. A child's response to this psychological manipulation may destroy the child's once-positive relationship with that parent. The psychological literature refers to the child's response as *parental alienation syndrome (PAS)*. If a custodial parent deliberately disparages and badmouths the noncustodial parent to the point where the child no longer wants to visit or spend time with that parent, the courts may intervene by awarding custody to the noncustodial parent. Diagnosis of PAS is made by a mental health professional who may be called into court as an expert witness. An expert opposing the diagnosis may also be called to the stand, resulting in a battle of the experts. Not all jurisdictions accept PAS as a recognized psychiatric condition as it is not set forth in the American

Psychiatric Association's current *Diagnostic and Statistical Manual* (*DSM-IV*). However, many of those courts will still make a factual finding of parental alienation and act accordingly.

- In 1974, Congress passed the *Child Abuse Prevention and Treatment Act (CAPTA)*, 42 U.S.C.A. Section 5101. Prior to the passage of this law, child abuse remained in the closet. The act required the states to adopt child abuse prevention laws or risk losing federal funding. Professionals who deal with children are mandated to report suspected child abuse and receive immunity for reports of suspected child abuse or neglect made in good faith. Mandated reporters include medical professionals, school personnel, police officers, mental health professionals, social workers, and members of the clergy. There is a lot of pressure on professionals to report suspected child abuse. Many feel that it is better to err on the side of caution rather than risk the possibility that their failure to report could result in a child's continued mistreatment or even death. Given this environment, a parent falsely alleging child abuse knows that such a claim will get an immediate reaction, not only from mandated reporters but also the court system. There are, unfortunately, many divorce litigants who falsely accuse their spouses of child sexual abuse. The mental health profession calls this *SAID*, which stands for *sexual allegations in divorce*. SAID is a type of parental alienation syndrome and occurs when one parent uses psychological manipulation to encourage the child to fabricate allegations of child sexual abuse. States have passed legislation to punish false accusers; however, the small penalties associated with such activity pale in comparison to the consequences suffered by someone who is wrongly accused. Great damage is also done to true victims of child sexual abuse, who may be looked upon with greater suspicion.

- A client who feels he or she is being falsely accused of child sexual abuse should retain counsel immediately. Generally, the state child protection department or police initiate an investigation. It is very important for clients to be represented at every stage of the case, including administrative intervention, no matter how benign it may look, especially if the parties are going through a divorce.

- **In the Matter of John A. v. Bridget M, 791 N.Y.S.2d 421, 16 AD.3D 234 (1st DEPT 2005) Appellate Division of the Supreme Court of New York First Department. (2005)[3]**

"Aylsworth, and the Twins" On June 1, 2004, the issue of parental alienation made national news in the case of Bridget Marks and John Aylsworth. Marks, an actress and former Playboy model, had an affair with a married casino executive named John Aylsworth. The affair resulted in Marks giving birth to twin daughters and a bitter custody fight. The trial court gave custody to Aylsworth on the basis that Marks sought to prevent the four-year-old twins from seeing their father by falsely accusing him of child sexual abuse, and that the mother had coached the children to make these allegations. The appellate court, however, returned custody of the children to Marks.

Reproductive Technology and Custody Disputes

Traditionally, the children in the center of a custody battle were conceived through the sexual union of their parents. As if the courts did not have enough problems deciphering these cases, enter the world of creating families through reproductive technology. Issues involving in vitro fertilization, artificial insemination, and

Child Abuse Prevention and Treatment Act of 1974 (CAPTA)
Federal government's most comprehensive effort to address the issue of child protection that provides federal funding to states to support child protective services that respond to cases of abuse, neglect, and sexual abuse.

SAID, or sexual allegations in divorce
An acronym for "sexual allegations in divorce"; a type of parental alienation syndrome that occurs when one parent uses psychological manipulation to encourage the child to fabricate allegations of child sexual abuse.

---

[3]791 N.Y.S.2a 421, 16 A.D.3a 324 (1st Dept 2005), Appellate Division of the Supreme Court of New York, First Department, New York State Unified Court System.

surrogacy are increasingly making their way into the family courts. The need to reproduce and create a family is not only an avenue sought by heterosexual couples who cannot conceive, but also by gay and lesbian couples who wish to have children but find procreation impossible due to biological impediments.

In vitro fertilization

The process of conceiving a human embryo outside the biological parents' physical body.

In Vitro Fertilization ***In vitro fertilization*** is the process of conceiving a human embryo outside the biological parents' physical bodies. Eggs or ova are removed from the female, sperm is taken from the father, and the two substances are joined together in a petri dish and then transplanted into the mother's or surrogate mother's uterus to facilitate the natural development of the fetus. A nonmedical term used to describe a child conceived through in vitro fertilization is *test tube baby*.

Sometimes, the embryos are frozen for later use. This practice can lead to problems later on. There are legal issues associated with in vitro fertilization, especially when the couple decides to divorce. While it is relatively easy to divide up fine china, furniture, and knickknacks, it is not so easy to divide the frozen embryos. If the mother chooses to have the embryos implanted in her uterus or the father chooses to have them implanted in a surrogate's uterus after the divorce, this will raise custody, visitation, and child support issues for all parties involved. If one parent wants the embryos destroyed, this raises ethical and religious concerns, especially among those whose faith views destruction of the embryos in the same manner as it views abortion.

The law regarding custody of frozen embryos varies from state to state, with some jurisdictions providing no statutory or judicial guidance on the subject. The parties involved in conceiving through in vitro fertilization sign a contract delineating what is to be done with the frozen embryos. While some states will uphold the agreement under contract law theory, the state of Louisiana forbids destruction of the frozen embryos regardless of any agreements entered into by the parties. There are three judicial rulings of importance in the United States regarding custody of frozen embryos:

- ***Davis v. Davis*, 842 S.W. 2d 588 (1992).** Mr. and Mrs. Davis were unable to have children, so they sought the services of a fertility clinic in Knoxville. With the clinic's assistance, they produced nine embryos. Two of the embryos were implanted in Mrs. Davis, but did not develop. The remaining seven were frozen in the clinic's cold-storage unit. The in vitro fertilization agreement signed by the parties did not include any provisions on what to do with any unused embryos. When Mr. Davis filed for divorce, there was a dispute over what to do with the frozen embryos and how to legally characterize them. Mr. Davis argued that the embryos were not alive and, as a result, the court had to apply the same principles it used to resolve issues over joint property. He wanted to have the embryos destroyed. The trial court declared that "life begins at conception" and the frozen embryos were children and not property. Once the court characterized the frozen embryos as children, it applied the best interest standard and awarded the seven remaining embryos to Mrs. Davis, who originally wanted to try to conceive a child. If Mrs. Davis did conceive and ultimately gave birth, the issues of child custody, support, and visitation would be decided at a later time. Mr. Davis's appeal had eventually reached the Tennessee Supreme Court. By this time, Mrs. Davis had remarried, moved out of state, and wished to donate the frozen embryos to a childless couple. The Tennessee Supreme Court ruled in favor of Mr. Davis since Mrs. Davis no longer wanted the frozen embryos and he wished to have them discarded. Justice Martha Craig Daughtrey summarized the court's ruling on how to resolve disputes over frozen embryos in the following paragraph:

In summary, we hold that disputes involving the Disposition of pre-embryos produced by in vitro fertilization should be resolved, first, by looking to the preferences of the progenitors. If their wishes cannot be ascertained, or if there is dispute, then their prior agreement concerning Disposition should be carried out. If no prior agreement exists, then the relative interests of the parties in using or not using the preembryos must be weighed. Ordinarily, the party wishing to avoid procreation should prevail, assuming that the other party has a reasonable possibility of achieving parenthood by means other than use of the preembryos in question. If no other reasonable alternatives exist, then the argument in favor of using the preembryos to achieve pregnancy should be considered. However, if the party seeking control of the preembryos intends merely to donate them to another couple, the objecting party obviously has the greater interest and should prevail. (***Davis***, **604**)

- ***Kass v. Kass*, 91 N.Y. 2d 554, 696 N.E. 2d 174 (1998).** In this case, the couple divorced after nine unsuccessful attempts at in vitro fertilization and $75,000 dollars in fees. At the fertility clinic, the parties signed an agreement donating any unused eggs for research purposes by the clinic, which would then destroy them after their scientific use. The parties engaged in a custody battle when Mrs. Kass decided she wanted the frozen embryos for future implantation, a position opposed by her husband, who argued that the frozen embryos were property and that the contract signed by the parties was binding. The New York Court of Appeals agreed with Mr. Kass and enforced the contract.

- ***A.Z v. B.Z*, 431 Mass. 150, 725 N.E.2d 1051 (2000).** This case involved a custody battle over four frozen embryos that the wife wanted implanted, even though the parties were going through a divorce. The husband filed an injunction, asking the court to prevent her from proceeding with her plan. The parties had signed a consent agreeing that the embryos would be implanted even though the parties separated. The trial court judge held that the consent form was not binding because of the divorce, the father's unwillingness to become a parent, and the unfairness to the child, who would be unwanted by one of its parents. The Massachusetts Supreme Judicial Court agreed with the trial court and affirmed the lower court's decision on the basis that the consent forms were not enforceable against the father.

Artificial insemination is the technique of injecting a male's semen into a female's uterus through artificial means. The goal of artificial insemination is to impregnate the woman without physical contact with the male. Heterosexual couples use this method when conceiving in the natural way is not possible due to a physical or mental health condition. Lesbian couples who wish to create families also use artificial insemination. Gay men or heterosexuals who cannot conceive also use artificial insemination while employing the services of a surrogate mother.

A *surrogate mother* is a woman who agrees by contract to bear a child for a couple or an individual who cannot conceive in exchange for a fee. The surrogate mother is impregnated with either a male's sperm or in vitro fertilization. A couple who cannot conceive through natural means may implant an embryo created in a petri dish into a surrogate's uterus for development when the wife is unable to carry a fetus. This is known as gestational surrogacy. As part of the contract, the surrogate mother agrees to bear the child in exchange for a fee that will cover her medical and any other expenses related to the pregnancy as well as an adoption fee for her services. As part of the contract, the surrogate mother agrees to terminate her parental rights and give the child up for adoption to the other party in the contract.

The law regarding surrogacy contracts varies from state to state. Some jurisdictions have declared these contracts to be illegal, unenforceable, and void against public policy. Other jurisdictions may prohibit the payment of a fee above and beyond the surrogate mother's birth-related expenses. A ban on such fees takes the profit motive out of the equation and may in some sense discourage women from going through the nine-month pregnancy without some sort of compensation above and beyond medically related expenses. Courts and legislatures confronted with this issue are particularly concerned with preventing baby selling and the exploitation of women. Many state surrogacy laws have been crafted by judges who creatively applied the principles of contract law, paternity law, family law, and criminal law and public policy considerations in forging a solution to disputes before them. The applicable law in a surrogacy case depends on the law of the state where the child is born.

Surrogacy agreements are potential landmines for custody disputes, especially when the surrogate mother changes her mind and refuses to give up custody of the child. A surrogacy contract that received nationwide publicity in the late 1980s was the case of Baby M. Mary Beth Whitehead, who was also the biological mother in this case, agreed to be a surrogate for William and Elizabeth Stern. Due to a diabetic condition, Mrs. Stern could not have children, so she and her husband agreed that Ms. Whitehead would be artificially inseminated with his sperm. Mrs. Stern would then adopt the child. Mrs. Whitehead changed her mind and sued for custody of the baby. The Sterns won custody of Baby M after a New Jersey court applied the best interest standard in the case. Mrs. Whitehead did, however, receive visitation rights with the child.

GRANDPARENTS' RIGHTS AND THE RIGHTS OF THIRD PARTIES TO VISITATION/ACCESS AND CUSTODY

Third-Party Visitation/Access Rights

As a rule, a court may not enter an order permitting a third-party legally enforceable visitation/access rights. As with most rules, however, exceptions exist.

In a divorce case, the husband and wife are the only legally recognizable parties to the action. When an individual who is neither mother nor father seeks to have visitation/access, if the family unit is intact, a third party has no standing to bring an action in court.

Standing
A term that describes whether a party has a legal right to request an adjudication of the issues in a legal dispute.

Standing is a legal term. It determines whether a party has a legal right to request an adjudication of the issues in a legal dispute. However, where the family unit is no longer intact, there are instances where a third party has standing to petition the court for custody or visitation/access. Every jurisdiction has enacted statutes permitting grandparents to intervene in divorce cases and request visitation or custody of the minor children. Once the court grants third parties a legal right to be heard in the proceedings, they are considered *third-party intervenors*.

Third-party intervenor
A party who is not one of the main parties in a dispute.

Protecting the Intact Family The *Castagno* case outlines the common law and statutory changes that allowed grandparents into divorce court. The courts, however, will not intrude on an intact family and will allow parents to make the decision regarding the grandparents' access to the children.

The general rule is that no third party may petition for access when the family is intact. This is a common law rule based on the presumption that parents have a constitutional right to raise their children as they see fit, free from the interference of third parties. This right, however, is not absolute. The state may intervene on behalf of abused and neglected children, and courts have the power to give visitation/access or custody to third parties when they deem it is in the child's best interest. This is known as the doctrine of parens patriae. ***Parens patriae*** is Latin term that describes the power of the state to protect and care for children when the parents are unwilling or unable to do so.

Grandparents may obtain visitation/access or custody rights under the following circumstances:

- Statutes and court procedures allowing grandparents to request visitation when the children's parents are getting divorced or when one of the parent dies.
- When there is a breakdown in the parent–child relationship; for example, removal of the children from the parent's care by state social workers due to abuse and neglect and the grandparents' petition for custody or guardianship. There are many grandparents, as well as aunts and uncles, who have come to the rescue of children under these circumstances and provide them with a stable and loving environment.
- With the consent of the parents in cases where the biological parents can no longer care for the children.
- Through informal family arrangements where the parents voluntarily maintain contact with the grandparents despite death, divorce, or other breakdown in the parents' relationship.

Parens patriae
The Latin term for the legal doctrine empowering the state to intervene to protect children when parents or guardians fail to do so.

Figure 7-4 Every jurisdiction has enacted statutes that permit grandparents to seek visitation or custody rights with minor grandchildren, where the family unit is no longer intact.

Soul/Photodisc/Getty Images.

From the early 1970s to 1980s, every state enacted some type of statute giving grandparents visitation when the court determined that it was in the children's best interest. These statutes varied from state to state. In the late 1990s, many state courts invalidated third-party visitation statutes, claiming they violated a parent's constitutional right to raise their children without influence or interference from others. Courts thus were declaring that it was unconstitutional to intrude on an intact family.

JEAN T. CASTAGNO, ET AL. v. TINA WHOLEAN, ET AL.

239 CONN. 336, 684 A.2D 1181 (CONN. 1996)
SUPREME COURT OF CONNECTICUT

KATZ, J.

The sole issue in this appeal is whether, pursuant to General Statutes § 46b-59,[4] the trial court had subject matter jurisdiction to entertain a petition by grandparents for visitation rights with their minor grandchildren when the grandchildren and their parents were not involved in any case or controversy currently before the court and there was no claim that the family unit was no longer intact. We conclude that although § 46b-59 lacks specific language imposing any threshold requirement, established rules of statutory construction, the context of the statute and its legislative history support the incorporation of a requirement that plaintiffs must demonstrate disruption of the family sufficient to justify state intervention. In the absence of any attempt by the plaintiffs here to satisfy this threshold requirement, we conclude that the trial court lacked jurisdiction to decide the issue of visitation and, therefore, properly dismissed the plaintiffs' action (footnote omitted). Accordingly, we affirm the judgment of the trial court. . . .

. . . The plaintiffs argue that the trial court misconstrued § 46b-59 to contain threshold requirements not expressed in the plain language of the statute. Specifically, the plaintiffs claim that the application of § 46b-59 is not limited by any threshold requirements, and that the sole criterion for application of the statute is the best interest of the child. Accordingly, the plaintiffs argue that any third party who seeks state intervention, in the form of a court's grant of visitation rights, may petition the court at any time, and need not present any allegations that the minor child's family is no longer intact. The plaintiffs further maintain that, because the language of § 46b-59 is clear and unambiguous, it was inappropriate for the trial court to rely on the legislative history of the statute to establish any threshold requirements. We disagree.

We begin with the common law background against which the visitation statutes were enacted. At common law, grandparents, or third parties in general, have no right to visitation. Rather, the decision as to who may or may not have access to a minor child has been deemed an issue of parental prerogative (citations and footnote omitted). The common law reflects the belief that the family unit should be respected, and its autonomy and privacy invaded through court action only in the most pressing circumstances. "That right [of the parents to determine the care, custody, and control of their children] is recognized because it reflects a strong civilization, and because the parental role is now established beyond debate as an enduring American tradi-

---

[4]General Statute §46b-59 provides: "the superior court may grant the right of visitation with respect to any minor child or children to any person, upon an application of such person. Such order shall be according to the court's best judgment upon the facts of the case and subject to such conditions and limitations as it deems equitable, provided the grant of such visitation rights shall not be contingent upon any order of financial support by the court. In making, modifying or terminating such an order, the court shall be guided by the best interest of the child, giving consideration to the wishes of such child if he is of sufficient age and capable of forming an intelligent opinion. Visitation rights granted in accordance with this section shall not be deemed to have created parental rights in the person or persons to whom such visitation rights are granted. The grant of such visitation rights shall not prevent any court of competent jurisdiction from thereafter acting upon the custody of such child, the parental rights with respect to such child or the adoption of such child and any such court may include in its decree an order terminating such visitation rights.

tion" (citation and footnote omitted). All families may have, at one time or another, unhappy conflicts and disputes among adult relatives that might result in an absence of contact between those adults and their minor relatives—be they grandchildren, nieces or nephews, cousins, etc.—but longstanding tradition holds that, absent compelling circumstances justifying some state intervention in the form or a judicial order, the parents' decision, whether wise or not, prevails. . . .

. . . The right to family autonomy and privacy acknowledged in the common law has been recognized as so fundamental as to merit constitutional protection. Consequently, any legislation affecting it is strictly scrutinized (citation omitted). . . .

. . . The plaintiffs' construction of § 46b-59 would allow the court to intrude upon an intact family that has not already opened itself to such intrusion. . . .

Source: 239 CONN. 336, 684 A.2D 1181 (CONN. 1996), Supreme Court of Connecticut.

Troxel V. Granville: U.S. Supreme Court Sets New Standard for Third-Party Visitation Grandparent visitation/access becomes problematic when parents refuse to maintain the children's relationship with the grandparents after a bitter divorce, breakup, or a parent's death. In the year 2000, the U.S. Supreme Court addressed the issue of the rights of third parties seeking visitation with children in the case of *Troxel v. Granville* (530 US 57, 120 S Ct. 2054,147 L.Ed 29). The case began with a relationship between Tommie Granville and Brad Troxel, an unmarried couple who had two daughters. Their relationship ended in 1991. Brad Troxel moved out and went to live with his parents, Jenifer and Gary Troxel. During this time, the children visited their father on weekends, as well as spent time with their grandparents. Tragically, Brad Troxel committed suicide in 1993. After Brad's suicide, Tommie Granville informed the paternal grandparents that she wanted to reduce their visits with the children to once a month. Granville had since remarried and was in the process of rebuilding her family.

- The Troxels petitioned for visitation under a Washington statute. The statute, Revised Code of Washington, Section 26.10.160 (3), at the time allowed "any person" to petition for visitation rights "at any time," whenever the court determined that such visitation was in the children's best interest. While Granville did not oppose the petition, she did not agree with the amount of time the Troxels were seeking for visitation. She argued that in the absence of a custody dispute or challenge regarding her fitness as a parent, she should have the right to decide issues involving her children. In 1995, the Washington Superior Court ruled in favor of the grandparents, giving them more visitation rights because, in the court's opinion, it was in the children's best interest. The Washington Court of Appeals reversed the decision and held that nonparents lacked standing to sue under the Washington law. The Washington Supreme Court affirmed, declaring the Washington statute unconstitutional because it interfered with her Fourteenth Amendment right to privacy and child-rearing authority. The grandparents disagreed and appealed their case to the U.S. Supreme Court.

- The issue on appeal before the Supreme Court was whether the Washington statute, which allowed any person to petition for court-ordered visitation over a parent's objection if the visitation was in the child's best interest, interfered with a parent's constitutional right to raise his or her children. In a 6–3 decision written by Justice Sandra Day O'Connor, the Supreme Court held that the Washington statute was too broad and unconstitutional as applied. The Court held that it violated a parent's right under the Due Process Clause of the Fourteenth Amendment to make decisions concerning the care of their children and went on to write that the "the liberty interest at issue in this case—the interest of parents in the care, custody, and control of their children—is perhaps the oldest of the fundamental liberty interests recognized by this Court."

State Response to Troxel After the *Troxel* decision, states either revised their visitation/access statute or waited for the courts to find their respective state statute unconstitutional under the *Troxel* decision.

Some of the statutes or court decisions bringing their state law in line with the *Troxel* decision require a two-prong test:

1. A break in the relationship of the child's parents; and
2. Proof by grandparents (or a third party) by clear and convincing evidence that visitation is in the child's best interest.

Some constitutional scholars argue that the *Troxel* decision may also require grandparents and third parties to demonstrate that the child will suffer harm from the lack of access. Several states, either through legislative action or court decisions, have adopted this requirement.

In *Roth v. Weston*, the Connecticut Supreme Court held that for it to have subject matter jurisdiction, the third party filing a petition for visitation must allege that he or she has a relationship with the child akin to a parent-child relationship, and that real and significant harm would come to the child if visitation is denied. Only if these assertions are alleged in the petition, will the parties have standing and only then will the court have jurisdiction to consider the merits of the petition.

As the *Roth* case also demonstrates, the decision in *Troxel* applies to any third party seeking time with a child. This includes not only grandparents but also other relatives and unmarried partners.

State Application of Troxel

- ***Roth v. Weston*, 259 Conn. 202 (2002)** A father refused to permit any contact between his children and their maternal grandmother and aunt after the death of the children's mother. The maternal relatives went to court. The trial court, in accordance with the current visitation statute, determined that visitation would be in the children's best interest and granted the petition for visitation. The father appealed.

  The Supreme Court of Connecticut reversed the trial court's judgment and remanded the case for dismissal. The court, in light of the decision in *Troxel*, found the Connecticut statute to be unconstitutional as applied to the extent that the court permitted third-party visitation contrary to the desires of a fit parent and in the absence of a showing that the children would suffer actual, significant harm, if deprived of visitation.

  The court did not declare the Connecticut visitation statute to be *facially unconstitutional* (meaning unconstitutional under any circumstances). The court acknowledged that there could be situations when denial of visitation to a person who previously had a strong parent-like relationship with the child would so seriously harm the child to justify state intervention:

  > . . . We are persuaded therefore that an allegation, along with proof thereof, that the parent's decision regarding visitation will cause the child to suffer real and substantial emotional harm likewise presents a compelling state interest that will permit interference with parental rights, provided the petitioner has established a parent-like relationship with the child. (*Roth*, 205)

- *Wickham v. Byrne*, **199 Ill.2d 309 (2002)** A child's widowed father filed a motion to dismiss the maternal grandmother's petition for overnight visitation. Basing his argument on the *Troxel v. Granville* decision, he alleged that the Illinois visitation statute violated due process rights under the U.S. Constitution and the constitution of Illinois. The trial court denied his motion. Following an evidentiary hearing, but prior to ruling, the court stated that:

> . . . the standard, to be used in grandparent's visitation is the best interest of the child. Generally, it's presumed that a relationship with a grandparent is in the best interest of child. (*Wickham*, 310).

The court denied overnight visits due to the grandmother's attempts to undermine the father's relationship with his son, but ordered four hours of supervised visitation each week. The father renewed his argument in an amended motion to dismiss which the court also denied, and the father appealed.

The Illinois Supreme Court reversed the trial court's order and, declared provisions 607 (b)(1) and 607 (b)(3) of the Illinois Marriage and Dissolution of Marriage Act, commonly known as the grandparent visitation statute, to be *facially unconstitutional* (unconstitutional under any set of facts).

Section 607 (b)(1) authorized a court to grant a grandparent's petition for reasonable visitation if the court determined it to be in the best interests and welfare of the child and one of the parents was deceased.

Section 607 (b)(3) provided: "When one parent is deceased, the surviving parent shall not interfere with the visitation rights of the grandparents."

The Illinois Supreme Court noted that under *Troxel*, the Fourteenth Amendment protects the right of parents to make decisions concerning the care, custody, and control of their children without unwarranted state intrusion, and that state interference should only occur when the health, safety, or welfare of a child is at risk. The court found that like the statute in *Troxel*, Section 607 (b)(1) contravened the traditional presumption that parents are fit and act in the best interest of their children, and concluded that:

> Section 607 (b)(1) exposes the decision of a fit parent to the unfettered value judgment of a judge and the intrusive micromanaging of the state. Because we can conceive of no set of circumstances under which section 607 (b) (1) of the Act would be valid, we hold that it is unconstitutional on its face. For the same reasons, we hold that section 607 (b)(3) is facially unconstitutional. . . . (*Wickham*, 315)

After the former Illinois grandparent statute was held unconstitutional in *Wickham*, the legislature enacted a new version of the statute which contained a provision establishing a rebuttable presumption that a fit parent's decisions regarding grandparent visitation are not harmful to the child's mental, physical, or emotional health and placing the burden on the grandparent to prove that the parent's denial of visitation harmed the child.

In *Flynn v. Henkel*, the Illinois Supreme Court relied on this section to reverse the rulings of both the trial and appellate courts and clarified the requirements that grandparents must meet to overcome this presumption.

- *Flynn v. Henkel*, **227 ILL.2D 176 (2007)** The child's paternal grandmother filed a motion for visitation which the trial court granted. The child's mother, a single parent, appealed. While the appellate court affirmed the lower court's decision, the Supreme Court of Illinois reversed the decision. Applying the new rebuttable presumption of the revised statute, Illinois Supreme Court found that the trial court's unsupported oral pronouncement, that the petitioner, grandmother, had met her burden of proof, was against the weight of the evidence where it did not make any specific findings as to how the grandmother had overcome the statutory presumption that the mother's decisions regarding the grandmother's visitation were not harmful to the child's mental, physical or emotional health. The appellate court had rejected the mother's argument that the grandmother failed to prove that denying grandparent visitation was harmful to the child as required by the revised statute. The appellate court stated that the harm the child suffered would suffer from the denial of visitation "can be inferred from the evidence." The Illinois Supreme Court reviewing the rationales of the lower courts found that neither " 'the denial of an opportunity for grandparent visitation,' as the trial court found, nor 'a child never knowing a grandparent who loved him, and who did not undermine the child's relationship with his mother' as the appellate court held is 'harm' that will rebut the presumption state in section 607 (a-5) (3) that a fit parent's denial of a grandparent's visitation is not harmful to the child's mental, physical or emotional health. (*Flynn*, 181).

THIRD-PARTY CUSTODY

While following *Troxell*, many states through case law decisions and statutory law revisions embraced rigorous standards to allow third parties standing to petition the court for visitation similar to the standard articulated in *Roth*, courts in various jurisdictions did not apply such a stringent standard in third-party intervention acts in custody proceedings. Instead, courts advocated a less stringent standard to determine custody actions because an action for custody not only affects the parent's constitutional rights but also the child's welfare.

FISH V. FISH, 285 CONN. 24 (CONN. 2008)

In *Fish v. Fish*, the defendant father appealed the lower court's ruling awarding joint custody to the child's mother and the child's paternal aunt. The father alleged that the standard applied in *Roth* should be the standard in third-party custody actions. He argued that this standard should apply because custody intrudes upon the rights of a fit parent at least as much as visitation. The Connecticut Supreme Court held that it would not apply the same standard articulated in *Roth*. The Court noted that the heightened pleading requirements and burden of persuasion set forth in *Roth* did not apply to third-party intervention petitions and custody awards. The Court noted that the standard for permitting grandparent visitation against a fit parent is a high one in order to preserve the parent's constitutional right to care for their children as they see fit. Conversely, the standard for awarding custody to a grandparent or other third party is less stringent because it affects not only the parent's constitutional rights but also the child's welfare. The Court held that where a third-party custody petition directly challenges the overall competence of a parent to care for the child, the standard employed to protect the liberty interest of the parent must be more flexible and responsive to the child's welfare than the standard applied in visitation cases in which the underlying parent-child relationship is not contested. However, the Court agreed with the defendant that third-party custody decisions require the application of "a standard more demanding than the best interest of the child." The Court held that for the standard to be applied when a third party seeks to intervene in a custody proceeding, the third party must prove, by a preponderance of the evidence: (1) that he or she has a relationship akin to that of a parent and (2) that to allow custody to remain with the challenged parent would clearly be detrimental to the child. Upon a finding of detriment, the award of third-party custody would be in the child's best interest.

Jurisdictional Issues in Child Custody and Visitation Cases

Before legislation was adopted addressing interstate jurisdiction over child custody and visitation matters, noncustodial parents would take children over state lines for the purpose of "forum shopping." This means that they looked for a court that would grant them custody of their children contrary to the order entered by the original court hearing the custody dispute. In response to this problem, the National Conference of Commissioners on Uniform State Laws drafted the Uniform Child Custody and Jurisdiction Act (UCCJA) to dissuade parents from kidnapping their own children. Every jurisdiction in the country passed a state version of the UCCJA by the year 1981. In that same year, Congress passed a federal law addressing the issue of interstate custody jurisdiction called the Parental Kidnapping Prevention Act (PKPA).

Problems quickly arose in the application of these two conflicting statutes. The UCCJA discouraged parents from running off to another jurisdiction with the child for the purpose of modifying an existing court order by establishing jurisdiction over child custody in one state alone and prohibiting modification of that order as long as the original state retains jurisdiction. The UCCJA did not give the child's home state priority in determining which state had jurisdiction to hear a custody case, in direct contradiction to the PKPA. The term *home state* is defined as the state where a child has resided for a period of six months. In addition to giving the child's home state priority in custody cases, it also stated that once a state exercised jurisdiction over a custody case, it had continuing jurisdiction until both parents and the children were no longer in that state. The UCCJA and PKPA also lacked enforcement of interstate custody and visitation orders.

Acknowledging these differences and the conflicts that arose, the Uniform Law Commissioners drafted the **Uniform Child Custody Jurisdiction and Enforcement Act (UCCJEA)** of 1997. The UCCJEA replaced the UCCJA by conforming the UCCJA to the PKPA, and added interstate enforcement of child custody and visitation orders. Following are some significant highlights of the UCCJEA. Lawyers and paralegals must read not only the UCCJEA but also the case law interpreting the statute from jurisdiction to jurisdiction. The UCCJEA:

Uniform Child Custody Jurisdiction and Enforcement Act (UCCJEA)
An act drafted by a national commission and enacted by many state legislatures to enforce on an interstate basis the rights of custodial parents and prevent parental kidnapping and custodial interference.

- Requires courts to honor the orders of the home state in determining which state has jurisdiction in interstate child custody and visitation cases. This is the most significant provision in the UCCJEA. A new state court may only modify another state's previous child custody or visitation order if the child resided in the new state for six months.
- Allows a state to retain continuing exclusive jurisdiction once it has taken jurisdiction over a case and retained such jurisdiction until all of the parties involved in the dispute moved out of the state. This prevents a parent from removing the child to another state and then seeking a more favorable custody order in the new state. In applying the UCCJEA, the new state is required to decline jurisdiction over the case.
- In cases where the child is abandoned, abused, or neglected and is present in a state other than the home state, the UCCJEA allows the new state to take temporary emergency jurisdiction over the case. While the new state

may not have jurisdiction because it is not the home state of the child, it may make a temporary emergency order for the protection of the child until the appropriate jurisdiction may be determined. It is possible that the new state may retain continuing jurisdiction if no other state has the authority to continue jurisdiction or refuses continued jurisdiction.

- Prohibits simultaneous proceedings in cases where one parent files a custody or visitation in one state, while another is filed in a different jurisdiction.
- Requires states to enforce custody and visitation orders from states that conform to the UCCJEA, which currently includes all fifty states. The parent must register the domestic order in the new state, unless it is contested. If not contested, the court has the authority to enforce the order through its contempt powers.

Concept Review and Reinforcement

KEY TERMS

access	legal custody	SAID
best interest of the child	noncustodial parent	sole custody
Child Abuse Prevention and	*parens patriae*	shared physical custody
Treatment Act of 1974 (CAPTA)	parent-child relationship	split custody
custodial parent	parental alienation	standing
expert witness	parental alienation syndrome	supervised visitation
family relations unit	parenting plan	tender years doctrine
family services division	*patria potestas*	third-party intervenor
fixed schedule	physical custody	Uniform Child Custody Jurisdiction
in vitro fertilization	primary caretaker	and Enforcement Act (UCCJEA)
joint custody	psychological parent	unsupervised visitation
joint legal and physical custody	reasonable rights of visitation	visitation rights

REVIEW OF KEY CONCEPTS

1. List and define the different types of custody arrangements discussed in this chapter.
2. Why do most courts presume that joint legal custody is in the best interest of the children?
3. When is a joint custody arrangement not in the best interest of the children?
4. What is the purpose of requiring divorcing parents to attend mandatory parenting education programs? What is a parenting plan, and what issues does it normally address?
5. What is the most significant feature of the Uniform Child Custody Jurisdiction and Enforcement Act, and why?

BUILDING YOUR PARALEGAL SKILLS

CASE FOR BRIEFING

ROTH v. WESTON, 259 CONN. 289 A.D 431 (2002)

Critical Thinking and Legal Analysis Applications

1. You work as a paralegal at the Law Office of Patricia H. Garner. She is a solo practitioner and extremely busy divorce attorney with absolutely no time to spend doing legal research. Mr. Hitendar Patel and his wife Lata have an

appointment late this afternoon for advice regarding their rights as grandparents. Their son and his wife are going to file for divorce and they assume the wife will get custody of the two minor children, aged three and four. The Patels are very involved with the children. Their daughter-in-law is a science professor at the local community college and works Monday through Thursday from 8:00 A.M. to 4:30 P.M., and on Tuesday and Thursday nights from 7:00 P.M. to 9:15 P.M. The Patels care for the children on a daily basis and have done so since birth. The children are very close to their grandparents. Their son works a full forty-hour week as an engineer. They want to know their rights in the event their daughter-in-law refuses to let them see the children. As it stands now, they plan to continue caring for the children after the couple separates, but they don't want to take any chances. Attorney Garner asks you to research the status of grandparents' rights in your state. She heard some lawyers talking about the *Troxel* case, but she doesn't know much about it.

A. Using the Internet or state-specific materials, determine the status of grandparents' rights in your state after the U.S. Supreme Court decision in *Troxel v. Granville*. Prepare an interoffice memorandum for your supervisor, citing any changes in your state statute and/or case law reflecting any changes.

B. Using the holding in *West v. Roth,* above, how would this issue be decided in Connecticut? Do the requirements in *West v. Roth* differ from the burden imposed in *Flynn v. Henkel?* If so, how?

2. You work as a paralegal for Raymond Jackson, a well-known father's rights advocate in the state of Wisconsin. Attorney Jackson represents client Frank Reed in a divorce case. Mr. Reed is a traveling salesman for a pharmaceutical company and is out of town at the company headquarters for several weeks of the year. He wishes to visit his children via Skype. You are in the process of completing the parenting plan, and Attorney Jackson asks you to draft a virtual visitation clause in accordance with Wisconsin's statute to facilitate virtual visitation when Mr. Reed is away from home. To find the governing provisions, go to your favorite search engine (e.g., Google) and type in **Wisconsin Statutes**; then, using the phrase **virtual visitation**, find the statute that addresses this form of access. In addition to drafting the clause, use the Internet to find a website on online visitation and see if you can learn how to set the virtual visitation aspect of the parenting plan. Draft a letter to the client explaining the process.

3. You work as a paralegal for the law firm of Schultz, Berkowitz, and Seeley in your state. The office represents Lucille Chen, who is in the midst of a bitter custody battle. Mr. Chen has threatened to "take the children away" from her because she is a "psycho." Mrs. Chen is taking medication for a chemical imbalance. She sees a therapist regularly and a psychiatrist to monitor her prescriptions. She has always taken good care of her children and has been their primary caretaker. She sought help for her mental health issues voluntarily, getting help from the outpatient psychiatric clinic at the local hospital. Her condition was exacerbated when Mr. Chen started having an affair at work with the receptionist in his office building. She is worried about losing her children. What is your opinion regarding Mrs. Chen's concerns?

4. You work as a paralegal in the law office of Elaine Coker in the State of Oregon. Your office represents Jonathan Arthur, the petitioner in a divorce case against his wife, Renee. Mr. Arthur has had temporary custody of their seven-year-old son Justin (date of birth January 10, 2000) and has been his primary caretaker for all of Justin's life. Mrs. Arthur plans to be discharged from an inpatient drug rehabilitation program just before the divorce becomes final. She has been in the program for six months and is doing very well. She and Mr. Arthur are in agreement over all issues of the divorce. Mr. Arthur will

continued

have sole legal and residential custody of the child. Mrs. Arthur suggested unsupervised visits, but Mr. Arthur thinks it's too much too soon and he is not quite ready to leave her alone with the child. Mrs. Arthur agreed to supervised parenting time from 10:00 A.M. to 5:00 P.M. on Saturdays, and her parents Nicholas and Catherine Bedell have agreed to supervise the visits at their home at 649 Ferris Lane in Elmira, Oregon. Mr. or Mrs. Bedell will transport the child to and from the visits, and their car is equipped with a child safety seat. Mrs. Arthur may attend the child's baseball games and any school activities as long as she is sober. She cannot be intoxicated during visits or phone calls with her child and will attend outpatient treatment and support groups to maintain her sobriety. There are no firearms in the Bedell household, and her parents have assured Mr. Arthur that alcohol and drugs are not on the premises. They have also agreed not to allow her into the home if she is "high" and will immediately contact Mr. Arthur. Mrs. Arthur may call the child on any day and at any time before 7:30 P.M. as long as she is sober.

Go to the Internet and read about safety-focused parenting plans. Find a safety-focused parenting plan for supervised visits and draft an agreement on behalf of Mr. Arthur.

Building a Professional Portfolio

PORTFOLIO **EXERCISES**

1. Using a paper or electronic calendar, prepare a visitation/access grid showing a mother and father's time with their child in accordance with their agreed-to parenting plan, which provides that Mother shall have primary physical custody of the child and that Father will have access every Tuesday and Thursday evenings from 5 P.M. until 9 P.M., and every other weekend from Friday 6 P.M. until Sunday 6 P.M.

Chapter **eight**
CHILD SUPPORT

The marital obligation to financially support and maintain minor children who are issue of a marriage does not cease for either parent upon dissolution of the marriage. Both parents are expected to provide economic support for their children. The dissolution decree will include an order for financial support of each child until such child reaches age eighteen, the age of majority.

Traditionally, when parents divorced, the father was usually the primary or sole breadwinner. Sole custody was awarded to the mother while support came from the noncustodial parent, usually the father. Today, the noncustodial parent continues to have an obligation for child support. In addition, even where parents have joint custody, courts will order the parent with whom the child does not make his or her primary residence to make child support payments to the parent with whom the child resides.

LEARNING OBJECTIVES

After studying this chapter, you should be able to:

1. Understand the rationale behind implementation of the child support guidelines.

2. Describe the purpose of deviation criteria and identify the factors a court may take into consideration when deviating from the guidelines.

3. Understand the basis for modification of child support orders.

4. Describe the child support enforcement process.

CHILD SUPPORT GUIDELINES: FEDERALLY MANDATED REQUIREMENTS

In the mid-1980s the federal government through its appropriate agencies studied court-ordered child support awards made in various jurisdictions throughout the country. In response to this problem, Congress passed the *Family Support Act of 1988*. This federal law requires every state to adopt numerical child support guidelines based on the income of the parties. The act mandates that the guidelines establish a rebuttable presumption in favor of a numerical computation of the child support obligation—in essence, taking it out of the trial judge's discretion. The states may establish their own *deviation criteria* after showing that application of the guideline figure would create an injustice or would be inappropriate under the circumstances. The federal study revealed that the amounts that many, if not most, courts ordered noncustodial parents to pay toward the support of their children were far too low to keep up with then-spiraling inflation and too little to meet the children's needs. Absent any uniform and rational guidelines, the amounts set for child support rested on the judge's discretion. Many judges set arbitrary amounts that were usually too low to make much of a difference in the custodial parent's ability to financially maintain the children in the family. Many judges ordered minimal child support payments because of their belief that the noncustodial parent would not pay anything substantial.

As a result of this practice, many single-parent homes existed at or below the poverty line. Single parents, usually single mothers, were forced to rely on government assistance for survival. The federal government, by mandating each state to adopt uniform and rational child support guidelines, sought to return the child support obligation back where it belonged, namely, with both parents—noncustodial as well as custodial. States were required to base child support awards on numerical guidelines rather than judicial whims. State legislatures enacted laws to require a uniform method of determining child support, and formula tables and child support guideline worksheets were created by each jurisdiction to execute these legislative enactments.

Today many courts apply statutorily enacted formulas to determine the amount the noncustodial parent must pay for the support of each child. These are known as *child support guidelines*. Appendix C of this book contains "State-by-State Child Support Enforcement Resources," which includes Internet websites for child support guidelines and worksheets for every jurisdiction in the country. Statutes establishing these guidelines were passed by state legislatures as a result of federal mandates to do so.

This Arizona statute legislates the state's child support guidelines and sets forth the criteria for establishing those guidelines.

Deviation criteria
The court may deviate from the child support guidelines upon a showing that application of the guideline figure would create an injustice or would be inappropriate under the circumstances.

Child support guidelines
Statutorily enacted formulas for determining the amount the noncustodial parent must pay for the support of each child.

Statutes

Arizona Revised Statutes § 25-320(D)

The supreme court shall establish guidelines for determining the amount of child support. The amount resulting from the application of these guidelines is the amount of child support ordered unless a written finding is made, based on criteria approved by the supreme court, that application of the guidelines would be inappropriate or unjust in a particular case. The supreme court shall review the guidelines at least once every four years to ensure that their application results in the determination of appropriate child support amounts. The supreme court shall base the guidelines and criteria for deviation from them on all relevant factors, considered together and weighed in conjunction with each other, including:

1. The financial resources and needs of the child.

2. The financial resources and needs of the custodial parent.

3. The standard of living the child would have enjoyed if the child lived in an intact home with both parents to the extent it is economically feasible considering the resources of each parent and each parent's need to maintain a home and to provide support for the child when the child is with that parent.

4. The physical and emotional condition of the child, and the child's educational needs.

5. The financial resources and needs of the noncustodial parent.

6. The medical support plan for the child. The plan should include the child's medical support needs, the availability of medical insurance or services provided by the Arizona health care cost containment system and whether a cash medical support order is necessary.

7. Excessive or abnormal expenditures, destruction, concealment or fraudulent disposition of community, joint tenancy and other property held in common.

8. The duration of parenting time and related expenses.

Source: Chapter 3—Dissolution of Marriage, Article 2, Sec 25-320—Child Support; Factors; Methods of Payment; Additional Enforcement Provisions; Definitions, State of Arizona.

DETERMINING EACH PARENT'S OBLIGATION FOR CHILD SUPPORT

Most jurisdictions in the United States have complied with the federal mandate and have a system for determining the exact amount a noncustodial parent must pay, given that parent's financial circumstances and the financial circumstances of the custodial parent. In addition, the states complying with the federal mandate have developed child support worksheets that assist parties in the calculation of this obligation. Each parent's income is a factor, as is the cost of living in the geographical area and the age and needs of each child. Each parent's net income is added together to arrive at a **combined net income** or **total net income** figure. A preset percentage is applied to this figure to establish how much of this combined income should be allocated for the financial maintenance of the child or for each of the children. The amount arrived at is often termed the *child maintenance figure.* Then, *a formula is applied to determine how much of this amount must be paid by the noncustodial parent.* For instance, if each parent has the same amount of net income, the court, upon applying the guidelines, will order the noncustodial parent to pay child support equal to one-half of the child maintenance figure. Similarly, if a noncustodial parent's net income is three times as high as that of the custodial parent, the noncustodial parent must pay three-fourths of the child maintenance figure, leaving the custodial parent to supply the other one-fourth needed.

Some states consider each parent's gross income as a starting point, rather than net income. Some states also consider other factors in addition to income to determine child support obligations.

Determining a Parent's Income The *Rosenbloom* case involves a father's appeal of the trial court's increase in his child support obligation pursuant to the mother's postjudgment motion to modify. After the divorce, the mother remarried. The Louisiana Court of Appeal held that, under Louisiana law, a court may

Combined net income
The figure arrived at when each parent's net income is added together to determine child support; also known as total net income.

Total net income
The figure arrived at when each parent's net income is added to determine child support; also known as combined net income.

D. STEPHEN ROSENBLOOM v. RENEE BAUCHET (KUTCHER), WIFE OF D. STEPHEN ROSENBLOOM

654 So. 2d 877 (La. App. 4 Cir. 1995)
COURT OF APPEAL OF LOUISIANA, FOURTH DISTRICT

... Mr. Rosenbloom next argues that the trial judge erred in calculating the award. Specifically, he argues that she erred in extrapolating a figure where the combined monthly income for the parties exceeded the maximum under the child support guidelines set forth at LSA-R.S. 9:315.10(B), resulting in an excessive award. Mr. Rosenbloom also contends that the award is excessive because the trial judge failed to consider that Mrs. Kutcher's circumstances had improved after her marriage to Mr. Kutcher.

With regard to the children of the marriage, both the father and the mother have the obligation to support. Support is to be granted considering the needs of the person to whom it is due, and the circumstances of those who are obligated to pay it (citation omitted). The court may consider as income the benefits a party derives from remarriage, expense-sharing, or other sources. LSA-R.S. 9:315(6)(c). In arriving at an award, the totality of relevant circumstances must be considered (citation omitted).

LSA-R.S. 9:315.10(B) provides:

If the combined adjusted gross income of the parties exceeds the highest level specified in the schedule contained in R.S. 9:315.14, the court shall use its discretion in setting the amount of the basic child support obligation, but in no event shall it be less than the highest amount set forth in the schedule.

Under the clear provisions of LSA-R.S. 9:315.10(B), the trial court has discretion in setting the amount of child support when the combined adjusted gross income of the parties exceeds the highest figure provided in the schedule, and its judgment in such matters will not be disturbed in the absence of a showing of an abuse of that discretion (citation omitted).

In the instant case, the trial court used the combined monthly income of the parties in calculating the award. The trial judge determined that Mr. Rosenbloom's monthly income was $39,891.50, by dividing his 1993 gross income of $478,698.00 by 12. As to Mrs. Kutcher's monthly income, the trial judge correctly considered the living expenses incident to her second marriage. The trial judge stated:

[t]he Court notes that in the case of Mrs. Kutcher that she has no single source of income of her own other than approximately 5,000 dollars a year that she earns. The bulk of her income comes from (A) what the Court will describe as an expense sharing that she receives the benefits from her current spouse, Robert Kutcher. And under R.S. 9:315(6)(c)—the law tells us that the Court can only consider as income the benefits a party derives from expense sharing or other sources. However, in determining the benefits of expense sharing the Court shall not consider the income of another spouse regardless of the remarriage existence except to the extent that such income is used directly to reduce the costs of a party's actual expenses.

So, consequently, to determine what Mrs. Kutcher's income is, the Court has to make a determination as to the benefits she receives from Mr. Kutcher. And that part of the statute also says, with regard to the party's actual expenses, his contribution to her actual expenses would not come from his gross income but from his net income.

The judge then correctly determined that Mrs. Kutcher's monthly income was $9,040.12.

Source: 654 SO. 2D 877 (LA. APP. 4 CIR. 1995), Court of Appeal of Louisiana, Fourth District, State of Louisiana.

consider the benefits a parent derives from remarriage in determining the combined monthly income of the parties in arriving at the child support obligation.

By Agreement or by Court Order

A divorcing couple may wish to avoid a trial and enter an agreement on the amount of support to be paid by the noncustodial parent to the custodial parent for the support of the minor children. While family court judges prefer agreements to litigating domestic issues, the court will examine the amount agreed upon by the parties and compare it to the amount the custodial parent would have received under the state's child support guidelines. If the amount is less than the guidelines, the parties must convince the judge that awarding this figure would be in the best interest of the children. The court has the final say in the amount of child support and can override the agreement of the parties. The judge must enter the reasons for deviating from the guidelines on the court record.

If the parties cannot agree on the amount of child support to be paid by the noncustodial parent, the court will issue a figure based on the guidelines and will incorporate this figure into the court's order. The order typically requires the noncustodial parent to pay a sum to the custodial parent on a monthly or weekly basis and that the duty to pay support shall continue until the child reaches the age of majority or becomes emancipated by a court of law.

Utilizing Computer Software

Most states that have adopted child support guidelines use worksheets and legislated criteria to determine the exact amount of child support due. The family services units of many states also assist the parties in determining the figures. Computer programs have emerged in many states where the calculation of child support is complex. The use of software saves time and money when calculating child support obligations in a busy law office. The user collects the data from the client and spouse and inputs the information into the system.

The California guidelines, for example, are calculated using a complicated algebraic formula. To ensure the accuracy of the calculations, computer programs are used. The most commonly used program in this jurisdiction is called DISSOMASTER™. The attorney or paralegal inputs information such as the custody arrangement, income of the parties, mandatory payroll deductions, child care expenses, and so on, and the software generates a child support figure. DISSOMASTER™ may also be purchased as an app and downloaded onto the attorney's or paralegal's phone or tablet—for example, an iPad—for easy access when in the courthouse or during an interview in the client's home. A paralegal working in the state of California, for instance, would learn how to use DISSOMASTER™ by attending training sessions or by accessing the tutorial available on the company's website.

It is important for paralegals practicing in the field of family law to become familiar with the computer software most used by law firms in their state and to seek classes or tutorials that provide training in the software.

Deviation Criteria

In jurisdictions where child support guidelines are applied, statutory maximum and minimum limits usually exist for contributions by each parent. However, if the parties agree between themselves that one party or the other will pay more or less of the statutorily determined amount, frequently courts will allow this *deviation from the guidelines* providing that the parties present the court with a good reason for the departure and providing that allowing the deviation does not appear to financially deprive the child.

The parties may not always agree on a deviation from the guidelines. In these cases, the parties are allowed to argue their reasons for and against the proposed amount of child support. Here are some of the factors a court may take into consideration when deciding whether or not to deviate from the guidelines:

- The extraordinary expenses incurred for the care of a physically or mentally disabled child;
- The noncustodial parent's obligation to pay child support to dependents from a previous marriage or relationship;
- The earning capacity of a parent—a parent who has a license to practice medicine and decides to work as a medical assistant may be deemed to be underemployed by the court;
- Whether other assets are available to the parent but do not appear on the calculation under the child support guidelines;
- Extraordinary expenses incurred by the parents in traveling a significant distance to visit with the children or legitimate expenses associated with the parent's employment, business, or medical expenses;
- Shared custody arrangements where both parents have physical custody of the children for equal time; and
- Whether the noncustodial parent is highly compensated and such compensation exceeds the state's child support guidelines.

Tennis, Anyone? In this section, we revisit the *Evans* case with an excerpt that deals with determining child support obligation when the income of the parents exceeds the state's child support guidelines.

EDWIN E. EVANS v. CYNTHIA S. EVANS

1997 S.D. 16, 559 N.W.2D 240 (S.D. 1997)
SUPREME COURT OF SOUTH DAKOTA

...ANALYSIS AND DECISION

1 Did the trial court abuse its discretion in failing to consider the children's actual needs and standard of living in setting child support?

SDCL 25-7-6.2 provides guidelines that trial courts must follow in setting child support amounts. However, where the parties' income exceeds the statutory guidelines, SDCL 25-7-6.9 provides the child support obligation "shall be established at an appropriate level, taking into account the actual needs and standard of living of the child" (citation omitted)....

... Cyndy sought $5,000 per month in child support, however, she produced an exhibit which listed expenses of $4,410 per month. Itemized, this figure included:

$400	for food
580	for vehicle expenses
110	per month for medical expenses
550	per month for educational expenses
500	per month for vacations
100	per month for dining out
550	for entertainment and allowances
200	for clothing purchases
1,300	for tennis expenses (Kelsey only) (clothes, supplies, lessons, tournament travel)
60	for piano lessons
25	for beauty shop expenses
25	for cosmetics expenses
10	for newspapers and subscriptions
$4,410	

The trial court ruled at an interim hearing that $1,300 per month for tennis expenses was clearly excessive and Ed would not be required to pay this expense . . . .

. . . Subtracting the $1,300 per month tennis expense from Cyndy's itemized living expenses for the children leaves a balance of $2,185 per month. The trial court ordered Ed to pay child support in this amount, plus pay $500 per month in allowances directly to the children, pay $600 per month for their tuition at parochial school, and provide health insurance for each child, for a total child support obligation of $3,505 per month.[1] The trial court noted that Ed had agreed to pay the children's allowances, parochial school tuition, medical insurance, and college expenses. The trial court noted this child support award still provided a "luxurious lifestyle" for the two girls.[2]

On appeal, Cyndy notes the amount of Ed's child support obligation, as determined by the trial court, is approximately twelve percent of his $25,000 net monthly income. Cyndy argues the trial court made two errors: (1) It applied the wrong legal standard by focusing on the children's needs rather than their standard of living; and (2) it substituted its personal judgment of what the children's standard of living should be, for the standard set by the parties themselves during their marriage.

In the trial court's memorandum decision, it cited "the needs of the children and the father's ability to pay" as the standard for determining child support obligations above the statutory guidelines. It then stated that because the father's ability to pay was not at issue in this case, the only consideration need be the "reasonable needs of the children." This solitary consideration does not reflect the standard set by statute and prior case law. As noted above, the trial court's inquiry is to take into account the actual needs and standard of living of the children. However, the record reflects the trial court did not apply only the reasonable needs of the children and that it did consider their standard of living in making its determination. A trial court is not required to accept either party's claimed expenses. To do so would remove the trial court's discretion in setting child support obligations where the parties' income exceeds the guidelines set forth in SDCL 25-7-6.2. Cyndy has the burden of proving her claimed expenses reflect the children's needs and standard of living (citation omitted).

Cyndy's claim of $1,300 per month ($15,600 annually) for tennis expenses is a projected expense for only one of the couple's daughters, which includes Cyndy's traveling expenses to accompany her daughter. Ed points out, which Cyndy does not dispute, that this projected expense is $6,760 per year more than was spent in 1995 for Kelsey to travel and participate in tournaments in several states. Ed also notes, which Cyndy does not dispute, that this projection is based in part on daughter Ashley's involvement with tennis, which she severely curtailed after her sixteenth birthday. At the time of this appeal, Kelsey is fifteen years old. As such, Cyndy has failed to prove the $1,300 per month is reflective of Kelsey's standard of living prior to the couple's divorce (citation omitted). . . . The trial court did not abuse its discretion in ordering support in an amount that will adequately care for the children's actual needs and permit them to enjoy a standard of living commensurate with that prior to their parents' divorce (citation omitted). . . .

Source: Edwin E. Evans v. Cynthia S. Evans, 1997 S.D. 16, 559 N.W.2D 240 (S.D. 1997), Supreme Court of South Dakota.

---

[1]We note several of these items the trial court ordered Ed to pay *in addition* to the $2,185 total amount were already included in the $2,185 total in Cyndy's list of expenses. Therefore, the amount actually awarded is closer to the amount requested by Cyndy than she argues in her appeal to this Court.

[2]Supplemental information in Ed's brief to this Court notes his older daughter graduated from high school in May 1996 and is currently enrolled in a private college in Minnesota. Ed continues to pay Cyndy the amount ordered by the trial court for two children and has not moved for a reduction of that amount.

MODIFICATION OF CHILD SUPPORT ORDERS

The order for child support entered at the time of dissolution can be modified if there is a *substantial change* in the financial circumstances of either party. Some jurisdictions refer to this as a *significant variance to modify.* If the paying party suffers a downward shift in income, that party may file a motion with the court to modify the child support to reflect his or her decreased ability to pay. Sometimes a court will not decrease the amount and direct the financially strapped party to economize in other areas of life. This is frequently the case where the custodial parent's income was not substantial at the time of dissolution and has not increased or has in fact decreased. On the other hand, if the custodial parent's income has increased or was substantial to begin with, the court may grant the noncustodial parent's request for a lowering of the amount of periodic child support payments.

In the states where statutory guidelines are used, and a formula is applied to determine each parent's contribution toward the dollar amount needed for the support of the child, if the noncustodial parent's income has dropped, then the court may decide that a greater proportion of the custodial parent's income shall be dedicated to child support and that the noncustodial parent's financial obligation will decrease. Conversely, if the noncustodial parent's income has risen substantially, the custodial spouse may bring a ***motion for modification of child support*** requesting the court to order the noncustodial parent to pay higher periodic child support payments, so that less of the custodial parent's income will be needed for the child. The court will grant this motion if the custodial parent demonstrates the need for additional support. Even if the children are being adequately provided for under the prevailing order, if the noncustodial parent's income has risen dramatically and includes many discretionary income dollars, the court may see fit to order a higher support obligation providing the court is given proper information on how this extra money will be put to use for the child's benefit.

Motion for modification of child support
A document requesting the court to order the noncustodial parent to pay higher periodic child support payments, so that less of the custodial parent's income will be needed for the child.

The noncustodial parent may also have a substantial increase in income upon the death of a relative who has left him or her a large inheritance or has been lucky enough to win the lottery.

A noncustodial parent may seek a reduction in his or her child support obligations due to a loss of employment, illness, disability, or unforeseen economic circumstances. A noncustodial parent employed in the area of lower Manhattan when the Twin Towers came down or running a business in New Orleans after Hurricane Katrina would argue that these unforeseen occurrences created a substantial change in circumstances that required a change in the original support order.

The court may also order a change in the amount of child support when there are substantial changes in circumstances involving the children. This may include providing for the needs of a growing child who now needs more food, more expensive clothing, unreimbursed medical or dental expenses, and costs associated with school such as class trips, yearbook and class ring expenses, and the school prom.

"Shocking" Results

In the *Rossino* case, the husband is forced to resign from the police force after a sexual liaison with another woman while on duty. A new career as an electrician's apprentice and a subsequent on-the-job injury raise questions regarding the modifiability of child support.

IN THE MATTER OF VETA (GAGLIARDI) ROSSINO AND JOSEPH A. ROSSINO

153 N.H. 367 (2006)
SUPREME COURT OF NEW HAMPSHIRE

GALWAY, J.

The petitioner, Joseph A. Rossino, appeals an order of the Marital Master (Nancy J. Geiger, Esq.), as approved by the Superior Court (Barry, J.), denying his petition for modification of child support and granting respondent Veta Gagliardi's motion for contempt. We vacate and remand.

The record supports the following facts. The parties were married in 1987 and have one son, born in 1990. They divorced on January 17, 1992, based upon irreconcilable differences. The respondent was granted primary physical custody of their son, and the petitioner was ordered to pay child support in the amount of $110 per week.

In March 2003, the petitioner involuntarily resigned from his employment as a police officer in the Hudson Police Department following allegations that he had sexual relations with another woman while on duty during the previous year. The petitioner had been employed as a police officer for over seventeen years, since 1986. He earned an annual income of approximately $60,000, which included significant overtime. Though the petitioner denied having sexual relations while on duty, he did not deny that he had sexual relations with another woman in 2002. Despite initiating a grievance and an arbitration procedure, the petitioner was unable to return to work as a Hudson police officer.

After involuntarily resigning from the Hudson Police Department, the petitioner was unable to obtain employment in a law enforcement related field. He was intermittently employed as an electrician's apprentice with two companies at an annual income averaging approximately $36,000. After March 2003, the petitioner alleged that he was unable to make regular child support payments to the respondent.

In April 2004, the respondent sought payment of child support, and the State began garnishing the petitioner's wages in the amount of $132 per week, which reflected the weekly child support payment plus a portion of the arrearages. In June 2004, the petitioner filed for modification of child support based upon his loss of employment with the Hudson Police Department. The respondent countered by filing a motion for contempt for failure to make child support payments in accordance with the permanent stipulation. On November 17, 2004, the court conducted a hearing by offers of proof and considered all pending motions. However, on October 27, 2004, while employed as an electrician's apprentice, the petitioner was "electrocuted." Consequently, at the time of the hearing and the subsequent filing of this appeal, the petitioner was unemployed and receiving workers' compensation.

At the November 2004 hearing, the petitioner sought a reduction in his child support obligation based upon his reduced annual income and his inability to work after the October 27, 2004 accident.

In its December 2, 2004, ruling, the court in this case took judicial notice that the marital master found, in the related divorce case between the petitioner and Lucille Rossino, see In the Matter of Rossino & Rossino, 153 N.H. 282 (2006), that "the [Noddin] case applies since it was a result of Joseph A. Rossino's own inappropriate conduct and voluntary actions that brought about his loss of employment with the Hudson Police Department." See Noddin v. Noddin, 123 N.H. 73 (1983). The court also reviewed the evidence, specifically noting its consideration of the petitioner's "lengthy disciplinary index," his resignation from the Hudson Police Department, and the arbitrator's decision. The trial court ruled that Noddin applied in this case and attributed the higher earnings from the Hudson Police Department to the petitioner.

continued

> On appeal, the petitioner argues the trial court erred in applying Noddin to the instant case, asserting that (1) his improper conduct was not criminal and, therefore, did not rise to the level of fault; (2) he has no valuable assets; and (3) he is physically incapacitated as a result of the October 2004 work injury, and, therefore, RSA 458-C:2, IV(a) precludes imputing the higher income to him...
>
> ... The respondent counters that the trial court correctly determined that Noddin applies because the petitioner's termination of employment was based upon his own actions and his retirement benefit from the Hudson Police Department constitutes a valuable asset as contemplated by Noddin. The respondent also asserts that the petitioner's injury does not rise to the level of physical incapacitation pursuant to RSA 458-C:2, IV(a)...
>
> ... Here, the petitioner raised the issue of his physical incapacity at the November 2004 hearing. Furthermore, during the hearing, the respondent conceded that she was not contesting the legitimacy of the petitioner's claim that he had been "electrocuted" and was unable to work full time. Therefore, the trial court committed an unsustainable exercise of discretion when it failed to make a determination regarding the petitioner's alleged physical incapacity under RSA 458-C:2, IV(a). Only if it determined that the petitioner was not physically or mentally incapacitated would the trial court proceed to determine whether, under the terms of that statute, the petitioner voluntarily became "unemployed or underemployed" for the purposes of imputing income to him. Accordingly, we remand this case to the superior court for a determination consistent with RSA 458-C:2, IV(a) and this opinion.
>
> *Source:* In the Matter of Veta (Gagliardi) Rossino and Joseph A. Rossino, 153 N.H. 367 (2006), Supreme Court of New Hampshire.

Informal Agreements

Sometimes parents who have had a substantial change in circumstances attempt to work out informal agreements regarding the payment of child support. While the parties believe they are saving money on legal fees by resorting to self-help, the agreement is not enforceable in a court of law. Furthermore, there may be a misunderstanding of the terms of the modification between the parties that may create a "he said, she said" scenario that may result in costly litigation. Parties who agree to a modification should put the terms in writing and ask the court to enter an order on the terms. Under these circumstances, the order may be enforced in the event that one of the parties fails to fulfill his or her obligations.

CHILD SUPPORT ENFORCEMENT

A child support order is an enforceable judgment. A custodial parent who has a court order for child support and is not receiving funds from the noncustodial parent must resort to the legal system.

The process of enforcement can be quite frustrating for a custodial parent who is in need of money to support the children and must resort to the courts for help. A custodial parent who has access to enough funds to hire a private attorney and pursue the matter through civil enforcement of the order in the family courts may be at a greater advantage than a custodial parent who must rely on the overburdened administrative enforcement system.

Every jurisdiction has an administrative enforcement system in the form of a child support enforcement agency that assists custodial parents with collecting child support. These agencies collect child support on behalf of the state when the taxpayers provide the children with support in the form of public assistance.

When applying for state welfare, a custodial parent agrees to assist the state in identifying and locating the noncustodial parent, as well as assigning to the state rights of collection. The custodial parent is also required to pursue the collection of child support, and any monies collected are taken by the state as reimbursement for state welfare payments.

Custodial parents who are not receiving state welfare may also apply for administrative enforcement assistance for a small fee.

Civil Enforcement

If a noncustodial parent fails to pay all or part of the child support obligation, the custodial parent may file a ***motion for contempt***. This motion will alert the court to the other party's failure to comply with the court's earlier support order and will request that the court provide relief by ordering the other party to pay the back child support owed as well as the attorney's fees the custodial parent has expended to bring the deficiency to the court's attention. If the noncustodial parent does not appear at the contempt hearing, the court may order what is known as a ***capias***. A capias is a document empowering a sheriff to arrest the nonappearing, noncustodial parent and bring him or her to jail and to court. However, if the noncustodial parent cannot be located by a sheriff or other court officer, the custodial parent may turn to administrative enforcement. Administrative enforcement also comes into the picture when the custodial parent is receiving government assistance or when the noncustodial parent has left the jurisdiction.

Motion for contempt
A document that alerts the court to the other party's failure to comply with the court's earlier order and requests that the court provide relief.

Capias
A document empowering a sheriff to arrest a nonappearing, noncustodial parent and bring him or her to jail and to court.

Administrative Enforcement

The term ***administrative enforcement*** refers to action by a state or federal agency. Many states have *Bureaus of Support Enforcement* or *IV-D agencies* (pronounced "four-d agencies"). These agencies are state agencies mandated by federal law, pursuant to the *Child Support Enforcement and Establishment of Paternity Act* passed by Congress in 1974. Their purpose is to facilitate the entry and enforcement of child support orders on a state-by-state basis. These agencies provide four services: (1) location of noncustodial parents through parent locator services, which are statutorily empowered to search the records of state and federal agencies such as the state's department of motor vehicles or department of revenue services and/or the federal government's Social Security Administration and the Internal Revenue Service (IRS); (2) establishment of the paternity of children through testing of putative fathers; (3) facilitation of the entry of support orders following the location of the noncustodial parent or following the establishment of paternity; and (4) enforcement of existing orders.

Administrative enforcement
Action by a state or federal agency, rather than a court.

Means of Enforcement

Most jurisdictions allow for a variety of enforcement means when enforcing child support orders. They include the following:

- Wage garnishment—deducting payments from the noncustodial parent's paycheck. In order to obtain a wage garnishment, the custodial parent must obtain a court order for child support, which is then served on the noncustodial parent's employer. The employer is then obligated to deduct the child support payments from the noncustodial parent's check and send a check to the custodial parent.
- Filing a negative report with a credit-reporting agency. This tactic interferes with the noncustodial parent's ability to obtain credit.

Figure 8-1 If a parent continually neglects to pay child support, administrative enforcement may become the only solution.

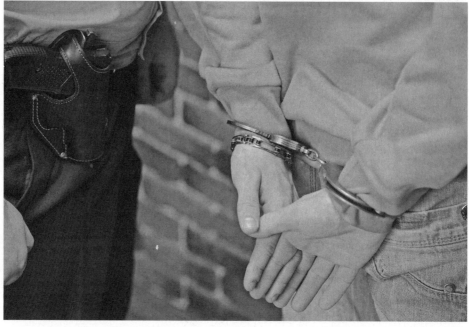

Fisun Ivan/Shutterstock.

- Intercepting federal and state tax refunds and unemployment compensation—for example, if a noncustodial parent owes child support, his or her state or federal tax refund or unemployment compensation may be intercepted to pay for the amounts owed.
- Denial of U.S. passport if the noncustodial parent owes more than $5,000 in child support.
- Obtaining a writ of execution—the custodial parent may enforce a child support order by obtaining a judgment and attaching the noncustodial parent's property, such as bank accounts, real estate, motor vehicles, and so on.
- Cash bond—a court order requiring the noncustodial parent to post a cash bond to secure the support payments.
- Denial or revocation of state-issued occupational and motor vehicle licenses.
- Obtaining a contempt order from the court that results in the incarceration of the noncustodial parent. If a noncustodial parent willfully fails to abide by a court order, he or she may be incarcerated on the grounds of civil contempt. The contempt petition is filed by the custodial parent, scheduled for a court hearing, and served on the noncustodial parent by a sheriff. During the hearing, the noncustodial parent must explain why he or she is in contempt. Very often, the filing of a contempt petition triggers the filing of a modification petition on behalf of the noncustodial parent. The noncustodial parent may have a legitimate reason for failing to make child support payments, such as loss of employment or illness. These two actions are often heard during the same hearing. If the noncustodial parent is found in contempt of court, the judge has the power to incarcerate the individual and not release the individual until a payment has been made. The noncustodial parent usually contacts a friend or relative to bring money for his or her release. In some cases, the threat of incarceration may be enough to motivate child support payments.

- Criminal prosecution—every jurisdiction has the statutory power to punish noncustodial parents who do not pay child support orders. In these cases, the noncustodial parent may be incarcerated or placed on probation as long as the child support is paid as scheduled. Indigent noncustodial parents facing incarceration under a contempt petition or criminal prosecution are entitled to a court-appointed attorney.
- Parent locator services—noncustodial parents who wish to avoid paying child support may leave the city or state or obtain jobs where they are paid "under the table." A custodial parent may have no other choice but to go on public assistance and have the taxpayers support the children. The federal and state governments have created parent locator services, whereby a search of IRS, Social Security, motor vehicle, and other records may be accessed for information on the noncustodial parent. Once the information is obtained, it can be used to help enforce pending orders.

Interstate Enforcement of Child Support Orders

One of the biggest problems facing custodial parents trying to enforce child support orders is doing so when the noncustodial parent has moved out of the state. Noncustodial parents may move to another jurisdiction under the mistaken belief that the original order cannot be enforced or that they may obtain a more favorable modification in another jurisdiction. For example, the child support guidelines in the state granting the original order may be much higher than the guideline amount in another state. This discrepancy in figures might encourage a parent to "forum shop" for a better deal.

The Full Faith and Credit Clause of the U.S. Constitution, however, mandates that each state honor final court orders entered by judges in other states and apply that particular state's laws. This mandate, however, does not include orders of a temporary nature. The Constitution requires the new state to apply the law of the jurisdiction where the original order was entered in order to determine whether the judgment is modifiable. This includes both *arrearages* (past-due payments) and any future payments.

A series of uniform acts passed by the states have been enacted to provide remedies to custodial parents seeking to enforce orders across state lines. The *Uniform Desertion and Non-Support Act* was published by the National Conference of Commissioners on Uniform State Laws (NCCUSL) in 1910 and made deserting or refusing to provide support to a spouse or child under the age of sixteen a punishable offense. The one major flaw of this act was that it did not allow for interstate enforcement of state support orders. Noncustodial parents who wished to avoid court orders simply left the state. Extradition of the offending parent was a long and often fruitless process. This left the state welfare departments with the expense of supporting children.

To remedy the flaws in the Uniform Desertion and Non-Support Act, the NCCUSL drafted the *Uniform Reciprocal Enforcement of Support Act (URESA)*. The purpose of the URESA was to improve enforcement of orders across state lines. The URESA included both criminal and civil enforcement provisions. Criminal enforcement was accomplished by the obligee state (the state where the custodial parent resides) demanding that the obligor state (the state where the noncustodial parent resides) extradite the noncustodial parent to the obligee state or, in the alternative, that the noncustodial parent submit himself or herself to the obligee state's jurisdiction.

Uniform Reciprocal Enforcement of Support Act (URESA)
A model act adopted by states designed to improve the enforcement of child support orders across state lines.

A custodial parent who chose civil enforcement of the child support order would bring an action in his or her state, and this jurisdiction would decide if the noncustodial parent had a duty to support the children. If the answer was in the affirmative, the court would enter an order of support and would then forward that order to the court in the noncustodial parent's state of residence. This state would now have jurisdiction over the noncustodial parent and have the authority to notify the noncustodial parent and conduct a hearing. The order could then be enforced in the noncustodial parent's state.

Revised Uniform Reciprocal Enforcement of Support Act of 1968 (RURESA)
Where a custodial parent may ultimately obtain child support from the noncustodial parent residing in another state by instituting certain procedures.

The URESA was amended in 1958, resulting in the ***Revised Uniform Reciprocal Enforcement of Support Act (RURESA)***. There were two very important changes to the URESA. The first was to facilitate the exchange of evidence from the obligee's state to the obligor's state. The purpose behind the URESA was being defeated because the obligor's state did not have the necessary evidence to enforce orders against the obligor, who very often walked out of court a winner. The RURESA now required the obligee's state to send any evidence available along with the obligee's file.

The second change in the RURESA was the ability of the obligee to take the initiative to register the court order in a court located in the obligor's state and bring the initial proceeding in that court. While this new provision enabled custodial parents to take more aggressive action against the noncustodial parent, the problem of multiple state orders emerged. For example, if a noncustodial parent moved from New York to Connecticut to New Hampshire and the custodial parent sought an order in each court, there would be three different state laws and original and modified orders to decipher.

Uniform Interstate Family Support Act (UIFSA)
Where the noncustodial parent's state must honor the original support and may not enter a new order or modify the existing order to conform to its guidelines for determining the amount of support.

In 1992, the NCCUSL replaced the URESA and the RURESA with the ***Uniform Interstate Family Support Act (UIFSA)***, and it has since been adopted by every state in the United States. (See Appendix D for Florida's version of the UIFSA.) The UIFSA is divided into five parts:

1. General Provisions
2. Establishing a Support Order
3. Enforcing a Support Order
4. Modifying a Support Order
5. Parentage

The UIFSA addressed the problem of multiple orders by allowing a child support order to be modified based on the law of the state with original jurisdiction. This is called *continuing exclusive jurisdiction.* So in the previous example, the Connecticut and New Hampshire courts could only modify the original order based on the law of the state of New York. Under the UIFSA, the noncustodial parent's state must honor the original support order and may not enter a new order or modify the existing order to conform to its guidelines for determining the amount of support. Only the custodial parent's state may modify its own order, unless the parties agree to the modification in writing or both parties have moved to the new state, thus giving the new state jurisdiction over the matter.

A custodial parent seeking relief under the UIFSA would file a petition in his or her own jurisdiction. The original court files the petition in a court where the obligor resides, where a hearing is held on the matter. An attorney employed by the state will represent the interest of the custodial parent at the hearing held in the obligor's state, unless the custodial parent has enough money to hire a private attorney to represent his or her interests and prosecute the petition. While state child support enforcement systems throughout the country are well intentioned, they are overwhelmed with a large volume of work. This makes the system frustrating for custodial parents trying to collect unpaid child support.

CHILD SUPPORT ORDER AND THE RIGHT TO VISITATION

Just as a noncustodial parent has an obligation to support his or her minor children, so must the custodial parent comply with the court's order giving the noncustodial parent reasonable visitation.

It is important to understand at the outset that the payment of child support and the right to access or visitation are disconnected issues. These obligations are separate obligations, independent of one another, and the default on one obligation by one parent will not excuse the default of the other parent on his or her obligation. If a noncustodial parent ceases to pay child support, the custodial parent may not withhold visitation; and if a custodial parent refuses to make the minor children available for visitation, the noncustodial parent is not excused from paying child support. A minority of states allow a noncustodial parent who is refused visitation to petition the court to temporarily cease child support payments.

Each party may seek to remedy the respective default by filing a motion for contempt of a court order. The injured party may request that the offending party be held in contempt of court and be ordered to resume his or her obligation. As mentioned, frequently the party bringing the motion for contempt will request and receive an order from the court that the offending party pay the costs and reasonable attorney's fees of the injured party. An attorney's fee award is made on the rationale that the party bringing the action would not have incurred the expense of representation had the other party fulfilled his or her legal obligation.

ADDITIONAL SUPPORT ORDERS

Sometimes support orders contain obligations beyond a periodic monetary payment. For instance, a judge may order a noncustodial parent to provide medical coverage to all children until they reach the age of majority. Also, when parties negotiate an agreement that one party shall pay private school tuition for all children during minority, this provision will be incorporated into the separation agreement. If the parent refuses to pay for tuition during minority, the other party may file a motion for contempt to enforce this agreed-to obligation. If the offending party counters this motion for contempt with a motion to modify the obligation for tuition because of changed financial circumstance, the court will not even consider a modification unless the separation agreement provided an accommodation for the event of changed circumstances. Further, the court will always order the party to pay the past-due amount. As noted, a past-due amount is termed an *arrearage*.

Supporting a Second Family

Noncustodial parents often create new families to support by either remarrying, cohabitating with a domestic partner, or engaging in intimate relations and choosing not to live with the other biological parent. In the past, family courts enforced the "first family first" rule; child support payments to the first family could not be reduced based on the argument that the noncustodial parent now had a second family to support. While some jurisdictions still adhere to this rule, the majority of states allow for some type of readjustment based on the best interest of the child theory. Though a noncustodial parent's obligation to support the first family is not diminished by the creation of a second family, a custodial parent who is receiving child support and remarries is still entitled to child support unless the new spouse adopts the child.

New Spouse or Domestic Partner's Income

What effect does a new spouse or domestic partner's income have on child support payments? While state child support guidelines do not consider a new spouse or domestic partner's income in calculating child support payments, their respective contributions to the family finances may affect child support payments in the form of a deviation from the child support guidelines. Remarriage or cohabitation may be considered a "substantial change in circumstances" that warrants another visit to family court for an adjustment in the amount of support paid.

If the obligor has remarried and has new children to support, he or she will inevitably file for a modification on the grounds that there is a change in circumstances because there are now more mouths to feed. The recipient spouse, on the other hand, may find that his or her child support payments will be reduced because the obligor has created a second family. The court makes the reduction because it must take into account the best interest of the children and must reallocate the income in order to cover both families.

If the recipient spouse has remarried or is cohabitating with a domestic partner who is making contributions to the household, including gifts to the children, the recipient spouse may find his or her child support reduced.

Nonbiological Parent's Duty to Support: The Doctrine of Equitable Estoppel

Courts across the United States have ordered nonbiological parents to pay child support on the basis of their relationship with the child. The problem usually arises when the relationship between the biological parent and friend, spouse, or lover terminates. This individual may have provided the child with financial support and may have interacted with a child as if the child were his or her own. The biological parent brings an action in the courts for child support relying on the *doctrine of equitable estoppel*. Under the doctrine of equitable estoppel, a court may hold that because the individual voluntarily assumed some type of parental role in the child's life and the child relied on this role, the individual is now obligated to provide the child with financial support.

Public policy arguments for holding nonbiological parents responsible when the relationship with the biological mother terminates include preventing the child from becoming a charge on the taxpayers and the child's need for support. Once the court has concluded that the doctrine of equitable estoppel applies in the case, the nonbiological parent is now barred from equitably denying a future obligation to pay child support. The court therefore creates a support obligation where none had existed. Once a promise is made to provide financial support to a child where no duty had previously existed, the doctrine of equitable estoppel arises. The biological parent, based on this promise, then fails to pursue the other biological parent for support based on the representations made by the nonbiological parent. Once the nonbiological parent stops paying, the biological parent has missed the opportunity to seek support from the legal parent.

In cases where the parties are legally married, the husband is presumed to be the father of any children born to the wife during the course of the marriage. This is called the presumption of paternity. If the wife conceived a child with another man during the course of the marriage, the husband is still legally and financially responsible for the child even though he is not the biological father. If the nonbiological father becomes aware of the wife's infidelity or is suspicious of the child's biological origins, he can demand a paternity test in the courts to determine if he is or is not the biological parent. In many states, if the courts find that he acted as a father, put his name on the child's birth certificate, provided emotional and financial support, and held himself out to the world as the child's father, as well as providing the child with support, he may be court ordered to pay support if, to the wife's detriment, she failed to pursue the biological father. This scenario often arises when the wife commits adultery and becomes pregnant as a result. The child then relies on the nonbiological father's representations, treats mother's husband as his or her father, and does not attempt to find the biological father.

Nice Guys Finish Last The case of *Nygard v. Nygard* illustrates that when a nonbiological parent voluntarily promises to provide financial support to a child, he may be barred from avoiding any future obligation if he stops paying, based on the theory that the child has now relied on his promise.

NYGARD v. NYGARD

156 Mich. app. 94, 401 N.W.2d 323 (1986)
Michigan Court of Appeals

T.M. Burns, P.J.

Defendant Dudley Neil Nygard appeals as of right from the provisions of a divorce judgment requiring defendant to contribute to the support and maintenance of Shuntelle Lee Nygard, a minor child.

Plaintiff Michael Ann Nygard met the defendant, Dudley Nygard, in July 1982, and began to spend a good deal of time with him thereafter. By October 1982, a strong relationship had developed between the two. In October 1982, plaintiff discovered that she was pregnant. It is undisputed that the pregnancy was not a result of plaintiff's relationship with defendant. Rather, plaintiff's pregnancy resulted from a short relationship with a man named "Tim" whom she had met in May 1982 during a stay in Florida. Plaintiff was shocked and upset when she discovered that she was pregnant and did not know how she would support a child.

In late October or early November 1982, plaintiff advised defendant that she was pregnant and that the child was not his. She told him that she planned to go to Alaska, where her brother lived, and give the baby up for adoption. Defendant asked plaintiff not to go to Alaska and stated that he did not want to lose her. Defendant wanted to marry plaintiff and thought that the mother and baby would be a "package deal." Defendant agreed to raise the child as his own. When he agreed to treat the baby as his own, he meant that he would buy her things, feed her, and house her.

Plaintiff decided not to go to Alaska and give the child up for adoption. She stressed that one of the main reasons she did not do so was because of defendant's statements.

On December 4, 1982, the parties were married. Defendant indicated that they married before the child was born so that the child would have defendant's name and so that no one would know that he had not fathered the child.

Shuntelle was born on February 14, 1983. Defendant was present in the delivery room during birth. He acknowledged to hospital personnel that he was the child's father and his name was placed on the birth certificate. Defendant treated Shuntelle as his own child during the marriage and encouraged her to call him "Papa."

The couple separated in May 1984. On June 6, 1984, plaintiff filed a complaint for divorce against defendant in Schoolcraft Circuit Court. On June 22, 1984, a temporary order of child support was entered by the circuit court. On October 11, 1984, defendant filed a motion to "remove the minor child from the divorce complaint and to discontinue child support" on the ground that he was not the biological father of

continued

the minor child. The circuit court denied defendant's motion. Defendant thereafter filed for leave to appeal, which this Court denied. On September 26, 1985, a judgment of divorce was entered. The judgment included provisions requiring defendant to contribute to the support and maintenance of the minor child. Because defendant was sick at the time, the judgment indicated that once defendant returned to work on a full-time basis, he was to pay support and maintenance of $99 per week. Defendant now appeals as of right. We believe that the trial court properly concluded that defendant could be held responsible for child support payments.

Defendant argues that the trial court erred in finding defendant estopped to deny parentage of the child and estopped to deny his obligation to support the child. We find that, under the facts of this case, defendant has an obligation to contribute to the support of this child.

It is generally recognized that the biological parents are obligated by law to maintain and support their children. The duty to support arises both from common law and from statutory law....

... In this case, there is no biological relationship from which a support obligation can arise. In most cases in which there is no biological relationship between the child and the adult, the adult is not required to support the child.... However, there are exceptional situations in which an adult who is not a biological parent of a child may be required to make payments to be used to support the child.

One such exceptional situation was referred to by this Court in Johnson v. Johnson, 93 Mich. App. 415; 286 N.W.2d 886 (1979). In that case, the plaintiff was a man who married the defendant knowing that she was carrying a child for whom he was only possibly the biological father. Plaintiff thereafter held himself out as the father and supporter of the child for several years. In Johnson, this Court stated,

> Even if plaintiff were not the biological father of the child, by marrying defendant he forecloses any action by her to seek support from the child's biological father. Actions under the paternity act are authorized only where the woman was unmarried from the conception to the date of birth of the child. MCL 722.711(a) and (b), 722.714(b); MSA 25.491(a) and (b), MSA 25.494(b). As the Ohio court observed in *Burse v. Burse,* 48 Ohio App.2d 244 248; 356 N.E.2d 755 (1976), "the man at the time he marries the woman, knowing the woman is pregnant by another man, should be cognizant that he is foreclosing the chance of the unborn child being legitimized by its natural father and is barring a bastardy action by the mother against the natural father."

Plaintiff assumed the status of father of this child when the child was born and continued as such for ten years until he amended his divorce complaint at trial. As the child was born during the marriage while the parties lived together as husband and wife, it was not necessary for plaintiff to go through adoption proceedings. Conversely, after plaintiff has represented himself as the father of this child for nine to ten years, he may not now say that he was not.

On the facts of this case the Court is compelled to hold that plaintiff is estopped by his conduct to deny paternity of this child. [93 Mich. App. 419-420.]

While the situation present in Johnson is somewhat different from the situation here, the policies and rationale of Johnson are sound and applicable in this case. We agree with Johnson that under certain circumstances a person other than a biological parent may be held responsible for child support. Such a concept is not novel or extraordinary. In this case, we find it equitable to hold defendant responsible for child support payments.

In addition, we believe that traditional notions of estoppel may provide a basis for plaintiff's requested relief. The facts of this case suggest either that plaintiff and defendant entered into an enforceable contract whereby defendant agreed to support the child or, if the statute of frauds prevents the contract from being enforceable, that defendant may be held responsible under the doctrine of "equitable estoppel" or "promissory estoppel."...

...The elements of equitable or promissory estoppel are (1) a promise; (2) that the promisor should reasonably have expected to induce action of a definite and substantial character on the part of the promisee; (3) which in fact produced reliance or forbearance of that nature; and (4) in circumstances such that the promise must be enforced if injustice is to be avoided....

... Each of these elements is clearly present in this case. The circumstances of this case are such that the promise must be enforced if injustice is to be avoided. Because of defendant's promise, an obligation arose both to plaintiff and to the child. We believe that this promise can be enforced by the circuit court in this divorce proceeding.

However, our de novo review leads us to the conclusion that payments of $99 per week may be inappropriate under the circumstances of this case. We remand to the circuit court for reconsideration of this amount. The circuit court may consider the fact that defendant is not the natural father of the child and may reduce defendant's required payments if the circumstances so indicate. Remanded. We do not retain jurisdiction. No costs.

Source: Nygard v. Nygard, 156 MICH. APP. 94, 401 N.W.2D 323 (1986), Michigan Court of Appeals, Michigan Courts.

Roe v. Wade and the Case for Men's Right to Reproductive Choice

On March 9, 2006, the National Center for Men filed a lawsuit in federal court on behalf of Matt Dubay, who challenged a court order requiring him to pay the sum of $500 per month in child support. Dubay alleged that he relied on his girlfriend's representations that due to a health problem, she was unable to get pregnant. Dubay also alleged that he made it clear to her that he did not want to father any children at this time in his life. As a result of their sexual relationship, the girlfriend gave birth to a daughter.

Dubay fought the court's child support order on the grounds that it was unconstitutional and violated his reproductive rights. He argued that the support order violated his right to equal protection under the Fourteenth Amendment of the U.S. Constitution by discriminating against him on the basis of gender. As a legal basis for his argument, Dubay cites *Roe v. Wade,* claiming that while women have the right to avoid procreating by having an abortion, men do not have equal rights in relieving themselves of fatherhood. He stated that the Michigan paternity laws were unconstitutional because they required fathers to pay child support for unwanted children. On July 19, 2006, the federal court dismissed Dubay's lawsuit, calling it frivolous, and awarded the state attorney's fees for defending the action.

POSTMAJORITY CHILD SUPPORT

A parent's obligation to support a child typically terminates when the child dies, reaches the age of majority, or becomes emancipated by a court of law.

Prior to 1970, the age of majority in most states was twenty-one. When parties agreed or when a judge ordered a parent to pay children's college costs, failure to do so constituted contempt as long as the child was under the age of twenty-one. This enabled courts to enforce at least two and often three years of college tuition.

In 1970, many states lowered the age of majority to eighteen, requiring parents to provide support until the age of majority or age nineteen if the child was still attending high school. Family courts charged with adjudicating disputes on payments for the minor child no longer had jurisdiction to enforce a provision in a separation agreement that obligated a noncustodial parent to pay college tuition for a child who had reached the age of eighteen. Because most children do not even start college until they are over the age of eighteen, this change wreaked havoc in splintered families where agreements long counted on were no longer worth the legal paper on which they were written.

To remedy this situation, eventually a number of state legislatures passed laws that provided henceforth—but not retroactively—that (1) divorcing parties could include a provision in their separation agreement for the postmajority support of children and (2) request that this provision along with the rest of the agreement be enacted into the divorce decree. The new statutes provided that if such a provision was enacted into the order of divorce or dissolution, then the family court had jurisdiction to enforce the clause.

Postmajority support agreements frequently address payment for college tuition or other postsecondary education, payment for the maintenance of postmajority adult children with special needs, and payment for medical and dental insurance coverage on dependent adult children while they are students or when they are newly employed but not yet eligible for coverage at work. These types of

Postmajority support agreements
Agreements that address payment for college tuition or other postsecondary education, payment for the maintenance of postmajority adult children with special needs, or payment for medical and dental insurance coverage on dependent adult children while they are students or when they are newly employed but not yet eligible for coverage at work.

Figure 8-2 Postmajority support agreements for college expenses came about as a result of the age of majority being lowered from twenty-one to eighteen during the 1970s.

Monkey Business Images/Shutterstock.

postmajority support provisions are realistic in our current society because young adults frequently continue to have the need for some form of financial support from their family of origin. It is important to note that with the passage of the Health Care Reform Bill of 2010, dependant children up to the age of twenty-six will be able to stay on their parents' health insurance. The Health Care Reform Bill also prohibits insurers from excluding children with preexisting conditions from coverage.

In instances where both the custodial and the noncustodial parent shared the support obligation during the child's minority, both parents should be required to continue with this obligation if they previously agreed to do so in their separation agreement.

Postmajority Educational Support Orders

Some states grant the family court judge the authority to order parents to pay a child's postsecondary or job training educational expenses past the age of majority.

Connecticut General Statutes **Sec. 46b-56c. Educational support orders.** (a) For purposes of this section, an educational support order is an order entered by a court requiring a parent to provide support for a child or children to attend for up to a total of four full academic years an institution of higher education or a private occupational school for the purpose of attaining a bachelor's or other undergraduate degree, or other appropriate vocational instruction. An educational support order may be entered with respect to any child who has not attained twenty-three years of age and shall terminate not later than the date on which the child attains twenty-three years of age.

In jurisdictions that do not recognize postmajority support either by legislative enactment or by judicial interpretation, parents may enter into settlement agreements or other contracts, addressing the issue of postmajority support. These agreements are enforced under contract law principles.

Postmajority support statutes are controversial in that intact parents are free to choose whether or not to pay for their children's college costs, while divorced parents may be forced to do so by law. Some state courts have even ruled that postmajority support laws or orders violate the Equal Protection Clause of the U.S. Constitution.

Tax Consequences of Child Support

While alimony is treated as income to the recipient spouse for tax purposes and deductible to the payor, the payment of child support is a tax-neutral event. Child support cannot be deducted from the payor's income taxes, nor must it be included as income on the recipient's tax return. A parent who pays more than fifty percent of the actual costs of child support may claim the child as a dependent on his or her tax return. It is advisable that clients deal with this matter at the time of the divorce and reach some type of agreement as to who will claim the child. Both parents claiming the child as a dependent is sure to trigger a red flag at the IRS and possibly subject the client to an audit.

Chapter Review and Reinforcement

KEY **TERMS**

administrative enforcement	motion for contempt	total net income
capias	motion for modification of child support	Uniform Interstate Family Support Act (UIFSA)
child support guidelines	postmajority support agreements	
combined net income	Revised Uniform Reciprocal Enforcement of Support Act (RURESA)	Uniform Reciprocal Enforcement of Support Act (URESA)
deviation criteria		

REVIEW OF **KEY CONCEPTS**

1. What is the rationale behind the federal mandate upon individual states to enact child support guidelines?

2. What are some of the factors that a court may consider when determining whether or not to deviate from the child support guidelines?

3. Based on your reading of Chapter 8, should a court modify a payor spouse's obligation to pay child support when that individual voluntarily left his or her job?

4. What are a client's options when seeking to enforce a child support order in a situation where the payor spouse has moved to another state?

5. In your opinion, is it fair for a family court to order divorced parents to provide their children with post-majority support when intact families are not subject to the same requirement?

BUILDING YOUR PARALEGAL SKILLS

CASE FOR BRIEFING

IN RE MARRIAGE OF DRYSCH, 314 ILL. APP.3D 640, 732 N.E.2D 125 (2000)

Critical Thinking and Legal Analysis Applications

1. You work as a paralegal in your state for the Law Office of Colton & Cuello. Your client, Alba Rivera, is currently receiving child support for her two minor sons from her former husband, Carlos. She plans on remarrying within the next few months and wants to know what effect, if any, her remarriage will have on her child support payments. Ms. Rivera plans on quitting her full-time job as a receptionist once she is married. Her fiancé is quite well off and has stated to her that she no longer has to work if she chooses not to do so.

Based on the case of IN RE MARRIAGE OF DRYSCH, 314 Ill. App.3d 640, 732 N.E.2d 125 (2000), how would the Illinois courts decide this case?

Based on the family law in your jurisdiction, how would the courts in your state decide this case?

Building a Professional Portfolio

PORTFOLIO **EXERCISES**

Robert and Andrea Lucas live in your jurisdiction and have been married for four years. The couple has one child, age three. The maternal grandmother babysits the child free of charge while the parents are at work, so the parties have no child-care costs. The parties have agreed upon joint legal custody, and on residential custody with the mother, Andrea. Robert, as the noncustodial parent, will be required to pay Andrea child support for the benefit of the minor child. Robert has agreed to carry the child on his health insurance plan, which is available to him through his employer. He owes no other support obligations.

Using the following information and your specific state information on the Internet, calculate the child support obligation and prepare a child support worksheet in this case.

	Andrea	Robert
Gross weekly income	$570	$668
Total weekly tax deductions	107.45	129.54
Federal income tax	63.84	78.47
Social Security tax	35.34	41.39
Medicare tax	8.27	9.68
Weekly cost for health insurance coverage for minor child		62.50
Weekly child care costs for minor child	0	0

Chapter **nine**

PATERNITY AND THE RIGHTS AND RESPONSIBILITIES OF UNMARRIED PARENTS

Many young couples are choosing to have a child together although they are not married nor are they necessarily contemplating marriage at any time in the near future. In other instances, a woman may discover that she is pregnant and decide to have the child and raise the child with or without the participation of the child's biological father. Alternately, a father who has not married his child's mother may bring an action in court seeking to obtain custody of his son or daughter. Although fifty or sixty years ago, these decisions would have been generally disparaged by a large portion of American society, today the idea of raising children outside the institution of marriage no longer shocks contemporary society.

This chapter addresses the legal rights and responsibilities of unmarried parents and also discusses reluctant fathers and the legal remedies available to help mothers to determine their child's paternity and establish the father's obligation to support his child.

LEARNING OBJECTIVES

After studying this chapter you should be able to:

1. Understand the rights and responsibilities of unmarried parents.
2. Understand the purpose of a parenting plan.
3. Learn how paternity is established.
4. Explain the role of the *de facto* father.

THE PREVIOUS STATUS OF THE CHILDREN OF UNMARRIED PARENTS—ILLEGITIMACY

Many unmarried parents of today do not know that in the not too far distant past, the children born to unmarried parents were not only subject to societal disapproval but also suffered an unfavorable legal status that deprived them of the rights available to the children of a legally valid marriage. Children born to unmarried parents were designated *illegitimate*. *Illegitimacy* was the term connoting a condition before the law, or the social status of a child whose parents were not married to each other at the time of his or her birth. The modern term used today when referring to a child that is not born to married parents is *nonmarital child*.

For many centuries, nonmarital children were stigmatized socially and legally were denied many rights available to the children of married parents. For instance, nonmarital children were denied the right to inherit from their fathers, and sometimes from both parents. In more recent times, for much of the twentieth century, nonmarital children could not bring a legal action for the wrongful death of a parent, and they were denied worker's compensation benefits and Social Security survivor benefits. Additionally, a nonmarital child had no right to receive support from his or her natural father. For many years, an unmarried mother had no standing to bring an action for child support against the nonmarital child's father.

The status of nonmarital children changed significantly following an opinion from the U.S. Supreme Court. In *Levy v. Louisiana,* 391 U.S. 68, 88 S.Ct. 1509, 20 L.Ed 436 (1968), the Court held that the Equal Protection Clause of the Fourteenth Amendment to the U.S. Constitution prohibited discriminating against individuals based on their birth status, and that illegitimate children were entitled to the same rights under the law as legitimate children. Shortly after that the Uniform Parentage Act was created. This act eliminated the distinction between legitimate and illegitimate children. Many states adopted this act or passed their own laws abolishing the distinction between legitimate and illegitimate children.

Following the changes in the law abolishing discrimination against the children born to unmarried parents, the stigma against these children and against their unmarried parents gradually diminished and now has mostly disappeared. American society has witnessed a dramatic increase in the number of births of children to unmarried parents. In the 1960s and 1970s unmarried couples started living together in increasing numbers. By the 1990s this arrangement had become commonplace. During these decades, and right up to the present time, more and more unmarried couples who were or are living together had or are having children together. Today, parenting by unmarried couples or by one unmarried individual is now also commonplace.

RIGHTS AND RESPONSIBILITIES OF UNMARRIED PARENTS

Unmarried parents have the same rights and responsibilities as married parents. When an unmarried couple is living together with their biological child, each parent is considered to be the *legal guardian* of the child, providing that the father has previously completed an *affidavit of paternity* or an *acknowledgement of paternity*. This can be done at the hospital shortly after the child's birth or may be at any time before the child reaches the age of majority. Signing this document provides the father with certain legal rights as the child's parent and imposes certain responsibilities upon him also.

Illegitimate
Born out of wedlock; the term given to a child born to parents who were not married to each other and who made no effort to legitimate the child afterward.

Nonmarital child
A child born to parents who are not married to each other and who do not legitimate the child; illegitimate child.

Legal guardian
A court appointed individual who is legally responsible for the care of a minor child.

Affidavit of paternity
A man's signed sworn statement containing facts that the man is the father of a child, often required if a man not married to the child's mother wishes to be listed on the child's birth certificate as the child's father; also known as acknowledgement of paternity.

Here Is a Sample of an Affidavit of Paternity

Exhibit 9-1 State of Louisiana Acknowledgment of Paternity Affidavit

STATE OF LOUISIANA

ACKNOWLEDGMENT OF PATERNITY AFFIDAVIT

CHILD BORN OF MARRIAGE

NOTICE: You must read and initial the NOTICE OF ALTERNATIVES, RIGHTS AND RESPONSIBILITIES before you sign the affidavit.

SECTION I. CHILD'S INFORMATION

This is a legal document. Complete in ink and do not alter.

Name of Child - First, Middle, Last (As it appears on birth certificate)

Date of Birth - (Month, Day, Year)

Place of Birth - City, State

Name of Hospital

Name of Child - First, Middle, Last (As the parents want it to appear on birth certificate)

SECTION II. MOTHER'S INFORMATION

Name of Mother - First, Middle, Last

(Maiden Name)

Date of Birth - (Month, Day, Year)

Mother's Address

Mother's Phone Number

Mother's Place of Birth - City, State

Race (Circle) American Indian, Black, White, Asian
If Other, List:

Mother's Social Security Number

Mother's Employer - Name & Address

Mother's Occupation

Was Mother Married at Time of Birth
Circle One: Yes   No

If Yes, Name and Address of Husband

Does Mother Have Health Insurance
Circle One: Yes   No

If Yes, Name of Insurance Company and Policy No.

State Medicaid:
Circle One: Yes   No

SECTION III. FATHER'S INFORMATION

Name of Father - First, Middle, Last

Date of Birth - (Month, Day, Year)

Father's Address

Father's Phone Number

Father's Place of Birth - City, State

Race (Circle) American Indian, Black, White, Asian
If Other, List:

Father's Social Security Number

Father's Employer - Name & Address

Father's Occupation

Father's Guardian (If Father under age 18) Print Name

Guardian's Address

Guardian's Signature

Does Father Have Health Insurance
Circle One: Yes   No

If Yes, Name of Insurance Company and Policy No.

MOTHER: I certify that I am the MOTHER of the child named above and that all statements made herein are true and correct to the best of my knowledge. I am signing this Affidavit voluntarily and of my own free will. I acknowledge that the man named above is the biological father of my child. I give my consent to have his name appear on the Certificate of Birth of my child. I declare and affirm that I lived separate and apart from the legal presumptive father for a minimum of one hundred and eighty days prior to the time of conception and have not reconciled since the beginning of the one hundred and eighty-day period.. I further acknowledge that I have received oral and written notice of the legal rights and consequences resulting from my acknowledging the paternity of my child and I understand this notice.

MOTHER'S SIGNATURE

DATE

WITNESS _____

WITNESS _____

State of Louisiana, Parish of _____

Signature then PRINT name of Notary

Signed and Affirmed before me on the _____ day of

_____, _____.

State Notary Registration Number

My Commission expires on

FATHER: I certify that I am the biological FATHER of the child named above and that all statements made herein are true and correct to the best of my knowledge. I am signing this Affidavit voluntarily and of my own free will. I acknowledge that I have received oral and written notice of the legal rights and consequences resulting from my acknowledging the paternity of my child and I understand this notice.

FATHER'S SIGNATURE

DATE

GUARDIAN'S SIGNATURE (If Father under age 18)

DATE

WITNESS _____

WITNESS _____

State of Louisiana, Parish of _____

Signature then PRINT name of Notary

Signed and Affirmed before me on the _____ day of

_____, _____.

State Notary Registration Number

My Commission expires on

HUSBAND/EX-HUSBAND OF THE MOTHER: I certify that I was married to the mother of this child at the time of conception or birth; however, I am not the biological father. Further, I declare and affirm that I lived separate and apart from the mother for a minimum of one hundred and eighty days prior to the time of conception and have not reconciled with her since the beginning of the one hundred and eighty-day period.

HUSBANS/EX-HUSBAN'S SIGNATURE

DATE

WITNESS _____

WITNESS _____

State of Louisiana, Parish of _____

Signature then PRINT name of Notary

Signed and Affirmed before me on the _____ day of

_____, _____.

State Notary Registration Number

My Commission expires on

DISTRIBUTION OF COPIES: Original to Registrar of Vital Records, Copies to Child Support, Mother, Father & Husband/ Ex-husband.

VRR-44 3-P 05/10

Page **1** of **2**

continued

Exhibit 9-1 Continued

NOTICE OF ALTERNATIVES, RIGHTS AND RESPONSIBILITIES

This is a legal document. Signing the form is voluntary. Since this form has legal consequences, you may want to consult an attorney before signing.

When this Acknowledgement is properly completed and signed, the biological father's name is entered on the birth certificate in place of the name of the husband of the mother and the man becomes the legal father of the child. This acknowledgement has the same effect as a court order establishing paternity and can be used as a basis for entering a child support order.

If either of you is not sure that this man is the biological father of this child, you should not sign the form. You should have a genetic test.

Mothers who are married to someone other than the biological father or were married to someone other than the father when the child was conceived, or have been divorced for less than three hundred days must have the agreement of their husband/ex-husband to execute this affidavit. Further, the use of this affidavit is limited to cases where the husband and the mother lived separate and apart continuously for a minimum of one hundred and eighty days prior to the conception of the child and have not reconciled since the beginning of the one hundred eighty-day period. If the agreement of the husband cannot be obtained or if the couple cannot meet the statutory requirements, this affidavit cannot be used. In order for the biological father's name to be added to the birth certificate, a court must establish paternity in accordance with R.S.40:34B.(1)(a)(vii)

RIGHTS AND RESPONSIBLITIES OF A PARENT

- Either party has the right to request a genetic test to determine if the alleged father is the biological father of the child.
- The alleged father has the right to consult an attorney before signing an acknowledgement of paternity.
- If the alleged father does not acknowledge the child, the mother has the right to file a paternity suit to establish paternity.
- After the alleged father signs an acknowledgement of paternity, he has the right to pursue visitation with the child and the right to petition for custody.
- Once an acknowledgement of paternity is signed, the father may be obligated to provide child support for the child.
- Once an acknowledgement of paternity is signed, the child will have inheritance rights and any rights afforded children born in wedlock.
- A party who executed a notarial act of acknowledgement may rescind the act, without cause, before the earlier of the following:

    - Sixty days after the signing of the act, in a court hearing for the limited purpose of rescinding the acknowledgment.
    - A court hearing relating to the child, including a child support proceeding, in which the father is involved.

Thereafter, the acknowledgement of paternity may be voided only upon proof, by clear and convincing evidence, that such act was induced by fraud, duress, or material mistake of fact, or that the father is not the biological father.

BENEFITS FOR YOUR CHILD

Every child has the right to know his or her mother and father and benefit from a relationship with both parents.

Both of your names will appear on the child's birth certificate.

It will be easier for your child to learn medical histories of both parents and to benefit from health care coverage available to you.

It will be easier for your child to receive benefits such as dependent or survivor's benefits from the Veteran's Administration or from the Social Security Administration as well as share any estate should you die.

To indicate that you have read and understood this notice of alternatives, rights and responsibilities, please initial below. If you require further assistance you may call us at (504) 593 - 5100.

Mother's Initials _____

Father's Initials _____

VRR-44 3-P (05/10)

Source: Acknowledgement of Paternity Affidavit, Department of Health and Hospitals, State of Louisiana.

When an unmarried couple splits up, each parent is still considered to be the child's legal guardian, unless one of the parents brings a legal action to obtain sole custody or joint legal custody. Most states have enacted statutes that authorize an unmarried parent to go into court and request that the court enter a custody order that both parents must honor. Usually the party bringing the action into court is the parent with whom the child is residing. That parent seeks to have the court invest him or her with either sole or joint legal custody with physical custody in that party. This petitioning party may also request that the court enter an order for payment of child support by the parent who does not reside with the child.

When a parent brings an action for custody and/or child support, the parent must arrange for legal service of the action on the other parent to give that parent notice that the action is taking place. When the other parent is served with legal process, that parent may obtain legal counsel to represent his or her interests, choose to represent himself or herself by entering a *pro se* appearance, or simply do nothing. Frequently, the parent served with a custody action, through counsel, will negotiate to have the petitioning parent agree to joint legal custody with physical custody with the petitioning parent and a parenting plan that includes considerable access time for the other parent. Occasionally, the other parent will seek sole custody, not as a strategic tactic but because the other parent wants the child to reside with him or her.

If parents cannot come to an agreement regarding custody, the court will usually refer the matter to the family relations division of the court. Family relations officers will conduct an investigation or study to decide what custodial disposition will best promote the child's best interest. Most states have statutes or case law providing that there is a presumption that joint legal custody with physical custody vested in one parent will best serve the child's interests. However, this is a **rebuttable presumption**. If family relations officers conclude that the parents are unable to communicate productively to make joint decisions for their child's health, education, and welfare, the family relations division will recommend that one parent have sole custody and that the other parent have access or visitation consistent with the child's best interest. In some instances, where previously there has been an order of joint legal custody, one or both of the parents may petition the court to modify the order and vest sole custody in one of the parents. The excerpt of the following case provides an example where the court found it to be in the child's best interest to modify the previous joint legal custody disposition and award sole custody to one of the parents, in this case the child's unmarried father.

Rebuttable presumption
An assumption or inference drawn from certain facts, known to be true, that will be disproved by introducing evidence that the assumption is false, such as the presumption that a man is the biological father of a child born to a woman he is married to, which could be rebutted by the introduction of uncontroverted evidence that another man is the child's father.

ANTHONY MM. v. JACQUELYN NN.

91 A.D.3rd 1036, 937 N.Y.S 2d 360
N.Y. A.D. Dept, 2012

Malone Jr., J.

Appeal from an order of the Family Court of Chenango County (DiStefano, J.) entered May 10, 2010, which among other things, granted petitioner's application, in two proceedings pursuant to Family Ct. Act article 6, to modify a prior order of custody.

Petitioner (hereinafter the father) and respondent (hereinafter the mother) are the unmarried parents of one child (born in 2007). In 2007, both parties filed petitions seeking custody of the child, and a temporary order granting custody to the mother was apparently entered. The mother thereafter sought to suspend the visitation, alleging, among other things, that she suspected that the father was sexually

continued

abusing the child. The matter was referred to the Supreme Court (Garry, J.) and, upon the parties consent, an order was entered granting the parties joint legal custody of the child and ordering them to submit to a family evaluation by a psychologist. After the evaluation was completed, a consent order was entered in April 2008 that continued shared custody of the child and required the mother to withdraw her allegations of sexual abuse due to a lack of evidence supporting them and seek counseling to address the issues raised in the psychologist's report.

In August 2009, the father commenced a proceeding seeking sole custody of the child, alleging that the mother continued to insinuate that he was sexually abusing the child. The mother thereafter filed a petition likewise seeking sole custody, alleging among other things that the father was disparaging her in front of the child. Following a fact-finding hearing, Family Court dismissed the mother's petition and awarded sole custody to the father. The mother opposes.

"An existing custody arrangement may be modified upon a showing that there has been a substantial change in circumstances and modification is required to ensure the best interests of the child." (Matter of Hayward v. Thurmond, 85 A.D.3d 1260, 1261, 925 N.Y.S. 2d. 209 [2011] [citations omitted]; see Matter of Dobies v. Brefka, 83 A.D.3d 1148, 1149, 921 N.Y.S.2d 349 [2011]. Although Family Court did not specifically make a finding of change in circumstances, upon our review of the record, we find that the evidence of the deterioration of the parties' relationship constituted a sufficient change in circumstances such that the court's consideration of whether a change in custody was necessary to protect the child's best interest was warranted ...
... To that end, the record contains substantial evidence to support the court's decision that an award of sole custody to the father is in the child's best interest.

The record establishes that, even after she agreed to withdraw her allegations, the mother continued to insinuate that the father was sexually abusing the child, despite the fact that no evidence of the alleged abuse was ever found by medical professionals who examined the child. The evidence also established that the mother was frequently hostile toward the father and his family, often made disparaging remarks about them in the child's presence and behaved inappropriately during the parties' visitation exchanges. A psychologist who evaluated the mother testified that she had personality disorders that caused her to, among other things, display little regard for the negative consequences that her action had on the father's relationship with the child and if left untreated, her disorders could result in the child being alienated from the father. Although a social worker with whom the mother had sought counseling stated that she disagreed with the psychologist's assessment, Family Court specifically found the social worker's testimony to be of little value because counseling did not address the personality disorders identified in the psychologist's report, as had been directed in the April 2008 consent order.

Although it is apparent that both parties are loving parents and capable of sufficiently providing for the child's physical needs, the father has demonstrated that he is currently better able to provide for the child's overall well-being and is more likely than the mother to encourage and nurture the child's relationship with the other parent, particularly considering the mother's repeated allegations and insinuations that the father sexually abused the child. (see Matter of Martinez v. Hyatt, 86 A.D.3d 571, 572, 927 N.Y.S.2d 375 [2011]; lv denied 17 N.Y.3d 713, 933 N.Y.S.2d 654, 957 N.E.2d 1158 [2011]; Young v. Young, 212 A.2d 114, 122, 628 N.Y.S.2d 957 [1995]. Such unfounded allegations, together with the persistent hostility that the mother demonstrates toward the father and his family, were appropriately viewed by Family Court as efforts to interfere with the child's relationship with the father (see Matter of Posporelis v. Posporelis, 41 A.D. 3d 986, 991, 838 N.Y.S.2d 603 [2006]). Considering the totality of the circumstances here, and according deference to Family Court's ability to assess the credibility of the witnesses and evaluate conflicting testimony (see Matter of Bush v. Bush, 74 A.D.3rd 1448, 1450, 902 N.Y.S.2d 697 [2010] lv denied 15 N.Y.3d 711 [2010]).

WL 4116959 [2010]; Matter of Siler v. Wright, 64 A.D.3d 926, 929, 882 N.Y.S.2d 574 [2009]) we find that the award of sole custody to the father is supported by substantial evidence. Finally, "although by no means determinative, this conclusion is in accord with the position advanced by the [attorney for the child]" (Matter of Siler v. Wright, 64 A.D.3d at 929, 882 N.Y.S.2d 574).

We have considered the mother's remaining contentions and find them to be unpersuasive.

ORDERED that the order is affirmed, without costs.

SPAIN, J.P., LAHTINEN, STEIN and EAGAN JR. JJ., concur.

Source: Anthony MM. V. Jacquelyn NN, 91 A.D.3rd 1036, 937 N.Y.S 2d 360 N.Y. A.D. Dept, 2012, New York State Unified Court System.

Whether the court awards one parent sole custody or enters an order of joint legal custody with the child's primary residence vested in one parent, the court, upon motion from the primary custodial parent, may order the other parent to pay child support. In states that have established uniform child support guidelines, these guidelines will be applied in the same manner they are applied to determine child support for divorcing parents, as discussed in detail in Chapter 8.

Sometimes when unmarried parents have been living together and then separate, typically the minor child remains with the mother. This is especially true if the child is young. If the parent with whom the child resides does not institute proceedings to formalize custody and support, the other parent may bring an action to legally confirm paternity and establish a parenting plan and the sharing of financial support for the child.

The following legal document provides the father the opportunity to confirm his status as the child's father, determine his financial obligation, and establish a ***parenting plan*** that will give him legally binding access to his child. A parenting plan is a written, detailed, legal document that outlines how parents will share the responsibility of caring for the children under circumstances where they are not living in the same household. The bringing of the following petition is the accepted procedure for resolving this issue in Florida, but it is also used in other states either in the form of a petition or a motion.

Parenting plan

A parenting plan is a written, detailed, legal document that outlines how parents will share the responsibility of caring for the children under circumstances where they are not living in the same household.

Exhibit 9-2 State of Florida Petition to Adjudicate Paternity, to Establish a Parenting Plan, and for Other Related Relief

IN THE CIRCUIT COURT OF THE ELEVENTH JUDICIAL CIRCUIT IN AND FOR MIAMI-DADE COUNTY, FLORIDA FAMILY DIVISION IN RE: THE MATTER OF:

BRENT LAWRENCE CASE NO. Petitioner/Father

and

ALICIA GARNER Respondent/Mother

_____   /____VERIFIED PETITION TO ADJUDICATE PATERNITY, TO ESTABLISH A PARENTING PLAN, AND FOR OTHER RELATED RELIEF

continued

Exhibit 9-2 Continued

Petitioner/Father, BRENT LAWRENCE ("Father"), being sworn, certifies that the following information is true:

1. This is an action to adjudicate paternity, to establish a parenting plan, determine parental responsibility, child support, and a time-sharing arrangement.
2. The Petitioner is the Father of the following minor child:

Name Place of Birth Birth Date Sex

MARK GARNER LAWRENCE Miami, Florida, May 5th, 2017, MALE

3. The Petitioner/Father currently resides as 331A Hyacinth Court, Miami, Florida.
4. The Respondent/Mother currently resides at 1030 Rivello Drive, Miami, Florida.
5. Both parties are over the age of 18, and neither is, nor has been, within a 30-day period, immediately, prior to this date, in the military service of the United States.
6. Neither Petitioner/Father nor Respondent/Mother is mentally incapacitated.
7. A completed **Uniform Child Custody Jurisdiction and Enforcement Act (UCCJEA) Affidavit,** Florida Supreme Court Approved Family Law Form 12.902(d), is being filed with this petition.
8. A completed **Family Law Financial Affidavit** will be filed.
9. **PATERNITY FACTS.** Paternity has previously been acknowledged set forth in the minor child's birth certificate; however, paternity has not been adjudicated by any Court in this, or any other jurisdiction.
10. **CHILD'S RESIDENCE.** Prior to and following the child's birth, the parties lived together until January 8, 2018, when the Respondent/Mother required the Petitioner/Father to vacate her residence.
11. Since then, the parties have lived separate and apart.
12. During the time the parties lived together, the Petitioner/Father fully participated in the child's daily care and upbringing, including, but not limited to, feeding the child at night. The Father has established a close relationship with the child and he has bonded with him.
13. **PARENTING PLAN AND TIMESHARING.** The Petitioner/Father seeks to have this Court approve a parenting plan that meets the child's best interests and includes an equal time-sharing plan.
14. There has been no set time-sharing schedule, temporary or otherwise, agreed to by the parties.
15. Since he vacated the Respondent/Mother's residence, the Petitioner/Father's contact with the minor child has been limited by the Respondent/Mother, who has set unilateral terms for time-sharing.
16. It is in the best interests of the minor child to have a time-sharing schedule ordered by this Court.
17. **PARENTAL RESPONSIBILITY.** The parties should have shared parental responsibility.
18. **CHILD SUPPORT.** Since before the parties separated, the Petitioner/Father has contributed substantially to the minor child's support and continues to do so.
19. The Petitioner/Father now requests that the Court award child support as determined by Florida Child Support Guidelines, taking into consideration the time-sharing schedule shared by the parties.
20. **ATTORNEY'S FEES AND COSTS.** The Petitioner/Father has retained undersigned counsel to represent him in this cause and has incurred reasonable attorney's fees and costs for his representation.
21. The Petitioner/Father has, in good faith, attempted, on several occasions, to reach an agreement with the Respondent/Mother without Court intervention, to no avail.

22. The Respondent/Mother's financial position is considerably superior to the Petitioner/Father's.

23. Should the Petitioner/Father have to incur additional reasonable attorney's fees and costs if the Respondent/Mother unnecessarily litigates this cause, the Petitioner/Father should be awarded the additional attorney's fees and costs

WHEREFORE, Petitioner respectfully requests a judgment adjudicating paternity, establishing a parenting plan that includes an equal time-sharing plan for the parties with their minor child; ordering shared parental responsibility, child support, and related obligations, and ordering such further relief as the Court deems proper under the facts of this case. Respectfully submitted on this 6th day of May 2018.

VERIFICATION I DECLARE UNDER PENALTY OF PERJURY, under the laws of the State of Florida, that the foregoing is true and correct and that this Petition to Adjudicate Paternity and for Other Related Relief is signed by me on May 6, 2018.

BRENT LAWRENCE

The Absent Parent

When a parent bringing a custody and child support action cannot locate the other parent, the requirement of providing that parent notice is met by publishing a legal notice of the action in a newspaper with a circulation in the geographical area in which the other parent was last known to reside. If the absent parent does not appear at the court proceeding, the court will usually enter an order of sole custody in favor of the petitioning party. Depending on the jurisdiction's rules, the court may or may not enter an order for child support. In states using the uniform child support guidelines and a formula based on each parent's income to determine the amount of child support payments, the court usually will not make a support order against a nonappearing parent.

Challenges to Child Support Orders

When a child's mother seeks child support from a man who hasn't signed an acknowledgement of paternity or a man to whom she was not married at the time the child was born, that man may deny that he is the child's biological father. This denial will sometimes lead to the mother instituting a paternity action. States generally have statutes that authorize the bringing of a ***paternity action*** and also specify the parameters under which the action may proceed.

Paternity action
Where the petitioning party, usually the child's mother but occasionally the father, requests that the court hold a hearing to establish whether a particular man is the child's biological father.

Statutes

Illustrated below is a North Carolina statute setting forth the procedures to be followed to establish parentage.

NORTH CAROLINA GENERAL STATUTES ANNOTATED

§ 49-14. Civil action to establish paternity

(a) The paternity of a child born out of wedlock may be established by civil action at any time prior to such child's eighteenth birthday. A copy of a certificate of birth of the child shall be attached to the complaint. The establishment of paternity shall not have the effect of legitimation. The social security numbers, if known, of the minor child's parents shall be placed in the record of the proceeding.

continued

(b) Proof of paternity pursuant to this section shall be by clear, cogent, and convincing evidence.

(c) No such action shall be commenced nor judgment entered after the death of the putative father, unless the action is commenced either: prior to the death of the putative father; Within one year after the date of death of the putative father, if a proceeding for administration of the estate of the putative father has not been commenced within one year of his death; or within the period specified in G.S. 28A-19-3(a) for presentation of claims against an estate, if a proceeding for administration of the estate of the putative father has been commenced within one year of his death.

Any judgment under this subsection establishing a decedent to be the father of a child shall be entered nunc pro tunc to the day preceding the date of the death of the father.

(d) If the action to establish paternity is brought more than three years after the birth of a child or is brought after the death of the putative father, paternity shall not be established in a contested case without evidence from a blood or genetic marker test.

(e) Either party to an action to establish paternity may request that the case be tried at the first session of the court after the case is docketed, but the presiding judge, in his discretion, may first try any pending case in which the rights of the parties or the public demand it.

(f) When a determination of paternity is pending in an IV-D case, the court shall enter a temporary order for child support upon motion and showing of clear, cogent and convincing evidence of paternity. For purposes of this subsection, the results of blood or genetic tests shall constitute clear, cogent and convincing evidence of paternity if the tests show that the probability of the alleged parent's parentage is ninety-seven percent (97%) or higher. If paternity is not thereafter established, then the putative father shall be reimbursed the full amount of temporary support paid under the order.

(g) Invoices for services rendered for pregnancy, childbirth, and blood or genetic testing are admissible as evidence without requiring third party foundation testimony and shall constitute prima facie evidence of the amounts incurred for the services or for testing on behalf of the child.

Source: Chapter 49—Bastardy, Article 3—Civil Actions Regarding Illegitimate Children, § 49-14. Civil Action to Establish Paternity; Motion to Set Aside Paternity, North Carolina General Assembly.

ESTABLISHING PATERNITY

Paternity is the legal and social acknowledgment of the paternal relationship between a father and his child. If a father wishes to be considered the child's father, he may sign an Affidavit Acknowledging Paternity, which establishes the legal relationship between the father and child. In order to be listed on a child's birth certificate, most states require unmarried fathers to sign an affidavit or acknowledgement of paternity. Frequently, this may be done in the hospital where the child is born.

DNA test
A genetic testing in which deoxyribonucleic acid is extracted from body cells to determine a relationship between two or more persons; this test is used to determine paternity.

Putative father
A man who is suspected of being or believed to be the biological father of a child born out of wedlock.

If a man denies that he is the father or is not sure, when the child's mother brings a child support action, the court may order a *DNA test* to determine paternity between the putative father and the child. This test uses several genetic markers to identify genetic similarities. If the test shows a likelihood of paternity of ninety-one percent or better, most courts make a determination that the *putative father* is the child's biological father.

If paternity is established, the court will order child support according to the Child Support Guidelines, and upon a motion from one or both parties, will rule on custody and visitation or time-sharing in accordance with the child's best interest.

Before the advent of DNA tissue analysis, a blood test to determine paternity was used, but it could only eliminate a man as a child's father. If the man was not eliminated, the court would then look at other factors to decide whether or not he was the father.

For married couples, most states had common law holdings that there was a rebuttable presumption that a child born to a woman during the existence of a legally valid marriage was the child of the husband. This presumption could be overcome upon a showing that during the period of conception, the ***presumed father*** had no access to the child's mother, or was sterile at the time or otherwise medically incapable of fathering a child.

For an unmarried mother, the task of proving paternity was much harder. Frequently the determination rested on the subjective opinion of the judge. Fortunately, the advent of DNA testing, which provides a scientific and nearly foolproof method of determining paternity, has eliminated arbitrary, subjective determinations by courts.

When a putative father is contesting paternity, either the father or the mother may petition the court to order a paternity test, or the court, on its own initiative, may enter such an order. In these instances, upon proof of paternity, the father will be ordered to pay child support. He will also have the right to reasonable access or visitation, and if he wishes, he may seek legal custody of the child then or at any future time during the child's minority.

Presumed father

The man presumed to be the father of a child for several reasons such as having been married to the child's mother when the child was born, or because he married the child's mother after the child was born and agreed to have his name be put on the birth certificate.

The Case of Mistaken Paternity

Many unmarried fathers play a significant part in their children's lives. If they do not reside with their child, they nevertheless wish to participate in the upbringing of their child as fully as possible. They are consistent with their child support payments, and they faithfully follow visitation schedules and parenting plans. Most of these men form very positive bonds with their children. They embrace fatherhood and willingly sign an acknowledgement of paternity at the time their child is born. A man who signs a child's birth certificate and/or completes an affidavit or acknowledgment of paternity is deemed to be the child's father before the law. At common law, this person was considered the ***de facto father***, and even if later, sufficient evidence was presented that another man was the child's biological father, the *de facto* father remained the child's legal father. When a state adopted the Uniform Parentage Act or a state passed legislation comparable to that act, the question arose whether the new statutory law preempted common law holdings on paternity, and if so whether the *de facto* father status established by the common law no longer applied.

In the following case, the Court of Appeals of the State of Washington recently addressed this issue where the acknowledged father, who had consistently participated in the minor child's life, wished to retain his status as the child's *de facto* father after the child's biological father's paternity was established in a court action.

De facto **father**

At common law, A man who signs a child's birth certificate and/or completes an affidavit or acknowledgment of paternity, is deemed to be the child's father before the law.

IN THE MATTER OF THE DE FACTO PARENTAGE AND *CUSTODY* OF M. J. M. FKA M. J. F. DOB 12/21/07 A MINOR CHILD RUSS FULTON, RESPONDENT AND FRANK JONATHAN MILLER AND MEGHAN COTTON, APPELLANTS

SCHINDLER, J.

The biological parents of M.J.M., Frank Miller and Meghan Cotton, contend the trial court erred in considering the petition of the acknowledged father to establish as a **de facto parent**, designating Russ Fulton as a de facto father of M.J.M.; and entering a parenting plan that allows Fulton visitation rights. Miller and Cotton claim that because the parentage statute, former Uniform Parentage Act (UPA), chapter 26.26 RCW (2002), expressly addressed the remedy available to an acknowledged father, the common law de facto parentage doctrine did not apply. We disagree. The

continued

legislature amended the UPA in 2011. Prior to the amendment to the UPAS in 2011, where a biological father challenged the paternity of an acknowledged father, the court could not hold a hearing to consider the best interest of the child. We affirm.

In early 2007, Meghan Cotton and Russ Fulton were dating. In February, Cotton and Fulton went on a week-long vacation together. Some time after that vacation, Cotton started living with her former boyfriend Frank Miller. In March, Cotton discovered she was pregnant. At first Cotton told Miller he was the child's father, but shortly thereafter, Cotton told Miller that "according to her doctor and the timing .... He couldn't be the father." Cotton then contacted Fulton and told him that she was pregnant and he was the child's father. Cotton moved in with Fulton and they started living together.

The child was born on December 21, 2007. On December 24, Cotton and Fulton signed a notarized affidavit of paternity. The affidavit of paternity states that Cotton is the mother and Fulton is the father of the child. The birth certificate also states that Fulton is the father of the child, and that the child's last name is Fulton.

For the first few months, Cotton stayed home to take care of the child. Fulton worked full time but also helped care for the child. After five or six months, Cotton went back to work as an exotic dancer. After Cotton returned to work, she "spent less and less time caring" for the child and Fulton assumed more responsibility taking care of the child.

Fulton and Cotton separated in December 2008. Cotton moved out and left the child with Fulton. Fulton continued to provide financial support and care for the child. Fulton filed a petition in superior court to adopt a parenting plan designating him as the primary residential parent and enter an order of child support. In answer to the petition, Cotton asserted that she should be designated the primary residential parent but agreed that as the child's biological father, the court should allow Fulton visitation rights. The court appointed a guardian ad litem (GA). The GAL filed a report recommending the court adopt a parenting plant designating Fulton as the primary residential parent.

In January 2009, the court entered a temporary parenting plan designating Fulton as the primary residential parent. The temporary parenting plan allowed Cotton to spend time with the child on weekends. The court scheduled a trial on April on the permanent parenting plan.

Sometime in early 2009, Cotton and Miller obtained genetic testing. The test established Miller was the biological father of the child. Because Miller "had not decided whether he wanted to be involved in [the child]'s life yet," for several weeks he took no action. Meanwhile Fulton continued to act as the primary parent and caregiver for the child.

PATERNITY ACTION

On April 7, Miller filed a petition to establish parentage based on the results of the genetic testing. Miller sought entry of an order declaring him the father of the child, amending the birth certificate and changing the surname of the child to Miller. Miller also requested entry of a parenting plan and a child support order. The petition identifies the respondents as Fulton as the acknowledged father and Cotton as the mother. Cotton joined the petition and agreed to the requested relief. The county appointed a GAL to represent the sixteen-month-old child.

Miller and Cotton filed a motion to dismiss Fulton from the paternity action. Miller and Cotton argued that the genetic test established that Miller was the child's biological father. Miller submitted an affidavit setting forth the chain of custody of the samples used for genetic testing and the results. Fulton stipulated to the genetic test. After the GAL filed a report stating that Fulton met the criteria as a *de facto* parent of the child, the parties submitted additional briefing.

The trial granted the motion to dismiss Fulton from the paternity action. The court ruled that Miller had timely filed the petition and established he was the biological father of the child. Accordingly, the court concluded, "[T]here is no need or justification for the Court to resort to a common law analysis or any determination of a *de facto* parent.

On August 20, the court entered a judgment and order on the paternity petition, findings of fact and conclusions of law, and an order dismissing Fulton from the action. The court also entered an agreed temporary parenting plan. The temporary parenting plan adopts a schedule to transition the care of the child from Fulton to Miller. The temporary parenting plan allows M.J.M. to continue to live with Fulton for six months while gradually increasing residential time with Miller. The court imposed restrictions on Cotton's residential time with M.J.M.

The mother's residential time with the child shall be limited based upon the mother's boyfriend engaging in domestic violence as alleged by the mother under King County 09-2-25480-0 KNT.

The court ruled that "Fulton's time after month 8 is reserved for agreement of the parties or court order. The guardian ad litem recommends that [the child] continue to have regular, consistent, weekly contact with Russ Fulton."

Fulton filed an appeal of the court's decision in the paternity action.

DE FACTO PARENTAGE ACTION

On November 9, Fulton filed a "Petition for Establishment of De Facto Parent status and/or Nonparental Custody. Miller and Cotton filed a motion to dismiss the petition on the grounds that the doctrine of res judicate barred the court from considering *de facto* parentage. The trial court denied the motion to dismiss on the grounds that "[t]he issue of *de facto* parentage as it was not previously litigated in the paternity action in [the paternity action]."

Fulton filed a motion to find adequate cause to establish the *de facto* parentage doctrine and nonparental custody. Fulton also requested entry of a temporary parenting plan to allow him to continue to have contact with M.J.M. On February 26, 2010, a superior court commissioner entered an "Order re Adequate Cause" granting the motion to proceed to trial on the petition to establish de facto parentage, but denied the motion as to "Third Party Custody." The commissioner entered a temporary parenting plan that allowed Fulton to spend residential time with M.J.M. Miller and Cotton filed a motion to revise the commissioner's decision.

A superior court judge denied the motion to revise the commissioner's decision. The court rejected the argument that the *de facto* parentage doctrine only applies to same-sex couples. The court also rejected the argument that Fulton was a stepparent.

Mr. Fulton was acknowledged as the biological father before the child's birth. After the child's birth, he continued to be part of the family unit consisting of himself as the father, Ms. Cotton as the mother, and the child. There was no parental relationship with Mr. Miller and the child at all until the child was more than a year old, during which time, Mr. Fulton had acted in all ways as the child's *de facto* parent.

Miller and Cotton filed a motion for discretionary review of the superior court's order on revision.... A commissioner of the court denied the motion for discretionary review.

On July 6, 2010, we issued an unpublished opinion in Fulton's appeal in the paternity action. We affirmed the trial court's motion to dismiss Fulton from the paternity action. *In re Parentage of M.J.M., 156 Wash.App. 1047, 2010 WL 26760676, at *1.* Trial On De Facto Parent Petition and Permanent Parenting Plan

On June 14, 2011, the superior court entered an order consolidating the paternity action and the *de facto* parentage action "for purposes of determining one final parenting plan for the child [M.J.M.] who is the subject of both actions....

Beginning in June, the court conducted a lengthy trial on the petition to establish *de facto* parentage and the permanent parenting plan. At the conclusion of trial, the court granted the *de facto* parentage petition.

After engaging in a "strict statutory inquiry," the court ruled that although the *de facto* parentage doctrine only applies in narrow circumstances, the evidence established that "those circumstances are present in this case." The court ruled in pertinent part: This case falls within the analysis of [*In re Parentage of L.B.,* 155 Wash.2d 679, 122 P.3d 161 (2005)], not [*In re Parentage of M.F.,* 168 Wash.2d 528, 228 P.3d 1270

continued

(2010)]. Mr. Fulton and Ms. Cotton formed the original family unit when [M.J.M.] was born. They intended Mr. Fulton act as [M.J.M.]'s real and only father from birth. Mr. Fulton also became [M.J.M.]'s actual original legal father at birth by virtue of him and Ms. Cotton signing the paternity acknowledgement. It was their intent that Mr. Fulton act as [M.J.M.]'s legal and biological father. Mr. Fulton was legally vested with all the rights and responsibilities of parenthood by statute. By statute, from birth Mr. Fulton and Ms. Cotton were the only two legal parents [M.J.M.] had. Mr. Fulton did not come to his relationship with [M.J.M.] as a later third party like a stepparent. He was the full original legal parent by statute. There was no physical, emotional, or legal relationship between [M.J.M.] and Mr. Miller at that time. Mr. Miller had established no legal rights regarding [M.J.M.] at that time and did not so for a year and a half thereafter. While Mr. Fulton was the acknowledged father and that acknowledgment was not contested by Mr. Miller, Mr. Miller had no established legal rights regarding {M.G.M.}.

The court set entered findings of fact and conclusions of law addressing each of the five factors that must be considered in determining whether the de facto parentage doctrine applied to Fulton. The court set forth extensive and detailed findings of fact in a fifteen-page attachment, "Exhibit A." ....

The court entered a *de facto* parentage custody decree, a final parenting plan, and an order of child support. The decree names Fulton as "a father to this child" and gives him visitation as set forth in the parenting plan. The parenting plan designates Miller as the primary residential parent but allows Cotton and Fulton to spend time with M.J.M. Miller and Cotton appeal. Fulton did not file a response. At our request, Legal Voice and the American Academy of Matrimonial Lawyers submitted briefs as amici curiae ....

Analysis

Miller and Cotton (collectively Miller) contend that the trial court erred in denying the motion to dismiss the petition to establish *de facto* parentage on the grounds that (1) the doctrine of res judicata barred the petition and (2) the statute former 2002 UPA expressly provided a statutory remedy.

Res Judicata

Miller argues that res judicata barred Fulton from filing an action to establish *de facto* parentage because the trial court in the paternity action rejected his *de facto* parentage claim.

Here Miller relies on the trial court's oral ruling in the paternity action to argue res judicata barred Fulton's *de facto* parentage action. But the court's oral ruling in the paternity action is not a final judgment on the merits of Fulton's *de facto* parentage claim.

The court in the paternity action ruled, in pertinent part: Because if the legislature has addressed the situation that is now before the Court, there is no need or justification for the Court to do a common law analysis and any determination of a de facto.

We hold that the doctrine of res judicata did not bar Fulton's de facto parentage action.

DE FACTO PARENTAGE DOCTRINE

Our Supreme Court first recognized the common law *de facto* parentage doctrine in *L.B.* In *L.B.*, the court addressed whether the former same-sex partner of the biological mother had standing to file a petition to establish parentage as a *de facto* parent. *L.B.*, 155 Wash.2d at 682-83, 122 P.3d 161 ....

The Supreme Court held that in the absence of a statutory remedy under the UPA, the same-sex partner had standing to file a petition for a determination of parentage under the equitable common law *de facto* parentage doctrine. *L.B.*, 155 Wash.2d at 683, 122 P.3d 161.

The court adopted the following criteria to establish de facto parentage: The natural or legal parent consented to and fostered the parent-like relationship, (2) the petitioner and the child lived together in the same household, (3) the petitioner assumed obligations of parenthood without expectation of financial compensation;

and (4) the petitioner has been in a parental role for a length of time sufficient to have established with the child a bonded, dependent relationship, parental in nature.

L.B., 155 Wash.2d at 708, 122 P.3d 161.

The court held that a *de facto* parent stands in legal parity with an otherwise legal parent, whether biological, adoptive, or otherwise; and as such, recognition of a person as a child's de facto parent necessarily "authorizes [a] court to consider an award of parental rights and responsibilities ... based on its determination of the best interest of the child." *L.B., 155* Wash ... 2d at 708, 122 P.3d 161 ...

[W]e adopted the de facto doctrine to correct a specific statutory shortcoming: the lack of remedy available to the respondent in *L.B.*, who was a parent in every way but legally.

M.F., 168 WASH.2D AT 533-34, 228 P.3D AT 1220.
Statutory Remedy

The dispositive question in this case is whether Fulton had a statutory remedy under former 2002 UPA to seek to preserve his parental relationship with the child. Miller contends that as in *M.F.,* the UPA unequivocally addresses the parental rights of an acknowledged father under former RCW 26.26.540 (20020 and former RCW 26.26.600 (2002). Contrary to Miller's contention, we conclude that while the former UPA required the court to consider a number of factors in determining whether allowing genetic testing was in the best interest of the child, the plain language of the statute did not provide the same remedy to an acknowledged father such as Fulton ... under former RCW 26.26.540(2). Miller could seek an adjudication of the child's paternity within two years of the effective date of the acknowledgment.

Under former RCW 26.26.600(1), [t]he paternity of a child having a presumed, acknowledged, or adjudicated father may be disproved only by admissible results of genetic testing, excluding that man as the father of the child or identifying another man to be the father of the child.

Under RCW 26.26.600, where the result of genetic testing is properly admitted, the man identified as the biological father must be adjudicated as the father of the child, and the "man excluded as the father of a child by genetic testing must be adjudicated not to be the father. RCW 26.26.600(2), (4) where there was a challenge to the paternity of a presumed father, former RCW26.26.535 (2002) required the court to hold an evidentiary hearing to determine whether genetic testing was in the best interests of the child. *In re Parentage of S.E.C.,* 160 Wash.App. 111, 112, 225 P.3d 327 (2010).

Former RCW 26.26.535 sets forth the factors the court must take into consideration in making this determination. The plain and unambiguous language of former RCW 26.26,535 makes clear that the statute applies only to a presumed father and does not apply to an acknowledged or adjudicated father. *In re Parentage of K.R.P.,* 160 Wash.App. 215, 225-226, 247 P.3d 491 (2011)....

In November 2002, NCCUSL amended the model UPA to address the disparate treatment of presumed, acknowledged, and adjudicated fathers and included an amendment that give the court direction not to allow genetic testing if an acknowledged father showed it was not in the best interest of the child....

This section incorporates the doctrine of paternity by estoppel, which extends equally to a child with a presumed father or an acknowledged father. In appropriate circumstances, the court may deny genetic testing and find the presumed or acknowledged father to be the father of the child.

Effective July 2011, the Washington State Legislature amended the UPA to incorporate the NCCUSL 2002 Model UPA.... As amended, RCW26.26.535 now provides in part:

Proceeding to adjudicate parentage-authority to deny genetic testing.

(1) In a proceeding to adjudicate parentage under the circumstances described in RCW 26.26.530 or in RCW 26.26.540, a court may deny a motion seeking an

continued

order fort genetic testing of the mother or father, the child, and the presumed or acknowledged father if the court determines that:

(a) (i) The conduct of the mother or father or the presumed or acknowledged parent estops that party from denying parentage; and

(ii) It would be inequitable to disprove the parent-child relationship between the child and the presumed or acknowledged parent; or the child was conceived through assisted reproduction.

In determining whether to deny a motion to seek an order for genetic test under subsection (1)(a) of this section, the court shall consider the best interest of the child, including the following factors:

The length of time between the proceeding to adjudicate parentage and the time that the presumed or acknowledged parent was placed on notice that he or she might not be the genetic parent;

The length of time during which the presumed or acknowledged parent has assumed the role of parent of the child:

The facts surrounding the presumed or acknowledged parent's discovery of his possible nonparentage;

The nature of the relationship between the child and the presumed or acknowledged parent;

The age of the child;

The harm that may result to the child if parentage is successfully disproved;

The nature of the relationship between the child and any alleged parent;

The extent to which the passage of time reduces the chances of establishing the parentage of another person and a child support obligation in favor of the child; and

Other factors that may affect the equities arising from the disruption of the parent-child relationship between the child and the presumed or acknowledged parent or the chance of other harm to the child.

The legislative history and the statutory language of the UPA makes clear that prior to July 2011, the court could not consider whether the admission of genetic testing was in the best interest of the child where there was a challenge to the paternity of an acknowledged father. We conclude the court did not err in considering Fulton's petition to establish de facto paternity, and AFFIRM.

WE CONCUR: COX and BECKER, JJ.

Source: Chapter 49—Bastardy, Article 3—Civil Actions Regarding Illegitimate Children, § 49-14. Civil Action to Establish Paternity; Motion to Set Aside Paternity, North Carolina General Assembly.

Concept Review and Reinforcement

KEY **TERMS**

acknowledgement of paternity
affidavit of paternity
de facto father
DNA test

illegitimate
legal guardian
nonmarital child
parenting plan

paternity action
presumed father
putative father
rebuttable presumption

REVIEW OF **KEY CONCEPTS**

1. What is the difference between a putative father and a presumed father?

2. Why is the DNA paternity test the most reliable method for establishing paternity?

3. What are the factors used to determine whether as man is a *de facto* father?

4. Why is it important for unmarried parents who no longer live together to take necessary steps to have the court enter orders for custody, a parenting plan, and child support?

5. If an unmarried father does not appear at a scheduled hearing for custody and child support, what are the likely outcomes for relief?

BUILDING YOUR PARALEGAL SKILLS

CASE FOR BRIEFING

ROBIN v. SALLA, 964 N.Y.S.2D 41, N.Y.A.D. 1 DEPT., 2013

Critical Thinking and Legal Analysis Applications

You work as a paralegal in your state for the Law Offices of Taylor & Tyson. Your firm's client, Mark Williams, lived with Marilyn Trent for eight years. Four years ago, Marilyn told Mark that she was pregnant with his child. When the child was born, Mark signed an affidavit of paternity and also signed the birth certificate. The child, Brian, was given Mark's last name. Mark, Marilyn, and Brian lived together for the next three years. During that time, Mark worked full-time during the week. On weekends, he cared for Mark while Marilyn, a Registered Nurse, worked two twelve-hour shifts.

Six months ago, Marilyn told Mark that she met someone at work, Greg, who is also a nurse, that she wanted to start seeing Greg, and that she wanted Mark to move out of the apartment they shared. Mark moved into his own apartment and on weekends, Brian stayed with him while Marilyn worked. Marilyn didn't ask Mark for any money to take care of Brian's needs, but Mark spent a considerable amount of his paycheck on Brian. When Brian visited he bought Brian clothing, took him for haircuts, and bought lots of toys for Brian to play with at the apartment.

Two weeks ago, Marilyn informed Mark that she and Greg are moving to a city in a nearby state that is 175 miles away. Mark became very upset over this news. He told her that unless she changed her mind and stayed here, he would go to court and seek custody of Brian. Marilyn laughed in his face and said he'd never get it since he is not Brian's biological father. In fact, she said that she was seeing Greg on the side when Brian was conceived and that he is Brian's father.

Mr. Taylor, your supervising attorney, wants you to prepare an interoffice memorandum for him that presents possible options for Mark. You will need to find out what legal effect an acknowledgement of paternity has in your state, and you will also have to find out what Marilyn must do to prove that Greg is Brian's natural father. In your memorandum discuss under what circumstances Mark might obtain custody of Brian and under what circumstances he might have court-ordered visitation. Also discuss whether Mark may have to pay child support to Marilyn or whether it will turn out that Marilyn will have to pay child support to Mark.

Building a Professional Portfolio

PORTFOLIO **EXERCISES**

Find out in your state what form must be used to acknowledge paternity. Go on the Internet, find the website for your state, and see if there is a form for acknowledgment of paternity or affidavit of paternity. If so, print it and keep in a folder where you will build a resource file on paternity.

Find the statute in your state that addresses the legal procedure for establishing paternity where the parents were not married when the child was born. Print a copy of the statute. At the end of the statute in the annotations section, look up some of the cases listed to see how the statute has been applied in cases that came before your state's trial courts and appellate courts.

Chapter **ten**

FAMILY VIOLENCE AND STATE INTERVENTION

LEARNING OBJECTIVES

After studying this chapter, you should be able to:

1. Describe the situations where the government intrudes into family matters.

2. Explain the concept of *parens patriae*.

3. Understand the basic steps in a child protection case.

4. Explain the difference between a protective order and restraining order.

5. Be familiar with the issues involved in representing clients in domestic violence cases.

The U.S. government has recognized the integrity of the family unit. In the Supreme Court case *Stanley v. Illinois, 405 U.S. 645, 92 S. Ct. 1208, 31 L. Ed. 2d 551 (1972)*, the Court maintained that family preservation is a priority and that the U.S. Constitution protects family integrity. However, this protection is not absolute, particularly when dealing with issues of child abuse and family violence.

INTRODUCTION: PROTECTING ABUSED AND NEGLECTED CHILDREN—A CHANGE IN PERCEPTION

Under English common law, children were considered the property of their fathers, and this practice was continued in America during the seventeenth and eighteen centuries. Children who were unfortunate enough to live in families that abused and mistreated them had little or no recourse or advocates to take up their cause. Abuse and neglect of children was considered a private matter. Intervention, whether individual or institutional, was unheard of. Turning away in silence was commonplace and was supported by societies' unwillingness to get involved with domestic affairs.

As with many major changes in the law, either past or present, a sacrificial lamb is needed to shake society out of its slumber and demand that something be done. In 1874, the case of Mary Ellen Wilson, a Civil War orphan, made national news and set the course for many reforms to protect children from abuse and neglect from the hands of those charged with their care. Mary Ellen found herself placed with the New York Department of Charities. She was eventually placed in the care of a very abusive woman who subjected Mary Ellen to severe beatings and whippings for close to seven years of her life. Finally, a neighbor tried to help, but authorities either lacked authority to intervene or refused to investigate. With nowhere to turn, this same neighbor sought help from Henry Bergh, founder of the American Society for the Prevention of Cruelty to Animals (ASPCA). Bergh enlisted the help of ASPCA attorneys who brought the case to court, sending the abusive foster mother to jail and removing Mary Ellen from her custody. As a result of their experience with Mary Ellen's case, Bergh and his associates created the New York Society for the Prevention of Cruelty to Children, the world's very first nongovernmental charity dedicated specifically to the protection of children. It was their efforts that led to the establishments of similar charities all across the United States.

In 1962, an article published in the *Journal of the American Medical Association* published a landmark article entitled "The Battered-Child Syndrome," which paved the way for evaluating suspected child abuse cases and the diagnosis of *battered child syndrome.* This syndrome, a frequent cause of permanent injury or death, has been defined by its authors as a "clinical condition in young children who have received serious physical abuse." The medical community was advised to consider the syndrome in cases where children suffered from bone fractures, subdural hematomas, bruising, soft tissue swelling, or failure to thrive, or where the history of the injury offered varied with the actual injuries. It also recommended that physicians owe a duty to the child to fully evaluate the problem and to make efforts that the trauma to the child would not be repeated.

Fortunately, societies' perceptions about children have come a long way from "spare the rod, spoil the child" and the old maxim which held that "children should be seen and not heard." What followed was mandatory reporting laws requiring those most frequently exposed to children in the community to report suspected child abuse and neglect, as well as federal and state laws addressing the protection of children.

CHILD PROTECTION LAW: FEDERAL AND STATE INTERVENTION

Child Abuse Prevention and Treatment Act of 1974

A disorganized system of sporadic services by the criminal justice system, private charitable organizations, and well-meaning family and neighbors was in desperate need of state and federal governmental intervention. The most comprehensive effort to address the issue of child protection came in 1974 when the U.S. Congress passed the ***Child Abuse Prevention and Treatment Act of 1974 (CAPTA)***. CAPTA, and its subsequent incarnations, provides federal funding to states to support child protective services that respond to cases of abuse, neglect, and sexual abuse. CAPTA requires states to establish services that focus on investigating allegations of child abuse and neglect, providing services to families, removing children in danger from the home, funding foster care services, contacting the police when criminal charges need to be filed against parents or guardians, and commencing abuse and neglect proceedings in the courts when necessary.

Armed with federal funding and mandates, every state now has a child protection agency charged with intervening in a family unit when neglect or abuse is known or suspected. In many states, this agency is known as the Department of Children and Families (DCF), the Department of Children and Youth Services (DCYS), the Department of Health and Rehabilitative Services (HRS), or a similar name.

The state possesses the authority to intervene in child protection matters under the legal doctrine of ***parens patriae***. This Latin term is literally translated as "the parent of the country." In reality, this doctrine gives the state the right to protect children and persons with disabilities when their parent or legal guardian has failed to do so. However, before the state acts, the state must have reason to believe that intervention is needed.

Mandatory Reporting Laws

The fact that a child needs protection must come to the state's attention, usually through a complaint or referral by a third party. The state child protection agency typically receives complaints from a variety of sources. Certain professionals and paraprofessionals are ***mandatory reporters***, meaning that by law, under penalty of law, they are required to report any signs of suspected child abuse or neglect. Statutes requiring designated professionals to report suspected child abuse and neglect are called ***mandatory reporting laws***. The initial report is made by a phone call to child protective services and is then followed up with a written report, which could include evidence such as photographs, x-rays, and medical reports. Mandated reporters include school personnel such as classroom teachers, school nurses, counselors, and social workers; and medical personnel, specifically pediatricians, general practitioners, emergency room personnel, medical social workers, and other hospital department staff. If a teacher sees a child with suspicious bruises, for example, the teacher must report this to the local child protection agency. Similarly, if a child is brought to the emergency room with a suspicious injury or illness, the local child protection agency must be called. Mandated reporters are immune from liability as long as their reports are made in good faith.

The following is a sample of a California Department of Justice suspected child abuse report to be filled out by mandated reporters.

Child Abuse Prevention and Treatment Act of 1974 (CAPTA)
Federal government's most comprehensive effort to address the issue of child protection, which provides federal funding to states to support child protective services that respond to cases of abuse, neglect, and sexual abuse.

Parens patriae
The Latin term for the legal doctrine empowering the state to intervene to protect children when parents or guardians fail to do so.

Mandatory reporter
A professional who is required by state statute to report suspected child abuse or neglect.

Mandatory reporting laws
Statutes requiring designated professionals to report suspected child abuse and neglect.

Exhibit 10-1 California Department of Justice Suspected Child Abuse Report.

STATE OF CALIFORNIA
BCIA 8572
(Rev. 04/2017)

DEPARTMENT OF JUSTICE
Page 1 of 2

SUSPECTED CHILD ABUSE REPORT
(Pursuant to Penal Code section 11166)

To Be Completed by Mandated Child Abuse Reporters
PLEASE PRINT OR TYPE

CASE NAME: _____

CASE NUMBER: _____

A. REPORTING PARTY

NAME OF MANDATED REPORTER	TITLE	MANDATED REPORTER CATEGORY

REPORTER'S BUSINESS/AGENCY NAME AND ADDRESS   Street   City   Zip

DID MANDATED REPORTER WITNESS THE INCIDENT?   ☐ YES   ☐ NO

REPORTER'S TELEPHONE (DAYTIME)   SIGNATURE   TODAY'S DATE

B. REPORT NOTIFICATION

☐ LAW ENFORCEMENT   ☐ COUNTY PROBATION   AGENCY
☐ COUNTY WELFARE / CPS (Child Protective Services)

ADDRESS   Street   City   Zip   DATE/TIME OF PHONE CALL

OFFICIAL CONTACTED - NAME AND TITLE   TELEPHONE

C. VICTIM
One report per victim

NAME (LAST, FIRST, MIDDLE)   BIRTHDATE OR APPROX. AGE   SEX   ETHNICITY

ADDRESS   Street   City   Zip   TELEPHONE

PRESENT LOCATION OF VICTIM   SCHOOL   CLASS   GRADE

PHYSICALLY DISABLED? ☐ YES ☐ NO   DEVELOPMENTALLY DISABLED? ☐ YES ☐ NO   OTHER DISABILITY (SPECIFY)   PRIMARY LANGUAGE SPOKEN IN HOME

IN FOSTER CARE? ☐ YES ☐ NO

IF VICTIM WAS IN OUT-OF-HOME CARE AT TIME OF INCIDENT, CHECK TYPE OF CARE:
☐ DAY CARE   ☐ CHILD CARE CENTER   ☐ FOSTER FAMILY HOME
☐ FAMILY FRIEND   ☐ GROUP HOME OR INSTITUTION   ☐ RELATIVE'S HOME

TYPE OF ABUSE (CHECK ONE OR MORE):
☐ PHYSICAL   ☐ MENTAL
☐ SEXUAL   ☐ NEGLECT
☐ OTHER (SPECIFY) _____

RELATIONSHIP TO SUSPECT   PHOTOS TAKEN? ☐ YES ☐ NO   DID THE INCIDENT RESULT IN THIS VICTIM'S DEATH? ☐ YES ☐ NO ☐ UNK

D. INVOLVED PARTIES

VICTIM'S SIBLINGS

	NAME	BIRTHDATE	SEX	ETHNICITY		NAME	BIRTHDATE	SEX	ETHNICITY
1.					3.				
2.					4.				

VICTIM'S PARENTS/GUARDIANS

NAME (LAST, FIRST. MIDDLE)   BIRTHDATE OR APPROX. AGE   SEX   ETHNICITY

ADDRESS   Street   City   Zip   HOME PHONE   BUSINESS PHONE

NAME (LAST, FIRST. MIDDLE)   BIRTHDATE OR APPROX. AGE   SEX   ETHNICITY

ADDRESS   Street   City   Zip   HOME PHONE   BUSINESS PHONE

SUSPECT

SUSPECT'S NAME (LAST, FIRST. MIDDLE)   BIRTHDATE OR APPROX. AGE   SEX   ETHNICITY

ADDRESS   Street   City   Zip   TELEPHONE

OTHER RELEVANT INFORMATION

E. INCIDENT INFORMATION

IF NECESSARY, ATTACH EXTRA SHEET(S) OR OTHER FORM(S) AND CHECK THIS BOX ☐   IF MULTIPLE VICTIMS, INDICATE NUMBER: _____

DATE/TIME OF INCIDENT   PLACE OF INCIDENT

NARRATIVE DESCRIPTION (What victim(s) said/what the mandated reporter observed/what person accompanying the victim(s) said/similar or past incident's involving the victim(s) or suspect)

DO NOT submit a copy of this form to the Department of Justice (DOJ). The investigating agency is required under Penal Code section 11169 to submit to DOJ a Child Abuse or Severe Neglect Indexing Form BCIA 8583 if (1) an active investigation was conducted and (2) the incident was determined to be substantiated.

Source: Suspected Child Abuse Report, State of California Department of Justice.

Permissive reporter
An individual who reports suspected child abuse and neglect, but is not legally obligated by statute to do so.

Adoption Assistance and Child Welfare Act of 1980 (CWA)
Major federal child protection statute passed by Congress that requires that state child protective services make reasonable efforts to maintain children with their families or reunify them.

Family preservation
The legal requirement that state child protection services must make reasonable efforts to maintain children with their families or reunify them.

Reasonable efforts
Such efforts must be made to maintain children with their families, or to reunify them, once the parents have received short-term, family-focused, and community-based services.

Sometimes a neighbor or a family member will report suspected child neglect or abuse by calling the child protection agency's emergency hotline. These individuals are called ***permissive reporters***, who, while not legally obligated to report suspected child abuse and neglect, feel a sense of moral responsibility to call the case in to the authorities. These voluntary reports may be made on an anonymous basis to the state child protection services. States have established central hotlines that provide a twenty-four-hour toll-free number for reporting suspected child abuse. Occasionally, the caller to a hotline will identify himself or herself, especially if the caller is a blood relative and wants to serve as a placement resource for the child if removal from the home becomes an option. More frequently, the caller may wish to remain anonymous and refuse to give his or her name. If the anonymous caller sounds credible, the child protection agency will investigate the complaint.

Adoption Assistance and Child Welfare Act of 1980

The next major federal child protection statute passed by Congress was the ***Adoption Assistance and Child Welfare Act of 1980 (CWA)***. CWA was enacted because by the late 1970s there were approximately 503,000 children languishing in foster care and the mistaken belief by some that poverty issues were synonymous with neglect. The goal of CWA is ***family preservation***, which requires that state child protective services make ***reasonable efforts*** to maintain children with their families, or to reunify them once the parents have received short-term, family-focused, and community-based services. The federal government has not defined the term *reasonable efforts*, but some states have.

Family-centered services are adapted to the individual needs of a family in regard to the specific services and other support provided to the child's family and the intensity and duration of service delivery. Family-centered services are intended to preserve a child's connections to the child's neighborhood, community,

Figure 10-1 States have established central hotlines that provide a twenty-four-hour toll-free number for reporting suspected child abuse.

David P. Smith/Shutterstock.

and family and to improve the overall capacity of the child's family to provide for the needs of the children in the family.

CWA also limits the amount of time that a child may stay in foster care to eighteen months. During this time, child protective services must make "reasonable efforts" to keep families together and then must have a plan to either return children to their families or free them for adoption.

Adoption and Safe families Act of 1997

CWA was amended in 1997 with the passage of the *Adoption and Safe Families Act (ASFA)*, in response to numerous highly publicized cases where children were left in the home with the goal of preserving the family and instead ended up dead or abused even further. Additionally, children who had been placed in foster care were spending more time there while parents attempted to remedy the issues that caused the removal in the first place. Parents with difficult issues such as drug addiction, mental health issues, domestic violence, or criminal behavior increasingly extended the child's time in foster care by seeking extensions of the process as they dealt with the starts and stops that come with making major changes in their lives. While ASFA did not do away with family preservation and reunification efforts, it did make child welfare and safety a top priority. ASFA does establish the requirement that a permanency planning hearing must be held within twelve months of the child's placement in foster care for the purpose of assessing whether the child should be returned home or whether termination of parental rights proceedings should commence for the purpose of making the child available for adoption. ASFA also eliminates reunification efforts in cases of chronic physical abuse and sexual abuse. Such cases directly proceed to termination proceedings.

Adoption and Safe Families Act (ASFA)
A federal law that established the requirement that a permanency planning hearing must be held within twelve months of the child's placement in foster care for the purpose of assessing whether the child should be returned home or whether termination of parental rights proceedings should commence for the purpose of making the child available for adoption.

Investigation of a Complaint of Child Neglect or Child Abuse

When a child protection agency determines that an incoming complaint warrants follow-up, an investigative child protection worker will visit the family, unannounced, and assess the physical living conditions and the emotional environment of the family. Through asking questions and observing the premises and condition of the children, the worker will decide whether or not the allegations can be substantiated.

If the allegations are not substantiated, no action is taken. However, the complaint is documented so that if another complaint is made in the future, knowledge of the previous complaint may alert the worker to move quickly and to conduct a more intensive investigation. If allegations are substantiated, the state will intervene. The type and degree of intervention will be determined by the seriousness of the situation.

SERVICE AGREEMENT APPROACH

If a worker goes to a home and finds that the children are at risk of not being properly cared for, the investigative worker may recommend that the children remain in the home but that a case be opened with the agency and that a treatment worker be assigned to the case and family. The treatment worker will meet with the parents and the children and communicate to the parents what they must do so that their children will not be removed from their home.

The worker may make a list of things that must be corrected. These items will be incorporated into a service agreement or performance agreement that the worker will ask the parent or parents to sign. For instance, the worker will indicate that the parents must take their children to the doctor and keep current with immunizations. If the parents indicate that they have a substance abuse problem, the worker will indicate that the parents must go through a treatment program; if food or clothing for the children is not sufficient, the worker may try to help the clients budget and also put them in touch with social service providers and government agencies for financial assistance, the Supplemental Assistance Nutrition Program (SNAP), medical insurance, and other benefits.

After the agreement is in place, the worker will visit the family regularly, and if the problems are corrected and all is well, the case will be closed. As long as the worker has concerns, the case will remain open, and if at any time the situation worsens and the risk to the children's health and safety increases, the worker may initiate a more intense intervention.

ORDER OF TEMPORARY CUSTODY

If at any time a worker suspects that children may be in a situation of imminent harm or danger, the worker will seek authorization from his or her supervisor to apply to the child protection court for an order that gives the child protection agency temporary custody of the children. This order enables the worker to remove the children from the home and place them in temporary foster care. The parents are then notified that within five to seven days a court hearing will be held to determine whether the children are to remain in the state's custody.

Frequently, at the same time the parents are notified of the impending court hearing, the parents are also served with a legal petition in which the child protection agency as the petitioner alleges that the children are being neglected and requests that the children be committed to the appropriate state agency for a statutorily mandated period of time. This petition usually contains a notice of a hearing on the neglect petition and the date of the hearing. This hearing date will be scheduled for a date after the date of the hearing on the order of temporary custody.

Prior to the temporary custody hearing, the child protection court appoints an attorney or guardian *ad litem* to represent the interests of the children. The parents are notified that they should obtain their own legal representation. If the parents cannot afford an attorney and if their income falls within certain guidelines, the court provides them with an attorney paid by the judicial system.

At the temporary custody hearing, the attorney for the child protection agency, usually an attorney from the state's attorney general's office, has to prove that the children would be placed in immediate, imminent harm if they were to be returned to their parents at that time. The parents' attorney introduces evidence and testimony to rebut the state's arguments. The children's attorney has a chance to cross-examine the witnesses of both the state and the parents and also may wish to present witnesses and evidence in support of either confirmation of the custody order or revocation, depending on what the children's attorney believes will best promote the children's interest.

After all evidence is presented and closing arguments are heard, the judge rules either to confirm the order of temporary custody or to revoke that order and allow the children to be returned to the parents. If the custody order is confirmed, the children will remain in the state's custody until the underlying neglect matter is adjudicated. If the order is revoked, the underlying neglect matter will remain. Although the children will be allowed to return home, the parents must return for further court proceedings, which may include a trial on the neglect petition. If the state prevails at the neglect trial or if the parents choose to forgo their right to a trial and either admit or plead no contest to the allegations of neglect, the children will be adjudicated as neglected children. The court then makes a disposition that could result in the children being committed for a statutory period or results in the children remaining in the home under state supervision for a period of several months.

EFFORTS FOR REUNIFICATION OF THE CHILD WITH THE PARENTS

When a court commits a child to the care and custody of the state's child protection agency, the court is frequently called on to order that specific requirements be met before the child may be returned to the parents. These requirements, which are often known as specific steps or expectations, are drawn up by the representative of the child protection agency. The parents sign the document containing these steps to acknowledge that they know what the court expects them to do and to acknowledge that they will participate in the activities the state requires in order to be reunified with their child.

Specific Steps

The expectations or specific steps may include requirements such as the parent completing a substance abuse treatment program, attending parenting classes, or undergoing domestic violence counseling. The steps usually include general requirements such as the requirement that the parents visit their child as frequently as the child protection agency permits; that the parents keep their whereabouts known to the child protection agency and to their attorney; that the parents obtain a means of legal income and adequate housing; and that the parents have no involvement or no further involvement with the criminal justice system. If a parent has completed all of the specific steps to the satisfaction of the child protection agency, the parent's attorney may bring a motion to revoke the commitment before the court before the statutory commitment period ends. If the state agrees that all expectations have been met or if the child's attorney demonstrates by a preponderance of the evidence that the parent has fulfilled all of the expectations, the court may revoke the commitment and order that arrangements be made to reunify the child and parent as soon as possible.

Extension of Commitment

If a parent is unable to meet the requirements set for reunification within the statutory twelve-month commitment period, the child protection agency will file a motion or a petition to extend the period of custodial commitment for an additional statutory period. The parent may oppose this extension of commitment. Unless an agreement or compromise is reached between the state and the parent, the parent's attorney may request an evidentiary hearing on the motion for extension. At that hearing, the state presents evidence that the parent has not completed the specific steps needed to be fulfilled for reunification. The parent's attorney presents evidence to the contrary, which demonstrates that the parent has complied with the child protection agency's requirements and that the child's best interest will be served by reunifying parent and child.

If the court is persuaded that the parent has completed all requirements for reunification and if the court is persuaded that it will be in the child's best interest to return the child home, the extension will be denied and the child protection agency will have to reunify the child with the parents before the state's custodial commitment expires. Conversely, if the child protection agency proves that the parent has not complied with the court-ordered specific steps and has failed to fulfill the expectations required for reunification, the court will extend the commitment.

If, following this period or perhaps even during this commitment period, the child protection agency has reason to believe that there is little chance that within a reasonable period of time the parent will be able to meet the conditions needed for reunification, the child protection agency will make a determination that reunification is no longer the agency's goal. At this point, the agency will look for other options. Such options include transferring guardianship of the child to one of either of the parents' relatives; placing the child in a long-term foster care arrangement, especially if the child is older or has special needs and requires considerable therapeutic treatment; or terminating the natural parents' rights and the placement of the child in the agency's preadoption program. The most drastic option the child protection agency may elect is bringing an action to terminate the parent's parental rights to the child.

Termination of Parental Rights

Termination of parental rights

A court proceeding that severs the legal bonds between a parent and his or her biological child.

A *termination of parental rights* is a court proceeding that severs the legal bond between a parent and his or her biological or legally adopted child. A court of appropriate jurisdiction may terminate or permanently remove all legal rights a parent possesses in connection with his or her child. Rights may be terminated as to both parents or only as to one parent. Specially, upon the effective date of termination, the parent will no longer have the following legal rights and responsibilities that are part of the parent–child relationship. The parent will no longer have a duty to support the child, nor will the parent have the right to inherit from the child or the legal right to participate in any decisions whatsoever regarding the health, education, or welfare of the child.

Voluntary Termination of Parental Rights

A voluntary termination of parental rights occurs when a natural parent or an adoptive parent consents to having a court of appropriate jurisdiction terminate all legal rights a parent possesses regarding his or her relationship to a minor child. An individual's parental rights may be terminated only through a court proceeding. If the parent consents to the termination, the court proceeding is fairly short and uncomplicated. The judge asks the parent whether he or she wishes to have his or her parental rights severed. The judge canvasses the parent to make sure that the parent's consent is being freely given, without the parent being pressured in any way to do so. The judge also informs the parent of each of the rights the parent will be relinquishing.

If the parent is represented by counsel in this matter, the judge may also ask the parent whether his or her attorney discussed the matter thoroughly with him or her and whether the parent is satisfied with the legal representation the attorney provided. Following this canvassing, the judge announces that the parent's rights have been terminated and the proceeding ends shortly thereafter.

Involuntary Termination of Parental Rights

An involuntary termination of parental rights proceeding involves a trial. The state or the child protection agency must bring a petition before the court seeking termination of parental rights. In this petition, the state will allege that one or more statutory grounds exist to provide the legal justification for the court to terminate the parent's rights.

Grounds for Termination of Parental Rights

Each state has its own set of statutory grounds for termination. Many states include grounds such as parental abandonment, absence of a parent–child relationship, and failure of the parent to rehabilitate to a degree where the parent can achieve a meaningful role in the child's care and upbringing. Parental consent is also usually a statutory ground. In order for the court to grant the state's petition for termination of parental rights, the state must prove at least one statutory ground by clear and convincing evidence. This term connotes a very high evidentiary standard of proof that requires a higher degree of certainty than the preponderance of the evidence standard required for a judicial finding of neglect.

Consideration of the Child's Best Interests

If the court finds that the state has met its evidentiary burden and that one or more of the necessary grounds have been proven, the court must then go one step further and determine through the evidence whether it is in the child's best interests to terminate the parent's rights or whether additional time should be allowed to give the parent time to rectify whatever situations gave rise to the existence of the grounds for termination.

If the court decides to allow a parent a specific additional amount of time in which to do what is necessary for reunification with the child, the child protection agency will retain custody during this time period, and the court will outline what requirements the parent will have to meet by the end of the additional time period. On the other hand, if the court decides that additional time is not warranted, the court will issue an order terminating the parent's rights. If the parental rights of both parents have been terminated, the child will be free to be adopted.

DOMESTIC VIOLENCE

Traditionally, the legal system did not interfere in domestic affairs. Once married, women were considered property of the husband. The husband was the head of the household and had the right, as well as the obligation, to physically correct his spouse. For many years, the courts, as well as law enforcement, regarded these matters as "private" and did not intrude on the "sanctity" of the family, regardless of what was going on in the home. Domestic violence knows no gender, as both men and women may be subjected to abuse by their spouses or partners. Once referred to as *wife* or *spousal abuse*, the term often used today is ***intimate partner violence***, which acknowledges the gender-neutral nature of the problem in our society. Intimate partner violence is defined as physical, sexual, or psychological harm by a current or former partner or spouse. What is of great importance is that our social and legal systems no longer turn a blind eye to these matters.

Intimate partner violence
A gender-neutral term used in place of "wife" or "spousal abuse."

The Landmark Case of Tracey Thurman In 1984, Tracey Thurman sued the City of Torrington, Connecticut, as well as various police officers for the failure to arrest her abusive husband and minimize the threats he made on her life. Thurman won a $2 million judgment against the city for serious injuries she suffered from her estranged husband as he repeatedly stabbed her while she waited for help from the Torrington Police Department. Thurman's husband was under a restraining order and forbidden to have any contact with her at the time the assault occurred. The *Thurman* case is the first federal case where a victim of domestic violence sued a city for failing to provide her with protection.[1]

SOCIAL AND LEGAL CHANGES

Today, domestic violence is a crime in all fifty states, and its definition varies from state to state. Here is an example of North Carolina's statute:

North Carolina General Statutes § 50B—1. Domestic violence; definition[2]

    (a) Domestic violence means the commission of one or more of the following acts upon an aggrieved party or upon a minor child residing with or in

---

[1]Tracey Thurman v. City of Torrington, 595 F.SUPP. 1521 (D.CONN. 1984), United States District Court, District of Connecticut.

[2]Chapter 50B—Domestic Violence, North Carolina General Assembly.

the custody of the aggrieved party by a person with whom the aggrieved party has or has had a personal relationship, but does not include acts of self-defense:

(1) Attempting to cause bodily injury, or intentionally causing bodily injury; or

(2) Placing the aggrieved party or a member of the aggrieved party's family or household in fear of imminent serious bodily injury or continued harassment, as defined in G.S. 14-277.3A, that rises to such a level as to inflict substantial emotional distress; or

(3) Committing any act defined in G.S. 14-27.21 through G.S. 14-27.33.

(b) For purposes of this section, the term "personal relationship" means a relationship wherein the parties involved:

(1) Are current or former spouses;

(2) Are persons of opposite sex who live together or have lived together;

(3) Are related as parents and children, including others acting in loco parentis to a minor child, or as grandparents and grandchildren. For purposes of this subdivision, an aggrieved party may not obtain an order of protection against a child or grandchild under the age of 16;

(4) Have a child in common;

(5) Are current or former household members;

(6) Are persons of the opposite sex who are in a dating relationship or have been in a dating relationship. For purposes of this subdivision, a dating relationship is one wherein the parties are romantically involved over time and on a continuous basis during the course of the relationship. A casual acquaintance or ordinary fraternization between persons in a business or social context is not a dating relationship.

Figure 10-2 Today, domestic violence is a crime in all fifty states.

Phase4Studios/Shuttertstock.

(c) As used in this chapter, the term "protective order" includes any order entered pursuant to this chapter upon hearing by the court or consent of the parties. (1979, c. 561, s. 1; 1985, c. 113, s. 1; 1987, c. 828; 1987 (Reg. Sess., 1988), c. 893, ss. 1, 3; 1995 (Reg. Sess., 1996), c. 591, s. 1; 1997-471, s. 1; 2001-518, s. 3; 2003-107, s. 1; 2009-58, s. 5; 2015-181, s. 36.)

The women's liberation movement in the 1960s created awareness in the area of spousal abuse and challenged the legal and social systems to become more responsive to situations that were once considered "private." Some of the changes over the years include:

- Ability to change Social Security number for victims of domestic violence through Social Security Administration
- Civil restraining or "no contact" orders issued by civil courts
- Criminal orders of protection issued by criminal courts
- Counseling and support groups for victims, abusers, and children
- Court advocates that inform victims of services available in community and what to expect in the court system
- Community education and outreach
- Federal law prohibiting abusers from having guns in their possession
- Financial assistance through State Victim's Compensation Boards
- GPS monitoring of offenders
- Legislative advocacy for victims' rights
- Mandatory arrest statutes
- Notification of status and release dates of abusers incarcerated in prisons
- Shelters and safe homes for victims and their children
- Specialized training for attorneys, law enforcement, and health-care professionals
- Toll-free, twenty-four-hour domestic violence hotlines

Civil Restraining Orders and Criminal Protective Orders

While the language may differ from jurisdiction to jurisdiction, all states provide some form of civil and criminal intervention to victims of intimate partner violence. Therefore, knowing state law is very important since vocabulary varies around the country. While there are many domestic violence organizations throughout the country that provide a myriad of services, the state legal system has responded with remedies available in both the civil and criminal courts. Two remedies for victims of domestic violence include criminal protective orders and civil restraining orders.

Both criminal protective orders and civil restraining orders may be obtained against "family or household members," the definition of which has been expanded over the years to include spouses or former spouses, regardless of whether they have resided together; cohabitants or those who have previously cohabitated within a certain period of statutory time; individuals who have a children in common, regardless of whether or not they reside in the same home; and parents, children, stepchildren, siblings, grandparents, grandchildren, and in-laws, regardless of whether they live in the same home. Violation of criminal protective orders and civil restraining orders is often a separate criminal offense punishable by law.

A ***criminal protective order*** is a court order issued by a judge in a criminal case against a defendant accused of a domestic violence–related crime. It requires the defendant to basically stay away from the victim; vacate the family residence; and refrain from threatening, assaulting, harassing, or contacting the victim in any manner, and it typically lasts for the duration of the case. Defendants in these

Criminal protective order
Is a court order issued by a judge in a criminal case against a defendant accused of a domestic-violence–related crime.

matters are often arrested for breach of peace, disorderly conduct, stalking, harassment, threatening, assault, battery, risk of injury, criminal mischief, sexual assault, burglary, and trespassing. If a child is injured or endangered in the course of a domestic violence crime, a companion charge of abuse and neglect will most likely be filed by the state child protection agency.

The criminal protective order is issued from the bench and served on the defendant right in the courtroom. The immediacy of the order is one of the main advantages of a protective order. The victim does not have to fill out paperwork or find a marshal or sheriff who will serve the defendant. It all takes place in the courtroom with the judge entering the order on the record. The defendant may be ordered to participate in anger-management or domestic-violence education programs, as well as drug or alcohol treatment if needed. Victims may also be offered services through the assistance of victims' advocates or the family services division of the court.

See **Appendix C, Rihanna and Chris Brown Search Warrant and Affidavit.**

While law enforcement's purpose for obtaining a search warrant was to access the cell phone records of Rihanna (aka Robyn Fenty), her personal assistant, and Chris Brown regarding a domestic violence matter that took place on February 8, 2009, the document reveals the details of the altercation between the two pop stars. As a result, Brown was arrested for felony assault and ordered to stay fifty yards away from Rihanna, or ten yards if they were both at an entertainment industry function. Ultimately, Brown completed a court-ordered domestic violence education program, as well as 180 days of community service, and was placed on five years of probation. The criminal protective order issued by the judge was extended to five years, the length of Brown's probation period. In February 2011, the judge lifted the criminal protective order against Brown with Rihanna's consent.

A *civil restraining order*, on the other hand, is obtained by the victim in a family (civil) court. The advantage of a civil restraining order is that the family court can award child custody and support and visitation. Obtaining a restraining order takes much more effort on the part of the victim. The victim, or petitioner, initially files a petition for a ***temporary restraining order (TRO)*** in family court alleging that the petitioner and/or members of the household are in immediate physical danger. An *ex parte* hearing is scheduled on the same day. This means that the respondent is not in court; therefore, the petitioner may only obtain a temporary order until the respondent has been given notice and a date to appear and be heard on the matter. At the ***ex parte*** hearing, the petitioner is required, under oath, to testify as to the statement filed along with the restraining order. If the judge determines that the petitioner and/or members of the household are in immediate physical danger, the judge will sign the temporary restraining order and schedule a full hearing, usually within two weeks. This allows the respondent to be served with the temporary restraining order and appear at a full hearing on the matter. At the full hearing, the respondent is given the opportunity to appear and present evidence, along with the petitioner, who may request that the orders continue for a statutory period of time. If the judge rules in favor of the petitioner, then a full restraining order will be issued against the respondent. The orders typically issued under a civil restraining order include orders to refrain from any contact with the petitioner, ***stay away orders***, which prohibit the respondent from coming to the home, workplace, school, or other premises of the petitioner; ***no contact orders***, which prohibit any type of physical or electronic contact with the victim and may specify the actual distance in terms of feet; and orders to vacate the premises if the parties reside together, as well as custody, visitation, and alimony orders, which are typically not granted by a criminal court in the case of a criminal protective order. Criminal protective orders may be modified or rescinded and typically last for the duration of the criminal case. Therefore, obtaining a civil restraining order may be advisable if necessary.

Civil restraining order
A court order obtained by a victim of domestic violence in a family (civil) court.

Temporary restraining order (TRO)
The petition filed by a victim of domestic violence in a civil court where the victim alleges that the petitioner and/or members of the household are in immediate physical danger and, as such, are requesting relief from the court.

Ex parte
A Latin term meaning "by one party" or "for one party."

Stay away orders
Prohibit the respondent in a domestic violence case from coming to the home, workplace, school, or other premises of the petitioner.

No contact orders
A court order issued in a domestic violence case that prohibits any type of physical or electronic contact with the victim.

Exhibit 10-2 California's Request for Domestic Violence Restraining Order.

DV-100

Request for Domestic Violence Restraining Order

Clerk stamps date here when form is filed.

You must also complete form CLETS-001, Confidential CLETS Information, and give it to the clerk when you file this Request.

(1) Name of Person Asking for Protection:

_____ Age: _____

Your lawyer in this case *(if you have one):*

Name: _____ State Bar No.: _____

Firm Name: _____

Address *(If you have a lawyer for this case, give your lawyer's information. If you do not have a lawyer and want to keep your home address private, give a different mailing address instead. You do not have to give your telephone, fax, or e-mail.):*

Address: _____

City: _____ State: _____ Zip: _____

Telephone: _____ Fax: _____

E-Mail Address: _____

Fill in court name and street address:

Superior Court of California, County of

Court fills in case number when form is filed.

(2) Name of Person You Want Protection From:

_____

Description of person you want protection from:

Case Number:

Sex: ☐ M ☐ F   Height: _____   Weight: _____   Hair Color: _____   Eye Color: _____
Race: _____   Age: _____   Date of Birth: _____
Address *(if known):* _____
City: _____   State: _____   Zip: _____

(3) Do you want an order to protect family or household members?   ☐ Yes ☐ No

If yes, list them:

Full name	Sex	Age	Lives with you?	Relationship to you
_____	_____	_____	☐ Yes ☐ No	_____
_____	_____	_____	☐ Yes ☐ No	_____
_____	_____	_____	☐ Yes ☐ No	_____

☐ *Check here if you need more space. Attach a sheet of paper and write "DV-100, Protected People" for a title.*

(4) What is your relationship to the person in (2) ? *(Check all that apply):*

a. ☐ We are now married or registered domestic partners.
b. ☐ We used to be married or registered domestic partners.
c. ☐ We live together.
d. ☐ We used to live together.
e. ☐ We are related by blood, marriage, or adoption *(specify relationship):* _____
f. ☐ We are dating or used to date, or we are or used to be engaged to be married.
g. ☐ We are the parents together of a child or children under 18:

If you do not have one of these relationships, the court may not be able to consider your request. Read form DV-500-INFO for help.

Child's Name: _____ Date of Birth: _____
Child's Name: _____ Date of Birth: _____
Child's Name: _____ Date of Birth: _____

☐ *Check here if you need more space. Attach a sheet of paper and write "DV-100, Additional Children" for a title.*

h. ☐ We have signed a Voluntary Declaration of Paternity for our child or children. *(Attach a copy if you have one).*

This is not a Court Order.

Judicial Council of California, www.courts.ca.gov
Revised July 1, 2016, Mandatory Form
Family Code, § 6200 et seq.

Request for Domestic Violence Restraining Order
(Domestic Violence Prevention)

DV-100, Page 1 of 6

→

continued

Exhibit 10-2 Continued

Case Number:

(5) Other Restraining Orders and Court Cases

a. Are there any restraining/protective orders currently in place OR that have expired in the last six months (emergency protective orders, criminal, juvenile, family)?

☐ No ☐ Yes *(date of order):*   and *(expiration date):*   *(Attach a copy if you have one).*

b. Have you or any other person named in **(3)** been involved in another court case with the person in **(2)**?

☐ No ☐ Yes *If yes, check each kind of case and indicate where and when each was filed:*

Kind of Case	County or Tribe Where Filed	Year Filed	Case Number *(if known)*
☐ Divorce, Nullity, Legal Separation	_____	_____	_____
☐ Civil Harassment	_____	_____	_____
☐ Domestic Violence	_____	_____	_____
☐ Criminal	_____	_____	_____
☐ Juvenile, Dependency, Guardianship	_____	_____	_____
☐ Child Support	_____	_____	_____
☐ Parentage, Paternity	_____	_____	_____
☐ Other *(specify):* _____	_____	_____	_____

☐ *Check here if you need more space. Attach a sheet of paper and write "DV-100, Other Court Cases" for a title.*

Check the orders you want. ☑

(6) ☐ Personal Conduct Orders

I ask the court to order the person in **(2)** not to do the following things to me or anyone listed in **(3)**:

a. ☐ Harass, attack, strike, threaten, assault (sexually or otherwise), hit, follow, stalk, molest, destroy personal property, disturb the peace, keep under surveillance, impersonate (on the Internet, electronically or otherwise), or block movements

b. ☐ Contact, either directly or indirectly, in any way, including but not limited to, by telephone, mail or e-mail or other electronic means

The person in **(2)** *will be ordered not to take any action to get the addresses or locations of any protected person unless the court finds good cause not to make the order.*

(7) ☐ Stay-Away Order

a. I ask the court to order the person in **(2)** to stay at least _____ yards away from *(check all that apply):*

☐ Me   ☐ My school
☐ My home   ☐ Each person listed in **(3)**
☐ My job or workplace   ☐ The child(ren)'s school or child care
☐ My vehicle   ☐ Other *(specify):* _____

b. If the person listed in **(2)** is ordered to stay away from all the places listed above, will he or she still be able to get to his or her home, school, job, workplace, or vehicle?   ☐ Yes ☐ No *(If no, explain):*

_____

(8) ☐ Move-Out Order

(If the person in **(2)** *lives with you and you want that person to stay away from your home, you must ask for this move-out order.)*

I ask the court to order the person in **(2)** to move out from and not return to *(address):*

_____

_____

I have the right to live at the above address because (explain):

_____

_____

This is not a Court Order.

Case Number:

(9) Guns or Other Firearms or Ammunition

I believe the person in (2) owns or possesses guns, firearms, or ammunition. ☐ Yes ☐ No ☐ I don't know
If the judge approves the order, the person in (2) will be ordered not to own, possess, purchase, or receive a firearm or ammunition. The person will be ordered to sell to, or store with, a licensed gun dealer, or turn in to law enforcement, any guns or firearms that he or she owns or possesses.

(10) ☐ Record Unlawful Communications

I ask for the right to record communications made to me by the person in (2) that violate the judge's orders.

(11) ☐ Care of Animals

I ask for the sole possession, care, and control of the animals listed below. I ask the court to order the person in (2) to stay at least _____ yards away from and not take, sell, transfer, encumber, conceal, molest, attack, strike, threaten, harm, or otherwise dispose of the following animals:

_____
_____
_____

I ask for the animals to be with me because:

_____
_____
_____

(12) ☐ Child Custody and Visitation

a. ☐ I do not have a child custody or visitation order and I want one.
b. ☐ I have a child custody or visitation order and I want it changed.

If you ask for orders, you must fill out and attach form DV-105, Request for Child Custody and Visitation Orders. You and the other parent may tell the court that you want to be legal parents of the children (use form DV-180, Agreement and Judgment of Parentage).

(13) ☐ Child Support *(Check all that apply):*

a. ☐ I do not have a child support order and I want one.
b. ☐ I have a child support order and I want it changed.
c. ☐ I now receive or have applied for TANF, Welfare, CalWORKS, or Medi-Cal.

If you ask for child support orders, you must fill out and attach form FL-150, Income and Expense Declaration *or form FL-155,* Financial Statement (Simplified).

(14) ☐ Property Control

I ask the court to give *only* me temporary use, possession, and control of the property listed here:

_____
_____

(15) ☐ Debt Payment

I ask the court to order the person in (2) to make these payments while the order is in effect:
☐ *Check here if you need more space. Attach a sheet of paper and write "DV-100, Debt Payment" for a title.*
Pay to: _____ For: _____ Amount: $ _____ Due date: _____

(16) ☐ Property Restraint

I am married to or have a registered domestic partnership with the person in (2). I ask the judge to order that the person in (2) not borrow against, sell, hide, or get rid of or destroy any possessions or property, except in the usual course of business or for necessities of life. I also ask the judge to order the person in (2) to notify me of any new or big expenses and to explain them to the court.

(17) ☐ Spousal Support

I am married to or have a registered domestic partnership with the person in (2) and no spousal support order exists. I ask the court to order the person in (2) to pay spousal support. *(You must complete, file, and serve form FL-150,* Income and Expense Declaration, *before your hearing).*

This is not a Court Order.

Revised July 1, 2016

Request for Domestic Violence Restraining Order
(Domestic Violence Prevention)

DV-100, Page 3 of 6
→

continued

Exhibit 10-2 Continued

Case Number: _____

(18) ☐ **Rights to Mobile Device and Wireless Phone Account**

a. ☐ **Property control of mobile device and wireless phone account**
I ask the court to give **only** me temporary use, possession, and control of the following mobile devices:
_____ and the wireless phone account for the
following wireless phone numbers because the account currently belongs to the person in **(2)** :
(including area code): _____ ☐ my number ☐ number of child in my care
(including area code): _____ ☐ my number ☐ number of child in my care
(including area code): _____ ☐ my number ☐ number of child in my care
☐ *Check here if you need more space. Attach a sheet of paper and write "DV-100, Rights to Mobile Device
and Wireless Phone Account" for a title.*

b. ☐ **Debt Payment**
I ask the court to order the person in **(2)** to make the payments for the wireless phone accounts listed in 18a
because: _____
Name of the wireless service provider is: _____ Amount: $ _____ Due Date: _____
*If you are requesting this order, you must complete, file, and serve form FL-150, Income and Expense
Declaration, before your hearing.*

c. ☐ **Transfer of Wireless Phone Account**
I ask the court to order the wireless service provider to transfer the billing responsibility and rights to the
wireless phone numbers listed in 18a to me because the account currently belongs to the person in **(2)** .
*If the judge makes this order, you will be financially responsible for these accounts, including monthly service
fees and costs of any mobile devices connected to these phone numbers. You may be responsible for other fees.
You must contact the wireless service provider to find out what fees you will be responsible for and whether you
are eligible for an account.*

(19) ☐ **Insurance**
I ask the court to order the person in **(2)** NOT to cash, borrow against, cancel, transfer, dispose of, or change the
beneficiaries of any insurance or coverage held for the benefit of me or the person in **(2)**, or our child(ren), for
whom support may be ordered, or both.

(20) ☐ **Lawyer's Fees and Costs**
I ask that the person in **(2)** pay some or all of my lawyer's fees and costs.
You must complete, file, and serve form FL-150, Income and Expense Declaration, before your hearing.

(21) ☐ **Payments for Costs and Services**
I ask the court to order the person in **(2)** to pay the following:
*You can ask for lost earnings or your costs for services caused directly by the person in **(2)** (damaged property,
medical care, counseling, temporary housing, etc.). You must bring proof of these expenses to your hearing.*
Pay to: _____ For: _____ Amount: $ _____
Pay to: _____ For: _____ Amount: $ _____

(22) ☐ **Batterer Intervention Program**
I ask the court to order the person listed in **(2)** to go to a 52-week batterer intervention program and show proof
of completion to the court.

(23) ☐ **Other Orders**
What other orders are you asking for? _____
_____
_____
_____

☐ *Check here if you need more space. Attach a sheet of paper and write "DV-100, Other Orders" for a title.*

This is not a Court Order.

Case Number:

(24) ☐ **Time for Service (Notice)**

The papers must be personally served on the person in **(2)** *at least five days before the hearing, unless the court orders a shorter time for service. If you want there to be fewer than five days between service and the hearing, explain why below. For help, read form DV-200-INFO, "What Is Proof of Personal Service"?*

_____

_____

(25) **No Fee to Serve (Notify) Restrained Person**

If you want the sheriff or marshal to serve (notify) the restrained person about the orders for free, ask the court clerk what you need to do.

(26) **Court Hearing**

The court will schedule a hearing on your request. If the judge does not make the orders effective right away ("temporary restraining orders"), the judge may still make the orders after the hearing. If the judge does not make the orders effective right away, you can ask the court to cancel the hearing. Read form DV-112, *Waiver of Hearing on Denied Request for Temporary Restraining Order,* for more information.

(27) **Describe Abuse**

Describe how the person in **(2)** abused you. Abuse means to intentionally or recklessly cause or attempt to cause bodily injury to you; or to place you or another person in reasonable fear of imminent serious bodily injury; or to harass, attack, strike, threaten, assault (sexually or otherwise), hit, follow, stalk, molest, keep you under surveillance, impersonate (on the Internet, electronically or otherwise), batter, telephone, or contact you; or to disturb your peace; or to destroy your personal property. (For a complete definition, see Fam. Code, §§ 6203, 6320.)

a. Date of most recent abuse: _____

  1. Who was there? _____

  2. Describe how the person in **(2)** abused you or your child(ren):

  _____

  _____

  _____

  _____

  _____

   ☐ *Check here if you need more space. Attach a sheet of paper and write "DV-100, Recent Abuse" for a title.*

  3. Did the person in **(2)** use or threaten to use a gun or any other weapon? ☐ No ☐ Yes *(If yes, describe):*

  _____

  _____

  4. Describe any injuries: _____

  _____

  _____

  5. Did the police come? ☐ No ☐ Yes

   If yes, did they give you or the person in **(2)** an Emergency Protective Order? ☐ Yes ☐ No ☐ I don't know
   Attach a copy if you have one.
   The order protects ☐ you or   ☐ the person in **(2)**

This is not a Court Order.

Revised July 1, 2016   **Request for Domestic Violence Restraining Order**   DV-100, Page 5 of 6
                             (Domestic Violence Prevention)   →

continued

Exhibit 10-2 Continued

Case Number:

(27) Describe Abuse (continued)

Has the person in (2) abused you (or your child(ren)) other times?

b. Date of abuse: _____

1. Who was there? _____

2. Describe how the person in (2) abused you or your child(ren):

_____

_____

_____

_____

_____

☐ *Check here if you need more space. Attach a sheet of paper and write "DV-100, Recent Abuse" for a title.*

3. Did the person in (2) use or threaten to use a gun or any other weapon? ☐ No ☐ Yes *(If yes, describe):*

_____

4. Describe any injuries: _____

_____

5. Did the police come? ☐ No ☐ Yes

If yes, did they give you or the person in (2) an Emergency Protective Order?

☐ Yes ☐ No ☐ I don't know *Attach a copy if you have one.*

The order protects ☐ you or   ☐ the person in (2)

If the person in (2) abused other times, check here ☐ and use Form DV-101, Description of Abuse or describe any previous abuse on an attached sheet of paper and write "DV-100, Previous Abuse" for a title.

(28) Other Persons to Be Protected

The persons listed in item (3) need an order for protection because *(describe):* _____

_____

_____

_____

_____

_____

_____

(29) Number of pages attached to this form, if any: _____

I declare under penalty of perjury under the laws of the State of California that the information above is true and correct.

Date: _____

_____   ▶ _____

Type or print your name   *Sign your name*

Date: _____

_____   ▶ _____

Lawyer's name, if you have one   *Lawyer's signature*

This is not a Court Order.

For your protection and privacy, please press the clear This Form button after you have printed the form.

Source: DV-100, Request for Domestic Violence Restraining Order, Judicial Council of Califor

California's Request for Domestic Violence Restraining Order

In 2005, the United States Supreme Court ruled in ***Castle Rock v. Gonzales, 545 U.S. 748 (2005)*** that the police did not have a constitutional duty to protect a person from harm, even though that individual had obtained a court-issued protective order against a defendant pursuant to a mandatory arrest authorized by state law. In this case, Jessica Gonzales made repeated attempts to have the Castle Rock police arrest her husband, who had violated a stay away order and had kidnapped their three daughters as they played outside in the front yard. Despite her pleas, the police did nothing. Hours later, her husband arrived at the police station firing a gun and was killed at the scene by police. Unfortunately for the girls, they were found dead in the trunk of his car. The Court reasoned that Gonzales did not have a recognized property interest protected under the Due Process Clause of the U.S. Constitution because the entitlement to enforcement of a restraining order had no monetary value and did not qualify as property.

Mandatory Arrests It has taken many years for law enforcement to treat domestic violence as a crime. Thanks to the efforts of the women's rights movement, which resulted in legislature and societal reforms, victims are no longer asked "Do you want to press charges?" because many states now require ***mandatory arrests*** in domestic-violence–related crimes. This means that the police must make an arrest if ***probable cause*** exists, thus removing police discretion in making an arrest. Probable cause means that a crime has been committed by the person sought to be arrested. For example, if a law enforcement officer responds to a 911 call where the victim is crying for help and, upon arrival at the home, finds the apartment is in disarray, broken glass on the floor, the complainant with a bruised eye and bloody lip, and a report from the victim that so and so did this, there is enough probable cause to arrest the individual.

In the past, the abuser might be asked by the police to "take a walk around the block to cool off," or the victim would be asked to stay with a friend or family for the night. The call for mandatory arrests in these cases is a far cry from the legal system's unwillingness to interfere in domestic affairs. And while mandatory arrests are a step in the right direction, in many cases both parties are arrested, without a determination of who perpetrated the crime. This practice is called ***dual arrests***. According to the U.S. Department of Justice, dual arrests are more common in states with mandatory arrest laws. Many victims of domestic violence have complained that inflicting even a scratch in self-defense on their abuser resulted in an arrest at the abuser's insistence. While it is often easier for law enforcement to arrest everyone and let the courts sort out the details, the argument on behalf of victims of domestic violence is that the victim is further victimized by the judicial system in the case of dual arrests. States like New York, New Jersey, and Rhode Island have tried to remedy the problem of dual arrests by enacting ***primary (or predominant) aggressor laws***. These statutes require police officers to attempt to identify the "primary aggressor" when deciding whether to arrest both parties in domestic violence cases where both parties claim injuries.

Violence Against Women Act of 1994

In 1994, Congress passed landmark federal legislation aimed at improving the criminal justice system and social programs in their responses to domestic violence, sexual assault, teen dating violence, and stalking. The ***Violence Against Women Act of 1994*** and its subsequent reauthorizations in 2000, 2005, and most recently in 2013 fund services to both adult and teen victims of domestic

Mandatory arrests
A law that requires police officers in domestic-violence–related crimes to make an arrest if probable cause exists, thus removing police discretion in making an arrest.

Probable cause
The legal requirement that must exist for the police to make an arrest. It means that based on the evidence, the arresting officers have determined that a crime has been committed by the person sought to be arrested.

Dual arrests
Where both parties involved in a domestic violence case are arrested, without a determination of who perpetrated the crime.

Primary (or predominant) aggressor laws
Statutes that require police officers to attempt to identify the "primary aggressor" when deciding whether to arrest both parties in domestic violence cases where both parties claim injuries.

Violence Against Women Act of 1994
A Federal law that provides for education on the cycle of violence and prevention of abuse, protection of victims in the areas of housing and employment, changes to immigration law allowing immigrant victims of domestic violence to apply for permanent residency, funding for Indian tribal governments to help prevent violence amongst the Native American population, encourages states to implement mandatory arrests, and mandates that orders of protection granted in one state be recognized in all other jurisdictions.

violence and emphasize a coordinated community response involving the court system, attorneys, law enforcement agencies, domestic violence and sexual assault services, and victim advocates. It also provides funding for education on the cycle of violence and prevention of abuse, protection of victims in the areas of housing and employment, changes to immigration law allowing immigrant victims of domestic violence to apply for permanent residency, and funding for Indian tribal governments to help prevent violence among the Native American population; provides more care, assistance, and protection for victims of the LGBTQ community; encourages states to implement mandatory arrests; and mandates that orders of protection granted in one state be recognized in all other jurisdictions. The act also provides that individuals subject to a protective order are prohibited from possessing firearms or ammunition, which must be surrendered to law enforcement. The Violence Against Women Act is up for reauthorization in 2018.

Possession of Firearm While Subject to Order of Protection, 18 U.S.C. §922(g)(8)

It is illegal for a person to possess a firearm while subject to a court order restraining such person from harassing, stalking, or threatening an intimate partner or the child of an intimate partner. The protection order must have been issued following an evidentiary hearing in which the defendant had notice and an opportunity to appear. The protection order must also include a specific finding that the defendant represents a credible threat to the physical safety of the victim, or must include an explicit prohibition against the use of force that would reasonably be expected to cause injury. The statutory language of Section 922(g)(8), in addition to the language of Section 2262, provides additional justification for review of a jurisdiction's protection order form to determine if they conform with the federal requirements. Again, refer any questions about the applicability of this statute to the United States Attorney's Office in that district.[3]

The act was amended and reauthorized in 2013, expanding funding and protections for immigrants; the lesbian, gay, bisexual, and transgender community; Native Americans; college students; and public housing residents. Despite its title, the language of the act equally protects male victims of violence.

Representing the Parties in Domestic Violence Cases

Because the law varies from state to state, it is important for legal professionals to become familiar with the domestic violence laws in their jurisdictions. A number of domestic violence cases that the law office handles may involve dual arrests, which occur when both of the parties are arrested. Sometimes, identifying the abused and abuser is not so simple, as dynamics in relationships are very complex. Knowledge of the services available to clients, whether they are victims, alleged abusers, or children, is crucial, since you never know who your supervising attorney will be representing.

Victims, for instance, often require the basics, like food, clothing, and shelter, if they are leaving an abusive environment. They also may need assistance in obtaining orders of protection, divorces, child support, custody, and exclusive possession of the marital residence and in enforcing existing court orders. The office may also wish to recommend individual counseling services or support groups for the client. Marriage counseling or mediation services for couples with domestic violence issues are often not recommended by many mental health professionals because of the imbalance of power, the inability of victims to speak freely during

---

[3]Title 18—Crimes and Criminal Procedures, part 1—Crimes, Chapter 44—Firearms, Office of the Law Revision Counsel.

the session, and the fear of repercussions after the session is over. It is also a good idea to keep a camera in the office so that the staff can photograph the victim's injuries as possible evidence. The client's safety is also a priority as the office arranges for face-to-face interviews as well as protection for the client going to and from court and while in the courthouse awaiting hearings.

When representing the alleged abuser, it is important that the attorney emphasize to the client that he or she must be protected from any further allegations or arrests. Contact with the spouse or ex-spouse should be minimized, especially when picking up or dropping off the children for visitation. It is also best to make child support payments through either wage withholding or mail, thus avoiding any unnecessary interactions between the parties. If the alleged abuser admits to having a problem, then it is important to seek out any services available such as one-on-one counseling, support groups, or anger management classes. Many states mandate anger management classes when such cases have entered into the criminal justice system. One of the hardest clients to represent is one that has a problem but does not care to address it and continues to engage in antisocial behavior. In these situations, an attorney may have to engage in a lot of damage control as the client suffers the consequences of his or her actions. It is also important in these situations, as in all matters, that attorneys and paralegals be vigilant in documenting all phone calls, court appearances, and any other efforts made on behalf of the client, including letters memorializing conversations and legal advice. Abusive clients and opposing parties may turn around and abuse the attorney with grievances and lawsuits.

Children are often caught in the middle of the crossfire. Children who have grown up in abusive households may also need counseling services, so it is important to become familiar with the services available for children in the community. Problems may also arise during visitation exchange, where parents are forced to interact with one another; therefore, it is important that a safe environment is created. If the situation warrants, the attorney may ask for supervised visitation. Many states also have state-approved visitation centers or visitation exchange centers to facilitate access to the children in a safe, structured environment.

Concept Review and Reinforcement

KEY **TERMS**

Adoption Assistance and Child Welfare
    Act of 1980 (CWA)
Adoption and Safe Families Act (ASFA)
Child Abuse Prevention and Treatment
    Act of 1974 (CAPTA)
civil restraining order
criminal protective order
dual arrests

ex parte
family preservation
intimate partner violence
mandatory arrests
mandatory reporter
mandatory reporting laws
no contact orders
parens patriae

permissive reporters
primary (or predominant) aggressor law
probable cause
reasonable efforts
stay away orders
temporary restraining order (TRO)
termination of parental rights
Violence Against Women Act of 1994

BUILDING YOUR PARALEGAL SKILLS

CASE FOR BRIEFING

UNITED STATES v. MORRISON, 529 U.S. 598 (2000)

Based on your reading of this U. S. Supreme Court case, what are the limitations of the Violence Against Women Act of 1994?

1. Go to a Web site that gives you state-by-state links to court-ordered protection for victims. What is available in your jurisdiction?

2. Using the Internet, find your state's statute on mandatory reporters. What persons in your jurisdiction are required to report suspected child abuse and neglect? What is the penalty in your state for failure of a mandatory reporter to file a report of suspected child abuse and neglect? Must the report be in writing? What is the time frame for filing a report?

3. Using the Internet, find out some of the problems that abused men face when they try to get help from the system. What services are available in your community for male victims of domestic violence?

4. Using the Internet or local hotline services, find out what services are available for victims of domestic violence in the state and city in which you intend to work as a paralegal.

5. Using the Internet, determine if your state has mandatory arrests in domestic violence cases and whether it has adopted a primary aggressor law.

6. Using the Internet, determine if your state has defined the term *reasonable efforts* in its child protection statute.

Building a Professional Portfolio

REVIEW OF **KEY CONCEPTS**

1. Does the U.S. Constitution guarantee absolute protection of the integrity of the family?

2. What is the function of a state child protection agency?

3. What is the state social worker's role in investigating allegations of child abuse and neglect?

4. What are the legal grounds for terminating a parent's parental rights?

5. What is the difference between a protective order and a restraining order?

6. What is the purpose of the Violence Against Women Act?

7. What happened in the *Tracey Thurman* case, and what is its significance to victims of domestic violence?

8. What is a mandatory arrest, and what problem has surfaced because of this practice? What steps have some states taken to remedy this issue?

Chapter **eleven**

ADOPTION AND SURROGACY CONTRACTS

A doption is the legal procedure that makes a person or persons the legal parent or parents of a minor child who is not their natural child. The legal procedure for adopting a child may vary from state to state; however, there are some basic principles that most jurisdictions share in common. The most important principle is that court approval is needed in any adoption case. Additionally, adoption laws and procedures must be strictly followed to ensure that both the termination of the rights of biological parents and the transfer of those rights to the adoptive parents are properly executed. When the law is not strictly followed, there is a risk that the court at a later date and at the request of an aggrieved party may invalidate the adoption. It is the children who then suffer from a transfer of custody as they are torn from a family they have bonded with and have grown to love.

LEARNING OBJECTIVES

After studying this chapter, you should be able to:

1. Distinguish between a voluntary and involuntary adoption.

2. Identify the various types of adoptions.

3. Determine the issues to consider when drafting an open adoption agreement.

4. Identify and describe the different types of surrogacy contracts.

ADOPTION

The Legal Adoption Process

Adoption

A legal procedure that makes a person or persons the legal parent or parents of a minor child who is not their natural child.

Voluntary adoption

An adoption where biological parents willingly relinquish their parental rights so another parent or parents may adopt their children.

Involuntary adoption

Where parental rights are terminated by court order without parental consent.

Safe haven laws

State statutes that allow parents to anonymously surrender infants to designated locations in the community without fear of criminal prosecution.

Adoptions are either voluntary or involuntary. A **voluntary adoption** takes place when parents willingly relinquish their parental rights to another parent or parents. An **involuntary adoption** occurs when parental rights are terminated by court order without parental consent.

Voluntary Adoption

Parents voluntarily terminate or relinquish their rights to the custody of their children when they are unable to take care of them in one way or another. According to the Administration for Children and Families, a division of the Department of Health & Human Services that promotes the economic and social well-being of families, children, individuals, and communities, the most common reason for putting a child up for adoption is that the biological parents are just too young to take on the responsibility. Young parents may lack the life skills, maturity, and money to raise a child and may also be pressured by families to resort to adoption.

All states have enacted what is known as *safe haven laws*. Safe haven laws allow parents to anonymously surrender infants to designated locations in the community without fear of criminal prosecution. The goal of safe haven laws is to prevent desperate parents from discarding unwanted infants in dumpsters or garbage cans. These statutes typically include an age limit for the child, since their intent is to eliminate the discarding of infants by parents in crisis. Legislators must carefully craft these statutes, however, or there may be some unintended consequences. In 2008, Nebraska intentionally omitted an age limit in the state's safe haven law in response to concerns from a number of legislators to provide for the protection of older children. This resulted in a large number of parents dropping off teenagers with behavioral problems at emergency rooms throughout the state. One mother drove her fourteen-year-old son all the way from California and dropped him off at a hospital on the Wyoming–Nebraska border before the state could close the loophole and set a thirty-day limit in the statute. Here is Nebraska's quickly revised 2008 safe haven statute complete with age limit:

Nebraska Revised Statute § 29-121

In Nebraska, any person leaving a child not older than 30 days in the custody of an employee on duty at a hospital licensed by the State of Nebraska shall not be prosecuted for any crime based solely upon the act of relinquishment. After accepting custody, the hospital shall contact the concerned authorities to transfer custody of the child.[1]

While the stigma of being an unwed mother has waned significantly since the days of sending a daughter off to a "home for wayward girls," the reality is that a child raising a child is not an easy task, nor are extended family members often willing to assume the responsibility. Some children are given up for adoption because their parents may lack the funds and just cannot afford another mouth to feed. A government report, *Expenditures on Children by Families, 2011*, issued by the Agriculture Department's Center for Nutrition Policy and Promotion estimates that it costs a middle-class family approximately $235,000 to raise a child to eighteen. The burden is much harder on poor families who come to the sad realization that raising another child is far beyond their means. Whatever the reason, relinquishing parental rights is never an easy decision and is one that the parent will also carry with them long after they have left the courthouse.

---

[1]Nebraska Safe Haven Laws, R.R.S. Neb. § 29-121.

A voluntary termination begins with the decision by the biological parents to surrender their parental rights and place the child for adoption. Parents will seek the assistance of either a state agency or a licensed private adoption service. Parents must provide a health history so that nonidentifying information may be passed along to the adoptive parents. Children may be adopted either by parties that have been identified to the biological parents, as in relative adoptions or open adoptions, or by unidentified adoptions where the parties involved do not know each other.

The legal process actually begins with the filing of a petition, signed by the parents of their own free will. While the child actually has to be born before a consent may be signed by the parents, the biological mother may begin the adoption process during her pregnancy for the purpose of finding suitable adoptive parents and beginning the placement process. If the biological father is not available to sign the consent, a diligent effort must be made to find the father and serve him with notice of the adoption proceedings. It is crucial that a diligent search be made to protect the father's rights regardless of the personal issues between the biological parents.

Adoptive parents must participate in a preplacement assessment known as a **home study**. A home study is conducted by a licensed social worker who works for the state or a licensed adoption agency. It consists of interviews with the prospective parents and family members, an autobiographical statement where the parents tell their life story, home visits, a review of health records, a medical exam, income statements, references, comprehensive background checks, and employment verifications. Adoptive parents will also be required to take adoption preparation classes to prepare for assuming their rights as legal parents. Once the adoptive parents have been approved, they may proceed by filing a petition for adoption with the court, along with any other documentation that may be required under state law. The biological parents are served with any petitions made by the adoptive parents, and a hearing is eventually set for the adoption to be finalized by the court. The judge must first terminate the parental rights of the biological parents before granting the adoptive parents rights to the child. As in any child custody proceeding, the presiding judge must determine that the adoption is in the best interest of the child. The child is issued a new birth certificate along with a name change to complete the process. It is important to note that there are some circumstances where a court may deny a termination of parental rights, particularly in cases where a parent is trying to avoid paying child support.

Home study

A preplacement assessment of prospective adoptive parents conducted by a licensed social worker who works for the state or a licensed adoption agency.

Involuntary Adoption

An involuntary adoption occurs when the biological parents' rights have been terminated by a court because the parents were found by a court of law to be unfit and the child would be endangered if returned home. Every state has statutes determining the legal grounds for involuntary termination of parental rights. Typical grounds include abuse, neglect, abandonment, severe mental illness, excessive use of drugs and alcohol, inability to rehabilitate, failure to maintain consistent contact and communication with the child, lack of effort to meet the child's needs, parental rights to a sibling of the child having been involuntarily terminated, imprisonment, or conviction of the murder or manslaughter of the other parent or siblings or other crimes. The involuntary adoption process begins with the state child protection agency filing a petition for termination of parental rights with the court. Notice must be provided to the biological parents so they can be served with the proceedings and be allowed the opportunity to contest the termination. The state must prove that it has made reasonable efforts to reunify the family, which requires documentation of efforts made beginning from the date of the initial contact. If the biological parents' rights are terminated, the state assumes legal custody of the child until suitable adoptive parents are available. Prospective adoptive parents go through the same preplacement assessment before the adoption can be finalized by the court.

TYPES OF ADOPTIONS

Agency Adoptions

There are two types of adoption agencies: public adoption agencies and private adoption agencies. Public agencies are usually a component of the state government's child protection agency. For instance, when parental rights to a minor child have been severed in response to a petition brought by a state's child protection agency, frequently, the child protection agency itself facilitates the child's adoption through the branch of the agency specializing in adoptions. When the parents voluntarily consent to termination of their parental rights and the state child protection agency is not directly involved, the adoption is often handled by a private agency, sometimes one that the parents themselves have selected.

Public Adoption Agencies

A public agency adoption usually addresses the adoption of children already committed to the state's custody. These children have been placed in foster care following court proceedings. Upon the termination of parental rights, the state becomes the statutory parent of the child and remains the child's statutory parent until the child is adopted. Sometimes, the child's foster parents may seek to adopt the child. If the foster parents meet the criteria for adopting the child, they are frequently given preference, especially if the child has been in their care for a period of time and has bonded with the foster family. If the foster family is unwilling or unable to adopt the child, the agency will transfer the child's file to the agency's preadoption unit, where an assigned worker will attempt to find suitable adoptive parents from the list of individuals and couples who have registered to be considered as adoptive parents.

Public agencies have many older children who have been in foster care for months or even years. Some of these children are available for adoption. A prospective adoptive parent who is willing to adopt an older child may face a shorter wait than the prospective parent who is seeking an infant or a very young child.

The children who are involuntarily committed to the care of a child protection agency are not available for adoption while the agency's goal for the child is reunification with the natural parents, and, as discussed, the natural parents are usually given a reasonable period of time in which to complete the court-ordered steps required for reunification. Individuals seeking to adopt infants are more likely to have success by going to a private adoption agency or seeking private adoption opportunities.

Private Adoption Agencies

A private adoption agency must be licensed and follow certain statutory and administrative regulations that govern the adoption process. Individuals and couples who register with either public or private adoption agencies must undergo rigorous examinations. Agency workers conduct home visits to assess the physical and emotional environment the prospective adoptive parents can provide for a child. Many agencies conduct intensive home studies to determine the appropriateness of placing a particular child with a particular family.

Once the decision is made to place a child with a family, the agency monitors the placement for several months to ensure that the placement meets the child's needs. When this provisional period ends and the agency approves the placement as permanent, the prospective adoptive parents file a petition to adopt or a similar document in probate or surrogates court. The court will request that the agency file a report. If the agency report is favorable and supports the adoption, the court will grant the adoption petition.

Private Adoptions

A private adoption is an adoption that takes place without the intervention of an agency. In a private adoption, the child's natural parents agree voluntarily to sever their parental rights so that a particular person or couple may adopt their child. The adoption is frequently facilitated by an attorney or by the natural parents' doctor.

The private adoption must be approved by the court, and many states require that a state agency child protection worker investigate the proposed adoption and file a report with the court as to the advisability of permitting the adoption. The court reviews the report prior to making a decision and will usually not approve the adoption unless the report is favorable.

Stepparent Adoption

One of the most common types of adoption is a ***stepparent adoption***. This is where an individual who marries a divorced or widowed person adopts his or her spouse's children. In these cases, the noncustodial parent relinquishes his or her parental rights. This includes the right to inherit from a child's estate; the right to visitation; the right to make decisions regarding health, education, and religious upbringing; and the obligation to pay child support. The procedures for a stepparent adoption are similar to those of independent adoptions in general, except that some courts have streamlined the process by eliminating waiting periods and the necessity for a home study conducted by state officials. The home study screening in a stepparent adoption is not as extensive as that conducted in an independent adoption.

Stepparent adoption
Where an individual who marries a divorced or widowed person adopts his or her spouse's children.

In order to adopt a stepchild, a stepparent must obtain consent from both biological parents. Consent is needed so the court can terminate the noncustodial parent's rights and legalize the adoption with the stepparent. The custodial parent's rights remain intact in a stepparent adoption. While obtaining consent from the custodial parent may be easy, as he or she is generally in favor of the adoption, the same may not be said of the noncustodial parent. A stepparent's attempt to adopt a stepchild may be unsuccessful if the biological, noncustodial parent raises an objection. There may be legal grounds in some jurisdictions for a stepparent to prevail—such as the noncustodial parent's willful failure to pay child support, abandonment, or parental abuse or neglect of the child. Legal abandonment is defined in many states as failure to have contact with a child or provide that child with support for one continuous year. If the noncustodial parent calls the child sporadically and sends cards or visits occasionally, this does not satisfy the definition of abandonment. The procedure is relatively easy when the noncustodial parent is deceased, since the parental rights are terminated by death.

Not all stepparent adoptions are heard in a state's family court. In the state of Connecticut, for example, the state's probate courts have jurisdiction over these matters. In other states, adoptions may be heard by the surrogacy courts. It is important to determine which court in the state may hear a stepparent adoption.

The next step in processing a stepparent adoption through the state courts is to file a petition in the appropriate court. Laws and forms to process stepparent adoptions vary from state to state. It is also important to give notice to all the parties involved. This includes conducting a diligent search for the noncustodial parent, who may have been absent from the child's life. It is best to exhaust all avenues to find the noncustodial parent and provide him or her with notice. This will spare any emotional trauma and legal challenges later on should the noncustodial parent raise any objections.

In the landmark U.S. Supreme Court case of *Armstrong v. Manzo*, 380 U.S. 545 (1965), the Court held that lack of notice to the noncustodial father violated his rights to due process. In *Armstrong*, the mother, who had custody of the minor child, remarried. Two years later, her new husband filed stepparent adoption papers. The mother informed the juvenile court that the biological father had not financially supported the child during this two-year period. The mother also told the court that she was not aware of his whereabouts. Based on her representations, the juvenile court granted the stepparent's petition for adoption. When the biological father heard of the news, he filed a petition to annul the adoption and, at a hearing before the juvenile court, also presented evidence that he had in fact met his child support obligations. The juvenile court denied his petition, the Texas Appellate Court affirmed the lower court decision, and the Texas Supreme Court refused to hear the case. The father's appeal to the U.S. Supreme Court proved successful. The Court agreed with the father's argument that his right to due process was violated. The Court held that father's due process rights would be protected by vacating the order and granting him a new hearing.

The Court must also determine that a stepparent adoption is in the child's best interest. If the child is old enough to be involved in the decision process, he or she should be involved. The child's opinion is very important. If the child has a relationship with the noncustodial parent, that child may be conflicted about the adoption. The child may feel less conflicted if there is little or no relationship with the noncustodial parent. In some jurisdictions, a child who is of sufficient statutory age must also consent to the adoption in writing.

Figure 11-1 The U.S. Supreme Court has held that lack of notice to the noncustodial father violated his rights to due process.

Steve Heap/Shutterstock.

Gay Adoption

Same-sex couples, in one way or another, have always created families that have included children. Some gay men or lesbians leave heterosexual marriages with custody of their children and form family units with their partners without legal protections. Lesbians may use artificial insemination, and gay men may hire surrogates to carry and deliver a child on their behalf. In the past, when sexual orientation was an issue kept in the closet, gay and lesbian parents adopted as "single persons" and explained away the same-sex partner as a roommate or member of the family. Perjury or lying under oath is a crime, so this type of subterfuge should never be recommended to a client. More and more same-sex couples are adopting children through the same channels used by heterosexual couples. Some couples have gone the traditional route of adopting through a state agency, while others have become parents through international adoptions. Their ability to adopt depends largely on state or international laws, as well as the attitudes of social workers, lawyers, judges, and adoption agency personnel.

Legal custody of a child protects both the rights of the parent and the rights of the child in the event of the dissolution of the relationship between the parents, intrusion by other relatives or the state, or death of one of the same-sex parents. In the wake of the 2015 U.S. Supreme Court decision of *Obergefell v. Hodges*, married same-sex couples who wish to adopt children may petition for a joint adoption in all fifty states. A ***joint adoption*** is when both partners adopt a child together at the same time. There are situations where one of the parties to the marriage has a child either from a previous relationship, as a result of a single-parent adoption, or artificial insemination. In these cases, the non-legal parent may be without legal protection in the event of divorce, death, or third-party intervention. It is highly recommended by attorneys representing LGBTQ parents in this situation to petition for a ***second-parent adoption***. This is where one partner adopts the other partner's child, similar to a stepparent adoption. Once a legal bond has been created through a second parent or joint adoption, a same-sex partner now has the right to make decisions regarding the child's health, education, and welfare, as well as the responsibility of providing the child with financial support. While married same-sex couples may petition for joint adoption, the same is not true for unmarried same-sex couples. Some states permit the non-legal parent in an unmarried same-sex relationship to petition for a second-parent adoption, while others that do permit such adoptions may make the administrative process long and onerous.

While the *Obergefell* decision makes it unconstitutional for married same-sex couples to be denied the right to adopt by a state agency, some states have proposed or passed laws allowing religiously affiliated adoption agencies to refuse to consider married or unmarried LGBTQ couples as adoptive or foster parents. For example, on April 5, 2016, Mississippi Governor Phil Bryant signed the *Protecting Freedom of Conscience from Government Discrimination Act* or House Bill (HB) 1523. Portions of the Act related to adoption and foster care applicable to same-sex couples read as follows:

SECTION 1. This act shall be known and may be cited as the "Protecting Freedom of Conscience from Government Discrimination Act."

SECTION 2. The sincerely held religious beliefs or moral convictions protected by this act are the belief or conviction that:

(a) Marriage is or should be recognized as the union of one man and one woman;

(b) Sexual relations are properly reserved to such a marriage; and...

Joint adoption
When both partners adopt a child together at the same time.

Second-parent adoption
A form of adoption where one partner of a same-sex couple adopts the child and the other partner files for co-parent status.

(1) …The state government shall not take any discriminatory action against a religious organization that advertises, provides or facilitates adoption or foster care, wholly or partially on the basis that such organization has provided or declined to provide any adoption or foster care service, or related service, based upon or in a manner consistent with a sincerely held religious belief or moral conviction described in Section 2 of this act.

(2) The state government shall not take any discriminatory action against a person who the state grants custody of a foster or adoptive child, or who seeks from the state custody of a foster or adoptive child, wholly or partially on the basis that the person guides, instructs or raises a child, or intends to guide, instruct, or raise a child based upon or in a manner consistent with a sincerely held religious belief or moral conviction described in Section 2 of this act.

The Mississippi law was challenged in *Barber v. Bryant* and *Campaign for Southern Equality v. Bryant*. The plaintiffs in this case prevailed on the trial court level on the grounds that HB 1523 violated the Establishment and Equal Protection Clauses of the U.S. Constitution. The Fifth Circuit Court of Appeals, however, held that the plaintiffs challenging the law had no standing because they failed to demonstrate that HB 1523 would violate their rights in any manner. On January 8, 2018, the U.S. Supreme Court declined to hear the plaintiffs' challenge to the Circuit Court of Appeals decision, leaving Mississippi's HB 1523 intact.

Open Adoption

Open adoption
An adoption where the biological parents, the adoptive parents, and sometimes the children are known to each other.

An *open adoption* is an adoption where the biological parents, the adoptive parents, and sometimes the children are known to each other. This is contrary to an independent adoption where the parties have no knowledge of the others' identity. The advantages of an open adoption are to maintain a child's relationship with the birth family, as long as doing so is in the child's best interest. Most adopted children, at some point in their lives, want the truth about their family of origin, which may include the desire to reconnect with their parents and other relatives. Open adoptions provide the adoptive parents and the child with an extensive medical history of the child's birth family. This information is necessary for the child to receive adequate health-care treatment throughout his or her life.

Informal open adoptions have existed since the beginning of time, where relatives have stepped in to care for the children of family members when they are unable to do so. The biological and adoptive parents may be aware of the others' identity under the following circumstances:

1. The biological parents may have specifically chosen the adoptive parents to adopt their children and therefore may know them personally. For example, biological parents who cannot care for their children or have had their parental rights terminated due to the abuse, neglect, or abandonment of a child may identify relatives who are willing and able to assume legal responsibility of the child.

2. The biological parents may have chosen an adoptive couple after having been provided with information about the prospective parents and their ability to provide the child with a loving home. This is usually done through a private or state agency. While the parties do not know each other by identity, the biological parents receive some personal assurances that they have chosen a good home for their child.

3. Another situation is where there is contact between the biological and adoptive parents and possibly the child. The degree of contact between the parties depends on the level of comfort of the parties. The degree of contact, arranged by agreement, may take the form of

(a) a picture of the child sent by the adoptive parents to the biological parents once or twice a year;
(b) letters, phone calls, or e-mails sent by the adoptive parents regarding the child;
(c) in-person visits with the children; and
(d) contact with the child.

The Open Adoption Agreement Biological parents who enter into an open adoption are not the child's legal parent because their parental rights have been severed by a court of law. The adoptive parents now have legal custody and guardianship of the child. The *open adoption agreement* is a contract entered into between one or both biological parents and the adoptive parents, prior to the adoption proceeding, that grants the biological parent(s) the right to continue some type of relationship with the child or to have information regarding the child's development and well-being. The first step in drafting an open adoption agreement is to determine the state law regarding these contracts.

Some states allow the parties to enter into an enforceable agreement regarding postadoption contact with the child or adoptive parents. The state of Washington, for example, has legislated that the parties may enter into a legally binding open adoption contract.

Other jurisdictions, such as the state of Oregon, for example, may allow the parties to enter into nonbinding agreements.

The paralegal may be given the task of drafting the open adoption agreement. In addition to becoming familiar with any state law on the subject, the paralegal must

Open adoption agreement
A contract entered into between one or both biological parents and the adoptive parents, prior to the adoption proceeding, that grants the biological parent(s) the right to continue some type of relationship with the child or have access to information regarding the child's development and well-being.

Figure 11-2 A paralegal must be clear regarding the terms agreed upon by the parties before drafting the open adoption agreement.

Lenetstan/Shutterstock.

also review the relevant case law interpreting the statute to get further insight on how to draft a valid open adoption agreement. A paralegal may also review an open adoption agreement on behalf of a client at the attorney's request. Knowledge of the law is equally important regardless of whether the office represents the biological parents, the adoptive parents, or the child. When reviewing the document on behalf of the minor child, the guiding principle is always the best interest of the child.

Once the relevant law of the jurisdiction is reviewed, the biological parents and their respective attorneys should establish the terms of the contract by determining the type of open adoption, the frequency of the contact, and the duration of the visits or phone calls. A paralegal must be clear regarding the terms agreed upon by the parties before drafting the open adoption agreement.

International Adoptions

International adoption

A legal process by which an individual or a couple becomes the legal parent of a child who is a citizen of another country and then brings that child to their home country to live with them permanently.

International adoptions, sometimes referred to as intercountry or transnational adoption, are a legal process by which an individual or a couple become the legal parent of a child who is a citizen of another country and then bring that child to their home country to live with them permanently. According to the U.S. Department of State, Americans have adopted over 250,000 children through international adoption since 1999. Some of the most popular countries represented in these cases were China, Ethiopia, Russia, South Korea, Ukraine, the Philippines, India, Columbia, Uganda, and Taiwan. The process is long, expensive, and stressful, with no guarantees. According to *Stuck*, the award-winning documentary film on international adoption released in 2013, the process can take up to 896 days and cost roughly $28,000. From a legal standpoint, international adoptions are very complex. The adoptive parent must engage the services of an agency that will assist the parent in the international adoption process and choose a country from which to adopt the child. When adopting children from other countries, prospective U.S. parents must comply with the laws of the country where the child resides. Additionally, bringing the child to the United States also involves proceedings with U.S. Citizenship and Immigration Services (USCIS). USCIS determines the eligibility and suitability of the prospective adoptive parents and the eligibility of the child to immigrate to the United States. The adoption then must be finalized in the state court where the adoptive parents are domiciled. International adoptions may also be governed by international law. Depending on the country where the child resides, there are three international adoption processes; they include the Hague process, non-Hague process, and in the event the child is a relative, an immediate relative petition with USCIS. The **Hague Adoption Convention** requires member countries to establish a central authority and point of contract in the country (in the United States it is the Department of State); ensure that international adoptions are in the best interest of the children by banning the abduction, sale, or trafficking of children; offer international adoptions in cases where a suitable home in the child's native country cannot be found; and provide for international and intergovernmental recognition of international adoptions. This all depends on whether both countries (of the prospective adoptive parents and child) are members of the Convention. The United States is a member of the Hague Adoption Convention and must follow the Convention requirements or Hague process when adopting a child who resides in a country that is also a member of the treaty. The Hague requirements are very strict and, according to some critics, are the reasons why international adoptions are on the decline. The non-Hague process, which does not include the strict requirements of the Hague process, requires USCIS to prove that the child qualifies as an orphan under the laws of the United States before the adoption takes place.

Hague Adoption Convention

An international treaty that requires member countries to establish a central authority and point of contract in the country (in the United States it is the Department of State); ensure that international adoptions are in the best interest of the children by banning the abduction, sale, or trafficking of children; offer international adoptions in cases where a suitable home in the child's native country cannot be found; and provide for international and intergovernmental recognition of international adoptions.

Tribal Adoptions

In 1978, Congress passed the *Indian Child Welfare Act (ICWA)* to address the overrepresentation of Native American children in the foster care system. Children were being placed in non–Native American homes, and it was feared that over time they would lose their cultural identity. ICWA was passed to prevent breaking up Native American families in cases where the state court has determined that, but for the adoption, the child would have been raised with strong ties to the Native American tribe and culture. While ICWA is a federal law, states are required to apply it in cases that involve Native American children in child custody proceedings. The intent of ICWA is to "protect the best interests of Indian children and to promote the stability and security of Indian tribes and families." In an effort to preserve Native American culture, ICWA maintains tribal jurisdiction in cases involving children of recognized tribes and establishing guidelines regarding child custody proceedings such as foster care, preadoptive placements, and adoption placements or termination of parental rights, but excludes divorce cases and juvenile delinquency matters. ICWA applies to children who are members of a federally recognized Native American tribe *or* are eligible for membership in the tribe. The act requires that the state and tribe must make "active efforts" to keep children with extended family members. If extended family is not available, then children may be placed in the homes of tribal members. If tribal members are not available, then Native American families from other tribes are considered for placement.

Indian Child Welfare Act (ICWA)

Federal law passed by Congress in 1978 to address the overrepresentation of Native American children in the foster care system.

Transracial and Transcultural Adoptions

Transracial (also known as interracial) *or transcultural adoptions* involve placing children who belong to one race or ethnic/cultural group with adoptive parents of another race or ethnic/cultural group. Approximately 50,000 black and biracial children were adopted by white parents between the years of 1968 and 1972 due to the increasing number of these children in foster care. The rationale for this was that there were not enough black families available to act as adoptive parents. In September 1972, the National Association of Black Social Workers openly rejected this practice and the reasons cited for it, and issued a *Position Paper on Trans-Racial Adoption*, which began with the following statement:

Transracial or transcultural adoption

(also known as interracial adoption) Involves placing children who belong to one race or ethnic/cultural group with adoptive parents of another race or ethnic/cultural group

> The National Association of Black Social Workers has taken a vehement stand against the placement of black children in white homes for any reason. We affirm the inviolable position of black children in black families where they belong physically, psychologically and culturally in order that they receive the total sense of themselves and develop a sound projection of their future.

Agencies responded to this position paper by reducing the number of transracial placements. The result was that while white foster parents could care for transracial children in the foster care system, they could not adopt. Some states even went so far as prohibiting adoptions of transracial children to white parents.

When placing a child in a foster or adoptive home, however, the race of the foster or adoptive parents *may* be considered, but it is not the determining factor. A federal statute called the *Multi-Ethnic Placement Act of 1994 (MEPA)* and its 1996 amendments prohibit discrimination on the basis of race, color, or national origin. Specifically, MEPA "prohibits the delay or denial of any adoption or placement in foster care due to the race, color, or national origin of the child or of the foster or adoptive parents and requires states to provide for diligent recruitment of potential foster and adoptive families who reflect the ethnic and racial

Multi-Ethnic Placement Act of 1994 (MEPA)

A federal statute that prohibits the delay or denial of any adoption or placement in foster care due to the race, color, or national origin of the child or of the foster or adoptive parents and requires states to provide for diligent recruitment of potential foster and adoptive families who reflect the ethnic and racial diversity of children for whom homes are needed.

Inter-Ethnic Adoption Provisions

Amendments to Multi-Ethnic Placement Act of 1994 passed in 1996.

Surrogacy contract

An agreement between a woman who will bear a child for a person or a couple who intend to adopt the child once he or she is born. The surrogate mother agrees to relinquish custody of the child so the contracting parents are free to proceed with the adoption.

Gestational surrogacy contract

Also called the host method, is an arrangement used when the intended mother cannot conceive or carry the child for health-related reasons. Therefore, the child is conceived through in vitro fertilization, a process where the intended mother's egg and the father's sperm are fertilized outside the body and then implanted into the surrogate mother. The surrogate in a gestational surrogacy agreement is not considered the legal biological parent of the child.

Altruistic surrogacy

A contract where the surrogate mother receives no financial reward for carrying the child or relinquishing her rights upon birth.

Commercial surrogacy

An agreement whereby the surrogate mother receives a fee for carrying the child to term.

diversity of children for whom homes are needed." Its 1996 amendment, *Inter-Ethnic Adoption Provisions*, "affirms the prohibition against delaying or denying the placement of a child for adoption or foster care on the basis of race, color or national origin of the foster or adoptive parents or of the child involved." It is important to note, however, that neither of these statutes have any effect on ICWA.

SURROGACY CONTRACTS

There are situations in which a couple or single person wants to have children but cannot conceive a child in the traditional way. In these cases, some may wish to enter into a surrogacy contract. A **surrogacy contract** is an agreement between a woman who will bear a child for a person or a couple who intend to adopt the child once he or she is born. The surrogate mother agrees to relinquish custody of the child so the contracting parents are free to proceed with the adoption.

The California Supreme Court in 1993 issued a landmark decision in the case of *Johnson v. Calvert*, 5 Cal. 4th 84, 19 Cal. Rptr. 2d 494, 851 P.2d 776, where it declared surrogacy contracts legal and enforceable in the state of California. In this case, the intended parents, the Calverts, entered into a surrogacy agreement with Anna Johnson, who agreed to serve as a host and carry an embryo created through in vitro fertilization, utilizing the Calverts' sperm and ovum. Conflicts arose between the parties, and Johnson sued for custody of the child even though she was not biologically related. The California Supreme Court upheld the validity of surrogacy agreements under federal and state law. The U.S. Supreme Court denied Johnson certiorari and refused to hear her case.

The validity of surrogacy contracts varies from state to state. Some states are considered "surrogacy-friendly" and have either passed laws permitting surrogacy arrangements or have established precedent decisions that recognize such agreements. Other jurisdictions do not recognize or enforce surrogacy contracts and may even prohibit compensated surrogacy by state statute or court decisions. Laws also differ in the protection offered to the surrogate and the intended parents.

There are different types of surrogacy arrangements. A traditional surrogacy contract is where the husband or gay male partner's sperm is implanted into the surrogate through a process called artificial insemination. The surrogate mother in this case is the biological parent and agrees to relinquish her rights under the surrogacy contract. A **gestational surrogacy contract**, or the host method, is an arrangement used when the intended mother cannot conceive or carry the child for health-related reasons. Therefore, the child is conceived through in vitro fertilization, a process where the intended mother's egg and the father's sperm are fertilized outside the body and then implanted into the surrogate mother. The surrogate in a gestational surrogacy agreement is not considered the legal biological parent of the child.

Surrogacy contracts may be either altruistic or commercial. An **altruistic surrogacy** contract is where the surrogate mother receives no financial reward for carrying the child or relinquishing her rights upon birth. The surrogate mother, however, will be paid for any expenses incurred during the course of the pregnancy such as medical expenses, health insurance, prenatal vitamins, maternity clothing, prenatal exercise classes, and any other pregnancy-related expenses. A situation like this may arise when a sister, for example, agrees to act as a surrogate for a sibling who cannot carry or conceive a child in the traditional manner. A **commercial surrogacy** is an agreement whereby the surrogate mother receives a fee for carrying the child to term.

The Battle over Baby M In 1987, the case of Baby M received national attention when the surrogate mother had a change of heart and withdrew her consent for adoption. Baby M, the topic of conversation at every water cooler and kitchen table, was the case that prompted many state legislatures to enact laws declaring commercial surrogate contracts unenforceable. The national conversation ran the gamut from whether it is ethical to legalize what amounted to "baby selling" to who should have custody of Baby M.

IN THE MATTER OF BABY M

537 A.2d 1227, 109 N.J. 396, 1988.NJ.41301
New Jersey Supreme Court
February 3, 1988

... In February 1985, William Stern and Mary Beth Whitehead entered into a surrogacy contract. It recited that Stern's wife, Elizabeth, was infertile, that they wanted a child, and that Mrs. Whitehead was willing to provide that child as the mother with Mr. Stern as the father ... The contract provided that through artificial insemination using Mr. Stern's sperm, Mrs. Whitehead would become pregnant, carry the child to term, bear it, deliver it to the Sterns, and thereafter do whatever was necessary to terminate her maternal rights so that Mrs. Stern could thereafter adopt the child. Mrs. Whitehead's husband, Richard, was also a party to the contract; Mrs. Stern was not. Mr. Whitehead promised to do all acts necessary to rebut the presumption of paternity under the Parentage Act. N.J.S.A. 9:17-43a(1), -44a. Although Mrs. Stern was not a party to the surrogate agreement, the contract gave her sole custody of the child in the event of Mr. Stern's death. Mrs. Stern's status as a nonparty to the surrogate parenting agreement presumably was to avoid the application of the baby-selling statute to this arrangement. N.J.S.A. 9:3-54.

Mr. Stern, on his part, agreed to attempt the artificial insemination and to pay Mrs. Whitehead $10,000 after the child's birth, on its delivery to him. In a separate contract, Mr. Stern agreed to pay $7,500 to the Infertility Center of New York ("ICNY"). The Center's advertising campaigns solicit surrogate mothers and encourage infertile couples to consider surrogacy. ICNY arranged for the surrogacy contract by bringing the parties together, explaining the process to them, furnishing the contractual form, and providing legal counsel ...

... Mrs. Whitehead realized, almost from the moment of birth, that she could not part with this child. She had felt a bond with it even during pregnancy. Some indication of the attachment was conveyed to the Sterns at the hospital when they told Mrs. Whitehead what they were going to name the baby. She apparently broke into tears and indicated that she did not know if she could give up the child. She talked about how the baby looked like her other daughter, and made it clear that she was experiencing great difficulty with the decision.

Nonetheless, Mrs. Whitehead was, for the moment, true to her word. Despite powerful inclinations to the contrary, she turned her child over to the Sterns on March 30 at the Whiteheads' home ... Later in the evening of March 30, Mrs. Whitehead became deeply disturbed, disconsolate, stricken with unbearable sadness. She had to have her child. She could not eat, sleep, or concentrate on anything other than her need for her baby. The next day she went to the Sterns' home and told them how much she was suffering ... The depth of Mrs. Whitehead's despair surprised and frightened the Sterns. She told them that she could not live without her baby, that she must have her, even if only for one week, that thereafter she would surrender her child. The Sterns, concerned that Mrs. Whitehead might indeed commit suicide, not

continued

wanting under any circumstances to risk that, and in any event believing that Mrs. Whitehead would keep her word, turned the child over to her. It was not until four months later, after a series of attempts to regain possession of the child, that Melissa was returned to the Sterns, having been forcibly removed from the home where she was then living with Mr. and Mrs. Whitehead, the home in Florida owned by Mary Beth Whitehead's parents.

... The struggle over Baby M began when it became apparent that Mrs. Whitehead could not return the child to Mr. Stern ... Eventually the Sterns discovered where the Whiteheads were staying, commenced supplementary proceedings in Florida, and obtained an order requiring the Whiteheads to turn over the child. Police in Florida enforced the order, forcibly removing the child from her grandparents' home. She was soon thereafter brought to New Jersey and turned over to the Sterns ... Pending final judgment, Mrs. Whitehead was awarded limited visitation with Baby M.

The Sterns' complaint, in addition to seeking possession and ultimately custody of the child, sought enforcement of the surrogacy contract. Pursuant to the contract, it asked that the child be permanently placed in their custody, that Mrs. Whitehead's parental rights be terminated, and that Mrs. Stern be allowed to adopt the child; that is, for all purposes, Melissa become the Sterns' child.

INVALIDITY AND UNENFORCEABILITY OF SURROGACY CONTRACT

... Considerable care was taken in this case to structure the surrogacy arrangement so as not to violate this prohibition. The arrangement was structured as follows: the adopting parent, Mrs. Stern, was not a party to the surrogacy contract; the money paid to Mrs. Whitehead was stated to be for her services—not for the adoption; the sole purpose of the contract was stated as being that "of giving a child to William Stern, its natural and biological father"; the money was purported to be "compensation for services and expenses and in no way ... a fee for termination of parental rights or a payment in exchange for consent to surrender a child for adoption"; the fee to the Infertility Center ($7,500) was stated to be for legal representation, advice, administrative work, and other "services." Nevertheless, it seems clear that the money was paid and accepted in connection with an adoption.

... The prohibition of our statute is strong. Violation constitutes a high misdemeanor, N.J.S.A. 9:3-54c, a third-degree crime, N.J.S.A. 2C:43-1b, carrying a penalty of three to five years imprisonment. N.J.S.A. 2C:43-6a(3). The evils inherent in baby-bartering are loathsome for a myriad of reasons. The child is sold without regard for whether the purchasers will be suitable parents. N. Baker, Baby Selling: The Scandal of Black Market Adoption 7 (1978). The natural mother does not receive the benefit of counseling and guidance to assist her in making a decision that may affect her for a lifetime. In fact, the monetary incentive to sell her child may, depending on her financial circumstances, make her decision less voluntary. Id. at 44. Furthermore, the adoptive parents may not be fully informed of the natural parents' medical history ...

... The surrogacy contract's invalidity, resulting from its direct conflict with the above statutory provisions, is further underlined when its goals and means are measured against New Jersey's public policy. The contract's basic premise, that the natural parents can decide in advance of birth which one is to have custody of the child, bears no relationship to the settled law that the child's best interests shall determine custody. See *Fantony v. Fantony*, 21 N.J. 525, 536–37 (1956); see also *Sheehan v. Sheehan*, 38 N.J. Super. 120, 125 (App.Div.1955) ...

TERMINATION

… We have already noted that under our laws termination of parental rights cannot be based on contract, but may be granted only on proof of the statutory requirements. That conclusion was one of the bases for invalidating the surrogacy contract. Although excluding the contract as a basis for parental termination, we did not explicitly deal with the question of whether the statutory bases for termination existed. We do so here …

… As noted before, if termination of Mrs. Whitehead's parental rights is justified, Mrs. Whitehead will have no further claim either to custody or to visitation, and adoption by Mrs. Stern may proceed pursuant to the private placement adoption statute, N.J.S.A. 9:3–48. If termination is not justified, Mrs. Whitehead remains the legal mother, and even if not entitled to custody, she would ordinarily be expected to have some rights of visitation. *Wilke v. Culp*, supra, 196 N.J. Super. at 496 …

… Nothing in this record justifies a finding that would allow a court to terminate Mary Beth Whitehead's parental rights under the statutory standard. It is not simply that obviously there was no "intentional abandonment or very substantial neglect of parental duties without a reasonable expectation of reversal of that conduct in the future," N.J.S.A. 9:3–48c(1), quite the contrary, but furthermore that the trial court never found Mrs. Whitehead an unfit mother and indeed affirmatively stated that Mary Beth Whitehead had been a good mother to her other children. 217 N.J. Super. at 397 …

CUSTODY

… Having decided that the surrogacy contract is illegal and unenforceable, we now must decide the custody question without regard to the provisions of the surrogacy contract that would give Mr. Stern sole and permanent custody. (That does not mean that the existence of the contract and the circumstances under which it was entered may not be considered to the extent deemed relevant to the child's best interests.) With the surrogacy contract disposed of, the legal framework becomes a dispute between two couples over the custody of a child produced by the artificial insemination of one couple's wife by the other's husband. Under the Parentage Act the claims of the natural father and the natural mother are entitled to equal weight, i.e., one is not preferred over the other solely because he or she is the father or the mother. N.J.S.A. 9:17-40. The applicable rule given these circumstances is clear: the child's best interests determine custody …

… Our custody conclusion is based on strongly persuasive testimony contrasting both the family life of the Whiteheads and the Sterns and the personalities and characters of the individuals. The stability of the Whitehead family life was doubtful at the time of trial. Their finances were in serious trouble (foreclosure by Mrs. Whitehead's sister on a second mortgage was in process). Mr. Whitehead's employment, though relatively steady, was always at risk because of his alcoholism, a condition that he seems not to have been able to confront effectively. Mrs. Whitehead had not worked for quite some time, her last two employments having been part-time …

… One of the Whiteheads' positive attributes was their ability to bring up two children, and apparently well, even in so vulnerable a household. Yet substantial question was raised even about that aspect of their home life. The expert testimony contained criticism of Mrs. Whitehead's handling of her son's educational difficulties. Certain of the experts noted that Mrs. Whitehead perceived herself as omnipotent and omniscient concerning her children. She knew what they were thinking, what they wanted, and she spoke for them. As to Melissa, Mrs. Whitehead expressed the view that she alone knew what that child's cries and sounds meant. Her inconsistent stories about various things engendered grave doubts about her ability to explain honestly and sensitively to Baby M—and at the right time—the nature of her origin. Although

continued

faith in professional counseling is not a sine qua non of parenting, several experts believed that Mrs. Whitehead's contempt for professional help, especially professional psychological help, coincided with her feelings of omnipotence in a way that could be devastating to a child who most likely will need such help. In short, while love and affection there would be, Baby M's life with the Whiteheads promised to be too closely controlled by Mrs. Whitehead. The prospects for wholesome, independent psychological growth and development would be at serious risk …

… The Sterns have no other children, but all indications are that their household and their personalities promise a much more likely foundation for Melissa to grow and thrive. There is a track record of sorts—during the one-and-a-half years of custody Baby M has done very well, and the relationship between both Mr. and Mrs. Stern and the baby has become very strong. The household is stable, and likely to remain so. Their finances are more than adequate, their circle of friends supportive, and their marriage happy. Most important, they are loving, giving, nurturing, and open-minded people. They have demonstrated the wish and ability to nurture and protect Melissa, yet at the same time to encourage her independence. Their lack of experience is more than made up for by a willingness to learn and to listen, a willingness that is enhanced by their professional training, especially Mrs. Stern's experience as a pediatrician. They are honest; they can recognize error, deal with it, and learn from it. They will try to determine rationally the best way to cope with problems in their relationship with Melissa. When the time comes to tell her about her origins, they will probably have found a means of doing so that accords with the best interests of Baby M. All in all, Melissa's future appears solid, happy, and promising with them …

Source: In The Matter Of Baby M, 537 A.2D 1227, 109 N.J. 396, 1988.NJ.41301, New Jersey Supreme Court.

Concept Review and Reinforcement

KEY TERMS

adoption	Inter-Ethnic Adoption Provisions	open adoption agreement
altruistic surrogacy	international adoption	safe haven law
commercial surrogacy	involuntary adoption	second-parent adoption
gestational surrogacy contract	joint adoption	stepparent adoption
Hague Adoption Convention	Multi-Ethnic Placement Act of 1994	surrogacy contract
home study	(MEPA)	transracial/transcultural adoption
Indian Child Welfare Act (ICWA)	open adoption	voluntary adoption

REVIEW OF KEY CONCEPTS

1. Define the various types of adoptions described in this chapter.

2. What is the difference between an agency adoption and a private adoption?

3. What is a safe haven law? Look up your state's safe haven law and explain how a mother with an unwanted child would go about surrendering her child.

4. What issues should be considered when drafting an open adoption agreement?

5. Explain the difference between a voluntary and involuntary adoption.

6. What is a surrogacy contract?

7. Define the different types of surrogacy contracts described in this chapter.

8. What happened in the Baby M case?

BUILDING YOUR PARALEGAL SKILLS

CASE FOR BRIEFING

IN RE CHRISTOPHER G., 118 CONN. APP. 569 (2009)

Critical Thinking and Legal Analysis Applications

1. Ann Sullivan gave birth to a son two years ago. Due to serious drug and mental health issues, her child was removed from her custody and placed by the state with foster parents, Sylvia and Jerrod Frankel. The Frankels want to adopt the child. Ann realizes that she is unable to care for her son and that adoption is in his best interest. She agrees to relinquish her rights as long as she can have a yearly visit with the child and receive periodic photographs throughout the year. At the final court hearing, her attorney arrives late and the parties are being rushed into court. Her lawyer hands her a pen and tells her to sign the agreement. While Ann had discussed the terms of the agreement with her attorney on the telephone several days prior to the hearing, she never had the opportunity to review the document. Believing that it included the terms she previously agreed to, she signs the paperwork and proceeds to terminate her parental rights to make the way clear for the child's adoption. A month later, she contacts the now adoptive mother, Mrs. Frankel, and asks for photographs of the child. Mrs. Frankel hangs up and tells her never to call there again. Ann contacts her attorney, who upon looking at the adoption agreement is shocked to find out that the terms of the open adoption were never included in the document. She now wishes to file a motion to open the judgment of the voluntary termination of her parental rights.

   Based on the case of *In re Christopher G.*, 118 Conn. App. 569 (2009), how would the Connecticut courts decide this case?

   Based on the adoption laws in your jurisdiction, how would the courts in your state decide this case?

Building a Professional Portfolio

PORTFOLIO **EXERCISES**

You work as a paralegal in the Law Firm of Capone, Ulto, & Torello in your state. Monique Fallon and Thomas Gallagher are clients of the firm. Monique Fallon was divorced three years ago and has two boys, ages eight and nine. Her ex-husband, William Fallon, moved out of state after the divorce and has not had any contact with either the ex-wife or the children. He does, however, pay child support, which is deducted from his paycheck under a wage withholding order. Ms. Fallon married Mr. Gallagher two years ago. He is wonderful with the children and treats them as if they were his own. The children call him "Dad." Mr. Gallagher

wants to adopt the children; Ms. Fallon is in full agreement with this idea and so are the children.

After researching your state law through an Internet legal research website, determine the procedure for processing a stepparent adoption and determine which court has jurisdiction over these matters. If Mr. Fallon does not consent to the stepparent adoption, what are the chances that his parental rights will be terminated under your jurisdiction's statute? Prepare an interoffice memorandum for your supervising attorney, Lori Ulto.

Part two

INTRODUCTION TO PART TWO: FAMILY PRACTICE

The traditional family unit, namely the marriage, cannot be dissolved without the involvement of the judicial system. Processing a client's case through the courts involves various steps and procedures that vary from state to state. The resolution of issues such as alimony, child support, property and debt distribution, child custody, and visitation are effectuated through court proceedings and are memorialized in the court's final judgment containing its orders on these matters. There are also judicial procedures available when any aspect of these orders is violated or needs to be modified afterward. The pages that follow delineate an illustration of some of the basic procedures and documents used to accomplish the post-dissolution process, with the understanding that there will be differences among the fifty states.

Chapter **twelve**

ETHICS IN FAMILY LAW

uring the course of a typical workday, the family law paralegal will come in contact with a variety of people: clients, supervising attorneys, office staff, opposing counsel and their staff, sheriffs, lay and expert witnesses, and court personnel. In addition, they will also encounter a variety of situations in which they will have to make decisions regarding their professional conduct. Whatever paralegals do or say during the course of their employment will impact the client, their supervisor, and themselves. The statutes regulating the unauthorized practice of law and the rules of ethics are two aspects of the law that paralegals must become familiar with in order to conduct themselves properly on a daily basis. This chapter addresses the principles regulating paralegal conduct and provides paralegals with guidelines that will help them maneuver confidently through their busy schedules.

LEARNING OBJECTIVES

After studying this chapter, you should be able to:

1. Describe the impact of electronic mail and the precautions that must be taken to avoid breaches of client confidentiality.

2. Explain the ethical issues involved in dealing with *pro se* or *pro per* litigants.

3. Explain the consequences of practicing law without a license.

4. Identify and describe the activities that constitute the unauthorized practice of law.

Rules of ethics
Standards of conduct that a profession demands from its members.

Freelance paralegal
Independent contractor who works for a number of attorneys on an as-needed basis.

Code
A set of written rules that establishes the guidelines for attorneys in their interactions with clients, courts, and staff and their obligations to the general public.

Model Rules of Professional Conduct (MRPC)
A prototype for attorney's ethics written by the American Bar Association as a model for states that wish to adopt them.

Integrated bar associations
Affiliations of state bar associations where membership is mandatory.

Grievance committees
State bar associations that regulate the legal profession through disciplinary bodies.

Disciplinary board
Bodies that may sanction or punish attorneys for engaging in conduct that violates the state's code of professional conduct.

Sanctions
Punishment issued to attorneys for engaging in conduct that violates the state's code of professional conduct.

Complaint
A grievance filed with a disciplinary body against an attorney; also, a document that commences an action when the opposing party is served; also known as a petition.

Grievance
A complaint filed with a disciplinary body against an attorney.

National Association of Legal Assistants (NALA)
Voluntary national, state, and local paralegal association that has established its own ethical codes.

National Federation of Paralegal Associations (NFPA)
Voluntary national, state, and local paralegal association that has established its own ethical codes.

OVERVIEW OF BASIC ETHICAL PRINCIPLES

Every profession has *rules of ethics*. Rules of ethics are standards of conduct that a profession demands from its members. Adherence to these standards of conduct is not limited only to attorneys. Attorneys often employ other attorneys, law students, paralegals, secretaries, clerks, and investigators to assist them in rendering legal services to clients. Supervising attorneys are obligated to see to it that all those employed by them are cognizant of the rules of ethics. Attorneys also hire *freelance paralegals* who are not employees of the attorney but are independent contractors who work for a number of attorneys on an as-needed basis. Attorneys supervise freelance paralegals in the course of performing each particular assignment. Freelance paralegals are also responsible for knowledge of the rules of ethics.

Attorneys and paralegals must work within the confines of the professional rules of ethics. Rules of ethics govern the manner in which the members of a profession conduct themselves. The legal profession holds itself to a high standard of conduct in order to facilitate a sense of trust and confidence among the general public and to preserve the integrity and respectability of the profession. The legal profession has a set of written rules called a *code* that establishes the guidelines for attorneys in their interactions with clients, courts, staff, and their obligations to the general public.

The American Bar Association (ABA) has established the *Model Rules of Professional Conduct (MRPC)* as a prototype for attorney ethics. Because the ABA is a national, voluntary bar association that does not have jurisdiction to oversee the legal profession, it has written the MRPC as a model for states that wish to adopt them. A majority of the states have adopted the MRPC as their ethical code. Some states have not adopted the MRPC but follow the Model Rules of Professional Responsibility, which is the ABA's older model code.

The legal profession and licensed attorneys are under the control of the state's highest court, commonly referred to in most jurisdictions as the supreme court. Some states have *integrated bar associations* in which membership is mandatory. Other states require attorneys to register and pay fees to state bar associations or to the court or designated agency. State bar associations regulate the legal profession through disciplinary bodies known as *grievance committees* or *disciplinary boards*. These disciplinary bodies may *sanction* or punish attorneys for engaging in conduct that violates the state's code of professional conduct.

If a *complaint* or *grievance* is filed with the disciplinary body, attorneys have the right to a hearing and to an appeals process in order to defend their privilege to practice law in that jurisdiction. Attorney grievance proceedings may result in a variety of dispositions. If the allegations against an attorney are unsubstantiated, the grievance committee may dismiss the complaint. This is equivalent to "dropping the charges." If the allegations against an attorney are substantiated, the attorney may be reprimanded, put on probation, suspended, or even disbarred, depending on the seriousness of the offense.

Paralegals are not members of the bar and cannot join, vote, or hold office. In some jurisdictions, paralegals may become associate members. The state agency or authority responsible for disciplining attorneys for unethical conduct does not have the same authority to impose sanctions on paralegals for engaging in unethical behavior. Therefore, it is important for paralegals to have a thorough knowledge of their jurisdiction's rules of professional conduct, which regulate attorneys, and of any ethical guidelines their state has established for paralegals. While national, state, and local paralegal associations such as the *National Association of Legal Assistants, Inc. (NALA)* and the *National Federation of Paralegal Associations (NFPA)* have established their own ethical codes, membership in these organizations is voluntary. These organizations do not have any disciplinary authority over paralegals. The most that one of these paralegal associations can do is revoke a paralegal's membership in the association.

While the state bar association cannot discipline paralegals for violating the rules of ethics, their supervisors will be held responsible for any unethical conduct by paralegals. Attorneys who employ paralegals are obligated to supervise their employees' conduct and **work product**. Work product consists of the notes, materials, memoranda, and written records generated by the attorney, as well as the written records of the attorney's mental impressions and legal theories concerning the case. Attorneys are also ultimately responsible for the quality and accuracy of their paralegals' work product.

As mentioned, if paralegals violate an ethical rule, it is the attorneys who have to answer to the state disciplinary body, not the paralegals. Although grievance committees can punish only attorneys for unethical conduct, violation of certain ethical rules may expose not only the attorney but also the paralegal to civil lawsuits and/or criminal prosecution.

Work product
The notes, materials, memoranda, and written records generated by an attorney, as well as the written records of the attorney's mental impressions and legal theories concerning a case.

Practice Tip
A paralegal should always disclose his or her professional status when communicating with clients, court personnel, opposing counsel and support staff, and other third parties. Such an introduction will clearly identify the paralegal's role and ensure that others are not under the impression that he or she is an attorney.

EXAMPLE 1

Johnny Swift, Esq., and his paralegal, Nona Williams, get bored one afternoon. They conspire to raid the Mary Smith Client Trust Account and go gambling in Atlantic City. They withdraw $50,000 from the account and take off for the casino. They lose the entire $50,000 at the roulette wheel. Mary finds out that her money was stolen by Swift and Williams.

What are Mary's remedies?

1. **Grievance.** Smith may file a grievance against Swift with the state disciplinary body. A lawyer is obligated under the ethical rules to keep his client's property safe and to maintain a fiduciary relationship of trust and confidence with the client. Although the grievance committee can reprimand, suspend, or disbar Swift, it has no authority to discipline the paralegal, Nona Williams. The consequences of a grievance will affect the attorney's privilege to practice law.

2. **Criminal.** Because Williams and Swift conspired to take the client's money, they committed a crime and may be subject to criminal prosecution. If a paralegal knowingly assists an attorney in committing a crime during the course of representation, both the paralegal and the attorney can be prosecuted. If a paralegal commits a crime on her own during the course of employment, both she and the attorney may be prosecuted. The consequence of a criminal prosecution is a fine, imprisonment, or both, or at the very least a criminal record.

3. **Civil.** Smith may also bring civil action against Swift and Williams alleging both the torts of civil conversion of Smith's money and malpractice. An aggrieved client may sue the attorney for injuries caused by the attorney or paralegal. An attorney and his staff owe a duty to effectively and ethically represent a client. In addition, an attorney is in a fiduciary relationship with the client. In this case, Swift owed Smith a fiduciary duty to keep her money safe. When the attorney breaches that duty and in the course of that breach the client suffers some type of loss, the client can sue the attorney for damages. The duty to Smith was breached when the money was removed from the client's trust account for personal use without the client's consent. Because the client's money was lost and the client was damaged,

Vicarious liability
Where an employer is responsible for negligence and other torts committed by his or her employees when the acts are committed during the scope of their employment.

Respondeat superior
The doctrine that states an employer is responsible for negligence and other torts committed by his or her employees when the acts are committed during the scope of their employment.

Deep pocket
The term applied to characterize the defendant in a lawsuit who has the financial resources to absorb a civil suit for monetary damages.

Premium
A monetary sum paid on an annual or installment basis for malpractice insurance coverage.

Smith can sue both Swift and Williams. The consequence of a civil suit is the payment of money damages to the client, if she prevails in the case.

What if Williams acted on her own in this case? Would attorney Swift be civilly responsible for her actions? The answer is yes. An employer is *vicariously liable* or responsible for the negligence and other torts committed by his employees when the acts are committed during the scope of their employment. This is known as the doctrine of *respondeat superior*. Even if Williams acted alone in this scenario, Smith may bring a civil action naming both the attorney and paralegal as defendants.

Although the client may sue both the attorney and the paralegal, the attorney is eventually the best defendant in the case because of his deep pocket. *Deep pocket* is the term applied to characterize the defendant in a lawsuit who has the financial resources to absorb a civil suit for monetary damages. Attorneys ordinarily carry malpractice insurance, which will cover them in civil lawsuits brought by their clients for their negligent acts or mistakes. However, malpractice insurance will not cover an attorney in a civil action based on a criminal act or for an intentional tort. Some states, such as Connecticut and New Jersey, require contributions from attorneys to fund accounts to reimburse clients in this type of situation.

Malpractice insurance usually covers the negligent acts of attorneys and sometimes the negligent actions of the attorney's staff; however, this is not always the case. Paralegals should inquire as to whether or not they are covered under a firm's malpractice insurance. Attorneys pay a *premium*, which is a monetary sum paid on an annual or installment basis for malpractice insurance coverage. The policy is renewable on a yearly basis. Attorneys must notify their malpractice carrier immediately on becoming aware that they have committed an act, error, or omission that could result in a civil lawsuit.

This chapter does not intend to exhaust all of the ethical rules that apply to attorneys. It only provides a general overview of the basic ethical principles with which paralegals must become familiar in the course of a family law practice. As stated earlier, paralegals must become thoroughly familiar with the rules of ethics that apply to attorneys in their jurisdiction and any ethical guidelines the state bar associations of their states have developed for them. Ethical codes established by paralegal associations also provide excellent guidelines. Paralegals should review the ethical rules on a regular basis in order to refresh their knowledge and update themselves on any changes in the rules or opinions interpreting them. If a paralegal has even the slightest concern about an ethical issue, the paralegal should always consult with the supervising attorney before taking action. Communication is a good way to minimize problems that could expose the firm to a grievance or malpractice suit. While supervising styles differ in the legal profession, conscientious attorneys will appreciate the paralegal's attention and cautiousness.

There are many ethical challenges in the area of family law practice. This area of the law is emotionally draining because it thrusts two people who once shared a life together into an adversarial system that is normally not conducive to amicable resolutions. Almost fifty percent of today's marriages end in divorce, and the proceedings involved may represent the first time a client is exposed to the legal system. Their expectations of what the legal system can do may be based on bad legal advice obtained from talk shows, magazine articles, or friends. When the results of a dissolution case do not live up to these expectations, an attorney may become the target of a disgruntled client. Paralegals should keep this in mind when performing their daily activities, and their conduct should conform to a strict adherence to the rules of ethics and unauthorized practice of law (UPL) statutes.

In addition to knowing and observing ethical boundaries, the following office procedure tips will assist paralegals in protecting their supervising attorneys from malpractice claims and grievance proceedings:

1. Promptly return client phone calls, log client contact in the client file, and reduce client conversations to writing to avoid any misunderstandings that can later be used against the attorney or paralegal. The attorney should review the file entries and client correspondence and maintain the attorney–client relationship.
2. Perform assignments in a timely fashion to avoid delays.
3. Identify professional status at all times and explain to those unfamiliar with the paralegal profession the limitations the law has placed on nonattorneys.
4. Keep track of all important court dates and make sure they are promptly and appropriately marked in the office master calendar and the attorney's personal calendar.
5. Disclose any conflicts of interest relating to the paralegal to the attorney.
6. Promptly relay client information to the attorney so action can be taken on a client's case.

Confidentiality

The ethical rule of *confidentiality* protects communications between attorneys and their clients. Paralegals working for attorneys, either as employees or freelance independent contractors, are equally obligated to be guardians of client information revealed during the course of representation. Attorneys cannot disclose information related to the representation of a client. There are several exceptions to this rule:

- The attorney may reveal such information after obtaining the client's consent. This means that the client has given his or her attorney permission to disclose information to another party. This permission should always be obtained in writing, in the form of a document called a *release*, which the paralegal may be asked to draft. Paralegals should also be very careful when disclosing information under the consent exception. The file should be consulted at all times to verify the existence of a release, to whom the information may be disclosed, and to what extent. Under most circumstances, the attorney may disclose most information to the paralegal who is working on the client's file. The paralegal, as an employee of the attorney or law firm, will have the same obligation to maintain client confidentiality.
- The attorney may also reveal information when the disclosure is impliedly authorized in order to carry out the representation. For example, if a client hires a family lawyer for the purpose of seeking an increase in alimony, the attorney is impliedly authorized to discuss the client's finances as it relates to the upward modification.
- Attorneys *shall* reveal client confidences when they have a reasonable belief that clients will engage in conduct that is likely to result in substantial bodily harm or death. The purpose of this rule is to prevent such crimes from occurring rather than reporting them to the authorities after the fact.

Confidentiality
The ethical rule that protects communications between attorneys and their clients.

Release
A document that indicates the client has given his or her attorneys permission to disclose information to another party.

EXAMPLE 2

During an office visit with his attorney, a very distraught client pulls out a .357 magnum pistol and reveals his plans to kill his wife.

In this scenario, if the attorney reasonably believes that her client will engage in conduct that may result in death or a serious physical injury, she may have an ethical obligation to inform the authorities of her client's plans for the purpose of stopping the crime before it takes place. If, however, the client first committed the murder and then broke down and confessed his crime to the lawyer, the attorney is under no ethical obligation to notify anyone! The communications between the attorney and client are protected by law.

Attorneys *may* reveal information relating to the representation of the client:

1. When the client is engaged in conduct that could result in an injury to the financial interests or property of another;
2. When the client grieves, sues, or charges the attorney with a crime. The attorney has the right to speak to his or her attorney for the purpose of defending the client's allegations;
3. Relating to the representation of a client to comply with a court order; or
4. Relating to the representation of a client to the court about any breach of fiduciary responsibility when the client is serving as a court-appointed fiduciary such as an executor, trustee, guardian, or receiver.

Paralegals must take special precautions to protect client confidentiality. If clients arrive early for an office appointment and start talking about their case in the reception area, paralegals should politely instruct clients to wait until they have privacy with the attorney before they discuss their case. Other clients or delivery or repair persons may be within earshot of the client's personal business, and once clients have disclosed information in the presence of a third party, that disclosure is not protected by the rules of confidentiality.

Paralegals should also be protective of client files, correspondence, or other materials and should not leave them in open view where other clients or visitors may see them. Therefore, reception areas, interview rooms, and any other area where clients or visitors may roam should be free of client information.

Paralegals should also avoid taking calls from clients while in the presence of other clients. If it is an emergency, the paralegal should use a separate room

Figure 12-1 Paralegals should refrain from engaging in unethical conduct such as gossiping about clients' cases.

Jupiterimages/Stockbyte/Getty images.

that lends itself to privacy. If no separate room is available, the call should be very short and paralegals should not reveal the caller's name or any other information. Care should also be taken when visitors such as repair, delivery, or cleaning personnel are in the office. Again, client documents should be kept out of sight, and oral communications should be brief and discreet.

The paralegal who works in a family law practice office will often be privy to the most intimate details of a client's marital relationship. Sometimes these details may be shocking, scandalous, or simply humorous or ridiculously funny. The paralegal may be tempted to share with friends or family some of the spicier portions of clients' files. Paralegals should avoid doing so at all costs!

Attorney–Client Privilege

The attorney–client privilege is often confused with the principle of confidentiality. The *attorney–client privilege* is a rule of evidence and applies to court or other proceedings where an attorney may be compelled to provide evidence concerning communications with a client. The client owns the communication and is the only one who may actually waive this privilege. For example, the attorney may be called as a witness or required to divulge evidence in a proceeding regarding client communications. In the family law realm, an attorney may be ordered by a court to reveal the client's whereabouts in a situation where the client has left the state with the minor children in cases of domestic violence. There have actually been attorneys who were incarcerated for refusing to reveal the client's whereabouts under order of the court. This privilege attaches upon formation of the attorney–client relationship and extends to members of the attorney's legal staff. Any disclosures made before the creation of the attorney–client relationship, however, may not be protected under the privilege rule. The attorney–client privilege rule may not apply where the client intends to commit a crime, the client is seeking the attorney's help in any way, or if the disclosure is made in front of third parties. The principle of confidentiality, on the other hand, is an ethical rule and applies in situations other than those requiring the divulging of client communications as evidence in a court of law.

> **Attorney–client privilege**
> The ethical rule stating that attorneys cannot disclose information related to the representation of a client, with certain exceptions.

Communicating Confidential Information in the Electronic Age

Electronic mail, or e-mail, has made correspondence with clients, coworkers, attorneys, opposing counsel, and other third parties easy, convenient, and cost effective. There are, however, many concerns regarding breaches of client confidentiality, so care should be taken when sending confidential, sensitive information through this medium. Many law offices use a secure website where a link to the website along with a password is e-mailed to the intended party. The individual who needs to view the confidential information can safely log onto and access the information through this password-protected website. If the law office intends to transmit client and/or case information via the Internet, the precautions in the following paragraphs should be observed.

Double-Check

Busy law offices can be hectic and fast-paced. Errors are likely to occur when professionals are multitasking and rushing to produce work to fulfill case timelines. Double-check addresses when sending e-mail correspondence. Relying on the "address book" in e-mail programs may sometimes lead to sending information to the wrong person. This error may lead to potential breach of confidentiality lawsuits. Always check to be sure the correspondence is being transmitted to the intended addressee before clicking the "Send" button.

The Intended Recipient: To:, Bcc:, and Cc:

Before copy machines and word processors were invented, if you wanted to send a copy of a letter to someone other than the original recipient, you placed a sheet of something called carbon paper between two or more sheets of paper. Whatever you typed on the front page was reproduced on subsequent pages. Once the typist hit a key on the typewriter, the character was reproduced on all the other pages because the carbon paper contained a layer of ink that caused a letter to be made.

When creating a new outgoing message, the standard procedure is to place the intended recipient's address in the section marked *To:*. It is very important to double-check this box and make sure that the e-mail is addressed to the actual individual it is intended to reach. A legal professional working in a busy office, if not careful, can accidentally place the wrong e-mail address in this box, so the rule is "check before you click." E-mailing to only one individual requires placing the recipient's e-mail address in the To: box. Two other e-mail address features are used when other recipients are intended.

Cc means "carbon copy." When you "cc" someone, it means that they receive the same e-mail that you sent your original addressee. When you carbon copy another individual, all of the other recipients can see who received a copy of the message. Cc is often used when we want to forward a copy of the e-mail to another person for information purposes only.

Bcc means "blind carbon copy" and is used when you want to hide the addresses of the other recipients of the e-mail message. Only the address of the original intended recipient you indicated in the To: box will appear. Recipients of the blind carbon copies cannot be seen by the original recipient. If you send an e-mail message To: marysmith@aol.com, for example, and Bcc: johnsmith@yahoo.com, Mary Smith will see herself as the only recipient of the e-mail. John Smith, however, is able to see that the original recipient is Mary Smith and that he was sent a "blind carbon copy." Using Bcc: instead of cc: is important when you do not want others to know the e-mail address of the individual who is receiving the blind copy.

Reply All?

Careful thought should be given before clicking the Reply All button when sending e-mail. It is possible that some original recipients of the initial e-mail received, including the Bcc recipients, were not intended to see the reply. When forwarding an e-mail or a chain of e-mails, be sure you know everyone included in that chain and edit text as necessary so that the information being sent is meant for *all* the intended parties.

E-mail Address Privacy

Treat a client's e-mail address as you would their other personal identifying information, such as a home address or phone number. Do not disclose a client's e-mail address without their consent.

E-mail Disclaimers

E-mail messages sent by a law office should always include a legal disclaimer. Legal disclaimers are essential to warn the recipient that the content of the e-mail is confidential and that if an accidental recipient receives it, they are bound by confidentiality laws not to disseminate the information to third parties. They are a good defense to breach of confidentiality claims made by clients whose information has accidentally gotten into the wrong hands. A generic legal disclaimer often contains the following language:

> This message contains confidential information and is intended only for the individual or entity to which it is addressed. If you are not the named addressee you should not disseminate, distribute, or copy this e-mail. If you are not the intended recipient you are notified that disclosing, copying, distributing, or taking any action in reliance on the contents of this information is strictly prohibited. Please notify the sender immediately if you have received this e-mail by mistake and delete this e-mail from your system. Finally, the recipient should check this e-mail and any attachments for the presence of viruses. Our firm accepts no liability for any damage caused by any virus transmitted by this e-mail.

The following Internal Revenue Service (IRS) Circular 230 disclaimer must also be included in *any* correspondence relating to IRS Code matter. The government's goal in requiring this language is to discourage tax fraud. Compliance is especially important for attorneys who practice before the IRS, as failure to include the disclaimer will result in suspension or disbarment from practice before the IRS, fine, or public censure. Avoid these severe consequences by adding the following disclaimer:

> Any U.S. tax advice contained in the body of this e-mail was not intended or written to be used, and cannot be used, by the recipient for the purpose of avoiding penalties that may be imposed under the Internal Revenue Code or applicable state or local tax law provisions.

Conflict of Interest

"You can't serve two masters" best describes this rule of ethics. Attorneys owe their clients a duty of loyalty and must exercise their independent judgment in the course of representation. Any activity that may divide an attorney's loyalty and compromise professional independent judgment is a ***conflict of interest***. Law offices routinely perform conflicts checks before accepting clients for the very purpose of avoiding ethical breaches. The following subsections present an overview of the various activities that might result in a conflict-of-interest situation.

Conflict of interest
Any activity that may divide the attorney's loyalty and compromise his or her independent judgment.

Multiple Representation Sometimes, divorcing couples decide to save money by hiring one lawyer to represent both spouses. This is known as ***multiple representation*** and presents unique ethical problems for attorneys.

Multiple representation
Where one lawyer is hired to represent both parties to a case.

Although attorneys may represent two opposing parties, provided that both parties consent, this could be disastrous in cases involving family relations. Parties may wish to retain a single lawyer's services on the promise that they have come to an agreement as to the distribution of their assets, the disposition of custody, and so on. The parties may represent that they merely need someone to act as a scribe for their agreement and to get them through the court system. The problem is that the amicable divorce of today can turn into the World War III of tomorrow. In addition, a client may find that after having consulted an attorney and learning of his or her legal rights, the agreement originally made with the other spouse may not be in his or her best interest. This puts the lawyer in an awkward position as both an advocate and as a counselor.

The parties may also have revealed confidential information to one attorney that can be used against them later. If attorneys have heard confidential information regarding the case, it would be unethical for them to represent one spouse versus the other. Before hearing any confidential information, attorneys may take on the representation of one spouse and direct the other spouse to obtain independent representation.

Former client–current opponent

Upon an attorney or paralegal switching jobs, discovering that his or her new employer is representing the opponent in a former client's case.

Ethical wall

When a paralegal cannot discuss a case with anyone in the office or have access to the file because of the possibility of conflict of interest.

Costs of litigation

Include filing fees, sheriff's fees, deposition costs, expert witness fees, and excessive photocopying and mailing costs.

Living expenses

Any monies for the client's personal use; may not be advanced to a client by the attorney.

Former Client–Current Opponent Attorneys and paralegals who switch jobs and go from one firm to another present special ethical problems. Freelance attorneys and paralegals working as independent contractors should also screen for conflicts where they are working for multiple attorneys. During their course of employment, attorneys and paralegals are privy to clients' confidential information. Upon switching jobs, an attorney or paralegal may discover that a former client is now the adversary of one of the clients in the new firm, termed ***former client–current opponent***.

EXAMPLE 3

John Doe is a paralegal who works at Law Firm A. Law Firm A represents Mrs. Smith in the divorce matter of Smith v. Smith. John Doe leaves Law Firm A and is now employed at Law Firm B, which represents Mr. Smith in the divorce case. John must immediately inform his new supervisor of the existence of a conflict. Because he previously worked on this case at Law Firm A, he cannot work on the same case in Law Firm B.

If John were allowed to work on the case, the danger exists that he could use the confidential information obtained in Mrs. Smith's case against her interests, in favor of Mr. Smith. Law Firm B must now build an ***ethical wall*** around John. This means that John cannot discuss the case with anyone in the office, nor can he have access to the file.

Another activity that may raise a conflict of interest is the tactic commonly used by one spouse seeking a divorce to obtain a free consultation from a variety of well-known divorce attorneys in the community. Confidential information is then revealed during the course of these initial consultations so as to preclude their spouses from retaining those attorneys' services. The unscrupulous spouse will then raise a conflict-of-interest claim alleging that he is the former client of the attorney and request that the attorney be disqualified from representing his spouse. The paralegal should carefully log the names of all clients, even if they just come to the office for an initial consultation, to avoid any conflict-of-interest challenges.

Sexual Relations with Clients Attorneys and paralegals should not engage in sexual relations with clients during the course of the client's representation! Clients going through a divorce may be very vulnerable and emotionally devastated. Unfortunately, unscrupulous attorneys take advantage of clients in this position and may engage in romantic relations or actual sexual harassment. Such a dynamic may influence attorneys to act contrary to a client's best interest. Sometimes paralegals work very closely with divorce clients over an extended period of time. The intimacy of working together may lead to a mutual personal attraction. If this attraction is acted on during the course of the representation of the client, the paralegal has put herself in an ethically precarious position. Only after representation has been completed should a paralegal consider having any sort of personal relationship with a client.

Sex and the Legal Assistant The following *Logan* case illustrates the serious breach of client confidentiality and conflict of interest problems involved when a legal assistant has an affair with a client's husband.

Loaning Money to a Client Attorneys may advance the ***costs of litigation*** to a client. These costs include filing fees, sheriff's fees, deposition costs, expert witness fees, and excessive photocopying and mailing costs. ***Living expenses***, however, may not be advanced to a client. This includes any monies for a client's personal use.

Gifts from a Client Clients may often show their appreciation by making a gift to attorneys or paralegals. There is nothing wrong with accepting a gift from a client as long as the transferring of that gift does not include the preparation of legal documents such as a deed, will, trust, or letter. An attorney may prepare a document that includes in it a bequest or transfer of property to that attorney if the attorney is re-lated to the donor. If the attorney is not related to the donor, it is best for the attorney to send the donor to another lawyer to avoid later allegations of undue influence.

Communicating with Opposing Party

Attorneys and paralegals may not communicate directly with the opposing party if that party is represented by legal counsel. It is unethical to communicate di-rectly with a represented adversary without the opposing attorney's permission, which is rarely obtained. This ethical rule protects represented individuals from being approached by the opposing party and gathering information to be used against them.

GERALDINE L. LOGAN v. HYATT LEGAL PLANS, INC.

874 S.W.2d 548(Mo. App. W.D. 1994)
Missouri Court of Appeals, Western District

PER CURIAM:

Geraldine Logan appeals from the trial court's order dismissing with prejudice her first amended petition for damages against Hyatt Legal Plans, Inc., a Delaware cor-poration. Her petition asserted that Hyatt Legal Plans, Inc., is liable for the tortious conduct of Dori Dolinar, a secretary and legal assistant who worked in the "Hyatt Legal Services" office during the time that an attorney in that office represented Lo-gan in an action for dissolution of marriage. The trial court, concluding there could be no basis of vicarious liability against Hyatt Legal Plans, Inc., dismissed the action with prejudice. We now reverse and remand.

Prior to and during the time of her dissolution proceeding in October 1991, Logan was employed by American Telephone & Telegraph (AT&T). One of the ben-efits offered to eligible non-management AT&T employees was a group legal ser-vices plan which provided prepaid personal legal services. . . .

. . . Logan claims that she was referred to Jay Crotchett of "Hyatt Legal Ser-vices" in Kansas City after calling the 800 number listed in the plan. Crotchett was employed in the law office operating under the name "Hyatt Legal Services." Logan apparently assumed that Crotchett was employed by Hyatt.

On May 16, 1991, Logan retained Crotchett as her attorney to represent her in a dissolution proceeding. Although she and her husband, John Gragg, were sepa-rated, they both attended the initial meeting at the Hyatt Legal Services office. At that meeting, Logan and Gragg met Dori Dolinar, a secretary and legal assistant, employed by the law firm. Shortly thereafter, Dolinar allegedly began a sexual rela-tionship with Gragg that continued throughout the dissolution proceedings. There is no allegation in the petition that either Jay Crotchett or Allen Lebovitz were aware of Dolinar's involvement with Gragg during Crotchett's representation of Logan. Logan alleges that during the time she was being represented by Crotchett, Dolinar secretly disclosed to Gragg various confidential communications between Logan and her attorney as to her negotiating posture, and that Dolinar counseled and en-couraged Gragg to refuse to pay certain portions of the marital debt, to renege on previous commitments, to threaten bankruptcy, and to refuse any offers of reconcili-ation with his wife.[1]

---

[1]Logan alleges Dolinar was guilty of various acts of a tortious nature. Some of the alleged tortious conduct is no longer cognizable in Missouri. See Thomas v. Siddiqui, 869 S.W.2d 740 (Mo. banc 1994) (where the Missouri Supreme Court abolished the tort of criminal conversation). Stripped to its basics, the claim would seem to be essentially a claim of legal malpractice based on Dolinar's conduct, which was disloyal to Logan.

continued

Following the dissolution of her marriage, Logan learned of Dolinar's involvement with Gragg and brought suit against Hyatt alleging that the corporation was vicariously liable for the tortious conduct of Dolinar. Hyatt filed a motion to dismiss, contending that Hyatt could have no liability because "Hyatt Legal Services" was a separate entity from Hyatt and that neither Dolinar nor Crotchett were agents or employees of Hyatt. The motion to dismiss was sustained by the court and Logan was granted thirty days to file an amended petition. . . .

. . . An employer may be held liable for the negligent acts or omissions of his employee under the doctrine of respondeat superior if those acts are committed within the scope of employment. *Studebaker v. Nettie's Flower Garden, Inc.,* 842 S.W.2d 227, 229 (Mo. App. 1992). In this case, all of the alleged misconduct of which Logan complains is attributed to Dolinar. The affidavit of Andrew Kohn, General Counsel of Hyatt, asserts that at the time of the alleged misconduct, Dolinar was employed by Allen Lebovitz, a sole proprietor of a law firm using the trade name "Hyatt Legal Services." The affidavit states that Dolinar was not paid and had never been an employee or agent of Hyatt and offers the conclusion that Hyatt had no actual control or right to control the activities of Ms. Dolinar. . . .

. . . On this appeal, Plaintiff argues that, based on the content of the summary plan booklet, defendant is estopped from denying liability for Dolinar's conduct. Plaintiff essentially argues that the content of the summary plan booklet created an impression, upon which plaintiff reasonably relied, that the legal services would be provided by an employee of Hyatt Legal Plans. ... At this early stage of the case, we will give plaintiff's pleadings (and proposed pleadings) the broadest possible intendment for purposes of our review, in view of the finality of a disposition by summary judgment.

A provision in the plan booklet states that "Hyatt Legal Plans or the law firms providing services under the plan are responsible for all services provided by their attorneys." This provision could be interpreted as a statement that Hyatt *is at least contingently responsible* for legal services provided under the plan. Also, the plan booklet states that service of process "concerning legal services provided under the plan should be directed to" Hyatt. Another provision of the booklet, which concerns liability with regard to legal services and attorney conduct, states: "[y]ou should understand that AT&T, the unions, the Plan and their directors, officers, and employees have no liability for the conduct of any plan attorney or the services provided." This sentence does *not* say that *Hyatt Legal Plans, Inc.,* has no liability in connection with such services, and the term "the Plan" is not synonymous with Hyatt Legal Plans, Inc., in the definitions set forth in the booklet (footnote omitted). Since the summary plan booklet is not entirely supportive of the idea that Hyatt has no relationship to Dolinar upon which liability could be imputed, there remained some reasonable question as to the nature of the relationship between Hyatt Legal Plans, Inc. and "Hyatt Legal Services."

Plaintiff's intention to plead a theory of vicarious liability was cut short by the action of the court in dismissing the case without prior notice to plaintiff that the court was considering, in effect, a summary judgment ruling. . . . It is difficult to imagine how plaintiff intends to show that Dolinar's actions were within the scope of her employment or agency when there is no apparent reason to believe that Dolinar's actions were undertaken in the interest of her employer, or were encouraged or tolerated by her employer. Crotchett, who was engaged in representing Logan, ordinarily would have no reason to countenance Dolinar's involvement with Gragg, which was disloyal to Logan and could have interfered with Crotchett's ability to secure a favorable result for Logan. However, we cannot say that it is impossible to imagine a set of facts in which Crotchett or Lebovitz could hypothetically have involved themselves in the matter to such a degree that vicarious liability is appropriate. . . . Plaintiff should be given an opportunity to explore the possibility of any malfeasance by Crotchett or Lebovitz, and to explore the relationship between Hyatt and "Hyatt Legal Services." Consequently, we reverse and remand the case. We conclude that there remain some genuine issues of material fact.

Source: Geraldine L. Logan v. Hyatt legal plans, Inc., 874 S.W.2d 548 (MO. APP. W.D. 1994), Missouri Court of Appeals.

Sometimes defendants who have been served with "divorce papers" may call the plaintiff's attorney and demand to speak to someone. If an opposing party contacts the office by telephone, paralegals should instruct that party to have his or her attorney contact the office. The conversation should go no further.

If an opposing party contacts the office in writing, the paralegal should inform the supervising attorney immediately.

The *Pro Se* (Self-Represented) Litigant

As you learned in the previous section, legal professionals cannot communicate with opposing parties if they are represented by counsel; instead they must communicate directly with the opposing party's legal representative. Sometimes, an individual may elect to represent themselves, acting as a *pro se* or *pro per* litigant in order to save money, or he may just wish to handle his own representation. It is important to navigate carefully when dealing with persons who are not represented by counsel. First, it is prudent to ask the *pro se* party to forward a letter confirming the self-representation. In addition, if there is a pending proceeding, the opposing party must file an appearance with the court indicating self-representation. The office should request a copy of the appearance from the *pro se* party and verification of its filing through the clerk's office. While this procedure may seem like a cumbersome formality, it enables attorneys to formally confirm the opposing party's status as a *pro se* litigant.

It is also prudent to communicate with a *pro se* party in writing when at all possible so that the office has a record of the communication. While many *pro se* litigants represent themselves with dignity and a high degree of professionalism, some *pro se* litigants abuse the legal system and resort to unethical conduct. Having communications in writing avoids the "he said, she said" situations that can occur when the office relies on telephone communications as opposed to written documentation. When telephone communications do occur, paralegals must carefully log all phone calls to keep the file current.

Attorneys and paralegals must also take care not to offer legal advice to *pro se* parties or take unfair advantage of them because of their lack of knowledge of the legal system. Paralegals should also avoid engaging the *pro se* party in any unnecessary communications.

Pro Se Resources and Unbundled Legal Services Read any family court docket and you will find that half of the appearances filed belong to *pro se* parties. Many have no choice. Many appear as *pro se* litigants because they are unable to afford the high cost of divorce, while a small number of *pro se* litigants don't trust attorneys, judges, and the entire system. The increase in *pro se* litigants presents special problems for the judicial system:

- Lack of legal knowledge (e.g., regarding substantive family law, court procedure, and rules of evidence)
- Inability to preserve a record for appeal
- Constant need to ask for legal advice or help from clerks, judges, or opposing counsel
- Inability to navigate in an increasingly complex field
- Execution of mistakes that will cost them later on
- Abusive behavior and an "axe" to grind against the spouse and/or the legal system
- Slowdown for the court system

Many jurisdictions have responded to the growing number of *pro se* litigants by offering a variety of self-help resources. In some jurisdictions, paralegals, under attorney supervision, may volunteer at legal aid clinics to assist *pro se* litigants in preparing the legal documents necessary to process a divorce case. Many jurisdictions offer simplified and standardized family law forms and how-to guides online, as well as self-help centers in courthouses and self-help seminars offered by local bar associations, to help alleviate the *pro se* burden.

Unbundled legal services (discrete tasks representation)
Clients purchase legal services on a task-by-task basis; the client and attorney agree by contract as to what services the lawyer will provide in exchange for a fee.

Another form of assistance for *pro se* parties is called **unbundled legal services**. Traditionally, a client who hires a divorce attorney is entitled to a full bundle of services. This means that the attorney, along with the assistance of his or her paralegal, will interview the client, gather the relevant facts of the case, prepare and file relevant documents, conduct discovery, research relevant legal issues, go to court, and do whatever is necessary to process the client's case from start to finish. Attorneys enjoy this method because it allows them to control all aspects of the case. Unbundled legal services, or *discrete tasks representation*, allow the client to purchase legal services on a task-by-task basis, sort of a pick-and-choose menu approach to legal representation. The client and attorney agree by contract as to what services the lawyer will provide in exchange for a fee. A list of unbundled legal services may consist of:

- Advising the client regarding the feasibility of self-representation depending on the complexity of the case
- Advising the client on maneuvering through the court system
- Educating the client on the divorce process
- Ghostwriting or preparation of legal documents as well as monitoring deadlines for filing
- Advising the client on legal issues impacting the case
- Coaching the client through the process by providing information on an as-needed basis
- Reviewing and responding to documents
- Conducting legal research on relevant issues
- Developing strategy for the case
- Introducing or objecting to evidence
- Dissecting and resolving legal problems
- Preparation for trial
- Advising the client on how to negotiate a settlement
- Advising the client on alternative dispute resolution options

For clients, unbundled legal services allow clients to represent themselves while providing legal expertise in certain areas without a large financial commitment. For legal professionals, unbundled legal services serve as a new source of revenue, as well as raise some ethical worries. Many state ethical codes allow an attorney to limit the scope of representation if the client consents after consultation. This means that the attorney must explain to the client the services she will and will not provide and how this arrangement may affect the client's case. While the ethical rules may provide some leeway, attorneys are concerned that performing small tasks could eventually lead to responsibility for the whole matter. Clients can also be very demanding and expect the attorney and his or her staff to take on more services than originally contracted for. A client may, for example, purchase the preparation of the initial documents from the attorney and then call constantly for information on how to proceed in the case. Attorneys are also worried that clients who rely on unbundled legal services may do more harm because of lack of knowledge in how to maneuver strategically or misuse of the services they purchased. States such as Colorado, Oregon, New York, Alaska, and California have addressed the matter of unbundled legal services and provide some guidance to the bar in how to proceed ethically. Due to the large number of *pro se* litigants dominating court dockets, we foresee unbundled legal services as the wave of the future in divorce litigation.

Under the supervision of a licensed attorney, paralegals will play an integral part in offering unbundled legal services. It is important to check your state bar association's rules on the topic and determine if your state allows attorneys to offer such services and integrate such rules into practice. Most state rules of professional conduct indicate that an attorney owes a duty of candor toward the tribunal. Basically, this means that an attorney must be truthful to the court. In Iowa, for example, "ghostwriting," or an attorney preparing documents for a *pro se* client without signing the pleadings, is a "deception on the court" (Iowa Opinion 94-35, May 23, 1995). In New York, pleadings prepared by attorneys for *pro se* litigants require the words *prepared by counsel* to be on the document (New York Bar Association Opinion 1987-2). In Maine and Alaska, no disclosure is necessary (Maine Ethics Commission No. 89, 8/31/88, Alaska Bar Association No. 93-1, 3/19/93).

The paralegal may also assist the attorney by preparing a contract for legal services or engagement letter for the client to sign. In cases where the attorney is providing unbundled legal services, this agreement is called a ***limited scope retainer agreement***. This is a contract for legal services between the attorney and client where the attorney limits the scope of representation with the client's consent. This is vital, especially in clarifying the role of the attorney and his or her office. The contract may contain:

Limited scope retainer agreement
A contract for legal services between the attorney and client where the attorney limits the scope of representation with the client's consent.

- An explanation of the client's options—full bundled services, unbundled services, alternative dispute resolution (ADR) options, risks of *pro se* representation—and that the attorney explained these options to the client.
- Explicit details concerning what the lawyer will do for the client and the limits of the attorney's representation. Here, we must be clear to indicate that the attorney will not be filing a court appearance on behalf of the client and that we are assisting a *pro se* litigant by providing unbundled legal services. Remember, once an attorney files an appearance, he or she may "own" the case. This means that an attorney will be responsible for the whole case and the judge will require his or her appearance at every court hearing.
- Fee for services. Usually, unbundled legal services are paid for by the client at the time of service and the attorney charges a flat or fixed fee per session to control costs.
- A clause that says the client has fully disclosed the facts of the case to the attorney.
- An option for client to go from an unbundled service agreement to full bundled representation and how much this will cost.
- A notice that client will be responsible for all expenses.
- It may also be a good idea to prepare a state-specific list of the steps in the divorce process as well as a timeline for filing various forms.

Finally, remember that attorneys who engage in offering unbundled legal services are just as open to malpractice allegations as any other attorney. Make sure to keep very good notes regarding all interactions with the client—they may one day prove to be crucial in a grievance procedure against your supervising attorney.

Competence

Attorneys have a duty to render competent legal representation to their clients. ***Competency*** is the duty to exercise a reasonable degree of care and skill commonly used by other attorneys engaged in a similar area of practice. Paralegals must also deliver competent services in assisting attorneys in client representation.

Competency is attained by engaging in activities that educate attorneys as to the most efficient and effective manner of representing a particular client. The following activities help educate attorneys:

Competency
The duty to exercise a reasonable degree of care and skill commonly used by other attorneys engaged in a similar area of practice.

1. **Attendance at continuing legal education seminars.** Such seminars are provided by local bar associations, local paralegal associations, and private entities.
2. **Associating with more experienced attorneys.** Experienced attorneys who possess adequate knowledge and skill in their particular area of practice frequently, either informally or through organized legal mentor programs, share their knowledge and expertise with attorneys who are new to their area of practice.
3. **Consulting statutes, case law, legal periodicals, journals, and other legal publications.** The practice of law is flexible in that attorneys can practice in a variety of areas as long as they become competent in those areas. Paralegals also enjoy this flexibility and work in different areas of practice as long as they, too, become competent and are supervised by attorneys. The ethical duty of competency is ongoing and imposes on attorneys and paralegals the obligation of continually educating themselves and upgrading their skills.

It is important for paralegals involved in family law practice to review their jurisdiction's domestic relations statutes and relevant case law and to attain familiarity with the forms used in their state. State bar associations and local paralegal associations may periodically offer seminars in family law practice, of which the paralegal should take full advantage. In addition, state bar publications and legal periodicals focusing on the jurisdictional law and procedures should be read on a regular basis to keep current on changing legal developments.

Fees

Attorneys should charge "reasonable" ***fees***. The factors considered when determining what is reasonable are the skill and experience of the attorney, the simplicity or complexity of the client's matter, the cost of similar service in the community, the result obtained, the reputation of the attorney, and whether the matter is contested or uncontested.

Fees
The amount the attorney will charge the client, based on the skill and experience of the attorney, the simplicity or complexity of the client's matter, cost of similar service in the community, the result obtained, the reputation of the attorney, and whether the matter is contested or uncontested.

Divorce attorneys may be compensated for their legal services by employing any one of the following fee arrangements:

Flat fee
An arrangement whereby a fixed dollar amount is agreed on and charged for the entire case.

Flat Fee Under a ***flat fee*** arrangement, a fixed dollar amount is agreed on and charged for the entire case. Flat fees are sometimes charged in uncontested divorce cases where the parties have no children, no property, and no disputed issues between them.

Hourly basis
Billing the client for each hour of time spent working on a client's file, including but not limited to research, drafting documents, phone calls, travel, office visits, trial preparation, and interviewing witnesses.

Hourly Rates Attorneys may also charge clients on an ***hourly basis***. This means that they will bill the client for each hour of time spent working on a client's file, including but not limited to research, drafting documents, phone calls, travel, office visits, trial preparation, and interviewing witnesses. Attorneys often bill in tenth or quarter hours.

Attorneys will also charge for expenses or costs, such as filing fees, sheriff's fees, and court reporter fees for transcripts and depositions.

Retainer
Payment made in advance to an attorney.

Retainer Arrangement Another type of fee arrangement is the requiring of a ***retainer*** prior to the attorney committing himself or herself to representation of a client. A retainer is a payment made in advance to an attorney. The attorney will deposit the retainer in a client trust account and withdraw amounts from the retainer in proportion to the amount of work expended on the client's file. For example, a client gives his attorney a retainer of $2,000 to represent him in a divorce matter. The attorney bills at the rate of $200 an hour. Once the attorney has completed ten hours of work on the case, he is entitled to withdraw the ***earned retainer***. If the attorney spent only five hours on the client's case, the attorney would be entitled to an earned retainer of $1,000 and would be obligated to return the ***unearned retainer*** to the client.

Contingent Fee Arrangement Attorneys may also be paid under a ***contingent fee*** arrangement, which entitles attorneys to a percentage of the financial outcome of the case, be it a judgment or settlement. Contingent fee arrangements are frequently used in personal injury cases and in other areas of civil litigation where the plaintiff lacks the financial resources to provide a retainer or pay the customary hourly rates. Many contingent fee arrangements provide that the attorney will receive one-third of the judgment or settlement amount the client recovers. Contingent fees are unethical in divorce cases because they discourage attorneys from accepting a settlement if they do not feel that the offer is adequate enough to cover their fee. They may push the parties to trial in order to seek a better disposition. Under these circumstances, they are acting in their best interests, not the client's.

Fee Agreements: Putting It in Writing Attorneys should always enter into written fee agreements with their clients so as to avoid any confusion regarding the attorney's billing practices. In fact, many jurisdictions require fee agreements between attorneys and clients to be in writing.

The fee agreement should specify the services to be performed by the attorney, the charge to the client, and the costs of litigation to be paid by the client. If the attorney uses paralegals in her law practice, the attorney should specify the paralegal's hourly rate for the performance of paralegal duties and the hourly rate for routine clinical tasks such as excessive photocopying, typing, and filing. Charging a client the attorney's rate for performing paralegal or clerical tasks is unethical.

Earned retainer
Amount from the retainer that the attorney may keep in proportion to the amount of work expended on the client's file.

Unearned retainer
Any part of a retainer left over after the attorney has completed his or her work; must be returned to the client.

Contingent fees
An arrangement that entitles attorneys to a percentage of the financial outcome of the case, be it a judgment or settlement.

Figure 12-2 It is important for family law paralegals to review their state's domestic relations law and attain familiarity with the forms used in their jurisdiction.

Kzenon/Shutterstock.

Billable hours
The amount of time expended on a particular case, which can later be billed to that client.

Paralegal Fees The following *McMacklin* case outlines the criteria for setting paralegal fees and the importance of differentiating among attorney, paralegal, and secretarial work in client billing practices.

In a law office, time is money; therefore, much emphasis is placed on **billable hours**. This is the amount of time expended on a particular case, which

---

Exhibit 12-1 Sample time sheet.

CLIENT _____   PHONE_____

ADDRESS _____

File #_____ DOCKET # _____ IN RE: _____ TYPE OF CASE _____

NOTES _____

_____

_____

Date	In	Out	Hrs	Description of Services
	:	:		
	:	:		
	:	:		
	:	:		
	:	:		
	:	:		
	:	:		
	:	:		
	:	:		
	:	:		
	:	:		
	:	:		
	:	:		
	:	:		
	:	:		
	:	:		
	:	:		
	:	:		
	:	:		
	:	:		
	:	:		
	:	:		
	:	:		
	:	:		
		Total Hrs _____		

can later be billed to that client. There is a lot of pressure in many firms to achieve a certain number of billable hours on a yearly basis. Attorneys and even paralegals are under similar pressure to produce billable hours. This pressure may lead some attorneys and paralegals to engage in unethical billing practices.

Traditionally, paralegals recorded the time spent working on client files on forms called **time sheets** or **time slips**. Today, paralegals can perform this function much more efficiently by using computerized billing software such as PC Law, AbacusLaw, or Timeslips Law. Many legal malpractice carriers, however, require a paper backup, so it is important to still use the traditional time sheets and time slips as a record of work performed on behalf of a client that will be billed to them on a periodic basis (see Exhibit 12-1).

These documents should include the client's name, file number, spaces to log the date, activity performed on the client's file, and time actually spent. Every time the paralegal performs a task on the client's file, it is important to log the appropriate information on the client's time sheet. The time sheet should be completed at the same time the work is done. Several risks arise if time sheets are not completed in a timely manner. The paralegal may forget to include tasks performed, which would cheat the law firm out of earned revenue. Conversely, the paralegal may increase the time spent on a particular task, which would cheat the client and risk engaging in the unethical practice of **padding**. Padding means unjustifiably increasing the number of hours actually spent on a client's case. Padding is not only fraudulent but also illegal since you are, in effect, stealing from the client.

Time sheet
A record of work performed on behalf of a client that will be billed to the client on a periodic basis; also known as a time slip.

Time slip
See time sheet.

Padding
Unjustifiably increasing the number of hours actually spent on a client's case.

JAMES H. MCMACKLIN v. MARIANNE C. MCMACKLIN

651 A.2D 778 (1993)

FAMILY COURT OF DELAWARE, NEW CASTLE COUNTY

OPINION

CROMPTON, JUDGE

The following is my decision regarding attorney's fees in the above-entitled matter. I have reviewed Affidavits for Fees submitted by counsel for both James H. McMacklin (hereinafter "Husband") and Marianne C. McMacklin (hereinafter "Wife"). Wife's total attorney's fees, paralegal fees and costs amount to $12,785.50. Husband's total attorney fees, paralegal fees and costs are $9,768.35.

. . . In the past, Family Court Judges have treated paralegal fees in a variety of ways. Some Judges have permitted them. Others have steadfastly denied them. In my view, paralegal costs should be uniformly allowed, so long as certain information is specifically addressed by the supervising attorney in the fee affidavit presented to the Court.

13 *Del.C* § 1515 is the controlling statute regarding an award of fees following a division of marital assets and debts. That statute reads as follows:

The Court from time to time after considering the financial resources of both parties may order a party to pay all or part of the cost to the other party of maintaining or defending any proceeding under this title and for attorney's fees, including sums for legal services rendered and costs incurred prior to the commencement of the proceeding or after the entry of judgment. The Court may order that the amount be paid directly to the attorney, who may enforce the order in his name.

The phrase "all or part of the costs of the other party of maintaining or defending" has previously been found broad enough to include fees incurred by a legal assistant or paralegal (citation omitted). . . .

. . . The United States Supreme Court has found that the term "attorney's fee" refers not only to the work performed by members of the Bar but also to reasonable fees for the work product of an attorney, which includes the work of paralegals, law clerks and recent law graduates at market rates for their services. *Missouri v. Jenkins,* 491 U.S. 274, 109 S. Ct. 2463, 105 L. Ed. 2d 229 (1989). . . .

continued

. . . Paralegal fees are not a part of the overall overhead of a law firm. Paralegal services are billed separately by attorneys, and these legal assistants have the potential for greatly decreasing litigation expenses and, for that matter, greatly increasing the efficiency of many attorneys. By permitting paralegal fees, the danger of charging these fees off as the attorney's work is hopefully extinguished. By the same token, the danger of charging off a secretary's services as those of a paralegal is very real and present, thereby mandating that certain information be provided by the supervising attorney before paralegal fees can be awarded by this Court in the future. Those criteria are as follows:

1. The time spent by the person in question on the task;
2. The hourly rate as charged to clients (will vary based on expertise and years of experience);
3. The education, training or work experience of the person which enabled him or her to acquire sufficient knowledge of legal concepts. The Court recognizes that not all those who work in a paralegal capacity have a paralegal degree or license, but many of these people do possess expertise, which should be recognized in family law matters;
4. The type of work involved in detail. The work must *not* be purely clerical or secretarial in nature. Such work would fall under costs and may not be charged as paralegal fees at the market rate. The task must contain substantive legal work under the direction or supervision of an attorney such that if that assistant were not present, the work would be performed by the attorney and not a secretary. However, the assistant may not do work that only an attorney is allowed to do under the rules of practice and ethics. Substantive legal work which may be performed by legal assistants and billed at the market rate includes, but is not limited to, such activities as:

   a. Factual investigation, including locating and interviewing witnesses;
   b. Assistance with depositions, interrogations and document preparation;
   c. Compilation of statistical and financial data;
   d. Checking legal citations;
   e. Correspondence with clients/opposing counsel/courts; and
   f. Preparing/reviewing/answering petitions and other pleadings.

. . . Applying the above standards to the two Affidavits received in the matters *sub judice*, it is evident that both of them contain the required information. Both affidavits clearly comply with all four criteria previously discussed. For example, they describe the time spent by the paralegal, the hourly rate, and the education, training or work experience of the paralegal. The type of affidavit submitted by Husband's counsel is exactly what this Court expects when reviewing fees. The affidavit of Wife's counsel leaves a bit to be desired in that it merely attaches invoices sent to the client. These invoices are very difficult to read and should be consolidated into one document with a separate affidavit attached by the paralegal. Husband's affidavit complies in every respect, but Wife's affidavit is certainly within the guidelines. Both attorneys have described in detail the type of work performed by the paralegal. This work includes such activities as reviewing depositions, preparing subpoenas, reviewing discovery, assisting in preparing Rule 52(d) Submissions, conferences with clients and correspondence. Clearly the type of work involved is that which would normally have been prepared or accomplished by the attorney and not a secretary.

Having made the decision that paralegal fees are and will be henceforth permissible by this Court, and having also decided that the Affidavits presented by counsel in this specific case rise to the required standards, I nevertheless must make a determination of counsel fees in accordance with 13 *Del. C.* § 1515, supra. . . .

. . . Husband has stated in his answer to Wife's Motion for Counsel Fees that he has no cash available to pay her fees. It is my opinion that his substantial income of approximately $82,000.00 per year versus Wife's income of approximately $35,000.00 per year mandates that he pay 60% of her fees or $7,671.30. This amount is to be added to the lump sum which Husband owes to Wife and is to be paid at the same time.

IT IS SO ORDERED.

Source: James H. Mcmacklin v. Marianne C. Mcmacklin, 651 A.2D 778 (1993), State of Delaware.

Establishing Legal Fees   Just as it is the attorney's role to accept or reject cases, the attorney is also the only one who may set legal fees. Paralegals cannot set legal fees. This is for the attorney to determine after he has consulted with the client. Attorneys are also prohibited from splitting fees with nonattorneys. For example, attorneys and paralegals may not enter into an agreement whereby the paralegal is paid a percentage on each client file. Attorneys may compensate paralegals through a weekly salary or on an hourly basis. In addition, the attorney may also offer the paralegal fringe benefits such as bonuses, retirement plans, and health insurance coverage.

Solicitation

Paralegals cannot be paid for cases that they refer to the office. While paralegals may hand out the attorney's business cards and be a source of referral, they cannot be compensated for the cases referred. The ethical rule prohibiting this practice is called *solicitation*. The public commonly uses the phrase *ambulance chasing* to describe this conduct. Attorneys cannot actively seek out persons they know are in need of legal services, either by mail or in person, unless there already exists an attorney–client relationship or a family relationship. There is an exception, however, in personal injury cases. In some jurisdictions, attorneys must wait thirty days before they may contact accident victims or their families by direct mail. Attorneys also may solicit clients if they wish to volunteer their legal services for free.

Solicitation
Actively seeking persons in need of legal services, either by mail or in person, unless there already exists an attorney–client relationship or a family relationship.

In addition, attorneys may advertise their services to the general public through the media, by having listings and advertisements in the telephone directory and on the Internet, and by having advertising spots on television and the radio.

Advertising

The practice of law has become very competitive over the years due to the increase in lawyers. Advertising is a key component in any law firm, and survival demands methods that go far beyond the traditional Yellow Pages ad. Advances in technology, social networking, online marketing, and the importance of creating a "brand" are just a few of the tools used by attorneys to attract new business.

For many years, attorneys did not advertise. This practice of advertising was viewed as unethical and strictly prohibited by the profession, which banned all advertising except for business cards and phone book listings. Attorneys were supposed to find clients through word of mouth. This all changed in 1977 when the United States Supreme Court in *Bates v. State Bar of Arizona*, 433 U.S. 350 (1977) ruled that such bans were unconstitutional. In *Bates*, two Arizona attorneys who ran a legal clinic for low-income clients decided to place an ad in the newspaper to increase business. The Court held that prohibiting attorneys from advertising restricted the flow of information to consumers, which is the traditional means for enterprises to inform the public of their services. The Court, however, did allow state bar associations to regulate attorney advertising and restrict ads that are deceptive or misleading.

In 2007, a Chicago family law firm, Fetman, Garland & Associates, created a billboard advertisement that included a scantily clad woman from the neck down and a muscular male torso, with a caption that read "Life's Short. Get a Divorce." While the ad did bring in a lot of business, it drew criticism from the legal community because it was in poor taste and encouraged the breakdown of a marriage. While sexually provocative, the ad was not false or misleading and there were no grounds to discipline the firm. State bar associations have to walk a thin line not to violate attorneys' First Amendment free speech rights.

A paralegal may be assigned the task of reviewing office advertisements to determine if they comply with the state's Rules of Professional Responsibility. A good working knowledge of the relevant code sections and cases interpreting attorney advertising issues are a must for spotting questionable advertising practices.

Authorized Practice of Law

Authorized practice of law
General criteria for obtaining a license to practice law required by state statute.

Reciprocity
Where one state may extend to attorneys in a different state the right to practice law in its jurisdiction in exchange for the other state's granting the same privilege to attorneys in their state.

Pro hac vice
Where a state may grant an attorney special permission to handle one particular case.

Every state has enacted statutes that establish the requirements necessary to obtain a license to practice law in that jurisdiction. The general criteria for obtaining a license to practice law are that an individual should be a graduate of an accredited law school, possess a good moral character, and successfully pass the state bar exam. Once all statutory requirements have been met, the individual is admitted to the bar of that state for *authorized practice of law* in that state only. If he or she wishes to practice law in another jurisdiction, he or she must meet that particular state's requirements for admission to the bar. This may include taking another bar exam. Some states do not require an attorney licensed to practice in another jurisdiction to take the state bar exam. One state may extend to attorneys in a different state the right to practice law in its jurisdiction in exchange for the other state's granting the same privilege to attorneys in their state. This is called *reciprocity*.

A state may allow out-of-state attorneys to practice law in its jurisdiction as long as the attorney has been practicing law in another state for a specified time and is a member in good standing of that state's bar. Other requirements must also be met, but they vary from state to state. A state may also grant an attorney special permission to handle one particular case. This is known as appearing *pro hac vice*.

Figure 12-3 Statutory requirements for obtaining a license to practice law are imposed to protect the public from unqualified legal representation.

Junial Enterprises/Shutterstock.

UNAUTHORIZED PRACTICE OF LAW

Statutory requirements for obtaining a license to practice law are imposed to protect the public from unqualified legal representation. Although there has been considerable discussion about licensing paralegals, as of 2006, California is the only jurisdiction that makes it illegal to identify oneself as a paralegal unless one has met certain educational standards. Even if paralegals were to be licensed by the state, they could not engage in the practice of law. Only those individuals who have met the state's statutory criteria may engage in the activities that constitute the practice of law.

In addition to statutes regulating the practice of law, most jurisdictions have enacted laws prohibiting the **unauthorized practice of law (UPL)**, or "UPL statutes," as they are commonly referred to in the paralegal profession. These statutes define the unauthorized practice of law. Violation of the UPL statutes is a criminal offense. This means that a nonattorney can be prosecuted in criminal court for engaging in any activity that a UPL statute prohibits.

UPL Violations

Violations of the UPL statute may have additional consequences for the paralegal, including civil liability, and may give rise to disciplinary proceedings against the supervising attorney, which are addressed later in this chapter. The paralegal may also suffer loss of employment and experience difficulty finding a new job if word gets around in the legal community that the paralegal has engaged in the unauthorized practice of law.

The following sections illustrate activities that are considered the unauthorized practice of law in most states when performed by those without a legal license. This includes paralegals and other nonattorneys, as well as attorneys who no longer have a license to practice law.

Representing Someone in Court or at Administrative Proceedings Only attorneys are allowed to represent clients in court proceedings or administrative proceedings unless a specific state or federal statute or regulation allows a nonattorney to appear. There are limited circumstances in which a nonattorney may represent another person. The **Administrative Procedure Act**, 5 U.S.C.A. § 555 (1967), is a federal statute that allows a person appearing before a federal administrative agency to be represented by an attorney or, if the agency permits, "by other qualified individual." This means that you must consult the federal statutes and regulations to determine (1) if the particular agency allows nonattorneys to practice before it and, if so, (2) what requirements the nonattorney must meet in order to be deemed a "qualified representative" (e.g., testing, applications). Examples of agencies that allow nonattorneys to practice before them on an administrative level are the Internal Revenue Service, Social Security Administration, and Immigration and Naturalization Service and, in some jurisdictions, state workers compensation commissions.

Many states have similar statutes that allow nonattorneys to represent individuals before state agencies. In addition, nonattorneys are always allowed to represent themselves before any court or administrative body. These individuals who represent themselves are known as **pro se** or **pro per litigants**.

Legal Advice This involves advising a client of his or her specific legal rights and responsibilities and either predicting an outcome or recommending that the client pursue a particular course of action. Paralegals must be very careful so that they do not render **legal advice**, either to clients or to the public in general. A paralegal may experience pressure from family, friends, or clients to render a legal opinion. The best way to avoid this is to tell the individual that the rendering of legal advice by a nonattorney is a violation of the law and that the paralegal may be subject to criminal prosecution.

Unauthorized practice of law (UPL)
When a nonattorney engages in any activity that the state UPL statute prohibits. Anyone engaging in UPL can be prosecuted in criminal court.

Administrative Procedure Act
A federal statute that allows a person appearing before a federal administrative agency to be represented by an attorney or, if the agency permits, "by other qualified individual."

Pro se litigants
Individuals who represent themselves in legal proceedings; see *pro per.*

Pro per
Individuals who represent themselves in court; also known as *pro se* litigants.

Legal advice
Advising a client of his or her specific legal rights and responsibilities and either predicting an outcome or recommending that the client pursue a particular course of action.

Figure 12-4 Paralegals may prepare legal documents under the supervision of attorneys.

Wavebreakmedia/Shutterstock.

Paralegals are allowed to relay legal advice from the attorney to the client but must be careful not to add any additional advice to the clients that was not mentioned by the attorney. Paralegals must also be careful not to put legal advice in letters to a client that are signed by the paralegal and not the attorney.

Preparation of Legal Documents and Pleadings Paralegals may prepare legal documents and pleadings under the supervision of attorneys. It is the responsibility of the attorney to review the documents and make sure they have been drafted correctly. The attorney is also responsible for signing legal documents and pleadings. Paralegals may sign a letter but must indicate their paralegal status at the end of the letter. Preparation of legal documents without attorney supervision constitutes the unauthorized practice of law.

Lawyer's Supervision Required In the following case, a paralegal advertised to prepare uncontested divorce papers for clients. The U.S. District Court was not swayed by the paralegal's constitutional arguments.

NADINE O. MONROE v. DANIEL B. HORWITCH ET AL.

820 F. Supp. 682 (D. Conn. 1993)
UNITED STATES DISTRICT COURT, CONNECTICUT
RULING ON PENDING MOTIONS

DORSEY, DISTRICT JUDGE

Plaintiff sues under 42 U.S.C. § 1983 alleging deprivation of her rights under the United States Constitution. Defendants move to dismiss.

I. BACKGROUND

Facts alleged in the complaint are assumed for purposes of a motion to dismiss. Plaintiff alleges that Conn. Gen. Stat. § 51–88,[1] forbidding the unauthorized practice of law, violates the First Amendment, freedom of speech, and the Fourteenth

Amendment, equal protection and due process. Plaintiff further alleges that Conn. Gen. Stat. § 51–90a(2) and § 51–90c(b)[2] unconstitutionally grant defendants, the Statewide Grievance Committee (SGC) and the Statewide Bar Counsel (SBC), respectively, criminal jurisdiction.

In October 1991, plaintiff, a paralegal, advertised an offer to prepare papers for parties representing themselves in uncontested divorce actions. In November 1991, defendant Horwitch, acting for SGC was investigating her, under Conn. Gen. Stat. § 51–88, for the unauthorized practice of law. Plaintiff did not testify at a March 1993 hearing, refusing to recognize the SGC's authority to conduct or to subpoena her to said hearing.

The SGC found, based on her advertisement, that plaintiff's actions constituted the unauthorized practice of law. Because plaintiff had ceased running the advertisement and had not served any clientele, the SGC recommended dismissing the complaint without prejudice. It recommended pursuit of the complaint under Practice Book 31(c) if she resumes offering the services.[3] In June 1992, defendant informed plaintiff of the SGC's decision. Plaintiff alleges that since that time, Horwitch has threatened her with prosecution for criminal contempt if she resumes the practice in question. . . .

1. FIRST AMENDMENT FREEDOM OF EXPRESSION

The prohibition against unauthorized practice of law does not violate plaintiff's First Amendment right to freedom of speech ... (citation omitted). "The practice of law is above that of a mere privilege. It cannot be treated as a matter of grace or favor. But it may be granted only upon fulfillment of certain rigid qualifications established by this court. The defendant had not fulfilled these qualifications and he is not therefore entitled to exercise the privilege bestowed upon those who have . . ." (citation omitted).

FOURTEENTH AMENDMENT

Due Process Statutes forbidding the "unauthorized practice of law" are "sufficiently definite" to withstand constitutional scrutiny . . . (citation omitted). An activity on the "outer boundaries" of the "practice of law" might be impermissibly vague. *Hackin,* 102 Ariz. at 221, 427 P.2d at 913. [P]reparation "of legal documents fall squarely within the boundaries."

. . . Plaintiff's vulnerability to Conn. Gen. Stat. § 51–88 arises from her offer to prepare court documents in uncontested divorce actions. Preparation of legal documents is "commonly understood to be the practice of law." *Grievance Committee v. Dacey,* 222 A.2d at 349. What constitutes "preparation of legal documents" is construed broadly. Preparation of instruments, even with *pre-printed forms* involves more than a "mere scrivener's duties" and, therefore, constitutes the practice of law. *State v. Buyers Service Co.,* 292 S.C. 426, 357 S.E.2d 15, 17 (1987). *See also Pulse v. North Am. Land Title Co.,* 218 Mont. 275, 707 P.2d 1105, 1109 (1985) ("drafting or filling in of blanks in printed forms of instruments dealing with land" constitutes the practice of law); *Kennedy v. Bar Ass'n,* 316 Md. 646, 561 A.2d 200, 208 (1989) (preparation of legal documents in patent case constitutes the practice of law). Legal documents purport to allocate legal obligation.

The preparation of documents in simple divorce actions unequivocally constitutes the practice of law. *See United States v. Hardy,* 681 F. Supp, 1326, 1328–29 (N.D. Ill. 1988) ("Common sense dictates that the drafting of even a simple complaint or an uncomplicated petition for dissolution of marriage requires at least some degree of legal knowledge or skill"); *McGiffert v. State ex rel. Stowe,* 366 So. 2d 680, 683 (Ala.1979) ("It would seem to be clear that only a licensed lawyer may obtain an uncontested divorce for another person without violating the statute"); *Florida Bar v. Brumbaugh,* 355 So. 2d. 1186, 1194 (Fla.1978) (assistance in preparation of dissolution of marriage forms constitutes the practice of law); *State Bar v. Cramer,* 399 Mich. 116, 249 N.W.2d 1, 9 (1976) (preparation of a client's no-fault divorce documents constitutes the practice of law). Such documents may assert, fail to assert or acknowledge legal rights.

Equal Protection . . . The states have a "compelling interest" in the practice of professions. *Goldfarb v. Virginia State Bar,* 421 U.S. 773,793, 95 S. Ct. 2004, 2015–16, 44 L. Ed. 2d. 572 (1975). "As part of their power to protect the public health, safety and other valid interests they have broad power to establish standards for licensing practitioners and regulating the practice of professions." *Id.* The limitation of the practice of law to bar members "protects the public against rendition of legal services by unqualified persons." Conn. Prac. Book Rule 5.5 (comment). Such a limitation constitutes "protection" in that "the public can better be assured of the requisite responsibility and competence if the practice of law is confined to those who are subject to the requirements and regulations imposed upon members of the legal profession." ABA Model Code of Professional Responsibility, EC3-1 (1987).

A lawyer may delegate functions to a paralegal "so long as the lawyer supervises the delegated work and retains responsibility for their work." Conn. Prac. Book Rule 5.5 (comment). Oversight and accountability guarantee, so far as practicable, that the "requirements and regulations" imposed on lawyers will also ensure the quality of work of supervised paralegals (footnotes omitted). Prohibiting unsupervised paralegals from work with legal consequences is rationally related to public protection. *See Lawline v. American Bar Ass'n,* 956 F.2d 1378, 1385–86 (7th Cir. 1992). . . .

VI. CONCLUSION

Defendant's motion to dismiss (document #10) is granted.

Source: Nadine O. Monroe v. Daniel B. Horwitch et al., 820 F. SUPP. 682 (D. CONN. 1993), United States District Court.

---

[1]Conn. Gen. Stat. § 51–88 proscribes the practice of law by persons not attorneys. Subsection (b) provides: "Any person who violates any provision of this section shall be fined not more than two hundred and fifty dollars or imprisoned not more than two months or both."

[2]Conn. Gen. Stat. §§ 51–90a and 51–90c(b) each delineate the powers and duties of the Statewide Bar Committee and Counsel, respectively, to include "investigate and prosecute complaints involving the violation by any person of any provision of section 51–88."

[3]Conn. Prac. Book 31(c) provides in part: "A petition to restrain any person from engaging in the unauthorized practice of law not occurring in the actual presence of the court may be made by written complaint to the superior court in the judicial district where the violation occurs . . . Such complaint may be prosecuted by the state's attorney, by the statewide bar counsel, or by any member of the bar by direction of the court . . . Such complaints shall be proceeded with as civil action."

Negotiating with Opposing Attorney in Pending Litigation It is the attorney's job to negotiate with the opposing party's attorney in pending litigation. Paralegals may relay messages between their supervising attorney and opposing counsel but must be careful not to use their independent judgment in making or accepting offers.

Accepting and Rejecting Cases Only the attorney can determine whether or not to accept or reject cases. The paralegal must leave this task up to the attorney and cannot use independent judgment in deciding whether or not to accept a case. Paralegals may screen prospective clients upon instruction by attorneys in limited and specific instances. For instance, if a person calls the law office requesting representation in a personal injury matter, and the law office limits its practice to family law, the paralegal may communicate this information to the caller without referring the call to the attorney.

Setting and Collecting Fees It is the attorney's responsibility to set or establish fees for legal services or collect fees from delinquent clients. While a paralegal may not determine the actual fee charged for a specific legal service, a paralegal may, in jurisdictions where permitted, quote standard legal fees where the attorney has already established the price. This may be permissible in situations where flat or fixed fees are charged. A paralegal may also quote fees to prospective clients with the attorney's permission to pass on such information. The paralegal should inform the client, however, that only the attorney can enter into a contract for representation with the client and that the standard fee quoted may be subject to change depending on the needs of the case. It is important to know your state's rules regarding a paralegal's ability to quote fees as well as engaging in a discussion with your supervising attorney as to whether he or she will permit this practice in your office.

Client billing and collection of fees from delinquent clients is considered by most attorneys to be an administrative or clerical task that is often delegated to paralegals, secretaries, or office managers. Interestingly, most grievances filed by clients to state bar associations, especially those involving family law matters, are over fee disputes. Therefore, as a protective measure, attorneys must supervise collections and delegate the function only to those in the office who can handle the process within the boundaries of the rules of ethics and state and federal fair debt collections practices. It is highly advisable for paralegals and other legal support staff who handle these functions to attend a continuing legal education course on understanding relevant laws and practices to avoid liability.

Maintaining an Office to Render Legal Services Only attorneys may operate an office for the practice of law. Many paralegals run paralegal services companies, which generally provide paralegal services to attorneys or law firms on an as-needed basis. When a paralegal is retained, the attorney or firm that hired the paralegal will supervise him or her. In some jurisdictions, paralegal businesses may prepare legal documents for nonattorney individuals but must be careful not to render legal advice in the course of providing this service.

Duty to Disclose Nonattorney Status It is the attorney's responsibility to identify the nonattorney status of his or her paralegals when introducing them to clients, opposing counsel, judges, and any other third parties. Conversely, a paralegal has the duty to identify his or her nonattorney status whenever meeting a third party for the first time. The reason for this requirement is so third parties do not assume that the paralegal is an attorney who is authorized to give legal advice. Paralegals in family law offices have a lot of client contact, and it is common for clients to find the paralegal much more accessible than the attorney. A family law practitioner is often in court trying cases or arguing motions, so the paralegal is often in the position of liaison between the two. It is very important for paralegals to make it clear to clients that they are unauthorized to give legal advice.

EXAMPLE: FLORIDA'S UPL STATUTE

Florida Statutes Annotated[*]

454.23 Penalties.—Any person not licensed or otherwise authorized to practice law in this state who practices law in this state or holds himself or herself out to the public as qualified to practice law in this state, or who willfully pretends to be, or willfully takes or uses any name, title, addition, or description implying that he or she is qualified, or recognized by law as qualified, to practice law in this state, commits a felony of the third degree, punishable as provided in s. 775.082, s. 775.083, or s. 775.084.

---

[*]Florida Statutes Annotated, 454.23. Penalties, Title XXXII—Regulation of Professions and Occupations, Chapter 454—Attorneys at Law, State of Florida.

Concept Review and Reinforcement

KEY TERMS

Administrative Procedure Act
attorney–client privilege
authorized practice of law
billable hours
code
competency
complaint
confidentiality
conflict of interest
contingent fees
costs of litigation
deep pocket
disciplinary board
earned retainer
ethical wall
fees
flat fee
former client–current opponent

freelance paralegal
grievance
grievance committees
hourly basis
integrated bar association
legal advice
limited scope retainer agreement
living expenses
Model Rules of Professional
    Conduct (MRPC)
multiple representation
National Association of Legal
    Assistants (NALA)
National Federation of Paralegal
    Associations (NFPA)
padding
premium
pro hac vice

pro per
pro se
reciprocity
release
respondeat superior
retainer
rules of ethics
sanction
solicitation
time sheet
time slip
unauthorized practice of
    law (UPL)
unbundled legal services
    (discrete tasks representation)
unearned retainer
vicariously liable
work product

REVIEW OF KEY CONCEPTS

1. What are some of the ethical issues that arise in the area of family law practice?

2. What is the unauthorized practice of law, and what steps can the paralegal take to avoid practicing law without a license?

3. What are some of the ethical considerations that a family law practitioner must take into account when dealing with a *pro se* or *pro per* litigant as the opposing party?

4. What are the ethical issues involved in performing unbundled legal services for clients?

5. What is the difference between client confidentiality and the attorney–client privilege?

6. What precautions must a paralegal take when using electronic mail to avoid breaches of client confidentiality?

BUILDING YOUR PARALEGAL SKILLS

CASE FOR BRIEFING

OHIO STATE BAR ASSN. v. COHEN, 107 OHIO

Critical Thinking and Legal Analysis Applications

1. Using the Internet or a legal research website, look up your state's UPL statute. Based on the events recited in *Ohio State Bar Assn. v. Cohen*, 107 Ohio St.3d 98, 836 N.E.2d 1219 (2005) and your state's UPL statute, write a judicial opinion indicating how a court in your state would decide this case.

2. You have been hired as a paralegal for the law office of Eileen Strauss. Attorney Strauss has a busy family law practice and asks you to go to court and argue a motion to modify child support on behalf of Mrs. Wanda Martinez. She also wants you to ask for a continuance in the matter of *Sykes v. Sykes,* which is also scheduled to be heard that morning. Based on the UPL statute and relevant case law in your jurisdiction, does your state law permit a nonattorney to represent a client in court? Explain your answer.

Building a Professional Portfolio

PORTFOLIO **EXERCISES**

1. You work as a paralegal for the law office of Jonathan Coleman. Attorney Coleman just interviewed Lorraine Newsome, a client who wants to represent herself *pro se* in a divorce matter. She would like to hire attorney Coleman for the limited purpose of giving her legal advice at different stages of the case. She is a businesswoman and has enough savvy to see the case through. Attorney Coleman has asked you to prepare a limited scope retainer agreement in which he agrees to give Mrs. Newsome legal advice on an as-needed basis for a fixed fee of $250.00 per hour. You have never drafted one of these documents, so you may want to check out the Internet as a starting point.

2. You work as a paralegal for Marie Chase, an attorney who was just admitted to the Texas bar. She wants to include you on her letterhead and business cards. Read the following ethics opinion and write attorney Chase a memo regarding your findings on this issue. Go to the Internet and read Opinion 403 (Tex. Comm. on Professional Ethics, Op. 403, V. 45 Tex. B.J. 78 [1982]).

Chapter **thirteen**

THE CLIENT INTERVIEW

LEARNING OBJECTIVES

After studying this chapter, you should be able to:

1. Understand the emotional aspects of family law practice.

2. Recognize the importance of referring clients to appropriate support services when necessary.

3. Describe the role of the paralegal in the client interview process.

4. Identify and describe the essential information that must be obtained from a client during the initial interview.

The family law legal process begins with a potential client contacting the law office for the purpose of obtaining legal representation. Clients seek the assistance of an attorney in obtaining dissolutions of marriage, custody, visitation, child support, adoptions, relief from domestic violence, appeals, and very often postjudgment remedies such as contempt and modification proceedings. A good understanding of the emotionality involved in family matters is also essential in approaching client relations with patience and understanding.

PRELIMINARY PRACTICE ESSENTIALS

Developing a Relationship of Trust and Confidence

One of the most important goals of the client interview is developing a relationship of trust and confidence with the client. At the beginning of the interview, the client should be assured that all communications with the office are strictly confidential. While the ethical standard of confidentiality applies to any situation in which an attorney–client relationship has been established, it is particularly important to verbally explain this duty to a client, especially a family law client. Divorce or family-related matters may present very sensitive issues that a client may be too embarrassed to discuss with an attorney or paralegal. Assure the client that the information will not be disclosed to third parties unless the client has consented or the disclosure is required by one of the exceptions to the confidentiality rule. A thorough knowledge of your state's confidentiality rule is extremely important.

An efficiently managed law office and a competent staff responding to clients' needs also help inspire trust and confidence. Returning phone calls and following through on promises made to clients are essential. If you have told a client that documents will be forwarded for her review, do so. Take good notes when speaking with a client, either in person or on the telephone. Transfer any tasks to be completed on behalf of the client to your "Things to Do" list. This will ensure that this information will not get lost and that these tasks will be completed. Attorneys are very busy and may also need to be reminded to complete certain tasks or return a client's phone call.

Maintaining a High Degree of Professionalism

At all times during *any* client contact, the paralegal should maintain a professional demeanor. There may be a tendency on the part of attorneys and paralegals to want to befriend a client going through a difficult process; however, it is important that boundaries be set with the client to keep the relationship on a professional level. Paralegals should never discuss personal information with the client, either about themselves, the attorney, or the law firm. This includes home phone numbers, home addresses, and personal information irrelevant to the client's case.

Paralegals should also refrain from making moral judgments about clients and telling them what to do with their lives. The paralegal must always remember that the goal of the law office is to process the client's matter and achieve the client's ultimate legal goals. Mental health professionals or the client's support network should provide for the client's other needs.

Developing Good Listening Skills

A good interviewer develops good interviewing and listening skills over time with a variety of clients. It is impossible for a legal professional to prepare a scripted interview, since a client's recitation of their legal matter can take many turns. Such an approach can sound "canned" and lacks authenticity, which will be very transparent and insulting to the client. There are, however, some techniques that are worth discussing and applying when interviewing a client. One such technique is active listening. When interviewing a client, it is important to pay close attention to what he or she is saying and to convey to him or her that you are actually listening. If the interviewer is not engaged in the interview, the mind may wander and vital information that could be useful to the client's case will be missed. The following are some guidelines to help you develop active listening skills:

1. **Refrain from passing judgment on your clients.** You will encounter clients with a wide range of life experiences and backgrounds that may conflict with your own values. It is not your function to judge the client but rather to assist the attorney in the client's representation. You may empathize with the client, if appropriate, but refrain from expressing an opinion on his or her choices or lifestyle.

2. **Be aware of your body language.** We communicate nonverbally through the use of our bodies. As interviewers, it is important that we maintain eye contact with the client. If you keep looking at the clock, for instance, it may show that you are either bored or in a rush. Maintaining eye contact shows that you are interested in what the client has to say. Another way to show a client that you are engaged in the conversation is to be conscious of your body position. Avoid placing barriers (i.e., a desk) between you and the client. Sit across from the client at a reasonable distance and lean forward to show interest. Clients also communicate with body language. There are numerous books on the market that can help you learn how to interpret visual cues and how to respond to them.

3. **Provide feedback.** Repeat some key facts back to the client or summarize a series of events. Politely do this during a break in the conversation. This conveys that you are actually hearing what the client is saying and gives him or her the opportunity to correct any misunderstandings.

4. **Empathize with your clients.** Be sensitive to your client's emotional needs and acknowledge his or her feelings. Do not, however, share your personal experiences. Not only is this unprofessional, but getting too personal also will disrupt your professional relationships. If you find that interviewing divorce clients raises certain issues in your own life, seek professional help or a support group.

Understanding the Emotional Aspects of Family Law

Before proceeding further with a discussion of the interview process, it is important for the paralegal to comprehend the emotional aspects of divorce. Marriages, marriage alternatives, and romantic relationships are entered into with high expectations. They can range from mutual promises to be faithful to each other and stay together forever, to somber resolves to maintain a sober and responsible lifestyle, to undying pledges to always be there for each other to provide emotional support, financial support, intimacy, companionship, love, caring, and mutual respect. When a client is at the threshold of seeking representation in a legal matter, it is important to understand that some of the expectations of marriage have been shattered in one way or another.

An impending divorce or breakup signals the rupture of a dream. This event can literally turn a client's life upside down and start the client on an emotional roller coaster. Throughout the process, clients experience everything from anger, jealousy, rage, and hopelessness to depression, frustration, and distrust. Furthermore, the adversarial nature of our legal system and litigious family law practitioners can exacerbate an already volatile situation.

Referring Clients to Support Services

Paralegals will have contact with clients at various stages in the legal process, either by phone or in person. The paralegal should provide emotional support for a stressed-out client in a professional and limited manner. While a paralegal should acknowledge clients' feelings and give them an opportunity to express themselves, it may be appropriate, in some cases, to refer a client to a therapist or support group. It is not the function of the law office to provide therapeutic services to clients. The law office must remain within the confines of its role to provide legal services efficiently and competently and to refer clients to therapists when they are in need of professional mental health services.

A discussion with the supervising attorney is essential when there is a concern on the part of the paralegal regarding the client's need for support services. Referring a client to a therapist or support group must be done in a sensitive, diplomatic manner to avoid insulting or talking down to a client. Fortunately, the stigma of consulting a counseling professional or support group has waned in recent years, but it still may be difficult for some clients to accept. A good way to broach the subject is to ask clients if they think it would help them to talk to someone about their feelings. It is also helpful to convey to the client that during periods of extreme stress, many individuals seek the professional help of an objective person who can provide them with some healing advice.

Encouraging a client to seek counseling can also help the client cope throughout the legal process, which will have its ups and downs. The client who is getting professional help and has a sounding board will be stronger and better emotionally able to handle the legal process. This client will rely less on the divorce process to solve his or her emotional problems. This client will also rely less on the legal staff to address his or her emotional needs, thus allowing the law office to concentrate on the client's legal matter.

A family law paralegal should become familiar with the local services available to clients. Internet websites, local newspapers, hotline telephone information lines, and hospitals can provide appropriate referrals. A client should also be encouraged to explore his or her medical insurance coverage to determine whether or not such services are provided under his or her plan. If insurance will not cover therapy or the client is without insurance and cannot afford to pay a private therapist, the law office can make the client aware of agencies that offer sliding-scale counseling services and of community support groups that are free or charge a nominal fee to help defray the cost of the meeting space.

The paralegal should create a list of resources in the firm's database, updating it regularly, that provides a quick reference for client referrals in the law office's database. The list should include a variety of services for an array of client needs such as domestic violence services, twelve-step groups, substance abuse counselors, support groups, displaced homemaker services, mental health clinics, pastoral counselors, and private mental health counselors. Clients themselves may also have resources available to them that they have not considered. They may have had a friend who went through a family-related legal matter and can recommend either a therapist or support group. Other clients may be in the position to take advantage of employee assistance programs at their place of employment. If a client has religious affiliations, these institutions may also provide services or referrals to the client.

The paralegal should keep the following client information in the law office's database:

- name of agency,
- address,
- phone number,
- name of contact person, and
- what services are provided and their dates, times, and cost.

In addition to assisting and encouraging the client to seek professional help, an inquiry should also be made regarding the status of the children. Divorce and family

Figure 13-1 Many clients' first contact with a law office will be made via telephone.

Phovoir/Shutterstock.

conflicts are devastating for most children, and their needs should be addressed. These stressful events may have long-term effects on the children. In addition to information hotlines, schools may also provide resources such as support groups or art therapy for children whose parents are going through a divorce or breakup.

Many organizations or professionals may also provide the office with business cards or brochures describing their services, which can be distributed to clients.

THE PARALEGAL'S ROLE IN THE INITIAL SCREENING PROCESS

The client's first contact with the law office will ordinarily be through the telephone. Family law paralegals may often find themselves answering the phone and fielding phone calls from prospective clients. Clients may also make initial inquiries through the "Contact Us" section of a law firm's website. It is good business practice to contact the client by phone within a timely fashion in order to establish a personal connection.

Use of an *initial client intake form* will help the paralegal obtain important information during the prospective client's first call to the family law office (see Exhibit 13-1).

The initial client intake form will aid the paralegal in obtaining data from the client and relaying information to the client. In addition to the prospective client's name, address, phone number, and reasons for seeking an attorney, the paralegal may:

1. Schedule an appointment for the client with the attorney, and log the appointment in the office's master calendar system such as Abacus, and in the attorney's individual daily diary, desk calendar, Blackberry, iPhone, or other portable electronic device. Even though we are in the electronic age,

Exhibit 13-1 Sample initial telephone interview.

Client Intake Form Initial Telephone Interview/Family Matters

Date: _____

Interviewed by: _____

Referred by: _____Friend/coworker/relative
                _____Legal referral source
                _____Yellow Pages
                _____Website
                _____Bar association
                _____Other:_____

1. Client's Name: _____
   Address: _____
   City/State/Zip: _____
   Phone: Work _____   Home _____

2. Reason for Calling: Dissolution _____   Postjudgment _____

3. Client's Occupation: _____
   Employer: _____
   Yearly income: _____

4. Length of Marriage: _____   Date Married: _____

5. Number of Children and Ages: _____

6. Brief Description of Assets: _____

7. Are there issues of: _____ adultery _____ alcoholism/drug abuse _____ domestic violence _____ gambling

8. Initial appointment scheduled for: Date: _____ Time: _____
                                With Attorney: _____

   Inform the client of the following:
        Directions to the office and parking instructions
        Bring the following documents: _____ Marriage certificate
                                        _____ Copy of deed
                                        _____ Current pay stub
                                        _____ Income tax returns
                                        _____ Police incident reports
                                        _____ List of assets and debts
                                        _____ Certified copy of judgment (if postjudgment)
                                        _____ Separation agreement (if postjudgment)

---

legal malpractice carriers still require attorneys to have some type of paper backup system for emergencies.
2. Ask the prospective client to identify the names of all of the participants involved in the case. In family matters, the parties are usually spouses, unmarried couples/parents, and in some situations, third parties seeking custody of the children. The client should be informed that the firm will

Conflict of interest
Any activity that may divide the attorney's loyalty and compromise his or her independent judgment.

Conflicting out
Where a prospective divorce client engages in the practice of interviewing all the available family law attorneys in a geographical area for the purpose of disqualifying them from representing the other spouse.

be checking for *conflicts of interest*. If your supervising attorney or the law firm has either consulted or represented with another party involved in the case, he or she may be unable to represent this prospective client. This rule also applies to attorneys or paralegals who may have worked on cases in other firms and now the former client becomes the current opponent. The reasoning behind this requirement is once a client reveals confidential information, an attorney–client relationship is created, and it is unethical to represent another client where such representation could adversely affect a current or former client. A very common practice in divorce cases is called *conflicting out* the top family attorneys in the area for the sole purpose of making it difficult for a spouse to hire one of the best practitioners. For example, in January 2012, it was reported in the popular press that fashion model Heidi Klum conducted interviews with Hollywood's top divorce attorneys, well known for representing celebrity clients. Seal, Klum's husband, could not hire any of these attorneys to represent him in their divorce. The confidential information obtained during Klum's interview created an attorney–client relationship, and that information could potentially be used against *her* if Seal were taken on as client. Therefore, the client should be informed that a conflict-of-interest check will be done to determine if representation is possible. Conflict checks are often conducted by the paralegals in the office.

3. Inform the client of the cost of an initial consultation (which is determined by the attorney). If the initial consultation is free, inform the client of the time limits of this initial meeting. If there is any charge for any portion of the interview, the client should know in advance.

4. Give the client travel instructions to the office and tell the client where to park. Many law firm websites include directions to the office or a link to travel-related websites such as MapQuest. Be courteous and ask the client if they would like directions over the phone. Not all clients have access to computers, and some may be annoyed at being referred to the website for directions.

5. If the prospective client was served with legal papers or has received any correspondence regarding possible litigation, tell the client to bring this material to the initial interview.

6. Confirm the client's appointment with the attorney with an appointment confirmation. Make sure to check with the client regarding the best avenue for contacting the client before the appointment. Does the client mind a phone call, snail mail, or e-mail? It is important to check so that client confidentiality is not breached in the process.

PREPARING FOR THE INITIAL CLIENT INTERVIEW

Initial client interview
The first meeting between a client and an attorney or paralegal at which basic information to start work on a case is gathered.

Assuming there are no conflicts of interest that would bar representation of the prospective client, the next step in the divorce process is the *initial client interview*. The initial interview is the first meeting between the client and the attorney.

The purposes of the initial interview are as follows:

1. To give the client the opportunity to meet the attorney
2. To give the client some preliminary legal advice regarding his problem
3. To give the attorney and the attorney's support staff (the attorney's secretary, paralegal, and law clerks) an opportunity to become acquainted with the client
4. To enable the attorney to establish a relationship of trust and confidence with the client

5. To give the attorney the opportunity to discuss fees and fee payment arrangements with the client, and to determine and communicate to the client the scope of the attorney's representation

6. To give the attorney the chance to assess the client's needs and determine whether he or she is willing and able to represent this particular client

7. To enable the attorney to obtain enough information to commence the client's legal action

No set rule dictates who should conduct the initial client interview. It will depend on the preference of the supervising attorney or, in an emergency situation, who is available. In some offices, the attorney will conduct the initial interview; in others, the paralegal will be the first person with whom the client has contact. The most ideal situation is to have both the attorney and the paralegal available for the client.

The presence of the attorney during the initial client interview is extremely important. Attorneys can perform a function that a paralegal cannot: give *legal advice*. Clients seeking a divorce from a spouse will have many questions regarding how the law will impact *their* particular case and how it will affect *their* family. *Legal advice can be provided only by an attorney.* Giving legal advice means that you are applying the law to a particular client's particular circumstances and either predicting an outcome or advising the client to take a particular course of action. A paralegal may relay legal advice from the lawyer to the client, may provide nonlegal advice, and may give information by describing the law. Once the paralegal has applied the specific facts of the client's case, the paralegal has crossed the line into the unauthorized practice of law. Any paralegal conducting *any* client interview must be very careful to refrain from giving legal advice to the client.

Legal advice
Advising a client of his or her specific legal rights and responsibilities and either predicting an outcome or recommending that the client pursue a particular course of action.

In offices where the attorney conducts the initial interview, the attorney will obtain enough information to commence the representation of the client. This information will then be passed on to the paralegal, who will begin the drafting of the initial pleadings. Sometimes the attorney will introduce the paralegal to the client so they may become acquainted and the role of the paralegal in the representation of the client can be explained.

In some law offices, both the attorney and paralegal are present at the initial interview. This enables the client to observe the attorney and paralegal as a team working toward the client's representation. The attorney can explain the paralegal's role and allow the client and paralegal to form a professional relationship that will benefit the client. Because family attorneys are often in court representing clients, the client may find the paralegal more accessible. The paralegal will have a considerable amount of contact with the client during the divorce process for purposes of gathering information, drafting documents, answering client phone calls, and relaying messages from the attorney. A client's ability to communicate with the attorney, even through the paralegal, will increase the client's satisfaction and decrease his or her level of anxiety. A client who has to wait until the attorney gets around to answering his or her phone calls or attending to his or her case will be a frustrated and dissatisfied customer.

In some law offices, the paralegal will conduct the initial interview. In this situation, the paralegal must be ever so careful not to render legal advice in the course of the interview. Even though a paralegal may know the answer to the client's question and be 100 percent correct, he or she must resist the temptation. In some instances, either unexpected or planned, the paralegal may be conducting the initial interview alone. For instance, a client will have a scheduled appointment with the attorney and the attorney is delayed in court. If this happens, the paralegal should contact the client to reschedule the appointment. If the client is already en route to the office, the paralegal will have to take over the initial interview. The paralegal should politely explain that the attorney has been delayed and that he or she will instead obtain all the necessary information, but that the client will be contacted later that day by the attorney, who will answer all legal questions.

The paralegal should make adequate preparations for the client interview. Determine the scope of the interview with your supervisor. Is the client seeking a divorce, child custody, child support, or visitation, or is it a postjudgment matter? Next, make sure that the interviewing room or area is private, neat, and free from confidential information pertaining to other clients. Facial tissues are also important to have on hand in case the client becomes emotional. You will also need a copy of the preprinted form used by your office, a legal pad for notes, and any releases or other documents necessary.

The actual time and date of the interview will have been set in advance at the time the client made the initial contact with the office. The paralegal should check the office calendar in order to refresh his recollection as to the name of the client and the date and time of the appointment.

THE CLIENT INTERVIEW

The Client's Arrival

When the client arrives, make sure that you are not interrupted. Greet the client with a smile and a handshake. Introduce yourself and identify your paralegal status. Take the client's coat and engage in small talk in order to put the client at ease. Chatting about the weather or asking if the client had difficulty locating the office are some ways of initiating a conversation. Many offices keep hot and cold beverages for their clients' enjoyment. Offer the client something to drink if this is the procedure in your office.

The Actual Interview

At the outset of the interview, the paralegal should explain his or her role in the family law office. Some clients will not be familiar with the paralegal profession and will need to be educated on what services the paralegal provides under the supervision of an attorney. The paralegal should also make it clear to the client that he or she cannot give legal advice. The issue of confidentiality should also be addressed. The client should be ensured that all communications made to any law office personnel are confidential, barring certain exceptions particular to the jurisdiction's rules of ethics.

It is also important to encourage the client to disclose all information, whether positive or negative, to the attorney and paralegal. Clients will often withhold embarrassing or damaging information for fear of being judged by the interviewer. It is imperative that the client disclose any information that can impact the divorce proceedings. If the attorney is made aware of this information in advance, he or she will be better equipped to deal with it instead of being surprised on the day of trial or having the opposing side ambush him or her in the course of negotiation. Learning about negative information at an advanced stage in the proceedings may be too late, and the attorney may be unable to counteract its effects.

Once the client is comfortably seated, the paralegal may encourage him or her to give a brief synopsis of the problem. At this time, the paralegal should not take notes, because it is important to actively listen and develop a trust relationship with the client. The paralegal should get a general idea of what caused the breakdown of the marriage, the extent of the marital estate, and the number and ages of the children. The use of recording devices should be avoided because the interviewer tends to relax and be less active if he or she is aware that a machine is preserving the data. This will make him or her less interactive with the client, and he or she may fail to ask probing questions.

Once some general information has been exchanged, the paralegal should tell the client that he or she will have to obtain some essential information in order for the office to adequately represent the client. Then the paralegal can use a pre-printed form as a guideline for obtaining the necessary information. Moving to the use of a form too quickly may insult a client and give him or her the impression that the office is sterile and uncaring.

The client's communication level will dictate how you approach the interview. Some clients are more verbal than others. For clients who talk too much, it is important to focus them on the purpose of the interview. Others are very nervous and need to be prompted with a lot of questions. Give the client an overview of the interview process and tell him or her that it is important that you hear his or her story and collect the necessary data. Tell the client that you will be taking notes so that you can preserve the information for the file.

Gathering Information Start with open-ended questions that will elicit more than a one-word response. For instance:

- "You contacted us about a divorce matter. Could you tell me what is going on in your marriage?"
- "What can we help you with today?"

These questions will encourage the client to start talking.

Figure 13-2 A paralegal may conduct the initial interview but must refrain from ever giving legal advice.

Wavebreakmedia/Shutterstock.

Jot down notes about questions or areas on which you may want the client to elaborate.

Narrowing Issues   Once you have a general idea of the client's situation, it is time to focus on specific issues. For example:

- "Can you elaborate on your child's educational problems?"
- "You mentioned that your wife was unfaithful during your marriage. Can you be more specific?"

Once you have a general picture of the marriage and the causes of the breakdown, it is now time to focus on the preprinted form. Say to the client, "I think I have enough for now. I'd like to go through our questionnaire so that we can take down some important information the attorney will need in order to adequately represent you."

Concluding the Interview Tell the client what will happen next: "I'll pass this information on to Attorney Jones" or "We'll draft the initial document and send you a copy." Take care of any documents that need to be signed at this time, such as releases or retainer agreements. (Retainer agreements are discussed later in this chapter.)

Explain to the clients what is expected from them. Do they need to gather additional information? Do they need to perform certain tasks? Ask the clients if they have any questions and tell them to feel free to call the office.

Whenever conducting a client interview, the interviewer must remember to obtain the essential information: where, when, who, what, why, and how. If a client has trouble remembering specific facts such as date, time, and place, it may be helpful to have the client go through his or her personal calendar, which may jar his or her memory. In addition to the initial interview, paralegals will often conduct subsequent follow-up interviews with the client during the course of the attorney's representation of the client. The basic skills of listening, actively asking questions, and gathering information from the client are equally as important in follow-up interviews.

OBTAINING ESSENTIAL INFORMATION FROM THE CLIENT

One of the primary purposes of the initial interview is to obtain enough information to commence representation of the client in his or her family matter. Most family law offices use preprinted initial intake sheets to garner these facts from the client (see Exhibit 13-2).

The advantage of a preprinted form is that the paralegal will not miss obtaining any relevant information because the form serves as a guideline. A legal pad should also be kept on hand to jot down other notes in the course of the interview.

Some paralegals may find themselves working for new attorneys or attorneys with very busy schedules who have not had the opportunity to draft preprinted forms. In such a case, the following is an overview of what information the initial interview should elicit about both spouses:

1. **Name.** The names of both the client spouse and the other spouse should be obtained and spelled correctly. The wife's maiden name should also be elicited.
2. **Current address.** Physical address is important for the purpose of personal or abode service. Post office boxes or mailbox services are not sufficient for service, but the client may request that correspondence be forwarded to a P.O. box for security purposes. For example, the client may fear that

Exhibit 13-2 Sample preprinted initial client interview form.

Client Intake Form
Initial Interview/Family Matters

Date: _____

Check one: _____ Dissolution of Marriage   Representing: _____ Plaintiff

_____ Legal Separation   _____ Defendant

_____ Annulment   _____ Third party

_____ Postjudgment   Intervenor

_____ Access for Unmarried Parent

_____ Child Support by Unmarried Parent

I. *General Information:*

  A. Client's Name: _____   Maiden Name: _____

     Address: _____

     City/State/Zip: _____

     Phone: (Home) _____ (Work) _____ Best time to call: _____

     DOB: _____ Place of birth: _____

     SSN: _____ Race: _____

     Education: _____ Military Service: _____

  B. Spouse's/Partner's Name: _____ Maiden Name: _____

     Address: _____

     City/State/Zip: _____

     Phone: (Home) _____ (Work) _____

     Best time to call: _____

     DOB: _____ Place of birth: _____

     SSN: _____ Race: _____

     Education: _____ Military Service: _____

     Represented by: _____

                     _____

                     _____

II. *History of the Marriage:*

  A. Place of marriage: _____

     Date of marriage: _____ Date of separation: _____

     Reason for breakdown: _____

  B. Children born of the marriage/relationship:

     Name   D.O.B.   Birthplace

     _____

     _____

     _____

     Is wife currently pregnant? _____ Yes _____ No

continued

Exhibit 13-2 Continued

C. Public Assistance:

Have you or your spouse ever received public assistance? _____

Are you or your spouse currently receiving public assistance? _____

D. Employment:

Client's Employer: _____

    Address: _____

    City/State/Zip: _____

Occupation: _____

Years Employed: _____ Salary: _____

Benefits: _____

Spouse's Employer: _____

    Address: _____

    City/State/Zip: _____

Occupation: _____

Years Employed: _____ Salary: _____

Benefits: _____

E. What would you describe as the cause of the breakdown of your marriage?

    Have you or your spouse/partner sought professional counseling?

    Is there any hope of reconciliation?

    Did you sign a prenuptial agreement?

F. Have you or your spouse had any prior marriages?

G. Disability/Illness (either spouse/children): _____

H. How long have you resided in this state?

III. *Client Claims:*

Pendente lite	*Final orders*
_____ Alimony	_____ Dissolution of marriage
_____ Child custody	_____ Legal separation
_____ Child support	_____ Annulment
_____ Access/Visitation	_____ Alimony
_____ Attorney's fees	_____ Property division
_____ Exclusive possession of the marital residence	_____ Child custody _____ Sole
	_____ Joint
_____ Restraining order	_____ Access/Visitation
_____ Other	_____ Attorney's fees
_____	_____ Name change to: _____
	_____ Contempt citation
	_____ Modification
	_____ Other:
	_____

IV. *Postjudgment Matters*

Contempt Citations

Date of the original order: _____

Court where order entered: _____

Original order:_____

Date of last payment: _____

Modification:

Date of the original order: _____

Court where order entered: _____

Original order: _____

Modification sought: _____

Specify the substantial change in circumstances since the date of the original order:

V. *Service of Process*

Where to serve spouse: _____

Best time to serve: _____a.m./p.m.

Brief description of spouse: _____

_____

Description of spouse's car: _____

VI. *Documents to Prepare*

_____ Summons/complaint   ____ Financial affidavit

_____ Temporary motions   ____ *Lis pendens*

_____ Subpoena   ____ Contempt citation

_____ Reopen and modify judgment

_____ Other: _____

VII. *Legal Fees*

Fee quoted: $_____   Costs: $_____

Initial retainer amount required before services are commenced: $_____

Terms of payment: _____

Fee agreement signed? ____ Yes ____ No

VIII. *Referral Source*

_____Friend/coworker/relative   ____ Legal referral service

_____Yellow Pages   ____ Bar association

_____ Other: _____

his or her correspondence will be intercepted by his or her spouse or other third party. The office should have a system of alerting any office personnel who happen to pick up the file on any given day that care should be taken in terms of forwarding correspondence to the client, perhaps using a special colored sticker to serve as a "red flag." You may also wish to obtain the client's e-mail address and ask for permission to forward correspondence from the law office electronically.

3. **Telephone numbers.** Obtain home, cell, and work numbers. Sometimes clients cannot receive phone calls at work, so you should avoid making calls to their workplace, except in emergency situations. On the other hand, some clients may not be comfortable receiving calls at home if they are still residing with their spouse, especially in cases where domestic violence is a problem. Clients may also request that you leave phone messages with family members or friends to keep attorney communications confidential.

4. **Jurisdiction.** How long has the client resided in the state? Each state has a jurisdictional requirement indicating how long a party must reside in the state before the state courts have the power to dissolve the marriage or hear a family-related matter.

5. **Social Security numbers.** Social Security numbers are useful for many reasons. Some jurisdictions may require Social Security numbers on initial pleadings. They are also important for tax purposes or when engaging the services of an investigator to conduct asset searches or track down a "deadbeat" parent. Social Security numbers are also useful in debt collection proceedings against delinquent clients.

6. **Military service.** Did either spouse serve in the military? This question is important because military pensions may qualify as marital property. Also, if a spouse is currently in the military, care must be taken so service of process will be adequate.

7. **Employer.** Where is the client employed? What is the address? What is the client's occupation? How long has the client been employed in his or her current position? Similarly, where is the client's spouse employed, and what is his or her occupation? This information will be helpful for purposes of service, subpoenaing employment records, and obtaining pension information.

8. **Date and place of marriage.** This will establish where and when the marriage took place, if the client is seeking a divorce.

9. **Education, race, and age.** These data may be necessary for statistical information to be made available to the state's bureau of vital statistics. Education will also indicate how far a client has gone through school, which may be relevant in terms of his or her ability to earn income.

10. **City or state welfare assistance.** Has the state or city welfare system ever provided financial support for the spouse and the children? Many jurisdictions require this information and require that the governmental entity be notified of the proceedings and appear for purposes of collecting monies owed to them.

11. **Date of separation.** When did the parties separate, and what were the reasons for the separation?

12. **Cause of breakdown of the marriage.** All jurisdictions have adopted some form of no-fault divorce where the grounds for divorce are commonly referred to as irretrievable breakdown or irreconcilable differences. It is still important, however, to elicit the cause of the breakdown of the marriage from the client.

13. **Reconciliation.** Is there any hope of reconciliation? Divorce is a devastating life event, not only for the spouses but also, and more important, for the children. It is the ethical responsibility of the attorney or paralegal to make sure that a divorce is what the client wants. Most clients who have made their way to an attorney's office are confident in their decision to dissolve the marriage. A client who is reluctant or may be having second thoughts should be encouraged to seek professional counseling services.

14. **Children.** How many children were born during the marriage? What are their names and dates of birth? Were any children born to the spouses prior to their marriage? Were there any children born to the spouses during the marriage who are not issue of the marriage? Is the wife pregnant? It is also important to obtain information regarding the children's birthdates if the parties share a child in common. These questions are important to ask for the purpose of allocating child support responsibilities and determining the custody and visitation rights of the parents. Paternity may also be at issue if challenged.

15. **Previous marriage(s).** Was either of the parties previously married? How, why, and when did the previous marriage(s) end? Is the spouse or parent currently paying alimony or child support pursuant to a court order? What, if any, orders are in effect?

16. **Prenuptial agreement.** Did the parties sign a prenuptial agreement? If the answer is yes, be sure to obtain a copy from the client. The existence of a prenuptial agreement will raise several issues. Is the agreement valid? What rights did the parties give up? What did they obligate themselves to do? If the parties lived together and were not legally married, did they execute a cohabitation agreement or any other document binding the parties to any legal obligation? If so, it is important to obtain copies.

17. **Was a divorce action previously initiated in the course of this marriage?** If the client tells you that a divorce was previously initiated, the paralegal should review any paperwork the client may have. The paralegal should then follow it up with a review of the court file in the appropriate courthouse where the actions were filed. The client may be surprised to find out that he or she may already be divorced or that the initial pleadings may have been filed. If the file is still active, a client seeking a divorce may save on filing and sheriff's fees. If this is the case, the filing of responses will be sufficient.

18. **Disability/illness.** The interviewer should ask whether either spouse or children suffer from any disabilities or illnesses. Issues regarding medical care and expenses, insurance coverage, and support may require special attention.

19. **Date of the interview.** When did the interview take place?

20. **Name of the interviewer.** Who conducted the interview?

21. **Source of referral.** Who referred the client to the attorney? This will help track the attorney's advertising dollars and zero in on where business is being generated. Thank-you cards or letters should be sent to individuals and organizations who refer business to the office; however, permission of the client is necessary so there are no breaches of client confidentiality.

22. **Legal fees.** If the attorney is conducting the interview, he or she will quote the client a fee for his or her services. If the paralegal is conducting the interview, he or she cannot quote a fee. Remember that a paralegal cannot set fees; this is the attorney's responsibility. In this instance, inform the client that he or she can discuss the fee structure with the attorney.

23. **Type of relief.** The interviewer should ask the client what type of legal relief he or she is seeking as a result of the family action. First and foremost, the attorney must determine the legal cause of action to be filed. Does the client want a dissolution of marriage, legal separation, or annulment? An attorney's legal advice is essential in making this selection. Additional relief includes child custody, child support, property and debt distribution, alimony, and attorney's fees. If the parties are not married, the client may be seeking child custody, child support, visitation, relief from abuse, or a determination of paternity.

24. **Name change.** A wife may seek to resume the use of her maiden name as part of the final divorce decree. It was a long-standing custom for women to assume their husband's surname upon marriage. Some states went as far as requiring women to assume their husband's last names through court decisions. Gender discrimination laws, however, prohibit this judicial mandate. The Equal Protection Clause of the U.S. Constitution prohibits states from requiring women to assume the husband's surname since there is no rational basis for women, but not men, to change their last names upon marriage. Today, women are free to follow custom or to retain their own maiden names. Some couples create a new last name using the wife's maiden name and the husband's surname. A married woman's legal name is determined by what she actually calls herself *after* the marriage ceremony. She is basically free to use whatever she pleases as long as her choice is not intended to defraud her creditors or use her name for unlawful purposes. In preparing the initial divorce pleadings, the wife may include restoration of her maiden name in her prayer for relief. The court will automatically grant the wife's wishes despite objections from the husband. Some women choose to retain their husband's surname as a matter of preference. Many women with young children choose to retain their married name until the children have finished school and may later return to court to restore their maiden name. Change of name after the divorce is final is considered a postjudgment matter. The wife must file a petition in the proper state court. A hearing date is scheduled by the court and a notice is published in the legal section of the newspaper. Courts generally allow former spouses to change their names as long as the change is not being made to advance fraudulent or illegal purposes. The wife must then obtain a certified copy of the court's final decree and notify her creditors and the Social Security Administration of the change. The children of the marriage will also assume their biological father's last name. Problems arise when the wife remarries. Sometimes the children develop a close relationship with their new stepfather and wish to take his name. The mother may also push for a change of the children's last names for various reasons. Because the change of names, even for minor children, requires a court hearing, the biological father must be notified of the proceedings. If the parties disagree regarding the children's name change, the court will have to decide. The court will determine whether the name change is in the children's best interest. The court will focus on the wishes of the parents, stepparent, and children and on the name that has been historically used by the child. While the best-interest standard is often applied, many courts still believe that it is in the children's best interest to use their biological father's surname.

Whenever conducting any client interview, the interviewer must obtain the essential information: where, when, who, what, why, and how. If a client has trouble remembering specific facts such as date, time, and place, it may be helpful to have the client go through his personal calendar, which may jar his memory. In addition to the initial interview, paralegals will often conduct subsequent follow-up interviews with the client during the course of the attorney's representation of the client. The basic skills of listening, actively asking questions, and gathering information from the client are equally as important in follow-up interviews.

    Once the initial interview form has been completed, the attorney or paralegal may give the client a *financial worksheet* to take home and fill out (see Exhibit 13-3). This worksheet should focus on the client's income, expenses, assets, and liabilities, be they joint or separate. The financial worksheet will enable the attorney to begin assessing the extent of the marital estate.

Financial worksheet
Focuses on the client's income, expenses, assets, and liabilities, be they joint or separate; enables the attorney to begin assessing the extent of the marital estate.

Exhibit 13-3 Sample financial worksheet to determine assets and liabilities.

Financial Worksheet

Client's name: _____ Date: _____

I. *INCOME*
(Indicate weekly income and deductions. If paid monthly, divide monthly figure by 4.3 to determine weekly amount.)

A. Gross weekly income

Salary, wages, commissions	$_____
Bonuses	_____
Tips	_____
Pensions/retirement	_____
Public assistance	_____
Social Security	_____
Unemployment insurance	_____
Disability	_____
Dividends/interest	_____
Rental income	_____
Alimony/child support	_____
Other: _____	_____
TOTAL GROSS WEEKLY INCOME	$_____

B. Deductions

Federal withholding tax	$_____
State withholding tax	_____
F.I.C.A.	_____
Medicare	_____
Health insurance	_____
Union dues	_____
Credit union	_____
Pension	_____
Other: _____	_____

continued

Exhibit 13-3 Continued

TOTAL WEEKLY DEDUCTIONS $_____

TOTAL NET WEEKLY INCOME $_____
   (A minus B)

II. EXPENSES
Indicate weekly expenses. If expenses incurred on a monthly basis, divide monthly figure by 4.3 to determine weekly amount.)

A. Rent/Mortgage/Household

  1. Rent/mortgage $_____

  2. Homeowner's/renter's insurance   _____

  3. Property taxes   _____

  4. Household repairs   _____

  5. Trash collection   _____

  6. Other: _____   _____

TOTAL RENT/MORTGAGE/HOUSEHOLD $_____

B. Utilities

  1. Electricity $_____

  2. Heat   _____

  3. Gas   _____

  4. Telephone   _____

  5. Water   _____

  6. Cable TV   _____

  7. Other: _____ $_____

TOTAL UTILITIES $_____

C. Groceries $_____

D. Clothing $_____

E. Dry Cleaning/Laundry $_____

F. Transportation

  1. Car payments $_____

  2. Parking   _____

  3. Tolls   _____

  4. Gas/oil   _____

  5. Repairs   _____

  6. Car taxes   _____

  7. License/registration/emissions   _____

  8. Bus   _____

  9. Train   _____

  10. Car insurance   _____

  11. Other: _____   _____

TOTAL TRANSPORTATION $_____

G. Medical (out-of-pocket expenses)

    1. Medical insurance $_____

    2. Dental insurance   _____

    3. Doctor visits   _____

    4. Dentist visits   _____

    5. Prescriptions/medicine   _____

    6. Optometrist   _____

    7. Orthodontist   _____

    8. Counseling/therapy   _____

    9. Other:_____   _____

TOTAL MEDICAL $_____

H. Life Insurance Premium $_____

I. Children's Expenses

    1. School lunches $_____

    2. School books/school supplies   _____

    3. Tutors   _____

    4. School tuition   _____

    5. Camps   _____

    6. Class trips   _____

    7. Lessons (piano, karate, etc.)   _____

    8. Allowance   _____

    9. Religious instruction   _____

    10. Day care/babysitter   _____

TOTAL CHILDREN'S EXPENSES $_____

J. Payment on Outstanding Debts

    1. Credit cards: _____ $_____

                     _____   _____

                     _____   _____

                     _____   _____

    2. Student loans   _____

    3. Installment contracts   _____

    4. Personal loans   _____

TOTAL PAYMENTS ON OUTSTANDING DEBTS $_____

K. Miscellaneous Expenses

    1. Haircuts $_____

    2. Newspapers/magazines   _____

    3. Eyeglasses   _____

continued

Exhibit 13-3 Continued

    4. Charitable contributions   _____

    5. Subscriptions   _____

    6. Gifts   _____

    7. Bank fees   _____

    8. Postage   _____

    9. Vacations   _____

   10. Entertainment   _____

   11. Pet care   _____

   12. Cigarettes   _____

   13. Toiletries   _____

   14. Other:_____   _____

TOTAL MISCELLANEOUS EXPENSES $_____

TOTAL EXPENSES $_____

III. *ASSETS*

(Provide the following information for each home, vacation home, condominium, farm, or parcel of real estate.)

A. Real Estate:

1. Address: _____

    City/State/Zip: _____

2. Date acquired: _____

3. Mortgage institution: _____

4. How is property owned? (Specify exact names on deed.)

_____

_____

_____

5. Estimated value $_____

6. Outstanding mortgage   _____

7. Equity   _____

TOTAL REAL ESTATE $_____

(Include only your one-half undivided interest if property jointly owned.)

B. Bank/Checking Accounts

Name of Bank	Account Number	How Held (Joint or Individual)	Balance
			$_____
_____	_____	_____	_____
_____	_____	_____	_____
_____	_____	_____	_____
TOTAL BANK/CHECKING ACCOUNTS			$_____

C. Stocks and Bonds

Number of Shares	Company or Fund	Value
_____	_____	$_____
_____	_____	$_____
_____	_____	$_____
TOTAL STOCKS and BONDS		$_____

D. Deferred Compensation (401k, SEP, Keogh, IRA, etc.)

(Provide the following information for each plan.)

    1. Name of company: _____

    2. Name of plan: _____

    3. Account number: _____

    4. Estimated value: _____

    5. Name and address of plan administrator: _____

TOTAL DEFERRED COMPENSATION $ _____

E. Motor Vehicles (Provide the following information for each motor vehicle, including boats, airplanes, and motorcycles.)

    1. Year: _____

    2. Model: _____

    3. Estimated value $_____

    4. Loan balance   _____

    5. Equity   _____

TOTAL MOTOR VEHICLES $_____

F. Business Interests

    1. Name of business: _____

    2. Type of business: _____

    3. Type of business interest: _____ Sole proprietorship

                                                    _____ Partnership

                                                    _____ Limited liability corporation

                                                    _____ Professional corporation

                                                    _____ Joint venture

                                                    _____ Corporation

    4. Estimated value of your interest $_____

    TOTAL BUSINESS INTERESTS $_____

G. Insurance

Insured	Company	Beneficiary	Face Value	Cash Surrender Value
_____	_____	_____	$_____	$_____
_____	_____	_____	$_____	$_____
_____	_____	_____	$_____	$_____
TOTAL CASH SURRENDER VALUE (minus loans)				$_____

H. Personal Property

1. Household furniture $ _____

2. Antiques   _____

3. Jewelry   _____

4. Artwork   _____

5. Collectibles   _____

6. Stereo/electronic equipment   _____

7. Clothing   _____

8. Furs   _____

9. Family heirlooms   _____

10. Silver   _____

11. Crystal   _____

12. Other _____   _____

      _____   _____

      _____   _____

TOTAL PERSONAL PROPERTY $ _____

TOTAL ASSETS $ _____

IV. LIABILITIES

Outstanding Debts

Date Debt Incurred	Creditor	Incurred by Payment	Monthly	Current Balance
_____	_____	_____	$ _____	$ _____
_____	_____	_____	$ _____	$ _____
_____	_____	_____	$ _____	$ _____
_____	_____	_____	$ _____	$ _____
TOTAL LIABILITIES				$ _____

The client should also be instructed to write a history of the marriage, which will be helpful in illuminating issues that may be of relevance in the divorce action. The client should be instructed to complete these documents before the next meeting.

If the paralegal has conducted the interview without the attorney present, an appointment should be scheduled for a meeting with the attorney, which will enable the client to obtain legal advice and go over the material obtained by the paralegal at the initial interview. The attorney can also address the legal course of action to be taken and review the fee structure.

If the attorney has conducted the interview with or without the presence of the paralegal, he or she will now turn over the initial interview form to the paralegal for the purpose of having the paralegal draft the initial pleadings.

REPRESENTING THE DEFENDANT SPOUSE

In a family law practice, the office will be representing either the plaintiff or the defendant spouse. With a plaintiff spouse, the divorce proceedings are basically starting at square one, which requires the drafting and service of the writ, summons, and complaint. When representing the defendant spouse, the paralegal must make sure in the initial phone consultation to instruct the client to bring in any papers that were served on him or her and all correspondence received in conjunction with the divorce matter. At the initial interview, the paralegal must make sure to photocopy all paperwork the client brings, must determine whether service was properly made either through abode or in-hand service, and may also want to go over the complaint or petition with the client to determine whether the information contained is accurate. This will enable the paralegal to obtain the data necessary to prepare the responsive pleadings.

Preparing Releases

Another task the paralegal may be asked to perform is to prepare a release of information or have the client sign a preprinted release. As explained in Chapter 12, "Ethics in Family Law," the confidential relationship of the attorney and client, just as the doctor and patient relationship, prohibits the professional from disclosing information without the client's consent. In family matters, an attorney may need a client's consent to communicate with any one of the following:

- client's physician or therapist;
- children's pediatrician, teachers, or therapists;
- client's accountant;
- client's employer, physician, mental health service provider; and
- hospital or treatment centers.

The paralegal should be sure to check the federal and state statutes that concern the release of confidential information, especially when dealing with drug treatment or HIV- and AIDS-related information. Furthermore, the enactment of HIPAA, or the Health Insurance Portability and Accountability Act of 1996, has created a great deal of caution among many medical records departments. It is a good practice when seeking medical releases of client information to first contact the medical records department of the business entity where the client's records are located and inquire whether they require their own release form to be filled out rather than one scripted by the attorney's office. This will save a lot of time and delays in obtaining medical records that are necessary in family-related litigation. Medical releases drafted by law offices should also include HIPAA-compliant authorizations for release of patient information pursuant to 45 CFR 164.508.

THE RETAINER LETTER

Before the client interview ends, the supervising attorney will review the law office's fee schedule for providing legal services to clients. The law firm's projected costs for handling a dissolution matter or any other related family law matter should be disclosed, with realistic figures presented. The client should fully understand the financial obligation he or she is undertaking by retaining the law firm and must be willing to assume this obligation. The client must also feel comfortable in other respects with having that particular law firm provide representation. Similarly, the law firm and the individual attorney who will be in charge of the case must also feel comfortable taking on the client. Sometimes an attorney may have reservations about dealing with a particular client. The attorney may feel that the prospective client may not honor the financial arrangement to be made, or the attorney may sense that the client is not being honest in disclosing information about marital assets, in revealing events leading up to the dissolution, or in revealing events that could cause controversy about the client's fitness as a custodial parent. If, on the other hand, neither the attorney nor the prospective client has such reservations, then the relationship will be formalized. The law office will prepare a retainer letter for the prospective client to sign. Once this document is executed, the law firm will actively begin work on the client file.

A *retainer letter* or *retainer agreement* is a contract between the law firm and the client whereby the law firm agrees to provide specified legal services in exchange for monetary compensation (see Exhibit 13-4).

As discussed in an earlier chapter, there are different types of fee arrangements, such as flat fees, contingency fees, and hourly fees assessed for time spent working on the file.

Retainer letter
See retainer agreement.

Retainer agreement
A contract between the law firm and the client whereby the law firm agrees to provide specified legal services in exchange for monetary compensation; also known as a retainer letter.

Exhibit 13-4 Sample retainer agreement (author unknown).

Retainer Agreement

A. EVELYN BRONSON ("Client") hereby employs GRACE A. LUPPINO, an attorney licensed to practice law in the State of Connecticut ("Attorney"), to represent her in a dissolution of marriage action: RODNEY BRONSON v. EVELYN BRONSON, Docket No. FA 13-123456.

B. In consideration of the services rendered, the Client shall pay the Attorney in the following manner:

1. The Attorney shall commence work on the Client's dissolution matter upon receipt of an initial retainer of $3,000.00 (Three Thousand dollars) from the Client.

2. The total number of hours expended by the Attorney will be billed at a rate of $200.00 (Two Hundred dollars) per hour.

3. Upon expending the initial retainer, the Attorney shall bill the Client for any additional hours expended at a rate of $200.00 (Two Hundred dollars) per hour.

4. Upon completion or termination of the Attorney's representation of Client, the Attorney shall return any unearned retainer to the Client.

C. The Client shall pay for all costs and expenses incurred by the Attorney in the course of representing the Client. Costs and expenses include, but are not limited to, court entry fees, sheriff's fees, process server fees, transcripts, subpoenas, and expert witnesses.

D. The Client authorizes the Attorney to engage the services of accountants, appraisers, evaluators, investigators, court reporters, sheriffs, experts, and process servers deemed necessary by the Attorney in rendering legal services to the Client. (The Client shall be directly responsible for the fees and bills of these service providers.) The Attorney shall obtain the Client's approval prior to engaging the services of such persons or incurring such costs and expenses.

E. The Attorney shall bill the Client for all legal fees, costs, and expenses on a monthly basis. Such bill shall be paid by the Client within 30 days from the date of the invoice.

F. If this Agreement is terminated by the Client prior to completion of the Attorney's services, the Client shall pay any Attorney's fees, costs, and expenses accrued to that date.

G. The Attorney shall not be required to deliver any reports, investigations, appraisals, evaluations, or other documents prepared by third parties that have not been paid for by the Client.

H. In the event that the Attorney must enforce this Agreement through any legal collection proceedings, the Attorney shall be entitled to recover reasonable attorney's fees and court costs in conjunction with such proceeding.

The undersigned parties have read the above Agreement and agree to abide by its terms and conditions. Signed this _____ day of _____, 2018.

_____
Evelyn Bronson, Client

_____
Grace A. Luppino, Esq. Attorney

Most of the time, in a complex family matter, firms charge by the hour. When this is the case, the retainer letter will state the firm's hourly rate schedule. There may be one hourly rate specified for work done on the file by a partner, a different and lower hourly rate for work done by associates in the firm, and hourly rates listed for work done by paralegals and law clerks.

The retainer letter will also specify the terms of payment. If interest or late fees are to be charged for tardy payments, that fact will be stated and agreed to. Sometimes a retainer letter will state that if a client defaults on payment of a balance owed, the firm may take legal actions and the client will be responsible for attorney's fees and collection costs. The retainer letter, as a contract, is signed by both parties. Each party has rights and obligations. Like other legal contracts, if either party breaches the agreement by failing to execute their obligations, the injured party may seek relief in the court system.

Retainer letters should not be entered into lightly by either the client or the law firm. The client must consider whether he or she can afford the anticipated cost of representation. The attorney must gauge whether the prospective client actually has the financial means to pay for services. In addition, the attorney must decide whether his or her firm has the legal expertise and technical resources to properly handle a case of the complexity and time the matter requires.

If the prospective client and the law firm agree to go forward with representation of the client, the parties will sign the agreement. When the retainer letter is finalized, the attorney in charge of the file will assign a staff person to prepare the documents that will initiate the court action being contemplated.

Workplace Violence

Divorces deal with heavy emotional issues—love, anger, money. jealousy, possessiveness, shattered dreams, and expectations. Divorce-related anger can be dangerous because it is often fueled by rage, vindictiveness, and a desire to punish or get even. This anger is sometimes expressed in the courts and toward the attorneys.

Many divorce litigants feel as though their cases and lives are spinning out of control in the adversarial system designed to dissolve their marriage. Attorneys and paralegals practicing in this field should take any threats very seriously and take steps to diffuse an already combustible situation. Here are some suggestions:

- Practice civility. See law practice as a profession, not a grudge match between attorneys and litigants. Help clients get through the process fairly and sanely for the sake of themselves and their children.
- Take precautions at the office if you feel threatened. The entire staff should meet to develop a safety plan when dealing with highly volatile cases. If the attorney or staff has been threatened, call the police. Lock doors at all times and only admit clients with an appointment.
- Seek out court-ordered protection in the form of restraining orders.
- Ask if the client or spouse has a history of violence. Is there access to weapons? Drug or alcohol abuse? Stalking? Threats to hurt self or others?
- Inquire about client's and opposing party's ability to resolve conflicts. Do they resort to verbal or physical assaults or threats?
- You may have to arrange for court security personnel to escort clients to their cars. Don't do it yourself. It could be dangerous.
- It is also dangerous to give clients rides to court. Meet at the courthouse instead. If they are uncomfortable waiting for the attorney in the courthouse, have them wait near security personnel or near the metal detectors at the entrance. Avoid parking garages and isolated areas around the courthouse.

- Seat clients as far as possible from abusive persons while waiting for the case to be called. Alert court security personnel to potential problems.
- Encourage angry clients to keep tempers under control and to seek counseling for anger issues.
- Encourage participation in mediation or collaborative divorce to resolve problems with the help of mental health professionals. The goal should be to seek a resolution, and not endless litigation that will damage the parties and their children long after the case is over.

Finally, we must accept that there are many divorces where no amount of mediation, collaborative efforts, or counseling will help. Cases involving domestic violence are not appropriate for mediation because the abused spouse may be intimidated and unable to speak due to fear. Some cases involve mentally ill individuals or those with a deep distrust of the courts and the law, and attempts to reach a resolution in such cases are literally impossible. As long as there are divorces, these types of cases will exist and will always pose a potential threat.

Reasons for High Cost of Divorce

Why are divorce costs so high? One reason, and you will learn this quickly if you venture into the field of family law, is that the initial retainer is often all that a family lawyer will see in the course of representing a client. Many clients will not pay monies owed to the attorney, even in long, drawn-out cases where the attorney and staff have worked numerous hours on the client's file. Lawyers hesitate to sue clients for breach of contract over legal fees for fear that the client will file a grievance with the state bar association, or worse, sue the attorney for legal malpractice, which will result in an increase to his or her insurance premiums. If lawyers do get paid, it is after the divorce settlement, which requires the attorneys to carry the client's unpaid balance until the end of the case without interest. A piece of advice one of the authors of this book received from a legal mentor upon venturing into the family law arena was "Get all you can up front, because that's all you may ever see in this case!"

Society blames "shark" or "gladiator" attorneys for making divorces unbearable. While some divorce lawyers fit this profile, many reject this form of family law practice. As a paralegal, you may find that the reverse is true. Many clients contemplating divorce seek out attorneys who are aggressive at the recommendation of their friends, coworkers, and family. A lawyer who encourages settlements and does not advocate "scorched earth" tactics is perceived as weak. One of the authors of this book recalls a case where a prospective female client with children was contemplating divorce. She came to the office for an interview and was advised by the attorney to resolve the matter amicably and avoid a long case that would not only damage her financially but cause stress to the children. The next day, the prospective client called the attorney and said, "I've decided to hire someone tougher. I think you're nice, but way too soft." Surely enough, one year later, she and her husband were still on the short calendar docket, fighting over temporary orders.

Many divorce clients are very demanding and place a great burden on the lawyer and his or her staff. Clients who promise "this will be easy" or "my husband would never take my kids away from me," lull the novice attorney into a virtual Pandora's box of endless court hearings, failures to comply with discovery requests, contempt hearings, phone calls, negotiation attempts, failure to follow the lawyer's advice, and exposure to malpractice if things don't go their way.

Many divorce clients make a lot of phone calls to the office over trivial matters such as complaints about the father arriving five minutes late to pick up the kids, or the mother spending all the child support money on manicures and not on the children. And guess who has to deal with these calls when the lawyer doesn't want to hear it anymore? The paralegal! Clients also rely on the paralegal for moral as well as legal support. Clients may find the paralegal more accessible and cheaper to talk to than the lawyer since paralegals are billed out at lower rates.

Concept Review and Reinforcement

KEY **TERMS**

conflict of interest
conflicting out
financial worksheet

initial client interview
legal advice

retainer agreement
retainer letter

REVIEW OF **KEY CONCEPTS**

1. Why is it important for the family law paralegal to comprehend the emotional aspects of divorce?

2. Explain the importance of locating the appropriate support services for clients.

3. What steps should the paralegal take in preparing for the initial client interview?

4. What is the purpose of a retainer agreement? What terms should a retainer agreement include? Why is it important to have the client prepare a detailed financial worksheet?

5. Explain the differences between conducting an initial interview with a plaintiff spouse and a defendant spouse.

BUILDING YOUR PARALEGAL SKILLS

CASE FOR BRIEFING

DOE v. CONDON, 341 S.C. 22, 532 S.E. 2D 879 (2000)

Critical Thinking and Legal Analysis Applications

Attorney Renee Weston is tied up in court for the afternoon. She has a 1:30 p.m. appointment with a new divorce client. Attorney Weston knows for sure that she won't make it back to the office on time. She calls the office and instructs her paralegal, Jonathan Fontaine, to go ahead and conduct the initial interview and answer any questions the client has regarding the case.

Based on the case of *Doe v. Condon*, 341 S.C. 22, 532 S.E. 2d 879 (2000), how would the South Carolina courts decide this case?

Based on the unauthorized practice of law statute and case law in your jurisdiction, how would the courts in your state decide this case?

Building a Professional Portfolio

PORTFOLIO **EXERCISES**

1. Review the sample Client Intake Form (Exhibit 13-2). Draft an initial intake form using Exhibit 13-2 as a guide, but reduce your form to two pages, including only the bare essentials.

2. Draft a HIPAA-compliant authorization for the release of patient information for a fictitious client and law firm using a form found on the Internet.

Chapter **fourteen**

INITIAL PLEADINGS: STARTING THE PROCESS

LEARNING OBJECTIVES

After studying this chapter, you should be able to:

1. Understand the difference between *in rem* and *in personam jurisdiction.*

2. Learn the essential elements of a dissolution of marriage complaint or petition.

3. Determine the purpose of responsive pleadings.

4. Understand why it is important to file an answer and a cross-complaint.

5. Learn the basics of e-services and e-filing.

Following the client interview and the signing of the retainer letter, the supervising attorney on the file will delegate to an appropriate staff member the responsibility of preparing the documents that must be filed with the court to initiate the divorce proceeding or other desired family-related suit.

PROCESSING THE DISSOLUTION ACTION

Every jurisdiction has its own rules for the processing of a dissolution or divorce action. The paralegal must become thoroughly familiar with the jurisdictional procedural rules that govern the preparation and filing of dissolution documents, including the time frames specified for initiating and responding to each document. This information can be found in the jurisdiction's official publications containing the procedural rules of the jurisdiction, commonly known as the *rules of court*. Additional or supplemental information can also frequently be found in the state's official statutory code. State family-related statutes as well as rules of court can also be found on the state's judicial branch website.

A dissolution is a civil action. As with all civil lawsuits, the action is commenced when the opposing party is served with an initiating document known as either the *complaint* or the *petition*. Whether this document is called a complaint or a petition depends on the jurisdiction's preference for one term or the other. In the state of Connecticut, the initial document in a family action is called the complaint, whereas in New York the same document is called a petition. In jurisdictions where the term *complaint* is used, the party commencing the action is called the *plaintiff*, and the party against whom the action is brought is called the *defendant*. In jurisdictions where the term *petition* is used, the commencing party is called the *petitioner*, and the party against whom the action is being brought is called the *respondent*.

Divorce Jurisdiction

The term *jurisdiction* is used to describe the court's control or power over a specific geographic territory. It also refers to the power of the court to hear and resolve a dispute. State courts have jurisdiction or the power to hear and resolve divorce cases. Three types of jurisdictional issues are relevant to divorce cases: subject matter, in personam, and in rem.

Subject Matter Jurisdiction

When representing the plaintiff spouse, the first step in the divorce process is to determine whether the client meets the state's residency requirements. This will give the state court *subject matter jurisdiction* over the divorce. This is the court's power to actually hear a divorce case. If the state does not have subject matter jurisdiction over the divorce, any orders entered dissolving the marriage, as well as any other issues, will be void. In Pennsylvania, for example, either spouse must fulfill the statutory *residency* requirement for a Pennsylvania court to have jurisdiction over the case. The term *residency* refers to the *domicile* of the parties. *Domicile* is defined as residing in a state with the intent to permanently remain. The court has jurisdiction to hear the divorce case as long as one of the spouses meets the residency requirements. Residency requirements vary from state to state, so it is important for paralegals to become familiar with their state's laws.

23 PENNSYLVANIA COMMONWEALTH STATUTES ANNOTATED SECTION 3104. BASES OF JURISDICTION

(b) Residence and domicile of parties.—No spouse is entitled to commence an action for divorce or annulment under this part unless at least one of the parties has been a bona fide resident in this Commonwealth for at least six months immediately previous to the commencement of the action. Both parties shall be competent witnesses to prove their respective residence, and proof of actual residence within this Commonwealth for six months shall create a presumption of domicile within this Commonwealth.

Rules of court
A jurisdiction's official publication containing the procedural codes of the jurisdiction.

Complaint
A grievance filed with a disciplinary body against an attorney; also, a document that commences an action when the opposing party is served; also known as a petition.

Petition
A document that commences the action when the opposing party is served; also known as a complaint.

Plaintiff
The party who brings a court action against another; also known as the petitioner.

Defendant
The party against whom an action is brought.

Petitioner
The party who brings a court action against another; also known as the plaintiff.

Respondent
The party against whom an action is brought.

Jurisdiction
Describes the court's control or power over a specific geographic territory; it also refers to the power of the courts to hear and resolve a dispute.

Subject matter jurisdiction
The court's power to actually hear a divorce case.

Residency
The domicile of the parties.

Domicile
Residing in a state with the intent to permanently remain.

In Personam Jurisdiction/Resident Defendant

In personam jurisdiction
Personal service over the defendant; it means that once the defendant is served with the initial pleadings, the court may enter orders and enforce judgments against that individual.

Service of process
Formal delivery of the initial pleadings.

Abode service
Service on a defendant by leaving a copy of the pleadings at his or her home.

Service by publication
When a sheriff puts a legal notice in the newspaper in the city, town, or general area where the defendant was last known to reside or where the defendant is now thought to be residing.

All jurisdictions require that the defendant to a divorce action, even if he or she is not in the state, be given notice of the proceedings by service of the pleadings and an opportunity to be heard. *In personam jurisdiction* means that once the defendant is served with the initial pleadings, the court may enter orders and enforce judgments against that individual. In personam jurisdiction is obtained by *service of process* on the defendant.

Typically, service of process, or formal delivery of the initial pleadings, is easy when the defendant resides in the state. The initial pleadings are served on the defendant by a sheriff, marshal, process server, constable, or indifferent person. Service of process may be obtained by serving the defendant in hand. This is called *personal service*. The defendant may also be served by *abode service*, which means leaving a copy of the pleadings at his or her home. If the plaintiff does not know the defendant's current address, but the last known address is in the same state where the plaintiff resides, the plaintiff may seek permission from the court to serve the defendant through *service by publication*. Service by publication is accomplished by publishing a legal notice in a newspaper circulated in the city or town of the defendant's last known address, informing the defendant of the proceedings. Once the court has in personam jurisdiction over the defendant, the judge may enter orders on alimony, child support, and property distribution, which may be enforced against the defendant. If it is determined that the defendant spouse was not properly served, the court may not have jurisdiction and any orders entered may be subject to jurisdictional attack by the defendant's legal counsel.

In Personam Jurisdiction/Nonresident Defendant

When the defendant spouse resides out of state, state procedural rules must be followed for the court to obtain in personam jurisdiction over a nonresident defendant. In personam jurisdiction is necessary for the court to enter orders against a nonresident defendant. If the plaintiff knows where the nonresident defendant lives, the plaintiff may have to obtain permission from the court to serve the defendant at his or her residence in accordance with the laws of that particular jurisdiction. Service of process over a nonresident defendant may take the form of actual in-hand service of process in another state by an authorized person or through certified or registered mail. Service by registered and certified mail can present problems if the nonresident defendant does not sign for the documents or fails to enter an appearance in the divorce case. Under this scenario, the court may have limited power to enter certain orders against a nonresident defendant. Once the defendant files an appearance in the case, the court has in personam jurisdiction over that individual. In either case, obtaining actual notice is crucial to enable the court in the plaintiff's state to exercise jurisdiction and enter orders against the nonresident defendant. If the plaintiff does not have an address for a nonresident defendant but knows the jurisdiction of his or her last known address, the defendant may receive notice by service through publication.

Proper Venue

Venue
The proper divorce court within the state in which to file the initial divorce complaint or petition.

Once the residency requirement is fulfilled, the next step is to choose the proper divorce court within the state in which to file the initial pleadings. This is known as the proper *venue*. There may be a number of divorce courts situated in any given counties or districts within a state. Generally, the proper venue in which to file an action is the county or district where either one of the spouses resides. If both live in the same district, there is no problem. If both reside in separate districts, then it is a "race to the courthouse." If an improper venue is chosen—for instance, the district where the plaintiff is employed—as a matter of convenience, the defendant may move to dismiss the divorce action on the basis of improper venue. Pennsylvania law authorizes more than one venue in which to bring a dissolution or annulment action:

23 PENNSYLVANIA COMMONWEALTH STATUTES ANNOTATED SECTION 3104. BASES OF JURISDICTION

(e) **Venue.**–A proceeding for divorce or annulment may be brought in the county:
>   (1) where the defendant resides;
>   (2) if the defendant resides outside of this Commonwealth, where the plaintiff resides;
>   (3) of matrimonial domicile, if the plaintiff has continuously resided in the county;
>   (4) prior to six months after the date of final separation and with agreement of the defendant, where the plaintiff resides or, if neither party continues to reside in the county of matrimonial domicile, where either party resides; or
>   (5) after six months after the date of final separation, where either party resides.

In Rem Jurisdiction

Another type of jurisdiction commonly encountered in divorce cases is *in rem jurisdiction*. In rem jurisdiction is the power of the courts to actually dissolve the marriage. In order for the state court to have in rem jurisdiction, either one of the spouses must be domiciled in that jurisdiction. Lack of in rem jurisdiction prohibits a court from dissolving the marriage.

In rem jurisdiction
The power of the courts to actually dissolve the marriage.

It is important to note that in personam jurisdiction is not needed for the plaintiff to obtain a divorce. As long as the court has in rem jurisdiction, it has the authority to dissolve the marriage. The court, however, must have in personam jurisdiction over the defendant in order to enter financial orders such as alimony, property distribution, child custody and support, and visitation.

INITIAL PLEADINGS IN A DISSOLUTION ACTION

The Pleadings

The documents that state the plaintiff's claims giving rise to the dissolution action and the defendant's responses or defenses to such claims are documents known as *pleadings*. The pleadings in any litigation matter include a *summons* and *complaint* or *petition;* and an *answer, special defenses, counterclaims,* and *cross-claims.*

Pleading
Documents that state the plaintiff's claims giving rise to the dissolution action and the defendant's responses or defenses to such claims.

The Complaint

The initial pleading or initiating document filed in a dissolution matter is the *complaint.* As mentioned, sometimes the initial pleading is called the *petition.* However, because the more commonly used term is *complaint,* that term will be used here. A document known as a *summons* usually accompanies the complaint. In most jurisdictions, the summons is a one-page preprinted form on which the names and addresses of parties and the name and address of the court are inserted (see Exhibit 14-1).

Summons
A one-page preprinted form on which the names and addresses of parties and the name and address of the court are inserted and that directs the defendant to appear in court and answer allegations in a complaint.

Exhibit 14-1 New York summons.

1 **SUPREME COURT OF THE STATE OF NEW YORK**   Index No.:_____
2 3 **COUNTY OF** _____   Date Summons filed:_____
4 --X   Plaintiff designates _____
5   County as the place of trial
                                                                 The basis of venue is:
6   _____

                                             Plaintiff,

         -against-   **SUMMONS WITH NOTICE**
                                                                 Plaintiff/Defendant resides at:
7   _____
8   _____
                                            Defendant.   _____
--X

ACTION FOR A DIVORCE

To the above named Defendant:

9   **YOU ARE HEREBY SUMMONED** to serve a notice of appearance on the ❏ *Plaintiff*
OR ❏ *Plaintiff's Attorney(s)* within twenty (20) days after the service of this summons, exclusive
of the day of service (or within thirty (30) days after the service is complete if this summons is not
personally delivered to you within the State of New York); and in case of your failure to appear,
judgment will be taken against you by default for the relief demanded in the notice set forth below.

10, 11 Dated _____   ❏ *Plaintiff*
                                         ❏ *Attorney(s) for Plaintiff*
12   Phone No.:
                                         Address:

13   **NOTICE:**   The nature of this action is to dissolve the marriage between the parties, on the
                    grounds: **DRL §170 subd.____ - _____
                                                         _____

The relief sought is a judgment of absolute divorce in favor of the Plaintiff dissolving the marriage
between the parties in this action.
14   The nature of any ancillary or additional relief requested (see p.14 of Instructions) is:
_____
❏ Additional page describing ancillary relief requested is attached;
❏ Marital property to be distributed pursuant to separation agreement/stipulation;
❏ I waive distribution of Marital property;
For divorces commenced on or after 1/25/16 only: ❏ *I am not seeking maintenance as payee as
described in the Notice of Guideline Maintenance (the "Notice") other than what was already agreed
to in a written agreement/stipulation ; OR* ❏ *I seek maintenance as payee, as described in the Notice*
❏ **NONE** - I am not requesting any ancillary relief;
AND any other relief the court deems fit and proper
**Read pp. 3-5 of Instructions and insert the grounds for the divorce:
DRL §170(1) - cruel and inhuman treatment   DRL §170(4) - adultery
DRL §170(2) - abandonment   DRL §170(5) - living apart one year after separation decree or judgment of separation
DRL §170(3) - confinement in prison   DRL §170(6) - living apart one year after execution of a separation agreement
                                               DRL §170(7) - irretrievable breakdown in relationship

(UD-1 Rev. 1/25/16)

Source: New York Summons, New York State Unified Court System.

The summons directs the defendant to appear in court and answer the allegations in the complaint. The spouse bringing the dissolution of marriage action is designated as the *plaintiff spouse*. The spouse against whom the dissolution proceeding is brought is designated as the *defendant spouse*. The plaintiff spouse will initiate the legal proceeding.

The law firm representing the plaintiff spouse will file the pleading known as the complaint. In this document, the plaintiff spouse will allege that grounds exist for a divorce, recite these grounds, and request that the court grant a divorce and enter orders regarding the distribution of marital property and, when appropriate, orders relating to child custody, alimony, and child support and addressing any other form of relief the spouse has requested.

Form of the Dissolution Complaint

A dissolution or divorce complaint has distinct sections. They are the *caption*, the *body*, the *prayer*, and the *subscription* (some jurisdictions also require a *verification*).

The Caption The **caption** refers to the initial section of the complaint, which contains the names of the parties, the name and division of the court, the return date of the action, and the date the complaint was drawn up. The **return date** is a date in the near future by which the complaint must be returned to the court clerk's office and filed with the court, along with payment of the filing fee the jurisdiction requires to process the complaint. A heading is also included to indicate that the document being drafted is a complaint.

The Body The **body** of the complaint contains the necessary factual information that establishes the jurisdiction of the court and identifies the grounds on which the divorce is being sought. In addition, other mandatory information in the body of the complaint includes the names and addresses of the parties, their date and place of marriage, and the names of all minor children born during the period of the marriage.

Prayer for Relief The **prayer for relief** section of the complaint contains the plaintiff's request for a dissolution and for court orders, when appropriate, regarding property distribution, alimony, child custody, support of the minor children, and the wife's request for restoration of her maiden name. Certain jurisdictions require very specific detail regarding the nature and extent of relief sought, while others require a more general statement. In either case, however, it is always a good idea to include a "catch-all" phrase such as "and such other relief as the court deems fair and equitable."

The Subscription and Verification The **subscription** and/or **verification** section of the complaint are included to confirm the truth and accuracy of the allegations and to confirm the veracity of the party making these allegations. The subscription contains the signature of the attorney filing the complaint, along with the attorney's address, phone number, and license number, known in some jurisdictions as the **juris number**. When an attorney signs a complaint, the attorney is representing or *subscribing* that to the best of the attorney's knowledge, the facts contained within are true and accurate. In some jurisdictions, the plaintiff bringing the action is also required to sign the complaint and to attest to its veracity. In these instances, the plaintiff will sign a sworn statement, under oath, that the facts contained in the allegations are true. By so doing, the plaintiff claims that the information is accurate and true. Hence the plaintiff's swearing and signing are termed the *verification*. A verified complaint used in the state of New York is illustrated in Exhibit 14-2. Also illustrated in Exhibit 14-3 is a preprinted form from the state of Wisconsin illustrating a complaint for dissolution of marriage.

Caption
The initial section of a complaint that contains the names of the parties, the name and division of the court, the docket number or the return date of the action, and the date the complaint was drawn up.

Return date
A date in the near future by which the complaint must be returned to the court clerk's office and filed with the court.

Body
The part of a complaint that contains the necessary factual information that establishes the jurisdiction of the court and identifies the grounds on which the divorce is being sought.

Prayer for relief
The plaintiff's request for a dissolution and for court orders, when appropriate, regarding property distribution, alimony, child custody, and support of the minor children.

Subscription
Part of a court document that confirms the truth and accuracy of allegations and confirms the veracity of the party making these allegations; also known as the verification.

Verification
Part of a court document that confirms the truth and accuracy of allegations and confirms the veracity of the party making these allegations; also known as the subscription.

Juris number
The attorney's license number.

Exhibit 14-2 New York verified complaint.

1

SUPREME COURT OF THE STATE OF NEW YORK
COUNTY OF _____

--X

2 3
                          Plaintiff,   Index No.:

    -against-   **VERIFIED COMPLAINT**

                                            ACTION FOR DIVORCE

4
                        Defendant.

--X

5
FIRST:

Plaintiff *herein / by* _____, complaining of the Defendant, alleges that the parties are over the age of 18 years and;

6
SECOND:

A) ❑ The ❑ *Plaintiff* ❑ *Defendant* has resided in New York State for a continuous period of at least two

years immediately preceding the commencement of this divorce action.

===========================**OR**===========================

B) ❑ The ❑ *Plaintiff* ❑ *Defendant* resided in New York State on the date of commencement of this

divorce action and for a continuous period of one year immediately preceding the commencement of this divorce action

AND:

a. ❑ the parties were married in New York State.

or

b. ❑ the parties have resided as married people in New York State.

===========================**OR**===========================

C) ❑ The cause of action occurred in New York State and ❑ *Plaintiff* ❑ *Defendant* resided in New York

State for a continuous period of at least one year immediately preceding the commencement of this divorce action.

===========================**OR**===========================

D) ❑ The cause of action occurred in New York State and both parties were residents at the time of commencement of this divorce action.

7
THIRD: The Plaintiff and the Defendant were married on _____
in (city, town or village; and state or country) _____.

(Form UD-2 Rev. 1/25/16)

8   The marriage was   *not*   performed by a clergyman, minister or by a leader of the Society for Ethical Culture.

(If the word "not" is deleted above check the appropriate box below).

❑   *To the best of my knowledge I have taken all steps solely within my power to remove any barrier to the Defendant's remarriage.*   **OR**

❑   *I will take prior to the entry of final judgment all steps solely within my power to the best of my knowledge to remove any barrier to the Defendant's remarriage.*   **OR**

❑   *The Defendant has waived in writing the requirements of DRL §253 (Barriers to Remarriage).*

9   **FOURTH:**   ❑ There are no children of the marriage (see definition on p.7 of Instructions)

OR

❑ There *is (are)* _____ child(ren) of the marriage (see definitions on p.7 of Instructions), namely:

Name	Date of Birth	Address
_____	_____	_____
_____	_____	_____
_____	_____	_____
_____	_____	_____

10   The Plaintiff resides at _____.

The Defendant resides at _____.

11   The parties are covered by the following group health plans:

Plaintiff	**Defendant**
Group Health Plan:_____	Group Health Plan:_____
Address:_____	Address:_____
Identification Number:_____	Identification Number:_____
Plan Administrator:_____	Plan Administrator:_____
Type of Coverage:_____	Type of Coverage:_____

12   **FIFTH:**   The grounds for divorce that are alleged as follows:

Cruel and Inhuman Treatment (DRL §170(1)):

❑   At the following times Defendant committed the following act(s) which endangered the Plaintiff's physical or mental well being and rendered it unsafe or improper for Plaintiff to continue to reside with Defendant.

(State the facts that demonstrate cruel and inhuman conduct giving dates, places and specific acts. Conduct may include physical, verbal, sexual or emotional behavior.)

_____
_____
_____
_____
_____

(Attach an additional sheet, if necessary).

(Form UD-2 Rev. 1/25/16)

continued

Exhibit 14-2 Continued

Abandonment (DRL 170(2)):

❏   That commencing on or about _____, and continuing for a period of more than one (1) year immediately prior to commencement of this action, the Defendant left the marital residence of the parties located at _____, and did not return. Such absence was without cause or justification, and was without Plaintiff's consent.

❏   That commencing on or about _____, and continuing for a period of more than one (1) year immediately prior to commencement of this action, the Defendant refused to have sexual relations with the Plaintiff despite Plaintiff's repeated requests to resume such relations. Defendant does not suffer from any disability which would prevent *her / him* from engaging in such sexual relations with Plaintiff. The refusal to engage in sexual relations was without good cause or justification and occurred at the marital residence located at _____.

❏   That commencing on or about _____, and continuing for a period of more than one (1) year immediately prior to commencement of this action, the Defendant willfully and without cause or justification abandoned the Plaintiff, who had been a faithful and dutiful spouse, by depriving Plaintiff of access to the marital residence located at _____. This deprivation of access was without the consent of the Plaintiff and continued for a period of greater than one year.

Imprisonment (DRL §170(3)):

❏   That after the marriage of Plaintiff and Defendant, Defendant was confined in prison for a period of three or more consecutive years, to wit: that Defendant is/was confined in _____ prison on the

    _____ *Name of correctional facility*

    _____day of _____,____, and remained confined until the
            Month   *Year*

    _____day of_____,____; **OR** ❏ remains confined to this date.
            Month   *Year*

Adultery (DRL §170(4)):

❏   That on the____ day of_____,____, at _____
                      Month   *Year*   *Location*
    the Defendant voluntarily committed of an act of sexual or deviate sexual intercourse with a person other than the Plaintiff after the marriage of Plaintiff and Defendant.

Living Separate and Apart Pursuant to a Separation Decree or Judgment of Separation(DRL §170(5)):

❏   (a)   That the _____ Court, _____ County, _____ (Country or State) rendered a decree or judgment of separation on _____, under Index Number _____; and

    (b)   that the parties have lived separate and apart for a period of one year or longer after the granting of such decree; and

    (c)   that the Plaintiff has substantially complied with all the terms and conditions of such decree or judgment.

(Form UD-2 Rev. 1/25/16)

<u>Living Separate and Apart Pursuant to a Separation Agreement (DRL §170(6)):</u>

   ❏   (a)   That the Plaintiff and Defendant entered into a written agreement of separation, which they subscribed and acknowledged on _____, in the form required to entitle a deed to be recorded; and

              (b)   that the *agreement / memorandum of said agreement* was filed on _____ in the Office of the Clerk of the County of _____, wherein *Plaintiff / Defendant* resided; and

              (c)   that the parties have lived separate and apart for a period of one year or longer after the execution of said agreement; and

              (d)   that the Plaintiff has substantially complied with all terms and conditions of such agreement.

<u>Irretrievable Breakdown in Relationship for at Least Six Months (DRL §170(7)):</u>

   ❏   That the relationship between Plaintiff and Defendant has broken down irretrievably for a period of at least six months.

13   **SIXTH:** There is no judgment of divorce and no other matrimonial action between the parties pending in this court or in any other court of competent jurisdiction.

(Form UD-2 Rev. 1/25/16)

continued

Exhibit 14-2 Continued

WHEREFORE, Plaintiff demands judgment against the Defendant as follows:
A judgment dissolving the marriage between the parties

AND

14   The nature of any ancillary or additional relief requested (see p.16 of Instructions) is:

_____
_____

❏ Additional page describing ancillary relief requested is attached;
❏ Marital property to be distributed pursuant to separation agreement/stipulation;
❏ I waive distribution of Marital property;
For divorces commenced on or after 1/25/16 only:❏ *I am not seeking maintenance as payee as described in the Notice of Guideline Maintenance (the "Notice") other than what was already agreed to in a written agreement/stipulation* ; OR ❏ *I seek maintenance as payee, as described in the Notice.*
❏ **NONE** - I am not requesting any ancillary relief;
AND any other relief the court deems fit and proper

15   Dated:_____

16   ❏ *Plaintiff*
                                                             ❏ *Attorney(s) for Plaintiff*
                                                                Address:

17   STATE OF NEW YORK, COUNTY OF _____ ss:

I _____ (Print Name), am the Plaintiff in the within action for a divorce. I have read the foregoing complaint and know the contents thereof.   The contents are true to my own knowledge except as to matters therein stated to be alleged upon information and belief, and as to those matters I believe them to be true.

Subscribed and Sworn to
before me on

_____   _____
                                                          Plaintiff's Signature

_____
        NOTARY PUBLIC

(Form UD-2 Rev. 1/25/16)

Source: New York Verified Complaint, New York State Unified Court System.

Exhibit 14-3 Wisconsin preprinted form illustrating a complaint for dissolution of marriage.

Enter the name of the county in which you are filing this case.	**STATE OF WISCONSIN, CIRCUIT COURT,** _____ **COUNTY**
Enter your name (you are the petitioner).	IN RE: THE MARRIAGE OF **Petitioner**
Enter your address.	Name (First, Middle and Last) Address
On the far right, check divorce or legal separation.	Address City State Zip
	and
Enter your spouse's name (your spouse is the respondent).	**Respondent**
Enter your spouse's address.	Name (First, Middle and Last) Address
Note: Leave case number blank; the clerk will add this.	Address City State Zip

Summons
With Minor Children

☐ **Divorce-40101**
☐ **Legal Separation-40201**

Case No. _____

The State of Wisconsin, to the person named above as respondent:

You are notified that your spouse has filed a lawsuit or other legal action against you. The **Petition**, which is attached, states the nature and basis of the legal action.

Within 20 days of receiving this **Summons**, you must provide a written response, as that term is used in ch. 802, Wis. Stats., to the **Petition**. The court may reject or disregard a response that does not follow the requirements of the statutes.

The response must be sent or delivered to the following government offices:

Clerk of Court
Name of county   _____
Address   _____
Address   _____
City, State and Zip   _____

County Child Support Agency
Name of agency   _____
Address   _____
Address   _____
City, State and Zip   _____

Enter the name and address of the 2 identified government offices.
DO NOT leave these lines blank. You must obtain these addresses and fill them in, or your Summons will be incomplete and will harm your case. This information may be available in the local phone book under listings for the county or from your local Clerk of Court's office.

FA-4104V, 04/08 Summons-With Minor Children   §§767.215(2m) and 801.095, Wisconsin Statutes
This form shall not be modified. It may be supplemented with additional material.
Page 1 of 3

continued

Exhibit 14-3 Continued

The response must also be mailed or delivered within 20 days to the petitioner at the address above.

It is recommended, but not required, that you have an attorney help or represent you.

If you do not provide a proper response within 20 days, the court may grant judgment against you, and you may lose your right to object to anything that is or may be incorrect in the **Petition**.

A judgment may be enforced as provided by law. A judgment may become a lien against any real estate you own now or in the future, and may also be enforced by garnishment or seizure of property.

> If you require reasonable accommodations due to a disability to participate in the court process, please call _____ at least 10 working days prior to the scheduled court date. Please note that the court does not provide transportation.

Sign and print your name.	_____
Enter the date on which you signed your name.	Signature
	_____
Note: This signature does not need to be notarized.	Print or Type Name
	_____
	Date

IMPORTANT NOTICES

You are notified of the availability of information from the Family Court Commissioner as set forth in sec. 767.105 Wis. Stats.

767.105 Information from Family Court Commissioner.

(2) Upon the request of a party to an action affecting the family, including a revision of judgment or order under sec. 767.59 or 767.451:

(a) The Family Court Commissioner shall, with or without charge, provide the party with written information on the following, as appropriate to the action commenced:
   1. The procedure for obtaining a judgment or order in the action.
   2. The major issues usually addressed in such an action.
   3. Community resources and family court counseling services available to assist the parties.
   4. The procedure for setting, modifying, and enforcing child support awards, or modifying and enforcing legal custody or physical placement judgments or orders.
(b) The Family Court Commissioner shall provide a party, for inspection or purchase, with a copy of the statutory provisions in this chapter generally pertinent to the action.

You are notified that if the parties to the action have minor children, violation of the following criminal statute is punishable by fines and/or imprisonment as set forth in sec. 948.31 Wis. Stats.

948.31 Interference with custody by parent or others.

(1) (a) In this subsection, "legal custodian of a child" means:
1. A parent or other person having legal custody of the child under an order or judgment in an action for divorce, legal separation, annulment, child custody, paternity, guardianship or habeas corpus.

2. The department of children and families or the department of corrections or any person, county department under sec. 46.215, 46.22 or 46.23 or licensed child welfare agency, if custody or supervision of the child has been transferred under chapter 48 or chapter 938 to that department, person or agency.
(b) Except as provided under chs. 48 and 938, whoever intentionally causes a child to leave, takes a child away, or withholds a child for more than 12 hours beyond the court-approved period of physical placement or visitation period from a legal custodian with intent to deprive the custodian of his or her custody rights without the consent of the custodian is guilty of a Class F felony. This paragraph is not applicable if the court has entered an order authorizing the person to so take or withhold the child. The fact that joint legal custody has been awarded to both parents by a court does not preclude a court from finding that one parent has committed a violation of this paragraph.

(2) Whoever causes a child to leave, takes a child away or withholds a child for more than 12 hours from the child's parents, or in the case of a nonmarital child whose parents do not subsequently intermarry under sec. 767.803, from the child's mother, or if he has been granted legal custody, the child's father, without the consent of the parents, the mother or the father with legal custody, is guilty of a Class I felony. This subsection is not applicable if legal custody has been granted by court order to the person taking or withholding the child.

(3) Any parent, or any person acting pursuant to directions from the parent, who does any of the following is guilty of a Class F felony:
(a) Intentionally hides a child from the child's other parent.
(b) After being served with process in an action affecting the family but prior to the issuance of a temporary or final order determining child custody rights, takes the child or causes the child to leave with intent to deprive the other parent of physical custody as defined in sec. 822.02(9).
(c) After issuance of a temporary or final order specifying joint legal custody rights and periods of physical placement, takes a child from or causes a child to leave the other parent in violation of the order or withholds a child for more than 12 hours beyond the court-approved period of physical placement or visitation period.

(4) (a) It is an affirmative defense to prosecution for violation of this section if the action:

1. Is taken by a parent or by a person authorized by a parent to protect his or her child in a situation in which the parent or authorized person reasonably believes that there is a threat of physical harm or sexual assault to the child;
2. Is taken by a parent fleeing in a situation in which the parent reasonably believes that there is a threat of physical harm or sexual assault to himself or herself;
3. Is consented to by the other parent or any other person or agency having legal custody of the child; or
4. Is otherwise authorized by law.
(b) A defendant who raises an affirmative defense has the burden of proving the defense by a preponderance of the evidence.

(5) The venue of an action under this section is prescribed in sec. 971.19(8).

(6) In addition to any other penalties provided for violation of this section, a court may order a violator to pay restitution, regardless of whether the violator is placed on probation under s. 973.09, to provide reimbursement for any reasonable expenses incurred by any person or any governmental entity in locating and returning the child. Any such amounts paid by the violator shall be paid to the person or governmental entity which incurred the expense on a prorated basis. Upon the application of any interested party, the court shall hold an evidentiary hearing to determine the amount of reasonable expenses.

Source: Petition with Minor Children, Wisconsin Court System.

Another example of a dissolution of marriage complaint can be found in Appendix B, "Alexander Rodriquez' Petition for Dissolution of Marriage." A-Rod, as he is affectionately known by his fans, was a third baseman for the New York Yankees who also played for the Seattle Mariners and the Texas Rangers. In 2008, his wife Cynthia filed for divorce, accusing A-Rod of serial infidelity, which allegedly included an extramarital affair with "Material Girl" Madonna. The divorce, which initially appeared as though it was going to be "messy," ended in a negotiated settlement.

Pre-Return Date Relief

Sometimes, a plaintiff spouse needs and may seek immediate relief or court intervention known as **pre-return date relief**. The plaintiff spouse may have serious and real concerns that the act of serving the dissolution complaint on the defendant spouse may cause the defendant spouse to take certain immediate initiatives that will either damage the plaintiff spouse economically or harm the plaintiff physically and/or emotionally.

For instance, when the plaintiff spouse serves a dissolution complaint in which that spouse seeks, as part of the dissolution action, a division of the marital assets and/or alimony and child support, the defendant spouse may attempt to move, hide, or dispose of assets that would be considered assets of the marital union to avoid having to share them or split their value with the plaintiff spouse.

There may also be assets acquired during the marriage where title rests completely with one partner or the other. For example, title to each family car will usually be in the name of only one spouse. In many jurisdictions, inheritances bequeathed to one spouse or gifts given solely to one spouse are not marital assets. However, practically every other possession acquired during the marriage is a joint asset. The plaintiff spouse may have concerns that the defendant spouse will dispose of bona fide joint property that is not legally registered to both parties. For instance, the defendant spouse may sell an expensive car purchased with marital funds and pocket or bury the money. The defendant spouse who has equal signing power or a joint checking account, joint savings account, joint CD certificates, or joint stock accounts may attempt to withdraw the contents of these accounts upon being served with divorce papers. To avoid this **dissipation** or squandering of assets, the plaintiff spouse may file along with the dissolution complaint an **application for a prejudgment remedy** to attach marital assets during the period pending litigation.

In many jurisdictions, a plaintiff spouse may apply for an attachment of known joint assets. Sometimes the court will grant a temporary attachment until there is a hearing on the matter; at other times the hearing must occur before even a temporary or *pendente lite* order is issued.

Sometimes a defendant spouse owns a business that the plaintiff spouse has had little hands-on involvement with, and hence the plaintiff spouse does not know the actual value of the business. The plaintiff spouse may also serve on the defendant, along with a **request for an order attaching known assets**, a **motion for disclosure of assets** to be made under oath. If the plaintiff is not satisfied with the disclosure, later in the discovery phase of the dissolution suit the plaintiff may serve the defendant with a **notice to appear for a deposition to disclose assets**. In this deposition, the defendant spouse will be questioned, under oath, on the previous disclosure to determine whether it completely reveals all the defendant's assets.

Pre-return date relief
Where a plaintiff spouse needs and may seek immediate relief or court intervention as soon as the complaint is served.

Dissipation
Depletion of the marital assets by waste.

Application for a prejudgment remedy
Where a party asks the court to take some action before a judgment in the case is rendered.

Request for an order attaching known assets
A document asking the court to freeze the opposing party's property in order to prevent dissipation of those assets.

Motion for disclosure of assets
Requests disclosure of all real and personal property owned by a spouse either in his or her own name or owned jointly with the spouse or with another person or entity.

Notice to appear for a deposition to disclose assets
A document that requires a party to appear in order to be questioned, under oath, on the previous disclosure to determine whether it completely revealed all of the party's assets.

TEMPORARY RESTRAINING ORDER

Sometimes when a plaintiff spouse has decided to file a dissolution action, the plaintiff spouse fears that notice of this action will trigger a response in the defendant spouse that includes being physically and verbally abusive to the plaintiff and possibly to the children as well. A plaintiff spouse may be afraid to return to the family home while the defendant continues to reside there.

Under these circumstances, if the fear is justified, the plaintiff may seek pre-return date relief in the form of a court-ordered *temporary restraining order* to restrain the defendant spouse from entering the family home for a significant number of days. In the application for such a restraining order, the plaintiff spouse will include a signed, sworn statement known as an ***affidavit*** that certain prior events have occurred and support the plaintiff spouse's belief that a restraining order is needed to keep the spouse safe from grave harm the defendant would otherwise inflict. A set of specific legal documents must be filed with the court in order for the court to consider the plaintiff's request for a restraining order. A paralegal must know what documents are included in this set and be especially careful to include everything needed and to make sure each document is factually and procedurally correct.

Affidavit
A signed, sworn statement.

SERVICE OF PROCESS OF THE DIVORCE COMPLAINT

Once the law office has prepared the divorce or dissolution summons and complaint, the paralegal may be responsible for seeing that these documents are properly served on the defendant. In most jurisdictions, the divorce complaint, just like the complaint in a regular civil lawsuit, must be served on the defendant named in the action by a statutorily authorized process server. This is true whether or not the case is filed electronically or in the standard hard copy format.

A paralegal will contact the office of the sheriff or process server to confirm that the person is available and then forward the initiating documents to be served. If the case involves service on a nonresident defendant or an in-state defendant whose whereabouts are unknown, the paralegal may have to prepare motions to seek a court order to serve such persons through certified mail or publication.

The process server must locate the party to be served and complete service by delivering the true and attested copies of the initial pleadings. Once service is completed, the sheriff or process server will return to the law office the original summons and complaint along with his or her proof of service or return, which the sheriff affirms that, on a specified date, the sheriff served the defendant by leaving with the defendant in his or her hands, at his or her abode, or by mail a true and attested copy of the summons and complaint. Exhibit 14-4 illustrates a sample proof of service for the State of Wisconsin. The sheriff's or server's bill for services rendered normally accompanies the return, either by e-mail or traditional mail delivery.

After the sheriff or process server returns the summons and complaint to the law office, these documents must be filed either electronically, by traditional mail delivery, or by a quick trip to the clerk's office, along with a fee, known in most jurisdictions as a ***filing fee*** or a ***court-entry fee***. In addition, an increasing number of jurisdictions now require that accompanying documents be filed at the same time as the complaint. These accompanying documents may include a financial affidavit, a custody affidavit, and stipulations regarding the irretrievable breakdown of the marriage.

Filing fee
An amount of money required to file a complaint in court; also known as a court entry fee.

Court-entry fee
An amount of money required to file a complaint in court; also known as a filing fee.

Exhibit 14-4 Wisconsin proof of service document.

Petitioner/Joint Petitioner A: _____	
Respondent/Joint Petitioner B: _____	

Enter the name of the county in which this case is filed.	**STATE OF WISCONSIN, CIRCUIT COURT,** _____ **COUNTY**
Enter the name of the petitioner. If joint petitioners, enter the name of Petitioner/Joint Petitioner A.	IN RE: THE MARRIAGE OF **Petitioner/Joint Petitioner A** _____ Name (First, Middle and Last)
	and
Enter the name of the respondent. If joint petitioners, enter the name of Respondent/Joint Petitioner B.	**Respondent/Joint Petitioner B** _____ Name (First, Middle and Last)
Enter the case number.	

Admission of Service

Case No. _____

Check the box for each document that is being served.

If one of the documents is an Order to Show Cause, enter the date [month, day, year] the Order To Show Cause was signed by a court official.

On [Date] _____ I received a copy of the following documents:

☐ Authenticated **Summons** and **Petition**

☐ **Order to Show Cause and Affidavit for Temporary Order** [Dated] _____

☐ A blank **Financial Disclosure Statement**

☐ **Proposed Marital Settlement Agreement/Order** [Dated] _____

☐ **Order to Appear** [Dated] _____

☐ **Motion/Order to Show Cause for Contempt** [Dated] _____

☐ **Motion/Order to Show Cause to Change:** _____ [Dated] _____

☐ Requirement to attend parent education

If other, enter the name of the document.

☐ Other: _____

☐ Other: _____

☐ Other: _____

The party who is voluntarily accepting the documents must sign and print their name.

They must enter the date on which the Admission was signed.

Note: This signature does not need to be notarized.

► _____
Signature

_____
Name Printed or Typed

_____
Date

FA-4119V, 05/17 Admission of Service   §801.10(4)(c), Wisconsin Statutes
This form shall not be modified. It may be supplemented with additional material.
Page 1 of 1

Source: Affidavit of Service, Wisconsin Court System.

Once a complaint has been filed, the clerk will assign the case a docket or case number. In some states, the case number is assigned before the documents are served. This number will be used on all further communications from the court. In addition, the parties should now replace the return date category with the case number in the caption section of all future documents filed with the court in this matter.

RESPONSIVE PLEADINGS TO THE DISSOLUTION COMPLAINT

When a spouse is served with divorce or dissolution papers, the spouse must decide what type of responsive action to take or whether to respond at all. The dissolution summons will command the defendant spouse to appear before the court on or before a certain date, and to do so not by appearing in person but by filing a written appearance form or by having the defendant spouse's attorney file a written *appearance* on his or her behalf.

If the defendant spouse fails to file an appearance, depending on the court rules of the particular jurisdiction, the judicial system will handle this failure in one of two or three different ways. In many states, the defendant spouse's failure to file an appearance can result ultimately in a ***default judgment*** being entered against that person. This means that the plaintiff spouse will "win" the dissolution or divorce suit by default; that is, the plaintiff spouse will be granted a divorce. In addition, if the court has personal jurisdiction over the defendant spouse, the court, even in the absence of the defendant, may order both spousal support and child support. In this event, the defendant will be notified by mail of the court's orders. If the defendant does not make the court-ordered payments and is still within the jurisdiction, the plaintiff spouse may serve the defendant with additional legal papers. These papers, often collectively called an *order to show cause*, will require the defendant to appear under penalty of civil arrest and to show cause or offer a good reason why the defendant should not be penalized or held in ***contempt*** for not making the court-ordered payments. In this instance, if the defendant spouse again fails to appear in court, the court may and usually will order a *capias*, which is actually an arrest warrant for committing a civil violation, in this case a violation of a court order.

If a plaintiff spouse seeks a divorce from a spouse who has fled the jurisdiction or who may still be in the jurisdiction but is "whereabouts unknown" as far as a place of abode or place of employment, then the plaintiff spouse may have a sheriff or process server serve the defendant by publication. The sheriff will put a legal notice in the legal notices section of a newspaper in the city, town, or general area where the defendant was last known to reside or where the defendant is thought to be residing. This legal notice will, in fact, be a printing of the text of the divorce or dissolution complaint. Once the notice is published and the newspaper sends the sheriff its ***affidavit of publication***, the sheriff will make a return noting the service by publication and return the complaint to the law firm for filing in court. Under these circumstances, after the appropriate waiting period, the plaintiff may seek to have the court formally dissolve the marriage. The plaintiff will appear on a certain date; the court will note that the defendant, served by publication, has failed to appear. The defendant spouse will be defaulted and the divorce or dissolution will be granted. However, the court will not have the authority to enter orders for alimony or child support because the court has no personal jurisdiction over the defendant spouse.

Appearance
A document stating that a person has come into a court action as a party or an attorney representing a party.

Default judgment
Where one party "wins" the dissolution or divorce suit by failure of the other party to act.

Contempt
Where one party in an action does not comply with the court's order.

Affidavit of publication
A signed, sworn statement that a legal notice was printed.

The case of the nonappearing spouse is the exception rather than the rule. Most often, the defendant spouse obtains the services of an attorney who files an appearance on behalf of the defendant spouse and who also files responsive pleadings to the dissolution complaint. Naturally, the defendant spouse must contact an attorney or a law firm and have an initial interview with the attorney or firm's officer. The client interview of the defendant spouse will proceed in a manner that is similar to the interview process described for the plaintiff spouse in Chapter 13. If an agreement is reached regarding representation, the defendant spouse will sign a retainer letter with the law office and pay a retainer fee, and the office will prepare the responsive pleadings. This task will be delegated to the family law paralegal.

THE APPEARANCE AND THE ANSWER

As mentioned, the attorney or firm representing the defendant spouse must file an appearance. This appearance is a document that lists the name of the case, the return date, the name of the party being represented, the fact that the party is the defendant in the action, and the name, address, phone number, and juris number of the attorney or law firm. A sample of a typical appearance form is provided in Exhibit 14-5.

Answer
A document in which each allegation contained in the numbered paragraphs of a complaint is responded to.

The next document to be filed is the *answer*. The answer, like the complaint, will have a caption containing the name of the case and the return date. It will also have a body in which each allegation contained in the numbered paragraphs in the complaint is responded to. The defendant spouse will either admit to or deny each allegation or, in appropriate instances, will state that he or she lacks the necessary information or knowledge on which to form a response. Exhibit 14-6 illustrates a preprinted answer form.

The next section of the answer is the prayer section. In this section, the defendant spouse will make known his or her requests regarding alimony, child support, child custody, and/or visitation. For instance, a defendant spouse may admit that the marriage has broken down irretrievably in the response to the allegations section. However, in the prayer section, the defendant may signal his or her opposition to the plaintiff spouse's requests by requesting full custody of the minor child or children and by requesting child support and alimony. On the other hand, if the defendant spouse does not object to the plaintiff spouse's request for custody, the defendant spouse will request reasonable visitation rights. If the defendant spouse does not wish any alimony, the defendant will remain silent on this issue and deal with the question of the plaintiff spouse's requests for alimony and child support at a later time in the proceedings. The defendant spouse should always request an equitable division of marital property and should request such other relief as the court deems fair and equitable.

The answer, like the complaint, has a subscription section, which lists the defendant spouse's attorney's name and other identifying information. In some jurisdictions, the defendant spouse, like the plaintiff spouse in the complaint, may have to provide a signed and sworn-to verification of the answer.

SPECIAL DEFENSES

Special defenses
Part of a defendant's answer in which he or she cites unusual or extraordinary circumstances as part of his or her defense.

A defendant in any civil suit has the right to file a *special defense* or special defenses to the legal action brought against him or her. A divorce proceeding is a civil matter, and the defendant spouse may assert a special defenses or special defenses along with the answer to the divorce complaint. Because very few special

Exhibit 14-5 Maine appearance form.

STATE OF MAINE

☐ UNIFIED CRIMINAL DOCKET   County:_____

☐ SUPERIOR COURT   Location:_____

☐ DISTRICT COURT   Docket No:_____

_____ Plaintiff

      v.   **ENTRY OF APPEARANCE**

_____ Defendant

The Clerk will please enter my appearance as counsel for _____

_____

Plaintiff / Defendant

Date: _____   _____

Bar#:   _____

Address: _____

_____

_____

Telephone number: _____

Notice: This Appearance should be signed by a member of the Bar of Maine or by the party if appearing pro se, filed with the Clerk and a copy served upon each of the parties.

CV-CR-021, Rev. 01/17   Page 1 of 1

Source: Entry of Appearance, Wisconsin Court System.

Exhibit 14-6 Connecticut dissolution answer.

DISSOLUTION ANSWER
JD-FM-160 Rev. 6-14
P.B. § 25-9

STATE OF CONNECTICUT
SUPERIOR COURT
www.jud.ct.gov

COURT USE ONLY
ANSWER

Instructions

Fill out the form below and file it with the Court Clerk. If you are the defendant, you must also file an Appearance form (JD-CL-12). You may also file a Dissolution of Marriage Cross-Complaint (JD-FM-159) or Dissolution of Civil Union Cross-Complaint (JD-FM-159A) to tell the Court what you want the judge to order.

☐ Answer to Divorce (Dissolution of Marriage) Complaint
☐ Answer to Dissolution of Civil Union Complaint
☐ Answer to Divorce (Dissolution of Marriage) Cross-Complaint
☐ Answer to Dissolution of Civil Union Cross-Complaint

Judicial District of	At *(Town)*	Return date *(Month, day, year)*
Plaintiff's name *(Last, first, middle initial)*	Defendant's name *(Last, first, middle initial)*	Docket number

Number each line in the chart below to match the numbered paragraphs in the <u>Complaint</u> or <u>Cross-Complaint</u> *(example: 1, 2, 3, 4, 5a, 5b).* Use as many lines as you need. For each paragraph, mark an "X" for Agree, Disagree, or Do Not Know.

Paragraph number	Agree	Disagree	Do not know
	☐	☐	☐
	☐	☐	☐
	☐	☐	☐
	☐	☐	☐
	☐	☐	☐
	☐	☐	☐
	☐	☐	☐
	☐	☐	☐
	☐	☐	☐
	☐	☐	☐
	☐	☐	☐
	☐	☐	☐
	☐	☐	☐
	☐	☐	☐
	☐	☐	☐
	☐	☐	☐

I certify that a copy of this document was mailed or delivered electronically or non-electronically to all attorneys and self-represented parties of record and that written consent for electronic delivery was received from all attorneys and self-represented parties receiving electronic delivery on:

Date mailed or delivered	Signed *(Attorney or self-represented party)* ▶	Printed Name

Address *(Number, street, town or city, zip code)*

Name and address of each party and attorney that copy was mailed or delivered to*

*If necessary, attach additional sheet or sheets with name and address which the copy was mailed or delivered to.

The Judicial Branch of the State of Connecticut complies with the Americans with Disabilities Act (ADA). If you need a reasonable accommodation in accordance with the ADA, contact a court clerk or an ADA contact person listed at *www.jud.ct.gov/ADA.*

Source: Dissolution of Answer, State of Connecticut.

defenses (sometimes known as affirmative defenses) are available to a defendant spouse, it is unusual to see one asserted as part of the responsive pleadings. However, although the raising of a special defense is rare, it is not an unheard-of action. If a defendant spouse believes that a valid marriage never existed, he or she should certainly raise that belief as a special defense and request that the matter be dismissed. Similarly, if the person served is *not* the defendant spouse but someone else, that person has a perfect defense and should assert it to avoid being defaulted and possibly held in contempt.

THE CROSS-COMPLAINT

In most jurisdictions, the defendant spouse has the right to file an additional pleading called a ***cross-complaint***. In the cross-complaint, the defendant spouse assumes the role of a plaintiff by bringing a cross-action or countersuit for dissolution in which that party makes allegations and asks the court to grant him or her the relief of a dissolution or divorce and orders regarding custody, child support, alimony, and property division. Since the advent of no-fault divorce and the fault-neutral ground of irretrievable marital breakdown, cross-complaints have been rarities. Previously, when divorces were granted only on allegation and proof of a fault-based ground or grounds, a spouse sued for divorce on the grounds of mental cruelty or adultery or another negative ground and was frequently countersued by his or her spouse, who alleged a ground of equally negative conduct. This practice has virtually disappeared except in instances where the divorce is very bitter and where either the marital property is extensive or the custody of the children is hotly contested. A sample cross-complaint appears in Exhibit 14-7. This form serves the purpose for both complaints and cross-complaints in that it contains virtually the same information. If a cross-complaint is filed, then the original plaintiff spouse must file an answer to this pleading that responds to all allegations and contains its own request for relief.

> **Cross-complaint**
> See cross-claim.

Once all of the previously mentioned documents have been filed with the court, the pleadings are closed and the pleading phase of the dissolution process is over. Even if the parties have no areas of disagreement, there will be a statutory waiting period before the divorce is granted. In the meantime, whether the parties are in agreement or not, there will be hearings to provide for temporary relief to the parties while the divorce is pending. During this ***pendency period***, the court will entertain motions regarding alimony, child support, child custody, and other pertinent issues. These motions are known as **pendente lite** *motions* and are discussed in the next chapter.

> **Pendency period**
> The time during court proceedings before judgment is rendered.

> ***Pendente lite* motion**
> A motion granting relief only for the duration of the court action, before judgment is rendered.

Most but not all jurisdictions allow *pendente lite* proceedings. Where this option is not available, the parties, themselves or with the assistance of their attorneys, may be able to negotiate an interim agreement. If no type of agreement is possible, the remaining alternative is to proceed as swiftly as possible to trial and a final resolution.

THE ELECTRONIC COURTHOUSE

An Introduction to E-services

The technological age has led to the modernization of the manner in which legal information, documents, and access to court cases are made available to members of the public, the legal profession, and self-represented parties. Many state judicial branch websites now have a section called ***e-services***, the *e* being an abbreviation

> **E-services**
> Often used as the umbrella term to identify services available online.

Exhibit 14-7 Connecticut cross-complaint.

**DIVORCE COMPLAINT
(DISSOLUTION OF MARRIAGE)**
JD-FM-159   Rev. 3-17
C.G.S. §§ 46b-40, 46b-56c, 46b-84,
P.B. § 25-2, et seq.

STATE OF CONNECTICUT
SUPERIOR COURT
www.jud.ct.gov

CROSS COMPLAINT CODE ONLY
CRSCMP

ADA NOTICE
The Judicial Branch of the State of Connecticut complies with the Americans with Disabilities Act (ADA). If you need a reasonable accommodation in accordance with the ADA, contact a court clerk or an ADA contact person listed at *www.jud.ct.gov/ADA*.

☐ **Complaint:** Complete this form. Attach a completed Summons (JD-FM-3) and Notice of Automatic Court Orders (JD-FM-158).

☐ **Amended Complaint**

☐ **Cross Complaint:** Complete this form and attach to the Answer (JD-FM-160) unless it is already filed.

Judicial District of	At *(Town)*	Return date *(Month, day, year)*	Docket number

Plaintiff's name *(Last, First, Middle Initial)*	Defendant's name *(Last, First, Middle Initial)*

1. Plaintiff's birth name *(If different from above)*	2. Defendant's birth name *(If different from above)*

3. a. Date of marriage	3. b. Date of civil union that merged into marriage by subsequent ceremony or by operation of law	4. Town and State, or Country where marriage took place

5. *("X" all that apply)*
☐ The *("X" one)* ☐ plaintiff ☐ defendant has lived in Connecticut for at least 12 months immediately before the filing of this divorce complaint or before the divorce will become final.
☐ The *("X" one)* ☐ plaintiff ☐ defendant lived in Connecticut at the time of the marriage, moved away, and then returned to Connecticut, planning to live here permanently.
☐ The marriage broke down after the *("X" one)* ☐ plaintiff ☐ defendant moved to Connecticut.

6. A divorce is being sought because: *("X" all that apply)*
☐ This marriage has broken down irretrievably.
☐ Other *(must be reason(s) listed in section 46b-40(c) of the Connecticut General Statutes):*

_____
_____

"X" and complete all that apply for items 6-13. Attach additional sheets if needed.
7. ☐ No children were born to either the plaintiff or defendant after the date of this marriage.
8. ☐ There are no children of this marriage under the age of 23.
9. ☐ The following children are either: (a) the biological and/or adoptive children of both of the parties, or (b) have been born to one of the parties on or after the date of the marriage and are claimed to be children of the marriage.
(List only children who have not yet reached the age of 23.)

Name of child *(First, Middle Initial, Last)*	Date of birth *(Month, day, year)*

10. ☐ The following children were born on or after the date of the marriage to the *("X" all that apply)*
☐ plaintiff ☐ defendant and are not children of the other party to this marriage.
(List only children who have not yet reached the age of 23.)

Name of child *(First, Middle Initial, Last)*	Date of birth *(Month, day, year)*

Page 1 of 2

continued

Exhibit 14-7 Continued

11. If there is a court order regarding custody or support for any child listed above, name the child(ren) below and specify the person or agency awarded custody or ordered to pay support:

Child's name	Name of person or agency awarded custody	Name of person ordered to pay support
Child's name	Name of person or agency awarded custody	Name of person ordered to pay support
Child's name	Name of person or agency awarded custody	Name of person ordered to pay support

12. The *("X" all that apply)* ☐ plaintiff ☐ defendant or any of the child(ren) listed above have received from the State of Connecticut:

☐ financial support *("X" one)* ☐ Yes ☐ No ☐ Do not know

☐ HUSKY Health Insurance *("X" one)* ☐ Yes ☐ No ☐ Do not know

If yes, **you must** send a copy of the Summons, Complaint, Notice of Automatic Court Orders and any other documents filed with this Complaint to the Assistant Attorney General, 55 Elm Street, Hartford, CT 06106, and file the Certification of Notice *(JD-FM-175)* with the court clerk.

13. ☐ The *("X" all that apply)* ☐ plaintiff ☐ defendant is pregnant with a child due to be born on _____ .

The other parent of this unborn child is the ☐ plaintiff or ☐ defendant ☐ unknown   *(date)*

☐ not the plaintiff ☐ not the defendant.

14. The *("X" all that apply)* ☐ plaintiff ☐ defendant or any of the child(ren) listed above has received financial support from a city or town in Connecticut. *("X" one)* ☐ Yes *(City or town:_____)*

☐ No ☐ Do not know. If yes, send a copy of the Summons, Complaint, Notice of Automatic Court Orders and any other documents filed with this Complaint to the City Clerk of the town providing assistance and file the Certification of Notice *(JD-FM-175)* with the court clerk.

The Court is asked to order: *("X" all that apply)*

☐ A divorce (dissolution of marriage).

☐ A fair division of property and debts.

☐ Alimony.

☐ Child Support.

☐ An order regarding the post-majority educational support of the child(ren).

☐ Name change to:

Regarding Parental Decision-making Responsibility:

☐ Sole custody.

☐ Joint legal custody.

☐ A parenting responsibility plan which includes a plan for the parental decision-making regarding the minor child(ren).

AND

Regarding Physical Custody:

☐ Primary residence with: _____ _____

☐ Visitation.

☐ A parenting responsibility plan which includes a plan for the schedule of physical care of the minor child(ren).

_____

And anything else the Court deems fair.

Signature	Print name of person signing	Date signed
Address	Juris number *(If applicable)*	Telephone *(Area code first)*

- **• If this is a Complaint, attach a copy of the Automatic Court Orders before serving a copy on the Defendant.**

- **• If this is an Amended Complaint or a Cross Complaint, you must mail or deliver a copy to anyone who has filed an appearance and you must complete the certification below.**

Certification

I certify that a copy of this document was mailed or delivered electronically or non-electronically on *(date)* _____ to all attorneys and self-represented parties of record and that written consent for electronic delivery was received from all attorneys and self-represented parties receiving electronic delivery.

Name and address of each party and attorney that copy was mailed or delivered to*

*If necessary, attach additional sheet or sheets with name and address which the copy was mailed or delivered to.

Signed *(Signature of filer)* ▶	Print or type name of person signing	Date signed
Mailing address *(Number, street, town, state and zip code)*		Telephone number

JD-FM-159   Rev. 3-17   *Page 2 of 2*

for the word *electronic*. E-services is often used as the umbrella term to identify services available online. While the types of e-services vary from state to state, here are examples of some of the most common:

- *E-filing* is the electronic filing of legal pleadings and documents and has been implemented in many courts across the country, particularly in the areas of small claims, civil cases, complex civil litigation, and commercial cases. Some states are now adding family matters to the list of cases that may be filed through electronic means.
- *E-service* (in the singular, as opposed to the plural *e-services*) involves the process of officially delivering or "serving" a document or pleading on a party or other person or entity involved in a legal matter by electronic means.
- *Electronic notification* is the process of notifying a party to the case by e-mail that a document is served or filed and providing a hyperlink that will direct them to the document so it can be read or downloaded.
- *E-payment* is the online payment of court fees, tickets, fines, and taxes.
- Online search of court records
- Online attorney registration
- Access to online fillable, printable forms
- Online support for self-represented parties

E-Filing

Legal documents were traditionally mailed, fax filed, or hand delivered to the courthouse, opposing parties, and other individuals or agencies associated with family matters. Law firms looking for space often want offices conveniently situated near the courthouse because parking (or lack thereof) and parking tickets are always an issue in congested courthouse districts. With e-filing, however, case-related documents and pleadings can easily be filed from any computer with Internet access, eliminating those last-minute mad dashes to the clerk's office.

The Benefits of E-Filing

Attorneys and paralegals who work on federal cases are familiar with e-filing through *Public Access to Court Electronic Records*, commonly known by its acronym PACER. Some states have modeled their e-filing system after PACER, while others use alternative technologies. Implementing a state e-filing system is an expensive endeavor that can pay large dividends once it is in operation. The process begins with the blessing of the state judiciary as well as the drafting of ethical rules that set the parameters for access and protection of privacy. An e-filing system also requires the integration of an electronic filing system with the state's court case management system and public access system, as well as an electronic method for the payment of filing fees. It also must include technology that accommodates electronic signatures, notarizations, and certifications as well as a service and notification system. While PACER and many states have paved the way so the process does not have to be reinvented by states moving to an e-filing system, each state must tailor a system that suits its specific needs and budget requirements.

While the initial implementation of an e-filing system can be very costly, the long-term benefits to the taxpayers may be well worth it. On February 14, 2012, in his "State of the Judiciary Report," Chief Judge Jonathan Lippman of New York summed up the economic as well as ecological benefits of electronic filing. "Every year, the attorneys and litigants in our courts purchase hundreds of millions of pieces of paper, serve a mountain of paper on opposing parties, and file it with the courts. All this paper has to be transported, stored, retrieved as needed, and, ultimately, disposed. The waste, inefficiencies, and cost are enormous." He estimated that eventually the e-filing system in New York would save the courts, litigants, attorneys, and county clerks in excess of $300 million per year.

The benefits of e-filing for law firms include decreased costs of printing, postage, and paying for file storage. Quick access to documents is also an advantage. Pleadings, documents, and information may be reviewed at any time, and e-filing eliminates the attorney or assistant having to take time out to physically go to the courthouse to review files. There is also better control of case management because all the necessary documents can be accessed through the judicial branch's website. The convenience of filing documents after the courthouse closes and the ability to deliver the same electronically to opposing counsel and other interested parties is also a convenience.

E-filing also benefits the family law clerk's office and court staff. An effective e-filing system eliminates the manual input of data regarding each case because it can automatically populate data from the state's judiciary website into the state's case management system. Court clerks do not have to spend time entering and scanning documents since they are immediately filed through the e-filing process. It will also cut down on the visits made to the family law clerk's counter and relieve the clerks of the function of having to retrieve files, transport them, and pull them for the court hearings. Clerks do not have to go through the task of physically preparing the file for court because judges can review the file directly from the bench without having to wait for the clerk's office to bring the file to the actual courtroom. The courts can also eliminate or drastically reduce the need for maintaining and storing paper files.

The Basic E-Filing Process

While the family e-filing process varies from state to state, certain basic functions are common to most e-filing systems:

Creating an E-Filing Account The law office will have to create an e-filing account with the state's judicial branch; the account will include the attorney's bar identification number. It is important to create the account before a case has to actually be filed so that any technological glitches can be addressed without the pressure of an impending deadline. Once the account is created, the office will obtain a user ID and password that will permit the filing of new cases or representation of clients in matters that have already been filed.

The attorney's name and bar identification number must be included on all filings even though paralegals and other assistants are actually doing the filing. In some states, the attorney may add additional users to his or her account. In many others, however, only attorneys can e-file. The reality is that paralegals and other legal staff members, with their supervising attorney's consent, use the attorney's login information to file and monitor client cases. While this may be a common practice, the attorney is responsible for the filing, the content, and any of the consequences arising out of authorizing a member of the office staff to e-file on his or her behalf.

Initial Filing The initial pleadings in a family matter may not be submitted in electronic form until the actual paper documents have been personally served on the defendant. While procedures vary from state to state, often the initiating documents are first prepared by the plaintiff or his or her attorney, either in the traditional paper format or by completing fillable preprinted forms on the state's judicial branch website. In some states, the court clerk assigns a case or docket number before the documents are served on the defendant, while in other states, the number is assigned after the documents have been officially served.

Once the initiating documents are served, they can be electronically filed by the plaintiff, along with the sheriff or marshal's proof of service. In states where e-filing is voluntary, the parties have to agree to service by electronic means. The initiating documents may include some type of request for consent to electronic service that must be served on the defendant. In jurisdictions where e-filing is mandatory, the initiating documents may include a notice informing the defendant that the case will be filed electronically.

Pleadings may be uploaded onto the e-filing system as a PDF file or in a word-processing format that converts them to a PDF file. The court filing or entry fee is paid by credit card at the time the initial pleadings are filed, and the system should generate some type of acknowledgment or receipt.

When e-filing, the original documents are retained by the attorney's office and an electronic version is forwarded to the court. The attorney, as an officer of the court, may certify on the client's behalf that the client actually signed the original document that is in his or her possession.

Subsequent Pleadings Depending on the state, subsequent pleadings, except for those that must be personally served (such as subpoenas served on expert and lay witnesses) may be filed and e-served on the parties. In states where e-filing is voluntary, the parties must agree to accept service of the pleadings by electronic means. The electronic notification system sends an e-mail to the parties notifying them that a document has been filed in the case and a hyperlink where the document can be viewed or downloaded.

Learning the State's E-Filing Procedure

The varying family law rules and court procedures among the fifty states demand that attorneys and paralegals who work in states that have adopted e-filing become experts at electronically processing cases. There are several approaches to educating legal professionals in states that have adopted e-filing in family matters:

- Online tutorial videos and manuals
- Seminars offered by bar association or paralegal groups
- Online teleconferences
- WebEx training
- Training sessions offered by the courts

Learning about the state's electronic filing system will require some work and practice until lawyers and paralegals have used the system enough that it becomes routine.

E-Filers Beware: Precautions and Repercussions

The unlimited accessibility and the ease of just an instantaneous keystroke can lull an e-filer into a false sense of security. There are many pitfalls that if not anticipated can lead to disastrous repercussions if a legal professional is not forewarned. It is imperative that attorneys, paralegals, and anyone else in the office working on e-filing is aware of what can actually go wrong before beginning the process. As the old saying goes, to be forewarned is to be forearmed.

Failing to Meet Deadlines Traditionally, filing paper document at the last minute required a race to the courthouse before the doors closed. Now that more courts have adopted e-filing, it is imperative that the manner in which the particular court determines the close of business day is clearly understood. How does the court define the "close of business day"? Knowing the exact time, as well as date deadlines, is important not only for e-filing of documents but also for e-service to other parties involved in the case. Post reminders in the office of deadlines so they are always visible.

Filing the Wrong Document Make sure that the proper document or pleading is being filed by making it a habit to double- and triple-check before clicking on the "send" or "file" icon.

Inadvertently Deleting E-Mails All incoming e-mails should be checked for electronic notifications of pleadings and documents filed in pending cases. Make sure that junk e-mail and spam filters are not set to block court notices. Set these filters to allow court domain courts, clients, agencies, or any other entity where communication is necessary. Changes may need to be made with the ISP (Internet service provider) as well as the law office e-mail settings. It is also a good idea to check the junk e-mail folder to make sure anything relevant is not left unattended.

Checking Court Docket Checking the court docket on a daily basis is a good way to ensure that all electronically filed documents and pleadings have been properly uploaded and that cases are properly monitored for any changes that can occur.

Protecting Privacy in a Public Records Environment With the increase in electronic filing on the state and federal level, the trend to use technology for the purpose of convenience and cost savings is also creating serious privacy concerns. Divorces and any other type of family-related litigation present ethical and confidential challenges to the public accessibility inherent in electronic filing. There is much more anonymity to looking at a court file from the privacy of one's own computer, instead of publically going to the clerk's office, checking out a file, and reading it.

Many e-filed documents are publicly available at the touch of a button. Furthermore, no confidentiality police are sitting in the clerk's office ready to review filings for confidential information that will alert the attorney's office of potential problems. It is the responsibility of the attorney and his or her staff to ensure that confidentiality is maintained in the e-filing process.

Basically, federal and state law requires that personally identifiable information, or any information that can be used to identify a specific individual, must be protected from public view, whether the information is filed electronically or in paper form. This type of confidential, sensitive information must be omitted if unnecessary, or redacted or sealed if the law requires.

Redacting is defined as striking out the confidential words, phrases, or numbers by "blacking out" the information with a marker or using computer software that allows for this process to be performed through electronic means. Attorneys and paralegals working on their behalf and under their supervision are required to redact personally identifiable information from any electronic or paper filings. Failure to do so could potentially expose the attorney to a malpractice, administrative grievances, or invasion of privacy lawsuit.

Other documents must be *sealed*, which means that they cannot be viewed by the public and are available only to the court or able to be reviewed by the parties to the case. Documents encountered in family cases that are of a sensitive nature and are typically sealed from public view include:

- Juvenile records
- Health-care records
- Parenting evaluations
- Mental health records
- Alcohol and drug treatment records
- Reports prepared by a guardian ad litem
- Adoptions, guardianships, and conservatorships
- Reports prepared by child protective services

- Medical, psychiatric, and psychological evaluations
- Documents related to adoptions, guardianships, and child protection matters
- Custody and visitation studies prepared for court purposes by family court services personnel
- Financial affidavits, income tax records, bank statements, credit card statements, wage stubs, check registers, and retirement plan documents
- Documents identifying and related to victims of domestic violence, sexual assault, and child sexual abuse

Attorneys, paralegals, and those working under their supervision are responsible for protecting not only the personally identifiable information of their clients but also that of the opposing party and other parties involved in the case. Care should be taken to review all pleadings, documents, exhibits, and any other attachments that are being filed with the court to determine what should be redacted and what should be sealed by the court or filed under seal.

Federal Rules of Civil Procedure on Privacy Protection

Learning what qualifies as personally identifiable information and what needs to be sealed involves an understanding of federal and state law. A good starting point is *Federal Rule of Civil Procedure 5.2*. According to the Advisory Committee notes that explain this statute, Rule 5.2 was adopted to comply with Section 205(c) (3) of the E-Government Act of 2002, which required the U.S. Supreme Court to prescribe rules to address the issue privacy in conjunction with the electronic filing of documents and ease of public access to them.

Rule 5.2. Privacy Protection for Filings Made with the Court

(a) **Redacted Filings**. Unless the court orders otherwise, in an electronic or paper filing with the court that contains an individual's Social Security number, taxpayer-identification number, or birth date, the name of an individual known to be a minor, or a financial-account number, a party or nonparty making the filing may include only:

(1) the last four digits of the Social Security number and taxpayer-identification number;

(2) the year of the individual's birth;

(3) the minor's initials; and

(4) the last four digits of the financial account number.

(b) **Exemptions from the Redaction Requirement.** The redaction requirement does not apply to the following:

(1) a financial account number that identifies the property allegedly subject to forfeiture in a forfeiture proceeding;

(2) the record of an administrative or agency proceeding;

(3) the official record of a state-court proceeding;

(4) the record of a court or tribunal, if that record was not subject to the redaction requirement when originally filed;

(5) a filing covered by Rule 5.2(c) or (d); and

(6) a *pro se* filing in an action brought under 28 U.S.C. §§2241, 2254, or 2255.

(c) **Limitations on Remote Access to Electronic Files, Social Security Appeals, and Immigration Cases.** Unless the court orders otherwise, in an action for benefits under the Social Security Act, and in an action or proceeding relating to an order of removal, to relief from removal, or to immigration benefits or detention, access to an electronic file is authorized as follows:

(1) the parties and their attorneys may have remote electronic access to any part of the case file, including the administrative record;

(2) any other person may have electronic access to the full record at the courthouse, but may have remote electronic access only to:

    (A) the docket maintained by the court; and

    (B) an opinion, order, judgment, or other disposition of the court, but not any other part of the case file or the administrative record.

(d) **Filings Made under Seal.** The court may order that a filing be made under seal without redaction. The court may later unseal the filing or order the person who made the filing to file a redacted version for the public record.

(e) **Protective Orders.** For good cause, the court may by order in a case:

(1) require redaction of additional information; or

(2) limit or prohibit a nonparty's remote electronic access to a document filed with the court.

(f) **Option for Additional Unredacted Filing under Seal.** A person making a redacted filing may also file an unredacted copy under seal. The court must retain the unredacted copy as part of the record.

(g) **Option for Filing a Reference List.** A filing that contains redacted information may be filed together with a reference list that identifies each item of redacted information and specifies an appropriate identifier that uniquely corresponds to each item listed. The list must be filed under seal and may be amended as of right. Any reference in the case to a listed identifier will be construed to refer to the corresponding item of information.

(h) **Waiver of Protection of Identifiers.** A person waives the protection of Rule 5.2(a) as to the person's own information by filing it without redaction and not under seal.

State Rules Governing the Sealing and Redacting of Court Records

In addition to federal privacy rules, e-filers should learn the specific state rules related to the sealing and redacting of private information. While some states have specific court rules or statutes that mandate what personally identifiable information must be sealed or redacted from electronic filings, other states limit access to the e-filing system only to the parties and court personnel. Below is an example of Wyoming's judicial branch rules regarding the redaction of court records.

Wyoming Judicial Branch Rules Governing Redactions from Court Records*

Rule 1. Redacted Filings For any documents filed after January 1, 2011, unless otherwise ordered by the court, the parties shall refrain from including, or shall redact, where inclusion is necessary, the following four personal data identifiers from their pleadings, including exhibits thereto:

(a) Social Security Numbers. If an individual's Social Security number must be included, only the last four digits of that number should be used.

(b) Names of Minor Children. If the involvement of a minor child must be mentioned, only the initials of that child should be used. This does not

---

*Rules Governing Redactions from Court Records, Wyoming Supreme Court.

include cases where the minor is a party to the case, unless the statutes otherwise require.

(c) Dates of Birth. If an individual's date of birth must be included, only the year of birth should be used.

(d) Financial Account Numbers. If a financial account number is relevant, only the last four digits of such numbers should be used.

The responsibility for redacting these personal data identifiers rests solely with counsel and the persons filing the documents with the court. The Clerk will not review papers for compliance with these rules.

Rule 2. Protection Orders Pursuant to 18 USC 2265(d)(3), information regarding the registration, filing of a petition, or issuance of a protection order, restraining order or injunction, shall not be made available publicly on the Internet, if such publication would be likely to reveal the identity or location of the party protected under such order, except for court-generated and law enforcement-generated information contained in secure, governmental registries for protection order enforcement purposes.

Rule 3. Exemptions from Redaction Requirements The above redaction requirements do not apply to the following:

(a) Documents already made confidential by statute, administrative rule, court rule, or court order;

(b) The record of an administrative agency or court proceeding if that record was not subject to the redaction requirement when originally made;

(c) Citations; and

(d) Audio digital recordings.

Rule 4. Filings Made under Seal. The court may order that a filing be made under seal without redaction. The court may later unseal the filing or order the person who made the filing to file a redacted version for the public record.

Rule 5. Protective Orders For good cause, as set forth in Rule 8 of the Rules Governing Access to Court Records, the court may by order in a case:

(a) require redaction of additional information; or

(b) limit or prohibit a nonparty's remote electronic access to a document filed with the court.

Rule 6. Additional Unredacted Filing under Seal A party making a redacted filing shall also file an unredacted copy under separate cover and seal. Such an additional unredacted filing is required only in those cases where the entire personal data identifier listed in Rule 1 herein is required (e.g., charging documents). The court must retain the unredacted copy as part of the confidential record. If the redacted and nonredacted documents are not offered for filing contemporaneously, the missing document may be filed or postmarked within one business day. The Court may reject any paper filed not in compliance with these rules. When filing confidential or unredacted documents, the court will not accept fax filings.

Rule 7. Clerk Refusal to File Without regard to W.S. 5-7-103, the Clerk may refuse to file documents that are obviously not in compliance with these rules.

Rule 8. Transcripts In those cases already made confidential by statute, administrative rule, court rule, or court order, it is not necessary to redact transcripts. The responsibility for redacting official court transcripts rests solely with counsel and the parties. The court, clerk, and court reporter/transcriber will not review the transcript for compliance with these rules. Once a prepared transcript pursuant to Wyo. Stat. Ann. §§ 5-3-401 to 412 is delivered to the clerk's office for filing, and the court reporter/transcriber has given written notice by e-mail or traditional means to the parties that the transcript is completed, the attorneys in the case are (or, where there is a self-represented party, the party is) responsible for reviewing it for the personal data identifiers required by these rules to be redacted. Each party or counsel shall give prompt written notice of changes of address, telephone number, or e-mail address, if any, to the clerk and other parties.

Within eleven calendar days of the delivery by the court reporter/transcriber of the official transcript to the clerk's office, or longer if the court orders, each party must inform the court, by filing a Notice of Intent to Redact with the clerk, of his or her intent to direct the redaction of personal identifiers from the transcript of the court proceeding. A party is only allowed to request redaction of the four personal data identifiers specified in Rule 1 herein without further order of the court. If no such notice is filed within the allotted time, the court will assume redaction of the personal data identifiers from the transcript is not necessary, and the record completion process will proceed without further delay.

Within twenty-one calendar days of the transcript's filing with the clerk, or longer if the court orders, an attorney of record or self-represented party, who has previously filed a Notice of Intent to Redact, must file a Confidential Redaction Request. (See Appendix A to these rules.) A copy of this request must also be submitted simultaneously to the court reporter/transcriber. The request shall include the title of the transcript, the date it was filed, the case number and the items to be redacted, referencing them by page and line number and how they are to be redacted. For example, if a party wanted to redact the Social Security Number 123-45-6789 appearing on page 12, line 9 of the transcript, the Confidential Redaction Request would read: page 12, line 9: Social Security Number 123-45-6789 should be redacted to read xxx-xx-6789.

When a Confidential Redaction Request is filed, the court reporter/transcriber must within thirty-one calendar days from the filing of the transcript with the clerk of court, or longer if the court orders, perform the requested redactions, and file a redacted version of the transcript with the clerk of court. The original unredacted transcript will be sealed and retained by the clerk of court. The unredacted transcript will always remain as a sealed document and will not be available for review without further order of the court. The unredacted transcript may be withdrawn from the office of the clerk of the trial court without an order of that court, in accord with W.R.A.P. 3.09. The unredacted transcript shall also be available for transmission to the appellate court.

For all civil transcripts and for all criminal trial transcripts when the case is appealed, court reporters of the district courts are required to provide either a key-word index or a PDF electronic file for all parties to assist in redaction efforts. Upon request, court reporters of the district courts shall provide either a key-word index or a PDF electronic file for other criminal transcripts.

Rule 9. Rules Governing Access to Court Records Documents filed in court records shall also meet the confidentiality requirements of the Rules Governing Access to Court Records.

Excuses, Excuses...

Judges do not want to hear excuses from attorneys when it comes to mistakes made in filings, whether they are submitted on paper or, now, electronically. Attorneys and paralegals are expected to become electronically savvy and well versed in the e-filing process. It is also important to hire IT professionals, either on staff or on an as-needed basis, who can maintain the office computer systems and fix glitches. Legal professionals must learn the e-filing process in their jurisdictions and learn it well. Judges are not willing to accept excuses. The technological age is here and the practice of law has changed forever.

The court will ultimately hold the attorney responsible for mistakes made in the e-filing process no matter who committed the error. The malpractice lawsuit, grievances to the ethics committees, and sanctions will fall on the shoulders of the attorney; however, legal support staff can lose their jobs and their reputations in the legal community if care is not taken when e-filing.

Illinois Attorney Reprimanded

On January 29, 2013, the Illinois Attorney Registration and Disciplinary Commission Hearing Board reprimanded John A. Goudge for e-filing breach of confidentiality and failing to supervise one of the members of his legal staff. Regardless of who makes the mistake, it is the attorney who will bear the brunt and the embarrassment of a public grievance. Here are excerpts from the Board's disciplinary action.

BEFORE THE HEARING BOARD OF THE ILLINOIS ATTORNEY REGISTRATION AND DISCIPLINARY COMMISSION IN THE MATTER OF JOHN A. GOUDGE

No. 1024426
REPRIMAND
TO: JOHN A. GOUDGE

1. You are being reprimanded for engaging in conduct, in which you did not adequately supervise non-lawyer assistants in redacting personal identifying information, causing defendants' personal identifying information to be available and viewable to the public on the N.D. Ill. website home page. After being notified and informed of the redaction problems, you did not take steps to adequately supervise your non-lawyer assistants or review their work. By failing to adequately supervise your non-lawyer assistants' work, the defendants' personal identifying information was not redacted and continued to be available and viewable through the CM/ECF system. Had you adequately supervised your non-lawyer assistants, these disciplinary proceedings might have been avoided.

2. Your conduct undermines the public's confidence in the legal profession. Attorneys have an obligation to avoid all conduct that could bring the legal profession into disrepute.

3. Your conduct as described in this reprimand and in the stipulation was improper. You have violated Rules 5.3(b), 5.3(c)(2), and 8.4(d) of the Illinois Rules of Professional Conduct, and engaged in conduct which tends to defeat the administration of justice or bring the courts or the legal profession into disrepute. You are therefore reprimanded not to repeat the conduct which has resulted in the imposition of discipline.

4. You are further advised that while this reprimand is not formally presented to the Illinois Supreme Court, it is not to be taken lightly. This reprimand is a matter of public record and is on file with the Attorney Registration and Disciplinary Commission and may be admitted into evidence in subsequent disciplinary proceedings against you.

    WHEREFORE, John A. Goudge, you are hereby reprimanded. You are admonished not to engage in such misconduct in the future and to strictly comply with the rules of professional conduct. You are further admonished that this disciplinary action is a public record and will be considered in the event of any future disciplinary proceedings relating to you...

Concept Review and Reinforcement

KEY TERMS

abode service	domicile	prayer for relief
affidavit	e-services	pre-return date relief
affidavit of publication	filing fee	request for an order attaching
answer	in personam jurisdiction	known assets
appearance	in rem jurisdiction	residency
application for a	juris number	respondent
prejudgment remedy	jurisdiction	return date
body	motion for disclosure of assets	rules of court
caption	notice to appear for a	service by publication
complaint	deposition to disclose assets	service of process
contempt	pendency period	special defenses
court-entry fee	*pendente lite* motion	subject matter jurisdiction
cross-complaint	petition	subscription
default judgment	petitioner	summons
defendant	plaintiff	venue
dissipation	pleading	verification

REVIEW OF KEY CONCEPTS

1. Why is obtaining in personam jurisdiction over the defendant important in a divorce case?
2. What does the family law attorney represent to the court when he or she signs the complaint or petition? What is the signing called and where does it occur in the document?
3. What are the paralegal's responsibilities for arranging service of the divorce or dissolution complaint?
4. What is service by publication, and when is this form of service used in a divorce or dissolution action?
5. Why are special defenses rarely asserted in divorce proceedings?

BUILDING YOUR PARALEGAL SKILLS

CASE FOR BRIEFING

ZWERLING v. ZWERLING, 167 MISC.2D 782, 636 N.Y.S.2D 595 (1995)

Critical Thinking and Legal Analysis Applications

A prospective client, Emily Wright, has come to the New York law firm where you work as a paralegal. John Wright, her husband of ten years, has abandoned Emily and their five-year old daughter Allison and has been living and working in London, England, for the past year. John is a British citizen. Emily and Allison are American citizens. The couple was married in Brooklyn, New York. Emily has resided there continuously since their marriage. Emily wishes to divorce John but doesn't know how to go about it since John is in England. She also wants sole custody of Allison, child support, and full title to and ownership of the townhouse in Brooklyn the couple currently own together. Your supervisor wants you to review the New York case *Zwerling v. Zwerling*, review the precedents cited in it, and look at subsequent case law citing Zwerling to identify the requirement for serving John in England and acquiring in personam jurisdiction over him. Your supervisor wants you to write up the results of your research in an interoffice memorandum and also include in the memorandum the New York State requirements for obtaining a default divorce judgment and its limitations.

Building a Professional Portfolio

PORTFOLIO **EXERCISES**

1. Using the Internet, look up your state and find the residency requirements in your jurisdiction.

2. Go on the Internet and find a California petition for dissolution of marriage. Summarize the nine declarations in this petition.

3. Go on the Internet and find a California summons for a divorce case. Summarize the notice to the respondent.

4. Using the Internet or state-specific resources, find the procedure and forms necessary in your state to file the initial and responsive pleadings in a divorce action.

5. If you were going to file for divorce in your state, in which county or district would you file your case? Determine the proper venue.

6. Using the Internet, look up your state's judicial branch and determine if your state has e-services and e-filing in family matters.

Chapter **fifteen**
TEMPORARY RELIEF

In the United States, there is no such thing as an instant divorce. Every jurisdiction has some type of **cooling-off period** or waiting requirement that must elapse before a final divorce decree may be entered. The term cooling-off period *refers to the statutorily mandated time period following the initiation of divorce proceedings during which no final decree may be entered. This period usually runs for a number of months, depending on the jurisdiction.*

In many instances, the divorce decree is not issued immediately after the cooling-off period has expired. This is because divorce presents many complex issues that the parties must resolve or the court must resolve for them. In addition, the parties' respective attorneys' calendars must be accommodated and the court calendar must be considered. The judicial system provides vehicles through which the parties may seek and obtain court orders to determine how the obligations of the marriage partnership may be fulfilled during the time frame. One spouse or the other may use such vehicles to obtain relief on the issues of spousal support, maintenance and custody of the minor children, use of the family residence, protection from an abusive or violent spouse, and arrangements for paying bills to creditors for obligations the marital unit incurred.

It is important to note that in cases in which the parties are unmarried, petitions for child support, child custody, and visitation bypass the need for temporary motions. The parties in these cases may file their respective petitions in court for the specific relief sought without going through the temporary relief process.

The paralegal working in a family law practice plays an important role in facilitating relief for his or her client. Specific documents must be prepared and filed with the court to provide temporary relief for the client seeking such assistance. These documents are called temporary relief motions or petitions. For brevity purposes, the authors will refer to these documents as "motions" throughout the chapter.

TEMPORARY RELIEF

While a divorce action is pending, the court, upon a party's motion, will consider entering certain orders with which the parties must comply from the time the order is entered until the entry of final orders at the time of the divorce decree. This is known as a **temporary** or **pendente lite** relief motion. Pendente lite is a Latin term meaning "during the litigation." The family law division of every U.S. jurisdiction has certain requirements regarding the form and manner in which temporary relief motions should be filed. The local rules of practice provide guidelines and sometimes sample forms to follow. In addition, law offices typically have access to state-specific forms made available through the state's judicial branch website, or private publishers publish these documents along with instructions and annotations on CD-ROM, downloadable software, or online fillable documents.

Although specifics vary from jurisdiction to jurisdiction and from case to case, motions or petitions for temporary relief have general features common to all jurisdictions: Most include a *caption*, a *body,* and a *signature* or *subscription* section; further, most state court systems require a separate *order* page and a *certification* page.

- **Caption**

  The *caption* section of a motion must have the docket number, the names of the parties, the name of the court, its geographical location, and the date the motion was filed.

- **Body**

  The *body* of the motion identifies the party filing the motion, the relief specifically requested, and the grounds or basis on which relief is requested.

- **Subscription**

  The **signature** or **subscription** section lists in block form the designation given to the party in the lawsuit, namely, whether the party is the plaintiff or defendant in the action, the actual name of the party, a signature line, and the name of the attorney acting on the party's behalf, followed by the attorney's address, license number, and his or her phone number.

  If a party is bringing the action himself or herself without benefit of counsel, the party is said to be acting **pro se** or **pro per**. In such a case, the words *pro se* appear underneath the party's name and then the party's own address and phone number are listed.

- **Order**

  An **order** is a statement that sets forth the judge's decision on a particular motion before the court. When drafting a motion, an order is included for the convenience of the court and may even be required in many jurisdictions.

Subscription
Part of a court document that confirms the truth and accuracy of allegations and confirms the veracity of the party making these allegations; also known as the verification.

Pro se litigants
Individuals who represent themselves in legal proceedings, see *pro per*.

Pro per
Individuals who represent themselves in court; also known as pro se litigants.

Order
A statement that sets forth the judge's decision on a particular motion before the court.

In many areas of law, the order page of a motion simply contains the title "ORDER" and the following language: "The foregoing motion having been heard, it is hereby ORDERED: GRANTED/DENIED." In family law, the order page frequently contains more specific and more elaborate directives. For instance, the order page accompanying a motion for alimony may contain the statement that the defendant pay to the plaintiff spouse the sum of a specific dollar amount at a specific interval, such as $100 a week. The order for child support is usually similarly specific.

Motions for visitation frequently set the number of times for visiting each week and the house where such visits will take place. This is done if the parties have concerns about the duration, frequency, and location of visits and have not been able to work out these arrangements informally. Where parties have no differences on the issue, an order for reasonable visitation will suffice.

- **Certification**

All parties must receive notice of every motion filed with the court. Court systems recognize the need for efficient and economic service upon parties. Unlike the complaint in a lawsuit, courts do not require most motions to be served by a sheriff or other process server. The typical mode of serving a motion was to file the original of the motion with the clerk of the court either by hand-delivering it or mailing it to the clerk's court address and, on the same day, mailing a copy of the motion to the attorneys appearing for the other parties or to the *pro se* litigant. While some states still follow this method, many jurisdictions are now requiring litigants to file their motions or petitions electronically through the state's judicial branch "e-filing" systems. It is important to check the state's judicial branch website and court rules to determine how motions or petitions for temporary relief are to be filed.

The ***certification*** page of the motion states that a copy of the foregoing (motion and order) was sent on a specific date to all counsel of record and *pro se* appearing parties (if any). This page is signed by the moving party's attorney or by the party, if acting *pro se*. Some local practice rules require that the attorney for the moving party recite the names and addresses of all parties to whom the motion was sent.

Certification
Page accompanying a court document stating that a copy of the document was sent on a specific date to all counsel of record and *pro se* appearing parties (if any).

Certain motions have additional requirements. On rare occasions, a process server must serve a motion. However, this usually does not occur during the pendency of the proceeding. Some motions must be filed with an accompanying financial affidavit or an affidavit stating other facts. Others will not be accepted by the court for filing without an accompanying memorandum of law setting forth a legal argument for granting temporary relief. Some require descriptions of real and personal property when the ownership and location of such property are relevant.

MOST FREQUENTLY USED FAMILY LAW MOTIONS

A number of temporary motions are commonly used in family law practice, and the paralegal should be familiar with them. They are as follows:

- motion for alimony,
- motion for custody of minor children,
- motion for child support,
- motion for visitation,
- motion for counsel fees,
- motion for exclusive possession of the marital residence,

- motion for use of motor vehicle,
- motion for payment of mortgage payments and insurance premiums,
- motion to restrain party from entering the marital residence (restraining order), and
- motion to freeze marital assets.

In most family court jurisdictions, the motion practice rules are so flexible that a moving party can create motions to ask the court for an order on various items particular to the party's circumstances. For instance, one party may file a motion for payment of children's secondary school tuition or a motion for joint use of the parties' sailboat.

Many state judicial branch websites have included the necessary forms for parties to obtain temporary relief in family matters. For example, see:

- Connecticut Motion for Orders before Judgment (Pendente Lite) in Family Cases
- Colorado Motion for Temporary Orders
- New Jersey Temporary Support Order

Motion for Alimony

Motion for alimony
Where a party to a dissolution proceeding asks the court to grant support payments to him or her for the duration of the case.

A *motion for alimony* seeks the court to order one spouse to make payments of support to the other spouse. Temporary support payments enable the requesting spouse to meet his or her financial obligations during the pendency of the divorce. Motions for alimony are most common when one spouse has stayed in the home or has earned much less than the other spouse during the marriage.

The case of *Ard v. Ard* illustrates a dispute over a motion for temporary alimony relief.

MARK STEVEN ARD v. DONNA J. ARD

208 So.3d 1288 (2017)
District Court of Appeal of Florida, First District.

PER CURIAM:

In this dissolution of marriage proceeding, Mark Ard (the Husband) appeals from the nonfinal order awarding Donna Ard (the Wife) temporary support. Because the record does not contain competent, substantial evidence to support the Wife's need for temporary alimony, we reverse and remand for further proceedings.

Although temporary awards of alimony are within the trial court's broad discretion, they must be supported by competent, substantial evidence that demonstrates the need for support and the paying spouse's ability to pay. Breitenbach v. Breitenbach, 838 So.2d 1266, 1267 (Fla. 2d DCA 2003); Driscoll v. Driscoll, 915 So.2d 771, 773 (Fla. 2d DCA 2005); see § 61.071, Fla. Stat. (2016). The alimony award in this case was not accompanied by any findings concerning the Wife's need for support. Nevertheless, it appears that the award was based, in significant part, on "anticipated" household expenses the Wife testified she would incur when she moved from her mother's home, where she had been living rent free for almost four years since the parties' separation. The record is devoid of any evidence concerning when the Wife would actually move from her mother's home and begin incurring these expenses. Accordingly, we conclude that there is insufficient evidence in the record to support the Wife's present need for temporary alimony.

REVERSED and REMANDED.

Exhibit 15-1 Connecticut Motion for Orders before Judgment (Pendente Lite) in Family Cases.

MOTION FOR ORDERS BEFORE
JUDGMENT (Pendente Lite)
IN FAMILY CASES
JD-FM-176   Rev. 6-12
C.G.S. § 46b-56, P.B. § 25-24

STATE OF CONNECTICUT
SUPERIOR COURT
www.jud.ct.gov

COURT USE ONLY

MFORPLC   *Use this docket legend if the child custody box below is checked*

MFORPL   *Use this docket legend if the child custody box below is not checked*

Instructions to person filling out this form:
1. Fill out this form and keep a copy for your records.
2. Mail or deliver a copy to all attorneys and self-represented parties of record in this case.
3. File the form with the court clerk's office.
4. Carefully read and follow the instructions on the court calendar when you receive it.

Judicial District of	At *(Town)*	Return date *(Month, day, year)*	Docket number
Plaintiff's name *(Last, first, middle initial)*		Defendant's name *(Last, first, middle initial)*	
Plaintiff's address *(Number, street, town, state, zip code)*		Defendant's address *(Number, street, town, state, zip code)*	

The ☐ Plaintiff   ☐ Defendant   requests court orders concerning *(check all that apply)*:

☐ child custody

☐ child support

☐ child visitation *(parenting time)*

☐ alimony

☐ exclusive use of the family home

☐ appointment of an attorney for my child*(ren)* under 18

☐ genetic testing for paternity of child _____

☐ medical insurance/expenses

☐ other *(specify)* _____

Certification

I certify that a copy of this document was mailed or delivered electronically or non-electronically on _____ to all attorneys and self-represented parties of record and that written consent for electronic delivery was received from all attorneys and self-represented parties receiving electronic delivery.

Name and address of each party and attorney that copy was mailed or delivered to*

*If necessary, attach additional sheet or sheets with name and address which the copy was mailed or delivered to.

Signed *(Individual attorney or self-represented party)*	Print or type name of person signing
▶	

Order - To Be Completed By The Court

The above motion having been heard, it is ordered that:

By the Court	Signed *(Judge/Assistant Clerk)*	Print name	Date signed

The Judicial Branch of the State of Connecticut complies with the Americans with Disabilities Act (ADA). If you need a reasonable accommodation in accordance with the ADA, contact a court clerk or an ADA contact person listed at *www.jud.ct.gov/ADA.*

Source: Motion for Orders Before Judgment (Pendente Lite) In Family Cases, State of Connecticut.

Exhibit 15-2 Colorado Motion for Temporary Orders.

❑District Court ❑Denver Juvenile Court _____ County, Colorado Court Address: _____ In re: ❑The Marriage of: ❑The Civil Union of: ❑Parental Responsibilities concerning: _____ Petitioner: and Co-Petitioner/Respondent:	 ▲ **COURT USE ONLY** ▲
Attorney or Party Without Attorney (Name and Address): Phone Number: E-mail: FAX Number: Atty. Reg.#:	Case Number: Division Courtroom

MOTION FOR TEMPORARY ORDERS

The ❑Petitioner ❑Co-Petitioner/Respondent (check one) requests this Court to enter Temporary Orders. The Court authorized the filing of this motion on _____ (date). Temporary Orders are necessary for the following issues:

❑Allocation of parental responsibilities   ❑Parenting time

❑Child support   ❑Maintenance (spousal/partner support)

❑Possession/use of property   ❑Possession/use of residence

❑Responsibility for payment of debts   ❑Insurance coverage (❑medical ❑dental)

❑Other: _____

❑Other: _____

❑ By checking this box, I am acknowledging I am filling in the blanks and not changing anything else on the form.

❑ By checking this box, I am acknowledging that I have made a change to the original content of this form. (Checking this box requires you to remove JDF number and copyright at the bottom of the form.)

_____   _____   _____   _____
Petitioner Signature   Date   Co-Petitioner/Respondent Signature   Date

_____   _____   _____   _____
Petitioner's Attorney Signature, if any   Date   Co-Petitioner/Respondent's Attorney Signature, if any   Date

CERTIFICATE OF SERVICE

I certify that on _____ (date), a true and accurate copy of the **Motion for Temporary Orders** was served on the other party by:
❑Hand Delivery **or** ❑Faxed to this number _____   **or**
❑by placing it in the United States mail, postage pre-paid, and addressed to the following:

To: _____

_____

_____   _____
                                                            Your signature

JDF 1106   R8-17   MOTION FOR TEMPORARY ORDERS © 2017 Colorado Judicial Department for use in the Courts of Colorado

Source: Motion For Temporary Orders, State of Colorado.

Exhibit 15-3 New Jersey Temporary Support Order.

Superior Court Of New Jersey, Chancery Division, Family Part
TEMPORARY SUPPORT ORDER

Plaintiff:	Defendant:	Docket No.
		County:

Plaintiff's Attorney:	Defendant's Attorney:	Probation Account No.: CS

Pursuant to a proceeding before the Superior Court, Chancery Division, Family Part on this day, it is ordered that:

1. The ☐ Plaintiff ☐ Defendant make support payments and/or provide health care coverage as set forth below.

☐ 2. Support payments shall be paid through an income withholding issued pursuant to N.J.S.A. 2A:17-56.7a., et seq. The obligor must make support payments directly to the New Jersey Family Support Payment Center, Post Office Box 4880, Trenton, New Jersey 08650, until the support payments are withheld from the obligor's income. Payments shall commence on the effective date of this order and shall be administered and enforced by the _____ Probation Division.

☐ 3. Income withholding is not ordered. Support payments shall be administered and enforced by the _____ Probation Division. The obligor must make support payments directly to the New Jersey Family Support Payment Center, Post Office Box 4880, Trenton, New Jersey 08650. Payments shall commence on the effective date of this order.

☐ 4. Support payments shall be made by direct payments from the obligor to the obligee.

☐ 5. ☐ Plaintiff ☐ Defendant is required to provide health care coverage for the child(ren).

6. This Temporary Order shall remain in effect until the entry of a final judgment or a subsequent order in this matter is submitted to the above Probation Division. Parties paying support through the NJ Family Support Payment Center are also required to include a Confidential Litigant Information Statement unless one has been provided prior to the submission of this Temporary Support Order. R. 5:7-4(b).

Child Support Amount:	Spousal Support Amount:	Arrears Payment:

Effective Date:	Frequency ☐ weekly ☐ bi-weekly ☐ semi-monthly ☐ monthly		

Child's Name	Date of Birth	Child's Name	Date of Birth
1.		5.	
2.		6.	
3.		7.	
4.		8.	

☐ Arrears are to be calculated based upon the amounts and effective date noted above.

So ORDERED by the Court: Date:

_____ , J.S.C.

Promulgated 08/29/11 to be effective 09/01/2011, CN: 10487   Page 1

continued

Exhibit 15-3 Continued

NEW JERSEY UNIFORM SUPPORT NOTICES

PURSUANT TO R. 5:7-4(f), TAKE NOTICE THAT THE FOLLOWING PROVISIONS ARE TO BE CONSIDERED PART OF THIS ORDER AND ARE BINDING ON ALL PARTIES:

1. You must continue to make all payments until the court order is changed by another court order.

2. You must file a **WRITTEN** request to the Family Division in the county in which the order was entered in order for the court to consider a change in the support order. Contact the Family or Probation Division to find out how to do this. It is important that you request a change as soon as possible after your income or the child(ren)'s status changes. In most cases, if you delay making your request, and you are the obligor, you will have to pay the original amount of support until the date of your written request.

3. Payments must be made directly to the New Jersey Family Support Payment Center, P.O. Box 4880, Trenton, NJ 08650, unless the court directs otherwise. Payments may be made by money order, check, direct debit from your checking account, or credit card. Gifts, other purchases, or in-kind payments made directly to the obligee or child(ren) will not fulfill the support obligation. Credit for payments made directly to the obligee or child(ren) may not be given without a court order.

4. No payment or installment of an order for child support, or those portions of an order that are allocated for child support, shall be retroactively modified by the court except for the period during which the party seeking relief has pending an application for modification as provided in *N.J.S.A.* 2A:17-56.23a. (*R.* 5:7-4(e)).

5. The amount of child support and/or the addition of a health care coverage provision in Title IV-D cases shall be subject to review at least once every three years, on written request by either party to the Division of Family Development, P.O. Box 716, Trenton, NJ 08625-0716, as appropriate, or upon application to the court. (*N.J.S.A.* 2A: 17-56.9a; *R.* 5:7-4(e)).

6. In accordance with *N.J.S.A.* 2A:34-23b, the custodial parent may require the non-custodial parent's health care coverage provider to make payments directly to the health care provider by submitting a copy of the relevant sections of the order to the insurer. (*R.* 5:7-4(e)).

7. Social Security numbers are collected and used in accordance with section 205 of the Social Security Act (42 *U.S.C.* 405). Disclosure of an individual's Social Security number for Title IV-D purposes is mandatory. Social Security numbers are used to obtain income, employment, and benefit information on individuals through computer matching programs with federal and state agencies, and such information is used to establish and enforce child support under Title IV-D of the Social Security Act (42 *U.S.C.* 651 et seq.). Any person who willfully and with the intent to deceive, uses a Social Security number obtained on the basis of false information provided to Social Security Administration **or** provides a false or inaccurate Social Security number is subject to a fine or imprisonment. (42 *U.S.C.* 408(7); *R.* 5:7-4(e)).

8. The United States Secretary of State is required to refuse to issue or renew a passport to any person certified as owing a child support arrearage exceeding the statutory amount. In addition, the U.S. Secretary of State may take action to revoke, restrict or limit a passport previously issued to an individual owing such a child support arrearage. (42 *U.S.C.* 652(k)).

9. Failure to appear for a hearing to establish or to enforce an order, or failure to comply with the support provisions of this order may result in incarceration. The obligee and obligor shall notify the appropriate Probation Division of any changes in address, employment status, health care coverage, or a change in the address or status of the child(ren). Changes must be reported in writing to the Probation Division within 10 days of the change. Not providing this information is a violation of this Order. The last address you give to Probation will be used to send you notices. If you fail to appear, a default order may be entered against you or a warrant may be issued for your arrest (*R.* 5:7-4(e)).

10. Any payment or installment for child support shall be fully enforceable and entitled to full faith and credit and shall be a judgment by operation of law on or after the date it is due (*N.J.S.A.* 2A:17-56.23a). Any non-payment of child support you owe has the effect of a lien against your property. This child support lien may affect your ability to obtain credit or to sell your property. Failure to remit timely payment automatically

results in the entry of a judgment against the obligor and post-judgment interest may be charged. Judgments accrue interest at the rate prescribed by Rule 4:42- 11(a). (*R.* 5:7-4(e), 5:7-5(g)). Before the satisfaction of the child support judgment, any party to whom the child support is owed has the right to request assessment of post-judgment interest on child support judgments.

11. All child support obligations are payable by income withholding unless otherwise ordered. If immediate income withholding is not required when an order is entered or modified, the child support provisions of the order may be subject to income withholding when the amount due becomes equal to, or in excess of the amount of support due for 14 days. The withholding is effective against the obligor's current and future income from all sources authorized by law. (*R.* 5:7-4(e), *R.* 5:7-5).

12. The occupational, recreational, and professional licenses, including a license to practice law, held or applied for by the obligor may be denied, suspended or revoked if: 1) a child support arrearage accumulates that is equal to or exceeds the amount set by statute, or 2) the obligor fails to provide health care coverage for the child as ordered by the court, or 3) a warrant for the obligor's arrest has been issued by the court for obligor's failure to pay child support as ordered, or for obligor's failure to appear at a hearing to establish paternity or child support, or for obligor's failure to appear at a child support hearing to enforce a child support order and said warrant remains outstanding. (*R.* 5:7-4(e)).

13. The driver's license held or applied for by the obligor may be denied, suspended, or revoked if 1) a child support arrearage accumulates that is equal to or exceeds the amount set by statute, or 2) the obligor fails to provide health care coverage for the child as ordered by the court. The driver's license held or applied for by the obligor shall be denied, suspended, or revoked if the court issues a warrant for the obligor's arrest for failure to pay child support as ordered, or for failure to appear at a hearing to establish paternity or child support, or for failure to appear at a child support hearing to enforce a child support order and said warrant remains outstanding. (*R.* 5:7-4(e)).

14. The name of any delinquent obligor and the amount of overdue child support owed will be reported to consumer credit reporting agencies as a debt owed by the obligor, subject to all procedural due process required under State law. (*N.J.S.A.* 2A: 17-56.21).

15. Child support arrears may be reported to the Internal Revenue Service and the State Division of Taxation. Tax refunds/homestead rebates due the obligor may be taken to pay arrears (*N.J.S.A.* 2A:17-56.16).

16. Child support arrears shall be paid from the net proceeds of any lawsuit, settlement, civil judgment, civil arbitration award, inheritance or workers' compensation award to a prevailing party or beneficiary before any monies are disbursed. (*N.J.S.A.* 2A:17-56.23b).

17. Periodic or lump sum payments from State or local agencies, including lotteries, unemployment compensation, workers' compensation or other benefits, may be seized or intercepted to satisfy child support arrearages. (*N.J.S.A.* 2A:17-56.53).

18. If you owe past due child support, your public or private retirement benefits, and assets held in financial institutions may be attached to satisfy child support arrearages. (*N.J.S.A.* 2A:17-56.53).

19. A person under a child support obligation, who willfully fails to provide support, may be subject to criminal penalties under State and Federal law. Such criminal penalties may include imprisonment and/or fines. (*N.J.S.A.* 2C:24-5; *N.J.S.A.* 2C:62-1; 18 *U.S.C.A.* 22).

20. If this order contains any provision concerning custody and/or parenting time, both parties are advised: Failure to comply with the custody provisions of this court order may subject you to criminal penalties under *N.J.S.A.* 2C:13-4, **Interference with Custody**. Such criminal penalties include, but are not limited to, imprisonment, probation, and/or fines.
Si usted deja de cumplir con las clausulas de custodia de esta ordern del tribunal, puede estar sujeto (sujeta) a castigos criminales conforme a *N.J.S.A.* 2C:13-4, **Interference with Custody, (Obstruccion de la Custodia)**. Dichos castigos criminales incluyen pero no se limitan a encarcelamiento, libertad, multas o una combinacion de los tres.

Source: Superior Court Of New Jersey, Chancery Division, Family Part Temporary Support Order, New Jersey Judiciary.

Figure 15-1 Courts do not like to change a child's living arrangements once the child has become accustomed to living with one parent.

Martin Allinger/Shutterstock.

Motion for Custody of Minor Children

A **motion for custody** requests the court to order that one parent have the primary obligation for care and custody of the minor children and the authority to make decisions concerning how the care and maintenance of the children are to be administered. This motion must be taken very seriously by the party who wishes permanent custody of the children. If the pendency period is lengthy, the likelihood of a change in the custody from one parent to the other is very slight because courts do not make changes in the child's living arrangements after the child has adjusted to being primarily with one parent and is accustomed to that parent's style of parenting. Because the outcome of this motion is so significant, many attorneys pursue this phase of the divorce proceeding with meticulous care and great vigor. Whenever a party seeks to obtain custody of a child through a court proceeding, they may be required by state law to file a custody affidavit along with their motion for custody. In this document, signed under oath, the moving party swears that there are no other custody proceedings pending regarding the minor child or children in question.

Motion for custody
Where a party to a dissolution proceeding asks the court to have possession of the children for the duration of the case.

Motion for Child Support

The party filing a motion for custody frequently also files a **motion for child support**, which seeks an order from the court that the other parent—that is, the noncustodial parent—contribute to the financial support of the children. The court will order the noncustodial parent to pay a specific amount for each child. The court will determine this amount by referring to state-enacted **child support guidelines**, which impose a duty on a noncustodial parent for an amount based on his or her income and the age and number of the minor children. A more detailed discussion of the child support guidelines appears in Chapter 8. State guidelines typically establish an amount for the noncustodial parent to pay after also considering the custodial parent's income and ability to provide for the financial needs of the children.

Motion for child support
Where a party to a dissolution proceeding asks the court to have the other party pay child maintenance for the duration of the case.

Child support guidelines
Statutorily enacted formulas for determining the amount the noncustodial parent must pay for the support of each child.

The following case of *Eisenbaum v. Eisenbaum* illustrates an appeal of the trial court's award of temporary child support.

DONNA EISENBAUM v. ALAN EISENBAUM

44 Conn. App. 605, 691 A.2d 25(1997)
Appellate Court of Connecticut

HENNESSY, J.

The defendant appeals from the trial court's *pendente lite* order of child support. On appeal, the defendant claims that the trial court improperly (1) exceeded its jurisdiction in ordering the defendant to make payments other than child support, (2) awarded the plaintiff counsel fees, and (3) changed the effect of its order in its response to the plaintiff's motion for clarification.

The facts relevant to this appeal are as follows. The parties' marriage was dissolved in 1980. They later resumed living together and, in 1983, the parties had a child. They had a second child in 1986. The defendant has acknowledged paternity of both children. From November 1983 to September 1993, the parties lived together as husband and wife, although they were not legally married. Throughout the ten-year period, the plaintiff has not worked outside the home, by mutual agreement of the parties. She has, instead, attended to the children's needs and to household matters. The defendant, who terms himself an investor, has had an income averaging approximately $250,000 per year over the past five years.

continued

The parties separated in September 1993. After the separation, the defendant moved out of the house but continued to pay household expenses, credit card bills, gas charges, and expenses for the children, such as clothes, gymnastics, and soccer.

The plaintiff subsequently brought an action seeking, inter alia, support for the children. After a hearing on February 14, 1995, the trial court temporarily ordered the defendant to pay as child support $1,000 per week and to continue to pay the household expenses and the outstanding credit card balance. In its March 28, 1995, memorandum of decision and its May 4, 1995, response to the plaintiff's motion for clarification, the trial court stated that its prior temporary order would continue as the permanent *pendente lite* order.

On May 17, 1995, the defendant filed an appeal from the trial court's order regarding his obligation to pay the household and credit card expenses. On July 19, 1995, the trial court granted the plaintiff's motion to terminate the stay and awarded her $10,000 in counsel fees. Upon the defendant's motion for review, this court reinstated the appellate stay. On November 2, 1995, the trial court responded to the plaintiff's motion for clarification indicating that its March, 1995 order was a "combination child support order of cash and in kind necessary to maintain the family home for the benefit of the children." The defendant amended his appeal to include the issues regarding the trial court's award of counsel fees and its November 1995 response to the motion for clarification.

The defendant first claims that the trial court exceeded its jurisdiction by making a *pendente lite* order other than child support. He argues that the portion of the trial court's order requiring him to pay the household expenses and the credit card bill is a disguised alimony order and, therefore, the order was outside the court's jurisdiction.

General Statutes § 46b-61 allows the trial court to make any order as to the "custody, care, education, visitation and support of any minor child of the parties" in all cases in which the parents of the minor child live separately. "To determine the amount of support required by minor children, the court considers the needs of the children and the respective abilities of the parents to maintain them." *Whitney v. Whitney*, 171 Conn. 23, 29, 368A.2d 96 29, 368 A.2d 96 (1976); see also General Statutes § 46b-84(c).

"In determining whether a trial court has abused its broad discretion in domestic relations matters, [the reviewing court allows] every reasonable presumption in favor of the correctness of [the trial court's] action." *Ashton v. Ashton*, 31 Conn. App. 736, 742, 627 A.2d 943 (1993), cert. denied, 228 Conn. 901, 634 A.2d 295 (1994).

We conclude that the trial court did not abuse its discretion in ordering the defendant to pay the household expenses. We also conclude, however, that the court improperly ordered the defendant to pay the credit card balance.

In the plaintiff's financial affidavit, she listed her total weekly expenses for herself and her two children as approximately $1,843. We conclude that the trial court properly ordered the defendant to pay the household expenses in addition to $1,000 per week based on the needs of the children and the parties' ability to pay. The trial court, however, had no authority to order the defendant to pay the credit card debt as part of *pendente lite* child support. "Child support orders must be based on the statutory criteria enumerated in General Statutes § 46b-84 of which one of the most important is the needs of the child." *Brown v. Brown*, 190 Conn. 345, 349, 460 A.2d 1287 (1983). Here, the record contains no evidence that the payment of the credit card balance was necessary for the maintenance of the children.

This part of the support order was, therefore, improper....

Source: Donna Eisenbaum v. Alan Eisenbaum, 44 CONN. APP. 605, 691 A.2D 25 (1997), Appellate Court of Connecticut, State of Connecticut.

Motion for Visitation

The noncustodial parent has a right to visitation (or access) with the children. Upon motion, the court will address the noncustodial parent's desire for visitation and will tailor the provision in the visitation order to the best interests of the child. It is not unusual for a noncustodial parent's *motion for visitation* to request that the court enter an order for "reasonable visitation" without specifying the breadth or limits of this visitation. An order for "reasonable rights of visitation" leaves much to the discretion of the parties, and its success depends on the ability of the soon-to-be ex-spouses to communicate and negotiate a visitation schedule between themselves. When the parties are unable to do this, a more definite visitation schedule becomes necessary that spells out frequency and duration of visitation, with dates and times of pickup and return specified. Upon a motion for visitation with a detailed schedule, if the court finds that good cause exists, it will order such an arrangement.

Motion for Counsel Fees

The court has the power, upon motion for counsel fees of one of the parties, to order the spouse to pay the reasonable attorney's fees of the moving party. If the court orders reasonable counsel fees, the court will usually specify a dollar amount it deems reasonable. This amount may or may not reflect the actual amount the party will have to pay his or her attorney. Often the court's estimate of "reasonable" falls far below what the client is actually charged.

Sometimes courts choose to deny a motion for temporary counsel and instead indicate that a decision on counsel fees will only be made at the final hearing. Further, when both parties have ample funds or other assets in their own right, the court will not order one party to pay for the other party's legal fees associated with the divorce.

Motion for Exclusive Possession of the Marital Residence

The court has the power upon ***motion for exclusive possession of the marital residence*** by either spouse to order temporary possession of the marital home to the moving spouse. While most couples who own a house own it jointly, the motion is just for possession during the pendency of the lawsuit. This motion determines which of the spouses will live in the family residence until the final divorce decree is entered. At the time of the final decree, the court will recognize each spouse's interest in the property and make equitable orders for the disposition to the residence. Courts are reluctant to order either spouse to leave the family home during the pendency period because of the financial burden it imposes on the spouse having to leave. However, the court will make such an order if the spouses are in agreement as to one spouse leaving or if there are issues of family violence.

Motion for exclusive possession of the marital residence
Where a party to a dissolution proceeding asks the court to allow him or her to stay in the home, without the other party, for the duration of the case.

Motion for Use of Motor Vehicle

Sometimes household automobiles are titled jointly or in the name of one spouse only. Therefore, the spouse without legal title or sharing title may find it necessary to motion the court to order that one of the family automobiles be designated for his or her use. This motion, a *motion for use of motor vehicle*, like the others, typically has an order page attached and is presented to the court usually at the same time other temporary relief motions for alimony, child support, use of the family home, custody, and visitation are addressed.

Motion for Payment of Mortgage Payments and Insurance Premiums

One spouse may make a ***motion for payment of mortgage payments and insurance premiums***, which asks the court to order the other spouse to make all or part

Motion for payment of mortgage payments and insurance premiums
Where a party to a dissolution proceeding asks the court to have the other party pay for certain bills for the duration of the case.

of the mortgage payment on the family home and also to pay all or part of the insurance premiums needed to keep in effect policies that insure family assets or policies that provide medical or life insurance coverage for the spouses and minor children.

Restraining Orders

Motion to freeze marital assets
Where a party asks the court to stop any transactions of the marital property from taking place.

Motion to restrain party from entering marital residence
Where a party asks the court to order that the other party be forbidden to enter the home where that party is living.

Ex parte
A Latin term meaning "by one party" or "for one party."

Ex parte proceeding
A court hearing conducted in response to one party's *ex parte* motion or petition. The opposing party is not present during an *ex parte* proceeding because such proceedings are generally filed in an emergency situation.

Many judicial systems permit spouses to file a legal document, called a *restraining order*, that requests the court order the other party to refrain from certain actions or types of conduct or behavior. These orders include a **motion to freeze marital assets**, that is, a restraining order not to deplete the family assets, or sell the family home or any of the family motor vehicles, boats, or other significant articles of personal property; a restraining order freezing the savings or checking account so that neither party may subsequently race to the bank and empty such joint accounts of funds; and a restraining order preventing one party or the other from entering the family home (a **motion to restrain party from entering marital residence**) or harassing or assaulting the other spouse.

Ex Parte Proceedings

The U.S. Constitution and its state counterparts protect defendants from someone walking into a court without their knowledge, accusing them of some wrongdoing, and obtaining a court order. The general rule is that defendants have a right to procedural due process. This is the right to notice of the proceedings as well as the opportunity to be heard. *Ex parte* proceedings are an exception to this rule. **Ex parte** is a Latin term meaning "by one party" or "for one party." An **ex parte proceeding** is a court hearing conducted in response to a moving party's *ex parte* motion or petition. The opposing party is not present during an *ex parte* proceeding because these documents are generally filed in an emergency situation. The most common type of *ex parte* order is a restraining order in a domestic violence case. For example, an abused spouse who feels that she is in imminent physical danger may file an *ex parte* motion to order her husband out of the marital home. Another example would be learning that a spouse is preparing to leave the country or move to another state and take the minor children with her. The father in this case would file an *ex parte* motion to restrain her actions. *Ex parte* motions are also filed to prevent the transfer or hiding of assets.

Ex parte orders are temporary in nature because the defendant has not had an opportunity to be heard. The moving party must file an application for *ex parte* relief as well as an affidavit supporting the reasons for the action. If the moving party is aware that the defendant has an attorney, defendant's counsel should be contacted. The moving party goes to court without the other party present, and the judge hears only one side of the story. While the court may grant an *ex parte* order immediately upon determining that there is good cause to do so, a hearing is scheduled within a matter of days to allow the defendant to appear and be heard by the court. Notice of this second proceeding will be sent to the defendant informing him or her of the opportunity to be heard on that date. At the second hearing, the defendant will have the opportunity to present his or her own evidence. The moving party may also present further evidence. At the close of this hearing, the judge will continue, modify, or vacate the order.

The following case of *Ex Parte K.N.L.* illustrates an "emergency motion" as well as issues involving military parents.

EX PARTE K.N.L.

872 SO.2D 868 (ALA.CIV.APP. 2003)
COURT OF CIVIL APPEALS OF ALABAMA

CRAWLEY, JUDGE

K.N.L., the mother of B.D.P., petitions this court for a writ of mandamus directing the Baldwin Juvenile Court to grant her motion to stay a *pendente lite* child custody proceeding. We deny the petition.

The mother is a member of a U.S. Army Reserve unit that was called to active duty on February 10, 2003, for deployment overseas as a part of "Operation Enduring Freedom." The mother sought a stay of the pendente lite child custody proceeding pursuant to the Soldiers' and Sailors' Civil Relief Act of 1940, 50 App. U.S.C. § 501 et seq. ("the Act").

K.N.L. ("the mother") and W.D.P. ("the father") are the parents of B.D.P. ("the child"), a ten-year-old girl. The parents have never been married. They lived together for the first six years of the child's life and then broke up in 1999, with the father taking up residence in Alabama and the mother taking up residence in Pennsylvania. For the next two years, the child, by agreement of the parties, lived with the father in Alabama during the school year and with the mother in Pennsylvania during the summer. In May 2000, the mother executed a power of attorney in favor of the father, allowing him to assume and maintain guardianship of the child during a time when the mother's reserve unit had been activated.

On May 2, 2002, the father filed in the Baldwin Juvenile Court a petition seeking sole physical custody of the child and requesting child support from the mother. The mother alleges that she was not served with the father's petition until nearly two months after the petition was filed. On May 20, 2002, as the parties had previously agreed, the child left for summer visitation with the mother in Pennsylvania. On July 28, 2002, the mother filed a motion for a thirty-day extension of time to answer the father's petition. Three days later, the mother filed an appearance for the limited purpose of filing a motion to dismiss the father's petition based upon her belief that the Alabama court had no personal jurisdiction over her. The mother did not return the child to the father at the end of the summer visitation.

On November 7, 2002, following a hearing, the juvenile court denied the mother's motion to dismiss. On November 14, 2002, the mother filed a "Contest of Paternity," alleging that W.D.P. was not the child's biological father and requesting that the court order paternity testing. On December 13, 2002, the father, alleging that the mother had failed to return the child at the beginning of the school year and had denied him any physical contact with the child, filed a petition for pendente lite custody of the child, or, in the alternative, for visitation with the child pending a final hearing on his custody and support petition.

On January 17, 2003, the juvenile court determined, based on an affidavit of paternity signed by the parties, that the issue of paternity was precluded by the doctrine of res judicata; therefore, the court denied the mother's request for paternity testing. The juvenile court set the father's custody and child support petition for a hearing on April 14, 2003.

On February 26, 2003, the father filed an emergency motion for pendente lite custody of the child, alleging that the mother had filed a number of baseless motions in an attempt to delay the custody proceedings; that the mother had failed to return the child at the beginning of the school year according to the parties' agreement; that he had reason to believe that the mother's military unit had recently been activated; that the mother had given legal guardianship of the child to the maternal grandmother in Florida; and that the mother had set up a child support allotment payable to the maternal grandmother. The juvenile court set the father's emergency motion for pendente lite custody for a hearing on March 19, 2003. On the morning set for the hearing, the mother moved to stay the proceedings, alleging that, because of her

continued

military orders, it was impossible for her to attend any custody hearing—final or pendente lite—and seeking a postponement under the Act until she returned from her overseas assignment. The mother attached to her motion a letter from her commanding officer and a copy of her activation orders, dated February 10, 2003, from the Department of the Army. The father filed an affidavit on April 21, 2003, stating that he had been informed by the child that, one week before the scheduled March 19, 2003, hearing, the mother's new husband had traveled to the home of the maternal grandmother in Florida to retrieve the child and to take her back to Pennsylvania to live with him while the mother was on active duty.

In Ex parte Integon Corp., 672 So.2d 497 (Ala. 1995), our supreme court reiterated what a petitioner must establish in order to be entitled to the issuance of a writ of mandamus.

> Mandamus is a drastic and extraordinary writ, to be issued only where there is (1) a clear legal right in the petitioner to the order sought; (2) an imperative duty upon the respondent to perform, accompanied by a refusal to do so; (3) the lack of another adequate remedy; and (4) properly invoked jurisdiction of the court.

672 So.2d at 499. The applicable portion of the Act provides:

> At any stage thereof any action or proceeding in any court in which a person in military service is involved, either as plaintiff or defendant, during the period of such service or within sixty days thereafter may, in the discretion of the court in which it is pending, on its own motion, and shall, on application to it by such person or some person on his behalf, be stayed as provided in this Act [Sections 501 to 591 of this Appendix], unless, in the opinion of the court, the ability of the plaintiff to prosecute the action or the defendant to conduct his defense is not materially affected by reason of his military service. 50 App. U.S.C. § 521.

In *Richardson v. First National Bank of Columbus,* 46 Ala.App. 366. 242 So.2d 676 (Ala.Civ.App. 1970), this court explained the purpose of the Act:

> The Soldiers' and Sailors' Civil Relief Act of 1940 (in like manner with all similar previous acts in our history) was prompted by at least two considerations, first, the maintenance in the armed forces of a reasonable measure of that unbothered serenity and security in respect of personal responsibilities which effectively promotes military efficiency and the national defense; and secondly, the assurance that in the field of individual justice no advantage in judicial proceedings by or against a soldier or sailor will result from his absorption in his country's defense....

... The Act "places upon the trial judge a wide discretion; and, in determining whether a service [member] is entitled to relief, each case must stand upon its own merits." 247 Ala. at 315, 24 So.2d at 222. "Whether to grant a continuance or stay pursuant to the act is a matter which rests in the sound discretion of the trial court and will not be disturbed on appeal absent an abuse of that discretion." ...

... Decisions construing the Act indicate that when a military parent seeks a stay of a child-custody or visitation proceeding, the trial judge should consider the impact of such a stay on the other parent's right to visit and communicate with the children. *See, e.g., Henneke v. Young,* 145 Ohio App.3d 111, 115, 761 N.E.2d 1140, 1143 (2001). In *Henneke,* the divorce judgment awarded the father, who was stationed in Korea, custody of the parties' three children and gave the mother "[v]isitation ... as agreed upon between the parties." 145 Ohio App.3d at 112, 761 N.E.2d at 1141. In response to the mother's motion to set a specific visitation schedule, the trial court awarded the mother one week of visitation in August. When the father indicated his inability to comply with the visitation order, the mother filed a petition seeking to hold the father in contempt. The father moved to have the contempt proceeding stayed until he was "relieved from his current assignment in Korea." 145 Ohio App.3d at 113, 761 N.E.2d at 1141. The trial court granted the stay, the mother appealed, and the Ohio appellate court reversed. The court stated,

> [W]hen exercising its discretion in this matter, the trial court should have considered the nature of the civil action at issue here. The dispute between the parties involves their children—the oldest of whom was nine years old at the time the proceedings were stayed—and the right of their natural mother to visit and communicate with them. Under the trial court's ruling, [the father] could prevent [the mother] from seeing her children for a substantial period of time while he is serving in Korea, without [the mother's] being able to do anything to vindicate her right, pursuant to the orders of the trial court, to visit and to communicate with her children. Under these circumstances, we conclude that the trial court acted unreasonably by suspending the proceedings in this matter, during the entire time that [the father] will serve in Korea, pursuant to the Soldiers' and Sailors' Civil Relief Act. 145 Ohio App.3d at 115, 761 N.E.2d at 1143.

> ... The juvenile court would have been well within its discretion in determining that the mother had intentionally delayed the custody proceedings and had used her active-duty orders in an eleventh-hour attempt to effect a long-term denial of the father's rights to visitation and custody. The Act "'is not to be employed as a vehicle of oppression or abuse....' Such statutes were enacted ... for the protection of the service [member's] rights and remedies, but not to be unjustly taken advantage of." ...

> ... The juvenile court would also have been within its discretion in deciding that the best interests of the child would be served by having her reside, pending a final hearing on the merits of the custody issue, with her natural father rather than with a third party such as the maternal grandmother or the mother's new husband.

> Finding that the mother had no clear legal right to a stay and that the juvenile court did not abuse its discretion in denying the stay, we conclude that the petition for the writ of mandamus is due to be denied.

Source: Ex parte K.N.L., 872 SO.2D 868 (ALA.CIV.APP. 2003), Court of Civil Appeals of Alabama, State of Alabama.

THE PARALEGAL'S ROLE IN FACILITATING TEMPORARY RELIEF MATTERS

The paralegal in a family law practice will perform many of the steps needed to bring temporary relief motions before the court. Frequently, the paralegal will draft all temporary relief motions for review by the attorney handling the file and any other documents that must accompany the motions in their respective jurisdiction.

After such review and any possible editing, the paralegal finalizes the motions for filing and makes sure that the appropriate number of copies is created. The paralegal ensures that the motions are filed with the proper court and copies are properly mailed to all necessary parties. The paralegal must make sure that he or she mails or electronically files the motion to the right court and to the proper division of the court handling family matters.

After the motion is filed with the court, the court clerk will assign the motion date for a court hearing. The clerk will send a *court calendar* to each attorney or *pro se* party. The court calendar is a small printed booklet or a set of pages that shows a number of cases listed according to parties and docket number. Each case

Court calendar
An official resource published by the court that contains a number of cases listed according to parties and docket number and indicates the order in which cases will be heard.

has a number, which indicates the order in which cases will be heard. However, the court calendar lists only a starting time for the court day, not for each case, so all attorneys must be there for the call of cases at that starting time even if their case is one of the last to be heard. In many jurisdictions, courts set aside one or two specific days of the week to hear motions brought before the court. Some court systems refer to these times as motion days, while other jurisdictions call the designated times a *short calendar*.

In every law office at least one staff person has the responsibility of keeping track of when each attorney must be in court. Often this function is delegated to the paralegal. The need to keep track of or docket all court dates is obvious. Failure to appear at a hearing may seriously disadvantage a client, drag out proceedings, and sometimes subject an attorney to a malpractice suit. The need for a *docket control system* is imperative.

Short calendar

One or two days of the week that courts set aside to hear motions brought before the court; also known as motion day.

Docket control system

A system of one or more calendars that helps an attorney keep track of the various court dates and deadlines.

DOCKET CONTROL SYSTEM

Dates for document filings, motions, trials, and other types of hearings come from different sources. In a law office in which general litigation is practiced as well as family law, the attorneys may receive electronic calendar notifications from both state and federal courts throughout the state. Calendaring these dates immediately is essential to avoid harm to a client's case as well as malpractice lawsuits. As soon as these notifications arrive or are retrieved, the paralegal must make sure that these dates are entered on the office's docket control system.

Every law office should have a master calendar through some type of case management and docket control software or online resource. Many law offices use either Microsoft's Outlook, Google Calendar, or a more sophisticated case management program designed specifically for family law firms. In addition to a docket control system, specialized case management software may also include such features as:

- Calculation of child and spousal support payments
- Determination of tax implications of property division
- Creation and tracking of child custody and visitation arrangements
- Record and track documents to be filed in courts and with other agencies
- New client/matter intake forms
- Timekeeping and client billing

In addition, many case management programs include downloadable apps for phones and tablets so that attorneys and paralegals may have instant access to case information.

As mentioned previously, the person bringing the motion is known as the *moving party*. The moving party will decide whether to go forward with the motion, that is, appear to argue the motion on the date the court has scheduled. On receipt of a court calendar, the paralegal must first determine whether the motion was brought by an attorney in the firm or by an opposing party. If the motion originated in the paralegal's firm, the paralegal should ask the attorney who brought the motion whether they plan to proceed with the motion on the date assigned. If this is the case, the paralegal may also be required to confirm that the attorney is "going forward" with the motion through online confirmation with the state's judicial branch. If the motion came from an opposing party, the paralegal must find out if the attorney handling the matter for the firm is available to appear at the motion hearing and whether he or she wishes to be there on that date.

Moving party

The person bringing the motion to court.

If the attorney in the paralegal's firm brought the motion and plans to argue it on the date assigned, the paralegal should contact the client to confirm the party's availability for court on that date if the client is needed at the hearing. A letter or e-mail should be sent to the client confirming the date of the hearing and the necessity of his or her presence. Then the paralegal must call the office of opposing counsel to notify that attorney that the motion will go forward. If the moving party is the opposing party, the opposing party will notify the paralegal's firm of their intention to go forward or postpone the hearing, and the paralegal will communicate this information to necessary individuals.

If the motion is going forward, the paralegal should locate the file prior to the hearing date and make sure that all recently received documents and other pieces of correspondence are appropriately filed. The file should be reviewed and updated on the day before the hearing, and the motion should be placed in the front of the court documents section of the file so it will be readily available to the attorney. In addition, the paralegal should confer with the attorney to ensure that other supporting documentation needed at the hearing is put with the file in a manner that is readily available to the attorney at the hearing. The paralegal should prepare the file so that the attorney may review it before the proceeding.

If the parties can reach an agreement on the temporary relief motions, they will prepare an agreement, or stipulation, outlining the terms and present it to the court. If the parties cannot agree, they may be required to meet with the court's family services division to assist them in arriving at an agreement. If this is unsuccessful, the court will hold a hearing on the motion. At the hearing the judge will either **grant** or **deny** the motion. If the motion is granted, the court will enter the appropriate orders. The parties are now required to follow the court's order. When the attorney returns from court, the paralegal should review the file to make sure that the motion with orders filled in is properly replaced in the file in the appropriate section.

Grant
In a court proceeding, when the judge decides to allow a party's request or motion.

Deny
In a court proceeding, where the judge refuses to grant the motion of one of the parties.

MOTIONS FOR CONTEMPT AND MODIFICATION

Contempt

When either party does not comply with a court order made in response to a previous motion, the opposing party may seek to have the party comply by filing what is known as a **motion for contempt**. The moving party must prove that the noncompliant party willfully violated the court's order. For example, suppose that upon the filing of the husband's motion for visitation, the court enters an order granting him reasonable rights of visitation with his minor children. A problem arises when the husband attempts to exercise his rights pursuant to the order and his wife refuses to allow him access to the children. The husband's recourse at this stage will be the motion for contempt.

Before drafting the motion for contempt, the paralegal must review the file in order to determine the court's original orders regarding the husband's motion for visitation. The motion for contempt must recite the court's original orders, when they were entered, the judge who entered such orders, and that the noncompliant party is willfully in violation of such order. The motion for contempt must also specify the type of relief sought, which may include a finding of contempt, payment of counsel fees and costs, and possible incarceration. If the motion for contempt addresses financial matters, the paralegal must also include a request for payment of any arrearages due by the spouse in contempt.

Motion for contempt
A document that alerts the court to the other party's failure to comply with the court's earlier order and requests that the court provide relief.

Modification

Sometimes temporary relief orders entered by the court are changed when a substantial change in the parties' circumstances occurs from the time the original order was entered. The legal vehicle for making such changes during the temporary relief phase is known as the ***motion for modification***.

Motion for modification
Where a party asks that orders entered by the court be changed when there has been a substantial change in one of the party's circumstances from the time the original order was entered; also known as a motion to modify.

For example, suppose that on August 15, 2018, the court grants the wife her motion for alimony pendente lite and orders the husband to pay her $275 per week. The husband makes weekly payments up to August 22, 2018. On August 25, 2018, the husband loses his job and is not employed again until September 20, 2018. At his new job, the husband earns far less than he did at his previous job. To change the existing order, the husband must file a motion for modification.

Note that while the husband was in the process of job hunting, the wife was probably on the phone to her attorney, and that office has responded with a motion for contempt against her spouse. It is very common for motions for modification and motions for contempt to be filed and addressed simultaneously before the court by the respective parties.

Many state judicial branch websites have included the necessary forms for parties to obtain temporary contempt and modification relief in family matters. For example, see:

Connecticut Motion for Contempt
Connecticut Motion for Modification
New York Petition for Violation of Support Order
New York Petition for Support

The following case illustrates a motion for modification of child support.

ROBERT PAUL HARRIS, III v. MELANIE HARRIS

No. 32A01-1702-DR-302
COURT OF APPEALS OF INDIANA
AUGUST 31, 2017

… ISSUE

Father raises one issue, which we restate as whether the trial court properly imputed income to him and denied his request for modification of child support.

FACTS

Father and Melanie Harris ("Mother") were married in 2000 and had three children. When they divorced in 2009, Father was ordered to pay $362.00 per week in child support. At that time, Father was working as an airline pilot.

On October 2, 2016, Father was arrested for operating a vehicle while intoxicated, and he was fired from his job. Father learned that, to resume flying as an airline pilot, he would have to pass a medical evaluation, see a psychiatrist, and provide the FAA with his police reports and court records. Father found temporary employment at a Wal-Mart warehouse making $361.00 a week, and he began working on December 9, 2016.

On December 21, 2016, Father filed a petition to modify his child support obligation as a result of his lower income. On January 4, 2017, Father pled guilty to Class A misdemeanor operating a vehicle while intoxicated, and he was sentenced to 361 days of probation. The trial court held an evidentiary hearing on the child support modification petition on January 13, 2017. The trial court entered findings of fact and conclusions thereon as follows:

6. The evidence established that [Father] was earning weekly gross income of $1,712.00, or approximately $89,000/yr at the time of the Decree.

7. [Father] is now earning $361.00 per week as a result of losing his job. The evidence established that [Father] was employed full time as a pilot with Republic Airways but was terminated on October 2, 2016, by his employer as a result of an operating while intoxicated charge. [Father] subsequently pled guilty on January 4, 2017, under case number 32D02-1610-CM-1510.

8. [Mother] was earning $460.00 per week at the time of the Decree, or approximately $23,920/yr. Currently, [Mother] works full-time and earns approximately $38,000/yr or $731/week.

9. [Mother] provides health insurance for the minor children at a weekly cost of $22.00. This is another substantial change since the Decree in that [Father] was previously providing health insurance.

10. The evidence established that [Father] does not spend more than 76 overnights per year with the minor children.

11. Based upon the foregoing, the Court finds and orders:

    a. [Father's] request to modify his support based upon a weekly gross income of $361.00 is denied. [Father's] reduction in income was as a result of a personal choice on his part to drink and drive. [Father] failed to demonstrate what reductions in personal expenses he has undertaken. Specifically, the evidence established that he continues to pay a monthly mortgage of $1,300.00 despite a reduction in income. Moreover, [Father] testified that it remains possible for him to work as a pilot again in the future after he completes several requirements which he has not fulfilled at this time;

    b. While [Father's] support should not be reduced based upon his personal choice to drink and drive, there have been other circumstances that have changed and that the Court considered for purposes of a modification. For example, [Mother's] income has increased; she has been paying the cost of health insurance; and, [Father's] overnight parenting time credit has decreased. Considering these changed circumstances, the new recommended weekly child support obligation is $343.00 per week. (Exhibit A). However, this is a change of only $19.00 per week and less than the 20% reduction threshold set forth in Ind. Code 31-16-8-1(b)(2);

    c. Even calculating support based upon an increase in [Father's] annual income to $100,000.00, taking into account all the other changes, the recommended support obligation only changes to $366.00 (Exhibit B), an increase of $4.00 per week which is also less than 20%;

    d. Based upon the foregoing, the Court finds that the current support order is not an unreasonable order. [Father's] request to modify child support is denied[.] ... Father now appeals.

Source: Robert Paul Harris, III, Appellant-Petitioner, v. Melanie Harris, Appellee-Respondent, August 31, 2017 Court of Appeals Case No. 32A01-1702-DR-302. https://www.in.gov/judiciary/opinions/pdf/08311701mb.pdf

Exhibit 15-4 Connecticut Motion for Contempt.

Clicking on the question marks (⍰) will give you information about that section of the form.

MOTION FOR CONTEMPT/ ⍰ CONTEMPT CITATION ⍰ JD-FM-173 Rev. 2-15 C.G.S. § 46b-87; 46b-220 P.B. § 25-27	STATE OF CONNECTICUT **SUPERIOR COURT** www.jud.ct.gov	COURT USE ONLY	
		MFCONTP	Use this docket legend when the Certification has been filled out, but there is no Order to Attend Hearing and Notice.
		CONTCPL	Use this docket legend when the Order to Attend Hearing and Notice has been filled out and the "Before Judgment" box is checked.
		CONTCIT	Use this docket legend when the Order to Attend Hearing and Notice has been filled out and the "After Judgment" box is checked.

ADA NOTICE
The Judicial Branch of the State of Connecticut complies with the Americans with Disabilities Act (ADA). If you need a reasonable accommodation in accordance with the ADA, contact a court clerk or an ADA contact person listed at *www.jud.ct.gov/ADA.*

(Check one) ☐ Before Judgment (pendente lite) ☐ After Judgment ⍰

Judicial District of ⍰   At *(Town)*   Docket number ⍰

Plaintiff's name *(Last, first, middle initial)* ⍰   Defendant's name *(Last, first, middle initial)* ⍰

Plaintiff's address *(Number, street, city, state, zip code)*   Defendant's address *(Number, street, city, state, zip code)*

I, the ☐ Plaintiff ☐ Defendant, respectfully represent that this Court issued an order on ⍰ _____ directing the ⍰
_____ *(month, day, year)*

☐ plaintiff ☐ defendant to *(fill out **only** the box (or boxes) below for the order (or orders) you are claiming was (or were) disobeyed):*

Pay child support in the amount of ⍰ per	Pay alimony in the amount of ⍰ per	Pay arrearages in the amount of ⍰ per	Total balance owed ⍰	As of *(Date)* ⍰

Have visitation or parenting time as follows: *(Attach a copy of the visitation schedule if available)* ⍰

Pay medical bills or provide health insurance as follows: ⍰

Other: ⍰

The ☐ plaintiff or ☐ defendant has disobeyed the court order in the following ways. ⍰ *(Please be specific. Include the amount of any past due amount you claim is due as of the date of this motion or another specific date.)*

I ask the Court to find the ☐ plaintiff ☐ defendant in contempt. ⍰ I certify that the above information is true to the best of my knowledge. ⍰

Signature* ⍰	Date	Telephone *(Area code first)*
Name of attorney or self-represented litigant ⍰	Address of attorney or self-represented litigant	

Certification *(Complete if motion is filed before judgment (pendente lite))*

I certify that a copy of this document was or will immediately be mailed or delivered electronically or non-electronically on *(date)* _____
to all attorneys and self-represented parties of record and that written consent for electronic delivery was received from all attorneys and self-represented parties of record who were or will immediately be electronically served.

Name and address of each party and attorney that copy was mailed or delivered to*

*If necessary, attach additional sheet or sheets with name and address which the copy was mailed or delivered to.

Signed *(Signature of filer)* ▶	Print or type name of person signing	Date signed
Mailing address *(Number, street, town, state and zip code)*		Telephone number

Order To Attend Hearing and Notice *(To be completed by the Court)* ⍰

The court orders ☐ the plaintiff ☐ the defendant to attend a hearing at the time and place shown below to show why you are not in contempt. The Court also orders the ☐ plaintiff ☐ the defendant to give notice to the opposing party of the Motion and of the time and place where the Court will hear it, by having a true and attested copy of the Motion and this Order mailed or delivered to the opposing party by any proper officer at least **12 days** before the date of the hearing. ⍰ Proof of mailing or delivery must be made to this Court at least **6 days** before the hearing. ⍰

By the Court *(Judge/Assistant Clerk)*	Date signed	Court Use Only

Hearing To Be Held At	Superior Court, Judicial District of	Date	Time	
	Court address	Room number *(If known)*	Telephone *(Area code first)*	

If you do not come to the court hearing, a civil arrest order (capias) may be issued against you.

(Continued on page 2)   *Check appropriate court: ☐ Superior Court ☐ Family Support Magistrate Division

Clicking on the question marks (?) will give you information about that section of the form.

Summons[?]

TO ANY PROPER OFFICER:

By the Authority of the State of Connecticut, you must serve a true and attested copy of the above Motion and Order to Attend Hearing on the below named person in one of the ways required by law at least **12 days** before the date of the hearing, and file proof of service with this Court at least **six days** before the hearing.

Person to be served	Address	
Assistant Clerk		Date signed

Order[?]

The Court has heard the above Motion and finds that the ☐ plaintiff ☐ defendant:

☐ **is not in contempt.**   ☐ **is in contempt in the following way(s):**[?]

☐ owes past due amount (arrears) as of _____ [?]in the amount of _____[?]

☐ other *(specify)* :[?] _____

_____

It is ordered:[?]

☐ payment in the amount of _____ for current support and _____ on past due by *(date)* _____[?]

☐ income withholding in the amount of _____[?]

☐ incarceration[?]

☐ attorney's fees[?]

☐ marshal's fees[?]

☐ this matter is continued to _____ at _____[?]
  (date)   *(time)*

☐ other *(specify):*[?] _____

_____

_____

_____

By the Court *(Judge/Family Support Magistrate)*	Signed *(Assistant Clerk)*	Date of order

Return of Service[?]

I left a true and attested copy of the Motion for Contempt ☐ in the hands of the defendant ☐ in the hands of the plaintiff

☐ at the current home of the ☐ defendant or ☐ plaintiff at _____
  (Number, street, town or city)

The original Motion is attached.

Name and title	County	Date of service

For Use By Any Proper Officer As Defined by C.G.S. § 52-50(a) Only

Fee information:

Copy _____

Endorsement _____

Service _____

Travel _____

Total _____

JD-FM-173   Rev. 2-15   **Page 2**

Source: Motion for Contempt, State of Connecticut.

Exhibit 15-5 Connecticut Motion for Modification.

Clicking on the question marks (⁇) will give you information about that section of the form.

MOTION FOR MODIFICATION ⁇
JD-FM-174   Rev. 2-13
C.G.S. §§ 46b-84, 46b-86
P.B. §§ 25-26, 25-30, 25-57, 25a-18, 25a-30
(Check one)

STATE OF CONNECTICUT
SUPERIOR COURT
www.jud.ct.gov

COURT USE ONLY
MFMOD

☐ **Before judgment** ⁇   ☐ **After judgment** ⁇ *(If the court has ordered you to attach a request for leave with a motion for modification of a final custody or visitation order, you must complete and attach a Request for Leave form (JD-FM-202) to this motion.)* ⁇

Judicial District of ⁇	At *(Town)*	Docket Number ⁇

Plaintiff's Name *(Last, first, middle initial)* ⁇	Plaintiff's Address *(Number, street, city, state, zip code)*

Defendant's Name *(Last, first, middle initial)* ⁇	Defendant's Address *(Number, street, city, state, zip code)*

Type of Motion to Modify ⁇
☐ Child Support   ☐ Alimony   ☐ Custody   ☐ Visitation   ☐ Other *(Specify):* _____

I, _____ , ☐ **the Plaintiff**   ☐ **the Defendant**   ☐ **a Support Enforcement Officer,**
         (Name)

respectfully represent that:

1. This Court issued an order dated _____ directing _____, residing at
                                                                              (Name)

_____, to: *(Complete the boxes that apply to your motion)* ⁇
         (Number, street, city, state, zip code)

Pay current support in the amount of:	Pay alimony in the amount of:
$ _____ every (per) _____	$ _____ every (per) _____

Pay arrearages as follows:	
$ _____ every (per) _____	on the total arrearage owed of $ _____ as of *(date)* _____

Have custody of the child/children: *(Check one)*	Have visitation or parenting time as follows:	Primary residence of children with:
☐ Joint legal custody ☐ Sole custody		

Provide health insurance coverage		Provide HUSKY/cash medical
☐ No ☐ Yes	Pay ____ % of unreimbursed medical expenses	$ _____ every (per) _____

Contribute to child care	Other *(Specify):*
____ % or $ _____	

2. You must explain briefly the facts that are the reasons why you are asking for this modification. *(Check appropriate box or boxes. Attach additional sheet or sheets if necessary.)*

   ☐ Since the date of the order, the circumstances concerning this case have changed substantially as follows:

   _____

   ☐ The order for current child support is substantially different from the current child support and arrearage guidelines presumptive child support order as follows:

   _____

3. The ☐ plaintiff ☐ defendant is a "deploying parent" of the armed forces. The facts about that deployment or mobilization are:

   _____

4.a. I am receiving state assistance or HUSKY health insurance, or I have received it in the past.   ☐ Yes   ☐ No
4.b. Any child that this motion is about is receiving state assistance or HUSKY health insurance, or has received it in the past.   ☐ Yes ☐ No
   If you answered "Yes" to either of these questions, you must send a copy of this motion to: The Office of the Attorney General, 55 Elm Street, Hartford, CT 06106. If you don't give the Attorney General's Office a copy, your motion may take longer to decide.

I ask the Court to modify the existing order or orders as follows: ⁇ *(Check all that apply)*

a. Child Support *(You must file a sworn to Financial Affidavit (JD-FM-6) at least 5 days before the hearing. You must also file an Affidavit Concerning Children (JD-FM-164), a completed Worksheet for the Connecticut Child Support and Arrearage Guidelines (CCSG-1, JD-FM-220), and an Advisement of Rights Re: Income Withholding (JD-FM-71) on your hearing date.)*
☐ Order current support   ☐ Find arrearage and order payment   ☐ Order immediate income withholding
☐ Increase current support   ☐ Provide HUSKY/cash medical   ☐ Provide health insurance coverage
☐ Decrease current support   ☐ Contribute to child care   ☐ Other _____

b. Alimony *(You must file a sworn to Financial Affidavit (JD-FM-6) at least 5 days before the hearing. You must also file an Advisement of Rights Re: Income Withholding (JD-FM-71) on your hearing date.)*

☐ Increase   ☐ Decrease
the amount of alimony to be paid.

c. Custody *(You must file a sworn to Financial Affidavit (JD-FM-6) at least 5 days before the hearing. You must also file an Affidavit Concerning Children (JD-FM-164) and a completed Worksheet for the Connecticut Child Support and Arrearage Guidelines (CCSG-1, JD-FM-220) on your hearing date.)*

☐ Modify custody as follows:

_____

(Continued on back/page 2)   Check appropriate court. ⁇   ☐ Superior Court   ☐ Family Support Magistrate Division

Plaintiff's Name *(Last, first, middle initial)*	Defendant's Name *(Last, first, middle initial)*	Docket Number

(Continued from page 1)

d. Visitation/Parenting Time *(You must file a sworn to Financial Affidavit (JD-FM-6) at least 5 days before the hearing. You must also file an Affidavit Concerning Children (JD-FM-164) and a completed Worksheet for the Connecticut Child Support and Arrearage Guidelines (CCSG-1, JD-FM-220) on your hearing date).*

e. Other *(Please be specific):*

☐ _____

☐ Modify visitation (parenting time) as follows:

_____

Signature	Print Name	Title *(If applicable)*	Date Signed
Address *(Number, street, city, state, zip code)*			Telephone *(Area code first)*

Certification

I certify that a copy of this document was mailed or delivered electronically or non-electronically on *(date)* _____ to all attorneys and self-represented parties of record and that written consent for electronic delivery was received from all attorneys and self-represented parties receiving electronic delivery.

Name and address of each party and attorney that copy was mailed or delivered to*

*If necessary, attach additional sheet or sheets with name and address which the copy was mailed or delivered to.

Signed *(Signature of filer)* ▶	Print or type name of person signing	Date signed
Mailing address *(Number, street, town, state and zip code)*		Telephone number

Order For Hearing and Summons *(To be completed by clerk or support enforcement officer, if applicable)*

The Court orders that a hearing be held at the time and place shown below. The Court also orders the

☐ Plaintiff   ☐ Defendant   ☐ Support Enforcement Officer   to give notice to the opposing party of the Motion and of the time and place where the court will hear it, by having a true and attested copy of the Motion and this Order served on the opposing party by any proper officer at least **12 days** before the date of the hearing. Proof of service must be made to this Court at least **6 days** before the date of hearing.

Hearing to be held at ➡	Superior Court, Judicial District of		Date	
	Court Address		Room Number	Time

To any proper officer:

By the Authority of the State of Connecticut, you must serve a true and attested copy of the above Motion and Order For Hearing and Summons on the person named below in one of the ways required by law at least **12 days** before the date of the hearing, and file proof of service with this Court at least **6 days** before the hearing.

Person to be Served	Address
By the Court	Assistant Clerk/Support Enforcement Officer	Date Signed

Order   The court has heard this motion and orders it

☐ **Granted**   ☐ **Denied**   **and**   ☐ **Further orders** *(if applicable):*

_____

_____

_____

By the Court *(Judge/Family Support Magistrate/Assistant Clerk)*	Date Ordered

For Court Use Only

Fee for Motion to Modify: ☐ Paid   ☐ Waived

Source: Motion for Modification, State of Connecticut.

Exhibit 15-6 New York Petition for Violation of Support Order.

F.C.A. §§ 453, 454, 459, Art.5-B;   Form 4-12
C.P.L.R.5242; S.S.L. § 111-g   (Petition-Violation
[**NOTE**: Personal Information Form 4-5/5-1d,   of Support Order)
containing social security numbers of parties and   10/2016
dependents, must be filed with this Petition]

FAMILY COURT OF THE STATE OF NEW YORK
COUNTY OF
....
In the Matter of a Proceeding under
Article (4)(5-B) of the Family Court Act   Docket No.

(Commissioner of Social Services, Assignee
on behalf of   , Assignor)   PETITION
                                                              (Violation of
                          Petitioner,   Support Order)

          -against-

                          Respondent.
....
WARNING: **THE PURPOSE OF THE HEARING REQUESTED IN THIS
PETITION IS TO PUNISH [SPECIFY NAME]:
FOR CONTEMPT OF COURT, WHICH MAY INCLUDE SANCTIONS OF A
FINE OR IMPRISONMENT OR BOTH. YOUR FAILURE TO APPEAR IN
COURT MAY RESULT IN YOUR IMMEDIATE ARREST AND IMPRISONMENT
FOR CONTEMPT OF COURT.**

TO THE FAMILY COURT:

          The Petitioner respectfully alleges that:
          1. a. Petitioner, [check box]: ☐ an individual, is related to the child(ren) as follows [specify]:
                    and resides at [specify]:[1]
                                   ☐ assignee agency, has its place of business at [specify]:
             b. [Applicable where Petitioner is assignee]: Assignor resides at [specify]: [2]
             c. Respondent resides at [specify]:[3]

          2. The name(s) and date(s) of birth of the child(ren) involved are:

---

[1] Unless the Court has ordered the address to be confidential on the ground that disclosure would pose an unreasonable health or safety risk. *See* Family Court Act §154-b; Form 21 (available at www.nycourts.gov).
   [2] *See* note 1.
   [3] *See* note 1.

Page 2

CHILD'S NAME	DATE OF BIRTH

3. By order of this Court, dated   ,   , the Respondent was ordered to pay for the support of the above-named child(ren) and was directed to pay the sum of $ □ weekly □ every two weeks □ monthly □twice per month □ quarterly to the □Petitioner
□ Support Collection Unit   □ NYS Office of Temporary and Disability Assistance.

4. (Upon information and belief) a) Respondent has failed to obey the order of this Court in that [specify provision(s) of order alleged to be violated and nature of violation(s)]:

b) As a result of Respondent's violation of the support order, Respondent owes $_____.

c) [Check if applicable]: □ Respondent's failure to comply was willful.

5. [Applicable to individual petitioners; if agency, skip to ¶ 6: check a box only if applicable]:
I am hereby applying for child support services from the Support Collection Unit (the IV-D program pursuant to Title 6-A of the Social Services Law) through the filing of this Petition, unless:

□ I have already applied for child support services from the Support Collection Unit (the IV-D program pursuant to Title 6-A of the Social Services Law)
□ I do not need to apply now because I have continued to receive child support services after the public assistance or care case, or foster care case, for my family has closed.
□ I do not wish to apply for child support services.
□ I am not eligible to apply for child support services because I am petitioning for spousal support only.

6. YOU ARE HEREBY NOTIFIED that Petitioner may amend this Petition to include any additional arrears which shall have accrued from the commencement of this proceeding up to the date of the hearing or disposition.

7. No previous application has been made to any judge or court, including a Native American tribunal, or is presently pending before any judge or court, for the relief requested in this petition (except

continued

Exhibit 15-6 Continued

Page 3

WHEREFORE, Petitioner requests an order granting Petitioner relief as set forth in Section 454 and 458-a, 458-b of the Family Court Act and Section 5242 of the Civil Practice Law and Rules, together with such other or further relief as the Court may deem just and proper.

NOTE:[4]   (1) A COURT ORDER OF SUPPORT RESULTING FROM A PROCEEDING COMMENCED BY THIS APPLICATION (PETITION) SHALL BE ADJUSTED BY THE APPLICATION OF A COST OF LIVING ADJUSTMENT AT THE DIRECTION OF THE SUPPORT COLLECTION UNIT NO EARLIER THAN TWENTY-FOUR MONTHS AFTER SUCH ORDER IS ISSUED, LAST MODIFIED OR LAST ADJUSTED, UPON THE REQUEST OF ANY PARTY TO THE ORDER OR PURSUANT TO PARAGRAPH (2) BELOW. SUCH COST OF LIVING ADJUSTMENT SHALL BE ON NOTICE TO BOTH PARTIES WHO, IF THEY OBJECT TO THE COST OF LIVING ADJUSTMENT, SHALL HAVE THE RIGHT TO BE HEARD BY THE COURT AND TO PRESENT EVIDENCE WHICH THE COURT WILL CONSIDER IN ADJUSTING THE CHILD SUPPORT ORDER IN ACCORDANCE WITH SECTION FOUR HUNDRED THIRTEEN OF THE FAMILY COURT ACT, KNOWN AS THE CHILD SUPPORT STANDARDS ACT.

(2) A PARTY SEEKING SUPPORT FOR ANY CHILD(REN) RECEIVING FAMILY ASSISTANCE SHALL HAVE A CHILD SUPPORT ORDER REVIEWED AND ADJUSTED AT THE DIRECTION OF THE SUPPORT COLLECTION UNIT NO EARLIER THAN TWENTY-FOUR MONTHS AFTER SUCH ORDER IS ISSUED, LAST MODIFIED OR LAST ADJUSTED BY THE SUPPORT COLLECTION UNIT, WITHOUT FURTHER APPLICATION BY ANY PARTY. ALL PARTIES WILL RECEIVE A COPY OF THE ADJUSTED ORDER.

(3) WHERE ANY PARTY FAILS TO PROVIDE, AND UPDATE UPON ANY CHANGE, THE SUPPORT COLLECTION UNIT WITH A CURRENT ADDRESS TO WHICH AN ADJUSTED ORDER CAN BE SENT AS REQUIRED BY SECTION 443 OF THE FAMILY COURT ACT, THE SUPPORT OBLIGATION AMOUNT CONTAINED THEREIN SHALL BECOME DUE AND OWING ON THE DATE THE FIRST PAYMENT IS DUE UNDER THE TERMS OF THE ORDER OF SUPPORT WHICH WAS REVIEWED AND ADJUSTED OCCURRING ON OR AFTER THE EFFECTIVE DATE OF THE ADJUSTED ORDER, REGARDLESS OF WHETHER OR NOT THE PARTY HAS RECEIVED A COPY OF THE ADJUSTED ORDER.

Dated: _____

_____
Petitioner

_____
Print or type name

_____
Signature of Attorney, if any

_____

[4]Not applicable to out-of-state orders entered in New York State for enforcement purposes only.

_____
Attorney's Name (Print or Type)

_____

_____
Attorney's Address and Telephone Number

Source: Form 4-12 (Petition Violation of Support Order), New York State Unified Court System.

Exhibit 15-7 New York Petition for Support.

S.S.L§§ 111-g; F.C.A; 416, 421, 422,
423; CPLR 5242
[**NOTE**: Personal Information Form 4-5/5-1-d,
containing social security numbers of parties and
dependents, must be filed with this Petition]

Form 4-3
(Support–Petition–
Individual)
10/2016

FAMILY COURT OF THE STATE OF NEW YORK
COUNTY OF
....

In the Matter of a Proceeding for Support
Under Article 4 of the Family Court Act

Docket No.

Petitioner,

-against-

SUPPORT
PETITION
(Individual)

Respondent.
....

TO THE FAMILY COURT:

The undersigned Petitioner respectfully alleges that:

1. a. I reside at [specify]:[1]
b. Respondent resides at [specify]:[2]

2. I am authorized to originate this proceeding because [check applicable box(es)]:

   ☐ Respondent and I were married at   on
   ☐ Respondent and I have the child(ren) named below in common
   ☐ Other [specify Petitioner's relationship to child(ren)]:

3. Respondent is chargeable with the support of the following spouse and dependent(s):

NAME	DATE OF BIRTH
SPOUSE:	
CHILD(REN):	

---

[1] Unless the Court has ordered the address to be confidential on the ground that disclosure would pose an unreasonable health or safety risk. *See* Family Court Act §154-b; Form 21 (available at www.nycourts.gov).
[2] Unless the Court has ordered the address to be confidential on the ground that disclosure would pose an unreasonable health or safety risk. *See* Family Court Act §154-b; Form 21 (available at www.nycourts.gov).

continued

Exhibit 15-7 Continued

4. [Check applicable box(es); if children have different fathers, include separate paragraphs]:
    □ The father of the of the above-named child(ren) is [specify]:   .
    □ The father was married to the child(ren)'s mother at the time of the conception or birth.
    □ An order of filiation was made on [specify date and court and attach true copy]:

    □ An acknowledgment of paternity was signed on [specify date]:   by
    [specify who signed and attach a true copy]:
□ The father is deceased.
    □ The father of the below-named child(ren) has not been legally established.
    □ A paternity agreement or compromise was approved by the Family Court of [specify county]:
    County on   ,   , concerning [name parties to agreement or compromise and
    child(ren)]:   . A true copy of the agreement or compromise is
    attached.

5. [Applicable to cases in which mother is not a party]: The name and address of the mother is [indicate if deceased or if address ordered to be kept confidential pursuant to Family Court Act §154-b(2) or Domestic Relations Law §254]:

6. [Check applicable box(es); if not applicable, SKIP to ¶7]:
Respondent has an
□ employer   □ income payor, as defined in Civil Practice Law and Rules 5241(a), whose address is [specify]:   , as a source of income.

7. I am hereby applying for child support services from the Support Collection Unit (the IV-D program pursuant to Title 6-A of the Social Services Law) through the filing of this Petition, unless [check a box only if applicable]:
    □ I have already applied for child support services from the Support Collection Unit (the IV-D program pursuant to Title 6-A of the Social Services Law)
    □ I do not need to apply now because I have continued to receive child support services after the public assistance or care case, or foster care case, for my family has closed.
    □ I do not wish to apply for child support services.
    □ I am not eligible to apply for child support services because I am petitioning for spousal support only.

8. No previous application has been made to any judge or court, including a Native American tribunal, or is presently pending before any judge or court, for the relief requested in this petition (except

WHEREFORE, I am requesting that this Court issue an order of support directing Respondent to pay fair and reasonable support, that Respondent be required to exercise the option of additional coverage for health insurance in favor of (his) (her) spouse and above-named child(ren), and for such other and further relief as the law provides.

NOTE: (1) A COURT ORDER OF SUPPORT RESULTING FROM A PROCEEDING COMMENCED BY THIS APPLICATION (PETITION) SHALL BE ADJUSTED BY THE

Page 3

APPLICATION OF A COST OF LIVING ADJUSTMENT AT THE DIRECTION OF THE SUPPORT COLLECTION UNIT NO EARLIER THAN TWENTY-FOUR MONTHS AFTER SUCH ORDER IS ISSUED, LAST MODIFIED OR LAST ADJUSTED, UPON THE REQUEST OF ANY PARTY TO THE ORDER OR PURSUANT TO PARAGRAPH (2) BELOW. SUCH COST OF LIVING ADJUSTMENT SHALL BE ON NOTICE TO BOTH PARTIES WHO, IF THEY OBJECT TO THE COST OF LIVING ADJUSTMENT, SHALL HAVE THE RIGHT TO BE HEARD BY THE COURT AND TO PRESENT EVIDENCE WHICH THE COURT WILL CONSIDER IN ADJUSTING THE CHILD SUPPORT ORDER IN ACCORDANCE WITH SECTION FOUR HUNDRED THIRTEEN OF THE FAMILY COURT ACT, KNOWN AS THE CHILD SUPPORT STANDARDS ACT.

(2) A PARTY SEEKING SUPPORT FOR ANY CHILD(REN) RECEIVING FAMILY ASSISTANCE SHALL HAVE A CHILD SUPPORT ORDER REVIEWED AND ADJUSTED AT THE DIRECTION OF THE SUPPORT COLLECTION UNIT NO EARLIER THAN TWENTY-FOUR MONTHS AFTER SUCH ORDER IS ISSUED, LAST MODIFIED OR LAST ADJUSTED BY THE SUPPORT COLLECTION UNIT, WITHOUT FURTHER APPLICATION BY ANY PARTY. ALL PARTIES WILL RECEIVE A COPY OF THE ADJUSTED ORDER.

(3) WHERE ANY PARTY FAILS TO PROVIDE, AND UPDATE UPON ANY CHANGE, THE SUPPORT COLLECTION UNIT WITH A CURRENT ADDRESS, AS REQUIRED BY SECTION FOUR HUNDRED FORTY-THREE OF THE FAMILY COURT ACT, TO WHICH AN ADJUSTED ORDER CAN BE SENT, THE SUPPORT OBLIGATION AMOUNT CONTAINED THEREIN SHALL BECOME DUE AND OWING ON THE DATE THE FIRST PAYMENT IS DUE UNDER THE TERMS OF THE ORDER OF SUPPORT WHICH WAS REVIEWED AND ADJUSTED OCCURRING ON OR AFTER THE EFFECTIVE DATE OF THE ADJUSTED ORDER, REGARDLESS OF WHETHER OR NOT THE PARTY HAS RECEIVED A COPY OF THE ADJUSTED ORDER.

Dated:

_____
Petitioner

_____
Print or type name

_____
Signature of Attorney, if any

_____
Attorney's Name (Print or Type)

_____
_____
Attorney's Address and Telephone Number

Analysis

Father challenges the trial court's denial of his motion for a modification of child support. The trial court entered findings of fact and conclusions thereon sua sponte. Sua sponte findings only control issues that they cover, while a general judgment standard applies to issues upon which there are no findings. *In re Paternity of Pickett,* 44 N.E.3d 756, 762 (Ind. Ct. App. 2015). We may affirm a general judgment with findings on any legal theory supported by the evidence. *Id.* As for any findings that have been made, they will be set aside only if they are clearly erroneous. *Id.* A finding is clearly erroneous if there are no facts in the record to support it, either directly or by inference. *Id....* The trial court here found no showing of changed circumstances so substantial and continuing as to make the terms unreasonable or a showing of a twenty-percent difference. Father argues that the trial court erred in calculating his weekly gross income because the trial court imputed income to him rather than using his actual income. The Indiana Child Support Guidelines provide:

If a court finds a parent is voluntarily unemployed or underemployed without just cause, child support shall be calculated based on a determination of potential income. A determination of potential income shall be made by determining employment potential and probable earnings level based on the obligor's work history, occupational qualifications, prevailing job opportunities, and earnings levels in the community ....

... Father's misconduct, while disturbing and criminal, do not seem to rise to the level of "intentional deceit".... It is undisputed that Father has lost his job as an airline pilot and, although he still has the chance of regaining similar employment if he complies with the FAA requirements, it is unclear when or if an increase in his income will occur. Under these circumstances, we conclude that the trial court's imputation of income to Father is clearly erroneous ....

Reversed and remanded.

Concept Review and Reinforcement

KEY **TERMS**

cooling-off period
court calendar
certification
child support guidelines
deny
docket control system
ex parte
ex parte proceeding
grant

motion for alimony
motion for child support
motion for contempt
motion for custody
motion for exclusive possession of the marital residence
motion for modification
motion for payment of mortgage payments and insurance premiums
motion to freeze marital assets

motion to restrain party from entering marital residence
moving party
order
pro per
pro se litigant
short calendar
subscription
temporary relief (pendente lite) motions

REVIEW OF **KEY CONCEPTS**

1. What is a statutory waiting requirement or "cooling-off period" in a divorce case?
2. Explain the purpose of a temporary relief motion.
3. What is the paralegal's role in facilitating temporary relief motions?
4. Explain the purpose of motion days or a short calendar.
5. What is a docket control system? What is the importance of maintaining a docket control system in a law office?

BUILDING YOUR PARALEGAL SKILLS

CASE FOR BRIEFING

GRAF v. GRAF, 208 N.J. SUPER. 240, 505 A.2D 207(1985)

Critical Thinking and Legal Analysis Applications

Based on the facts in the case of *Graf v. Graf*, 208 N.J. Super. 240, 505 A.2d 207(1985), how would the courts in your state decide this case? Does the family court in your state have the power to order the sale of marital assets before the court has entered a judgment of divorce?

Building a Professional Portfolio

PORTFOLIO **EXERCISES**

1. You work as a paralegal for the law office of Barbra Naughton in your state. Merrill Van, a client, informs Attorney Naughton that he needs an emergency divorce from his wife who lives in the same state. Go to the Internet and find the mandatory waiting requirement in your jurisdiction.

   a. Draft a letter to Mr. Van, on behalf of Attorney Naughton, advising him of the mandatory waiting period in your state.

   b. Are there any other possible solutions for Mr. Van? A coworker heard that you could get a "quickie" divorce in the Dominican Republic. Are there any other alternatives? Using the Internet, determine if this is at all possible and draft an interoffice memo informing Attorney Van of your findings.

2. You work as a paralegal for the law firm Zullo, Kretsch, and Barinsky in your state. Your office represents Anthony Guttmann as the defendant in a divorce action against his wife, Lori Guttmann. He and his wife have been living separate and apart for over a month. During this time, Mrs. Guttmann was very cooperative in arranging visitation with Mr. Guttmann and their two children, Gunter and Alisa. Once the initial pleadings were served on Mr. Guttmann, Mrs. Guttmann would not let him see the children. There are currently no pending orders in this case. Using forms found on the Internet or state-specific resources, draft the appropriate temporary relief motion and order in response on behalf of Mr. Guttmann.

3. You work as a paralegal for the law office of Melissa M. Fae in your state. Attorney Fae represents Twanetta Gibbs as the plaintiff in a divorce action against her husband, Erik Gibbs. She recently filed for divorce. Upon being served with the initial pleadings, Mr. Gibbs moved out of the marital home into his sister's basement. Mrs. Gibbs works full-time but cannot make ends meet on her salary. Mr. Gibbs is also employed full-time but refuses to give her any money to help support the children and pay the bills on the marital home. Using forms found on the Internet or state-specific resources, draft the appropriate temporary relief motion and order in response on behalf of Mrs. Gibbs.*continued*

Chapter **sixteen**

DISCOVERY IN THE ELECTRONIC AGE

LEARNING OBJECTIVES

After studying this chapter, you should be able to:

1. Recognize the different types of discovery tools used in family law litigation.

2. Understand the importance of financial statements or affidavits in family law litigation.

3. Comprehend the basic principles of E-discovery.

4. Understand the relevant use of information obtained through social media in family law litigation.

The discovery process is an important part of any type of civil suit. Discovery is the term used to describe the process or stage in a civil litigation matter during which information is gathered by each party for use in his or her case against the other party. There are set procedures known as discovery tools that the court allows the parties to employ while conducting discovery. The court, upon a motion from one of the parties, may hold the other party in contempt and/or compel the other party to release information requested unless the reluctant party has asserted a valid objection or privilege.

In a dissolution action, discovery is used to acquire essential information that will lead to an equitable distribution of marital property and to accurately determine each party's income in order to set alimony and child support payments. Finally, discovery can provide the information needed to make wise decisions about what type of custody the court will award and what visitation arrangements are in the child's best interests.

In our fast-paced and ever-changing age of electronic information and communications, it is imperative for the family law professional to be aware of how technology can both aid and hinder the discovery process.

DISCOVERY TOOLS

In any type of lawsuit, each party has the right to use any or all of the following discovery vehicles:

- interrogatories,
- requests for the production of documents,
- requests for physical and mental examination,
- requests for admission, and
- depositions.

In litigation involving family law matters, most and sometimes all of these general discovery tools are used. Frequently, family law attorneys also employ additional discovery-oriented procedures designed to elicit specific information essential to the resolution of the particular issues involved in a family law matter. Examples include the motion for disclosure of assets and the parties' respective financial affidavits.

What follows is a description of both the general discovery tools common to all types of litigation and the subsidiary discovery vehicles commonly used in family matters. Accompanying each of these descriptions is a summary of the family law paralegal's role and duties in facilitating effective use of each discovery tool and procedure. It is important to remember that when complying with discovery requests, irrelevant, unnecessary, privileged, and *confidential information must be redacted* in accordance with the rules discussed in Chapter 14, "Initial Pleadings: Starting the Process," whether the information is being delivered through hard copies or the e-filing process. Word files are converted to PDF format, and hard copies can be scanned after manual redaction and converted in this same manner.

Interrogatories

Interrogatories are written questions that one party in a lawsuit serves on any opposing party or parties. The party on whom the interrogatories are served must answer the interrogatories under oath. A party may object to having to answer an interrogatory. Objections can be asserted on the grounds that the information sought is *irrelevant*, *overbroad*, or *duplicative*. A party may also refuse to answer by asserting a privilege. A *privilege* is a court-conferred right permitting parties in a lawsuit to keep confidential any information exchanged between themselves and another person in instances where there was a special type of relationship between themselves and the other person that generated an expectation of trust, confidentiality, and privacy. For instance, the court recognizes:

- spousal privilege,
- attorney/client privilege,
- physician/patient (therapist/client) privilege, and
- priest/penitent (clergy/parishioner) privilege.

Interrogatories in a family law proceeding may seek to have the other party identify all banks accounts, stock accounts, and real property held by that party jointly or in his or her name, solely. Interrogatories may contain questions about a spouse's current employment, earned income, bonuses, and health insurance and life insurance coverage. In this new age of technology, interrogatories must now include questions regarding whether the party in question has stored financial records regarding his or her personal or business concerns on a computer hard drive or other electronic storage device. The purpose of these types of interrogatories is to uncover all of the opposing party's assets and sources of earned and unearned income, as well as forms of nonmonetary employment compensation.

Interrogatories
Requests for disclosure of all real and personal property owned by a spouse either in his or her own name or owned jointly with the spouse or with another person or entity.

Irrelevant
Not having anything to do with the matter at hand.

Overbroad
Too general; not specific enough.

Duplicative
Referring to discovery, something that has already been requested.

Privilege
A court-conferred right permitting parties in a lawsuit to keep confidential any information exchanged between themselves and another person in instances where there was a special type of relationship between themselves and the other person that promoted an expectation of trust, confidentiality, and privacy.

Interrogatories may also seek to have the opposing party spouse reveal the names of parties residing with the spouse, the names and addresses of doctors who have treated the spouse or who have treated the minor children when in that spouse's care, and the names of day-care providers or other child-care workers who have cared for the child or children. Interrogatories must be answered in writing, under oath, and by the party on whom they have been served.

Preparation of Interrogatories The paralegal in a family law practice will often have the task of drafting interrogatories to be served on the opposing party. The paralegal should begin this process by reviewing the client's file and making a list of all areas where information will be needed from the opposing spouse. Then the paralegal, with the supervising attorney's approval, should schedule a meeting with the client.

Prior to the meeting, the paralegal prepares a rough draft of the interrogatories or questions to be posed and answered. Most states or private legal publishing companies produce sample interrogatories that cover the main areas of personal and financial concern in family law matters. These sample interrogatories provide a good framework to gather the essential information needed. Additions and revisions can be made to accommodate the specific facts and circumstances of the case. At the meeting, the client and paralegal review these questions, correct any inaccurate information, and add and delete questions they agree are appropriate or not. Following the initial meeting, the paralegal revises the draft of the interrogatories and presents this revised draft to the supervising attorney for review and further revision, if necessary.

Once the supervising attorney completes any needed revisions and signs off on the document, the paralegal prepares the final form of the interrogatories and returns the completed document to the supervising attorney for final review and signature. Once signed, the paralegal ensures that the document is sent to the opposing party's attorney. In most jurisdictions, interrogatories and responses are not filed with the court. Many states, however, require that parties file with the court a ***notice of filing of interrogatories*** and a ***notice of responding to and/or objecting to interrogatories***.

The paralegal may also have the responsibility of monitoring the opposing party's compliance in response to the interrogatories. In many jurisdictions, the rules of court provide that interrogatories must be answered or objected to within thirty days of receipt. It is not unusual for a party's attorney to file a motion for extension of time in which to reply or object to the interrogatories or to informally have an agreement with the opposing party's counsel to provide the responses within a reasonable amount of time after the thirty-day period. However, an informal agreement allowing for additional time does not exempt the responding party from the obligation of filing any objections to any of the interrogatories within the original thirty-day period.

Sometimes, the thirty-day period will pass without any communication from the party served. The paralegal will have the compliance date marked on his or her calendar. If the answers to the interrogatories do not arrive at the office by the date due or shortly thereafter, the paralegal will notify his or her supervising attorney and learn from the attorney whether he or she should prepare a *motion to compel discovery* for filing with the court. In some family law practices, the office will have a procedure whereby, upon the expiration of the thirty-day period, the paralegal will automatically prepare a motion to compel for the attorney's signature and filing with the court. Frequently, simply receiving a motion to compel will be enough to hasten the opposing party's provision of responses, and the motion will not have to be heard by the court. Again, though, because the thirty-day period has passed, the responding party will have lost his or her opportunity to object to any of the questions and must answer all of the interrogatories.

If objections to any of the interrogatories are filed in a timely manner, and if the parties' attorneys have conferred and are unable to resolve the issue of objections, the paralegal will prepare a *motion to compel answers to interrogatories*,

Notice of filing of interrogatories
A document that alerts the court that a party has asked the opposing party to answer a set of written questions.

Notice of responding to and/ or objecting to interrogatories
A document that alerts the court that the answering party has either answered the written questions or objects to one or more of the questions.

which will address the objections, dispute their validity, and request that the court overrule them. A hearing will take place. After hearing oral argument from the parties' respective attorneys, the court will decide whether any of the interrogatories objected to must be answered and whether any of the objections fall within the allowed exceptions for not complying.

Once all the required interrogatory responses are received by the office, the paralegal will review the document. If any of the answers reveal the need to request certain documents, previously not known of, the paralegal will relay this information to the supervising attorney and inquire whether such documents should be added to any forthcoming production requests that the paralegal will prepare.

Preparation of Responses to Interrogatories As mentioned, a party served with interrogatories must answer the interrogatories in writing and under oath, and within a specific time frame. In the oath, the party must state that his or her answers or responses are true and accurate to the best of his or her knowledge. This obligation to answer truthfully and accurately does not preclude the law firm from providing a client with assistance in forming and articulating accurate responses or from providing technical assistance in the manuscripting or transcribing of the answers or objections.

When a law firm receives a set of interrogatories for a particular client to answer, frequently the family law paralegal will see to it that the client provides the required responses within the appropriate time frame. The paralegal forwards the interrogatories and e-mails or makes available on the firm's secure, password-protected website a copy to the client with instructions explaining that the client should try to provide answers to all questions to the best of his or her ability. The paralegal will also tell the client to send back his or her responses as soon as possible. After the client has sent the responses to the law firm, the paralegal reviews the information and then, with the approval of the supervising attorney, calls the client and sets a date for the client to come to the office to finalize the responses.

At this meeting, the paralegal assists the client in reformulating any answers that are incomplete or that do not really answer the question asked. In addition, the paralegal helps the client delete any information in answers that should be objected to or that is privileged. The paralegal also helps the client delete any information that has not been requested, especially information that, if left in the response, would, in fact, help the other side with their case and hurt the client.

The paralegal may also be extremely helpful to the client by telling the client how to go about getting some information sought that is not in the client's possession but that only the client can obtain. There may be an interrogatory that asks for details about the client's health plan, such as whether it covers children who are over eighteen but are full-time students. Another interrogatory may ask whether any life insurance or disability income is available through employment. Another interrogatory may ask for the name of the plan administrator for the client's pension plan. Some clients may not have the know-how or patience to negotiate the various bureaucratic procedures required to obtain such information. An experienced family law paralegal, one who has been confronted with this type of situation before, will be able to help clients cut through the "red tape," find the individuals they need to speak to, and obtain the necessary information. Sometimes, the paralegal will ask the client to contact these individuals while the client is in the law office so that the paralegal can intervene if necessary to explain more precisely what information is needed.

After the responses have been finalized, the paralegal prepares a final document for review by the supervising attorney. If the supervising attorney requests further revisions, the paralegal incorporates these changes and the attorney then reviews the final work product.

If everything is in order, the paralegal again arranges for the client to come to the office and review the final document. Then, subject to any final revisions, the client signs the responses under oath in the presence of two witnesses, and a notary public or officer of the court acknowledges his or her oath. Once finalized, the paralegal sends the responsive document to the opposing party's counsel and files notice with the court, if such notice is required.

EXAMPLE 1

Interrogatories Regarding Parties' Pension

The plaintiff requests that the defendant answer under oath the following interrogatories within thirty days of the service hereof by serving the same upon counsel for the defendant of this action and that they can be provided by the defendant with substantially greater facility than they can otherwise be obtained by the plaintiff.

1. *State whether or not you have present or future interest in any pension plan, retirement plan, profit sharing plan, stock option plan, deferred income plan, or other similar type of plan, annuity, or fund.*
2. *If the answer to Interrogatory 1 is yes, please answer the following:*
   a. *The type of plan, annuity, or fund.*
   b. *Name of the plan, annuity, or fund.*
   c. *Account number of the plan, annuity, or fund.*
   d. *Name and address of the plan administrator, trustee, or custodian.*
   e. *Age of eligibility for each plan, annuity, or fund.*
   f. *Date when each plan, fund, or annuity will vest.*
   g. *Present value of each plan, fund, or annuity.*
   h. *Projected value of plan, fund, or annuity at eligibility age.*
   i. *Date of withdrawal for each plan, fund, or annuity.*
   j. *Amount of benefits upon retirement for each plan, fund, or annuity.*

Requests for Production

Request for production of documents
Where a party formally asks that the other party present certain papers for use in a case.

Requesting party
The party asking the court to take some action.

Responding party
The party who must produce discovery documents.

Confidential
Information that is privileged; that is, not everyone is allowed access to it.

Motion for protective order
Where a party asks the court to prevent the other party from coming in contact with him or her.

Confidentiality agreement
An arrangement between an attorney and a client that certain information the client may divulge will be kept secret.

Parties may request production and inspection, and often copying or scanning, of documents that are relevant to a dissolution action. For instance, by means of a *request for production of documents*, one party can request inspection of the other party's federal and state tax returns, canceled checks, computer hard drives and other electronic storage documents, bills for the minor children's summer camp or private school, copies of health insurance plans, insurance policies, copies of driver's licenses, pay stubs, and titles to cars, boats, or other recreational vehicles. The party asking to see, and most likely copy, these documents is called the *requesting party*. The party who must produce these documents is known as the *responding party*.

The responding party must produce all documents requested unless he or she has a valid objection or the documents are privileged, or *confidential*, or the responding party does not possess what has been requested and has no idea of where this information is located. Sometimes, a responding party may withhold a document on the grounds that it is confidential. In a family law matter, this issue might arise when the requesting party seeks information relating to the respondent's business, profession, or employment. For the respondent to produce this information, the respondent might be divulging a trade secret, classified work-related data, or even information about an invention for which the respondent is seeking a patent or about an artistic work the respondent wishes to have copyrighted before revealing it to the public. In instances like this, either or both parties may draft and file with the court a *motion for protective order* and a *confidentiality agreement*. This information will ensure that although certain confidential information will be disclosed to the opposing party, that party, under penalty of law, must limit disclosure of this information to the court and the parties only and must affirmatively act to protect the confidentiality of the material provided.

Frequently, in a complex family litigation matter, one party may request production of documents that the opposing party or their attorney considers privileged information or attorney work product. The failure to produce these documents or the filing of an objection regarding their production may give rise to a motion to compel disclosure from the requesting party.

Previously, when courts granted such a motion, they nevertheless accommodated the objecting party by granting the requesting party the right to inspect or review the documents at the opposing party's office. The burden was placed on the reviewing attorney or paralegal to make photocopies and reimburse the office for the expense. Today, a paralegal can scan a paper document and create a PDF file in response to a production request.

Responses to interrogatories may be made in either hard copy or electronic form, known as e-discovery. It may be necessary to hire a forensic expert in cases where one spouse may accuse the other of having deleted or not produced relevant information from their personal or business computer. The suspicious spouse may, upon the court's approval, request inspection of the other spouse's hard drive, since nothing is ever permanently deleted from a computer. A competent forensic expert can facilitate the process of uncovering deleted or omitted materials. It is helpful for the attorney to narrow down the span of time to be searched on the hard drive for the benefit of the forensic expert. The use of a forensic expert can be costly; however, a motion may be made to force a nondisclosing party to pay the cost of such a service, which may be necessary due to his or her deceptive practices.

Preparation of Requests for Production The family law paralegal is often the person who prepares the preliminary draft of production requests. The steps in this process are similar to the steps utilized for preparing interrogatories. The paralegal reviews the file, consults with the attorney and with the client, and also draws on models of production requests from previous similar types of family law actions.

When the opposing party remits documents in response to the request, the paralegal checks off these documents, catalogs them, and prepares a list of documents not produced so that the supervising attorney will know of and can respond to the opposing party's noncompliance.

Sometimes when documents are produced and the paralegal catalogs them, the paralegal will recognize that some of the documents suggest the presence of other documents that should be produced. For instance, canceled checks from a spouse's separate personal or business checking account may include checks written monthly to pay a bill on an unknown credit card. The paralegal may want to ask the supervising attorney whether there should be a second request for production asking for copies of the last twelve months' receipts for this credit card and for any other credit card the responding party may possess. If the responding party has not kept all of the receipts, copies can be obtained from the credit card companies. Once all of these receipts have been provided to the law office, the paralegal will have the task of organizing them both chronologically and according to category of expenditure (entertainment, recreation, food, clothing, gifts, gasoline, etc.). The paralegal may also add up the expenditures in each category and come up with a total of all charges. Breaking the receipts down in this fashion and providing a summary of the pattern of spending to the supervising attorney will help greatly when the supervising attorney questions the spouse in a deposition.

Preparation of Responses to Requests for Production The family law paralegal may also be responsible for orchestrating a client's response to the opposing side's production requests. When the law firm receives a request for the production of documents, the paralegal forwards a copy of the interrogatories to the client. Because there is only a thirty-day time limit in which to respond to both interrogatories and production requests, the paralegal follows up with the client and may offer assistance in helping the client to identify and find the requested information. The paralegal should also meet with the supervising attorney to discuss which documents the attorney wishes to withhold as privileged, which documents the attorney objects to producing, and which documents, if any, the attorney wishes to be shielded by a protective order and confidentiality agreement.

If the attorney is seeking either a protective order or a confidentiality agreement, the paralegal may have the responsibility of drafting a motion for protective order or a motion to approve confidentiality agreement. Some jurisdictions require the filing of a memorandum of law in support of this type of request. If the paralegal has been adequately trained to do legal research, the supervising attorney may delegate to the paralegal the task of doing the legal research necessary for identifying and articulating the legal standard that must be met for the granting of a protective order or a confidentiality agreement.

EXAMPLE 2

Request for Production Regarding Pension

The plaintiff requests that certain documents material to the pending action, which are not privileged or within the possession of the plaintiff, whose production would be of assistance in the prosecution of the action, can be provided by the defendant with substantially greater facility than they could otherwise be obtained by the plaintiff and therefore requests that the defendant produce for inspection and copying the following:

1. *Copies of any pension plan, retirement plan, profit sharing plan, stock option plan, deferred income plan, or other similar type plan, annuity, or fund.*
2. *Copies of all statements or accounts for the year 20__ through the present date, which indicates the amount of your interest and contributions to all said plans, annuities, or funds.*

Request for Physical or Psychiatric Examination

In a dissolution action, one party may request that the other party submit to a physical examination and/or a psychiatric evaluation. This may occur when the requesting party believes and alleges that the other party's physical or mental status should preclude awarding child custody or unsupervised visitation to the other party. A physical examination should also include a blood test to detect the presence of any recreational or prescription drugs present.

EXAMPLE 3

Request for Medical/Psychiatric Examination

The plaintiff requests the Court to order a psychiatric evaluation of the defendant. The plaintiff contends that the mother's ability to care for the children is at issue.

A party may also file a request for physical or mental examination if the opposing party has requested a high amount of alimony on the basis that he or she is physically unable to work or too emotionally unstable to work, or where the party on his or her financial affidavit reflects high weekly costs for mental health counseling or therapy.

Finally, in dissolutions involving minor children, the children's mother may request a physical examination of the male spouse to establish paternity of the child for purposes of support, custody, and visitation. The husband may also request a paternity test if he doubts that he is the natural father of one or more of the children born during the marriage. Sometimes, sadly, a spouse may request a physical or psychiatric evaluation of a minor child when that parent suspects sexual abuse of the child on the part of the other parent. Conversely, the accused parent may also make the same request to exonerate him or her of these allegations, if they deem them to be false. A parent accused of sexual abuse who feels that the accusations are false and simply a retaliatory measure may request a mental health evaluation of the accusing parent to support his or her defense.

Preparation of a Request for a Medical Examination   When a family law paralegal has an initial informational interview with a client, as discussed in an earlier section, the paralegal asks the client to complete a questionnaire that addresses many aspects of the client's marital history and each spouse's individual family background, educational attainments, and medical history. After reviewing the client's responses, the paralegal may immediately recognize the existence of one of the previously mentioned circumstances that gives rise to the need for a physical or mental examination of the opposing party. The paralegal should bring this to the attention of the supervising attorney. If the supervising attorney agrees with the paralegal's analysis, he or she will direct the paralegal to prepare the document for filing in court.

In most jurisdictions, the party desiring such an examination must file a document with the court known as a ***request*** rather than a motion. A request differs from a motion in that it is automatically granted by the court thirty days after filing, absent the opposing party's objection. The family paralegal files the original of the request document with the court and makes sure that proper service is made on the opposing party's counsel. If no objection is filed within the prescribed time limit and the time limit expires, the paralegal contacts opposing counsel requesting dates on which to schedule the requested examination or examinations. Absent the timely filing of an objection, the opposing party must submit to the examination

Request
A document that asks the court to take some type of action; it is automatically granted by the court thirty days after filing, absent the opposing party's objection.

Figure 16-1 In a dissolution action, one party may request that the other party submit to a physical examination and/or a psychiatric evaluation.

Alexander Raths/Shutterstock.

Motion to compel examination
A document that asks the court to force the opposing party to submit to an examination.

within a reasonable amount of time. If the party refuses to do so, the paralegal must alert the supervising attorney of this failure and, with the supervising attorney's approval, file a ***motion to compel examination***.

Frequently, an opposing party may object to an examination completely, or object unless there is agreement as to the choice of examiner and agreement as to the extent, nature, and exact purpose of the exam or the use to which the requesting party will allocate the results. When an objection is filed, the opposing attorneys may be willing to negotiate a compromise and avoid litigating the issue in open court.

If no agreement is reached, the matter is scheduled for a hearing and the paralegal keeps a watchful eye for the court calendar indicating the date of the hearing. In many jurisdictions, a hard copy of the court calendar is no longer mailed but is made available on the state's judicial websites. Once confirmed, the paralegal will docket the hearing on the office master calendar and on the attorney's personal calendar and/or handheld electronic device such as a smartphone and/or tablet.

The paralegal is responsible for notifying the client of the need to be in court on the hearing date. If the supervising attorney believes that the client needs to be present, the paralegal may schedule a meeting to prepare the client in the event he or she will have to take the witness stand.

Preparation of a Response to a Request for a Medical Examination
When the family law firm receives a request that a client be subjected to a physical examination or mental or psychological evaluation, the attorney handling the file may direct the paralegal to communicate the request to the party and arrange for a conference to discuss the request. After this meeting, the supervising attorney may decide to object to the request or negotiate with opposing counsel to allow the examination subject to agreed-on parameters.

Usually, a party's attorney will not allow a blanket assent to an examination. Rather, he or she will propose limits to which the results are put, unless the examination is limited by its own nature. The family law paralegal may have the task of drafting a letter to the opposing counsel memorializing the limiting terms to which the parties have agreed. If no agreement is reached, the paralegal will, within the thirty-day period, draft and see to the finalization of an objection or objections that must be filed with the court. Once filed, the paralegal will make sure that the court hearing date is docketed on the firm's and the attorney's calendar and that any need for a continuance is requested in a timely manner.

If a client must submit to a medical examination or mental or psychological evaluation, the paralegal may be the staff person who arranges for the client's appointment, notifies the client of this appointment, and reminds the client a day or two before the appointment of this obligation. After the examination, the paralegal should make sure that the firm receives a copy of the examining physician's report and/or a copy of the results of any laboratory tests.

If there has been a request for a client to submit to a paternity test, the supervising attorney will probably suggest to the client that he not oppose the request because, absent a compelling reason, the court will overrule his objection, especially since the test now consists merely of taking DNA from saliva through a quick swab. If there are compelling circumstances to oppose a determination of paternity at this time, the client should bring the situation before the court. For instance, a child or children who are older and who have had the client as their psychological father for their entire lives would undoubtedly be devastated to learn that at the same time that their parents are divorcing, their father is really not their biological parent. In this situation, especially if the client desires to continue with his parental obligations, a judge might decide that it is not in the children's best interest.

If a paternity test is to be done on the client, the paralegal may have the responsibility for setting it up. In most communities, there are public and quasi-public health organizations that offer such testing periodically at a low cost.

Request for Admission

Sometimes either party in a dissolution action may file a ***request for admission*** of certain facts or events. In civil suits, one party may request formally that an opposing party admit the truth of some fact or event that will inevitably be proved at trial. For instance, one party may request that the other party admit that although the other party receives child support for three minor children, the oldest child resides with the noncustodial parent. If one party files a request for admission with the court, and the other party does not object to this request within thirty days after it is filed, the facts or events requested to be admitted are deemed admitted. If the other party does file an objection, then the parties may negotiate a compromise of admissions or, if no compromise is reached, the parties' attorneys will argue their respective positions before the court.

Preparation of a Request for Admissions The family law paralegal is responsible for recognizing any circumstances listed on the client questionnaire that may necessitate the filing of a request for admission. The paralegal should apprise the supervising attorney of such circumstances, and if the supervising attorney agrees that a request for admission of certain facts is in order, then the paralegal may prepare the document, present it to the attorney for review and signing, and see that it is filed properly with the court and that a copy is sent to the opposing counsel in a timely manner.

Once such a document is filed, the paralegal should watch the calendar to ensure that any objections received from opposing counsel are filed within the thirty-day time limit. If objections are filed in a timely manner and the parties' attorneys reach a compromise, the paralegal prepares, for court filing, either a revised request for admissions negotiated and agreed to by both parties, which will be automatically granted after thirty days, or a *joint stipulation* in which the opposing party withdraws its objections subject to the modification of some aspect of the requested admissions.

Preparation of a Response to a Request for Admission Frequently, when an attorney receives a request for admission from opposing counsel, the attorney will ask the paralegal to contact the client, explain the purpose of a request for admission, describe the nature of the admissions sought, and inquire whether the facts the opposing counsel seeks to have admitted are true and accurate. The paralegal discusses the outcome of this conversation with the supervising attorney, who will decide how to respond to the request. If the paralegal feels that the client needs further explanation or clarification of the request for admissions, the paralegal should convey this to the attorney, who may wish to speak to the client without further proceeding. The attorney may direct the paralegal to forward to the client a copy of the request for admission as well as instructions to the client to contact the office and set up a meeting.

The paralegal must also monitor the running of the thirty-day objection deadline so that before the time period expires, the attorney confers with opposing counsel and decides whether to allow the admissions or prepare objections to the request for admission to be heard by the court. If objections are filed and the court schedules a hearing, the paralegal will be responsible for docketing the date and notifying the client.

Request for admission
Where a party formally asks that an opposing party admit the truth of some fact or event that will inevitably be proved at trial.

EXAMPLE 4

Request for Admission

The plaintiff hereby requests the defendant to admit the truth of the following statements:

That the defendant's employer provides health insurance coverage for all biological or adopted minor children of the insured employee, regardless of their place of residence.

Depositions

The need for depositions does not arise in every dissolution case. Depositions are employed primarily when there is a need to identify all of the opposing spouse's assets, when documentation is needed to support one parent's claim that the child's interest will be best served by investing sole custody in that parent, or when a parent wishes to establish the need to severely restrict the other party's visitation rights.

A **deposition** is a procedure in which one party's attorney orally questions an opposing party or a nonparty witness who has sworn under oath to answer all questions truthfully and accurately to the best of his or her knowledge and ability. The person being deposed is known as the **deponent**. The format of a deposition includes the initial questioning by the deposing party's attorney. This questioning is termed **direct examination**. After the deposing attorney conducts the direct examination, the opposing party's lawyer has the opportunity to cross-examine his or her client. After this **cross-examination**, the deposing attorney may question the deponent on any subject covered in the cross-examination testimony. This questioning is known as **redirect** questioning.

The following individuals must be present at a deposition: the deposing attorney, the opposing party, and the court reporter or videographer. The attorney for the opposing party *should* also be present. The deposing party's client may be present and, for practical reasons, should be present. If, however, the deposing party's client in a dissolution suit is terrified of the opposing party, and the deposing lawyer decides that the risks to his or her client's well-being outweigh the value of the client's presence at the deposition, the attorney may choose to depose the opposing party outside the client's presence. The deposing attorney may also decide to have his or her paralegal present to take notes or retrieve documents for direct questioning or cross-examination.

At the deposition of a nonparty witness, all parties must be invited, but their presence is not mandatory. Usually the opposing party's lawyer will attend and want the client also to attend. The court reporter must always be present at a deposition.

Deposition Expenses Depositions are expensive. Therefore, the need for a deposition must be great enough to justify the expense. An attorney will apprise a client of the availability of the deposition as a discovery tool and may strongly recommend deposing the opposing party or a witness or witnesses. However, the decision to depose ultimately rests with the client, who must pay the attorney for time spent preparing for and appearing at the deposition and who must pay the court reporter for transcription services at the deposition and for the typed transcript of the deposition.

Videotaped depositions may be used, especially in cases where the witnesses are unavailable to attend trial. Examples of unavailability include the following:

- Witness is too physically ill or infirm to come to court,
- Witness, such as an expert, is living in another jurisdiction and cannot be compelled by service of process to appear but is willing to submit to a videotaped deposition in his or her own home state. The travel costs associated to bring a willing witness within the jurisdiction may also be beyond the client's financial means.

Early in a client's representation, the attorney should make the client aware of the possible need for depositions and the anticipated costs. An attorney should also tell his or her client that the opposing spouse's attorney may require that he or she be deposed. A client may refuse to appear at a deposition once he or she is noticed. A **notice of deposition** is served on a party to a lawsuit by sending the notice via first-class mail or by facsimile transmission to the party's lawyer.

Deposition
A procedure in which one party's attorney orally questions an opposing party or a nonparty witness who has sworn under oath to answer all questions truthfully and accurately to the best of his or her knowledge and ability.

Deponent
The person who is being questioned at a deposition.

Direct examination
The initial questioning by the party's own attorney.

Cross-examination
When the opposing party's lawyer has the opportunity to question the opposing party.

Redirect
After cross-examination, where the party's attorney may question the witness on any subject covered in the cross-examination testimony.

Notice of deposition
A document that alerts a party that he or she will be required to submit to examination by the opposing attorney.

Once a party has been served, the party through his or her attorney has the following options:

1. Appear at the deposition at the noticed time and place,
2. Negotiate to reschedule the deposition to a time and/or place mutually agreeable to the deposing party and the party being deposed, or
3. Request to have the other party cancel the deposition by offering to negotiate or informally resolve the issue that has given rise to the noticing of a deposition.

If a deposing party's purpose for the deposition is to uncover the opposing party's hidden assets or hidden and ongoing source of income, the party noticed for deposition may decide to amend his or her financial affidavit to reflect these amounts, thus obviating the need, time, and expense of a deposition. In the alternative, the party may simply decide to give the opposing spouse a higher property settlement or agree to a higher amount of alimony or child support or both.

Sometimes the simple act of noticing a party for a deposition will produce one or another of these results. Doing so is considered an act of strategy!

The Paralegal's Role in the Deposition At a minimum, the paralegal in a family law practice is responsible for preparing the notice of deposition, determining the client's availability, and forwarding notice to all counsel and *pro se* parties. Because a deposition is usually held at the law offices of the deposing attorney, the paralegal must check the availability of the conference room.

Sometimes, either the attorney or the paralegal will contact the opposing attorney or his or her paralegal to agree and reserve in advance the date or dates for the deposition. These dates then appear on the notice of deposition, which must nevertheless be served even if the respective attorneys have agreed to the fact of the deposition and its place, time, and date.

The paralegal must also make arrangements for a court reporter or videographer to take the deponent's testimony. Sometimes when calling an agency or business that employs several court reporters, the agency contact person may request that the paralegal forward to that person a copy of the notice of deposition sent to opposing counsel. This practice helps the agency provide accurate information to the attending court reporter regarding time, place, and the names of the parties and attorneys. It also serves as documentation for billing purposes that the deposition was ordered. If for some reason the deposition is canceled or must be rescheduled, the paralegal should notify the individual court reporter or agency as soon as he or she knows of the change to avoid any charge to the client or firm and to reserve a court reporter for the new date if that date is known.

EXAMPLE 5

Notice of Deposition

The plaintiff hereby gives notice that his attorney intends to take the deposition of the defendant regarding her knowledge of the above-captioned matter on October 22, 2018, at 11:30 a.m., before court reporters at the law office of the plaintiff's counsel located at 22 Park Place, New Haven, Connecticut.

Noticing of Nonparty Witnesses

The paralegal is also often responsible for preparing the documents needed to bring a nonparty witness to a deposition.

To require a nonparty witness to appear at a deposition to be deposed, the deposing lawyer must serve a subpoena on the witness ordering his or her appearance. A *subpoena* is a legal document signed by an officer of the court that requires the person receiving it to appear under penalty of law at the time, date, and place indicated

Subpoena
A legal document signed by an officer of the court that requires the person receiving it to appear under penalty of law at the time, date, and place indicated on the document.

Subpoena duces tecum
A type of subpoena signed by an officer of the court at the request of one of the parties to a suit, requiring a witness to bring to court or to a deposition any relevant documents that are under the witnesses' control.

on the document (see Exhibit 16-1). A sheriff, process server, or other indifferent person serves the subpoena on the nonparty witness. In many jurisdictions, the statute requires the sheriff to give the nonparty witness cash or a check to reimburse the nonparty for a percentage of his or her travel expenses from his or her home to the site of the deposition. A *subpoena duces tecum* is a subpoena commanding a party or witness, who has in his or her possession documents that are relevant to a case, to produce them at a deposition, motion hearing, or trial.

Exhibit 16-1 Connecticut civil subpoena.

SUBPOENA — CIVIL/HOUSING/SMALL CLAIMS/FAMILY/ FAMILY SUPPORT MAGISTRATE/CRIMINAL/MOTOR VEHICLE
JD-CL-43 Rev. 12-15
C.G.S. § 52-143, 52-144; P.B. §§ 7-19, 24-22

STATE OF CONNECTICUT
SUPERIOR COURT
www.jud.ct.gov

Court Use Only
SUBISSU

Instructions:
1. Do **Not** use this subpoena if the witness is being summoned by the state or by the attorney general or an assistant attorney general or by any public defender or assistant public defender acting in his/her official capacity.

2. The person being subpoenaed and the items they are ordered to bring as listed below must be identical to the names and items as ordered on the Application for Issuance of Subpoena, form JD-CL-136 (if applicable).

Name of Case *(Full name of Plaintiff v. Full name of Defendant)*

Docket Number

☐ Judicial District   ☐ Housing Session   Geographical Area Number _____   ☐ Small Claims Area

Address of Court *(Number, street, town and zip code)*

To: *(Name and address)*

Date and time you are to come to court
Time
. m.

Report to
☐ Clerk's office
☐ Courtroom number _____
☐ Person requesting subpoena

By Authority of The State of Connecticut, you are commanded to come to the court at the Address of Court above on the Date and Time indicated above or to another day after (within 60 days of the Date indicated above) when the case will be tried; you must come to the court to testify what you know in the case.

You Are Further Commanded To Bring With You And Produce:

Hereof Fail Not, Under Penalty Of The Law.
To any proper officer or indifferent person to serve and return.

Name of person requesting subpoena

Phone number *(with area code)*

Signed *(Clerk, Commissioner of Superior Court)*   Print or type name   Date   At

Notice To The Person Summoned

If you do not come to court on the day and at the time stated, or on the day and at the time which your appearance may have been postponed or continued to by order of an officer of the court, the court may order that you be arrested. Also, if one day's attendance and traveling fees have been paid to you and you do not come to court and testify, without reasonable excuse, you will be fined not more than $25.00 (twenty-five dollars) and pay all damages to the aggrieved party. **The party requesting the subpoena is responsible for paying the witness fees.**

Any questions regarding this subpoena should be directed to the person who requested it.

Phone number *(with area code):* _____

ADA NOTICE
The Judicial Branch of the State of Connecticut complies with the Americans with Disabilities Act (ADA). If you need a reasonable accommodation in accordance with the ADA, contact a court clerk or an ADA contact person listed at *www.jud.ct.gov/ADA.*

Return Of Service

Judicial District of

ss.

Date

Then and there I made service of the within subpoena not less than eighteen hours prior to the time designated for the person summoned to appear, by reading the same in the presence and hearing/leaving a true and attested copy hereof in the hands/at the last usual place of abode of each of the within-named persons, viz:

Fees
Copy

Endorsement

Service

Travel *(Show miles & amount)*

Attest *(Signature of proper officer or indifferent person)*   Title *(If applicable)*   **Total**

Distribution: Original - Return to clerk after making service   Copy 1 - Witness   Copy 2 - Court file

---

Source: Subpoena/Civil, State of Connecticut.

Typically, the paralegal prepares the subpoena and arranges for the sheriff to pick up the subpoena and serve the witness. The paralegal is responsible for giving the sheriff the proper address and possibly a physical description of the witness or even better, a photograph. Also, the paralegal should later check with the sheriff to determine if service has indeed been made.

A subpoena must be served at least eighteen hours before the scheduled proceeding. Usually the subpoena is served earlier because most jurisdictions require the party issuing the deposition subpoena to give notice to the opposing party's counsel of the date and time of the deposition and invite the opposing counsel and opposing party to attend. Eighteen hours is not reasonable notice for the other counsel. On the other hand, the deposing party's attorney does not wish to give the witness too much time to either prepare or engage in a lengthy consultation with the opposing party's attorney. The paralegal will be responsible for sending opposing counsel a *notice of intent to depose nonparty witness* as well as for contacting a person authorized to serve the subpoena on the nonparty witness.

Motion for Disclosure of Assets

Frequently, in conjunction with the taking of a party's deposition, the deposing attorney will file with the court a ***motion for disclosure of assets***. In this motion, the moving attorney requests the court to order the opposing party to bring to the deposition detailed information on all existing assets and acceptable documentation to substantiate the value of such assets. The opposing attorney may object to the granting of this motion. However, if the motion is granted, the party must, under penalty of law, bring such materials to the deposition. There, the opposing counsel examines the documents and questions the party on their various aspects.

If a party's attorney is not deposing the opposing party, the party's attorney may still file a motion for disclosure of assets. If the motion is granted, the opposing party's attorney must see that a written disclosure is made, that it is accompanied by supporting documentation, and that the disclosure is made within the court-ordered time frame. If a party fails to fully disclose his or her assets, the opposing counsel may file a motion for contempt of court. If contempt is proven, the court may order immediate and full disclosure that, if not complied with, could result in the court issuing a ***capias***. A capias is a civil arrest warrant served by a sheriff ordering that officer to take physical custody of the party and bring him or her to *jail*, where he or she will remain incarcerated until he or she makes arrangements to comply with the court's order for disclosure.

A motion for disclosure of assets in a family law matter typically requests disclosure of all real and personal property owned by a spouse either in his or her own name or owned jointly with the other spouse or with another person or entity. Examples of such assets include bank accounts, certificates of deposit, mutual funds, stocks, boats, cars, and parcels of real estate.

Preparation of a Motion for Disclosure of Assets The family law paralegal drafts the motion for disclosure of assets. The paralegal should review the client intake form on which the client has listed assets he or she believes the other spouse owns. In addition, the paralegal should confer with the client to review the assets listed and determine whether disclosure of other assets should be requested. After a client conference, the paralegal drafts the motion and submits it to the supervising attorney for review and possible revision.

Motion for disclosure of assets
Requests disclosure of all real and personal property owned by a spouse either in his or her own name or owned jointly with the spouse or with another person or entity.

Capias
A document empowering a sheriff to arrest a nonappearing, noncustodial parent and bring him or her to jail and to court.

Once the final draft of the motion is approved and signed, the paralegal files the motion. The court then schedules the motion for a hearing that the paralegal will docket or, if necessary, reschedules. If the motion is granted, the paralegal monitors the compliance with the motion and drafts a motion for contempt if disclosure is not made or is incomplete.

When the paralegal drafts the contempt motion, the supervising attorney may also have the paralegal file a motion for sanctions and costs, providing the jurisdiction allows for such a motion. If so, the supervising attorney will prepare a listing of the number of hours he or she spent preparing the motion for sanctions and costs and the motion for contempt. He or she will also list tasks performed during these hours of preparation and give this information to the paralegal, who will prepare a formal *affidavit of fees and costs* to be submitted with the motion. This affidavit will include the activities the attorney undertook to prepare the motions and total up his or her hours, hourly rate, the fee for each task, and the total amount he or she must charge the client unless the court orders that the opposing party and/or his or her counsel to pay the amount since the work was required to facilitate the opposition's compliance.

EXAMPLE 6

Motion for Disclosure of Assets

The plaintiff in the above-captioned matter hereby requests the Court to order the defendant to disclose her assets.

Memorandum of law

A written document presented to the court that states a party's argument in a case and supports that argument with specific case law and statutes.

Preparation of a Response to a Motion for Disclosure of Assets If the opposing party serves the firm's client with a motion for disclosure of assets, the supervising attorney may decide to file a written objection, and may direct the paralegal to draft an objection and possibly draft a **memorandum of law** supporting the objection. After the supervising attorney reviews these documents, the paralegal will finalize them, obtain the attorney's signature, and ensure that the originals of the documents are filed with the court and that copies are properly noticed on opposing counsel.

If the court orders a client to disclose the enumerated assets, the paralegal may be given the task of helping the client list all of the assets and compile, assemble, and organize the substantiating documentation.

The Financial Statements or Affidavits

Certainly most, if not all, jurisdictions require that both parties in a dissolution or divorce proceeding file a financial affidavit with the court within a specified period of time after the commencement of the proceeding. A *financial statement or financial affidavit* is a sworn statement that enumerates the party's sources of income, earned and unearned; the party's expenses, necessary and optional; and all of the party's assets and liabilities.

Financial statement or financial affidavit

A sworn statement that enumerates the party's sources of income, earned and unearned, the party's expenses, necessary and optional, and all of the party's assets and liabilities.

The party completing the affidavit must provide either a weekly or monthly breakdown of income, expenses, and payments on debts. Whereas in years past the financial affidavit was drafted by a party's attorney, most jurisdictions now provide a fillable online form on the state's judicial branch website (see Exhibit 16-2). Most family law courts require the filing of this document before resolving any matters of any nature, financial or otherwise, in the pending proceeding. Financial affidavits must always be filed not only in dissolution matters but also in any subsequent matters involving a change in alimony and child support orders.

Exhibit 16-2 Connecticut financial affidavit.

Click here to get more information about the fields on this form.

FINANCIAL AFFIDAVIT
JD-FM-6-SHORT   Rev. 2-16
P.B. §§ 25-30, 25a-15

STATE OF CONNECTICUT
SUPERIOR COURT
www.jud.ct.gov

Court Use Only
FINAFFS

‖‖‖‖‖‖‖‖‖‖‖‖‖

ADA NOTICE
The Judicial Branch of the State of Connecticut complies with the Americans with Disabilities Act (ADA). If you need a reasonable accommodation in accordance with the ADA, contact a court clerk or an ADA contact person listed at *www.jud.ct.gov/ADA*.

Docket number

- FA -   -   - S

Instructions

*Use this short version if your **gross annual income is less than $75,000** (see Section I. Income) and your **total net assets are less than $75,000** (see Section IV. Assets). Otherwise, use the long version, form JD-FM-6-LONG.*

For the Judicial District of	At *(Address of Court)*

Name of case

Name of affiant *(Person submitting this form)*

☐ Plaintiff   ☐ Defendant

Certification

I understand that the information stated on this Financial Statement and the attached Schedules, if any, is complete, true, and accurate. **I understand that willful misrepresentation of any of the information provided will subject me to sanctions and may result in criminal charges being filed against me.**

I. Income

1) Gross Weekly Income/Monies and Benefits From All Sources

Computed based on year-to-date, but no less than the last 13 weeks. If computation is based on less than 13 weeks or if your computations are not reflective of current wages, explain:

_____

Paid: ☐ Weekly   ☐ Bi-weekly   ☐ Monthly   ☐ Semi-monthly   ☐ Annually

If income is not paid weekly, adjust the rate of pay to weekly as follows:

Bi-weekly → divide by 2	Semi-monthly → multiply by 2, multiply by 12, divide by 52
Monthly → multiply by 12, divide by 52	Annually → divide by 52

(a)   Employer   Address   Base Pay:

Job 1 _____   _____   ☐ Salary ☐ Wages $ _____

Job 2 _____   _____   ☐ Salary ☐ Wages $ _____

Job 3 _____   _____   ☐ Salary ☐ Wages $ _____

Total of base pay from salary and wages of all jobs.......................... $ _____

(b) Overtime .... $ _____   (j) Child Support *(Actually received)*............ $ _____
(c) Self-employment.................................. $ _____   (k) Alimony *(Actually received)* .... $ _____
(d) Tips... $ _____   (*l*) Rental and income producing property.... $ _____
(e) Social Security.................................... $ _____   (m) Contributions from household member(s) $ _____
(f) Disability... $ _____   (n) Cash income.. $ _____
(g) Unemployment .... $ _____   (o) Veterans Benefits .... $ _____
(h) Worker's compensation .... $ _____   (p) Other: _____ $ _____
(i) Public Assistance *(Welfare, TFA payments)* .... $ _____

(q) Total Gross Weekly Income/Monies and Benefits From All Sources *(Add items a through p)* $ _____

Hours worked per week _____
Gross yearly income from prior tax year. Provide amount of income, not copies of forms................................. $ _____
List here and explain any other income including but not limited to: non-reported income; and support provided by relatives, friends, and others:

_____
_____

(Page 1 of 4)

continued

Exhibit 16-2 Continued

2) Mandatory Deductions *(If consistent deductions don't occur every pay check **provide average amounts**.)*

	Job 1	Job 2	Job 3	Totals
(1) Federal income tax deductions *(claiming ___ exemptions)*	$	$	$	$
(2) Social Security or Mandatory Retirement	$	$	$	$
(3) State income tax deductions *(claiming ___ exemptions)*	$	$	$	$
(4) Medicare	$	$	$	$
(5) Health insurance	$	$	$	$
(6) Union dues	$	$	$	$
(7) Prior court order — child support or alimony	$	$	$	$
(8) Total Mandatory Deductions *(add items 1 through 7)*	$	$	$	$

3) Net Weekly Income.. $ _____

Subtract the Total Mandatory Deductions [see item I., 2), (8)] from the Total Gross Weekly Income/Monies and Benefits From All Sources [see item I., 1), q)]

II. Weekly Expenses Not Deducted From Pay

If expenses are not paid weekly, adjust the rate of payment to weekly as follows:

Bi-weekly → divide by 2	Semi-monthly → multiply by 2, multiply by 12, divide by 52
Monthly → multiply by 12, divide by 52	Annually → divide by 52

Insert an ("x") in the box if you are **not** currently paying the expense, or if someone else is paying the expense.

Home:

Rent or Mortgage *(Principal, Interest — Real Estate Taxes and Insurance if escrowed)* ☐ $_____   Property taxes and assessments .... ☐ $_____

Utilities:

Oil .... ☐ $_____   Telephone/Cell/Internet.......................... ☐ $_____
Electricity .... ☐ $_____   Trash Collection .... ☐ $_____
Gas .... ☐ $_____   T.V./Internet .... ☐ $_____
Water and Sewer........................ ☐ $_____

Groceries *(after food stamps):* Including household supplies, formula, diapers .... ☐ $_____

Transportation:

Gas/Oil .... ☐ $_____   Auto Loan or Lease .... ☐ $_____
Repairs/Maintenance .... ☐ $_____   Public Transportation............................ ☐ $_____
Automobile Insurance/Tax/Registration ... ☐ $_____

Insurance Premiums:

Medical/Dental *(Out-of-pocket expense after Health Savings Account/Plan).......* ☐ $_____   Life.. ☐ $_____

Uninsured Medical/Dental not paid by insurance .... ☐ $_____
Clothing .... ☐ $_____

Child(ren):

Child Support of this case .... ☐ $_____   Child Care Expense *(after deductions, credits and subsidies)*............................ ☐ $_____

Child Support of other children other than this case *(attach a copy of the order)* ... ☐ $_____   Child(ren)'s activities *(e.g., lessons, sports, etc.)* .... ☐ $_____

Alimony: Payable to this spouse .... ☐ $_____   Alimony: Payable to another spouse .... ☐ $_____

Extraordinary travel expenses for visitation with child(ren) .... ☐ $_____
Other *(Specify):* _____ ☐ $_____

Total Weekly Expenses Not Deducted From Pay .... $_____

III. Liabilities *(Debts)*

Do not include expenses listed above. Do not include mortgage current principal balance or loan balances that are listed under "Assets."

Creditor Name /Type of Debt		Balance Due	Date Debt Incurred/ Revolving	Weekly Payment
Credit Card, Consumer, Tax, Health Care, Other Debt				
	☐ Sole ☐ Joint	$		$
	☐ Sole ☐ Joint	$		$

JD-FM-6-SHORT   Rev. 2-16   (Page 2 of 4)

		Sole	Joint	$		$
		Sole	Joint	$		$
		Sole	Joint	$		$

(A). Total Liabilities *(Total Balance Due on Debts)* .... $

(B). Total Weekly Liabilities Expense .... $

IV. Assets

Note: Under "Ownership" indicate S for sole, JTS for joint with spouse, and JTO for joint with other.
You must complete the last column to the right "Value of Your Interest" in each applicable section.

A. Real Estate *(including time share)*

Address	Ownership S	JTS	JTO	a. Fair Market Value *(Estimate)*	b. Mortgage Current Principal Balance	c. Equity Line of Credit and Other Liens	d. Equity (d = a minus (b + c))	e. Value of Your Interest
Home								
	☐	☐	☐	$	$	$	$	$
Other								
	☐	☐	☐	$	$	$	$	$
	☐	☐	☐	$	$	$	$	$

Total Net Value of Real Estate: $

B. Motor Vehicles

Year	Make	Model	Ownership S	JTS	JTO	a. Value	b. Loan Balance	c. Equity (c = a minus b)	d. Value of Your Interest
1:			☐	☐	☐	$	$	$	$
2:			☐	☐	☐	$	$	$	$

Total Net Value of Motor Vehicles: $

C. Bank Accounts

Do not include custodial accounts or child(ren)'s assets — complete Section V. below.

Institution	Account Number *(last 4 numbers only)*	Ownership S	JTS	JTO	Current Balance/ Value	Value of Your Interest
Checking						
		☐	☐	☐	$	$
Savings						
		☐	☐	☐	$	$
Other						
		☐	☐	☐	$	$

Total Net Value of Bank Accounts: $

D. Stocks, Bonds, Mutual Funds

Company	Account Number *(last 4 numbers only)*	Listed Beneficiary	Current Balance/ Value
			$
			$

Total Net Value of Stocks, Bonds, Mutual Funds: $

E. Insurance *(exclude children)* D = Disability   L = Life

Name of Insured	D	L	Company	Account Number *(last 4 numbers only)*	Listed Beneficiary	Current Balance/ Value
						$
						$

Total Net Value of Insurance: $

F. Retirement Plans *(Pensions on Interest, Individual IRA, 401K, Keogh, etc.)*

Type of Plan	Name of Plan/Bank/Company	Account Number *(last 4 numbers only)*	Listed Beneficiary	Receiving Payments	Current Balance/ Value
				☐ Yes ☐ No	$
				☐ Yes ☐ No	$

Total Net Value of Retirement Plans: $

G. Business Interest/Self-Employment

If you own an interest in a business, or are self-employed, complete this section.

Name of Business	Percent Owned	Value
	%	$

Total Net Value of Business Interest/Self-Employment: $

JD-FM-6-SHORT   Rev. 2-16   (Page 3 of 4)

continued

Exhibit 16-2 Continued

H. Other Assets

Name of Asset	Current Balance/ Value	Name of Asset	Current Balance/ Value
	$		$
	$		$
	$		$
	$		$
		Total Net Value of Other Assets:	$

I. Total Net Value All Assets *(add items A through H)* .... | $ |

V. Child(ren)'s Assets

Include Uniform Gift to Minor Account, Uniform Trust to Minor Account, College Accounts/529 Account, Custodial Account, etc.

Institution	Account Number *(last 4 numbers only)*	Listed Beneficiary	Person Who Controls the Account *(Fiduciary)*	Current Balance/ Value
				$
				$
			Total Net Value of Child(ren)'s Assets:	$

VI. Health *(Medical and/or Dental Insurance)*

Company	Name of Insured Person(s) Covered by the Policy

Do you or any member of your family have HUSKY Health Insurance Coverage? ☐ Yes ☐ No ☐ I Don't Know

If Yes, whom?

_____

_____

_____

Important:

If you have other financial information that has not yet been disclosed, you have an affirmative duty to disclose that information. List additional information below:

_____

_____

_____

_____

Summary *(Use the amounts shown in Sections I. through IV.)*

Total Net Weekly Income *(See Section I. 3)* .... $ _____

Total Weekly Expenses and Liabilities *(Total From Section II. + III.(B))* .... $ _____

Total Cash Value of Assets *(See Section IV. I.)* .... $ _____

Total Liabilities *(Total Balance Due on Debts) (See Section III. (A))* .... $ _____

Certification

I certify under the penalties of perjury that the information stated on this Financial Statement and the attached Schedules, if any, is complete, true, and accurate. **I understand that willful misrepresentation of any of the information provided will subject me to sanctions and may result in criminal charges being filed against me.**

I, _____ the ☐ Plaintiff   ☐ Defendant herein, residing at

_____ , telephone number _____ , being duly

sworn, depose and say that the following is an accurate statement of my income from all sources, my liabilities, my assets and my net worth, from whatever sources, and whatever kind and nature, and wherever situated.

Signed *(Affiant)*	Date signed
Signed *(Notary, Commissioner of Superior Court, Assistant Clerk, Other Proper Officer under Section 1-24 of the Connecticut General Statutes)*	Print name and title of person signing at left	Date signed

Source: Financial Affidavit, State of Connecticut.

Preparation of a Financial Affidavit The family law office paralegal frequently assists the client in preparation of the financial affidavit. The amount of assistance needed will vary depending on the individual client's level of financial sophistication, his or her recordkeeping and organizational skills, the quantity and nature of the assets and liabilities involved, and the complexity or simplicity involved in calculating sources of income and essential and nonessential expenses. At the very least, the paralegal will transmit a copy of the financial affidavit form to the client with instructions to complete and return the form to the law office together with copies of applicable substantiating documentation. When the paralegal receives this information, he or she may have to see that the amounts reported are broken down into the periodic increments the court requires, such as in weekly or monthly amounts.

In instances where the parties in a dissolution proceeding each earn a moderate income from only one or two sources—for instance, employment compensation and bank account interest—the completion of the financial affidavit is fairly simple. However, when one or both of the divorcing parties have a very high earned income as well as considerable unearned income from several sources, and where the parties, together or separately, have accumulated valuable assets, both tangible and intangible, the completion of a financial affidavit in a manner that accurately and fully reflects each party's financial status is extremely challenging.

The paralegal may also have responsibilities involving the review of the opposing party. The paralegal may have to meet with the client to review the other party's affidavit. If the client believes that the opposing spouse has not fully disclosed all assets or sources and amounts of income or has misrepresented his or her financial position, the paralegal must report this to the supervising attorney immediately. Subsequently, the attorney may assign the paralegal various tasks designed to properly uncover the opposing party's hidden assets and/or unreported income.

It is extremely important that the financial information obtained be complete and accurate. The paralegal assigned to the file must perform his or her duties in a very thorough, responsible, and competent manner. Failure to do so could expose the client to allegations of fraud because the financial affidavit is signed under oath. The injured client who has provided honest and full disclosure to the firm handling the matter could seek redress against the firm through an action for professional malpractice and/or breach of fiduciary duty.

Avoiding Legal Malpractice

The paralegal must handle these assignments with the utmost care and professionalism. Failure to do so can mislead the supervising attorney, who may honestly "miss" identifying and locating all of the opposing party's assets and sources of income. If divorcing parties agree to a financial settlement based on wrong data, the party injured by lack of the right information can and may bring suit against his or her attorney for negligent legal representation, more commonly known as *malpractice*. The supervising attorney is ultimately responsible for the negligent actions of the law office staff persons. This attorney as well as the entire firm will suffer the consequences. If the attorney has instructed the paralegal in a clear and understandable manner to perform relatively standard procedures and the paralegal performs this work in a slipshod way, yet leads the supervising attorney to believe that the work has been done responsibly, the paralegal should and most likely will be terminated and may have difficulty obtaining employment elsewhere.

On the other hand, if an attorney assigns a paralegal work well beyond the paralegal's area of knowledge, training, and expertise and, further, fails to review the paralegal's work product before sending it out or relies on the paralegal to make decisions on the case, the paralegal is blameless. The attorney has committed

Malpractice
Negligent legal representation; representation that is below the standard of the professional community and could result in damage to the client.

malpractice and should be dismissed from the firm, but the paralegal should not be held responsible if he or she completed the assigned work to the best of his or her training and ability.

Sometimes an attorney will in good faith assign a paralegal work that is beyond his or her reach. In this instance, the paralegal should communicate his or her concerns about being able to complete the assignment adequately. The attorney is then put on notice and can modify the assignment or tell the paralegal to complete it to the best of his or her ability, knowing that the results cannot be relied on as a finished product.

THE LEGAL LANDSCAPE OF E-DISCOVERY

Electronic discovery (often referred to as e-discovery) is the process of obtaining, collecting, preparing, reviewing, and distributing information from the opposing party in a legal case that has been electronically stored. It is an extension of the traditional discovery process, the difference being that the information being sought is now electronic and not on paper. ESI, or electronically stored information, includes e-mail correspondence, databases, spreadsheets, instant messages, word processing files, Web pages, flash drives, voicemails, audio and video files, and content from social networking sites. This information can be stored on a home or work desktop computer, laptop, smartphone, network server, or any other form of electronic storage.

ESI differs from traditional hard copy paper discovery in that greater quantities of information can be stored electronically. More important, it is very easy to determine if the material was tampered with in anticipation of or during the course of litigation because electronic altering of information leaves a trail where it is possible to determine that date and time the changes were made and from where. The intentional act of destroying, mutilating, altering, or concealing evidence that is relevant to a legal proceeding is known as *spoliation*. Courts presume that if the evidence was tampered with in this manner, it was done because it dealt with matters that were unfavorable to the destroying party's legal position, and it was their intent to conceal them from the opposing party as well as the court. Attorneys representing parties involved in family matters should inform clients that the information requested during the discovery process should not be tampered with in any way.

The availability of surveillance technology and the anonymity of using these devices have made spying on a spouse or partner easier than ever. Suspicious clients have a myriad of gadgets at their fingertips, and many do not hesitate to use them when it means that stooping to these tactics will help catch someone "in the act." The problem for the law office is that clients will bring the fruits of their self-help searches to the attorney for use in their domestic battles. Because clients often resort to self-help methods when garnering fodder for a nasty court battle, legal professionals have an obligation of not only warning clients of the repercussions of their actions but also knowing the barriers of what is admissible in court and what is not. While a client may be enthusiastic about the information he or she has obtained through electronic means, use of the information and the manner in which it was obtained are of concern to the legal team. Knowledge of federal and state law as well as the case law interpreting those statutes may provide some guidance when confronted with issues regarding the admissibility of electronic evidence. This area of the law is constantly evolving given the innovative use of technology in litigation. Consulting with an attorney specializing in criminal matters may also be necessary when the client has engaged in behavior that could potentially expose him or her to crimes involving the intentional accessing of a computer and the disclosure of any information obtained without the owner's consent.

In 1968, Congress passed the ***Omnibus Crime Control and Safe Streets Acts of 1968***, commonly referred to as the *Wiretap Act*. This law prohibits the recording

Omnibus Crime Control and Safe Streets Acts of 1968 Commonly referred to as the *Wiretap Act*. This law prohibits the recording of private conversations by use of wiretaps on telephones or hidden microphones.

of private conversations by use of wiretaps on telephones or hidden microphones. Violation of the Wiretap Act requires that there must be (1) an "interception" of an electronic communication that is (2) without the prior consent of the party whose data was intercepted. This law, however, was no match for the technological advances that quickly outpaced this legislation. In response to the new world of microchip technology, wireless phones, radio transmissions, and fax machines, Congress passed *The Electronic Communications Privacy Act of 1986 (ECPA)*, which prohibits the intentional interception of wire, oral, or electronic communications and intentionally disclosing the contents without the person on the other end knowing or having a reason to know that the information is being intercepted.

The problem with this statute is that many courts have interpreted it to apply only in situations where the information is intercepted *as it is actually being transmitted*. So the wiretapping statute would not cover the retrieval of stored information such as photographs, e-mails, text messages, and voicemail because there was actually no interception as defined under the statute. Title II of the act is called the **Stored Communications Act**, which prohibit anyone but an *authorized* user from accessing electronically stored voicemails and e-mails.

Stored Communications Act
Federal law that prohibits anyone but an authorized user from accessing electronically stored voicemails and e-mails.

Spouses and domestic partners, however, typically share household computers, so any information obtained through shared passwords and from access to the "family computer" is not protected. Many family law clients are now becoming aware of this and may communicate or store information on work computers or on personal tablets. This facilitates secret communications without generating any suspicion; however, this type of information may be very relevant to the divorce proceedings. A judge compared the family computer to a file cabinet when the wife took her husband's work computer to her attorney for examination of the contents. "The real issue is not who possesses the computer but rather who has access to the computer's memory. The computer memory is akin to a file cabinet. Clearly, plaintiff could have access to the contents of a file cabinet left in the marital residence. In the same fashion she should have access to the content of the computer. Plaintiff seeks access to the computer memory on the grounds that defendant stored information concerning his finances and personal business records in it. Such material is obviously subject to discovery. Therefore, it is determined that plaintiff did nothing wrong by obtaining the physical custody of the notebook computer." *Byrne v. Byrne*, 650 N.Y.S.2d 499 (N.Y. Sup. Ct., Kings County 1996). Bottom line—if both spouses have access to the family computer and both have the password, any information may be downloaded and used as evidence in a divorce case. There is no expectation of privacy if the spouses know each other's passwords.

A spouse's e-mails can also be an important source of information relevant to a divorce case. The law, however, distinguishes between e-mails that have been not yet been read by the intended recipient and those that are stored on the family computer.

Some divorce litigants may have **spyware** installed on their home or business computers. Spyware is computer software that gathers information from a computer without the user's knowledge or permission. A spyware program allows the spying spouse to monitor the activities on his or her computer that are either saved in that particular computer or can be accessed from a remote location. One can monitor all websites visited, chats, instant messages, e-mails, and keystrokes, which can provide a lot of ammunition for divorce litigation. Intercepting e-mails with the use of spyware software, for example, is prohibited under the Wiretap Act, while reading stored e-mails may be permissible in some jurisdictions.

Spyware
Computer software that gathers information from a computer without the user's knowledge or permission. A spyware program allows the spying spouse to monitor the activities on his or her computer that are either saved on that particular computer or can be accessed from a remote location.

Global Positioning Systems or *GPS* tracking devices carefully placed in a spouse's cell phone or car allow clients the ability to track the physical location of the spouse and/or their vehicle in real time. For example, the unfaithful spouse's trips to the local "no-tell" motel can be easily monitored. A spouse who claims that he or she cannot pay his or her alimony or child support obligations, but is in reality working under the table, can be easily located with a few keystrokes. The information can be retrieved at a later time, and traveled routes can be downloaded for a trip to the lawyer's office. In some jurisdictions, however, GPS trackers may not be inadmissible in court and may violate state stalking statutes, exposing users to criminal prosecution.

While spyware and GPS tracking device evidence may not be admissible in court, a spouse may use these devices to gain information and, unbeknownst to his or her spouse, substantiate it through an independent source, such as a private investigator or actually catching a spouse in the act. There are, however, legal problems with the use of spyware that include not only inadmissibility of such evidence in court but also exposure to criminal prosecution. The admissibility of spyware may be left up to the discretion of the judge and may depend on whether the software was installed before or after the parties separated, or whether both spouses had access to the same family computer. Installing such software in one's own home for monitoring of children's activities, for example, is not illegal, but doing so on a spouse's computer at their place of employment would be illegal and inadmissible in court.

When You Stoop to Snooping …

In the following case, discovery of the husband's online chats with another woman through a spyware program was excluded as evidence even though the Florida wiretapping statute only barred the admission into evidence of intercepted oral or wire communications, not electronic communications. The District Court of Appeal of Florida, Fifth District, upheld the trial court's decision to exclude the evidence since it was illegally obtained.

BEVERLY ANN O'BRIEN v. JAMES KEVIN O'BRIEN

899 So.2d 1133 (2005)
District Court of Appeal of Florida, Fifth District

Sawaya, C.J.

Emanating from a rather contentious divorce proceeding is an issue we must resolve regarding application of certain provisions of the Security of Communications Act (the Act) found in Chapter 934, Florida Statutes (2003). Specifically, we must determine whether the trial court properly concluded that pursuant to section, 934.03(1), Florida Statutes (2003), certain communications were inadmissible because they were illegally intercepted by the Wife who, unbeknownst to the Husband, had installed a spyware program on a computer used by the Husband that copied and stored electronic communications between the Husband and another woman.

When marital discord erupted between the Husband and the Wife, the Wife secretly installed a spyware program called Spector on the Husband's computer. It is undisputed that the Husband engaged in private online chats with another woman while playing Yahoo Dominoes on his computer. The Spector spyware secretly took snapshots of what appeared on the computer screen, and the frequency of these snapshots allowed Spector to capture and record all chat conversations, instant messages, e-mails sent and received, and the websites visited by the user of the computer. When the Husband discovered the Wife's clandestine attempt to monitor and record his conversations with his Dominoes partner, the Husband uninstalled the Spector software and filed a Motion for Temporary Injunction, which was subsequently granted, to prevent the Wife from disclosing the communications. Thereafter, the Husband requested and received a permanent injunction to prevent the Wife's disclosure of the communications and to prevent her from engaging in this activity in the future. The latter motion also requested that the trial court preclude introduction of the communications into evidence in the divorce proceeding. This request was also granted. The trial court, without considering the communications, entered a final judgment of dissolution of marriage. The Wife moved for rehearing, which was subsequently denied.

The Wife appeals the order granting the permanent injunction, the final judgment, and the order denying the Wife's motion for rehearing on the narrow issue of whether the trial court erred in refusing to admit evidence of the Husband's computer activities obtained through the spyware the Wife secretly installed on the computer. The Wife argues that the electronic communications do not fall under the umbra of the Act because these communications were retrieved from storage and, therefore, are not "intercepted communications" as defined by the Act. In opposition, the Husband contends that the Spector spyware installed on the computer acquired his electronic communications real-time as they were in transmission and, therefore, are intercepts illegally obtained under the Act.

The trial court found that the electronic communications were illegally obtained in violation of section 934.03(1)(a)(e), and so we begin our analysis with the pertinent provisions of that statute . . .

The clear intent of the Legislature in enacting section 934.03 was to make it illegal for a person to intercept wire, oral, or electronic communications. It is beyond doubt that what the trial court excluded from evidence are "electronic communications." The core of the issue lies in whether the electronic communications were intercepted. The term intercept is defined by the Act as "the aural or other acquisition of the contents of any wire, electronic, or oral communication through the use of any electronic, mechanical, or other device." § 934.02(3), Fla. Stat. (2003). We discern that there is a rather fine distinction between what is transmitted as an electronic communication subject to interception and the storage of what has been previously communicated. It is here that we tread upon new ground. Because we have found no precedent rendered by the Florida courts that considers this distinction, and in light of the fact that the Act was modeled after the Federal Wiretap Act, we advert to decisions by the federal courts that have addressed this issue for guidance.

The federal courts have consistently held that electronic communications, in order to be intercepted, must be acquired contemporaneously with transmission and that electronic communications are not intercepted within the meaning of the Federal Wiretap Act if they are retrieved from storage . . . These courts arrived at this conclusion based on the federal law definitions of (1) the term intercept, which is very similar to the definition in the Florida Act, (2) the term wire communication, which provides for electronic storage, and (3) the term electronic communication, which does not provide for electronic storage. The fact that the definition of "wire communication" provides for electronic storage while the definition of "electronic communication" does not suggests to the federal courts that Congress intended "intercept" to include retrieval from storage of wire communications, but exclude retrieval from storage of electronic communications. The definition of "wire communication" in the Florida Act, unlike the Federal Wiretap Act, does not include a provision for retrieval from storage and, therefore, it is not clear whether the same rationale would be applied by the federal courts to provisions identical to the Florida Act. However, we need not decide whether electronic communications may never be intercepted from storage under the Florida Act because the particular facts and circumstances of the instant case reveal that the electronic communications were intercepted contemporaneously with transmission.

The Spector spyware program that the Wife surreptitiously installed on the computer used by the Husband intercepted and copied the electronic communications as they were transmitted. We believe that particular method constitutes interception within the meaning of the Florida Act . . . We conclude that because the spyware installed by the Wife intercepted the electronic communication contemporaneously with transmission, copied it, and routed the copy to a file in the computer's hard drive, the electronic communications were intercepted in violation of the Florida Act.

continued

> We must next determine whether the improperly intercepted electronic communications may be excluded from evidence under the Act. The exclusionary provisions of the Act are found in section 934.06, Florida Statutes (2003), which provides that "[w]henever any wire or oral communication has been intercepted, no part of the contents of such communication and no evidence derived therefrom may be received in evidence.... "Conspicuously absent from the provisions of this statute is any reference to electronic communications. The federal courts, which interpreted an identical statute contained in the Federal Wiretap Act, have held that because provision is not made for exclusion of intercepted electronic communications, Congress intended that such communications not be excluded under the Federal Wiretap Act ... We agree with this reasoning and conclude that the intercepted electronic communications in the instant case are not excludable under the Act. But this does not end the inquiry.
>
> Although not specifically excludable under the Act, it is illegal and punishable as a crime under the Act to intercept electronic communications. § 934.03, Fla. Stat. (2003). The trial court found that the electronic communications were illegally intercepted in violation of the Act and ordered that they not be admitted in evidence. Generally, the admission of evidence is a matter within the sound discretion of the trial court ... We affirm the orders and the final judgment under review in the instant case.
> AFFIRMED. MOTION FOR REHEARING DENIED.
>
> *Source:* Beverly Ann O'Brien v. James Kevin O'Brien, 899 SO.2D 1133 (2005), District Court of Appeal of Florida, Fifth District, State of Florida.

E-Discovery and Professional Ethics

While clients who have found damaging information against their spouses may expect the attorney to introduce the material in the client's court case, the use of illegally obtained evidence may subject the attorney to disciplinary action. Model Rules of Professional Conduct, Rule 8.4(c) precludes an attorney from engaging in conduct involving dishonesty, fraud, deceit, or misrepresentation. Here the attorney may be bound by client confidentiality not to disclose the client's conduct; however, as an officer of the court the attorney may not assist the client in perpetrating a fraud upon the court. The admissibility of evidence obtained by clients' actions should be scrutinized extremely carefully to avoid a potential professional grievance. Paralegals who receive information from clients about do-it-yourself surveillance activities should immediately notify the attorney.

Legal professionals also should not be counseling clients to engage in surveillance unless the activities are permissible under law, such as having access to the family computer. Lawyers as well as legal staff working under the lawyer's supervision are prohibited from knowingly counseling or assisting a client in committing a crime or fraudulent act. The lawyer can advise the client on the legality of his or her actions and the consequences of such conduct; however, this does not in and of itself make the lawyer a party to the client's illegal activities.

Clients violating ECPA may be subjected to criminal penalties of up to five years in jail or civil damages up to $10,000 per violation. They can also be civilly sued for actual damages, punitive damages, and attorney's fees under federal law, as well as criminal and civil violations of state law. If the government violates the ECPA, it cannot be sued for civil damages; however, the illegally gathered information is now the "fruit of the poisonous tree" and cannot be admitted into evidence.

Teddy Spy-Bear

A Nebraska woman, unhappy with the court awarding her husband unsupervised visitation, resorted to self-help surveillance by placing a digital recording device in her child's teddy bear. Her efforts backfired. Not only was the evidence inadmissible in the custody trial, her ex-husband sued her in federal court for violating the Wiretap Act as well as the Nebraska Telecommunications Consumer Privacy Protection Act. The verdict? The court ruled in favor of the plaintiffs and assessed a $120,000 damages award.

WILLIAM DUANE LEWTON v. DIANNA DIVINGNZZO

772 F. Supp.2d 1046 (2011)
UNITED STATES DISTRICT COURT, D. NEBRASKA.

MEMORANDUM AND ORDER

F.A. GOSSETT III, United States Magistrate Judge.... The court has considered the parties' legal arguments, together with over 6,000 pages of their evidentiary submissions. For the reasons discussed below, the court finds that defendants Dianna Divingnzzo, Sam M. Divingnzzo and William Bianco violated the provisions of Title III of the Omnibus Crime Control and Safe Streets Act of 1968, as amended by the Electronic Communications Privacy Act of 1986, 18 U.S.C. §§ 2510 et seq. (the "Wiretap Act" or "Title III"). Dianna Divingnzzo and Sam M. Divingnzzo are liable to the plaintiffs for statutory damages on the Wiretap Act claims. The court declines to assess damages against William Bianco on the Wiretap Act claims. Finally, the court declines to exercise supplemental jurisdiction over the plaintiff's state law claims.

I. BACKGROUND

The events giving rise to the plaintiffs' claims arose in conjunction with a dispute between William Duane ("Duke") Lewton and his ex-wife, Dianna Divingnzzo, over the custody of their minor child, Ellenna Divingnzzo-Lewton. Shortly after the state court granted Duke the right to have unsupervised visits with Ellenna, Dianna inserted a recording device inside Ellenna's teddy bear and secretly intercepted communications between or among Ellenna and the plaintiffs, and/or between or among the plaintiffs themselves without Ellenna's participation. The recordings were made without the plaintiffs' knowledge or consent and occurred over a period of several months. In May 2008, Dianna and her father, Sam Divingnzzo, presented the recordings to Dianna's attorney in a digital format, using CD-ROM data storage discs, for use as evidence in the custody dispute. Dianna's attorney had the recordings copied and transcribed, and supplied copies of the CDs and transcripts to Lewton's attorney and others involved in the state court case. The Sarpy County District Court held that the recordings were illegally obtained and were inadmissible. This federal lawsuit followed.

In the Amended Complaint, (Doc. 63), plaintiffs assert claims under the Federal Wiretap Act, *see* 18 U.S.C. §§ 2511 and 2520, together with state law claims for invasion of privacy, conspiracy to commit invasion of privacy, and violations of Neb. Rev. Stat. § 86-2,103. All defendants deny liability. Defendants Bianco, Perrone and Bianco, Perrone & Stroh, LLC affirmatively allege they are immune from liability because they had a privilege to disclose or use the recordings in the context of their legal representation of Dianna Divingnzzo. Dianna Divingnzzo and her father, Sam Divingnzzo, affirmatively allege that they are immune from liability based on Dianna's legal responsibility to protect Ellenna....

... **Federal Wiretap Act Claims 1. Liability** The civil damages provision of Title III of the Omnibus Crime Control and Safe Streets Act of 1968, as amended by the Electronic Communications Privacy Act of 1986, 18 U.S.C. §§ 2510 *et seq.* (the "Wiretap Act" or "Title III") affords a private right of action to "any person whose wire, oral, or electronic communication is intercepted, disclosed, or intentionally used in violation of this chapter[.]" 18 U.S.C. § 2520(a). The activities constituting violations of the Wiretap Act are described in 18 U.S.C. § 2511. Subject to certain exceptions not relevant in this case, § 2511(1) imposes liability for any person who — (a) intentionally intercepts, endeavors to intercept, or procures any other person to intercept or endeavor to intercept, any wire, oral, or electronic communication; (b) intentionally uses, endeavors to use,

continued

or procures any other person to use or endeavor to use any electronic, mechanical, or other device to intercept any oral communication when —(i) such device is affixed to, or otherwise transmits a signal through, a wire, cable, or other like connection used in wire communication; or (ii) such device transmits communications by radio, or interferes with the transmission of such communication; or (iii) such person knows, or has reason to know, that such device or any component thereof has been sent through the mail or transported in interstate or foreign commerce; or (iv) such use or endeavor to use (A) takes place on the premises of any business or other commercial establishment the operations of which affect interstate or foreign commerce; or (B) obtains or is for the purpose of obtaining information relating to the operations of any business or other commercial establishment the operations of which affect interstate or foreign commerce; or (v) such person acts in the District of Columbia, the Commonwealth of Puerto Rico, or any territory or possession of the United States; (c) intentionally discloses, or endeavors to disclose, to any other person the contents of any wire, oral, or electronic communication, *knowing or having reason to know that the information was obtained through the interception of a wire, oral, or electronic communication in violation of this subsection*; [or] (d) intentionally uses, or endeavors to use, the contents of any wire, oral, or electronic communication, *knowing or having reason to know that the information was obtained through the interception of a wire, oral, or electronic communication in violation of this subsection*[.] 18 U.S.C. § 2511(1) ... (emphasis added)....

... To prove an "interception" violation of the Wiretap Act, see 18 U.S.C. §§ 2511(a) & (b), a plaintiff need only show that the defendant intentionally, rather than inadvertently, intercepted the plaintiff's oral communication.... To establish liability for use or disclosure of the communications, *see* 18 U.S.C. §§ 2511(c) & (d), the plaintiffs must show that the defendants were aware of the factual circumstances that would violate the statute.... The record conclusively demonstrates that all of the defendants were fully aware of the facts of their conduct. There is no evidence whatsoever that either of the Divingnzzos sought the advice of counsel ... as to the legality of their course of action prior to bugging the teddy bear, intercepting the plaintiffs' oral communications, transcribing the plaintiffs' private conversations, and delivering the entire bundle to Mr. Bianco after the fact. Sam Divingnzzo admits that he signed a sworn affidavit stating that he and Dianna had a digital recording device placed in Ellenna's toy. He was given the opportunity to review the affidavit prior to signing it, and then signed it. To the extent the defendants are arguing that they should not be held liable because they believed that intercepting the plaintiffs' oral communications in this manner was lawful, "innocence cannot be asserted of an action which violates existing law, and ignorance of the law will not excuse."

Source: William Duane Lewton v. Dianna Divingnzzo, 772 F. Supp.2d 1046 (2011), United States District Court, District of Nebraska.

Social Networking Websites

Once upon a legal time, discovery in divorce cases was limited to the hiring of private investigators that tailed the opposing spouse and snapped pictures of various wrongdoings. The social networking era, however, has provided a wealth of free information for use in family law litigation.

Social networking websites are increasingly finding their way into family law cases. According to a survey conducted by the Academy of Matrimonial Lawyers in 2010, eighty-one percent of its members have either submitted or objected to evidence obtained on these websites, with sixty-six percent of the online evidence used coming from Facebook. A social networking website is an Internet website that facilitates the connection of groups and individuals with similar interests. Users create profiles and can interact with others through e-mail and instant messaging made available on the website. The most popular websites include Facebook,, Instagram, Snapchat, Twitter, YouTube, and LinkedIn.

Figure 16-2 Social networking websites reveal everything from marital infidelity to financial wrongdoing.

James Woodsen/Photodisc/Getty Images.

Social networking websites reveal information divorce lawyers could have only dreamed of in the old days:

- adulterous conduct
- addictions to drugs, alcohol, gambling, or Internet pornography
- criminal activity
- dissipation of marital assets
- a spouse's whereabouts on particular dates of interest
- new jobs, promotions, or overtime hours worked
- monitoring of spouse's activities through electronic surveillance

The following is a list of items that might be of interest to legal professionals in the process of collecting discovery in divorce cases:

- A married person listing themselves as "single" on their social networking website profile, as well as "interested in dating," or a spouse who is fighting his wife tooth and nail for custody of the children who lists himself on a dating website as being not only single but also "childless."
- Flirty or sexually explicit comments posted by a spouse or to a spouse or other individuals.
- Posts regarding their whereabouts, plans to attend certain events, or acceptance of invitations to various social gatherings.
- Pictures galore! Nothing says more than a spouse caught in the act on camera! Individuals using these sites love to post pictures of themselves and their friends in somewhat compromising and damaging positions. This can include a spouse, who swears up and down that he or she doesn't have an alcohol problem, sipping a beer. Or the wife who claims to have never engaged in marital infidelity caught kissing her husband's best friend on the lips while sitting on his lap at a summer picnic. Or the spouse with a gambling problem "tweeting" about his or her winnings at the crap table. More important, the comments made in relation to the photos can also be revealing.

- Learning that a former spouse who is in arrears in his or her child support and alimony payments just bought a new car or spent a fortune on a recent vacation.
- Dates related to comments, photos, and events attended may be of interest. Suppose it is the mother's weekend for visitation with the children and she abruptly cancels on Saturday morning claiming to be suffering from a migraine, but by Monday morning she has posted pictures of herself sunbathing on her boyfriend's boat.
- LinkedIn, a business social networking website, may include information regarding recent or hidden employment, job promotions, and potential earning capacity.
- Never forget that simple Google search. One never knows what surprises may emerge by just typing in someone's name. Do not forget to check Internet sex offender and judicial branch websites to determine if any of the parties involved in the case have criminal records or pending civil lawsuits. This information may be useful as leverage against the other spouse or damage control in cases where the client has forgotten to mention his or her social difficulties to the law office staff.
- Look for incriminating "wall messages" on Facebook.
- Twitter "tweets" are often posted under spontaneous, impulsive circumstances and may reveal the parties' "state of mind," which may be used as secondary evidence. In the midst of her divorce case, for example, the wife of recording artist Usher complained about her divorce lawyer and informed the world that she needed to look for a new attorney.
- Pay close attention to with whom the spouse is conversing on a social networking page. The "friends" section on Facebook may reveal, for instance, that the husband is conversing with way too many sexy coworkers or one in particular on a frequent basis.
- Venting, defaming, and making disparaging comments about a spouse or former spouse should be avoided at all costs. There is a tendency for clients going through the divorce process to want to vent about all the spouse's wrongdoings and shortcomings and provide blow-by-blow comments regarding the legal process. While a spouse may have removed the client from having access to his or her page, sympathetic friends and family who do have access may be more than happy to make copies for divorce court purposes. In 2008, Tricia Walsh-Smith posted several videos on YouTube trashing her husband, Philip Smith, president of the Shubert Organization, revealing intimate details about their marriage, premarital agreement, and divorce proceedings, as well as placing a call to his assistant regarding this information. Interestingly enough, the YouTube video became an instant sensation with over three million hits. Unfortunately, the judge sitting on the bench in divorce court did not share the same enthusiasm, awarding the husband a divorce on the grounds of cruel and inhuman treatment. The judge also found the terms of the premarital agreement Walsh-Smith signed valid and enforceable, and much to her disapproval, ordered her to vacate the couple's Park Avenue apartment. Walsh-Smith received the sum of $750,000 as previously agreed in a premarital agreement she signed prior to the marriage.
- Look for lies and contradictions. A mother seeking custody of her children who testifies that she can provide a stable home environment will not be well served by comments she makes on her Facebook page about her numerous boyfriends and her sexual escapades. The spouse who claims to be on a business trip but tweets that he is having a great time partying with his "new friend" also is not well served by social media. It is easier for the attorney to defend a client with human weaknesses than it is to defend a liar.

Clients should be warned that anything they post on a social networking website can be used as evidence in a divorce case, whether it is shown to a judge or used as leverage in settlement conferences. Once information is published in a public forum, it is admissible in a court of law and there is no expectation of privacy. Attorneys and paralegals should ask clients about the social networking websites that they use and ask to see the clients' page and profile. A review of this information and warnings from legal professionals could save the client a lot of problems later on. Clients should also be instructed to use the privacy settings on each of their social networking websites to limit the amount of access and information that is available. The law office may also obtain permission from the client to enter the client's social networking page and delete objectionable photographs and wall messages, as well as tightening the client's privacy settings. It is also important to be cautious regarding who has access to the client's information. Accepting new friends during a divorce is very risky and not a very good idea. One never knows who is connected to the opposing party and may be feeding them information from a client's Facebook page. Clients going through a divorce should also be advised to tell their friends not to post anything about the divorce proceedings or about the client that could potentially fall into the hands of the opposing spouse. This also includes the taking of photographs at social events, posting them on social media, and then "tagging" the spouse in the photograph—not a great idea, especially if the photographs are of an incriminating nature. Some lawyers even go so far as to advise clients to shut down all social networking websites. In others, the attorney may assign the paralegal the task of monitoring a certain client's social networks as a form of damage control.

See Appendix E, "David Voelkert Criminal Complaint and Dismissal of Criminal Complaint," as an illustration of how *not* to use social media in a divorce case.

If You Want It, Ask for It

The best way to obtain discovery from the opposing party is to ask for it. This can either be done with a request for production or a motion to compel. Access to laptop and desktop computers, iPhones, iPads, smartphones, and any other devices that transmit, store, and retrieve information from one party to another should be analyzed in divorce cases for crucial data that could bolster or defend the client's case. Family law judges are savvy to the workings of electronic communications and the reality that information may exist on these devices that is relevant to the case at hand. Even access to the parties' social media account may be obtained if requested, provided that the appropriate arguments may be made to justify a court order.

Connecticut Judge Orders Parties to Disclose Passwords

On September 30, 2011, Connecticut Superior Court Judge Kenneth Shluger ordered the parties to exchange passwords to social media sites that could potentially contain information relevant to their divorce and custody case. More judges are entering such orders as social media takes center stage in family matters.

STEPHEN GALLION v. COURTNEY GALLION

Docket No. FA114116955S

Connecticut Superior Court

CLARIFICATION OF ORDER

By way of a clarification of the court's September 29, 2011, oral order:

1. Counsel for each party shall exchange the password(s) of their client's Facebook and dating website passwords.

   - The parties themselves shall not be given the passwords of the other.
   - If either party already possesses the password of the other, the party whose password is in the possession of the other party may change their password and give the new password to opposing counsel only.
   - Neither party shall visit the website of the other's social network and post messages purporting to be the other.
   - Shluger, Kenneth L., J.

PROTECTING CLIENTS FROM ELECTRONIC SABOTAGE

For obvious reasons, family law practitioners are grateful when clients engage their services *before* installing spyware, GPS tracking devices, and transmitting damaging information into cyberspace. In a perfect world, clients should be warned in advance of the illegal nature pitfalls of installing such electronic devices. Therefore, it is important for clients to

- Change passwords on a regular basis. Passwords should also be well thought out, since a creative spouse can figure it out given the extensive knowledge one may have regarding a spouse's personal preferences.
- Stay out of Internet chat rooms, forums, instant messaging, and visits to incriminating websites.
- Never send confidential e-mails or messages through a computer shared by other members of the household. An Internet service provider can be subpoenaed and ordered to disclose not only the client's e-mails but also the contents of the trash or recycle bin.
- Install anti-spyware software on computers to protect from unwanted intrusions.

Remember, there is no expectation of privacy on a computer that a client shares with other individuals, so every piece of information may be fair game. There is, however, an expectation of privacy in one's place of business, and any information obtained from these sources through self-help methods may be inadmissible in family court, and the intruder may also face civil and criminal liability.

Concept Review and Reinforcement

KEY TERMS

capias	cross-examination	direct examination
confidential	deponent	duplicative
confidentiality agreement	deposition	financial affidavit

interrogatories
irrelevant
malpractice
memorandum of law
motion for disclosure of assets
motion for protective order
motion to compel examination
notice of deposition

notice of filing of interrogatories
notice of responding to and/or
    objecting to interrogatories
Omnibus Crime Control and Safe
    Streets Acts of 1968
overbroad
privilege
redirect
request

request for admission
request for production of documents
requesting party
responding party
spyware
Stored Communications Act
subpoena
subpoena duces tecum

REVIEW OF KEY CONCEPTS

1. List and describe the five discovery tools and explain how each of these tools can be used in a family law proceeding.

2. What is the difference between an objection and a privilege raised in the discovery process?

3. What types of interrogatories might be filed in a dissolution matter where the issue of child custody is contested?

4. What types of documents might either party request in a family law proceeding relating to a divorce matter for a modification of alimony, child support, or custody?

5. If a party does not furnish adequate financial information and records in response to interrogatories and production requests, what other means may the opposing party employ to obtain this information?

6. Give one example of when a party's attorney in a family law proceeding might decide to file a request for admission.

BUILDING YOUR PARALEGAL SKILLS

CASES FOR BRIEFING

GRAYSON v. WOFSEY, ROSEN, KWESKIN & KURIANSKY, 231 CONN. 168, 646 A.2D 195 (1994)

Critical Thinking and Legal Analysis Applications

1. You work as a paralegal in the law office of Jeffrey Abawi. Carla Pastore has hired Attorney Abawi to represent her in a divorce case against her husband, Angelo Pastore. In your interview with Mrs. Pastore, Attorney Abawi learns that the couple's assets include the marital home, the husband's pension, and several joint bank accounts. Mrs. Pastore also tells Attorney Abawi that her husband has quite an extensive baseball card collection that he started when he was a child and has continued adding to this collection over the years. She tells Attorney Abawi that he has spent a lot of time over the years going to baseball card shows where he purchased many autographed cards. Attorney Abawi glosses over the information provided by Mrs. Pastore regarding the baseball cards. He fails to pursue a valuation of the baseball card collection, dismissing it as a worthless child's play thing. Applying the holding in *Grayson v. Wofsey, Rosen, Kweskin & Kuriansky,* 231 Conn. 168, 646 A.2d 195 (1994), what advice would you give Attorney Abawi regarding the importance of the baseball card collection and the potential consequences of failing to pursue it as a marital asset?

2. Your firm represents Mrs. Church in her pending dissolution action, and the court has already issued *pendent lite* orders relating to support and custody. Your supervising attorney informs you that Mrs. Church just called to tell him that she has lost her job and will lose her medical benefits for herself and her children within thirty days unless she elects to pay a hefty monthly premium under COBRA for the next thirty-six months. She also indicated that she cannot

pay for health insurance or otherwise maintain the household without additional assistance from Mr. Church until she finds new employment. Your supervising attorney tells you to set up a meeting with Mrs. Church to obtain all information needed to bring the matter back to court. He also tells you to draft for his review all the documents that must be filed with the court to prepare for the modification hearing. Describe how you would go about completing this task, identify the information you would need from Mrs. Church, and identify the documents you would be preparing for filing with the court. What would you hope to be the outcome of the upcoming modification hearing?

Building a Professional Portfolio

PORTFOLIO **EXERCISES**

1. When you meet with Mrs. Church, she tells you that she suspects that Mr. Church has additional sources of income that he did not disclose on his financial affidavit and that he keeps the income from these other sources hidden in a separate bank account. When you mention this to your superior, he tells you to research your local practice book and family law statutes to see what avenues exist to expose these assets and to present your findings to him in an inter-office memorandum. Using your own jurisdiction's rules of family practice and family law statutes, determine what legal measures may be taken to discover these additional sources of income. Present your findings in an inter-office memorandum and make recommendations on how to proceed.

Chapter **seventeen**

SEPARATION AGREEMENTS

M any divorces are settled without a trial. With the help of their attorneys or a mediator, many spouses are able to resolve their issues through negotiation and compromise. Attorneys on opposing sides confer with each other and propose resolutions through telephone calls, e-mails, formal correspondence, and meetings. The attorneys' offices communicate proposals to their clients, and the parties often arrive at an agreement. This agreement will eventually result in the creation of a separation agreement.

LEARNING OBJECTIVES

After studying this chapter, you should be able to:

1. Understand the purpose of a proposal letter.

2. Understand the advantages of reaching an agreement.

3. Devise a parenting plan. Prepare a separation agreement.

PRELIMINARY PROPOSALS

Proposal

A formal written indication, from one party to the opposing party, that communicates what the first party is seeking in terms of a divorce settlement.

Proposal letter

Details the client's position on the various legal issues to be resolved, such as property division, alimony, child custody, visitation and support, maintenance of health and life insurance, distribution of debts and other liabilities, and counsel fees.

After discovery has been exchanged, reviewed, and analyzed, a picture of the marital estate emerges. The next step is for the parties to draft and exchange proposals. *Proposals* are formal written indications, from one party to the opposing party, that communicate what the first party is seeking in terms of a divorce settlement. Proposals are drafted after the attorney has consulted with the client. A client who is fully informed regarding the extent of the marital estate may determine, with the assistance of the attorney, what type of settlement he or she will seek. The *proposal letter* will detail the client's position on the various legal issues to be resolved: property division, alimony, child custody, visitation and support, maintenance of health and life insurance, distribution of debts and other liabilities, and, of course, counsel fees. Remember, the client determines what he or she is seeking in a divorce settlement, so any formal offer of settlement must be approved by the client before it is submitted to the opposing party. Similarly, any proposal or counterproposal received by an attorney should always be forwarded to the attorney's client for review and written approval before acceptance. After each client has had an opportunity to review the other client's proposal letter, the parties, through their attorneys, will try to reach an agreement on how each of the issues will be resolved and often arrive at a resolution. Sometimes, the parties will agree on many of the disputed issues but reach a stalemate on other issues. When this occurs, the court will decide the unresolved issues after a trial.

CREATING THE SEPARATION AGREEMENT

Separation agreement

A contract between spouses who are in the process of obtaining a divorce or a legal separation resolving the various legal issues that arise when a marriage is dissolving; also known as a marital settlement agreement, property settlement, or settlement agreement.

Once the parties have reached a resolution, one of the parties undertakes the responsibility of reducing the agreement to a writing known as a *separation agreement*. In some jurisdictions, this writing is referred to as a *property settlement, settlement agreement,* or *marital settlement agreement.* A separation agreement is a contract between spouses who are in the process of obtaining a divorce or a legal separation. This agreement resolves the various legal issues that arise when a marriage dissolves.

Traditionally, the public policy of the states has been to encourage and preserve marriage. Marriage and the family unit are the very foundation on which our society has been built. At one time courts were very reluctant to accept separation agreements in divorce cases since these agreements promoted the breakdown of the family. Even today, courts will validate separation agreements only when entered into, after one or both parties has instituted legal proceedings for divorce, or for a legal separation. If the marriage has deteriorated with no hope of reconciliation, the courts will be more likely to accept the separation agreement. If the parties to a failed marriage have amicably agreed to the terms of their dissolution, it is in the best interest of all parties involved for the court to accept the separation agreement rather than forcing an agonizing divorce trial. The parties must indicate in their agreement that their marriage has broken down, there is no hope of reconciliation, and the parties intend to live separate and apart.

Uncontested hearing

A judicial procedure where neither party objects to the court granting a divorce and entering an order of marital dissolution.

An agreement avoids the need for a contested divorce trial. The case will proceed as an *uncontested hearing* matter. When a matter is uncontested, it means that neither party objects to the court granting a divorce and entering an order of marital dissolution. However, even when a divorce action is uncontested, most jurisdictions require a formal court proceeding at which at least the petitioning spouse must appear. This proceeding is relatively short. The parties will arrive at court on the date of the uncontested hearing with the signed separation agreement. The document will be submitted to the court. The judge will review the agreement and determine if it is fair and equitable and if it has been entered into voluntarily.

Merger of Separation Agreement into the Court's Decree

As mentioned earlier, the separation agreement is a contract between the spouses. The language in the agreement will indicate if the parties want the agreement to *survive* as a contract or if the parties want it merged into the court's decree. If the agreement survives as a contract, the agreement cannot be modified unless both parties mutually consent. In the event that one of the parties fails to comply with the provisions of the agreement, the aggrieved party will be left with the traditional contractual remedies, such as breach of contract and specific performance. If the agreement is instead merged into the court's decree, the **merger** is no longer a contract between the two parties but rather a court order, which can be modified or enforced through contempt of court proceedings.

Merger
An agreement that is no longer a contract between the two parties but rather a court order, which can be modified or enforced through contempt of court proceedings.

ADVANTAGES OF REACHING AN AGREEMENT

A successfully negotiated separation agreement reflects the best efforts of both parties and their respective attorneys. Legal professionals should encourage agreements for many reasons: Agreements are quicker and more economical, and the parties are not subjected to an adversarial system that may destroy the little civility remaining between them. The ability to have some input regarding the resolution of the divorce affords the parties more control than they would have if the judge were to decide the case. Reaching an agreement, however, involves compromise on the part of both parties. **Compromise** involves meeting someone halfway or giving up a position in exchange for something else. By the very definition of compromise, parties doing so are generally not one hundred percent satisfied with a separation agreement. The degree of noncompliance with separation agreements is very high. Even the most carefully scripted and negotiated agreement may result in noncompliance even before the ink has dried.

Compromise
Meeting someone halfway or giving up a position in exchange for something else.

PARALEGAL'S ROLE IN DRAFTING THE SEPARATION AGREEMENT

Paralegals may be assigned the task of drafting a separation agreement under the attorney's supervision. To begin drafting the separation agreement, the paralegal must have a copy of the finalized proposal and a good understanding of the agreement between the parties. This is an essential element before commencing the initial draft.

The paralegal must next obtain a model separation agreement or several models to use in constructing one for the client. Standardized or *boilerplate* separation agreement forms or clauses may be available in the particular jurisdiction's practice book. Forms and clauses may also be found in loose-leaf legal publications specializing in family law. Model separation agreements may also be available in the local law library or in the law office library. In addition, the law office may maintain its own file of standard separation agreements, either on computer or as hard copies. Paralegals may also review closed divorce files that contain previously drafted separation agreements.

Boilerplate
Standardized agreement forms or clauses.

The paralegal may need to draw from several resources to obtain the necessary language to draft the agreement. Whenever using standardized forms or previously drafted separation agreements as models, the paralegal must proceed with a great deal of caution. The agreement should contain the particular provisions applicable to the underlying case—it should not be merely an exercise in filling in the blanks.

The paralegal may also have responsibilities related to reviewing an agreement drafted by the opposing party. In this case, the paralegal, under the attorney's supervision, reviews the separation agreement to make certain it reflects the agreement of the parties. If the document appears to depart from what was agreed to, the paralegal will bring this departure to the attorney's attention, and may also wish to offer suggested revisions to cure the discrepancies.

Whether on the drafting side or reviewing side, several drafts may be necessary to script an agreement that accurately reflects the intent of the parties. A separation agreement should be drafted with great care because the parties to it will have to live with this agreement long after they have left the courthouse. Agreements drafted too hastily, without adequate review and reflection by both attorneys and clients, set the stage for unnecessary future battles. Each party will hold the other to every letter, syllable, and punctuation mark in their agreement. Therefore, it is necessary to draft them carefully, make them clear and readable, and spell out any definitions or terms that could later cause confusion.

FINALIZING THE SEPARATION AGREEMENT

Once the attorney has approved a final draft, an office appointment with the client should be scheduled. At this meeting the attorney carefully reviews the agreement with the client and thoroughly answers any and all questions the client poses. If the client approves the agreement and the opposing side does likewise, the case will proceed as an uncontested divorce matter. If the parties are still in dispute over various sections, renegotiation and revisions may be appropriate.

We cannot stress the importance of careful drafting. Sometimes when dissolution actions have been particularly draining, the attorneys and paralegals may hurriedly draft an agreement with very little thought or reflection. The trap is that this agreement may continue to haunt both client and attorney as various sections become disputed in postjudgment battles.

BASIC CLAUSES AND STRUCTURE OF THE SEPARATION AGREEMENT

The paralegal should delineate the various subjects covered by the separation agreement by dividing them into "articles" or "sections" and using roman numerals or cardinal numbers in numerical sequence. It is important to organize the agreement in this manner for quick reference and logical sequence.

Heading

Every agreement should have a heading. As mentioned earlier, various headings can be used depending on your supervisor's wishes or the accepted local preference: *SEPARATION AGREEMENT, PROPERTY SETTLEMENT, PROPERTY SETTLEMENT AGREEMENT, MARITAL SETTLEMENT, MARITAL SETTLEMENT AGREEMENT,* or *AGREEMENT.*

Identification

The identification clause identifies the parties, their respective residences, and the respective label that will be used to refer to each spouse throughout the agreement, avoiding the need to spell out full names each time one is used. It also indicates the date on which the agreement was executed.

EXAMPLE

SEPARATION AGREEMENT[1]

THIS AGREEMENT, made and entered into this 8th day October, 2018, by and between Kayla Martin of North Haven, Connecticut (hereinafter referred to as "Wife"), and Troy Martin of Branford, Connecticut (hereinafter referred to as "Husband"):

Recitals

The recitals section indicates the date and place of the marriage, names and ages of the minor children, grounds for the dissolution, a declaration that the parties are living separate and apart, the pendency of an action for dissolution, and the intent to settle the spouses' rights and obligations pursuant to this action. Each sentence is often preceded by the word "WHEREAS."

EXAMPLE

WITNESSETH:

WHEREAS, the parties married each other on June 15, 2005, in Branford, Connecticut; and Whereas, said parties have three minor children born issue of this marriage:

> *Ariana Martin, born October 17, 2007*
> *Emma Martin, born November 3, 2009*
> *Jason Martin, born August 25, 2011*

No other minor children have been born to the Wife since the date of the marriage;

> *WHEREAS, irreconcilable differences have arisen between the parties as a result of which the marriage of the parties has broken down irretrievably and they are now and have been living separate and apart; and*

> *WHEREAS, the Wife has instituted an action against the Husband a dissolution of marriage, and further relief, which case is currently pending in the Superior Court for the Judicial District of New Haven at New Haven.*

> *WHEREAS, the parties wish to enter into an agreement under which they will continue living separate and apart and under which fair and reasonable provisions will be made for the support of each other and the minor children and for the settlement, adjustment and compromise of all property rights and obligations resulting from the marriage.*

> *NOW THEREFORE, in consideration of the premises and the mutual promises and undertaking therein set forth and for other good and valuable consideration paid over by each party to the other, the receipt and sufficiency of which is hereby acknowledged, it is covenanted and agreed as follows:*

Irretrievable Breakdown

This clause indicates that the marriage has broken down and there is no hope of the parties reconciling.

---

[1]The text of the separation agreement illustrated in this chapter has been constructed from provisions and portions of provisions of separation agreements that the authors of this book have accumulated during their years of practice, and as such reflects the work of anonymous authors.

ARTICLE I

Irretrievable Breakdown

The marriage of the parties has broken down irretrievably, and there is no prospect of reconciliation.

Separation of the Parties

This clause indicates that the parties intend to live separate and apart and will not interfere with each other. In addition, each one is free to dispose of his or her property upon death, as he or she sees fit.

ARTICLE II

Separation of the Parties

2.1 The parties may and shall at all times hereafter live separate and apart for the rest of their mutual lives. Each shall be free from interference, authority or control, direct or indirect, by the other as fully as if he or she were single and unmarried. Each may reside at such place or places as he or she may select. The parties shall not molest each other or compel or endeavor to compel the other to cohabit or dwell with him or her, by any legal or other proceedings for the restoration of conjugal rights or otherwise.

2.2 The Husband and Wife shall have the right to dispose of his or her property by will or otherwise in such manner as they may, in his or her uncontrolled discretion deem proper; and neither one will claim any interest in the estate of the other.

Alimony

The alimony clause addresses the payment of alimony, maintenance, or spousal support. The agreement should clearly spell out the type of alimony, frequency and mode of payment, modifiability, and termination. If the parties are waiving alimony, it should be spelled out in the agreement.

ARTICLE III

Spousal Support

3.1 The Husband shall pay to the Wife as periodic alimony the sum of $850.00 per week commencing October 15, 2018, for a NONMODIFIABLE period of 416 weeks/8 years up to, but not including, the week ending October 15, 2026, unless terminated earlier as provided herein.

3.2 Alimony shall terminate prior to October 15, 2026, upon the occurrence of the first of the following events: a) death of either party; b) remarriage of the Wife; or c) cohabitation of the Wife with an unrelated male over the age of 18 years. Cohabitation shall have the meaning from time to time, as per applicable Connecticut Statutes.

3.3 Alimony may be modified as to amount upon mutual agreement of the parties or upon a showing by either party of a substantial change in the circumstances of either party which warrants such modification.

3.4 For federal and state income tax purposes, the spousal support payments shall be reportable as income by the Wife and deductible by the Husband.

Real Property

The real property section deals with the parties' disposition of any real property owned. The most common asset to be dealt with is the marital home. The parties may agree to put the house up for sale and divide the proceeds after expenses have been paid. Another option is for one party to buy out the other party, or offset it with a pension. If the parties have minor children, the custodial parent may be allowed to live in the home until the emancipation of the children. Once the last child has reached age eighteen, the home can be sold.

EXAMPLE

ARTICLE IV

Real Property

4.1 *The parties agree that the Wife shall have exclusive possession of the marital residence located at 42 Willow Court, in North Haven, Connecticut, until such time as the youngest child graduates from high school or attains the age of 19 years, whichever occurs first. Within 30 days of the first of these occurrences, the Wife shall arrange for the parties to list the marital residence for sale with a mutually agreed-upon listing agent. The parties shall agree on the listing price. In the event that the parties cannot agree on the listing price, the property shall be listed at a price to be determined by the listing agent in accordance with the market values existing at that time. The parties agree to accept the first offer on the house that is at least 85% of the asking price.*

4.2 *When the house is sold, the parties agree that the Husband shall receive 1/3 of the net proceeds and the Wife shall receive 2/3 of the net proceeds. The parties shall contribute equally to the closing costs associated with the sale of the house.*

4.3 *While the Wife has exclusive possession of the marital residence, she shall be solely responsible for payment of the existing mortgage, property taxes, and home-owner's insurance as well as ordinary and necessary maintenance and repairs to the premises. The Wife shall have 100% of the tax deduction for mortgage interest and property taxes. If the Wife fails to fulfill the above-listed obligations, the Husband may seek relief from this court, including, but not limited to, an order for immediate sale of the property.*

4.4 *The Husband shall be responsible for 1/3 of any extraordinary and necessary maintenance, repair, or replacement costs associated with the marital residence, included but not limited to painting of the exterior of the residence, replacement of the heating system, and any major electrical or plumbing repairs.*

Personal Property

In the personal property clause, the parties address the division of their personal property. This includes motor vehicles; bank, pension, and retirement accounts; household furnishings; and miscellaneous matters.

EXAMPLE

ARTICLE V

Personal Property

5.1 *Motor Vehicles*
The Wife shall have sole title, possession, and ownership of the 2016 Honda HRV. The Husband shall have sole title, possession, and ownership of the 2013 Chrysler Pacifica Touring Car.

From and after the date of this Agreement, each party shall be responsible for any and all costs associated with said respective vehicles, and shall indemnify and hold the other harmless for all said costs.

This shall include any and all property taxes now due and owing for these vehicles.

5.2 Bank Accounts, Investments, Pension, and Retirement Accounts

The Wife shall retain sole right, title, and interest in and to the following:

(a) *Northern Imperial Bank checking account number 005340 50591, approximate value $7,200.00*

(b) *Hubbard Growth Fund, approximate value $10,059.00 and Long River Bank IRA, approximate value $12,000.00*

The Husband shall retain sole right, title, and interest in and to the following:

(a) *Northern Imperial Bank checking account number 00510066201, approximate value $4,240.00*

(b) *Manhattan Merchant's Bank IRA, approximate value $18,500.00*

(c) *Dominion Forklift, 330 shares (inherited from grandfather), approximate value $45,000.00*

The Husband and Wife will equally divide the following jointly held investments:

(a) *Northern Imperial Money Market, approximate value $34,000.00, Aquitaine Fund, approximate value $8,855.00*

The Husband and Wife shall divide the Husband's 401k plan as follows:

(a) *The Husband shall retain 100% of the amount existing in the plan at the time of the parties' marriage, approximate value $24,500.00*

(b) *The parties shall equally divide the remaining amount in the plan, approximate value $61,000.00.*

5.3 Furnishings, Appliances, Tools, and Miscellaneous Items at the Marital Residence

The Wife shall retain all of the furnishings, appliances, tools, and miscellaneous items located at the martial residence with the exception of the following items of personal property, which the Husband shall remove as soon as possible but in any event before October 8, 2018:

(a) *grape press*

(b) *power drill*

(c) *electric shrub clippers*

(d) *grandmother's sterling silver tea set*

(e) *Keurig K55 Coffee Maker*

(f) *framed Norman Rockwell print of Stockbridge, Massachusetts*

(g) *red kayak*

(h) *grandfather's mahogany clothes tree*

(i) *burgundy leather recliner in the family room*

(j) *42-inch HD TV in master bedroom*

(k) *all personal clothing, jewelry, and sports equipment*

5.4 Proceeds from Personal Injury Claim

The Husband waives any right, title interest in and to all proceeds, settlements, and judgments obtained by the Wife as a result of her personal injury suit arising from her 2011 automobile accident.

Custody and Access

The issues considered in the custody and access section involve the type of custody (sole, joint, split) arrangement agreed to by the parties. Access is also addressed either by a "reasonable access" clause or by a more detailed schedule. In some situations, access to the child may be supervised. The success of a "reasonable access" arrangement will depend on how well the parties can arrange visits between themselves. A more detailed schedule, now officially called a parenting plan, may or may not be mandatory in the jurisdiction. A parenting plan may typically specify particular days, times, transportation, place of pickup and drop-off, holidays, summer vacations, and birthdays. A clause requiring the custodial parent to contact the noncustodial parent may also be included to cover certain situations such as medical emergencies.

The issue of relocation by the custodial parent should also be addressed in this section.

EXAMPLE

ARTICLE VI

Child Custody and Access

The parties have developed the following Parenting Plan and agree to abide by its terms:

6.1 **Custody**

The parties shall have joint legal custody; primary residence shall be with the Wife.

6.2 **Parental Access**

WEEKENDS

The Husband shall have overnight weekend visitation every other weekend from Friday at 6:30 p.m. until Sunday at 6:30 p.m. The Husband shall pick up the children at the Wife's residence and return them there.

WEEKDAY VISITATION

The Husband shall have overnight weekday visitation every Wednesday from 5:30 p.m. until Thursday at 8:30 a.m. The Husband shall pick up the children at the Wife's residence on Wednesday evening and drop off the children at their school on Thursday morning.

WINTER HOLIDAY SCHOOL VACATION—CHRISTMAS DAY AND NEW YEAR'S DAY

The winter vacation is defined as the period from the end of the last school day before the start of the vacation to the morning of the first day school resumes after vacation.

In odd-numbered years, the children shall spend the winter holiday vacation with the Wife.

In even-numbered years, the children shall spend the winter holiday vacation with the Husband.

If either party wishes to take the children out of state for the vacation, that party must notify the other party thirty days before the anticipated departure date and provide the parent with the proposed travel itinerary, including flight numbers, travel destinations, and landline number and cell phone numbers at which the Wife and children may be reached.

If the children will be in the state on either Christmas Day or New Year's Day or on both days, the parent not sharing the winter vacation with the children may visit the children on either or both holidays for at least a four-hour period at a time and locations mutually agreed to by the parties.

FEBRUARY AND APRIL SCHOOL VACATION WEEKS

The February and April school vacations are defined as the period commencing at 6:30 p.m. on the Friday before the vacation week and ending at 6:30 p.m. on the Sunday before the Monday that school resumes.

The children will spend the February school vacation with the Husband in odd-numbered years and with the Wife in even-numbered years.

The children will spend the April school vacation with the Husband in even-numbered years and with the Wife in odd-numbered years.

This school vacation week schedule preempts the usual weekend visitation and weekday visitation schedule.

SUMMER VACATION SCHEDULE

The children will spend the month of July with the Husband in odd-numbered years and with the Wife in even-numbered years.

The children will spend the month of August with the Husband in even-numbered years and with the Wife in odd-numbered years.

This summer vacation schedule preempts the usual weekend and weekday visitation schedule.

MOTHER'S DAY AND FATHER'S DAY

The children shall spend every Mother's Day with the Wife and every Father's Day with the Husband. This arrangement preempts the Sunday portion of the usual weekend visitation schedule.

THE CHILDREN'S BIRTHDAYS

Each child shall spend at least four hours of the day on his or her birthday with each of his parents.

OTHER PERIODS OF ACCESS

The Husband and Wife may upon mutual agreement modify the periods of access when it is in any or all of the children's best interests.

6.3 In the event of a dispute, or the failure of one or both of the parties to abide by the terms of the parenting plan, the parties hereby agree to submit the matter to the Family Relations division of the court for mediation.

Child Support

The child support section should specify the amount of child support due and the date on which it is payable. It is very important to include the date on which the payments are to commence so as to avoid confusion.

Other matters that may be addressed in this section are whether support payments will extend beyond a child's majority. Some parties will agree to pay for a child's college education, which should be clearly expressed in the agreement and include any restrictions or conditions the parents may have regarding the choice of location or cost of the school.

This section should also address which parent will declare the children as dependants for federal and state income tax purposes.

EXAMPLE

ARTICLE VII

Child Support, Qualified Child-Care Expenses, and Costs of Extracurricular Activities

7.1 Commencing on October 8, 2018, the Husband shall pay to the Wife the sum of $750.00 per week as child support in accordance with the Child Support Guidelines. The Court may adjust this amount upward or downward in accordance with the guidelines until all of the children have reached their majority subject to any postmajority obligations either party may have under subsection 7.4 of this article.

7.2 The parties shall share the qualified child-care costs in accordance with the percentages established in the Child Support Guidelines. This provision shall include the cost of any summer camp fees that are incurred as summer child care.

7.3 The parties agree to be equally responsible for the costs of the agreed-upon extracurricular activities of the children.

7.4 The parties hereby agree that the Superior Court shall retain jurisdiction over issues of Post-Majority Educational Support pursuant to Conn. Gen. Stat. § 46b-56c.

7.5 The Husband shall claim Ariana Martin and Emma Martin as dependants on his state and federal income tax returns.

7.6 The Wife shall claim Jason Martin as a dependant on her state and federal income tax returns.

Life Insurance

Frequently parties agree that during the minority of the children, the parent who does not have physical custody of the children will carry life insurance for their benefit so that if he or she dies before the children reach their majority, the benefit will help the surviving parent to offset the loss of child support payments.

EXAMPLE

ARTICLE VIII

Life Insurance

8.1 The Husband agrees to maintain the existing life insurance policy on his life in the amount of $500,000 until the youngest child graduates from high school or attains the age of nineteen years, whichever occurs sooner.

8.2 The Husband agrees that the Wife shall remain as the beneficiary of this life insurance policy until the youngest child graduates from high school or attains the age of nineteen years, whichever occurs sooner.

8.3 On or about November 1 of each year, the Husband shall provide the Wife with verification that said life insurance policy is still in force in the amount of $500,000, and that the Wife is still the beneficiary of said life insurance policy.

Health Insurance

Many parties have health insurance coverage that is provided as a fringe benefit by their employer. Self-employed parties may carry their own health insurance, and those who cannot afford coverage simply go without or apply for government benefits. The health insurance section should spell out the health insurance coverage for both spouses and the minor children. It should also cover payment of unreimbursed expenses and how the parties plan to pay such costs.

EXAMPLE

ARTICLE IX

Health Insurance

9.1 The Husband has available and agrees to maintain health insurance coverage for himself and the minor children through his employer. Should the Husband leave his employment, the Husband agrees to continue to provide health insurance coverage for the minor children unless the Wife is employed and has health insurance coverage available to her for the minor children at a lower cost.

9.2 The parties agree that health insurance coverage through the Husband's employer is available to the Wife under COBRA and that the Husband shall pay the premium for the Wife's health insurance coverage for the statutory time period available, unless the Wife obtains employment before the statutory period ends and comparable coverage is available to her through her employment at no cost or at a cost to her that is much lower than the cost of COBRA.

9.3 The parties agree that after the statutory period for health insurance coverage for the Wife under COBRA expires, the Wife shall be responsible for obtaining and paying for her own health insurance coverage.

9.4 The parties shall equally share any unreimbursed medical expenses of the minor children, except that should any or all of the minor children require orthodontic care, the parties shall contribute to the cost of such care in accordance with the percentages established for their respective child support obligations under the Child Support Guidelines.

Liabilities

The debts and liabilities of the parties and who will be responsible for their payment must be covered in the separation agreement. The liabilities section should also include a *hold harmless provision* whereby the spouses indemnify each other from any debt incurred by the other.

EXAMPLE

ARTICLE X

Liabilities

10.1 The parties agree that they will each be responsible for the liabilities on their respective financial affidavits submitted in connection with this pending matter.

10.2 The Husband shall indemnify, defend, and hold Wife harmless from any and all other indebtedness, loans, obligations, claims, and causes of action that have, may now, or hereafter be made against Wife on her property as a result of any acts or omissions of Husband, judgments that may be obtained against Husband, debts, guarantees, or obligations incurred by Husband.

10.3 The Wife shall indemnify, defend, and hold Husband harmless from any and all other indebtedness, loans, obligations, claims, and causes of action that have, may now, or hereafter be made against Husband on his property as a result of any acts or omissions of Wife, judgments that may be obtained against Wife, debts, guarantees, or obligations incurred by Wife.

Taxes

The filing of federal and state tax returns is an important issue to be addressed in the agreement. In addition, the question of how the parties will share a refund or pay for an assessment should be determined to avoid surprises later.

EXAMPLE

ARTICLE XI

Taxes

11.1 With respect to the calendar year of 2017, the parties filed joint tax returns, both federal and state. Pursuant to these returns, the parties owed $1,045.00 in federal income tax and owed $0.00 in state income tax. The payment of $1,045.00 was tendered to the Connecticut Commissioner of Revenue Services, by the Husband and Wife.

11.2 The parties agree to equally pay any additional taxes which may hereafter be assessed in connection with either 2017 return and equally divide any refunds or rebates in connection with such returns.

11.3 For the calendar year of 2018, and thereafter, the parties shall file separate tax returns, both federal and state. Each party shall pay and be responsible for all taxes assessed against their respective separate incomes.

Disclosure

In the disclosure clause, the parties acknowledge that they have had the opportunity to fully discover any data regarding their spouse's income, assets, liabilities, and expenses; and that they have accurately disclosed the same.

EXAMPLE

ARTICLE XII

Disclosure

12.1 The parties acknowledge that they have had the opportunity for full discovery of any and all pertinent data with regard to income, assets, liabilities, and expenses of the other and that each waives his or her right to further discovery based upon the other's representation that they have fully and accurately disclosed to each other all their respective assets, income, and liabilities as set forth in their financial affidavits.

Representation of the Parties

In the representation section, the parties acknowledge that they have been represented by independent counsel and indicate the name of each attorney. This section may also deal with the issue of attorney's fees and who will be responsible for their payment.

EXAMPLE

ARTICLE XIII

Representation of the Parties

13.1 Each party to this AGREEMENT represents and acknowledges that he or she has been represented in negotiations for and in preparation of this AGREEMENT by counsel of his or her own choosing.

13.2 Each party has been fully advised by his or her respective attorney, Justine FitzGerald. Miller, Esq. of New Haven, Connecticut, for the Husband, and Grace A. Luppino, Esq. of New Haven, Connecticut, for the Wife, as to their respective rights and liabilities, each against the other, and to and upon the property and estate of the other in regard to the dissolution of their marriage.

13.3 Each party has read this AGREEMENT and has had it fully explained to him or her.

13.4 The Husband has agreed to pay his own attorney's fees in the present dissolution action, and he agrees to pay the outstanding balance of $6,750.00 which the Wife owes for her attorney's fees in the present dissolution action.

Miscellaneous Clauses

The miscellaneous section addresses matters of a general nature that might be anticipated to arise, such as questions of governing jurisdictional law, the parties' cooperation in executing documents necessary to facilitate the operation of the separation agreement, a waiver of rights in the other party's estate in the event of death, and provisions to address unexpected occurrences or events.

EXAMPLE

ARTICLE XIV

Miscellaneous

14.1 *Except as provided herein, the Husband and Wife each hereby waive any right at law or in equity to elect to take against any last will made by the other, including all rights of dower or of curtesy, and hereby waives, renounces, and relinquishes unto the other, their respective heirs, executors, administrators, and assigns forever, all and every interest of any kind or character which either may now have or may hereafter acquire in any real or personal property of the other, whether now owned or hereinafter acquired by either.*

14.2 *Except for any cause of action for divorce, legal separation, or dissolution of marriage or any action or proceeding to enforce the provisions of their Agreement, each party hereby releases and forever discharges the other, and by this Agreement does for himself or herself and his or her heirs, legal representatives, executors, administrators and assigns, release and discharge, and releases the other, with respect to matters arising out of the marital relationship from any and all causes of action, claims, rights, or demands whatsoever in law or in equity, which either of the parties ever had or now has against the other.*

14.3 *The Husband and Wife agree that they will, from time to time, at the request of the other, execute, acknowledge, and deliver any and all further instruments that may be reasonably required to give full force and effect to the provisions of this Agreement.*

14.4 *A waiver of any provision of this Agreement shall be effective only if made in writing and executed with the same formality as this Agreement. The failure of either party to insist upon strict enforcement of any provisions of this Agreement shall not be construed as a waiver of such terms, and such terms shall nevertheless continue in full force and effect.*

14.5 *If any provision of this Agreement is held to be invalid and unenforceable, all other provisions shall nevertheless continue in full force and effect.*

14.6 *This Agreement shall be construed and governed in accordance with the laws of the State of Connecticut.*

14.7 *The parties hereto agree and intend that the Agreement shall be incorporated in full by reference or otherwise in the dissolution proceedings. This Agreement shall merge with any decree of any Court affecting the parties.*

14.8 *This Agreement shall not be modified or altered except by an instrument signed and acknowledged by the Husband and Wife.*

14.9 *This Agreement is simultaneously executed in five (5) counterparts and each of said counterparts shall be original and each of said counterparts shall constitute but one and the same instrument.*

Signature Provisions

In the signatory section of the separation agreement, each party signs his or her legal signature, which should conform to the name used in the legal action before the court. Each party's signature is witnessed by two people.

EXAMPLE

IN WITNESS WHEREOF, the parties hereto have hereunto set their respective hands and seals on the day and year first above written.

_____	_____
Witness	*KAYLA MARTIN*
_____	
Witness	
_____	_____
Witness	*TROY MARTINA*
_____	
Witness	

Acknowledgment

The acknowledgment section follows the signing and witnessing of the separation agreement. In this section, a notary public or an officer of the court, if allowed to do so in the jurisdiction, will take the acknowledgment of each party. This means that the notary public or court officer will acknowledge that the party signed the document in the presence of witnesses, and acknowledge that he or she signed the document, and did so freely and without coercion.

EXAMPLE

STATE OF CONNECTICUT   )

*   )   ss._____*

COUNTY OF NEW HAVEN   )

On this the 8th day of October, 2018, personally appeared TROY MARTIN known to me to be the person whose name is subscribed to the within instrument and acknowledged that he executed the same, for the purposes therein contained, as his own free act and deed, before me.

IN WITNESS WHEREOF, I hereunto set my hand and official seal.

_____

JUSTINE FitzGerald MILLER
Commissioner of the Superior Court

STATE OF CONNECTICUT   )

*   )   ss._____*

COUNTY OF NEW HAVEN   )

On this the 8th day of October, 2018, personally appeared KAYLA MARTIN known to me to be the person whose name is subscribed to the within instrument and acknowledged that she executed the same, for the purposes therein contained, as her own free act and deed, before me.

IN WITNESS WHEREOF, I hereunto set my hand and official seal.

_____

GRACE A. LUPPINO
Commissioner of the Superior Court

Concept Review and Reinforcement

KEY TERMS

boilerplate
compromise
merger

proposal
proposal letter

separation agreement
uncontested hearing

REVIEW OF KEY CONCEPTS

1. What is a proposal letter?
2. How is a proposal letter different from a separation agreement?
3. Explain the concept of merging a separation agreement into a dissolution decree.

4. What is meant by the term *compromise?*
5. Describe the resources a paralegal might utilize when drafting a separation agreement.
6. What are boilerplate agreements, and why should the paralegal proceed with caution when using them?

BUILDING YOUR PARALEGAL SKILLS

CASE FOR BRIEFING

IN THE MATTER OF *ASCH v. ASCH*, 30 A. D. 3RD 513 (2D DEPT. 2006) (NY)

Critical Thinking and Legal Analysis Applications

1. Your work as a paralegal for Harvey Havermeyer, a highly acclaimed "household word" in the area of family law, who specializes in representing the heavy hitters in both the corporate world and the entertainment industry. One of Harvey's best-known clients is Lateisha L'Amour, a TV talk show personality. Lateisha and her husband John Harrington, a marine biology professor, share legal custody of their fifteen-year-old triplet sons. The children reside with John. The parties' separation agreement provides that Lateisha will pay the triplet's tuition at their exclusive preparatory school and two-thirds of the costs of their extracurricular activities. Lateisha has just received an e-mail from John telling her that she must pay for the boys to attend a school-related summer marine biology camp. This camp includes a six-week cruise to the Coral Sea and costs $60,000 per camper. Lateisha is furious. She thinks that the cost is ridiculously exorbitant and that the camp does not qualify as an extracurricular activity. Lateisha, John, and the triplets all live in Manhattan. Attorney Havermeyer wants you to look at the recent New York case law on separation agreements. You quickly find Asch v. Asch, which you believe will provide a short and sweet answer to the question of Lateisha L'Amour's obligations in this circumstance. Write up your results for Attorney Havermeyer in a brief interoffice memorandum. Don't forget to "global cite" Asch to make sure you're still on the right track.

Building a Professional Portfolio

PORTFOLIO EXERCISES

1. List the basic provisions of a separation agreement.
2. Develop a parenting plan for a newly divorced young couple who have a six-month-old daughter. The parties live and work within five city blocks of one another and both are fewer than ten minutes by car from the baby's day-care facility. Before the breakup, the father took the child to day care each day and the mother picked her up. The father wishes to continue to

do this. He also wants the child overnight two nights a week, and he wants overnight weekend visits every other weekend. The mother is happy to have the father take the baby to day care every morning but will not agree to any overnights until the baby is older. In this parenting plan, try to be creative in proposing some access time that the father will be happy with and that the mother will not oppose.

Chapter **eighteen**

ALTERNATIVE DISPUTE RESOLUTION AND THE DIVORCE TRIAL

T he prevailing trend in resolving divorce cases is to encourage the parties to work out their differences privately and amicably. The adversarial process, complete with battling lawyers and harmful words hurled from a witness box, is not the preferred environment for the parties to settle their differences. The reality is that most divorces do not allow the parties the luxury of going their separate ways. Former spouses who may despise each other must still function as parents. A divorce trial that leaves "scorched earth" behind may create wounds that will last long after the lawyers and judges have walked away from the case.

LEARNING OBJECTIVES

After studying this chapter, you should be able to:

1. Explain the various types of alternative dispute resolution options used to resolve family matters.

2. Understand the paralegal's role in the alternative dispute resolution process.

3. Distinguish between a contested and uncontested hearing.

4. Describe the role of the paralegal in trial preparation.

5. Understand the role of technology in family courts.

Alternative dispute resolution or ADR
A method of resolving disputes between parties without resorting to a trial.

Most jurisdictions now require the parties in a divorce action to participate in some type of *alternative dispute resolution,* or *ADR*. ADR is a method of resolving disputes between parties without resorting to a trial. While every marriage must be dissolved by a judge, the actual divorce trial will be either contested or uncontested. When the parties work out an agreement through ADR, the divorce trial is an uncontested proceeding, and it takes a judge matter of minutes to review the agreement and go through the legal motions of dissolving the marriage.

There are many benefits to ADR. The first is that an amicable divorce is less expensive. The cost of any form of ADR pales in comparison to the legal fees charged for a contested divorce case. Matters resolved through ADR take less time than countless court hearings. Staying out of court also helps reduce the emotional costs. This saves the parties from having to take the witness stand, facing harsh cross-examination and possibly saying something they will later regret or that will have long-lasting effects. A professional trained in ADR can sometimes help the parties get to the root of their dispute and encourage a "win-win" compromise. The ADR process also is better for the children. They are not stuck between two parents who are in the midst of litigation and may be spared an additional layer of stress in an already difficult situation. Trained professionals help the parties focus on their goals as parents and encourage them to make decisions that are in the best interest of the children. Another benefit to ADR is privacy, as these meetings are conducted in private. Courtrooms are open to the public, and divorce trial proceedings, as well as appeals, are published and easily accessible on the Internet. Some forms of ADR also give the parties some control over the outcome of their case, whereas the results of an adjudicated proceeding are in the hands of a judge.

TYPES OF ALTERNATIVE DISPUTE RESOLUTION IN FAMILY CASES

There are several types of ADR options available for divorce cases. Not all of these options work for every case, so the legal professionals have to determine which one is more suitable, given the client's needs and willingness to participate.

Settlement Conference

Settlement conference
A meeting with both lawyers and their respective clients, with the specific goal of settling the case without court intervention.

The first type of ADR is called a *settlement conference*. A settlement conference is a meeting with both lawyers and their respective clients, with the specific goal to settle the case without court intervention. During a settlement conference, the parties, with the assistance of their attorneys, attempt to reach an agreement by discussing the issues in their case and finding some type of resolution. This method is useful when the parties are able to at least be in the same room together, share equal bargaining power, and do not require the assistance of a mental health professional. The end goal is an amicable agreement in their case that will be presented to a judge on the day of the final hearing.

Divorce Mediation

Mediation
Where the parties meet and attempt to resolve the pending issues surrounding their dissolution of marriage action with the assistance of a trained third party, either court-provided and free, or privately engaged and paid.

Mediation is a confidential, structured process in which a neutral third party assists the parties in resolving their differences and reaching an agreement. Mediation is appropriate where the parties need help in resolving alimony, child custody, visitation, and complicated issues of property and debt distribution. Mediation is also appropriate for resolving postjudgment matters, such as changes in parenting plans and child support. Mediation is not marriage counseling or psychotherapy but rather a short-term conflict resolution alternative to court litigation.

Mediation is either voluntary or mandatory. Parties who choose voluntary mediation seek out such services on their own for the purpose of avoiding litigation and its inherent financial and emotional costs. Voluntary mediation requires the parties to seek private mediation services from a qualified professional. The respective parties pay for private mediation services. Courts in many states require mandatory mediation before the court will even hear a contested divorce case. A court-ordered private mediator or court personnel trained in such matters might conduct the mediation. Costs vary from state to state. Whether voluntary or mandatory, the divorce mediation process takes several sessions to complete. More sessions may be necessary depending on the complexity of the case.

A divorce mediator, the neutral third party in the mediation process, may be a mental health professional or lawyer trained in helping parties identify issues of mutual concern, discuss possible solutions, and work out an agreement that is mutually acceptable. There are attorneys and mental health counselors who work together as co-mediators, combining their respective areas of expertise. A mediator guides the parties toward arriving at their own solutions. The parties, not the mediator, determine the outcome. The purpose behind this practice is that parties who participate in decision making are happier with the outcome and more likely to honor such agreements. Paralegals may also become divorce mediators by participating in training courses focusing on mediation techniques and the relevant law. There are currently no states that certify or license divorce mediators. In addition to participating in training courses, persons interested in offering divorce mediation services should join a reputable professional organization. The Academy of Family Mediators, the Association of Family and Conciliation Courts, and the Society of Professionals in Dispute Resolution are national organizations. Individual states may also have comparable organizations that set professional standards, require a minimum level of training for membership, follow a code of ethics, and continue members' education through group-sponsored programs.

Lawyers who offer mediation services cannot act as counsel for one or both parties. Such representation would be considered a conflict of interest. The lawyer-mediator must make it clear to the parties that he or she will not represent either party but rather serve as a neutral facilitator in helping them resolve their issues. The distinction of the attorney's role as mediator and not advocate should be memorialized in writing in a contract between parties and the mediator.

Once the lawyer-mediator has facilitated the process, he or she will prepare a ***memorandum of understanding***, a plain-language, nonbinding document containing the agreement of the parties on the various issues relevant to their case. The parties must then take this document to their respective attorneys, who will prepare a formal separation agreement to be filed with the court and incorporated into the divorce decree. The separation agreement is binding on the parties once the court incorporates it into its decree. It is important for the parties to have their own attorneys who will explain the legal implications of the mediated agreement, advocate for any modifications, and process the case through the court system. It is not uncommon for one of the parties to file a *pro se* appearance where money is an issue. Sometimes, both parties will use a mediator, draft their own separation agreement, and appear before the judge *pro se*.

Memorandum of understanding
A written, plain-language, nonbinding document containing the tentative agreement of the parties on various issues relevant to their case.

As long as they are willing to submit to the process and their primary concern is the welfare of the children, many divorcing couples benefit from the voluntary mediation process. Some cases, however, are inappropriate for mediation services. Mediation will not work where:

- There is a history of physical, emotional, financial, or sexual abuse. In these cases, the abused spouse may be intimidated or fear the consequences of speaking his or her mind.

- There is a history of alcohol or substance abuse that would impair the afflicted party from participating in the process.
- One or both parties want things their way and are unwilling to compromise or work toward mutually agreeable solutions.
- Parties are hiding assets and are not truthful in their disclosures.
- One or both parties are extremely angry and want revenge. There is no way to mediate with such persons unless they can put their anger aside and work toward more noble goals.

Where the state's family courts mandate mediation services, an attorney representing a client with a history of domestic violence may request some type of *shuttle mediation*. In this process, the parties will meet separately with the mediator, who then shuttles between the parties in attempt to broker an agreement. If the client is not comfortable with this process, the attorney may make a motion to the court, arguing that the case is not appropriate for any type of ADR option and should proceed directly to trial.

Collaborative Law Divorce

Collaborative divorce
A team approach to divorce dispute resolution designed to protect the spouses and their children from the trauma of divorce litigation where both parties employ the services of a collaborate divorce attorney, financial planner, and mental health professional.

Collaborative divorce is a fairly new concept in comparison to other forms of ADR in family matters. In cases where the parties need the strong advocacy of an attorney but wish to protect themselves and their children from the emotional trauma inherent in divorce litigation and avoid lengthy proceedings and their high costs, the collaborative process is an option. It is a team approach to divorce dispute resolution where both parties employ the services of a collaborative divorce attorney, financial planner, and mental health professional. Other professionals may be hired, such as vocational experts, when the case warrants creative input from other disciplines. While the prospect of paying fees to each of these professionals may cause some to worry, the reality is that a long, protracted divorce will drain much more of the marital assets.

In a collaborative law divorce, the couple and their respective attorneys agree in advance of the collaborative process to collaborate on resolving the matter and that they will not litigate. The agreement signed by the couple and their attorneys will include a provision stating that in the event the couple fails to resolve their dispute, the attorneys will not represent them in a contested hearing and they must then find new counsel. This clause strongly encourages the parties to work on resolving their case. The agreement will also include a provision stating that all the experts who worked on the case are disqualified as witnesses and that their work product is inadmissible in court unless an agreement to the contrary is signed. The attorneys, however, will provide new counsel with the client file and any other relevant documents. The disclosures made by the parties during the collaborative process are confidential in nature, except for threats to harm another or claims of child abuse, which must be reported to the appropriate state child protection agency. The parties also agree in advance to make full and honest disclosures regarding their financial matters.

Attorneys who practice collaborative law should be trained in resolving matters in a nonadversarial manner and are an essential component to the process. The attorney's role in the process is to provide advice to his or her client on legal matters as well as work with the other attorney toward crafting an amicable separation or settlement agreement. The mental health professional is essential in helping the client through what can be a very emotional time. Financial planners are essential in helping the client determine how the divorce will affect his or her financial future and how to minimize problems before they materialize. The parties are free to bring whoever can assist the parties in creative problem solving. The emphasis of the teams is not adversarial but rather a search for "win-win" solutions.

Figure 18-1 Attorneys who practice collaborative law should be trained in resolving matters in a nonadversarial manner and are an essential component to the process.

ESB Professional/Shutterstock.

Divorce Arbitration

There are some divorce cases where resolution by settlement conference, mediation, or collaborative divorce is not an option. Though some parties are unable to work out a resolution and need a third party to decide their case, they do not want prolonged court proceedings. The parties may also want to save on legal fees as well as have their case heard in a more informal setting. This type of case may be suitable for arbitration.

In *divorce arbitration*, the parties present their evidence before a neutral third party who will render a decision in the case. The arbitrator is either a retired judge or an attorney experienced in divorce cases. The arbitrator renders an opinion called an *arbitration award*. Depending on the agreement of the parties or state law, the award will be either binding or nonbinding on the parties. If binding, the arbitration award will be filed with the court and treated as if the parties had tried their case before a judge. It is important to check state statutes regarding divorce arbitration. Most jurisdictions, with some variation, follow the *Uniform Arbitration Act*, which strictly limits appeals of arbitrated matters. The parties, however, may enter an agreement to the contrary prior to the arbitration proceeding to include certain appeal rights.

Shuttle Diplomacy In *Miller v. Miller*, the arbitrator conducted the hearing by positioning the parties in separate rooms and shuttling back and forth. Both spouses agreed to the use of this procedure. The wife later objected, filing a motion to set aside the award based on the argument that she did not have the opportunity to present evidence or take testimony. Applying Michigan's Domestic Relations Arbitration Act, the Supreme Court of that state held that arbitration and trial proceedings do not require the same formalities and that parties are free to agree to "shuttle" arbitration.

Divorce arbitration
An alternative to a divorce trial whereby parties, who are unable to work out a resolution, present their evidence before a neutral third party who will render a decision on the contested issues.

Arbitration award
The opinion rendered by an arbitrator, which depending on the prior agreement of the parties, may be either binding or nonbinding.

DEBRA LEA MILLER v. JOHN THOMAS MILLER

707 N.W.2D 341, 474 MICH. 27(2005)
SUPREME COURT OF MICHIGAN

This case presents the question whether the Domestic Relations Arbitration Act (DRAA) requires a formal hearing during arbitration comparable to that which occurs in traditional trial proceedings. We conclude that it does not.

Also at issue is whether a court order to which the parties have stipulated in writing can satisfy the act's requirement of a written agreement to arbitrate. We conclude that it can. Therefore, we reverse the judgment of the Court of Appeals, which ruled to the contrary on both issues, and we reinstate the arbitration award and the judgment of divorce.

THE FACTUAL AND PROCEDURAL HISTORY

Plaintiff filed for divorce in January 2001. After failed settlement conferences in the circuit court, on December 4, 2001, both parties stipulated in writing to entry of an order sending all issues in the case to binding arbitration.

The arbitrator put the parties in separate rooms during the arbitration proceedings. He shuttled between them, gathering the necessary information and hearing the respective arguments. Both parties agreed to this procedure.

At the end of the day, plaintiff asked the arbitrator for additional sessions. He denied the request, expressly noting in his written award that plaintiff had failed to raise anything new to justify further proceedings. When plaintiff made a second request, the arbitrator gave her three days to provide an outline of what she would present at the additional proceedings. She supplied, instead, voluminous material. Rather than schedule more hearings, the arbitrator reviewed plaintiff's material, modified the award, and issued the final binding arbitration award.

Plaintiff filed a motion in court to set aside the arbitration award on the basis that the arbitrator had failed to conduct a "hearing" as required by the DRAA. She also claimed that no arbitration agreement existed. The court rejected plaintiff's claims and entered a judgment of divorce. In a split published decision, the Court of Appeals reversed the judgment of the circuit court and vacated the arbitration award. It held that the DRAA required a formal hearing and that none occurred during the arbitration. *Miller v. Miller*, 264 Mich App 497; 691 NW2d 788 (2004).

THE APPROPRIATE STANDARD OF REVIEW

The two issues on appeal are matters of statutory interpretation that we review de novo. *People v. Kimble*, 470 Mich 305, 308–309; 684 NW2d 669 (2004). When interpreting a statute, our goal is to give effect to the Legislature's intent as determined from a review of the language of the statute. *People v. Koonce*, 466 Mich 515, 518; 684 NW2d 153 (2002).

Defendant asks us to review the Court of Appeals decision not to enforce the arbitration award. We review such decisions de novo to determine whether the arbitrators exceeded their powers. See *Gordon Sel-Way, Inc. v. Spence Bros, Inc.*, 438 Mich 488, 496–497; 475 NW2d 704 (1991). Arbitrators exceed their powers whenever they act beyond the material terms of the contract from which they draw their authority or in contravention of controlling law. *DAIIE v. Gavin*, 416 Mich 407, 433–434; 331 NW2d 418 (1982).

WHAT CONSTITUTES A HEARING UNDER THE DRAA

MCL 600.5081 is the statutory provision that governs vacation and modification of arbitration awards under the DRAA. MCL 600.5081(2) provides:

If a party applies under this section, the court shall vacate an award under any of the following circumstances:

a. The award was procured by corruption, fraud, or other undue means.

b. There was evident partiality by an arbitrator appointed as a neutral, corruption of an arbitrator, or misconduct prejudicing a party's rights.

c. The arbitrator exceeded his or her powers.

d. The arbitrator refused to postpone the hearing on a showing of sufficient cause, refused to hear evidence material to the controversy, or otherwise conducted the hearing to prejudice substantially a party's rights.

The Court of Appeals concluded that the arbitrator violated MCL 600.5081(2)(d). It reasoned that the informality of the hearing prejudiced plaintiff's rights. The question is whether, in proceedings under the DRAA, the statute precludes hearings being conducted as the hearing was conducted in this case.

In reaching its decision, the Court of Appeals majority relied primarily on MCL 600.5074(1), which provides:

> An arbitrator appointed under this chapter *shall hear* and make an award on each issue submitted for arbitration under the arbitration agreement subject to the provisions of the agreement. [Emphasis added.]

The DRAA does not define the term *hear* or *hearing*. Moreover, it sets no procedural requirements for arbitration. Rather, it specifically eschews them. For example, MCL 600.5077 requires, with certain exceptions, that the arbitrator not make an official record of most arbitration proceedings. This purposeful requirement of little or no record shows that the Legislature intended not to require specific procedures in arbitration proceedings. Without a record, reviewing courts cannot assess what procedures have been followed.

The Legislature's failure to provide specific arbitration procedures is consistent also with tradition. Historically, judicial review of arbitration awards is highly limited. *Gavin*, 416 Mich 433–434. This Court has characterized arbitration procedures as "informal and sometimes unorthodox. . . ." *Id.* at 429. Consequently, courts should not speculate why an arbitrator ruled in one particular manner. *Id.*

Rather than employ the formality required in courts, parties in arbitration are able to shape the parameters and procedures of the proceeding. The DRAA requires that they first sign an agreement for binding arbitration delineating the powers and duties of the arbitrator. MCL 600.5072(1)(e).

The act also contemplates that the parties will discuss with the arbitrator the scope of the issues and how information necessary for their resolution will be produced. MCL 600.5076. The act contemplates that the parties will decide what is best for their case. Nowhere in the DRAA are procedural formalities imposed that restrict this freedom.

This Court has consistently held that arbitration is a matter of contract. "It is the agreement that dictates the authority of the arbitrators." *Rowry v. Univ of Michigan*, 441 Mich 10; 490 NW2d 305 (1992). In this case, the Court of Appeals decision infringes on the parties' recognized freedom to contract for binding arbitration.

It restricts the parties' freedom to decide how the arbitration hearing should be conducted. Plaintiff presents no convincing argument that the Legislature intended all DRAA hearings to approximate traditional court hearings. We know of none. It is inappropriate for a court to read into a statute something that was not intended. *AFSCME v. Detroit*, 468 Mich 388, 412; 662 NW2d 695 (2003).

Significantly, in this case, the parties specifically agreed to allow the arbitrator to conduct the hearing in two separate rooms. If the parties and the arbitrator thought that this was the best way to hold their hearing, they were at liberty to make that agreement. Because it is the agreement of the parties that dictates arbitration, the Court of Appeals should not have altered the agreement. *Rowry*, 441 Mich 10.

THE SUFFICIENCY OF THE PARTIES' WRITTEN ARBITRATION AGREEMENT

Plaintiff argued below that no written arbitration agreement existed in this case. Defendant disagreed. Although the Court of Appeals majority did not reach this issue directly, it listed as alternative grounds for possible relief that the stipulated

continued

order did not constitute a written arbitration agreement. *Miller*, 264 Mich App 507 n. 12. We disagree.

As we noted earlier, the DRAA requires a written arbitration agreement setting out the subject of the arbitration and the arbitrator's powers. MCL 600.5071 and MCL 600.5072(1)(e). Here, the parties entered into a written agreement satisfying these requirements when they stipulated to entry of the particularized order for binding arbitration that the court in due course entered.

The order lists the issues for arbitration. It clearly delineates the arbitrator's powers and duties. Accordingly, it is sufficient to satisfy the requirements of MCL 600.5071 and MCL 600.5072 (1)(e).

Nothing in the DRAA mandates that there be an agreement separate from the stipulated order. This is consistent with the informal and sometimes unorthodox nature of arbitration. *Gavin*, 416 Mich 429. As long as the parties agree to some document that meets the minimal requirements of MCL. 600.5071 and MCL 600.5072 (1)(e), the agreement is sufficient. Therefore, we reverse the decision of the Court of Appeals that reached the contrary conclusion.

CONCLUSION

We hold that the DRAA does not require that the formality of a hearing in arbitration proceedings approximate that of a hearing in court. Arbitration is by its nature informal. The appropriate structure for an arbitration hearing is best decided by the parties and the arbitrator. A procedure by which the arbitrator shuttles between the parties in separate rooms questioning and listening to them satisfies the act's requirement of a hearing.

We also hold that no written agreement beyond the order for binding arbitration is required (1) if the parties stipulate to entry of the order and the order meets the criteria of MCL 600.5071 and MCL 600.5072 (1)(e), and (2) if the parties satisfy MCL 600.5072 (1)(a) to (d) on the record.

Therefore, we reverse the judgment of the Court of Appeals and reinstate the arbitration award and the judgment of divorce.

Source: Debra Lea Miller v. John Thomas Miller, 707 N.W.2D 341, 474 MICH. 27 (2005), Michigan Supreme Court.

The Paralegal's Role in Alternative Dispute Resolution

In all forms of ADR, the most important role for the paralegal is that of information gathering and analysis. Family law is a fact-driven field of practice. Divorce cases are decided on a case-by-case basis because every family and its particular financial and social structure are different. Paralegals may assist the attorney in the ADR process by:

- having knowledge of all forms of ADR available in their jurisdiction.
- compiling files on various reputable and reliable ADR professionals.
- preparing state-specific forms required for mandatory ADR procedures.
- monitoring clients who are required by state law to attend mandatory mediation and parenting classes and following up on their compliance.
- scheduling ADR conferences with the relevant parties.
- preparing and processing discovery requests.
- helping the client respond to discovery requests.
- reviewing the client's discovery as well as that of the opposing party.
- assisting the attorney at settlement conferences and collaborative law sessions.
- drafting mediation agreements between the lawyer-mediator and clients.
- drafting memorandums of understanding in mediation cases.

- drafting collaborative law agreements between the attorney and client.
- drafting separation agreements in accordance with agreements reached through settlement conferences, mediation, or collaborative law sessions.

The Divorce Trial

At this stage, the parties have either reached an agreement or plan to litigate some or all of their issues in a *divorce trial*, the process in which both parties present their case to the court for its final hearing. Divorce trials are for the most part *bench trials*, which means that the trial is conducted before a judge, not a jury. In some jurisdictions, such as New York and Texas, the parties can demand a jury trial in divorce cases. In a bench trial the judge is the trier of both fact and law. The family court judge is knowledgeable in the area of domestic relations, and his or her role is to apply the law, which includes statutory and case law, to the particular facts in the case before him or her and render a decision that is fair to both parties.

Divorce trials are open to the public, so anyone can sit in and observe the case. Courtrooms may be sealed upon motion of the parties to protect children of the marriage when the trial issues are of a particularly sensitive nature. Divorce files are also open to the public and may be viewed in local courthouses at the clerk's office.

Divorce trials are either uncontested or contested. Whether the case is contested or uncontested, the paralegal must send a formal notice to the court indicating that the case is ready for the trial list.

Uncontested Hearing

In an *uncontested hearing*, either the parties have reached an agreement regarding the issues surrounding the dissolution of their marriage (i.e., alimony, property division, child custody and support, attorney's fees), or one party is defaulted for failure to appear. A *default trial* takes place when one of the parties to an action

Divorce trial
A trial in which both parties present their case to the court for its final hearing.

Uncontested hearing
A judicial procedure where neither party objects to the court granting a divorce and entering an order of marital dissolution.

Default trial
Where one of the parties to an action has failed to appear at the scheduled trial date even though he or she has received proper notice of the proceedings; the court proceeds with a hearing and severs the marriage.

Figure 18-2 Divorce trials are for the most part bench trials, which means that the trial is conducted before a judge, not a jury.

Sirtravelalot/Shutterstock.

has failed to appear at the scheduled trial date even though he or she has received proper notice of the proceedings. In this case, the court will proceed with a default hearing and sever the marriage. It is important that the respondent/defendant file a cross-complaint so in the event the petitioner/plaintiff does not appear, the court can proceed on the respondent/defendant's cross-complaint.

Most divorce cases proceed as uncontested matters. Many couples resolve their major issues through negotiations between themselves, through their respective attorneys, or with a professional mediator. The parties then preserve their agreement in writing. The case must then be put on the court calendar as an uncontested hearing.

Every jurisdiction has specific procedures for requesting a trial date in either an uncontested or contested dissolution matter. The paralegal should become familiar with his or her particular state's requirements for getting a case on the court calendar. In addition, some jurisdictions may also provide preprinted forms to facilitate this process.

Uncontested divorce trials are very brief in duration. The court will first confirm service of process on the defendant spouse. This means that the judge determines whether service of the divorce complaint/petition was adequately made on the defendant/respondent. In the case where there is a nonappearing defendant, the moving party must provide the court with a ***military affidavit*** in accordance with the Soldiers and Sailors Relief Act 50 USC § 520 (1982) to prove that the defendant is currently not serving in one of the armed forces. This used to require contacting each branch of the military to determine whether or not the defendant is in the armed forces. Now this task can be accomplished online by accessing the United States Department of Defense website section on "Verifying Active Duty Military Status." If there is any doubt that the individual found online is the defendant, then the military affidavit may have to be obtained in the traditional manner of notifying each branch of the military. When requesting a military affidavit, either online or by contacting the individual branches, the paralegal should provide the defendant's name, address, Social Security number, and date of birth. In addition, a small fee must accompany each request.

Some jurisdictions do not require the parties to appear in court if the divorce is uncontested or if there is a default. In these jurisdictions the parties are merely required to file the appropriate paperwork with the court.

In matters where the parties have worked out a settlement or separation agreement, the plaintiff/petitioner will be called to the witness stand and put under oath. The plaintiff's attorney will question him or her briefly on the allegations made in the complaint/petition, which is necessary to establish the statutory grounds for a dissolution of marriage. The judge may also direct some questions to the parties.

If the parties have executed the separation agreement, the original is presented to the court and reviewed by the judge. Separation agreements are usually approved by the court unless the terms of the agreement are deemed by the court to be ***unconscionable***, unfair, or one sided. The court must determine if the parties are aware of the contents of the agreement, that they understand it, that it is their free and voluntary act, that it was not made under fraud or duress, and that the assets have been fully disclosed. Provisions regarding alimony and property division will not be scrutinized as carefully as those provisions dealing with child custody, support, or visitation. The court also has an interest in determining the economic position of the parties after the divorce. If the court finds the agreement unconscionable, it will order the parties to go back to the drawing board and reconsider certain provisions.

If the court accepts the parties' agreement by finding it to be fair and equitable, the court will first dissolve the marriage and then, upon request of the

Military affidavit
A sworn statement that serves as proof that the defendant is currently not serving in one of the armed forces.

Unconscionable
An agreement that is so unfair to one party that the court will refuse to enforce it.

parties, will either "merge" the separation agreement into the divorce decree or "incorporate, but not merge" the separation agreement into the divorce decree. Whether the separation agreement is merged or incorporated, both parties are required to fulfill their obligations under the agreement. The main difference is that when the separation agreement is merged, it becomes a court order, while the incorporated agreement does not and must be enforced on contractual grounds.

A *merger* affords the parties with the postjudgment remedies of contempt and modification. If a spouse fails to comply with the terms of a separation agreement that has been merged into the divorce decree, the aggrieved spouse may seek contempt of court proceedings to enforce its provisions. A merger also allows parties to seek modification of certain provisions as long as they can prove that there has been a substantial change in circumstances since the entry of the original decree.

Unlike a merged separation agreement which may be modified upon a showing of a substantial change in circumstances, an agreement that has survived the divorce decree requires a higher standard to be met for modification purposes. The moving party must prove that there are "countervailing equities" that support a change. A countervailing equity is an interest that conflicts with another interest or right. For example, let's say that a wife is receiving alimony for a three-year period pursuant to a separation agreement that survived the divorce decree by incorporation, not merger. After three years, the wife goes back to court seeking an extension of alimony. Proving a substantial change in circumstances will not be enough to modify the agreement. The wife may have to prove that she risks becoming a charge on the taxpayers if the alimony will not be extended. It is then up to the court to determine whether the higher standard of protecting the public from having to add to the public assistance rolls has been met. A separation agreement that has been "incorporated and not merged," however, does not prohibit the modification of child support payments since "[p]arents may not bargain away the rights of their children to support from either one of them." *Knox v. Remick*, 371 Mass. 433, 437 (1976); *DeCristofaro v. DeCristofaro*, 24 Mass. App. Ct. 231 (1987).

Merger
An agreement that is no longer a contract between the two parties, but rather a court order, which can be modified or enforced through contempt of court proceedings.

CONTESTED HEARING

Parties that have been unable to reach an agreement regarding issues of alimony, property division, visitation, and child custody and support will have to let the judge make those decisions. A disputed divorce trial is known as a *contested hearing*. Although contested trials give the client their "day in court," they can also be very stressful and their outcome uncertain.

Parties who have negotiated a settlement agreement are more likely to be content with the final results because they actually had some degree of participation in its formation and are more likely to cooperate with its terms because it was agreed to voluntarily. Once a case has been turned over to a judge, there is no telling what the result will be.

Contested hearings may also increase the parties' hostility toward each other. This has a particularly devastating result when children are caught in the middle. Contested hearings can also be very expensive. Clients incur additional legal fees and expenses such as sheriff's fees, expert witness fees, court costs, transcript fees, appraisal reports, investigations, or evaluations prepared by third parties.

Why, then, despite these consequences, do some divorces end up in a contested trial? The trial process provides a forum where opposing parties can vigorously

Contested hearing
A disputed divorce trial arising from the parties' failure to resolve disputed issues without judicial intervention.

litigate issues of law and fact before an impartial third party. Unfortunately, the hostility surrounding a broken marriage can often spill into the courts. Some parties find that a proposed settlement is unfair and refuse to accept it. The other spouse refuses to change or modify his or her position; hence, the parties reach a stalemate. Sometimes clients have unrealistic expectations of what the legal system can do for them and insist on going to trial. Others wish to use the threat of trial to intimidate a spouse who may not wish to have every sordid detail of the marriage exposed in public. Others still play out their anger toward their spouse in the legal system by refusing to cooperate or compromise on anything and instead contest every single issue possible.

If the case cannot be settled and it looks like it will proceed as a contested matter, the appropriate forms must be filed to request a trial date.

Judicial pretrial conference
A conference that takes place before a judge, not a trial, to help the parties try to come to an agreement before the trial starts; also known as a pretrial conference.

Some jurisdictions require that parties in contested matters attend a ***judicial pretrial conference***. The pretrial conference takes place before a judge. It is not a trial. The purpose of the judicial pretrial conference is to help parties come to an agreement. The judge's role is to tell the parties how he or she would rule if this matter were to be tried before him or her. If parties agree to the judge's proposal, an agreement will be drafted and the parties will bring the agreement before the court. Another function of the judicial pretrial conference is to narrow the issues to be litigated in cases where there is no agreement in sight.

Pretrial conference
A meeting that takes place before a judge, not a trial, to help the parties try to come to an agreement before the trial starts; also known as a judicial pretrial.

If the case cannot be resolved and instead heads for trial, a ***pretrial conference***, or mandatory settlement conference, may be scheduled. The purpose of the pretrial conference is to streamline the trial process. At the pretrial conference, the parties will:

1. **Exchange witness lists.** This will assist the parties in preparation of cross-examination and impeachment of the opposing party's witnesses. It will also help anticipate witnesses' testimony.
2. **Disclose exhibits to be filed.** Parties can review in advance exhibits that will be entered as evidence and determine which exhibits may be entered into evidence by agreement and which ones will be opposed.
3. **Narrow the issues to be tried.** Even though the divorce is contested, there may be issues that the parties can agree on or can stipulate to.
4. **Establish if an interpreter is needed for the proceedings.** A party may not be able to speak or understand the English language or may require sign language to be used. The pretrial conference serves to give court personnel advance notice of such needs so they can make arrangements to have an interpreter present.
5. **Establish if a habeas corpus is needed.** A writ of ***habeas corpus*** may be necessary so that an incarcerated party may be transported by the state's correction department for trial.
6. **Determine the role of the child's attorney.**
7. **Determine whether children will testify and under what circumstances.**

Habeas corpus
A document that allows an incarcerated party to be transported by a state's correctional department for trial.

If disagreements still exist after a pretrial conference, a trial date will be scheduled. The goal of the trial process is to arrive at the truth. The way we arrive at the truth in our American system of jurisprudence is through the adversarial system. Both parties, represented by competent counsel, battle it out before an impartial third party known as a judge. The rules of evidence dictate which information can be admitted and which excluded so that evidence offered at trial is reliable and untainted. The problem with the adversarial system is that it assumes that both lawyers are equally competent, that the judge has no biases or prejudices, and that both sides have enough funds in their war chest to afford expert witnesses, evaluations, appraisals, investigators, and every legal maneuver available to present their case.

Unfortunately, this is not always the case. Some attorneys are better than others, and just because a judge puts on a black robe does not mean that he or she is saturated with the wisdom of Solomon. Clients do not always possess the funds to pay for the presentation of a perfect case and may have to settle for what is realistic.

As mentioned earlier, parties who go to trial take a risk when turning their decision-making power over to the judge. They have now lost the ability to control their destiny in terms of the dissolution of their marriage.

THE PARALEGAL'S ROLE IN TRIAL PREPARATION

The process of trial preparation begins on the day of the initial client interview. Only a clairvoyant will know whether or not a case will go to trial. Clients will, at times, inform the attorney that the parties have worked out an agreement and there are no problems. This, however, is never a sure thing. The amicable agreement of today can turn into the contested bloodbath of tomorrow.

The attorney will need to develop the theory of the case. The ***theory of the case*** is the legal justification for the client's position and for the relief he or she is seeking. A thorough review of the discovery materials will help formulate some type of case strategy.

Theory of the case
The legal justification for a client's position and for the relief he or she is seeking.

Family court dockets can be extremely crowded, and judges appreciate a well-prepared, well-researched, and well-organized case that does not take up time with matters that have already been resolved.

Once a theory of the case has been developed, the lawyer and paralegal must assemble the necessary evidence to present the client's case to the court. A client's case is proven by presenting evidence that will support the client's claim. The client's case is developed through the evidentiary vehicles of testimony and documents.

At trial, the petitioner or plaintiff spouse, through his or her attorney, will be the first to present evidence at the final dissolution hearing. The attorney for the petitioner or plaintiff spouse will call the plaintiff to the stand, as well as other witnesses if necessary, to testify and support the claims in the divorce complaint or petition. The attorney may wish to enter evidentiary exhibits to support and bolster the client's case. The opposing party will have the opportunity to cross-examine the plaintiff and any other witnesses, and to challenge the evidence being presented in court. Once the attorney for the plaintiff spouse rests his or her case, the defendant or respondent spouse has the opportunity to present testimonial and documentary evidence on behalf of the client.

Testimony is often given during a divorce trial. A list of witnesses is prepared to determine who will testify at trial. In a divorce case, the client spouse will be the primary witness, and he or she will tell his or her story to the court. Other witnesses may also be called to testify: expert witnesses such as physicians and mental health professionals, social workers, teachers, appraisers, accountants, and investigators. Lay witnesses such as family members, friends, neighbors, coworkers, employers, and/or supervisors may also testify.

Testimony
Evidence given by a witness under oath or affirmation.

When calling a witness other than a client, it is necessary for the party calling that witness to subpoena the witness to trial. A subpoena is a document ordering a witness to appear under penalty of law to provide testimony at a legal proceeding. A paralegal may be in charge of preparing the subpoenas and arranging for service of these orders by a sheriff. The paralegal must also keep track of subpoenas to make sure they have been properly served. Failure to subpoena a party may result in his or her not appearing for trial. Records also need to be subpoenaed. Witnesses also need to be prepared by the attorney to testify.

Documents that may be used as evidence at trial include the following:

- financial records of parties already produced through discovery,
- any court-ordered evaluations that are part of the court file,
- additional psychological or psychiatric reports that either party seeks to have admitted in support of his or her position,
- appraisals of assets, an independent financial evaluation of business interests, licenses, goodwill, and pensions,
- children's school, pediatrician, and counseling records,
- electronic evidence from social networking websites such as Twitter and Facebook, word processing and database files, e-mail correspondence, spreadsheets, financial management programs, browser history files, and calendars,
- photographs,
- deeds and mortgages, and
- state, federal, and local tax returns.

Trial notebook

A method of organizing the materials prepared for trial in a manner that makes them readily available for use at trial.

Once the attorney has determined which types of evidence will be used at trial, the next step is to prepare the *trial notebook*. The trial notebook provides a way to organize materials important to the case in a manner that makes them readily available for use at trial. There is nothing more embarrassing for an attorney than having to fumble and leaf through stacks of unorganized documents during a trial. It gives the client and the court the impression that the attorney did not prepare adequately.

The trial notebook is not necessarily a physical notebook, although a notebook can be used if preferred. Some attorneys organize their trial notebooks by designating a series of file folders to contain certain information. These file folders will then be placed in a large folder or box to facilitate easy access during trial. Other attorneys may prefer to use commercial or self-prepared trial notebooks. The trial notebook may contain a variety of subfiles organized such that they facilitate easy access to the information.

Financial disclosure affidavit

A sworn statement indicating the income, expenses, assets, and liabilities of a client.

Custody affidavit

An affidavit indicating that there is no other proceeding pending in another court that affects the custody of the minor children.

The parties may also be required to submit certain documents to the court at the time of trial that may be prepared by the paralegal. Please note that filing requirements vary from state to state. These documents include the following:

1. An updated sworn *financial disclosure affidavit*, indicating the income, expenses, assets, and liabilities of the client.
2. A *custody affidavit*, indicating that there is no other proceeding pending in another court that affects the custody of the minor children. If a proceeding is pending, the paralegal must indicate where and the nature of the proceedings.
3. A *claim for relief*, which is a statement filed by a party indicating what he or she wants in terms of a disposition in the case.
4. *Wage execution* forms for the purpose of facilitating alimony and child support payments through automatic deductions from the obligor's paycheck.
5. State-specific *Bureau of Vital Statistics forms* designed for the purpose of collecting statistical information on divorcing couples.
6. *Stipulations*, which are written agreements in which parties agree that certain facts are true or that certain procedures are to be followed.

Claim for relief

A statement filed by a party indicating what he or she wants in terms of a disposition in the case.

Wage execution

Serves the purpose of facilitating alimony and child support payments through automatic deductions from the obligor's paycheck.

Bureau of Vital Statistics form

A form that is filled out and sent to the state in order to keep track of certain information regarding divorcing couples.

Stipulations

Written agreements where parties agree that certain facts are true, or that certain procedures will be followed.

The client should be notified by phone and then in writing regarding the trial date. The attorney should set up an appointment with the client prior to trial for the purpose of reviewing testimony and explaining the trial process to the client. The attorney should also review the exhibits he or she intends to introduce through the client so the client becomes familiar with them and will be prepared to testify. The client should be given directions either to the courthouse or to meet the attorney at the office. The client should also be informed to dress conservatively as if he or she were attending a religious service. A conservative appearance conveys reverence and respect for the court.

DAY OF THE TRIAL

Some attorneys allow their paralegals to assist at trial. Although a paralegal may not question witnesses, argue motions, make opening and closing arguments, or raise objections, paralegals can perform many important tasks at trial. At trial, the paralegal will sit at the counsel table with the attorney and client. Remember that the paralegal's status must be communicated to the court so that neither the judge nor opposing party is under the impression that the paralegal is an attorney.

The divorce trial will be heard by a judge, who will preside over the hearing. Parties may be referred to a hearing officer, referee, or a special master in courts that utilize these alternative decision makers to resolve the overflow of cases. As mentioned earlier, a divorce trial is open to the public unless the court has ordered the courtroom sealed to protect particularly sensitive cases, and in some jurisdictions, the parties can demand a jury trial.

The plaintiff or petitioner will be the first to put on his or her case and call his or her witnesses to the stand. The opposing party will then have the opportunity to cross-examine the plaintiff's witnesses. Once the plaintiff has rested his or her case, the defendant/respondent will be able to proceed with his or her case and present his or her witnesses. During the course of the trial, the paralegal may make notes during each witness's testimony. This is one of the most important functions of a paralegal during the trial. It is important that the lawyer focus his or her attention on the testimony in order to make the appropriate objections or argue with opposing counsel regarding the admission or exclusion of evidence. If the note-taking process is delegated to the paralegal, then the attorney can concentrate on the trial. Taking notes during testimony is essential for the purpose of preparing closing arguments and cross-examination. A paralegal may also assist at trial by dealing with the client. A client should be given a legal pad and pen and instructed to write down any questions or comments that arise during trial. This lets the client express himself or herself without distracting the attorney.

The paralegal may also help keep track of exhibits, pass materials to the attorney, and deal with impatient witnesses waiting to testify. Paralegals may also run errands such as photocopying, making quick legal research trips to the court library, and making phone calls to witnesses or the office.

After testimony, each attorney argues why the court should rule in his or her client's favor. This is known as *final argument*. The court may decide the case immediately or render its decision at a later date. Sometimes the court will require the parties to prepare briefs or a memorandum of law on particular issues to assist the court in making its decision.

If the court renders its decision immediately after trial, the court must first *dissolve* the marriage—that is, declare that the spouses are no longer married. The court will then rule on the issue of child support, property division, alimony, attorney's fees, and debts. One of the parties will be ordered to prepare the judgment, which will be signed by the opposing party and the court. The *judgment* delineates the orders made by the court pursuant to the court's decision after trial and becomes a permanent part of the court file.

A *transcript* of the trial may be necessary if the decision was rendered at the close of trial to facilitate the preparation of the judgment or the preparation of

Final argument
Where each attorney argues why the court should rule in his or her client's favor.

Judgment
An order made by the court pursuant to the court's decision after a trial; it becomes a permanent part of the court file.

Transcript
An official copy of the record of proceedings in a trial or hearing.

an *appeal* of the case to a higher court. The paralegal may have the responsibility of ordering the transcript and dealing with the court reporter's office that will be responsible for its preparation. The paralegal may also be required to draft the judgment in accordance with local rules.

Use of Technology in the Family Courtroom

Family courts are increasingly modernizing their operations by implementing new technology in the courtroom. The following are examples of how family courts around the United States are using technology to expedite their caseload, increase productivity, save money by going paperless, and improve communications with both attorneys and litigants:

- Advanced audio-recording equipment
- Assistive-listening devices for the hearing-impaired
- Audio-visual conferencing for remote appearances and remote interpreting
- Computer "dashboards" permitting judges and court personnel to review the family court docket and details of cases in a spreadsheet format that can be filtered by age of case, attorney name, case type, court part, judge, next appearance date, and party name
- Court social media presence for the dissemination of access to court resources, news, and services
- DIY (do-it-yourself) electronic resources for self-represented litigants
- E-mail notification to attorneys and self-represented litigants of court filings and court orders document attachments
- E-track systems allowing attorneys to track *all* their cases
- Evidence presentation systems for displaying physical and electronic evidence
- File accessibility for attorneys of record through e-filing systems
- Instant voice-to-text transcriptions
- Recommendation of OurFamilyWizard co-parenting app, a software program that centralizes communications and information related to children in custody and visitation cases
- Installation of computer monitors for judges
- Open Internet access for the public
- Secure Wi-Fi access for laptops and tablets issued to judges and court personnel
- Skype visitation for access to children in custody and relocation cases
- Social media accounts for announcing emergency court closures
- Text message reminders to litigants before their court appearance date
- Updated sound systems that ensure proper sound levels
- Use of evidence from social media in family law cases

Cell Phones in the Courtroom

When it comes to lawyers and paralegals entering the courtroom with various forms of modern-day technology, it is crucial to become familiar with the state's court rules regarding the use of electronic devices in the courthouse. The state's judicial branch website is the best place to start and will most likely include guidelines regarding what can be brought into the courtroom, in the same way the court has for years dealt with the issues of televising, photographing, or any other form of media coverage at trials. For example, The State of Maine Supreme Judicial Court, Administrative Order JB-05-16 (A. 5-08) states that:

"All cellular phones, pagers, computers, and other electronic devices shall be turned off prior to entering the courtroom, unless otherwise authorized by the

Figure 18-3 It is important to check local court rules as many courts prohibit the general public from entering the courthouse with cell phones.

Felix Mizioznikov/Shutterstock.

presiding judge, justice, or magistrate. . . . Any camera, cell phone, computer, or other electronic device that also contains a camera or is equipped to take photographs in a courthouse may be subject to confiscation, unless use is authorized pursuant to JB-05-15."

The most common technological device used by both legal professionals and clients in the courtroom is the cell phone. Cell phones are helpful for keeping in touch with clients, law office personnel, and opposing counsel. In family court, continuances, trial dates, and other important appointments can be immediately entered into the attorney's cell phone calendar and serve as a reminder as the hearing approaches. Many states allow legal professionals to bring cell phones into court but require that all phones be turned off and prohibit the taking of photographs. It is important to check local court rules as many courts prohibit the general public from entering the courthouse with cell phones. Illinois, for example, bans visitors from bringing "cell phones, smartphones, laptop computers, tablet computers, and all other electronic devices capable of connecting to the Internet or making audio or video recordings" into the courtroom. Clients may have to leave their phones in their cars, so it is helpful to know the court's electronic device policies in advance. A paralegal may wish to include this information in correspondence sent to the client when reminding them of their next court hearing. While technology has improved the flow of information in the courtroom, it is not without its disadvantages. Ringing cell phones often interrupt courtroom proceedings. It is important for legal professionals to turn off their phones so they do not ring accidentally while in the courtroom. Forgetting to set the phone on "off" can result in anything from an admonishment from the judge, to sanctions, or confiscation of the device. In some states, the public is also banned from bringing cell phones into the courtroom to discourage the spread of information through social networking websites such as Facebook and Twitter.

Concept Review and Reinforcement

KEY **TERMS**

alternative dispute resolution or ADR
arbitration award
Bureau of Vital Statistics forms
claim for relief
collaborative divorce
contested hearing
custody affidavit
default trial
divorce arbitration
divorce trial

final argument
financial disclosure affidavit
habeas corpus
judicial pretrial conference
mediation
memorandum of understanding
merger
military affidavit
pretrial conference

settlement conference
stipulation
testimony
theory of the case
transcript
trial notebook
unconscionable
uncontested hearing
wage execution

REVIEW OF **KEY CONCEPTS**

1. Name and describe the forms of alternative dispute resolution discussed in this chapter.

2. If you and your spouse were getting divorced, what form of dispute resolution would you use? Explain your reasons for choosing this option.

3. What is the paralegal's role in alternative dispute resolution?

4. What is the paralegal's role at the trial?

5. How does the trial notebook assist the attorney at trial?

6. Explain the role technology plays in the divorce trial.

BUILDING YOUR PARALEGAL SKILLS

CASE FOR BRIEFING

PATEL v. PATEL, 359 S.C. 515, 599 S.E.2D 114 (2004) (AN INTERESTING CASE THAT TOOK EIGHT YEARS AND THOUSANDS OF DOLLARS TO RESOLVE!)

Critical Thinking and Legal Analysis Applications

1. Based on the facts in the case of *Patel v. Patel*, 359 S.C. 515, 599 S.E.2d 114 (2004), how would a family court resolve the matter of attorney's fees in this case? Is the law regarding the awarding of attorney's fees in your jurisdiction similar to South Carolina's, or does your state have a different approach?

2. Go to the Internet and read "Deconstructing the Divorce Mediation Process: One Practitioner's Approach," by Anju D. Jessani. Based on your reading of this article, explain what actually happens during the divorce mediation process.

Building a Professional Portfolio

PORTFOLIO **EXERCISES**

1. You work as a paralegal for the law office of Peter Panzarella, an attorney and divorce mediator in your state. Delores and Arthur Fleming have retained the services of Attorney Panzarella to mediate their custody issues. Both parties wish to avoid the costs of a contested divorce trial and resolve their dispute amicably for their children's sake. Using a sample mediation agreement found online, draft a mediation agreement in this case.

Chapter **nineteen**

POSTJUDGMENT DIVORCE MATTERS

The entry of a final dissolution decree does not always end the litigation in a particular case. A spouse ordered to pay alimony or child support may cease making payments, either voluntarily or involuntarily. The circumstances of the parties may have changed substantially in a number of areas since the date of the original divorce decree.

A large part of a family lawyer's practice involves **postjudgment matters**. Postjudgment matters are court proceedings that arise after the case has gone to final judgment. They often address the modification of existing court orders or their enforcement when parties fail to meet their obligations. A glance at the family law calendar of any state confirms the reality that postjudgment motions dealing with the failure to comply with existing court orders, and motions seeking modifications of such orders far outnumber the motions on the calendar relating to pending dissolution matters. This chapter is essential to acquiring a complete understanding of the ongoing effect of divorce on a previously intact family unit. It focuses on postjudgment matters, which consist of modifications of the original order, enforcement of existing orders, and motions to reopen the divorce judgment. Appeals are also postjudgment matters, but because appeals are covered in basic civil litigation courses, they are not addressed here.

LEARNING OBJECTIVES

After studying this chapter, you should be able to:

1. Identify the modifiable and nonmodifiable portions of a dissolution decree.

2. Describe the events that give rise to the changed circumstances needed to modify alimony, child support, custody, and access/visitation.

3. Understand the issues surrounding parental relocation cases.

4. Identify the options some states provide to assist a spouse in recovering unpaid alimony or child support payments.

Postjudgment matters
Court proceedings that arise after the case has gone to final judgment. They often address the modification of existing court orders or their enforcement when parties fail to meet their obligations.

NONMODIFIABLE TERMS OF THE DISSOLUTION DECREE

The dissolution decree contains some provisions that constitute the final resolution of an issue and hence cannot be modified. Other provisions are modifiable and are subject to the court's continuing jurisdiction until certain events occur.

A final decree of dissolution usually contains a section that deals with the distribution of marital assets or property. The separation agreement, signed by the parties, approved by the court, and incorporated into the divorce decree, sets forth a final disposition of assets. If the parties are unable to agree on how the assets are to be divided, then the court makes the property division determination. The court's ruling may be appealed. However, if the appellate court upholds or affirms the trial court's decision, then the property distribution award remains intact and final, or *nonmodifiable*. Most property distribution awards are *nonmodifiable*. If parties agree that one spouse will transfer all of his or her right and title to the family residence, once this agreement is made a part of the divorce judgment, the transferring party usually may not come back at a later date to modify or reverse this arrangement. Only if a spouse alleges and can prove fraud in the making of the divorce agreement will the court consider reopening and modifying the disposition of issues deemed final and nonmodifiable. This will require the aggrieved spouse to file a *motion to reopen judgment*, requesting that a new trial be granted.

If alimony is awarded as a one-time lump sum and is labeled nonmodifiable in the divorce decree, then the spouse paying the lump sum is released from any future obligation to provide maintenance or support for the ex-spouse regardless of his or her future need for assistance, no matter how urgent. Lump sum alimony is nonmodifiable even if it is to be paid in installments. If lump sum alimony is to be paid in installments, and the separation agreement or judgment of the court specifies the number of installments to be paid and the amount of each such installment, the court, upon hearing a spouse's motion to modify, may determine that a modification of the payment arrangement is necessary to avoid substantial financial hardship for the payer. In making that determination, the courts will look for a substantial change in the circumstances of the payer. Such changes include loss of employment, loss of income-generating assets that are not the result of the payer's intentional alienation or dissipation of these assets, or changes in a child support obligation based upon a change in the circumstances of the party or the "deviation" criteria that result in an upward deviation of the child support obligation.

Nonmodifiable
Orders issued by a court that cannot be changed, regardless of the circumstances.

Motion to reopen judgment
The legal procedure necessary to seek the reopening of a divorce case that has already gone to final judgment. Its purpose is to modify the disposition of issues that were deemed final and nonmodifiable.

EXCEPTIONAL CIRCUMSTANCES UNDER WHICH NONMODIFIABLE TERMS OF THE DISSOLUTION DECREE HAVE BEEN MODIFIED

There have been infrequent but significant instances where a court has granted a party's motion to modify a clause or term of the separation agreement or dissolution decree that was originally deemed nonmodifiable.

This is especially true where a separation agreement has provided that the alimony obligation is nonmodifiable as to the amount. Either a substantial change in the circumstances of one of the parties or a significant increase in the cost of living since the entry of the judgment would be a compelling reason for the court to override the nonmodifiability provision of an alimony order. There have also been instances where the court has overridden the clause regarding nonmodifiability of the term of alimony when the payee spouse has developed a severe medical problem, can no longer work, and still has minor children. Some courts will not approve the inclusion of a nonmodifiable periodic alimony provision in a separation agreement. These courts assume this position to prevent the possible future ordeal of filing a motion to reopen the divorce judgment. If this is the case, then the spouse requiring an increase or decrease in the alimony obligation need only file a motion to modify alimony.

Controlling Provisions of State or Federal Law and the Effect on Nonmodifiability of Changes in These Laws

The operation of provisions in federal or state law or changes in federal or state law may result in the modifiability of provisions of a dissolution judgment that previously was nonmodifiable.

In the early 1980s the U.S. Supreme Court held that federal law precluded state courts from dividing military retirement benefits under state community property laws. See *McCarty v. McCarty*, 453 U.S. 210, 101 S.Ct. 2728, 69 L.Ed.2d 589 (1981). Subsequently, the Uniformed Services Former Spouses Protection Act (USFSPA), 10 U.S.C. § 1 408, was enacted by Congress. Contained within the USFSPA was a specific provision that allowed for the retroactive application of the law, changing the status of military retirement benefits to divisible. As a result, those individuals whose judgments of dissolution had entered between the time *McCarty* was decided and the enactment of the USFSPA were granted the right to seek a portion of the military retirement benefits. However, it is noted that it remains within the sound discretion of the court to determine whether such a modification should be granted. Though this is an extremely rare circumstance, it may occur again in the future.

Statutory Provisions That Control in the Absence of a Specific Waiver

In any situation regarding the obligations of one spouse to another for alimony that fails to include a triggering event that would terminate said alimony, statutory provisions relating to the modification or termination of alimony shall control. In *In Re: Marriage of Thornton*, 95 Cal. App. 4th 251 (2002), the court held that the omission of express language regarding the termination of alimony upon remarriage did not prevent the payer husband from obtaining an order terminating the alimony obligation as of the date of the wife's remarriage because California law specifically requires that any waiver of the statutory provisions must be in writing.

MODIFIABLE TERMS OF THE DISSOLUTION DECREE

Let's now take a look at the terms of a dissolution decree that can be modified.

Modification of Alimony

In determining the modifiability of alimony, the parties must look to the original alimony award. The original award was either agreed on by the parties in a separation agreement or ordered by the court in a contested hearing where the parties could not agree on the issue of alimony. The court can modify alimony unless it is barred from doing so under the separation agreement or decree of dissolution.

If an order for alimony requires a spouse to pay the other spouse a fixed amount of money periodically, such as every week or every month, either the

Substantial change in circumstances
An actual or assumed alteration in the financial status or capability of either party.

Modification
A change or adjustment to a previous court order.

Arrearage
Amount due by court order but unpaid; also known as back alimony.

Motion to modify
Where a party asks that orders entered by the court be changed when there has been a substantial change in one of the party's circumstances from the time the original order was entered; also known as a motion for modification.

Motion to modify alimony
Where a party asks that orders for spousal support entered by the court be changed when there has been a substantial change in one of the party's circumstances from the time the original order was entered; also known as a motion to modify support.

paying spouse or the receiving spouse may bring the matter back to the court to request either an increase or a decrease in the periodic amount ordered. In either case, the moving party will usually allege, as grounds, a change in his or her circumstances or a change in the other party's circumstances. The moving party must prove that since the date of the original order, there has been a *substantial change in circumstances* requiring a *modification* of the original order.

If either party waived alimony at the time of the dissolution, they are forever barred from returning to court and asking for alimony in the future. If a party was awarded nominal alimony of one dollar per year, this will allow the recipient spouse to return to court at a later date and request a modification of the original one-dollar alimony award. If a party was awarded rehabilitative alimony, either the separation agreement or court order after trial will indicate its modifiability. Reimbursement alimony is typically nonmodifiable since modifiability would defeat the purpose of "reimbursing" a spouse.

Arrearages, or amounts of unpaid alimony due to the recipient spouse, are nonmodifiable. A recipient spouse has a vested property right in the arrearage that cannot be changed by the court. For instance, if a spouse seeks a decrease in the amount of his or her periodic alimony or support payment, even if the court grants the motion, the spouse will usually be responsible for paying the unpaid amount due under the previously existing order.

Motion to Modify Alimony A party brings his or her request to the court's attention by filing a *motion to modify*, or petition to change the court's previous alimony order (see Exhibits 19-1 and 19-2). In this motion, the moving party alleges that a substantial change in circumstances has occurred since the date of the original decree, requiring the court to reopen the case and modify its original order.

In many jurisdictions, if a party files this motion within six months after the entry of the dissolution decree, the party need only file the motion with the court and serve, by mail, a copy of the motion to the attorney who represented the other spouse in the dissolution action. This avoids the need for service of the motion by a sheriff. The attorney must also serve by mail a copy on the attorney for the children if the children were represented by counsel in the action.

If more than six months have elapsed, the moving party must serve additional documents on the ex-spouse, along with the motion to modify. In many jurisdictions, the moving spouse must serve an order to show cause on the ex-spouse. This document must usually be personally served by a sheriff or other individual authorized to serve process. The *motion to modify alimony* will accompany the rule to show cause, which will already have identified a hearing date set by the court clerk. Some courts have preprinted forms and simplified procedures, allowing parties to appear *pro se*.

After service is complete, the papers must be filed with the court and an entry fee must be paid, the amount of which depends on the jurisdiction. Sheriff's fees and attorney's fees must also be paid by the client. Therefore, bringing an action to modify parts of the divorce judgment can be costly.

Grounds for Modification of Alimony Grounds for all modifications are broadly known as a substantial change in circumstance. What constitutes a substantial change? In matters relating to alimony, changed circumstances refer to an actual or assumed change in the financial status or capability of either party. For instance, if a spouse-husband was earning a high salary when the alimony order was entered and he subsequently loses his job and now works for a much lower rate, he can move to have the court lower the amount previously ordered based on his loss of ability to pay. Similarly, if a spouse-wife was receiving alimony and had a high-paying job that she had to leave because of illness, she may petition the court to increase the amount her ex-husband must pay her.

Exhibit 19-1 New Hampshire petition to change court order.

THE STATE OF NEW HAMPSHIRE
JUDICIAL BRANCH
http://www.courts.state.nh.us

Court Name: _____

Case Name: _____

Case Number: _____

PETITION TO CHANGE COURT ORDER

☐ No agreement   ☐ Agreement

1. Your Name _____

   Date of Birth _____ E-mail Address (optional) _____

   Residence Address _____

   Mailing Address (if different) _____

   Telephone Number (Home) _____ (Work) _____

2. Other Party's Name _____

   Date of Birth _____ E-mail Address (optional) _____

   Residence Address _____

   Mailing Address (if different) _____

   Telephone Number (Home) _____ (Work) _____

3. List minor children born to or adopted by the parties:

Name	Date of Birth	Current Address

If there are minor children born to or adopted by the parties, complete questions 4 – 8. This information is required under RSA 458-A, the Uniform Child Custody Jurisdiction and Enforcement Act (UCCJEA).

It is important that you answer these questions with as much detail and accuracy as possible. Lack of adequate information could significantly delay orders being issued in your case.

There are several situations that might result in New Hampshire exercising jurisdiction over child/ren. The continuous presence of the child/ren in New Hampshire for six (6) months is not the only basis for jurisdiction. In some emergency situations, the court may be able to exercise jurisdiction on a temporary basis.

continued

Exhibit 19-1 Continued

Case Name: _____

Case Number: _____

PETITION TO CHANGE COURT ORDER

4. List the places where the minor child/ren of the parties has/have lived in the last **five (5) years** and the names of the people they lived with at that time, if you know. Start with where the child lives now and work backward in time.

Dates From/To	Town/City, State	Parent(s)/Caretaker	Current Address/Contact Address of Parent/Caretaker	Which Child/ren

If more space is needed, attach Extra Page (Form NHJB-2656-FPS).
☐ **I have attached Form NHJB-2656-FPS because additional space was needed.**

5. Are there any person(s), not a party to this proceeding, who have physical custody of the child/ren or who claim to have custody, physical custody or parenting time rights? ☐ Yes ☐ No
    If yes, list name(s) and address(es) of person(s):

_____

_____

_____

_____

6. Check one of the following:
    ☐ I **have not** participated in any court case(s) concerning the custody, visitation, parenting time or placement of the child/ren in this or any other state.
    OR
    ☐ I **have** participated in court case(s) concerning the custody, visitation, parenting time or placement of the child/ren in this or any other state. I have participated in the following:

Name of Court	State	Case No.	Date of Court Order

7. Are there any actions for enforcement, or proceedings relating to domestic violence, domestic relations, protective orders, marriage dissolution, paternity, legitimation, custody, parental rights and responsibilities, termination of parental rights, adoption, juvenile, or other proceedings in any court in any state affecting any children named in this petition or parents of those children? ☐ Yes ☐ No If yes, complete the following:

Name of Court	State	Case No.	Type of Court Case

Case Name: _____

Case Number: _____

PETITION TO CHANGE COURT ORDER

8. Optional: ☐ I am alleging, under oath, that my or my child/ren's health, safety, or liberty would be jeopardized by the disclosure of identifying information set forth in this Petition. To support my allegation, I state as follows:

_____

_____

_____

_____

9. What part of the court order(s) do you want the court to change? **(Check any that apply)**
   The date of the most recent court order (if known): _____

   ☐ Child Support Only   ☐ Child Support and Parenting Plan

   ☐ Legal Separation to Divorce   ☐ Alimony

   ☐ Parenting Plan   ☐ Other _____

10. ☐ I have tried to resolve the issue(s) raised in this petition with the other party. We are unable to resolve the issue(s) and have sought the help of a neutral third party (such as a mediator or neutral evaluator) to assist us. We are unable to work out the disagreement after seeking third party assistance.
    OR
    ☐ I have **not** tried to resolve the issue(s) raised in this petition because:

    a. ☐ There is a domestic violence protective order in effect **OR**

    b. ☐ Other (State reasons you did not try to resolve issue(s) with other party):

    _____

    _____

11. What, specifically, do you want the court to order? **(Please attach additional page(s) if necessary.)**

_____

_____

_____

_____

12. Why should the court change the current orders? **(List each reason separately.)**

_____

_____

_____

_____

13. Please check one of the following regarding public assistance.
    ☐ No public assistance (TANF) is now being or has within the last 6 months been provided, nor is medical assistance (Medicaid) presently being provided, for any minor child of the parties.

    ☐ The N. H. Department of Health and Human Services is providing or has provided within the last 6 months public assistance (TANF) and/or medical assistance (Medicaid) for a minor child or children of the parties. If you check this box, you must mail copies of this petition and the Personal Data Sheet (NHJB-2077-FS) to DHHS at:

    New Hampshire Department of Health and Human Services
    Division of Child Support Services - Legal Unit
    129 Pleasant Street
    Concord, NH 03301

NHJB-2062-F (04/11/2014)   Page 3 of 4

continued

Exhibit 19-1 Continued

Case Name: _____

Case Number: _____

PETITION TO CHANGE COURT ORDER

14. By filing this petition, you are asking that the Court:

☐   Change the current orders as stated above;

☐   Schedule a hearing;

☐   Other:

_____

_____

☐   Grant any other orders which may be appropriate.

I acknowledge that I have a continuing duty to inform the court of any court action in this or any other state that could affect the child/ren in this case.

I swear or affirm that the foregoing information is true and correct to the best of my knowledge.

_____   _____
Date   Signature of Party Filing Petition to Change Court Order

State of _____, County of _____

This instrument was acknowledged before me on _____ by _____

My Commission Expires _____

Affix Seal, if any   _____
                                                               Signature of Notarial Officer / Title

_____
Signature of Attorney

_____
Printed Name, Address and Phone Number of Attorney   Bar #

Source: The State of New Hampshire Judicial Branch, New Hampshire Judicial Branch.

Exhibit 19-2 Connecticut preprinted form requesting a modification to a divorce decree.

Clicking on the question marks (?) will give you information about that section of the form.

MOTION FOR MODIFICATION ?
JD-FM-174   Rev. 2-13
C.G.S. §§ 46b-84, 46b-86
P.B. §§ 25-26, 25-30, 25-57, 25a-18, 25a-30
(Check one)

**STATE OF CONNECTICUT
SUPERIOR COURT**
www.jud.ct.gov

COURT USE ONLY
MFMOD

☐ **Before judgment** ? ☐ **After judgment** ? *(If the court has ordered you to attach a request for leave with a motion for modification of a final custody or visitation order, you must complete and attach a Request for Leave form (JD-FM-202) to this motion.)* ?

Judicial District of ?	At *(Town)*	Docket Number ?
Plaintiff's Name *(Last, first, middle initial)* ?		Plaintiff's Address *(Number, street, city, state, zip code)*
Defendant's Name *(Last, first, middle initial)* ?		Defendant's Address *(Number, street, city, state, zip code)*

Type of Motion to Modify ?

☐ Child Support ☐ Alimony ☐ Custody ☐ Visitation ☐ Other *(Specify):* ? _____

I, _____, ☐ the Plaintiff ☐ the Defendant ☐ a Support Enforcement Officer,
(Name)

respectfully represent that:

1. This Court issued an order dated _____ directing _____, residing at
(Name) ?

_____, to: *(Complete the boxes that apply to your motion)* ?
(Number, street, city, state, zip code) ?

Pay current support in the amount of:	Pay alimony in the amount of:	
$ _____ every (per) _____ ?	$ _____ every (per) _____ ?	
Pay arrearages as follows:		
$ _____ every (per) _____ ?	on the total arrearage owed of $ _____ ?	as of *(date)* _____ ?
Have custody of the child/children: *(Check one)*	Have visitation or parenting time as follows: ?	Primary residence of children with: ?
☐ Joint legal custody ? ☐ Sole custody ?		
Provide health insurance coverage		Provide HUSKY/cash medical ?
☐ No ☐ Yes ?	Pay _____ % of unreimbursed medical expenses ?	$ _____ every (per) _____
Contribute to child care	Other *(Specify):* ?	
_____ % or $ _____		

2. You must explain briefly the facts that are the reasons why you are asking for this modification. *(Check appropriate box or boxes. Attach additional sheet or sheets if necessary.)*

☐ Since the date of the order, the circumstances concerning this case have changed substantially as follows: ?

_____

☐ The order for current child support is substantially different from the current child support and arrearage guidelines ? presumptive child support order as follows: ?

_____

3. The ☐ plaintiff ☐ defendant is a "deploying parent" ? of the armed forces. The facts about that deployment or mobilization are: ?

_____

4.a. I am receiving state assistance or HUSKY health insurance, or I have received it in the past.   ☐ Yes ☐ No
4.b. Any child that this motion is about is receiving state assistance or HUSKY health insurance, or has received it in the past. ☐ Yes ☐ No
If you answered "Yes" to either of these questions, you must send a copy of this motion to: The Office of the Attorney General, 55 Elm Street, Hartford, CT 06106. If you don't give the Attorney General's Office a copy, your motion may take longer to decide.

I ask the Court to modify the existing order or orders as follows: ? *(Check all that apply)*

a. Child Support *(You must file a sworn to Financial Affidavit (JD-FM-6) at least 5 days before the hearing. You must also file an Affidavit Concerning Children (JD-FM-164), a completed Worksheet for the Connecticut Child Support and Arrearage Guidelines (CCSG-1, JD-FM-220), and an Advisement of Rights Re: Income Withholding (JD-FM-71) on your hearing date).*

☐ Order current support ☐ Find arrearage and order payment ? ☐ Order immediate income withholding
☐ Increase current support ☐ Provide HUSKY/cash medical ☐ Provide health insurance coverage
☐ Decrease current support ☐ Contribute to child care ☐ Other _____

b. Alimony *(You must file a sworn to Financial Affidavit (JD-FM-6) at least 5 days before the hearing. You must also file an Advisement of Rights Re: Income Withholding (JD-FM-71) on your hearing date).*

c. Custody *(You must file a sworn to Financial Affidavit (JD-FM-6) at least 5 days before the hearing. You must also file an Affidavit Concerning Children (JD-FM-164) and a completed Worksheet for the Connecticut Child Support and Arrearage Guidelines (CCSG-1, JD-FM-220) on your hearing date).*

☐ Increase ☐ Decrease
the amount of alimony to be paid.

☐ Modify custody as follows:

_____

(Continued on back/page 2)   Check appropriate court. ?   ☐ Superior Court   ☐ Family Support Magistrate Division

continued

Exhibit 19-2 Continued

Plaintiff's Name *(Last, first, middle initial)*	Defendant's Name *(Last, first, middle initial)*	Docket Number

(Continued from page 1)

d. Visitation/Parenting Time *(You must file a sworn to Financial Affidavit (JD-FM-6) at least 5 days before the hearing.* You must also file an Affidavit Concerning Children (JD-FM-164) and a completed Worksheet for the Connecticut Child Support and Arrearage Guidelines (CCSG-1, JD-FM-220) on your hearing date).

☐ Modify visitation (parenting time) as follows:

e. Other *(Please be specific):*

☐ _____

Signature	Print Name	Title *(If applicable)*	Date Signed
Address *(Number, street, city, state, zip code)*			Telephone *(Area code first)*

Certification

I certify that a copy of this document was mailed or delivered electronically or non-electronically on *(date)* _____ to all attorneys and self-represented parties of record and that written consent for electronic delivery was received from all attorneys and self-represented parties receiving electronic delivery.

Name and address of each party and attorney that copy was mailed or delivered to*

*If necessary, attach additional sheet or sheets with name and address which the copy was mailed or delivered to.

Signed *(Signature of filer)* ►	Print or type name of person signing	Date signed
Mailing address *(Number, street, town, state and zip code)*		Telephone number

Order For Hearing and Summons *(To be completed by clerk or support enforcement officer, if applicable)*

The Court orders that a hearing be held at the time and place shown below. The Court also orders the

☐ Plaintiff   ☐ Defendant   ☐ Support Enforcement Officer   to give notice to the opposing party of the Motion and of the time and place where the court will hear it, by having a true and attested copy of the Motion and this Order served on the opposing party by any proper officer at least **12 days** before the date of the hearing. Proof of service must be made to this Court at least **6 days** before the date of hearing.

Hearing to be held at ►	Superior Court, Judicial District of		Date
	Court Address	Room Number	Time

To any proper officer:
By the Authority of the State of Connecticut, you must serve a true and attested copy of the above Motion and Order For Hearing and Summons on the person named below in one of the ways required by law at least **12 days** before the date of the hearing, and file proof of service with this Court at least **6 days** before the hearing.

Person to be Served	Address	
By the Court	Assistant Clerk/Support Enforcement Officer	Date Signed

Order   The court has heard this motion and orders it

☐ **Granted**   ☐ **Denied**   **and**   ☐ **Further orders** *(if applicable):*

_____

By the Court *(Judge/Family Support Magistrate/Assistant Clerk)*	Date Ordered

For Court Use Only
Fee for Motion to Modify: ☐ Paid   ☐ Waived

JD-FM-174 (Back/Page 2) Rev. 2-13

Source: Motion for Modification, State of Connecticut.

When the court addresses a request to modify alimony, the court looks at the financial status of each of the parties and tries to make a decision that is reasonable under the circumstances. Both spouses are expected to provide for themselves according to ability to do so. If a spouse, male or female, has been making alimony payments consistent with the court order to an able-bodied nonworking spouse and the paying spouse suddenly—say, through a significant job promotion—experiences a large increase in earned income, the nonworking spouse may bring a motion to modify alimony upward. The court, however, may find that since the nonworking spouse never sought employment, the previous award sufficiently satisfied the spouse's financial need and that the other spouse should not be penalized because his or her ability and hard work have resulted in greater financial remuneration.

The change in circumstances must also be involuntary. If, for example, a husband ordered to pay alimony voluntarily quits his job and then shows up in court with a motion to modify alimony, the court will not be very sympathetic. If a recipient spouse runs up charges on a credit card, she cannot later come in to court and ask for a modification, since she created the financial problem.

The following circumstances may constitute sufficient grounds for modification of alimony:

- deteriorating health of the payer or recipient spouse,
- increased cost of living,
- loss of employment,
- remarriage or cohabitation of recipient spouse,
- pay raises,
- winning the lottery,
- retirement,
- employment changes (i.e., downsizing),
- rehabilitation of recipient spouse, and
- unforeseen economic circumstances.

Modification of Child Support

The court has continuing jurisdiction in child support matters and may entertain modifications until its jurisdiction ends. The family court has the right to order child support for each child until the child reaches the age of majority. As with alimony, a custodial parent may file a *motion to modify child support* if that spouse can prove a substantial change in circumstances since the date of the original order. A noncustodial parent paying child support may also move to modify an existing court order if he or she can prove a change in circumstances. The moving party must file motions similar to those discussed in the earlier section regarding modification of alimony. If a modification is warranted, the court will make the change in the child support award pursuant to that jurisdiction's child support guidelines. Child support arrearages, however, are unmodifiable.

When addressing a motion to decrease the amount obligated to pay, the court usually does not extinguish the arrearage and will order that continuing payments, whether the same or lower, include an additional amount to pay off any unpaid back alimony or child support. Alternatively, the court may order that the total of the arrearage owed be paid to the recipient spouse within a reasonable time, such as thirty or sixty days.

The following circumstances may constitute sufficient grounds for modification of child support:

- increase in the cost of living—as children grow, their expenses increase (i.e., clothing, food, extracurricular activities),
- custody change—if the noncustodial parent moves for custody and prevails,
- an increase or decrease in either parent's income,

- change in the child's health requiring unusual or extraordinary expenses, and
- increased or onset of costs for special education, tutoring, or day care.

Substantial Change in Circumstances and Child Support Orders

The state of Connecticut has established a "rule of thumb" to determine whether a party seeking a modification of child support orders has met the "substantial change of circumstances" criteria for a modification. The rule of thumb is that there must be a fifteen percent change in the support obligation itself, not the income of either or both of the parties. It would be advisable for a paralegal to know whether the state in which he or she is practicing has such a rule of thumb and, if so, what the rule says.

Modification of Custody and Visitation

Custody and visitation orders are always modifiable. The courts, however, will not disturb a custody or visitation order unless the moving party can prove that there has been a substantial change in circumstances *and* that a modification to the existing custody or visitation situation is in the best interest of the child or that the court did not have certain facts available at the time of entering the original order of custody. The substantial change of circumstances must have occurred after the date of the original order. The court will not entertain any evidence that has already been introduced at the divorce trial. New evidence must be such that it justifies a ***motion to modify custody*** or a ***motion to modify visitation***; the court will not tolerate a disgruntled parent retrying the custody matter through the mask of a modification.

The following circumstances may constitute sufficient grounds for modification of custody or visitation:

- the child becomes old enough to choose a custodian,
- either parent's remarriage or cohabitation,
- a change in the child's needs,
- the parent's lifestyle adversely affecting the child,
- a parent's or child's health issues,
- abuse or neglect, and
- the custodial parent's relocation.

In some states, a guardian *ad litem* or attorney for the minor child, appointed or retained during the *pendent lite* period, may be ordered to continue in that capacity for so long as the court shall have jurisdiction over issues of custody and visitation.

In January 2006, the state of Connecticut added to its rules of court a requirement that a party seeking postjudgment modification of orders relating to custody, visitation, or parental responsibility shall append a request for leave to the motion. In addition, the rules require that a sworn statement of the moving party or other individual having personal knowledge reciting the factual and legal basis for the requested modification also be filed (see Conn. Rules of Court § 25-26[g]). This was enacted in order to allow the court to make a preliminary determination of whether the motion for modification had merit, thereby stemming the tide of frivolous motions.

RELOCATION OF CUSTODIAL PARENT

Because mobility is a characteristic of our society today, many dissolution decrees anticipate the possible relocation of a custodial parent and the consequences. Many dissolution decrees provide that a custodial parent may not move out of the jurisdiction without giving the noncustodial parent sufficient advance notice so that the noncustodial parent will have sufficient time if he or she desires to bring this proposed move to the attention of the court and object to this move as being contrary to the child's best

Motion to modify custody
Where a party asks that orders regarding child custody entered by the court be changed when there has been a substantial change in one of the party's circumstances from the time the original order was entered.

Motion to modify visitation
Where a party asks that orders for child visitation entered by the court be changed when there has been a substantial change in one of the party's circumstances from the time the original order was entered.

interest. If the noncustodial parent brings such a motion before the court, the matter may be referred to the family relations division for a study and recommendation to the court. The noncustodial parent's chances of prevailing will be greater if that parent demonstrates the strength and value of the child's relationship with the noncustodial parent and with other significant individuals within the jurisdiction, such as grandparents or uncles and aunts. On the other hand, if the noncustodial parent has played only an inconsistent and erratic role in the child's life, the court may not find that the child's best interests will be compromised by an out-of-state move.

In the past, in a decree for divorce or dissolution, a judge would sometimes order the custodial parent not to move out of the state with the children. While the parent was free to travel as he or she pleased, the children could not be moved out of the jurisdiction. Unfortunately, life isn't that simple, and circumstances arise requiring a return to court to address the original order barring relocation. Let's say the mother is the custodial parent and her original decree states that she shall not remove the children from the state. Mother remarries, and her new spouse is offered a job in another state. Mother must return to court to get permission to take the children out of the state, or she will be in contempt of court. The court now must address the issue of relocation pursuant to a two-prong test:

1. Is the original decree modifiable?
2. If modifiable, is the relocation in the best interest of the children?

The court must look at the original decree and determine if the court-ordered limitation on the custodial parent's freedom to relocate with the children is modifiable or whether the original order was a final, nonmodifiable, nonappealable part of the judgment, as is the case with the distribution of marital assets. While child custody is always modifiable, the issue of one parent relocating with the children may be limited by the court in that it deprives the other parent of contact and access to the children. The burden is on the moving party to prove to the court whether the original decree is modifiable. A review of the original decree and/or transcript may reveal that the issue is explicitly addressed and there is no dispute as to its modifiability. If the issue is unclear, then the court must make a decision based on the evidence offered and arguments of the parties. In the case illustrated earlier, if the decree is deemed nonmodifiable, the relocation of the children is barred. If modifiable, then the court moves to the second prong of the test, which is determining if the relocation is in the best interest of the children.

If the custodial parent prevails on the argument that the limitation on the custodial parent's freedom to have the child take up residence out of state is modifiable, then the burden falls on the noncustodial parent to demonstrate that such a move would not be in the child's best interest. At this point, the custodial parent may offer evidence to refute the noncustodial parent's evidence that such a move would compromise the child's best interest, and the custodial parent may introduce evidence that such a move will enhance the child's best interest.

EXAMPLES OF PARENTAL RELOCATION STATUTES

CONNECTICUT GENERAL STATUTES SEC. 46B-56D. RELOCATION OF PARENT WITH MINOR CHILD. BURDEN OF PROOF. FACTORS CONSIDERED BY COURT.

(a) In any proceeding before the Superior Court arising after the entry of a judgment awarding custody of a minor child and involving the relocation of either parent with the child, where such relocation would have a significant impact

continued

on an existing parenting plan, the relocating parent shall bear the burden of proving, by a preponderance of the evidence, that (1) the relocation is for a legitimate purpose, (2) the proposed location is reasonable in light of such purpose, and (3) the relocation is in the best interests of the child.

(b) In determining whether to approve the relocation of the child under subsection (a) of this section, the court shall consider, but such consideration shall not be limited to: (1) Each parent's reasons for seeking or opposing the relocation; (2) the quality of the relationships between the child and each parent; (3) the impact of the relocation on the quantity and the quality of the child's future contact with the nonrelocating parent; (4) the degree to which the relocating parent's and the child's life may be enhanced economically, emotionally, and educationally by the relocation; and (5) the feasibility of preserving the relationship between the nonrelocating parent and the child through suitable visitation arrangements.

WEST VIRGINIA CODE §48-9-403. RELOCATION OF A PARENT.

(a) The relocation of a parent constitutes a substantial change in the circumstances under subsection 9-401(a) of the child only when it significantly impairs either parent's ability to exercise responsibilities that the parent has been exercising.

(b) Unless otherwise ordered by the court, a parent who has responsibility under a parenting plan who changes, or intends to change, residences for more than ninety days must give a minimum of sixty days' advance notice, or the most notice practicable under the circumstances, to any other parent with responsibility under the same parenting plan. Notice shall include:
  (1) The relocation date;
  (2) The address of the intended new residence;
  (3) The specific reasons for the proposed relocation;
  (4) A proposal for how custodial responsibility shall be modified, in light of the intended move; and
  (5) Information for the other parent as to how he or she may respond to the proposed relocation or modification of custodial responsibility.

Failure to comply with the notice requirements of this section without good cause may be a factor in the determination of whether the relocation is in good faith under subsection (d) of this section and is a basis for an award of reasonable expenses and reasonable attorney's fees to another parent that are attributable to such failure.

The Supreme Court of Appeals shall make available through the offices of the circuit clerks and the secretary-clerks of the family courts a form notice that complies with the provisions of this subsection. The Supreme Court of Appeals shall promulgate procedural rules that provide for an expedited hearing process to resolve issues arising from a relocation or proposed relocation.

(c) When changed circumstances are shown under subsection (a) of this section, the court shall, if practical, revise the parenting plan so as to both accommodate the relocation and maintain the same proportion of custodial responsibility being exercised by each of the parents. In making such revision, the court may consider the additional costs that a relocation imposes upon the respective parties for transportation and communication, and may equitably allocate such costs between the parties.

(d) When the relocation constituting changed circumstances under subsection (a) of this section renders it impractical to maintain the same proportion of custodial responsibility as that being exercised by each parent, the court shall modify the parenting plan in accordance with the child's best interests and in accordance with the following principles:
  (1) A parent who has been exercising a significant majority of the custodial responsibility for the child should be allowed to relocate with the child so long as that parent shows that the relocation is in good faith for a legitimate

purpose and to a location that is reasonable in light of the purpose. The percentage of custodial responsibility that constitutes a significant majority of custodial responsibility is seventy percent or more. A relocation is for a legitimate purpose if it is to be close to significant family or other support networks, for significant health reasons, to protect the safety of the child or another member of the child's household from significant risk of harm, to pursue a significant employment or educational opportunity or to be with one's spouse who is established, or who is pursuing a significant employment or educational opportunity, in another location. The relocating parent has the burden of proving of the legitimacy of any other purpose. A move with a legitimate purpose is reasonable unless its purpose is shown to be substantially achievable without moving or by moving to a location that is substantially less disruptive of the other parent's relationship to the child.

(2) If a relocation of the parent is in good faith for legitimate purpose and to a location that is reasonable in light of the purpose and if neither has been exercising a significant majority of custodial responsibility for the child, the court shall reallocate custodial responsibility based on the best interest of the child, taking into account all relevant factors, including the effects of the relocation on the child.

(3) If a parent does not establish that the purpose for that parent's relocation is in good faith for a legitimate purpose into a location that is reasonable in light of the purpose, the court may modify the parenting plan in accordance with the child's best interests and the effects of the relocation on the child. Among the modifications the court may consider is a reallocation of primary custodial responsibility, effective if and when the relocation occurs, but such a reallocation shall not be ordered if the relocating parent demonstrates that the child's best interests would be served by the relocation.

(4) The court shall attempt to minimize impairment to a parent-child relationship caused by a parent's relocation through alternative arrangements for the exercise of custodial responsibility appropriate to the parents' resources and circumstances and the developmental level of the child.

(e) In determining the proportion of caretaking functions each parent previously performed for the child under the parenting plan before relocation, the court may not consider a division of functions arising from any arrangements made after a relocation but before a modification hearing on the issues related to relocation.

(f) In determining the effect of the relocation or proposed relocation on a child, any interviewing or questioning of the child shall be conducted in accordance with the provisions of rule 17 of the rules of practice and procedure for family law as promulgated by the Supreme Court of Appeals.

A judge who enters a family court order binds all of the parties involved to its terms. If either of the parties fails to abide by the judge's order, the court has the authority to enforce its ruling. The term *contempt* refers to a party's refusal to obey the judge's order and as a consequence, the court's authority to enforce that order. There are two different types of contempt: civil and criminal.

Civil Contempt

A *civil contempt* proceeding is often described as "remedial" or "coercive" in nature. Its purpose is to bring noncompliant parties before the court and convince them to comply with the court order. Civil contempt must be proven by a preponderance of the evidence and if established, gives the court the authority to incarcerate the noncompliant party until the court-ordered alimony or child support is paid.

Contempt
A party's refusal to obey the judge's order and as a consequence, the court's authority to enforce that order.

Civil contempt
A "coercive" remedy used by courts to bring noncompliant parties before the judge and convince them to comply with an existing court order.

Criminal Contempt

Criminal contempt

A "punitive" remedy used by courts where a noncompliant party may be incarcerated if it is proven beyond a reasonable doubt that the court's order was *willfully violated.*

While a civil contempt proceeding is coercive in nature, a ***criminal contempt*** proceeding is punitive. This means that the noncompliant party may be incarcerated if it is proven beyond a reasonable doubt that the court's order was *willfully violated.* While a noncompliant party who is found in civil contempt has the opportunity to be released from incarceration if he or she complies with the court order, the same is not true in a case of criminal contempt. In these cases, they may face a criminal contempt conviction that may result in fines or incarceration. There is no opportunity to rehabilitate through compliance with the court order in criminal contempt cases.

If the court has ordered a spouse to make periodic payments of alimony or child support and the spouse ceases to make these payments, the other spouse may file a motion for contempt to bring this matter to the court's attention. Enforcement of child support orders is addressed in Chapter 9.

Motion for contempt

A document that alerts the court to the other party's failure to comply with the court's earlier order and requests that the court provide relief.

If a party fails to make court-ordered payments, the receiving spouse should first write a letter to the paying spouse stating the arrearage owed and demanding payment of that arrearage. If that does not get a response and the party continues to fail to comply with a court order, the receiving spouse may bring this to the court's attention by filing a ***motion for contempt***, *contempt citation*, or *petition for contempt* (see Exhibit 19-3). In family law disputes, common motions for contempt include motions for contempt for failure to pay alimony or child support; motions for contempt against the custodial parent for withholding visitation from the noncustodial parent; or motions for contempt against the noncustodial parent for not complying with visitation orders by bringing the child back late, picking the child up late, or engaging in inappropriate activities while the child is visiting.

Sometimes, one or the other party may not be happy with the visitation arrangements under a court order that provided only for the "right of reasonable visitation." What is "reasonable" is a subjective judgment—what one party thinks is reasonable, the other party may not. Therefore, the unhappy party may not be successful in proving that the other party is in contempt of the court order. Therefore, a motion for contempt is not the appropriate legal vehicle to use in resolving this matter. Instead, one party or the other may file a motion to modify visitation and ask the court to modify its ruling from "reasonable visitation" to a definite schedule for weekly visitation and a specific visitation schedule for holidays, school year vacations, and summer vacations. This is usually needed when the parties are unable to resolve these types of issues on their own. Many jurisdictions now attempt to avoid this situation by requiring that a parenting plan be submitted as part of the separation agreement. The parenting plan specifies, in detail, the terms of the noncustodial parent's access to the minor child or children and includes not only the regularly scheduled visits, such as weekends and major holidays, but also includes sharing of all national and state holidays, the family's religious holidays, school vacations, the child's or children's birthdays, each parent's birthday, and Mother's Day and Father's Day.

Obligor

The party responsible for money that is owed; also known as a debtor.

Child Support Enforcement Remedies

Many states have enacted legislation whereby nonpayment of support can result in a criminal contempt proceeding against the delinquent ***obligor***.

Uniform Interstate Family Support Act (UIFSA)

Where the noncustodial parent's state must honor the original support and may not enter a new order or modify the existing order to conform to its guidelines for determining the amount of support.

In 1997 the federal government enacted the ***Uniform Interstate Family Support Act (UIFSA)*** (see Appendix D), which has been adopted by all fifty states, Washington, D.C., and most territories. As a result of this act, questions regarding jurisdiction, "choice of law," and "authority to modify in support matters" have been virtually eliminated. One of the most important provisions of the UIFSA is the adoption of a uniform Wage Assignment Form. The failure of an employer to respond to a wage assignment will mean that it will be subject to federal jurisdiction and severe penalties for the failure to comply.

Exhibit 19-3 West Virginia preprinted form of a petition for contempt.

IN THE FAMILY COURT OF _____ **COUNTY, WEST VIRGINIA**

In Re:
The Marriage / Children of: **Civil Action No.** _____

_____, and   _____.
Petitioner   Respondent

_____   _____

_____   _____
Address   Address

_____   _____
Daytime phone   Daytime phone

<u>**PETITION FOR CONTEMPT**</u>

1.   Your name: _____. List any other name(s) you were known by

during this case. _____

Your current address: _____

2.   Name of the person you want the court to hold in contempt: _____

Address: _____

Daytime telephone number: _____ Social Security number: _____

3. <u>Your Reasons for Making this Contempt Petition</u>

___**A.** <u>Failure to Make Payments of Money</u>

___ I believe the person I want the court to hold in contempt has failed to make court ordered

payments of:

___ Child support

___ Spousal support

___ Separate maintenance

___ Equitable distribution

___ Medical support

___ Other (List, and be <u>specific</u>.) _____

You must attach a copy of the order requiring these payments.

List the due dates and amounts for all payments that have not been made.

_____

_____

continued

Exhibit 19-3 Continued

_____ _____

_____

_____

List the total amount due and unpaid on the date you sign this petition: $_____ .

__**B.**   Failure to Obey Court Ordered Parenting Plan

___ I believe the person I want the court to hold in contempt has failed to abide by the terms and conditions of a court ordered Parenting Plan. For each instance you believe the person has failed to abide by the Parenting Plan, you must list the date, and explain *specifically* how the person failed to abide by the plan; and you MUST attach a copy of the Parenting Plan.

_____

_____

_____

_____

_____

_____

__**C.**   Failure to Obey *Other* Terms, Conditions, or Requirements of a Court Order

___ I believe the person I want the court to hold in contempt has failed to abide by the terms, conditions, or requirements of a court order in some way other than those listed in items A. and B. above. For each instance you believe the person has failed to abide by the terms, conditions, or requirements of an order, you must list the date, and explain *specifically* how the person failed to abide by the order; and you MUST attach a copy of the order.

_____

_____

_____

_____

_____

4.   I have attached to this Petition documents I believe prove the person I have named has failed to obey a court order. The documents I have attached are:

_____

_____

_____

For the reasons stated above, I request that the Court issue a Notice of Contempt Hearing / Rule to Show Cause setting a hearing to determine if the person named in this Petition should be held in Contempt of Court.

_____   _____
Your Signature / Petitioner   Date

VERIFICATION of CONTEMPT PETITION

I, _____, after making an oath or affirmation to tell the truth, say that the facts I have stated in this Contempt Petition are true of my personal knowledge; and if I have set forth matters upon information given to me by others, I believe that information to be true.

_____   _____
Signature   Date

This Verification was sworn to or affirmed before me on the ____ day of _____, 200__.

_____
Notary Public / Other Official

My commission expires:_____.

Suspension of Passport The UIFSA provides for the suspension of an obligor's passport when the arrearage owed exceeds $5,000. The information is provided by the individual states to the State Department. In the event that an obligor owes more than $5,000, he or she will not be permitted to leave the country until such time as the obligation has been paid to an amount such that it is less than $5,000. A well-paid business professional who must travel abroad on a regular basis as part of his or her job may find that failure to remain current with child support may result in suddenly not being able to leave the country due to suspension. This is an embarrassing but effective way to see that affluent obligors who neglect to support their children will experience curtailment of significant activities unless they pay their child support.

Other Sanctions Among the sanctions that may be imposed upon a delinquent child support obligor are the following: driver's license suspension, professional and occupational license suspension, seizure of bank accounts, seizure of workers' compensation or personal injury awards, conversion of child support arrearages to judgments and levying of liens upon personal and real property, reporting of child support arrearages to credit bureaus, federal and/or state income tax refund offsets, seizure of lottery winnings, and incarceration. In addition to utilizing these sanctions, some states, including the state of California, charge interest on the child support arrearage.

Wage Withholding Orders (Executions) Pursuant to federal law, a wage withholding order for support enters in all cases that involve state assistance. Whether to obtain such an order when state assistance is not involved is a matter of decision for the court and/or the parties.

A wage withholding order is executed by the court and served upon the obligor's employer, who must then begin to withhold from the obligor's pay the court-ordered support amount. The employer must send it directly to the state's enforcement agency or the payee. This method works reasonably well, provided an obligor remains with the same employer. Problems with this system include delays in the receipt of payments by the payee as a result of delays in forwarding payment by the employer and the processing of payments by the state enforcement agency. Additionally, because a wage execution does not automatically follow an obligor, in many states the duty to notify a new employer of a support obligation falls upon the obligor. This can present great difficulties if the obligor does not disclose to his or her new employer the existence of a wage withholding order.

Fortunately, some states have developed a system that allows the wage withholding order to follow the obligor. California, for instance, has instituted a tracking system whereby each employer must report the Social Security number of each new hire to a central child support agency. If the new hire is included in the database, the agency will automatically forward notice of the wage withholding order to the employer, and the order will become effective upon the new employer.

Though this method is highly controversial, it is also very effective because (1) it is successful in tracking the employment movements of obligors, and (2) it provides a cost-effective way for the state to be reimbursed for assistance payments made for the benefit of the children of obligors.

Suspension of Driver's Licenses and Professional Licenses Many states now permit suspension of the driver's licenses and professional licenses of delinquent obligors. The trigger for reinstatement of the various licenses varies from state to state; however, the result is the same. The license is suspended and the obligor may not engage in those activities for which the license is required until such time as a specified percentage or dollar amount of the child support or alimony arrearage is paid. In some instances, a history of current payments is maintained for a specified period.

Federal and/or State Income Tax Offsets In accordance with the Welfare Reform Act of 1998, all states are required to report to the Internal Revenue Service all those who are delinquent in their child support and/or alimony payments. In accordance with federal law, the Internal Revenue Service will, upon the meeting of certain criteria, divert payment of any refund due to the delinquent obligor to the state agency charged with collection of child support. This is known as a federal income tax offset. Many states have also developed a similar system for the diversion of state income tax refunds to the state agency charged with the collection of child support payments.

Incarceration In some states, delinquent obligors face incarceration when they are found in contempt of court for ignoring a support order. However, the delinquent obligor is frequently given the opportunity to "purge" himself or herself of the contempt by paying a certain amount of the past-due child support. This amount is within the sound discretion of the court. In order to purge oneself of the contempt, the delinquent obligor is given a certain date by which he or she must make the ordered payment or face incarceration. Alternatively, upon a finding of contempt, the delinquent obligor may be incarcerated immediately and remain so until the ordered payment is made. In extreme circumstances, where a delinquent obligor has a significant history of willful noncompliance and cannot show that he or she was unable to pay the child support as it became due, a court may simply order the delinquent obligor incarcerated until such time as the arrearage is paid in full.

KIDNAPPING AND CROSSING STATE LINES

Occasionally, a parent flees with a child from the jurisdiction to parts unknown. A custodial parent may abruptly move out of state and fail to give the noncustodial parent information as to where the custodial parent and children are now living. Sometimes, a noncustodial parent may have the child legally in his or her possession during an agreed-on visitation period but then refuse to return the child at the end of the visiting period.

For instance, in one case a noncustodial father had the right to take his children to his residence in a neighboring state for a school vacation visitation. When the visitation period ended, the father refused to return the children. The mother sought legal counsel only to find that the father was not guilty of kidnapping because when he took the children, he had the legal right to do so. Instead, under the laws of the custodial parent's state, the noncustodial parent was merely guilty of a misdemeanor known as interference with custodial rights, or simply custodial interference, and the state would not seek extradition on such a minor criminal violation.

The custodial parent was forced to obtain the services of a lawyer in the neighboring state, who had to bring an action there to enforce an out-of-state decree. The noncustodial parent countered by bringing a custodial action in that jurisdiction, and a custody trial was held several months later in the neighboring state. During the entire period, the children remained with the parent who kept them away from the custodial parent, and by the time of the trial had become so attached to that parent and the extended family members that they did not wish to leave that parent. Thus, the court deemed that it was in the children's best interest to remain where they were.

The advent of the *Uniform Child Custody Jurisdiction Act (UCCJA)* of 1968 changed this situation. Under this act, if a noncustodial parent took a child while under the custodial parent's control, and then failed to return the child after a visitation period ended, the custodial parent had the right to have law enforcement officials in the other jurisdiction arrest the noncustodial parent and arrange for the children's return to the custodial parent. This new law has resulted in fewer kidnapping and custodial interference cases—when the whereabouts of the noncustodial parent and children are known. However, where a noncustodial parent simply disappears, the custodial parent will receive no relief until the noncustodial parent and the children are located.

Many children who are kidnapped have been kidnapped by noncustodial parents. Alternatively, sometimes a custodial parent and children will simply disappear or vanish to avoid having to deal with an abusive or difficult noncustodial parent. In several cases, mothers or fathers have disappeared with children when they believed that the noncustodial parent was sexually abusing the children. In at least one instance, a mother who came out of hiding with her child was willing to go to jail because her infraction had allowed her to successfully protect her child from the child's sexually abusive father.

All fifty states have adopted the UCCJA. As an additional response to the parental kidnapping dilemma, the federal government passed the *Parental Kidnapping Prevention Act (PKPA)*, U.S.C. § 1 738A, in 1980. The PKPA was enacted by Congress because states had very different laws regarding the enforcement of another jurisdiction's custody decrees. Lack of a uniform system throughout the country encouraged parents dissatisfied with an original custody order to flee the jurisdiction and seek modification of the original order in another state. This is known as *forum shopping*. Under the PKPA, a new state court must give full faith and credit to a custody order entered in another state and cannot modify that order as long as one of the child's parents resides in that jurisdiction.

Uniform Child Custody Jurisdiction and Enforcement Act (UCCJEA)
An act drafted by a national commission and enacted by many state legislatures to enforce on an interstate basis the rights of custodial parents and prevent parental kidnapping and custodial interference.

The PKPA and the UCCJA had conflicting provisions that caused much confusion and litigation in the legal community. In 1997, the ***Uniform Child Custody Jurisdiction and Enforcement Act (UCCJEA)*** was drafted by the National Conference of Commissioners on Uniform State Laws in hopes of rectifying the inconsistencies between the PKPA and the UCCJA. Some of the highlights of the UCCJEA include the following:

- simplification of the procedures necessary for registering an original state's order in a new state,
- prohibiting a new state (enforcing state) from modifying an original state's custody decision; the new state can only enforce the original order,
- a *habeas corpus* remedy requiring return of the child by the parent violating a custody or visitation order,
- granting the enforcing court the authority to issue a warrant to physically take the child into custody if there are fears that the parent will harm the child or flee the state, and
- assistance of state prosecutors or attorneys general in the enforcement of the orders in civil proceedings and in locating the child. Prosecutors can pursue criminal actions if the parent violated a criminal law in the process.

Concept Review and Reinforcement

KEY TERMS

arrearage
civil contempt
contempt
criminal contempt
modification
motion for contempt

motion to modify
motion to modify alimony
motion to modify custody
motion to modify visitation
motion to reopen judgment
nonmodifiable

obligor
postjudgment matters
substantial change in circumstances
Uniform Child Custody Jurisdiction and Enforcement Act (UCCJEA)
Uniform Interstate Family Support Act (UIFSA)

REVIEW OF KEY CONCEPTS

1. What parts of a dissolution decree are modifiable, and what parts are not modifiable? Why are some parts modifiable and others not?

2. What facts might constitute "changed circumstances" in terms of a modification of alimony or child support?

3. What are some changes in circumstances that could merit a modification of a custody order or a modification of a visitation order?

4. What is an arrearage?

5. What are some of the measures various states provide to "encourage" a delinquent obligor to pay the outstanding arrearage and remain current on alimony and child support payments?

6. Discuss the remedies available to a custodial parent when the noncustodial parent leaves the jurisdiction and ceases to pay child support.

7. Discuss the remedies available to a custodial parent when the noncustodial parent has fled the jurisdiction with a minor child.

8. What factors does a court consider when allowing a custodial parent to move out of the jurisdiction with a minor child?

9. What is the difference between parental kidnapping and the misdemeanor known as custodial interference?

BUILDING YOUR PARALEGAL SKILLS

CASE FOR BRIEFING

IN RE: MARRIAGE OF O'DANIEL, 382 ILL. APP. 3RD 845 (2008)

Critical Thinking and Legal Analysis Application

1. You work for a family law practice in Evanston, Illinois. You have just met with Mary Marvin, a former client whom the firm represented in her divorce six years ago. Under the terms of the dissolution decree, Mary's former husband, James, was to pay $400.00 a week for child support. Mary tells you that James has made only intermittent payments for the past two years and owes her approximately $150,000.00. James lost his job in the financial services industry when the stock market crashed in 2008. He collected unemployment for eight months, then obtained and lost two other jobs. However, four months ago, James began working for the state of Illinois and has passed his ninety-day probationary period. Although his monthly income from this job is $2,000.00 less than his financial services job, this position appears to be a stable one. Mary tells you that she tried to be understanding and patient with James when he was out of work, but now she wants to go to court and collect the child support arrearage. James has offered Mary $8,000.00 to settle the arrearage, and he wants to go back to court to lower his child support obligation. Mary is not sure of what to do and is seeking the firm's advice. She does not really want to settle for a lower arrearage amount because she recently learned that while James was unemployed, he received a bequest from his uncle of $50,000.00. Mary feels that James could have used some of that money to keep his child support current. Now she wants him to use whatever is left of his inheritance to pay the entire arrearage. She knows that James will go back to court and should be able to get his support amount lowered, but she believes that she is entitled to full payment by him of the child support money due under the current order.

   a. Your supervising attorney is concerned that the court may not make James pay all of the arrearage because the court may find that his contempt of court was not "willful contempt." Your supervisor wants you to review the 2008 case *In Re: Marriage of O'Daniel* and any subsequent case citing *O'Daniel* to see how the appellate court's reasoning might affect Mary Marvin's claim. Then he wants you to present your conclusions in a draft of an opinion letter which he will review, finalize, and send to Mrs. Marvin.

   b. Using your firm's online legal research service, you should have no trouble locating your case. Click on CASE LAW; then click on ILLINOIS; next enter either the CASE NAME or CASE CITATION; after you have read the case, click on GLOBAL CITE or a comparable title to see how subsequent cases have applied *O'Daniel*.

2. You work as a paralegal for a firm in Louisiana. Your supervising attorney asks you to research the state's position regarding the enforcement of the Uniformed Services Former Spouse's Protection Act, in which a separation agreement provides that the nonmilitary spouse will take no share of the other spouse's pension.

3. Your firm represented Mr. Collier in a dissolution proceeding three years ago. This morning he called the office very upset because he just received a notice from the Department of Motor Vehicles stating that the registration for his recreational motor home has been revoked because he has not paid his child support in a year and owes more than $8,000. He tells you that his former spouse had not let the children visit him since Thanksgiving, which was over eight months ago, and that because of this he has not been motivated to pay child support. He also

continued

tells you that recently, his former spouse told him that he may take his three children for two weeks' vacation as soon as school ends, which will be in less than a month. He planned to take the children to Disneyworld in his recreational vehicle and they would camp in a nearby state park. He has already told the children and they are elated. He cannot afford airfare and hotel accommodations for himself and the children, so if he does not get his registration reinstated, they will not be able to go and the children will be heartbroken. He doesn't understand how the state can do this to him, and he wants to know what he can do about it.

You relay this information to your supervising attorney. She asks you to research the background on this state initiative and also to research what steps Mr. Collier must take to get his registration back. Prepare an interoffice memorandum for your supervisor that includes this information.

Building a Professional Portfolio

PORTFOLIO **EXERCISES**

1. Research your state's case law and statutes to see what criteria the family courts use to decide whether a parent with physical custody of the minor children may move out of the state. Present a fact pattern under which the court is likely to grant the parent's request.

2. Locate and review your state's statutory provision or the state's controlling case law that enumerates the events that will precipitate an end to the payment of alimony, and make a list of these events.

Appendix A

ARIZONA AND CALIFORNIA PREMARITAL AGREEMENT ACTS

ARIZONA UNIFORM PREMARITAL AGREEMENT ACT

Ariz. Rev. Stat. § 25-201 *et seq.*[*]

25-201. Definitions In this article, unless the context otherwise requires:
1. "Premarital agreement" means an agreement between prospective spouses that is made in contemplation of marriage and that is effective on marriage.
2. "Property" means an interest, present or future, legal or equitable, vested or contingent, in real or personal property, including income and earnings.

25-202 Enforcement of premarital agreements; exception
A. A premarital agreement must be in writing and signed by both parties. The agreement is enforceable without consideration.
B. The agreement becomes effective on marriage of the parties.
C. The agreement is not enforceable if the person against whom enforcement is sought proves either of the following:
   1. The person did not execute the agreement voluntarily.
   2. The agreement was unconscionable when it was executed and before execution of the agreement that person:
      (a) Was not provided a fair and reasonable disclosure of the property or financial obligations of the other party.
      (b) Did not voluntarily and expressly waive, in writing, any right to disclosure of the property or financial obligations of the other party beyond the disclosure provided.
      (c) Did not have, or reasonably could not have had, an adequate knowledge of the property or financial obligations of the other party.
D. If a provision of a premarital agreement modifies or eliminates spousal support and that modification or elimination causes one party to the agreement to be eligible for support under a program of public assistance at the time of separation or marital dissolution, a court, notwithstanding the terms of the agreement, may require the other party to provide support to the extent necessary to avoid that eligibility.

---

[*]Chapter 2—Husband and Wife, Property and Contract Rights, Article 1—Arizona Uniform Premarital Agreement Act, State of Arizona.

E. An issue of unconscionability of a premarital agreement shall be decided by the court as a matter of law.

F. If a marriage is determined to be void, an agreement that would otherwise have been a premarital agreement is enforceable only to the extent necessary to avoid an inequitable result.

25-203. Scope of agreement

A. Parties to a premarital agreement may contract with respect to:
1. The rights and obligations of each of the parties in any of the property of either or both of them whenever and wherever acquired or located.
2. The right to buy, sell, use, transfer, exchange, abandon, lease, consume, expend, assign or create a security interest in, mortgage, encumber, dispose of, or otherwise manage and control property.
3. The disposition of property on separation, marital dissolution, death, or the occurrence or nonoccurrence of any other event.
4. The modification or elimination of spousal support.
5. The making of a will, trust, or other arrangement to carry out the provisions of the agreement.
6. The ownership rights in and disposition of the death benefit from a life insurance policy.
7. The choice of law governing the construction of the agreement.
8. Any other matter, including their personal rights and obligations, not in violation of public policy or a statute imposing a criminal penalty.

B. The right of a child to support may not be adversely affected by a premarital agreement.

25-204. Amendment or revocation of agreement
After marriage, a premarital agreement may be amended or revoked only by a written agreement signed by the parties. The amended agreement or the revocation is enforceable without consideration.

25-205. Limitation of actions
A statute of limitations applicable to an action asserting a claim for relief under a premarital agreement is tolled during the marriage of the parties to the agreement. However, equitable defenses limiting the time for enforcement, including laches and estoppel, are available to either party.

CALIFORNIA PREMARITAL AGREEMENT ACT
California Family Law Code Sections 1600–1601, 1610–1617[*]

§ 1600 Fam. This chapter may be cited as the Uniform Premarital Agreement Act.

§ 1601 Fam. This chapter is effective on and after January 1, 1986, and applies to any premarital agreement executed on or after that date.

§ 1610 Fam. As used in this chapter:

(a) "Premarital agreement" means an agreement between prospective spouses made in contemplation of marriage and to be effective upon marriage.

(b) "Property" means an interest, present or future, legal or equitable, vested or contingent, in real or personal property, including income and earnings.

§ 1611 Fam. A premarital agreement shall be in writing and signed by both parties. It is enforceable without consideration.

---

[*]Chapter 2—Uniform Premarital Agreement Act, Article 1 and 2, State of California.

§ 1612 Fam.

(a) Parties to a premarital agreement may contract with respect to all of the following:
   (1) The rights and obligations of each of the parties in any of the property of either or both of them whenever and wherever acquired or located.
   (2) The right to buy, sell, use, transfer, exchange, abandon, lease, consume, expend, assign, create a security interest in, mortgage, encumber, dispose of, or otherwise manage and control property.
   (3) The disposition of property upon separation, marital dissolution, death, or the occurrence or nonoccurrence of any other event.
   (4) The making of a will, trust, or other arrangement to carry out the provisions of the agreement.
   (5) The ownership rights in and disposition of the death benefit from a life insurance policy.
   (6) The choice of law governing the construction of the agreement.
   (7) Any other matter, including their personal rights and obligations, not in violation of public policy or a statute imposing a criminal penalty.
(b) The right of a child to support may not be adversely affected by a premarital agreement.
(c) Any provision in a premarital agreement regarding spousal support, including, but not limited to, a waiver of it, is not enforceable if the party against whom enforcement of the spousal support provision is sought was not represented by independent counsel at the time the agreement containing the provision was signed, or if the provision regarding spousal support is unconscionable at the time of enforcement. An otherwise unenforceable provision in a premarital agreement regarding spousal support may not become enforceable solely because the party against whom enforcement is sought was represented by independent counsel.

§ 1613 Fam. A premarital agreement becomes effective upon marriage.

§ 1614 Fam. After marriage, a premarital agreement may be amended or revoked only by a written agreement signed by the parties. The amended agreement or the revocation is enforceable without consideration.

§ 1615 Fam.

(a) A premarital agreement is not enforceable if the party against whom enforcement is sought proves either of the following:
   (1) That party did not execute the agreement voluntarily.
   (2) The agreement was unconscionable when it was executed and, before execution of the agreement, all of the following applied to that party:
      A. That party was not provided a fair, reasonable, and full disclosure of the property or financial obligations of the other party.
      B. That party did not voluntarily and expressly waive, in writing, any right to disclosure of the property or financial obligations of the other party beyond the disclosure provided.
      C. That party did not have, or reasonably could not have had, an adequate knowledge of the property or financial obligations of the other party.
(b) An issue of unconscionability of a premarital agreement shall be decided by the court as a matter of law.

(c) For the purposes of subdivision (a), it shall be deemed that a premarital agreement was not executed voluntarily unless the court finds in writing or on the record all of the following:

(1) The party against whom enforcement is sought was represented by independent legal counsel at the time of signing the agreement or, after being advised to seek independent legal counsel, expressly waived, in a separate writing, representation by independent legal counsel.

(2) The party against whom enforcement is sought had not less than seven calendar days between the time that party was first presented with the agreement and advised to seek independent legal counsel and the time the agreement was signed.

(3) The party against whom enforcement is sought, if unrepresented by legal counsel, was fully informed of the terms and basic effect of the agreement as well as the rights and obligations he or she was giving up by signing the agreement, and was proficient in the language in which the explanation of the party's rights was conducted and in which the agreement was written. The explanation of the rights and obligations relinquished shall be memorialized in writing and delivered to the party prior to signing the agreement. The unrepresented party shall, on or before the signing of the premarital agreement, execute a document declaring that he or she received the information required by this paragraph and indicating who provided that information.

(4) The agreement and the writings executed pursuant to paragraphs (1) and (3) were not executed under duress, fraud, or undue influence, and the parties did not lack capacity to enter into the agreement.

(5) Any other factors the court deems relevant.

§ 1616 Fam. If a marriage is determined to be void, an agreement that would otherwise have been a premarital agreement is enforceable only to the extent necessary to avoid an inequitable result.

§ 1617 Fam. Any statute of limitations applicable to an action asserting a claim for relief under a premarital agreement is tolled during the marriage of the parties to the agreement. However, equitable defenses limiting the time for enforcement, including laches and estoppel, are available to either party.

ALEXANDER RODRIGUEZ PETITION FOR DISSOLUTION OF MARRIAGE

IN THE CIRCUIT COURT OF THE 11TH JUDICIAL CIRCUIT IN AND FOR MIAMI-DADE COUNTY, FLORIDA

FAMILY DIVISION

CASE NO.   06_16475FC16

IN RE: THE MARRIAGE OF

CYNTHIA A. RODRIGUEZ,

    Petitioner-Wife,

and

ALEXANDER E. RODRIGUEZ,

    Respondent-Husband.

PETITION FOR DISSOLUTION OF MARRIAGE

For her Petition for Dissolution of Marriage, the Wife states:

1. <u>ACTION FOR DISSOLUTION</u>: This is an action for dissolution of marriage, which is being filed only after the Petitioner has exhausted every effort to salvage the marriage of the parties. However, "Alex" has emotionally abandoned his wife and children and has left her with no choice but to divorce him.

2. <u>JURISDICTION</u>: The Court has jurisdiction over the parties and subject matter of this action.

3. <u>RESIDENCY</u>: Both parties have been residents of the State of Florida for more than six months prior to the filing date of this petition.

4. <u>MARRIAGE</u>: The parties were married to each other on November 2, 2002, in Dallas, Texas.

5. <u>IRRETRIEVABLY BROKEN</u>: The marriage of the parties is irretrievably broken because of the Husband's extra marital affairs and other marital misconduct.

[Rodriguez v. Rodriguez, Petition for Dissolution of Marriage]

6. <u>CHILDREN</u>: There are two children born of this marriage: Natasha A. Rodriguez, D/O/B: November 18, 2004 and Ella A. Rodriguez, D/O/B: April 21, 2008.

7. <u>SHARED PARENTAL RESPONSIBILITY</u>: The Husband and Wife should share parental responsibility of the children.

8. <u>RESIDENTIAL PARENT</u>: The Wife desires and it is in the children's best interest that she be the primary residential parent of the minor children, *pendente lite* and permanently.

9. <u>CHILD SUPPORT</u>: The children need temporary and permanent support from the Husband, and the Husband has the ability to pay. The lifestyle and background of the parties and the children is such that the Husband should provide life insurance, health insurance, private school; and, continue to maintain the existing lifestyle of the children.

10. <u>STANDARD OF LIVING</u>: The Husband is a prominent athlete and has, due to his substantial earning power, provided the parties and their children with a lavish lifestyle. The Husband has provided his family with a residence that is compatible with his great wealth and high standard of living. The Husband has the fiscal capacity to continue his high style of living, but the Wife does not.

11. <u>ALIMONY</u>: The Wife needs and is entitled to temporary, rehabilitative, permanent, periodic and lump sum alimony, and the Husband is well able to pay all forms of alimony.

12. <u>MARITAL RESIDENCE AND CONTENTS AS LUMP SUM ALIMONY</u>: The parties jointly own, as their former marital home, the real property located at 181 East

-2-

[Rodriguez v. Rodriguez, Petition for Dissolution of Marriage]

Sunrise Avenue, Coral Gables, Florida 33133. The Wife is entitled to receive, the marital home and contents, as lump sum alimony and partial equitable distribution.

13. **EXCLUSIVE POSSESSION:** The Wife is entitled to continuing temporary and permanent exclusive possession of the marital residence, to provide a home for herself and the minor children.

14. **EQUITABLE DISTRIBUTION:** The Wife claims and is entitled to an equitable distribution of all assets acquired during the marriage, pursuant to Section 61.075, *Florida Statutes.*

15. **AUTOMOBILE FOR THE WIFE:** The Wife needs and is entitled to possession and title to the automobile she is presently driving.

16. **PERSONAL PROPERTY:** The Wife is in need of and entitled to exclusive possession of and title to the real and personal property now in her possession. This includes the personal property contained in the marital residence.

17. **LIFE AND MEDICAL INSURANCE:** The Husband has and is maintaining life and medical insurance for the benefit of the Wife and minor children. He should be required to continue to maintain that or comparable insurance.

18. **DEBTS:** The parties have incurred certain debts, which the Husband should be required to discharge.

19. **ATTORNEYS' FEES, SUIT MONIES, AND COSTS:** The Wife has obligated herself to pay reasonable attorneys' fees, suit monies, and costs to her attorneys and other professionals in this action and asks for a judgment against the Husband for a sum considered to be a reasonable fee for those services, based upon her need and his ability to pay.

-3-

[Rodriguez v. Rodriguez, Petition for Dissolution of Marriage]

20. **ANTENUPTIAL AGREEMENT:** On October 3, 2002, the parties executed a "document" titled "Antenuptial Agreement."[1] A determination as to the validity or enforceability of the agreement requires additional investigation and discovery.

WHEREFORE, it is requested that the Court grant relief consistent with this Petition for Dissolution of Marriage.

<table>
<tr><td>

LILLY LAW OFFICE[2]
4544 Post Oak Place - Suite 380
Houston, Texas 77027
Phone: (713) 966-4444
Fax: (713) 966-4466

</td><td>

KUTNER AND ASSOCIATES
11th Floor - Courthouse Tower
44 West Flagler Street
Miami, Florida 33130-1808
Phone: (305) 377-9411
Fax: (305) 377-4758

</td></tr>
<tr><td>

By: _____
    EARLE S. LILLY
    Texas Bar No.: 12356000

</td><td>

By: _____
    MAURICE JAY KUTNER
    Florida Bar No.: 44775

</td></tr>
<tr><td>

and

</td><td>

and

</td></tr>
<tr><td>

By: _____
    JOHN E. VAN NESS
    Texas Bar No.: 00792890

</td><td>

By: _____
    ANTHONY P. SABATINO
    Florida Bar No.: 185809

</td></tr>
</table>

and

---

[1] The Agreement has deliberately not been attached.

[2] The appearance of attorneys Lilly and Van Ness is subject to the Court granting the Motion to Appear Pro Hac Vice, which is being filed simultaneously with this Petition for Dissolution of Marriage.

-4-

REQUIRED INFORMATION

Petitioner:
Name:
Home Address:
City, State & Zip:

CYNTHIA A. RODRIGUEZ
181 East Sunrise Avenue
Coral Gables, Florida 33133

Home Telephone Number:
Cellular number:

(305) ▓▓▓▓▓
(305) ▓▓▓▓▓

Social Security No.:
Date of Birth:

▓▓▓▓▓
December 28, 1972

Attorneys:
Attorneys' Address:

MAURICE JAY KUTNER, ESQUIRE
KUTNER AND ASSOCIATES
11th Floor - Courthouse Tower
44 West Flagler Street

City, State & Zip:
Telephone Number:

Miami, Florida 33130-1808
(305) 377-9411

EARLE S. LILLY, ESQUIRE
LILLY LAW OFFICES
4544 Post Oak Place - Suite 380
Houston, Texas 77027
(713) 966-4444

Respondent:
Name:
Home Address:
City, State & Zip:

ALEXANDER E. RODRIGUEZ
502 Park Avenue - Apartment 4C
New York, N.Y. 10022

Social Security No.:
Date of Birth:

▓▓▓▓▓
July 27, 1975

Attorney (if known):
Attorney's Address:
City, State & Zip:

Unknown
Unknown
Unknown

Telephone Number:

Unknown

Minor Children:

1. Natasha A. Rodriguez   Date of Birth: November 18, 2004
2. Ella A. Rodriguez   Date of Birth: April 21, 2008

Source: Case No: 08-16475 FC 16, Eleventh Judicial Circuit of Florida.

Appendix C

RIHANNA AND CHRIS BROWN SEARCH WARRANT AND AFFIDAVIT

SEARCH WARRANT AND AFFIDAVIT

1 Your affiant, Detective De Shon Andrews, Serial No. 33208, has been a Police Officer for

2 the Los Angeles Police Department for the past twelve years. In January of 2003, your affiant

3 promoted to the rank of Detective. Since this promotion your affiant has worked various assignments

4 which include Autos, Homicide, Robbery, the Abused Child Unit and Force Investigation Division. Your

5 affiant is currently assigned as to Major Assault Crimes, Wilshire Division. While working these

6 assignments your affiant was responsible for investigating and assisting with the investigations of crimes

7 that range from simple battery, murder/manslaughter and the use of force pertaining to police officers. In

8 addition your affiant has attended the Los Angeles Police Departments Basic Detective School, the

9 Robert Presley Institute of Criminal Investigation Courses in Auto Theft and Major Assault Crimes,

10 the Los Angeles Police Department's Homicide Investigators School and the California Robbery

11 Investigators training seminar.

12

13 Christopher Brown and Robyn F. have been involved in a dating relationship for approximately

14 one and a half years. On Sunday February 8, 2009 at 0025 hours, Brown was driving a vehicle with

15 Robyn F. as the front passenger on an unknown street in Los Angeles. Robyn F. picked up Brown's

16 cellular telephone and observed a three page text message from a woman who Brown had a previous

17 sexual relationship with. A verbal argument ensued and Brown pulled the vehicle over on an unknown

18 street, reached over Robyn F. with his right hand, opened the car door and attempted to force her out.

19 Brown was unable to force Robyn F. out of the vehicle because she was wearing a seat belt. When he

20 could not force her to exit, he took his right hand and shoved her head against the passenger window of

21 the vehicle causing an approximate one inch raised circular contusion. Robyn F. turned to face Brown

22 and he punched her in the left eye with his right hand. He then drove away in the vehicle and continued

23 to punch her in the face with his right hand while steering the vehicle with his left hand. The assault

24 caused Robyn F's. mouth to fill with blood and blood to splatter all over her clothing and the interior of

25 the vehicle.

26

1 Brown looked at Robyn F. and stated, *"I'm going to beat the shit out of you when we get home! You*

2 *wait and see!"* Robyn F. picked up her cellular telephone and called her personal assistant, Jennifer

3 Rosales at (818) 523-████. Rosales did not answer the telephone but while her voicemail greeting was

4 playing, Robyn F. pretended to talk to her and stated, *"I'm on my way home. Make sure the cops are*

5 *there when I get there."* (This statement was made while the greeting was playing and was not captured

6 as a message). After Robyn F. faked the call, Brown looked at her and stated, *"You just did the*

7 *stupidest thing ever! Now I'm really going to kill you!* Brown resumed punching Robyn F. and she

8 interlocked her fingers behind her head and brought her elbows forward to protect her face. She then

9 bent over at the waist, placing her elbows and face near her lap in attempt to protect her face and head

10 from the barrage of punches being levied upon her by Brown. Brown continued to punch Robyn F. on

11 her left arm and hand causing her to suffer a contusion on her left triceps that was approximately two

12 inches in diameter and numerous contusions on her left hand. Robyn F. then attempted to send a text

13 message to her other personal assistant, Melissa Ford. Brown snatched the cellular telephone out of her

14 hand and threw it out of the window onto an unknown street.

15

16 Brown continued driving and Robyn F. observed his cellular telephone sitting in his lap. She picked up

17 the cellular telephone with her left hand and before she could make a call he placed her in a head lock

18 with his right hand and continued to drive the vehicle with his left hand. Brown pulled Robyn F. close to

19 him and bit her on her left ear. She was able to feel the vehicle swerving from right to left as Brown sped

20 away. He stopped the vehicle in front of 333 North June Street and Robyn F. turned off the car, removed

21 the key from the ignition and sat on it. Brown did not know what she did with the key and began

22 punching her in the face and arms. He then placed her in a head lock positioning the front of her throat

23 between his bicep and forearm. Brown began applying pressure to Robyn F's. left and right carotid

24 arteries causing her to be unable to breathe and she began to lose consciousness. She reached up with her

25 left hand and began attempting to gouge his eyes in an attempt to free herself. Brown bit her left ring and

26 middle fingers and then released her. While Brown continued to punch her, she turned around a placed

1 her back against the passenger door. She brought her knees to her chest, placed her feet against Brown's
2 body and began pushing him away. Brown continued to punch her on the legs and feet causing several
3 contusions. Robyn F. began screaming for help and Brown exited the vehicle and walked away. A
4 resident in the neighborhood heard Robyn F.'s plea for help and called 911, causing a police response.
5 An investigation was conducted and Robyn F. was issued a Domestic Violence Emergency Protective
6 Order (EPO).

8 Your affiant conducted an interview with witness Melissa Ford who advised that on February 8, 2009 at
9 approximately 0055 hours, she received a telephone call from Robyn F. from an unknown telephone
10 number, later identified as the cellular telephone of Police Officer III Chavez, Serial No. 32483. Robyn
11 F. advised Ford that she had been assaulted by Brown. At approximately 0100 hours, Brown called
12 Ford as if nothing had happened. Ford advised Brown that she had already talked to Robyn F. and was
13 aware of what happened. Ford advised Brown that the neighbors had called the police and that they were
14 with Robyn F. Brown asked Ford if Robyn F. had provided the police with his name and Ford advised
15 him that she had. Brown hung up the cellular telephone and did not call back.

17 On February 8, 2009 at 1900 hours, Brown surrendered himself to your affiant and was arrested for 422
18 PC, Criminal Threats. Brown was given a copy of the EPO and advised not to contact Robyn F.

20 On February 17, 2009, Ford advised your affiant that she had received text messages from telephone
21 number (804) 929-█████, a number that Ford recognizes as belonging to Brown. In the text message,
22 Brown apologized for what he had done to Robyn F. and advised Ford that he was going to get help.

STATE OF CALIFORNIA - COUNTY OF LOS ANGELES
SEARCH WARRANT AND AFFIDAVIT

1 Your affiant is requesting the telephone records and text message data stored on the cellular telephones of

2 Robyn F., (914) 316-█████, Ford, (914) 320-█████ and Brown, (804) 929-█████, in an attempt to establish a

3 time line of the events that occurred on the evening of February 8, 2008 and to further implicate Brown

4 as the person who assaulted Robyn F.

5

6

7

8

9

10

11

12

13

14

15

16

17

18

19

20

21

22

23

24

25

26

SW & A1

Source: Search Warrant and Affidavit, Los Angeles Superior Court.

Appendix D

BILL MAHER PALIMONY COMPLAINT

Cyrus John Nownejad, Esq. SBN: 207769
Roger Y. Muse, Esq. SBN: 147120
LAW OFFICES OF CYRUS & CYRUS, PLC
433 North Camden Drive, Suite 510
Beverly Hills, California 90210
Tel: 310.623.1676; Fax: 310.271.6893
Attorneys for: Coco Johnsen

1
2
3
4
5
6
7
8
9
10
11
12
13
14
15
16
17
18
19
20
21
22
23
24
25

SUPERIOR COURT OF THE STATE OF CALIFORNIA,

COUNTY OF LOS ANGELES-CENTRAL DISTRICT

NANCY JOHNSON a.k.a. "COCO
JOHNSEN", an individual,

v.

BILL MAHER, an individual; and DOES 1-50,
inclusive.

CASE NO.

COMPLAINT FOR:

1. BREACH OF CONTRACT
2. PROMISSORY ESTOPPEL
3. PROMISSORY FRAUD
4. BATTERY
5. ASSAULT

PARTIES

1.   NANCY JOHNSON a.k.a. "COCO JOHNSEN" (hereinafter referred to as "JOHNSEN")

is, and at all times mentioned herein, was an individual residing in Los Angeles County,

California.

2.   BILL MAHER (hereinafter referred to as "MAHER"), is, and all times mentioned herein,

was an individual residing in Los Angeles County, California.

3.   The true names and capacities of Defendants sued herein as DOES 1 through 50

(hereinafter collectively referred to as "DOES"), are unknown to JOHNSEN who therefore has

- 1 -

COMPLAINT

LAW OFFICES OF CYRUS
P.L.C.
433 North Camden Drive, Suite 510
Beverly Hills, California 90210
310-823-1676

sued said defendants by such fictitious names. JOHNSEN will seek leave to amend this Complaint to set forth their true names and capacities when the same are ascertained. JOHNSEN is informed and believes and thereon alleges that each of the defendants sued herein as a DOE is, and at all times material hereto was, legally responsible in some manner for one or more of the acts, omissions, breaches, occurrences, losses and damages herein complained of, and further, that each DOE is, and at all times material hereto was, acting as an agent, servant, employee, representative, managing agent, partner, principal, alter ego, affiliate, or co-conspirator of one or more of the other defendants, with the knowledge, consent, and ratification of such other defendants in causing or permitting the acts, omissions, breaches, occurrences, losses and damages herein complained of.

ALLEGATIONS COMMON TO ALL CAUSES OF ACTION

4. Venue is proper in this Court because the acts complained of took place in the County of Los Angeles.

5. Prior to October, 2003, JOHNSEN was employed as an airline attendant with DELTA AIRLINES, and, as of that date, had been so employed for more than twelve. As a consequence of that employment, JOHNSEN had accrued and enjoyed significant benefits including healthcare benefits, participation in a 401 K plan and more than twelve years of seniority. As a further consequence of her long term of employment, JOHNSEN received the highest salary pay rate paid to flight attendants by her employer.

6. In addition, JOHNSEN was a successful fashion and glamour model, represented by legitimate agencies, and earning substantial income.

///

LAW OFFICE... OF CYRUS & ...S
PLC
433 North ...nden Drive, Suite 510
Beverly Hills, California 90210
310 ...2-1676

FIRST CAUSES OF ACTION

(Breach of Contract; Against MAHER and DOES 1 through 50)

7.   JOHNSEN realleges and incorporates in this cause of action Paragraphs 1 through 6 hereof as though here fully set forth.

8.   On or about January 2003, JOHNSEN was introduced to MAHER. This meeting lead to a relationship which lasted for a period of approximately seventeen months, during which period JOHNSEN fell in love with MAHER, and during which period MAHER professed to be in love with JOHNSEN and made several promises to JOHNSEN as stated herein.

9.   On or about February 2003, MAHER represented to JOHNSEN that he was in love with her and that he wished to make her his fiancé and marry her. MAHER also advised JOHNSEN that he needed her help in pursuing his career in the entertainment industry. He indicated that it would be beneficial to his career if they were seen together as a "power couple" socially and otherwise, and asked that she always be available to accompany him to social, ceremonial and public events for that purpose.

10.   In asking that JOHNSEN be seen with MAHER as a couple and attend various social and events together, MAHER promised JOHNSEN that he would pay or reimburse JOHNSEN for all costs incurred for clothing, makeup or other accoutrements which JOHNSEN incurred in so accompanying MAHER. In addition, in return for JOHNSEN'S assistance with his career, MAHER promised to pay the rent on JOHNSEN'S apartment.

11.   Thereafter, JOHNSEN did accompany MAHER to numerous social and public events and publicly appeared with MAHER as a couple.

12.   Beginning on or about February, 2003, and on numerous occasions thereafter, MAHER asked that in order for him and JOHNSEN to be a true "power couple," that JOHNSEN quit her careers, both as an airline attendant and as a model, and devote her efforts fully to their

- 3 -

COMPLAINT

1   relationship and to the furtherance of MAHER'S career.

2   13.   In exchange for ceasing pursuit of her own career, MAHER promised to JOHNSEN:

3   a) that he would marry JOHNSEN and produce children with her;

4   b) that he would pay for all of the clothes and expenses which where required of her in

5   order to fulfill her commitments to helping out MAHER in his career, or would reimburse

6   her for those expenses.

7   c) that he would "support" and "take care of" JOHNSEN for the rest of her life;

8   d) that he would purchase for her in her name a house located at 9500 Cherokee Lane in

9   Beverly Hills, formerly inhabited by BEN AFFLECK and JENNIFER LOPEZ, or that in

10   the alternative he would give JOHNSEN sufficient funds to purchase a house of similar

11   value and appeal.

12

13   14.   In the months following MAHER'S making of the above-described promises, JOHNSEN

14   repeatedly sought assurances from MAHER regarding the sincerity of his feelings for her, as well

15   as the reliability of his promises to her. In seeking these assurances from MAHER, JOHNSEN

16   advised MAHER on several occasions that she lacked a formal education, and that her career as

17   an airline attendant had provided her with more than twelve years of seniority and a level of

18   income that would be difficult or impossible for her to repeat or match if she was forced to start

19   over. In addition, she advised MAHER that stopping all activities relating to her modeling career

20   would effectively end that career since all of the momentum she had generated for that career

21   would be lost.

22

23   15.   Each time such assurances were sought from MAHER, MAHER would profess his love

24   for JOHNSEN and restate his promises, and encourage her to quit her career to help him and

25   spend more time on his career. Each such time, MAHER assured JOHNSEN that her sacrifice

would be well rewarded, in light of the promises he had made to her.

- 4 -

COMPLAINT

16. On or about October 2003, in reliance on MAHER'S promises, JOHNSEN quit her job at DELTA AIRLINES, moved into MAHER'S house, and began to devote herself full-time to her relationship with MAHER and to the furtherance of MAHER'S career. JOHNSEN continued to make herself available to accompany MAHER to public events and did in fact so accompany him, and was seen publicly on numerous occasions with MAHER.

17. Thereafter, MAHER verbally abused JOHNSEN by making insulting, humiliating and degrading racial comments to JOHNSON (who is African American), and about JOHNSEN to others. As is described below, MAHER also physically threatened and physically abused JOHNSEN during this period. Additionally, although JOHNSEN came under increasing financial distress due to the loss of the income from her careers, MAHER refused to reimburse JOHNSEN for the costs she continued to incur in promoting MAHER'S career. MAHER also refused to buy JOHNSEN the house he had promised her, or to provide her with the funds for her to purchase a house. Finally, JOHNSON learned that MAHER had continued to date and have relations with at least one other woman even after JOHNSON had quit her careers and devoted herself to his career and their relationship. As a consequence of these facts, JOHNSEN came to realize that MAHER did not intend to keep any of the promises he had made to her and therefore, on or about May, 2004, JOHNSEN moved out of MAHER'S house and ceased to have contact with him.

18. Thus, in view of the above-described conduct of MAHER, JOHNSEN was prevented from continuing to play her part as a member of a "power couple" in the furtherance of MAHER'S career.

19. MAHER breached his oral agreements with JOHNSON by:

a) failing to reimburse JOHNSON for the costs she incurred for clothing, makeup, and other accoutrements which were required for her to accompany MAHER to public and social events as a "power couple";

- 5 -

COMPLAINT

b) by failing to pay the rent on JOHNSON'S apartment;

c) by failing to marry JOHNSON;

d) by failing to purchase the house in her name or to give her the funds to purchase the house; and,

e) by failing to financially support and "take care" of JOHNSEN.

20.   As a result of MAHER'S failure to perform according to his promises that he made to JOHNSEN, JOHNSEN has suffered damages in the total amount of $9,000,000.00 for the following items of damage;

    a. Loss of income from her modeling career;

    b. The loss of income from her career as flight attendant for DELTA AIRLINES including the loss of her 401K plan, medical, dental benefits, and unlimited worldwide travel benefit passes;

    c. Loss of the promised rent payments;

    d. Un-reimbursed costs for clothing, make-up, etc.;

    e. Loss of the promised house or equivalent house; and

    f. Loss of the promised lifelong financial support.

SECOND CAUSE OF ACTION

(Promissory Estoppel; Against MAHER and DOES 1 through 50)

21.   JOHNSEN realleges and incorporates in this cause of action Paragraphs 1 through 6 and 8 through 20 hereof as though here fully set forth.

22.   In quitting her careers as a flight attendant and as a model as described in Paragraph 16 hereof, JOHNSEN relied upon the above-described promises made by MAHER. JOHNSEN'S reliance was reasonable for the reasons, among others, that JOHNSON believed MAHER'S

- 6 -

COMPLAINT

LAW OFFICE OF CYRUS &c
- PLC
433 North Camden Drive, Suite 510
Beverly Hills, California 90210
310-623-4476

repeated professions of affection for and devotion to JOHNSON, MAHER was apparently

sufficiently wealthy to keep his financial promises, and JOHNSON was in love with MAHER.

23.   In making the promises herein alleged and repeatedly assuring her of his intent to carry

out those promises, MAHER knew and intended that JOHNSEN be induced to rely on those

promises by quitting her careers as a flight attendant and as a model.

24.   MAHER has not performed any part of his promises.

25.   As a result of MAHER'S failure to perform according to his promises that he made to

JOHNSEN, JOHNSEN has suffered damages in the total amount of $9,000,000.00 for the

following items of damage;

   a. Loss of income from her modeling career;

   b. The loss of income from her career as flight attendant for DELTA AIRLINES,

        including the loss of her 401K plan, medical, dental benefits, and unlimited

        worldwide travel benefit passes;

   c. Loss of the promised rent payments;

   d. Un-reimbursed costs for clothing, make-up, etc.;

   e. Loss of the promised house or equivalent house; and

   f. Loss of the promised lifelong financial support.

26.   Injustice can be avoided only by enforcing MAHER'S promises completely by means of

the award of damages to JOHNSEN.

THIRD CAUSE OF ACTION

(Promissory Fraud; Against MAHER and DOES 1 through 50)

27.   JOHNSEN realleges and incorporates in this cause of action Paragraphs 1 through 6, 8

through 20 and 22 through 26 hereof as though here fully set forth.

-7-

COMPLAINT

28.   At the time MAHER represented to JOHNSEN that he would give JOHNSEN the above-described house, or would give her funds with which to purchase a comparable house, MAHER did not intend to perform on that promise.

29.   The promise was made by MAHER with the intent to induce JOHNSEN to rely thereon.

30.   In reliance upon, and as a direct and proximate result of MAHER'S false promise, JOHNSON quit her job as a flight attendant and ceased to pursue her career as a model

31.   As a result of the loss of her careers as a flight attendant and as a model, JOHNSEN has sustained, and continues to sustain damages in an amount to be proven at trial.

32.   JOHNSEN'S reliance upon MAHER'S false promise was reasonable in that JOHNSEN had no reason to doubt thereby losing all of the income and benefits attendant with those careers, in an amount to be proven at trial.

33.   MAHER engaged in the above-described conduct in with the intent of thereby depriving JOHNSEN of property or legal rights or otherwise causing injury, and was despicable conduct that subjected JOHNSEN to a cruel and unjust hardship in conscious and reckless disregard of JOHNSEN'S rights, so as to justify an award of exemplary and punitive damages.

FOURTH CAUSE OF ACTION

(Battery; Against MAHER and DOES 1 through 50)

34.   JOHNSEN realleges and incorporates in this cause of action Paragraphs 1 through 6, 8 through 20, 22 through 26, 28 through 33, and 35 through 38 hereof as though here fully set forth.

35.   On or about May, 2004, JONHSEN and MAHER attended a party for JIM LEFKOWITZ. During that party, MAHER became very angry and shouted at JOHNSEN while pulling very aggressively at JOHNSEN'S arm.

36.   In pulling on JOHNSEN'S arm and shaking her, MAHER acted with the intent to make

- 8 -

COMPLAINT

1 contact with JOHNSEN'S person.

2 37.   At no time did JOHNSEN consent to this conduct of MAHER.

3 38.   As a direct and proximate result of MAHER'S conduct, JOHNSEN sustained injuries to

4 her back and neck. JOHNSEN has additionally suffered pain and mental anguish as a result of

5 the conduct of MAHER and has incurred medical expenses in the treatment of the injuries she

6 sustained as a result of MAHER'S conduct.

7 39.   The aforementioned conduct of MAHER, was despicable, willful and was intended to

8 cause injury to JOHNSEN. Such conduct warrants an award of punitive and exemplary damages

9 sufficient to punish MAHER, to make example of him, and to deter such conduct in the future.

10

11

12 **FIFTH CAUSE OF ACTION**

13 (Assault; Against MAHER and DOES 1 through 50)

14 40.   JOHNSEN realleges and incorporates in this cause of action Paragraphs 1 through 6, 8

15 through 20, 22 through 26, and 28 through 33 hereof as though here fully set forth.

16 41.   Later in the evening after returning to MAHER'S house from the party described in

17 Paragraph 35 above, MAHER picked up a hammer, held it toward JOHNSEN'S head and

18 indicated that he would strike her with it if she were to fail to be faithful to him.

19 42.   In engaging in that conduct, MAHER intended to place JOHNSEN in imminent

20 apprehension of unwelcome, harmful and injurious contact, and to place her in fear of her

21 wellbeing.

22

23 43.   As a result of MAHER'S acts as alleged above, JOHNSEN, in fact, was placed in great

24 apprehension of a harmful contact with her person.

25 44.   As a proximate result of the acts of MAHER, JOHNSEN experienced severe mental

shock, and fear for her wellbeing, and emotional distress.

- 9 -

COMPLAINT

LAW OFFICES OF CYRUS & [...]US
PLC
423 North [...]nden Drive, Suite 510
Beverly Hills, California 90210
310 [...]

45.   The aforementioned conduct of MAHER, was despicable, willful and was intended to cause injury to JOHNSEN. Such conduct warrants an award of punitive and exemplary damages sufficient to punish MAHER, to make example of him, and to deter such conduct in the future.

PRAYER

WHEREFORE, JOHNSEN prays judgment against Defendants as follows:

ON THE FIRST AND SECOND CAUSES OF ACTION

1. For compensatory damages in the sum of $ 9,000,000.00;

2. For interest on the sum of $ 9,000,000.00 from and after the date of the filing of this Complaint;

3. For costs of suit and

4. For such other and further relief as the court may deem proper.

ON THE THIRD CAUSE OF ACTION

1. For general damages according to proof;

2. For medical and related expenses according to proof;

3. For punitive damages;

4. For interest as allowed by law;

5. For costs of suit herein incurred; and

6. For such other and further relief as the court may deem proper.

ON THE FOURTH AND FIFTH CAUSES OF ACTION

1. For general damages according to proof;

2. For medical and related expenses according to proof;

3. For punitive damages;

4. For interest as allowed by law;

5. For costs of suit herein incurred; and

6. For such other and further relief as the court may deem proper.

Dated: November 9 , 2004   LAW OFFICES OF CYRUS & CYRUS, PLC

By: _____

Roger Y. Muse, Esq.,
Attorneys for Plaintiff, COCO JOHNSEN

- 10 -

COMPLAINT

Source: Superior Court of the State of California County of Los Angeles.

Appendix **E**

DAVID VOELKERT CRIMINAL COMPLAINT AND DISMISSAL OF CRIMINAL COMPLAINT

STATE OF INDIANA   )
) SS
COUNTY OF ST JOSEPH   )

I, Robert Dane, being duly sworn, depose and state:

1.   I am a Special Agent with the Federal Bureau of Investigation ("FBI"). I have been an FBI Agent for approximately one year. I am currently assigned to the Indianapolis Field Division in South Bend, Indiana, which is tasked with, among other investigative responsibilities, investigating murder for hire and illegal use of audio-interception devices.

2.   The information contained in this affidavit is based upon my participation in this investigation, including conversations with other law enforcement officers and my review of documents. This affidavit is submitted for the limited purpose of establishing probable cause in support of a criminal complaint filed against David Voelkert. This affidavit does not contain all the information known to me about this investigation.

Facebook Communication

3.   On approximately May 23, 2011, Angela Voelkert, herein referred to as "AV", created a fictional profile on Facebook. The profile is of a seventeen-year-old, white female named "Jessica Studebaker," and includes a photograph of "Jessica Studebaker." AV used the profile to "friend" her ex-husband Voelkert, on Facebook.

4.   Soon after "friending" Voelkert on Facebook, AV contacted a female friend, gave the female friend access to "Jessica Studebaker's" Facebook account, and asked her female friend to email Voelkert through Facebook. AV involved her female friend for fear that, if she (AV) were the one emailing Voelkert, he would guess her identity through the content of the emails and

1

AV's style of writing.

5.   After AV's female friend began emailing Voelkert through Facebook, Angela monitored the emails on "Jessica Studebaker's" Facebook account.

6.   AV's female friend, using "Jessica Studebaker's" Facebook account, and Voelkert began discussing Voelkert's children and ex-wife (AV) via emails sent to and from the Facebook accounts.

7.   On May 26, 2011, Voelkert wrote "Jessica" to tell her he had sold his business (Secured Alarms) and planned to move somewhere warm with his kids, that he was still going to his next court dates, and would take off soon after.

8.   Secured Alarms is a business owned by Voelkert in South Bend that sells and installs sophisticated video and audio equipment. Among Secured Alarms' customers are police departments.

9.   On May 31, 2011, at 12:14 a.m., Voelkert wrote to "Jessica", "Ok, here is the deal. I had a GPS tracker on my van and I took it off earlier, it was just installed on my ex-wife's van so I can track her and know where she goes. It is hidden very well and would take a lot for it to be found, but my helper is a mechanic and knows what he is doing." Voelkert went on to discuss what kind of trouble that they could get in for doing this and that he wants "Jessica" to delete the message so there is no trace of talking about it.

10.   On May 31, 2011, at 12:48 a.m., Voelkert wrote "Jessica", "I just got my brother in law to lend me the money to just leave. Here is the deal, I am going to try and pack up and be out of here by Friday the 3rd with my kids." Voelkert explains that his brother-in-law is getting everything in his house for lending him the money.

11.   On May 31, 2011, at 1:58 p.m., Voelkert wrote "Jessica", "I have a GPS on her van,

so I know where she is all the time.   I am going to find someone to take care of her and now it will be easier because I know where she is at all times.   The GPS unit is cool because I can call in on the phone number to it and listen in with a microphone, but he couldn't get the microphone hooked up, so that really sucks.   No worries, once she is gone I don't have to hide with my kids, I can do what I want and not have to worry about not seeing my family any more.   You should find someone at your school, there should be some gang bangers there that would put a cap in her ass for $10,000.   I am just done with her crap!"

12.   On May 31, 2011, at 2:03 p.m., Voelkert wrote "Jessica", "I just have to get my kids to where they are safe as I do not want anything happening around them with their mom, so after they are safe away, I will have her taken care of.   I finally have the money to do this, I can finally be free of her . . . See, I am taking care of everything!   I will finally be free, my kids can grow up and not be around all the hatred, it will be over.   With me gone with my kids, the police can't pin anything on me as I will be in another state, so I will be fine.   Will you be ready to go with me on the 10th?   Let me know baby! ;-)"

13.   On May 31, 2011, at 2:05 p.m., David Voelkert wrote "Jessica", "Oh, if you find someone for me I will not have the money until the 10th, but I can have cash . . . Make sure they know this as I do not want to get shot for oweing someone money!"

14.   On May 31, 2011, after corresponding via Facebook with Voelkert about the GPS unit he had place on her vehicle, AZ contacted her brother to come over and take a look in her van. He discovered a small black plastic box, approximately 2"X2"X1/4" stuck to the upper corner of the driver's side windshield.   A black cable ran from the plastic box directly to the fuse box. Attached to the black box was an antenna approximately 5 inches long.   AZ's brother removed the black box and cut the cable.

3

15.   On May 31, 2011, at 4:22 p.m., Voelkert wrote "Jessica", "I am pissed because I lost GPS signal on my ex's van, I need to find out why but I don't want to stir anything up.   I will just hope it pop back in.   I got a low battery alert, then it was gone, I think it lost power somehow. Grr, I am just so pissed and I am tired of getting walked on."

16.   Voelkert later wrote "Jessica", "The GPS is back working again, so I am just waiting for the data on it to come through, the battery is low, it has to charge and she has to drive it to charge it.   I set it so that it shuts off when she isn't driving so it will not kill the battey and when it gets power again, it comes back on, that is what was wrong with it . . ."

17.   Based on your affiant's investigation and research, no manufacturers of combined tracking and audio-intercept devices, such as that described by Voelkert in his Facebook emails and viewed on AV's vehicle, are located in Indiana.

18.   Based on the above factual information, your affiant respectfully submits that there is probable cause to believe that David Voelkert, intentionally used, endeavored to use, and procured another person to use and endeavor to use an electronic, mechanical, or other device to intercept an oral communication,   when he knew, and had reason to know, that such device or any component thereof had been sent through the mail and transported in interstate or foreign commerce, in violation of Title 18, United States Code, Section 2511(1)(b) and Title 18, United States Code, Section 2.

Further your affiant sayeth not.

_____
Robert Dane
Special Agent
Federal Bureau of Investigation

Sworn to before me, and subscribed in my presence this 3rd day of June, 2011.
S/Christopher A. Nuechterlein

_____
Honorable Christopher A. Nuechterlein
United States Magistrate Judge
Northern District of Indiana
South Bend Division

AO 91 (Rev. 08/09) Criminal Complaint

UNITED STATES DISTRICT COURT
for the
Northern District of Indiana

United States of America v. DAVID VOELKERT _____ *Defendant(s)*	))))))) Case No. 3:11MJ39

CRIMINAL COMPLAINT

I, the complainant in this case, state that the following is true to the best of my knowledge and belief.

On or about the date(s) of _____ May through June, 2011, _____ in the county of _____ St. Joseph _____ in the

_____ Northern _____ District of _____ Indiana _____ , the defendant(s) violated:

Code Section	Offense Description
18:2511	Intentionally used an electronic, mechanical, or other device to intercept an oral communication
18:2	Aiding and abetting
(See Attachment)	(See Attachment)

FILED

JUN -3 2011

At _____ M

STEPHEN R. LUDWIG, Clerk
U.S. DISTRICT COURT
NORTHERN DISTRICT OF INDIANA

This criminal complaint is based on these facts:

SEE ATTACHED AFFIDAVIT

☑ Continued on the attached sheet.

_____
Complainant's signature

Robert Dane, Special Agent, FBI
Printed name and title

Sworn to before me and signed in my presence.

Date: _____ 06/03/2011 _____

S/Christopher A. Nuechterlein
_____
Judge's signature

City and state: _____ South Bend, Indiana _____

Honorable Christopher A. Nuechterlein
Printed name and title

SWORN AFFIDAVIT

STATE OF INDIANA
COUNTY OF ST. JOSEPH

PERSONALLY came and appeared before me, the undersigned Notary, the within named David E. Voelkert, who is a resident of St. Joseph County, Indiana, and makes his statement and Sworn Affidavit upon oath and affirmation of belief and personal knowledge that the following matters, facts and things set forth are true and correct to the best of his knowledge:

May of 2011 I received a friend request from a one Jessica Studebaker. From the start of that friend request, I was under suspicion that it was not a real person, but my ex-wife or someone she knows. I am talking to this 'person' on Facebook via messages through the Facebook mail system. I am lying to this person in extent to gain positive proof that it is indeed my ex-wife trying to again tamper in my life. Anything said in the chat to her from me cannot be held as the truth and I am chatting to this person in attempts to prove to my court that my ex-wife will not leave my personal life alone. This AFFIDAVIT was to be done when I started chatting with this said person, but I think this is enough evidence that I think this person is no more than my ex-wife or someone that she knows and not a real person. The lies that I am placing in this chat is for her to bring such up in court on the 8th day of June, 2011. I need proof what my ex-wife has been doing, so this will be part of such. In no way do I have plans to leave with my children or do any harm to Angela Dawn Voelkert or anyone else. At the time of the AFFIDAVIT, I am not sure where I will go with this chat. It may go as far as the other person will take it, but if it starts to get to an illegal chat where people could get hurt, I will contact my local authorities right away. With this AFFIDAVIT, I am attesting to most of the things contained in the chat with Jessica Studebaker on Facebook to be false and everything being said is to try and have my ex-wife bring up the chat in court, thus, proving she is tampering with my life. **** NOTHING FURTHER ****

DATED this 25th day of May, 2011

David E. Voelkert

SWORN to subscribed before me, this 25th day of May, 2011.

NOTARY PUBLIC

OFFICIAL SEAL
JASON WAITE
NOTARY PUBLIC - INDIANA
ST. JOSEPH COUNTY
My Comm Expires July 5, 2017

i

UNITED STATES DISTRICT COURT
NORTHERN DISTRICT OF INDIANA
SOUTH BEND DIVISION

UNITED STATES OF AMERICA	)	
	)	
v.	)	CASE NO. 3:11-MJ-39 CAN
	)	
DAVID VOELKERT	)	

MOTION FOR DISMISSAL OF CRIMINAL COMPLAINT

Comes now David Capp, United States Attorney for the Northern District of Indiana, by Assistant United States Attorney Jesse M. Barrett, and represents to the Court the following:

1.   On June 3, 2011, Magistrate Judge Christopher A. Nuechterlein approved a one-count criminal complaint against the defendant David Voelkert charging him with intentionally using an electronic, mechanical, or other device to intercept an oral communication, in violation of 18 U.S.C. §§ 2511 and 2.

2.   The government requests the Court to dismiss the complaint in this case against defendant David Voelkert. This request is based upon information learned in the government's ongoing investigation of the case.

WHEREFORE, the government respectfully requests that the criminal complaint as to defendant David Voelkert be dismissed.

Respectfully submitted,

DAVID CAPP
UNITED STATES ATTORNEY

By: s/ Jesse M. Barrett
        Jesse M. Barrett
        Assistant United States Attorney

UNITED STATES DISTRICT COURT
NORTHERN DISTRICT OF INDIANA
SOUTH BEND DIVISION

UNITED STATES OF AMERICA   )
)
            v.   )   CASE NO. 3:11-MJ-39 CAN
)
DAVID VOELKERT   )

ORDER FOR DISMISSAL

Having considered the government's motion to dismiss the criminal complaint filed

against defendant David Voelkert, IT IS SO ORDERED:

The Court GRANTS the government's motion to dismiss the criminal complaint against

defendant David Voelkert.

Dated: __June 8, 2011_____.

                        s/Christopher A Nuechterlein_____
                        Magistrate Judge, United States District Court

Source: State of Indiana, County of St Joseph.

Glossary

A

Abode service   service on a defendant by leaving a copy of the pleadings at his or her home.

Access   the child's right to see the noncustodial parent.

Access Rights   right of a noncustodial parent to frequently spend time with the child unless the court finds that visitation in some way endangers the child's emotional, mental, moral, or physical health.

Administrative enforcement   action by a state or federal agency, rather than a court.

Administrative Procedure Act   a federal statute that allows a person appearing before a federal administrative agency to be represented by an attorney or, if the agency permits, "by other qualified individual."

Adoption   a legal procedure that makes a person or persons the legal parent or parents of a minor child who is not their natural child.

Adoption Assistance and Child Welfare Act of 1980 (CWA)   major federal child protection statute passed by Congress which requires that state child protective services make to maintain children with their families, or to reunify them, once the parents have received short-term, family-focused, and community-based services.

Adoption and Safe Families Act (ASFA)   a federal law that established the requirement that a permanency planning hearing must be held within twelve months of the child's placement in foster care for the purpose of assessing whether the child should be returned home or whether termination of parental rights proceedings should commence for the purpose of making the child available for adoption.

Adversary proceeding complaint   a civil case filed within a bankruptcy case filing it will permit the client to argue to the judge that discharging nonsupport obligations will have an adverse effect on the client.

Affidavit   a signed, sworn statement.

Affidavit of publication   a signed, sworn statement that a legal notice was printed.

Affidavit of paternity   a man's signed sworn statement containing facts that the man is the father of a child, often required if a man not married to the child's mother wishes to be listed on the child's birth certificate as the child's father; also known as acknowledgement of paternity.

Affinity   related by marriage.

Alimony   a sum of money, or other property, paid by a former spouse to the other former spouse for financial support, pursuant to a court order, temporary or final, in a divorce proceeding; also known as spousal maintenance or spousal support.

Alimony in gross or Alimony in solido   a support payment made in one single payment; also known as lump sum alimony.

Alternative dispute resolution or ADR   a method of resolving disputes between parties without resorting to a trial.

Altruistic surrogacy   a contract where the surrogate mother receives no financial reward for carrying the child or relinquishing her rights upon birth.

Annulment   a judicial decision that a valid marriage does not exist or never existed between a person and another party.

Answer   a document in which each of the allegations contained in the numbered paragraphs of a complaint is responded to.

Antenuptial agreement   a contract entered into by the prospective spouses regarding their rights during the marriage and in the event of a divorce; also known as a premarital or prenuptial agreement.

Appearance   a document stating that a person has come into a court action as a party or an attorney representing a party.

Application for a prejudgment remedy   where a party asks the court to take some action before a judgment in the case is rendered.

Arbitration award   the opinion rendered by an arbitrator which, depending on the prior agreement of the parties, may be either binding or nonbinding.

Arrearage   amount due by court order but unpaid; also known as back alimony.

Attorney–client privilege   the ethical rule stating that attorneys cannot disclose information related to the representation of a client, with certain exceptions.

Attorney's fees   the amount charged by a lawyer to a client for undertaking his or her case.

Authorized practice of law   general criteria for obtaining a license to practice law required by state statute.

Automatic stay   an injunction issued by the bankruptcy court that prohibits any collection activity against the debtor and it can only be lifted by an order of the bankruptcy court.

B

Bankruptcy   a legal proceeding in federal court that allows individuals or businesses that are unable to pay their debts to either discharge their obligations, or reorganize them to be paid over a period of time.

Bankruptcy Abuse Prevention and Consumer Protection Act   new federal bankruptcy law passed on April 20, 2005 (with most provisions effective October 17, 2005) legislating significant changes impacting divorce litigation.

Bankruptcy trustee   individual who administers the bankruptcy estate.

Best interest of the child   standard that opened the contest for custody not only to fathers but also to other potential caregivers when the child's well-being or interests could be best served by such a custody determination.

Bigamy   being married to two people at the same time.

Billable hours   the amount of time expended on a particular case, which can later be billed to that client.

Blended families   a term used to refer to couples marrying for the second time where the family comprises children of each spouse from a previous marriage or relationship, and children the couple have had together.

Body   the part of a complaint that contains the necessary factual information that establishes the jurisdiction of the court and identifies the grounds on which the divorce is being sought.

Boilerplate   standardized agreement forms or clauses.

Bridge-the-gap alimony   short-term, lump sum alimony awarded to a spouse for the purpose of transitioning from married to single status.

Bureau of Vital Statistics form   a form that is filled out and sent to the state in order to keep track of certain information regarding divorcing couples.

C

Canon law   the church's body of law or rules that determine man's moral obligations to man, to woman, and to God.

Capias   a document empowering a sheriff to arrest a nonappearing, noncustodial parent and bring him or her to jail and to court.

Caption   the initial section of a complaint that contains the names of the parties, the name and division of the court, the docket number or the return date of the action, and the date the complaint was drawn up.

Chapter 7   a form of bankruptcy that allows a debtor to discharge or liquidate a majority of their debts.

Chapter 13   a form of bankruptcy where instead of liquidating of the debt, the debtor is subject to reorganization. Reorganization requires the debtor to pay back their creditors under a plan approved by the Bankruptcy Court over a period of three to five years.

Certification   page accompanying a court document stating that a copy of the document was sent on a specific date to all counsel of record and *pro se* appearing parties (if any).

Chattel   a tangible, movable piece of personal property.

Child Abuse Prevention and Treatment Act of 1974 (CAPTA)   federal government's most comprehensive effort to address the issue of child protection, which provides federal funding to states to support child protective services that respond to cases of abuse, neglect, and sexual abuse.

Child Support Enforcement Amendments   federal laws passed to enable mothers to collect child support and ease the social welfare burden on the taxpayers.

Child support guidelines   statutorily enacted formulas for determining the amount the noncustodial parent must pay for the support of each child.

Civil code   the system of Spanish and French concepts of marital property law existing on the European mainland; also known as the *code civile*.

Civil contempt   a "coercive" remedy used by courts to bring noncompliant parties before the judge and convince them to comply with an existing court order.

Civil contempt proceeding   a proceeding that is "remedial" or "coercive" in nature. Its purpose is to bring the noncompliant party before the court and convince them to comply with the court order. Civil contempt must be proven by a preponderance of the evidence and if proven, gives the court the authority to incarcerate the noncompliant party until the court ordered alimony or child support is paid.

Civil marriage or civil ceremony   a legal status created by a state government when a state official, such as a judge or justice of the peace, performs a ceremony joining two single adults who have met the state's statutory qualifications in a marital union.

Civil restraining order   a court order obtained by a victim of domestic violence in a family (civil) court.

Civil union   a separate category of legal recognition that grants same-sex couples marriage rights available to heterosexual couples, in the states of Vermont and Connecticut; civil unions are a way for same-sex couples to formalize their relationship and take advantage of the same state rights afforded to heterosexual couples.

Claim for relief   a statement filed by a party indicating what he or she wants in terms of a disposition in the case.

Code   a set of written rules that establishes the guidelines for attorneys in their interactions with clients, courts, and staff and their obligations to the general public.

Cohabitation   unmarried parties living together as if married.

Collaborative divorce   a team approach to divorce dispute resolution designed to protect the spouses and their children from the trauma of divorce litigation where both parties employ the services of a collaborate divorce attorney, financial planner, and mental health professional.

Collaborative lawyering   a form of dispute resolution designed to bring together the respective parties, their attorneys, and other professionals with the goal of reaching an amicable settlement, thus avoiding costly litigation in family court.

Combined net income   the figure arrived at when each parent's net income is added together to determine child support; also known as total net income.

Commercial surrogacy   an agreement whereby the surrogate mother receives a fee for carrying the child to term.

Common law marriage   a marriage created without a license or ceremony.

Community property distribution   a system of property division that assumes that both husband and wife contributed to the accumulation of marital assets.

Competency   the duty to exercise a reasonable degree of care and skill commonly used by other attorneys engaged in a similar area of practice.

Complaint   a grievance filed with a disciplinary body against an attorney; also, a document that commences an action when the opposing party is served; also known as a petition.

Compromise   meeting someone halfway or giving up a position in exchange for something else.

Concurrent ownership   when property is held by two or more persons together; also known as joint ownership.

Confidential   information that is privileged; that is, not everyone is allowed access to it.

Confidentiality   the ethical rule that protects communications between attorneys and their clients.

Confidentiality agreement   an arrangement between an attorney and a client that certain information the client may divulge will be kept secret.

Confidentiality clause   a clause found in an agreement where the parties agree not to discuss the details of their relationship to the press.

Conflict of interest   any activity that may divide the attorney's loyalty and compromise his or her independent judgment.

Conflicting out   where a prospective divorce client engages in the practice of interviewing all the available family law attorneys in a geographical area for the purpose of disqualifying them from representing the other spouse.

Consanguinity   related by blood.

Consolidated Omnibus Budget Reconciliation Act (COBRA), 26 USC sec. 4980B(f)   a federal law that enables a nonemployee spouse to continue his or her health insurance coverage provided by his or her spouse's employer for a period of three years after a divorce, as long as the nonemployee spouse pays the premium.

Contempt   where one party in an action does not comply with the court's order; also party's refusal to obey the judge's order and as a consequence, the court's authority to enforce that order.

Contempt proceeding   a civil proceeding that a party may commence to force the payor spouse to comply with the court's order when the party entitled to alimony is not paid.

Contested hearing   a disputed divorce trial arising from the parties' failure to resolve disputed issues without judicial intervention.

Contingent fees   an arrangement that entitles attorneys to a percentage of the financial outcome of the case, be it a judgment or settlement.

Cooling-off period   the statutorily mandated time period following the initiation of divorce proceedings during which no final decree may be entered.

Cost-of-living clause   provides for increases in the alimony payments due to the increase of payor's income and an increase in the cost of living, which obviates the need for the parties to go back to court for modifications; also known as an escalation clause.

Costs of litigation   include filing fees, sheriff's fees, deposition costs, expert witness fees, and excessive photocopying and mailing costs.

Court calendar   An official resource published by the court that contains a number of cases listed according to parties and docket number and indicates the order in which cases will be heard.

Court-entry fee   an amount of money required to file a complaint in court; also known as a filing fee.

Covenant marriage   an alternative type of marriage that can be summarized as requiring premarital counseling, a return to fault-based grounds in order to dissolve the marriage, counseling before going through divorce, the signing of a covenant contract, and longer mandatory waiting periods.

Criminal contempt   a "punitive" remedy used by courts where a noncompliant party may be incarcerated if it is proven beyond a reasonable doubt that the court's order was *willfully violated*.

Criminal protective order   is a court order issued by a judge in a criminal case against a defendant accused of a domestic-violence–related crime.

Cross-complaint   see *cross-claim*.

Cross-examination   when the opposing party's lawyer has the opportunity to question the opposing party.

Custodial parent   the parent with whom the child primarily resides.

Custody affidavit   an affidavit indicating that there is no other proceeding pending in another court that affects the custody of the minor children.

D

Deep pocket   the term applied to characterize the defendant in a lawsuit who has the financial resources to absorb a civil suit for monetary damages.

***De facto* Father**   at common law, a man who signs a child's birth certificate and/or completes an affidavit or acknowledgment of paternity is deemed to be the child's father before the law.

Default judgment   where one party "wins" the dissolution or divorce suit by failure of the other party to act.

Default trial   where one of the parties to an action has failed to appear at the scheduled trial date even though he or she has received proper notice of the proceedings; the court proceeds with a hearing and severs the marriage.

Defendant   the party against whom an action is brought.

Defense of Marriage Act (DOMA)   a federal law passed in response to attempts on the part of gay-rights activists to require states to recognize same-sex marriages; DOMA defines marriage for federal purposes.

Deny   in a court proceeding, where the judge refuses to grant the motion of one of the parties.

Deponent   the person who is being questioned at a deposition.

Deposition   a procedure in which one party's attorney orally questions an opposing party or a nonparty witness who has sworn under oath to answer all questions truthfully and accurately to the best of his or her knowledge and ability.

Deviation criteria   special circumstances that allow the court to deviate from the child support guideline formula.

Direct examination   the initial questioning by the party's own attorney.

Disciplinary board   bodies that may sanction or punish attorneys for engaging in conduct that violates the state's code of professional conduct.

Dissipation   depletion of the marital assets.

Dissolution of marriage   the phrase many jurisdictions use to formally define the complete legal severance of the marital relationship.

Divorce   the complete legal severance of the marital relationship.

Divorce arbitration   an alternative to a divorce trial whereby parties, who are unable to work out a resolution, present their evidence before a neutral third party who will render a decision on the contested issues.

Divorce trial   a trial in which both parties present their case to the court for its final hearing.

DNA test   a genetic testing which deoxyribonucleic acid is extracted from body cells to determine a relationship between two or more persons; this test is used to determine paternity.

Docket control system   a system of one or more calendars that helps an attorney keep track of the various court dates and deadlines.

Domestic partners   a committed relationship between two persons of the same or opposite gender, who reside together and support each other, in a mutually exclusive partnership.

Domestic partnership   a committed relationship between two persons of the same gender, who reside together and support each other, in a mutually exclusive partnership.

Domestic support obligations (DSOs)   under bankruptcy law, the classification of alimony, maintenance, and child support payments as first priority in bankruptcy proceedings which means that other creditors cannot receive any payments owed to them by the creditor until the domestic support obligations are fulfilled and that these obligations cannot be discharged in bankruptcy under either a Chapter 7 or Chapter 13.

Domicile   residing in a state with the intent to permanently remain.

Dual arrests   where both parties involved in a domestic violence case are arrested, without a determination of who perpetrated the crime.

Duplicative   referring to discovery, something that has already been requested.

Durational alimony   a type of alimony that provides a spouse with financial assistance for a limited period of time following a short or moderate term marriage and the length of the support cannot exceed the length of the marriage.

E

Earned retainer   amount from the retainer that the attorney may keep in proportion to the amount of work expended on the client's file.

Ecclesiastical courts   courts that had the jurisdiction to hear some matters that could also be heard in the general state courts; however, they had exclusive jurisdiction over all family-related legal matters; also known as church courts.

Emancipation   acquiring adult status; a youth may be emancipated by operation of law, that is, on his or her birthday by reaching the age of majority or by court order at a younger age.

Employee Retirement Income Security Act (ERISA) is federal statute passed in 1974 to protect employees and their pensions in case an employer declares bankruptcy or goes out of business. This law also governs retirement pay and pension benefits.

Enterprise goodwill   the intangible but usually marketable existence in a business of established relationships with employees, customers and suppliers.

Equitable distribution   a system allowing family courts to distribute property acquired during marriage on the basis of fairness, as opposed to ownership.

Escalation clause   provides for increases in alimony payments due to the increase of payor's income and an increase in the cost of living, obviating the need for the parties to go back to court for modifications; also known as a cost of living clause.

E-services   often used as the umbrella term to identify services available online.

Ethical wall   when a paralegal cannot discuss a case with anyone in the office or have access to the file because of the possibility of conflict of interest.

Exclusive jurisdiction   a court's power to hear certain actions of classes of actions to the exclusion of all other courts.

Exemptions   the amount and type of property that a debtor may keep despite the bankruptcy proceedings.

Ex parte   a Latin term meaning "by one party" or "for one party."

Ex parte **proceeding**   a court hearing conducted in response to one party's *ex parte* motion or petition. The opposing party is not present during an *ex parte* proceeding because such proceedings are generally filed in an emergency situation.

Expert witness   a person with specialized knowledge who is called to testify in court.

F

Family counseling   a service or process that enables couples to evaluate the viability of their marriage.

Family preservation   the legal requirement that state child protection services must make reasonable efforts to maintain children with their families or reunify them.

Family relations unit   trained social workers who work for the court and conduct studies and apply child development and child psychology concepts to make custody and visitation recommendations; also known as the family services division.

Family services division   see *family relations unit.*

Family support payments (or unallocated support)   Terms given to regular, periodic payments made by a payer spouse for the financial maintenance of both the ex-spouse and children.

Fault   the responsibility for or cause of wrongdoing or failure; the wrongful conduct responsible for the failure or breakdown of a marriage.

Fees   the amount the attorney will charge the client, based on the skill and experience of the attorney, the simplicity or complexity of the client's matter, cost of similar service in the community, the result obtained, the reputation of the attorney, and whether the matter is contested or uncontested.

Filing fee   an amount of money required to file a complaint in court; also known as a court entry fee.

Final argument   where each attorney argues why the court should rule in his or her client's favor.

Financial disclosure affidavit   a sworn statement indicating the income, expenses, assets, and liabilities of a client.

Financial statement or financial affidavit   a sworn statement that enumerates the party's sources of income, earned and unearned; the party's expenses, necessary and optional; and all of the party's assets and liabilities.

Financial worksheet   focuses on the client's income, expenses, assets, and liabilities, be they joint or stable; enables the attorney to begin assessing the extent of the marital estate.

Fixed schedule   definite dates and time frames set aside for the purpose of allowing a noncustodial parent to visit with a child.

Flat fee   an arrangement whereby a fixed dollar amount is agreed on and charged for the entire case.

Foreclosure   a legal proceeding where the lender seeks to force the sale of real property secured by a mortgage in order to recover the money and interest due, plus the legal costs of the foreclosure, when the borrower failed to make payments.

Former client–current opponent   upon an attorney or paralegal switching jobs, discovering that his or her new employer is representing the opponent in a former client's case.

Freelance paralegal   independent contractor who works for a number of attorneys on an as-needed basis.

Front loading   where the majority of property settlements in a divorce case are made in the first three years after the divorce.

G

Gestational surrogacy contract   also called the host method, is an arrangement whereby the intended mother cannot conceive or carry the child for health-related reasons. Therefore, the child is conceived through in vitro fertilization, a process where the intended mother's egg and the father's sperm are fertilized outside the body and then implanted into the surrogate mother. The surrogate in a gestational surrogacy agreement is not considered the legal biological parent of the child.

Grant   in a court proceeding, when the judge decides to allow a party's request or motion.

Grievance   a complaint filed with a disciplinary body against an attorney.

Grievance committees   state bar associations that regulate the legal profession through disciplinary bodies.

H

Habeas corpus   a document that allows an incarcerated party to be transported by a state's correctional department for trial.

Hague Adoption Convention   an international treaty that requires member countries to establish a central authority and point of contract in the country (in the United States it is the Department of State), ensure that international adoptions are in the best interest of the children by banning the abduction, sale of, or traffic of children, offer international adoptions in cases where a suitable home in the child's native country cannot be found, and provide for international and intergovernmental recognition of international adoptions.

Home study   a preplacement assessment of prospective adoptive parents and conducted by a licensed social worker who works for the state or a licensed adoption agency.

Homestead exemption   determines the amount of equity the parties can keep in their homes and shield from the bankruptcy proceedings.

Hourly basis   billing the client for each hour of time spent working on a client's file, including, but not limited to, research, drafting documents, phone calls, travel, office visits, trial preparation, and interviewing witnesses.

I

Illegitimate   born out of wedlock; the term given to a child born to parents who were not married to each other and who made no effort to legitimate the child afterward.

Indian Child Welfare Act (ICWA)   federal law passed by Congress in 1978 to address the overrepresentation of Native American children in the foster care system.

Infidelity clause   an infidelity clause is triggered if one of the spouses commits adultery. Its purpose is to penalize the cheating spouse by affecting the divorce settlement.

Initial client interview   the first meeting between a client and an attorney or paralegal at which basic information to start work on a case is gathered.

Innocent spouse relief   an Internal Revenue Service rule that allows an aggrieved spouse to avoid full or partial liability arising from a joint tax return where a tax is assessed against his or her spouse.

In personam jurisdiction   personal service over the defendant; it means that once the defendant is served with the initial pleadings, the court may enter orders and enforce judgments against that individual.

In rem jurisdiction   the power of the courts to actually dissolve the marriage.

Integrated bar associations   affiliations of state bar associations where membership is mandatory.

Inter-Ethnic Adoption Provisions   amendments to Multi-Ethnic Placement Act of 1994 passed in 1996.

International adoption   a legal process by which an individual or a couple becomes the legal parent of a child who is a citizen of another country and then brings that child to their home country to live with them permanently.

Interrogatories   requests for disclosure of all real and personal property owned by a spouse either in his or her own name or owned jointly with the spouse or with another person or entity.

Intimate partner violence   a gender neutral term used in place of "wife" or "spousal abuse."

In vitro fertilization   the process of conceiving a human embryo outside the biological parents' physical body.

Involuntary adoption   where parental rights are terminated by court order without parental consent.

Irrelevant   not having anything to do with the matter at hand.

IRS recapture rule   applies when the parties do not wish to have alimony taxed as income or deducted; should be indicated in the settlement agreement.

J

Joint adoption   when both partners adopt a child together at the same time.

Joint custody   arrangement in which parents are equally responsible for the financial, emotional, educational, and health-related needs of their children.

Joint legal and physical custody   a custody arrangement where both parents share residential or physical custody of the children and make decisions regarding the children's health, education, and welfare.

Jointly and severally liable   where one or both parties may be held responsible for taxes due as well as any additions, penalties, or interest.

Judgment   an order made by the court pursuant to the court's decision after a trial; it becomes a permanent part of the court file.

Judicial pretrial conference   a conference that takes place before a judge, not a trial, to help the parties try to come to an agreement before the trial starts; also known as a pretrial conference.

Juris number   the attorney's license number.

Jurisdiction   describes the court's control or power over a specific geographic territory; it also refers to the power of the courts to hear and resolve a dispute.

L

Legal advice   advising a client of his or her specific legal rights and responsibilities, and either predicting an outcome or recommending that the client pursue a particular course of action.

Legal custody   where both parents are the children's legal guardians and, as such, have the right to make decisions regarding their children's health, education, and welfare.

Legal guardian   name given to the person who has the legal authority to care for another person; or as a parent has the legal right and responsibility to provide for their children's health, education, and welfare.

Legal separation   an action brought by a spouse who wishes to avoid the legal, social, or religious ramifications of a divorce but nevertheless wishes to live apart from his or her spouse.

Liquidate   to sell off assets and pay creditors with the proceeds.

Limited scope retainer agreement   a contract for legal services between the attorney and client where the attorney limits the scope of representation with the client's consent.

Living expenses   any monies for client's personal use that may not be advanced to a client by the attorney.

M

Malpractice   negligent legal representation; representation that is below the standard of the professional community and could result in damage to the client.

Mandatory arrests   a law that requires police officers in domestic-violence–related crimes to make an arrest if probable cause exists, thus removing police discretion in making an arrest.

Mandatory reporter   a professional who is required by state statute to report suspected child abuse or neglect.

Mandatory reporting laws   statutes requiring designated professionals to report suspected child abuse and neglect.

Marriage   the joining together of two adult individuals in a civil contract.

Marital assets   the property acquired during a marriage.

Marital debts   marital debts are the liabilities incurred by either spouse during the course of the marriage.

Marital property   real and personal property acquired during a marriage.

Marriage certificate   a document prepared by the official performing the marriage; most jurisdictions require the bride and groom, the person officiating the marriage, and one or two witnesses to sign the marriage certificate after the completion of the ceremony; in some jurisdictions, the marriage certificate is filed with the clerk upon completion of the marriage and in others it is incorporated into the marriage license.

Marriage license   a document issued by the county clerk that authorizes a couple to get married.

Married Women's Property Acts   statutes that eliminated the disadvantages of married women and gave them the right to control their own earnings, bring lawsuits, be sued, own their own property, enter into contracts, and function in a legal capacity.

Massachusetts Alimony Reform Act of 2011   a Massachusetts statute which became effective on March 1, 2012, for the purpose of reforming its alimony statute, taking into account women's increased participation in the workforce.

Means test   a calculation under bankruptcy law that determines whether a debtor has the ability to pay back debts. Debtors have to pass what is called a in order to determine if they can pay back their debts.

Mediation   a form of alternative dispute resolution, conducted by a neutral person, designed to avoid undue litigation and lessen the emotional trauma involved in a divorce; also where the parties meet and attempt to resolve the pending issues surrounding their dissolution of marriage action with the assistance of a trained third party, either court-provided and free, or privately engaged and paid.

Memorandum of law   a written document presented to the court that states a party's argument in a case and supports that argument with specific case law and statutes.

Memorandum of understanding   a written, plain-language, nonbinding document containing the tentative agreement of the parties on various issues relevant to their case.

Merger   an agreement that is no longer a contract between the two parties, but rather a court order, which can be modified or enforced through contempt of court proceedings.

Migratory divorces   people flocking to a particular jurisdiction to get divorced because of the short divorce residency requirements.

Military affidavit   a sworn statement that serves as proof that the defendant is currently not serving in one of the armed forces.

Model Rules of Professional Conduct (MRPC)   a prototype for attorney's ethics written by the American Bar Association as a model for states that wish to adopt them.

Modification   a change or adjustment to a previous court order.

Modification of alimony   the issue of whether spousal support may be either increased or decreased after the original order has been entered due to a substantial change in one spouse's circumstances.

Mortgage   a loan obtained for the purpose of purchasing a home.

Motion for alimony, pendente lite   where a party to a dissolution proceeding asks the court to grant support payments to him or her for the duration of the case.

Motion for child support, pendente lite   where a party to a dissolution proceeding asks the court to have the other party pay child maintenance for the duration of the case.

Motion for contempt   a document that alerts the court to the other party's failure to comply with the court's earlier order and requests that the court provide relief.

Motion for custody, pendente lite   where a party to a dissolution proceeding asks the court to have possession of the children for the duration of the case.

Motion for disclosure of assets   requests disclosure of all real and personal property owned by a spouse either in his or her own name or owned jointly with the spouse or with another person or entity.

Motion for exclusive possession of the marital residence, pendente lite   where a party to a dissolution proceeding asks the court to allow him or her to stay in the home, without the other party, for the duration of the case.

Motion for modification   where a party asks that orders entered by the court be changed when there has been a substantial change in the one of the party's circumstances from the time the original order was entered; also known as a motion to modify.

Motion for modification of child support   a document requesting the court to order the noncustodial parent to pay higher periodic child support payments, so that less of the custodial parent's income will be needed for the child.

Motion for payment of mortgage payments and insurance premiums, pendente lite   where a party to a dissolution proceeding asks the court to have the other party pay for certain bills for the duration of the case.

Motion for protective order   where a party asks the court to prevent the other party from coming in contact with him or her.

Motion to compel examination   a document that asks the court to force the opposing party to submit to an examination.

Motion to freeze marital assets   where a party asks the court to stop any transactions of the marital property from taking place.

Motion to modify   where a party asks that orders entered by the court be changed when there has been a substantial change in one of the party's circumstances from the time the original order was entered; also known as a motion for modification.

Motion to modify alimony   where a party asks that orders for spousal support entered by the court be changed when there has been a substantial change in one of the party's circumstances from the time the original order was entered; also known as a motion to modify support.

Motion to modify custody   where a party asks that orders regarding child custody entered by the court be changed when there has been a substantial change in one of the party's circumstances from the time the original order was entered.

Motion to modify visitation   where a party asks that orders for child visitation entered by the court be changed when there has been a substantial change in one of the party's circumstances from the time the original order was entered.

Motion to reopen judgment   the legal procedure necessary to seek the reopening of a divorce case that has already gone to final judgment. Its purpose is to modify the disposition of issues that were deemed final and nonmodifiable.

Motion to restrain party from entering marital residence   where a party asks the court to order that the other party be forbidden to enter the home where that party is living.

Moving party   the person bringing the motion to court.

Multi-Ethnic Placement Act of 1994 (MEPA)   a federal statute that prohibits the delay or denial of any adoption or placement in foster care due to the race, color, or national origin of the child or of the foster or adoptive parents and requires states to provide for diligent recruitment of potential foster and adoptive families who reflect the ethnic and racial diversity of children for whom homes are needed.

Multiple representation   where one lawyer is hired to represent both parties to a case.

N

National Association of Legal Assistants (NALA)   voluntary national, state, and local paralegal association that has established its own ethical codes.

National Federation of Paralegal Associations (NFPA)   voluntary national, state, and local paralegal association that has established its own ethical codes.

Nesting   An arrangement where the access afforded to the noncustodial parent occurs at the child or children's primary residence. During the access period, the noncustodial parent moves in with the child or children while the custodial parent leaves the residence for that period of time.

No contact orders   a court order issued in a domestic violence case that prohibits any type of physical or electronic contact with the victim.

No-fault divorce   in order to obtain a divorce, a litigant traditionally had to prove one of the statutory fault grounds or no divorce was granted; in 1969, the California legislature enacted the first no-fault divorce, which required parties only to prove that they had irreconcilable differences and there was no hope of reconciliation; currently, all fifty states have some form of no-fault divorce provisions where one of the parties only has to allege that the marriage has broken down and that there is no hope of reconciliation in order for the court to dissolve a marriage.

No-fault divorce laws   a modification of existing divorce laws to include the ground that the marital union or marital relationship had broken down irretrievably.

Nominal alimony   alimony in the amount of $1.00 per year; the purpose of nominal alimony is to allow the spouse to preserve his or her right to return to court in the event there is a change in circumstances.

Noncustodial parent   the parent who does the child living with him or her on a full-time basis.

Nonmarital child   a child born to parents who are not married to each other and who do not legitimate the child; illegitimate child.

Nonmodifiable   orders issued by a court that cannot be changed, regardless of the circumstances.

Non-recognition rule   Federal tax rule where the division or transfer of property made from an individual to a former spouse is not considered a taxable event as long as the transfer is incident to divorce.

Notice of default   a letter informing the homeowners that they have failed to comply with the terms of the mortgage and that if they do not bring their payments up to date, the lender may seek a court order to repossess the home.

Notice of deposition   a document that alerts a party that he or she will be required to submit to examination by the opposing attorney.

Notice of filing of interrogatories   a document that alerts the court that a party has asked the opposing party to answer a set of written questions.

Notice of responding to and/or objecting to interrogatories   a document that alerts the court that the answering party has either answered the written questions or objects to one or more of the questions.

Notice to appear for a deposition to disclose assets   a document that requires a party to appear in order to be questioned, under oath, on the previous disclosure to determine whether it completely revealed all of the party's assets.

Nuclear family   a term used to refer to the "typical American family," consisting of a mother, father, and their offspring.

O

Obligor   the party responsible for money that is owed; also known as a debtor.

Omnibus Crime Control and Safe Streets Acts of 1968   commonly referred to as the *Wiretap Act*. This law prohibits the recording of private conversations by use of wiretaps on telephones or hidden microphones.

Open adoption   an adoption where the biological parents, the adoptive parents, and sometimes the children are known to each other.

Open adoption agreement   a contract entered into between one or both biological parents and the adoptive parents, prior to the adoption proceeding, that grants the biological parent(s) the right to continue some type of relationship with the child or have access to information regarding the child's development and well-being.

Order   a statement that sets forth the judge's decision on a particular motion before the court.

Overbroad   too general; not specific enough.

P

Padding   unjustifiably increasing the number of hours actually spent on a client's case.

Parens patriae   the Latin term for the legal doctrine empowering the state to intervene to protect children when parents or guardians fail to do so.

Parental alienation   psychological manipulation that destroys the child's once-positive relationship with that parent.

Parental Alienation Syndrome   a child's response to this psychological manipulation that destroys the child's once-positive relationship with that parent.

Parenting plan   a parenting plan is a written, detailed, legal document that outlines how parents will share the responsibility of caring for the children under circumstances where they are not living in the same household.

Paternity action   where the petitioning party, usually the child's mother but occasionally the father, requests that the court hold a hearing to establish whether a particular man is the child's biological father.

Patria potestas   in ancient civilizations, where fathers possessed absolute right to the possession of their children and could even sell the children or put them to death if desired.

Pendency period   the time during court proceedings before judgment is rendered.

Pendente lite alimony   payments made during the pendency of the divorce with the purpose of providing temporary financial support for the spouse; also known as temporary alimony.

Pendente lite motion   a motion granting relief only for the duration of the court action, before judgment is rendered.

Periodic alimony or alimony in future   a term applied to court-ordered payments that are to be made to a spouse on a regular basis.

Permanent alimony   the term applied to court-ordered payments that are to be made to a spouse on a regular and periodic basis and that terminate only on the death, remarriage, or cohabitation of the other spouse or on court order.

Permissive reporter   an individual who reports suspected child abuse and neglect, but is not legally obligated by statute to do so.

Personal goodwill   the goodwill attributable to an individual's personal skill, training or reputation.

Personal property   anything other than real property that can be touched and is movable.

Petition   a document that commences the action when the opposing party is served; also known as a complaint.

Petitioner   the party who brings a court action against another; also known as the plaintiff.

Physical custody   when a parent has actual bodily possession of the children.

Plaintiff   the party who brings a court action against another; also known as the petitioner.

Pleading   documents that state the plaintiff's claims giving rise to the dissolution action and the defendant's responses or defenses to such claims.

Polygamy   having multiple spouses.

Postjudgment matters   court proceedings that arise after the case has gone to final judgment. They often address the modification of existing court orders or their enforcement when parties fail to meet their obligations.

Postmajority support agreements   agreements that frequently address payment for college tuition or other postsecondary education; payment for the maintenance of postmajority adult children with special needs; and payment of medical and dental insurance coverage for dependent adult children while they are students or when they are newly employed but not yet eligible for coverage at work.

Postnuptial agreement   agreements made *after* the marriage has been performed in which the elements are similar to those of prenuptial agreements.

Prayer for relief   the plaintiff's request for a dissolution and for court orders, when appropriate, regarding property distribution, alimony, child custody, and support of the minor children.

Premarital agreement   a contract entered into by the prospective spouses regarding their rights during the marriage and in the event of a divorce; also known as an antenuptial agreement or prenuptial agreement.

Premium   a monetary sum paid on an annual or installment basis for malpractice insurance coverage.

Prenuptial agreement   a contract entered into by the prospective spouses regarding their rights during the marriage and in the event of a divorce; also known as an antenuptial agreement or premarital agreement.

Pre-return date relief   where a plaintiff spouse needs and may seek immediate relief or court intervention as soon as the complaint is served.

Presumed father   the man presumed to be the father of a child for several reasons such as having been married to the child's mother when the child was born, or because he married the child's mother after the child was born and agreed to have his name be put on the birth certificate.

Pretrial conference   a meeting that takes place before a judge, not a trial, to help the parties try to come to an agreement before the trial starts; also known as a judicial pretrial.

Primary (or predominant) aggressor laws   statutes that require police officers to attempt to identify the "primary aggressor" when deciding whether to arrest both parties in domestic violence cases where both parties claim injuries.

Primary caregiver   the individual who has done most of the significant parenting of the child since birth or for the several preceding years.

Primary caretaker   the individual who has taken on the main responsibility for the daily care, rearing, and nurturing of a child.

Privilege   a court-conferred right permitting parties in a lawsuit to keep confidential any information exchanged between themselves and another person in instances where there was a special type of relationship between themselves and the other person that promoted an expectation of trust, confidentiality, and privacy.

Probable cause   the legal requirement that must exist for the police to make an arrest. It means that based on the evidence, the arresting officers have determined that a crime has been committed by the person sought to be arrested.

Pro hac vice   where a state may grant an attorney special permission to handle one particular case.

Pro per   individuals who represent themselves in court; also known as *pro se* litigants.

Property settlement   a contract between spouses who are in the process of obtaining a divorce or a legal separation resolving the various legal issues that arise when a marriage is dissolving; also known as a marital settlement agreement, separation agreement, or settlement agreement.

Proposal   a formal written indication, from one party to the opposing party, that communicates what the first party is seeking in terms of a divorce settlement.

Proposal letter   details the client's position on the various legal issues to be resolved, such as property division, alimony, child custody, visitation and support, maintenance of health and life insurance, distribution of debts and other liabilities, and counsel fees.

Pro se **litigants**   individuals who represent themselves in legal proceedings, see pro per.

Psychological parent   the parent who has had the child since the child's birth and/or who has spent the most meaningful time with the child, has bonded most fully with the child, and who has provided the most psychological nurturing of the child.

Public policy   a belief generally held by a majority of the public as to the desirability or rightness or wrongness or certain behavior.

Putative father   a man who is suspected of being or believed to be the biological father of a child born out of wedlock.

Putative spouse   the spouse in a second marriage where the first marriage has not yet been legally dissolved.

Q

Qualified Domestic Relations Order (QDRO)   a court order served on the pension administrator ordering the plan to distribute a specified portion of the pension funds to the nonemployee spouse.

R

Real property   land and anything affixed to it.

Reasonable efforts   such efforts must be made to maintain children with their families, or to reunify them, once the parents have received short-term, family-focused, and community-based services.

Reasonable rights of access   flexible arrangement that requires the parties to work out their own schedule for visitation with children.

Reasonable rights of visitation   a very flexible arrangement that requires the parties to work out their own schedule for visitation with children.

Rebuttable presumption   an assumption or inference drawn from certain facts, known to be true, that will be disproved by introducing evidence that the assumption is false, such as the presumption that a man is the biological father of a child born to a woman he is married to, which could rebutted by the introduction of uncontroverted evidence that another man is the child's father.

Reciprocity   where one state may extend to attorneys in a different state the right to practice law in its jurisdiction in exchange for the other state's granting the same privilege to attorneys in their state.

Redirect   after cross-examination, where the party's attorney may question the witness on any subject covered in the cross-examination testimony.

Rehabilitative alimony   spousal support that is awarded for a limited period of time to give the spouse the opportunity to become self-sufficient.

Reimbursement alimony   where a nondegreed spouse may be compensated for his or her contribution to the student spouse's attainment of an advanced degree that results in an enhanced earning capacity.

Release   a document that indicates the client has given his or her attorneys the permission to disclose information to another party.

Religious marriage   the religious solemnization of the union of two individuals according to the requirements of the particular faith in question.

Request   a document that asks the court to take some type of action; it is automatically granted by the court thirty days after filing, absent the opposing party's objection.

Request for admission   where a party formally asks that an opposing party admit the truth of some fact or event that will inevitably be proved at trial.

Request for an order attaching known assets   a document asking the court to freeze the opposing party's property in order to prevent dissipation of those assets.

Request for production of documents   where a party formally asks that the other party present certain papers for use in a case.

Requesting party   the party asking the court to take some action.

Residency   the domicile of the parties.

Respondeat superior   the doctrine that states an employer is responsible for negligence and other torts committed by his or her employees when the acts are committed during the scope of their employment.

Respondent   the party against whom an action is brought.

Responding party   the party who must produce discovery documents.

Retainer   payment made in advance to an attorney.

Retainer agreement   a contract between the law firm and the client whereby the law firm agrees to provide specified legal services in exchange for monetary compensation; also known as a retainer letter.

Retainer letter   see *retainer agreement*.

Return date   a date in the near future by which the complaint must be returned to the court clerk's office and filed with the court.

Revised Uniform Reciprocal Enforcement of Support Act of 1968 (RURESA)   where a custodial parent may ultimately obtain child support from the noncustodial parent residing in another state by instituting certain procedures.

Rules of court   a jurisdiction's official publication containing the procedural codes of the jurisdiction.

Rules of ethics   standards of conduct that a profession demands from its members.

S

Safe haven laws   state statutes that allow parents to anonymously surrender infants to designated locations in the community without fear of criminal prosecution.

SAID, or sexual allegations in divorce   an acronym for "sexual allegations in divorce"; a type of parental alienation syndrome that occurs when one parent uses psychological manipulation to encourage the child to fabricate allegations of child sexual abuse.

Sanctions   punishment issued to attorneys for engaging in conduct that violates the state's code of professional conduct.

Second glance doctrine   consideration of what circumstances exist at the time of enforcement of a prenuptial agreement in order to protect spouses from changes in circumstances that occurred since the date of the formation of the prenuptial agreement.

Second parent adoptions   a form of adoption where one partner of a same-sex couple adopts the child and the other partner files for co-parent status.

Separate maintenance   an action that affirms the continuation of a marriage and enforces the legal obligations of each spouse in the marriage.

Separate property   property acquired by a spouse *prior* to the marriage, or after the marriage by a gift, inheritance, or will, designated to that particular spouse alone.

Separation agreement   a contract between spouses who are in the process of obtaining a divorce or a legal separation resolving the various legal issues that arise when a marriage is dis-

solving; also known as a marital settlement agreement, property settlement, or settlement agreement.

Service by publication   when a sheriff puts a legal notice in the newspaper in the city, town, or general area where the defendant was last known to reside, or where the defendant is now thought to be residing.

Service of process   formal delivery of the initial pleadings.

Settlement   the practice of negotiating areas of disagreement and, through compromise, reaching an agreement to present to the court.

Settlement conference   a meeting with both lawyers and their respective clients with the specific goal of settling the case without court intervention.

Sham or green card marriage   a U.S. citizen agrees to a marriage for monetary compensation.

Shared physical custody   an arrangement where parents have both joint legal custody and joint physical custody and the child resides with one parent for a certain number of days a week and a certain number of days with the other parent.

Short calendar   one or two days of the week that courts set aside to hear motions brought before the court; also known as motion day.

Simplified divorce procedure   a form of low-cost divorce enacted by a number of states that is sometimes referred to as summary process or divorce by mutual consent; the parties in these states must appear before the court to dissolve their marriage.

Sole custody   where one parent has exclusive custody of a child.

Solicitation   actively seeking persons in need of legal services, either by mail or in person, unless there already exists an attorney–client relationship or a family relationship.

Special defenses   part of a defendant's answer in which he or she cites unusual or extraordinary circumstances as part of his or her defense.

Split custody   arrangement where one parent has sole custody for part of the calendar year each year, and the other parent has sole custody for the remaining portion of the year.

Spousal maintenance   a sum of money, or other property, paid by a former spouse to the other former spouse for financial support, pursuant to a court order, temporary or final, in a divorce proceeding; also known as alimony or spousal support.

Spousal support   see *spousal maintenance*.

Spyware   computer software that gathers information from a computer without the user's knowledge or permission. A spyware program allows the spying spouse to monitor the activities on his or her computer that are either saved on that particular computer or can be accessed from a remote location.

Standing   a term that describes whether a party has a legal right to request an adjudication of the issues in a legal dispute.

Stay away orders   prohibit the respondent in a domestic violence case from coming to the home, workplace, school, or other premises of the petitioner.

Stepparent adoption   where an individual who marries a divorced or widowed person adopts his or her spouse's children.

Stipulations   written agreements where parties agree that certain facts are true or that certain procedures will be followed.

Stored Communications Act   federal law that prohibits anyone but an authorized user from accessing electronically stored voicemails and e-mails.

Subject matter jurisdiction   the court's power to actually hear a divorce case.

Subpoena   a legal document signed by an officer of the court that requires the person receiving it to appear under penalty of law at the time, date, and place indicated on the document.

Subpoena duces tecum   a type of subpoena signed by an officer of the court at the request of one of the parties to a suit, requiring a witness to bring to court or to a deposition any relevant documents that are under the witnesses' control.

Subscription   part of a court document that confirms the truth and accuracy of allegations and confirms the veracity of the party making these allegations; also known as the verification.

Substantial change in circumstances   an actual or assumed alteration in the financial status or capability of either party.

Summary dissolution of marriage   simplified procedures for obtaining a divorce in cases where the parties have little or no assets, have no children, and were married for a relatively short period of time, and both want the divorce; all that is required in these jurisdictions, if you meet the requirements, is the filing of official documents with the appropriate court without the assistance of attorneys.

Summons   a one-page preprinted form on which the names and addresses of parties and the name and address of the court are inserted and that directs the defendant to appear in court and answer allegations in a complaint.

Supervised visitation   a type of visitation that limits or restricts a parent's visitation rights.

Surrogacy contract   an agreement between a woman who will bear a child for a person or a couple who intend to adopt the child once he or she is born. The surrogate mother agrees to relinquish custody of the child so the contracting parents are free to proceed with the adoption.

T

Taxpayer Relief Act of 1997   a federal tax law, as amended by subsequent legislation enacted in 1998, that allows homeowners who live in a home no fewer than two years in the five-year period prior to sale to deduct a gain of $250,000 each or $500,000 for couples before any tax on gain must be paid.

Temporary restraining order (TRO)   the petition filed by a victim of domestic violence in a civil court where the victim alleges that the petitioner and/or members of the household are in immediate physical danger and, as such, are requesting relief from the court.

Tender years doctrine   the theoretical justification for the placing of children with their mother.

Termination of parental rights   a court proceeding that severs the legal bonds between a parent and his or her biological child.

Testimony   evidence given by a witness under oath or affirmation.

Theory of the case   the legal justification for a client's position and for the relief he or she is seeking.

Third-party intervenor   a party who is not one of the main parties in a dispute.

Time sheet   a record of work performed on behalf of a client that will be billed to the client on a periodic basis; also known as a time slip.

Time slip   see *time sheet*.

Total net income   the figure arrived at when each parent's net income is added to determine child support; also known as combined net income.

Tracing   the process of tracking property during the course of a marriage so it retains its definition as separate property.

Transcript   an official copy of the record of proceedings in a trial or hearing.

Transitional alimony   short-term, lump-sum alimony awarded to a spouse for the purpose of transitioning from married to single status.

Transmutation   the transformation of separate property to marital property.

Transracial or transcultural adoption   (also known as interracial adoption) involves placing children who belong to one race or ethnic/cultural group with adoptive parents of another race or ethnic/cultural group.

Trial notebook   a method of organizing the materials prepared for trial in a manner that makes them readily available for use at trial.

U

Unauthorized practice of law (UPL)   when a nonattorney engages in any activity that the state UPL statute prohibits. Anyone engaging in the UPL can be prosecuted in criminal court.

Unbundled legal services or discrete tasks representation   clients purchase legal services on a task-by-task basis; the client and attorney agree by contract as to what services the lawyer will provide in exchange for a fee.

Unconscionable   an agreement that is so unfair to one party that the court will refuse to enforce it.

Uncontested hearing   a judicial procedure where neither party objects to the court granting a divorce and entering an order of marital dissolution.

Unearned retainer   any part of a retainer left over after the attorney has completed his or her work that must be returned to the client.

Uniform Child Custody Jurisdiction and Enforcement Act (UCCJEA)   an act drafted by a national commission and enacted by many state legislatures to enforce on an interstate basis the rights of custodial parents and prevent parental kidnapping and custodial interference.

Uniform Interstate Family Support Act (UIFSA)   where the noncustodial parent's state must honor the original support and may not enter a new order or modify the existing order to conform to its guidelines for determining the amount of support.

Uniform Premarital Agreement Act (UPAA)   a model act drafted by the National Conference of Commissioners on Uniform State Laws that provides states with model legislation addressing the issues necessary to create a valid premarital agreement.

Uniform Reciprocal Enforcement of Support Act (URESA)   a model act adopted by states that requires cooperation among the states in the collection and enforcement of child support and alimony.

Unity of spouses   the English common law system used to determine the division of marital property on dissolution of a marriage, which stated that, on marriage, a husband and wife merged into a single legal entity—the husband.

Unsupervised visitation   a type of visitation that permits a noncustodial parent to freely visit with the child without others present.

V

Venue   the proper divorce court within the state in which to file the initial divorce complaint on petition.

Verification   part of a court document that confirms the truth and accuracy of allegations and confirms the veracity of the party making these allegations; also known as the subscription.

Vicarious liability   where an employer is responsible for negligence and other torts committed by his or her employees when the acts are committed during the scope of their employment.

Violence Against Women Act of 1994   a Federal law that provides for education on the cycle of violence and prevention of abuse, protection of victims in the areas of housing and employment, changes to immigration law allowing immigrant victims of domestic violence to apply for permanent residency, funding for Indian tribal governments to help prevent violence amongst the Native American population, encourages states to implement mandatory arrests, and mandates that orders of protection granted in one state be recognized in all other jurisdictions.

Visitation rights   the right of a noncustodial parent to frequently spend time with the child unless the court finds that visitation in some way endangers the child's emotional, mental, moral, or physical health.

Void ab initio   invalid from its inception.

Void marriage   a marriage that is invalid at the time of its creation.

Voidable marriage   a marriage that is invalid at its inception but remains in effect unless the court terminates it.

Voluntary adoption   an adoption where biological parents willingly relinquish their parental rights so another parent or parents may adopt their children.

W

Wage execution   serves the purpose of facilitating alimony and child support payments through automatic deductions from the obligor's paycheck.

Waiver of alimony   one or both of the spouses may wish to waive or relinquish their right to ask for alimony.

Willful contempt   when the recipient spouse proves that the payor spouse has the means to make weekly payments but purposefully and deliberately fails to do so.

Work product   the notes, materials, memoranda, and written records generated by an attorney, as well as the written records of the attorney's mental impressions and legal theories concerning the case.

Index

Note: The letter 'f' following the locators refers to figures cited in the text.